Andrew Hudson
Paul Hudson

Fedora™

UNLEASHED

2008 Edition

SAMS | 800 East 96th Street, Indianapolis, Indiana 46240 USA

Fedora™ Unleashed, 2008 Edition

Copyright © 2008 by Sams Publishing

ISBN-13: 978-0-672-32977-7
ISBN-10: 0-672-32977-8

Library of Congress Cataloging-in-Publication Data

Hudson, Andrew, 1978-
    Fedora unleashed, 2008 edition / Andrew Hudson, Paul Hudson. – 8th ed.
        p. cm.
    ISBN 978-0-672-32977-7 (pbk. w/dvd)
    1. Linux. 2. Operating systems (Computers)   I. Hudson, Paul, 1979- II. Title.
QA76.76.O63H7945 2008
005.4'32–dc22
                            2007050344

Printed in the United States of America

First Printing February 2008

Trademarks

All terms mentioned in this book that are known to be trademarks or service marks have been appropriately capitalized. Sams Publishing cannot attest to the accuracy of this information. Use of a term in this book should not be regarded as affecting the validity of any trademark or service mark.

Warning and Disclaimer

Every effort has been made to make this book as complete and as accurate as possible, but no warranty or fitness is implied. The information provided is on an "as is" basis. The authors and the publisher shall have neither liability nor responsibility to any person or entity with respect to any loss or damages arising from the information contained in this book or from the use of the CD or programs accompanying it.

Bulk Sales

Sams Publishing offers excellent discounts on this book when ordered in quantity for bulk purchases or special sales. For more information, please contact

> **U.S. Corporate and Government Sales**
> **1-800-382-3419**
> **corpsales@pearsontechgroup.com**

For sales outside of the U.S., please contact

> **International Sales**
> **international@pearsoned.com**

Free Online Edition

When you buy this book, you get free access to the Safari online edition for 45 days.

Safari Bookshelf is an electronic reference library that lets you easily search thousands of technical books, find code samples, download chapters, and access technical information whenever and wherever you need it.

To gain 45-day access to the online edition of this book:

- Go to www.informit.com/onlineedition
- Complete the brief registration form
- Enter the coupon code IZL7-KS2M-4ZU6-GHMR-XMR8

If you have difficulty registering on Safari Bookshelf or accessing the online edition, please email customer-service@safaribooksonline.com.

Acquisitions Editor
Mark Taber

Development Editor
Michael Thurston

Managing Editor
Gina Kanouse

Project Editor
Anne Goebel

Copy Editor
Keith Cline

Indexers
Erika Millen
Lisa Stumpf

Proofreader
Water Crest
Publishing

Technical Editor
Dallas Releford

**Publishing
Coordinator**
Vanessa Evans

Multimedia Developer
Dan Scherf

Book Designer
Gary Adair

Composition
Bronkella Publishing

Contents at a Glance

Table of Contents

About the Authors

Andrew Hudson is a regular contributor to *Linux Format* magazine, the UK's largest Linux magazine. His particular area of expertise is Red Hat–based distributions, including Red Hat Enterprise Linux and The Fedora Project, having worked with the original Red Hat Linux since version 5. Seemingly obsessed with performance, he spends many an evening trying to squeeze more performance out of legacy hardware. Andrew lives in Wiltshire, England, with his wife Bernice and son John. Andrew does not like Emacs. Andrew can be contacted at andy.hudson@gmail.com.

Paul Hudson is a recognized expert in open-source technologies. He is Editor of *Linux Format* magazine, a professional developer, and full-time journalist for Future Publishing. His articles have appeared in *Mac Format*, *PC Answers*, *PC Format*, *PC Plus*, and *Linux Format*. Paul is passionate about free software in all its forms and uses a mix of Linux and BSD to power his desktops and servers. Paul likes Emacs. Paul can be contacted through http://hudzilla.org.

Dedications

To my family, for their love and support —Andrew

To Mum and Dad, for all their love, help, and support —Paul

Acknowledgments

Andrew Hudson

This is where I get to mention a few people, and I'd like to specifically thank Dallas Releford, Michael Thurston, and Mark Taber for keeping Paul and me going. My wife Bernice and son John allow me to shut myself away and write for endless evenings, but I do it all for them. Juggling a book, being a father and husband, and also working full-time is no mean feat, and it's all worth it.

Finally I want to thank God for the many blessings He has given me. My life would not be anything without Him, and I am eternally grateful for His grace.

Paul Hudson

Although only two names appear on the cover of this book, it is the culmination of many years of writing, refining, testing, rewriting, exploration, and passion from many people. I feel lucky to be part of the team and want to thank the others for their enthusiasm and humor—it makes a huge difference to know that everyone who works on this book enjoys the topic!

I'm grateful to the entire team at Pearson for their help and feedback—it's great to work with people who really care about free software and want to help others along that same journey. Of course, Andrew and I both owe a huge debt to our good friend Hoyt Duff, who we hope is somewhere sunny buffing up a classic car!

My family's contribution to this work has been immense. Andrew was brave in accepting the job of co-writing, but it turns out that we work in tandem very well—he has done a marvelous job, and we are both very proud of this end result. My wife, Ildiko, managed to put up with even more months of me doing no housework, although I think that the minute I am finished with this it is back to the grindstone for me (why do you think these acknowledgments are so long?). My parents have been immensely supportive throughout, and I love them dearly.

Finally, none of this work would have been possible without the grace of God. Andrew and I have been blessed to be able to write this book, and I pray it blesses you even more.

We Want to Hear from You!

As the reader of this book, *you* are our most important critic and commentator. We value your opinion and want to know what we're doing right, what we could do better, what areas you'd like to see us publish in, and any other words of wisdom you're willing to pass our way.

You can email or write me directly to let me know what you did or didn't like about this book—as well as what we can do to make our books stronger.

Please note that I cannot help you with technical problems related to the topic of this book, and that due to the high volume of mail I receive, I might not be able to reply to every message.

When you write, please be sure to include this book's title and author as well as your name and phone or email address. I will carefully review your comments and share them with the author and editors who worked on the book.

Email: opensource@samspublishing.com

Mail: Mark Taber
         Associate Publisher
         Sams Publishing
         800 East 96th Street
         Indianapolis, IN 46240 USA

Reader Services

Visit our website and register this book at **www.informit.com/sams** for convenient access to any updates, downloads, or errata that might be available for this book.

Introduction

Welcome to *Fedora Unleashed, 2008 Edition*! This book covers the free Linux distribution named Fedora and includes a fully functional and complete operating system produced by the Fedora Project, sponsored by Red Hat.

Fedora is directly descended from one of the most popular Linux distributions ever: Red Hat Linux. Those of you who know nothing about Linux might have heard of Red Hat; it is enough to know that it is the largest Linux vendor in North America. Fedora benefits directly from many Red Hat engineers as well as the wider contributions from free software developers across the world.

If you are new to Linux, you have made a great decision by choosing this book. Sams Publishing's *Unleashed* books offer an in-depth look at their subjects, taking in both beginner and advanced users and moving them to a new level in knowledge and expertise.

Fedora is a fast-changing distribution that can be updated at least twice a year. We have tracked the development of Fedora from very early on to make sure that the information contained in this book mirrors closely the development of the distribution. A full copy of Fedora is included on the DVD, making it possible for you to install Linux in less than an hour!

This book provides all the information that you need to get up and running with Fedora. It even tells you how to keep Fedora running in top shape, as well as how to adapt Fedora to changes in your needs and requirements. Fedora can be used at home, in the workplace, or, with permission, at your school and college. In fact, you might want to poke around your school's computer rooms: You will probably find that someone has already beaten you to the punch—Linux is commonly found in academic institutions. Feel free to make as many copies of the software as you want. No copyright lawyers are going to pound on your door, because Fedora is freely distributable all over the world.

After this brief introduction, you will get straight into the distribution, learning how to install and configure Fedora and find your way around the Gnome graphical interface and learning about the command line. We also take you through installing software, managing users, and other common administrative tasks. For the more technically minded, we cover some starting steps in programming across several languages—why not pick one and give it a go? Through the book, you will also find information on multimedia applications, digital graphics, and even gaming for after hours when you are finished tinkering. After you make it through the book, you will be well equipped with the knowledge needed to use Linux successfully. We do assume that you are at least familiar with an operating system already (even if it is not with Linux) and have some basic computer knowledge. We round off the book by giving you some reference points for you to access via the web, and we also explore the origins of Fedora and Linux.

Changes from Previous Editions

Readers who may already own previous editions of *Fedora Unleashed* might wonder what work has gone into this edition. Well, we've overhauled the entire structure of the book, making it far faster for you to get stuck into Fedora.

We have also substantially rewritten several chapters and introduced new ones, such as Chapter 4, "Command-Line Quick Start," and others. This book also looks at the three main ways in which you can obtain Fedora: by using the DVD, Live CD, and KDE Live CD media. There are many changes to this book, and it's taken a long time to come to fruition.

Licensing

An important thing to consider, given Linux's unique place in the market, is the licensing situation surrounding Fedora. Believe it or not, the software that you are about to install is 100% free in every sense of the word. You may have handed over your money for this book, but you can download the software itself for free from the Internet, or you can purchase a CD for a small price (usually to cover postage and packaging). Not only that, but you are able to examine the code behind all the packages and make changes yourself, if you want to. This is in stark contrast to other vendors, who charge you for the operating system and then prevent you from making any changes at the code level. It is this key difference that makes Linux into an open source operating system. Surprisingly enough, these vendors never actually sell you the software for you to own; rather, they give you only the right to use the software. As mentioned before, this is certainly not the case with the software included with this book. You are entirely free to make copies of the DVD, share them with friends, and install the software on as many computers as you want—we encourage you to purchase additional copies of this book to give them as gifts, however. Be sure to read the Read Me file on the DVD included with this book for important information regarding the included software and disc contents. Look under the /usr/share/doc/fedora-release-8 directory after you install Fedora to find a copy of the GNU GPL (along with copies of other software licenses). You will see that the GPL provides unrestricted freedom to use, duplicate, share, study, modify, improve, and even sell the software.

You can put your copy of Fedora to work right away in your home or at your place of business without worrying about software licensing, per-seat workstation or client licenses, software auditing, royalty payments, or any other types of payments to third parties. However, be aware that although much of the software included with Fedora is licensed under the GPL, some packages on this book's DVD are licensed under other terms. There is a variety of related software licenses, and many software packages fall under a broad definition known as *open source*. Some of these include the Artistic License, the BSD License, the Mozilla Public License, and the Q Public License.

For additional information about the various GNU software licenses, browse to http://www.gnu.org/. For a definition of open source and licensing guidelines, along with links to the terms of nearly three dozen open source licenses, browse to http://www.opensource.org/.

Who This Book Is For

This book is for anyone searching for guidance on using Fedora, and primarily focuses on Intel-based PC platforms. Although the contents are aimed at intermediate to advanced users, even new users with a bit of computer savvy will benefit from the advice, tips, tricks, traps, and techniques presented in each chapter. Pointers to more detailed or related information are also provided at the end of each chapter.

Fedora's installer program, named Anaconda, makes the job of installing Linux as easy as possible. However, if you are new to Linux, you might need to learn some new computer skills, such as how to research your computer's hardware, how to partition a hard drive, and occasionally how to use a command line. This book will help you learn these skills and show you how to learn more about your computer, Linux, and the software included with Fedora. System administrators with experience using other operating systems will be able to use the information presented in this book to install, set up, and run common Linux software services, such as the *Network File System (NFS)*, a *File Transfer Protocol (FTP)* server, and a web server (using Apache, among other web servers).

What This Book Contains

Fedora Unleashed is organized into seven parts, covering installation and configuration, Fedora on the desktop, system administration, Fedora as a server, programming and housekeeping, and a reference section. A DVD containing the entire distribution is included so that you will have everything you need to get started. This book starts by covering the initial and essential tasks required to get Fedora installed and running on a target system.

If you're new to Linux, and more specifically, Fedora, first read the chapters in Part I, "Installation and Configuration." You will get valuable information on the following:

- ▶ Detailed steps that take you by the hand through various types of installations

- ▶ Critical advice on key configuration steps to fully install and configure Linux to work with your system's subsystems or peripherals, such as pointers, keyboards, modems, USB devices, power management, and—for laptop users—PCMCIA devices

- ▶ Initial steps needed by new users transitioning from other computing environments

- ▶ Configuration and use of Gnome and X, the graphical interface for Linux

Part II, "Desktop Fedora," is aimed at users who want to get productive with Fedora and covers the following:

- ▶ Discovering the many productivity applications that come with Fedora

- ▶ Surfing the Internet and working with email and newsgroups

- ▶ Using Fedora to listen to music and watch video

- ▶ Using Fedora to download and manipulate images from digital cameras

- ▶ Setting up local printers for Fedora

- ▶ A look at the current state of gaming for Linux

Moving beyond the productivity and desktop areas of Fedora, Part III, "System Administration," covers the following:

- ▶ Managing users and groups

- ▶ Automating tasks and using shell scripts

- ▶ Monitoring system resources and availability

- ▶ Backup strategies and software

- ▶ Network connectivity, including sharing folders and securing the network

- ▶ Internet connectivity via dial-up and broadband connections

Part IV, "Fedora As a Server," looks at the opportunities provided by every Fedora system by covering the following:

- ▶ Building and deploying web servers

- ▶ Database creation, management, and manipulation

- ▶ File and print servers

- ▶ Using FTP for serving files across the Internet and local networks

- ▶ Building and deploying email servers with Postfix as well as managing mailing lists

- ▶ Creating remote access gateways and services

- ▶ Configuring DNS for your network

- ▶ Using LDAP for storing information on users and security

- ▶ Configuring a local news server

Part V, "Programming Linux," provides a great introduction into ways in which you can extend Fedora's capabilities even further, using the development tools supplied with it. This part covers the following:

- ▶ Programming in Perl, using variables and scripting

- ▶ An introduction to the Python language

- ▶ Writing PHP scripts and linking them to databases

- ▶ An introduction to the mono programming language

- ▶ C and C++ programming tools available with Fedora, and how to use the *GNU C Compiler* (gcc)

Part VI, "Fedora Housekeeping," looks at some of the more advanced skills you need to keep your system running in perfect condition, including the following:

- ▶ Securing your machine against attack from outsiders and viruses

- ▶ Performance tuning

- ▶ Command-line master class

- ▶ Advanced yum

- ▶ Kernel and module management and compilation

- ▶ Managing the file system

There is also an extensive reference in Part VII, "The Appendices," which gives you an opportunity to explore in even more depth some of the topics covered in this book. It also gives you some history on Fedora and Linux and an installation checklist.

Conventions Used in This Book

A lot of documentation is included with every Linux distribution, and Fedora is certainly no exception. Although the intent of *Fedora Unleashed* is to be as complete as possible, it is impossible to cover every option of every command included in the distribution. However, this book offers numerous tables of various options, commands, or keystrokes to help condense, organize, and present information about a variety of subjects.

This edition is also packed full of screenshots to illustrate nearly all Fedora-specific graphical utilities—especially those related to system administration or the configuration and administration of various system and network services.

To help you better understand code listing examples and sample command lines, several formatting techniques are used to show input and ownership. For example, if the command or code listing example shows typed input, the input is formatted in boldface like this:

```
$ ls
```

If typed input is required, as in response to a prompt, the sample typed input also is in boldface, like so:

```
Delete files? [Y/n] y
```

All statements, variables, and text that should appear on your display use the same boldface formatting. In addition, command lines that require root or super-user access are prefaced with a pound sign like this:

```
# printtool &
```

Command-line examples that can be run by any user are prefaced with a dollar sign ($), like so:

```
$ ls
```

The following elements provide you with useful tidbits of information that relate to the discussion of the text:

NOTE

A note provides additional information you might want to make note of as you are working, augment a discussion with ancillary details, or point you to an article, a whitepaper, or another online reference for more information about a specific topic.

TIP

A tip can contain special insight or a timesaving technique, as well as information about items of particular interest to you that you might not find elsewhere.

CAUTION

A caution warns you about pitfalls or problems before you run a command, edit a configuration file, or choose a setting when administering your system.

Sidebars Can Be Goldmines

Just because it is in a sidebar does not mean that you will not find something new here. Be sure to watch for these elements that bring in outside content that is an aside to the discussion in the text. You will read about other technologies, Linux-based hardware, or special procedures to make your system more robust and efficient.

Other formatting techniques used to increase readability include the use of italics for placeholders in computer command syntax. Computer terms or concepts also are italicized upon first introduction in text.

Finally, you should know that all text, sample code, and screenshots in *Fedora Unleashed* were developed using Fedora and open source tools.

Read on to start learning about and using the latest version of Fedora. Experienced users will want to consider the new information presented in this edition when planning or considering upgrades. New users, or users new to Fedora, will benefit from the details presented in this book.

PART I

Installation and Configuration

Installing Fedora

This chapter shows you how to get a basic installation of Fedora up and running. You will learn how to start installation and how specify certain configuration options during the install. Before you even insert the disc, you'll have a chance to consider choices that will affect how you install Fedora. It is impossible to take you through every single variation of the install, but you will get a step-by-step guide of a typical installation, including how to log in to your new system and shut down or reboot the system.

Before You Begin the Installation

It can be a big step to wipe off whatever was on your hard drive and replace it with Fedora. Before you even go near the CD/DVD drive, prepare for the installation by researching some basic information about your hardware. In Appendix B, "Installation Resources," you'll find a useful section on hardware specifications, with a list of hardware devices that you'll probably want. Fortunately, you can now take a test drive with Fedora without ever having to install it to your hard drive, as Fedora has created Live CD spins of the distribution.

Live CDs

If you've not come across Live CDs, you might be a bit unsure as to what they are. Basically, a *Live CD* is a single CD that enables you to boot into a fully functional operating system, in this case Fedora. The Live CD stores all the system files on the CD in a compressed format, uncompressing parts of the operating system as needed. The upshot of this is that you can give Fedora a try without having to repartition or otherwise modify your hard drive.

More important, however, the Live CD enables you to test your hardware to make sure that it is compatible with Fedora. When you are happy, you can use the Live CD to give you a base Fedora installation. Just double-click the Install icon on the desktop and follow the installation instructions found later in this chapter. For now, download and burn the Live CD ISO file to a blank CD using your favorite CD-burning application—it will come in handy later!

Planning Partition Strategies

If you are a diehard Windows user, partitioning is something that might never have entered your mind. Put simply, it is the efficient layout of information on your hard drive, and it is certainly worth giving thought ahead of the installation as to how you want to partition your drive.

What Is a Partition?

It can be difficult to explain to new users about *partitions*. A useful analogy is of a kitchen, in which there are many different drawers and cupboards. Imagine the kitchen is your hard drive, and the drawers and cupboards are partitions. In one cupboard, you may keep cups, another might hold ingredients, yet another may hold pots and pans. They are all part of the kitchen but have specific roles within the kitchen.

Taking this back to your hard drive, you may have a partition to hold your user information, another partition to hold the files you will use for serving web pages, and another for boot information.

Typically, Fedora creates three partitions on your drive: a /boot partition that stores information to help Fedora boot up, a /partition (or root partition) that stores the bulk of your information, and a swap partition that Fedora uses to temporarily store information when your RAM is full. For the majority of people this is fine, and many users go ahead and use the default partition options. However, there may be occasions when you want to store your /home? directory (which contains your user settings and documents) on a separate partition. This might be the case if you plan on upgrading your distribution fairly often and don't want to lose settings unique to you. You should be mindful of not only the current business requirements, but also any anticipated requirements, especially if you are in a growing company. It can be very painful when you are running out of storage space because you underestimated storage or partitioning requirements.

Knowing how software is allocated on your hard drive for Linux involves knowing how Fedora organizes its *file system*—its layout of directories on storage media. This knowledge can help you make the most out of hard drive space; and in some instances, such as planning to have user directories mounted via NFS or other means, it can help head off data loss, increase security, and accommodate future needs. Create a great system, and you'll be the hero of information services.

To plan the best partitioning scheme, research and know the answers to these questions:

► How much disk space does your system require?

► Do you expect your disk space needs to grow significantly in the future?

► Will the system boot just Fedora, or do you need a dual-boot system?

► How much data will require backup, and what backup system will work best? (See Chapter 13, "Backing Up," for more information on backing up your system.)

Most new users to Fedora will want to run a dual-boot system, meaning a system that will enable you to boot into Windows and Fedora. To do this, you need to make sure that you have allocated space on your hard drive for Fedora to use during installation. Unfortunately, Anaconda, the Fedora installation program, does not allow you to resize NTFS partitions, so you need to either use a program such as Partition Magic, or, if you don't want to spend money on an application that you might use only once or twice, download a copy of the Fedora Live CD and use gParted.

gParted is a simple GUI program that allows you to resize your NTFS partition to make room for Fedora. You can find gParted under the Applications, System Tools menu on the Live CD. Its simple interface is shown in Figure 1.1.

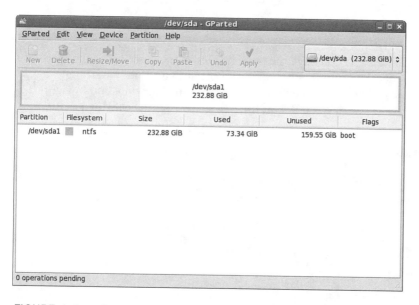

FIGURE 1.1   gParted enables you to work with the partitions on your hard drive to make room for Fedora.

To get started, right-click the main Windows partition shown and select Resize/Move to bring up the resizing options, as shown in Figure 1.2 and Figure 1.3.

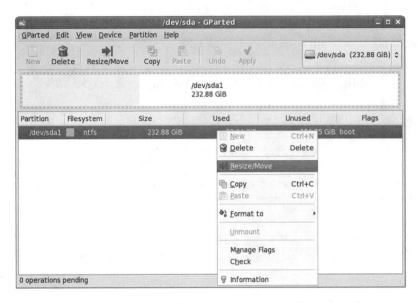

FIGURE 1.2   Select Resize/Move from the right-click menu to start the resizing process.

In Figure 1.3, you can see that you have the choice to resize the partition so that you have space free at either the beginning or end of the current partition. We strongly recommend that you add the free space following the existing partition, and in Figure 1.3 you can see that we have selected 8000MB as the free space after the existing partition.

Alternatively, you can click and drag either side of the partition bar shown to resize the partition accordingly.

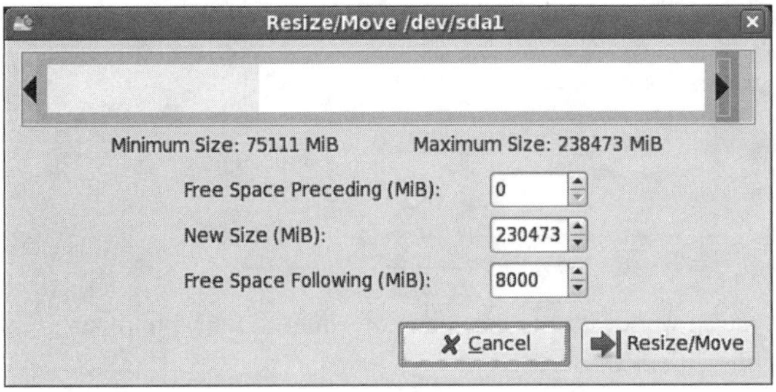

FIGURE 1.3   Either enter a value in the Free Space Following field, or click and drag the arrows to either side of the partition bar.

As soon as you are happy, click the Move/Resize button and gParted returns to the main screen, with the pending operation listed in the lower half of the screen, as shown in Figure 1.4. As you are working with file systems, gParted does not make the changes immediately because you may want to carry out other operations on the file system before committing the changes. In this case, however, you just want to resize the disk, so to commit the changes go to Edit, Apply All Operations, or click the Apply button in the toolbar to start the process. gParted asks you whether you are sure, so click Apply only if you are really ready to commit your changes.

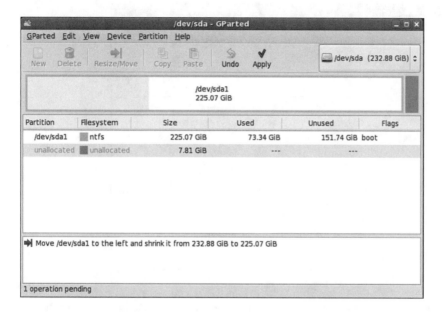

FIGURE 1.4   This is the point of no return. After you have clicked Apply, gParted prompts you one last time before it starts to resize your partition.

After a few minutes, gParted completes the operation and returns you to the main screen, as shown in Figure 1.5.

DVD Installation Jump-Start

To install Fedora from the DVD included with this book, you must have at least a Pentium-class CPU, 800MB hard drive, and 128MB RAM. You need at least 192MB to install with Fedora's graphical installer. A 10GB hard drive can easily host the entire distribution, leaving about 3GB free for other data. Most modern systems have significantly larger drives, but it is still a good idea to invest in more storage from your local computer store.

To begin the installation, you need to get into your computer's BIOS to set the boot sequence so that the CD/DVD drive is the first drive that is booted. Insert the DVD into the drive and let the system boot. When the boot: prompt appears, press the Enter key and follow through the various dialog boxes to install Fedora.

Make sure that you make a note (mental or otherwise) of the root password because you will need it later. When the installer is finished, the DVD ejects and you are asked to reboot the computer. A few more dialog boxes appear to allow you to do some more initial configuration of the system before you are greeted with a login prompt. Make sure to log in as the user you created during the installation and not as root. Finally, finish the install, remove the DVD from your computer, and reboot. Then log in and enjoy Fedora!

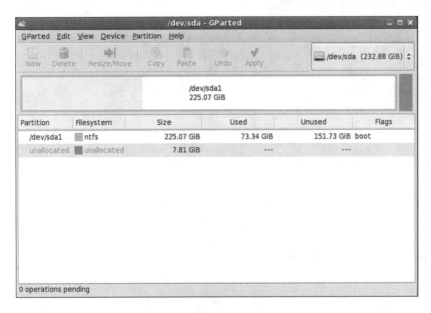

FIGURE 1.5   All done and ready for a Fedora install, you can see that gParted has created 7.81GB of unallocated space.

Choosing How to Install Fedora

Fedora can be installed in a variety of ways, using different techniques and hardware. Most users install Fedora by booting to the installation directly from a CD or DVD. Other options include the following:

▶ Booting to an installation and installing software over a network or even via the Internet, using FTP or HTTP protocols

▶ Booting to an installation and installing software from an NFS-mounted hard drive

How you choose to install (and use) Fedora depends on your system's hardware, networking capabilities, corporate information service policy, or personal preference. The following sections describe the issues surrounding each of these types of installation.

Installing from CD or DVD

Most PCs' BIOSes support booting directly from a CD or DVD drive, and offer the capability to set a specific order of devices (such as floppy, hard drive, CD-ROM, or USB) to search for bootable software. Turn on your PC, set its BIOS if required (usually accessed by pressing a function or Del key after powering on); then insert the Fedora installation disc, and boot to install Fedora.

To use this installation method, your computer must support booting from your optical drive, and the drive itself must be recognizable by the Linux kernel. You can verify this by checking your BIOS and then booting your PC.

The file `boot.iso` is a 8.5MB CD-ROM image found under the `images` directory on the Fedora DVD. The image can be burned onto a blank CD, and supports booting to a network install. This is a convenient way to boot to a network install on a PC with a bootable CD-ROM drive, but no installed floppy drive, or when you don't want to use multiple floppies during an install requiring driver disks.

You burn the image onto optical media by using the `wodim` command. For example, copy the file to your hard drive, insert a blank CD-R into your CD-RW drive, and then use a command line like so:

```
# wodim -v speed=40 dev=0,0,0 -data -eject boot.iso
```

This example creates a bootable CD-ROM, and then ejects the new CD-ROM after writing the image. The speed (`40`, in this example) depends on the capabilities of your CD-writing device. The device numbers are those returned by running `cdrecord` with its `scanbus` option, like so:

```
# wodim -scanbus
```

Installing Using a Network

Fedora can be installed from a local network (or even over the Internet if you have broadband access). You need access to a web, FTP, or NFS server hosting the installation packages. To boot to a network install, use the bootable CD-ROM created with the `boot.iso` boot image as described previously, or the Fedora DVD included with this book. Boot your PC with the boot floppy or, if you use CD-ROM, type **linux askmethod** at the boot prompt. Follow the prompts, and you will be asked to choose the type of network installation.

> **TIP**
>
> Just press Enter at the boot prompt if you boot to a network install by using a CD-R created with the `boot.iso` image. You will boot a graphical network install.

To install from an FTP location, select the network IP address assignment for your target PC, such as DHCP, or manually enter an IP address along with optional gateway IP address and nameserver addresses. You are then asked for the FTP site name. You can enter the name or IP address of a remote FTP server hosting the Fedora release. The name of the remote directory depends on where the Fedora install files are located on the remote server.

Using the *File Transfer Protocol (FTP)* to install Fedora requires access to an FTP server (see Chapter 20, "Remote File Serving with FTP," to see how to set up a server and use FTP). You have to know the hostname or IP address of the server, along with the path (directory) holding the Fedora software. One way to prepare a server to host installs is to follow these steps:

1. Create a directory named `Fedora` under the FTP server's `pub` directory. The directory is usually `/var/ftp/pub` on a Linux server.

2. Create a directory named `base` and a directory named `RPMS` underneath the `Fedora` directory.

3. Copy or download all RPM packages included with Fedora into the `pub/Fedora/RPMS` directory.

4. Copy all original base files (`comps.rpm`, `comps.xml`, `hdlist`, `hdlist2`, `hdstg2.img`, `netstg2.img`, `stage2.img`, `TRANS.TBL`) from the DVD's `base` directory into the `pub/Fedora/base` directory.

Using this approach, enter **pub** when asked for the name of the remote directory holding the Fedora install software.

Installing Fedora from a remotely mounted *Network File System (NFS)* is similar to a hard drive installation, but requires access to an NFS server. You need access permission, a permitted IP address or hostname for your computer, the hostname or IP address of the NFS server, and the path to the Fedora software. See Chapter 14, "Networking," for more information about NFS and network addressing.

To install Fedora with HTTP, you need the hostname or IP address of the remote web server, along with the directory containing Fedora's software. See Chapter 17, "Apache Web Server Management," to see how to set up a web server.

> **NOTE**
>
> See Chapter 20 for details on how to configure the `vsftpd` FTP server. Chapter 17 provides information on how to set up and configure Apache for web service. See Chapter 19, "File and Print," for Samba settings. Note that you can have your server perform all three duties.

Step-by-Step Installation

This section provides a basic step-by-step installation of Fedora from the DVD included with this book. There are many different ways to proceed with an install, and the installer can provide a graphical or text-based interface in a variety of modes.

NOTE

If you are using the Live CD, we assume that you have double-clicked the Install icon on the desktop. Pick up the instructions below at the Release Notes point.

This example installation prepares a computer for general duties as a desktop workstation, giving you access to office productivity applications and Internet applications.

CAUTION

If you are wanting to dual boot with Windows, make sure you have prepared your partitions, using the instructions detailed earlier.

Before you begin, ensure that your computer is not connected to the Internet. Although you can use the installer to set up network protection during the install, it is best to check your system settings after any install and before opening up any public services (see the section "Firstboot Configuration" later in this chapter).

TIP

If you are installing to a system that has an older display monitor, it is a good idea to have your monitor's manual handy during the installation. If the install does not detect your monitor settings, you might need to specify the monitor's vertical and horizontal frequencies. This does not happen often, but if it does, you will be prepared.

Starting the Install

To get started, insert the DVD into your drive and reboot your computer. You first see a boot screen that offers four options for booting (see Figure 1.6). You can pass options to the Linux install kernel by pressing **e** at this screen.

The basic options most often used are

- ▶ **Install or Upgrade an Existing System**—This starts the graphical installation, using Anaconda.

- ▶ **Install or Upgrade an Existing System (text mode)**—Starts the install, using a text interface.

- ▶ **Rescue Installed System**—Boots into rescue mode to enable you to rescue a "broken" system.

- ▶ **Boot from Local Drive**—Boots whatever operating system is present on your hard drive.

FIGURE 1.6   Select an installation option in this first Fedora boot screen.

TIP

The installer starts automatically in 60 seconds. Press the spacebar, reboot, or turn off your PC if you need to halt the install.

After you press Enter, the installer's kernel loads, and you're asked (in a text-based screen) whether you would like to perform a media check of your installation media, as shown in Figure 1.7.

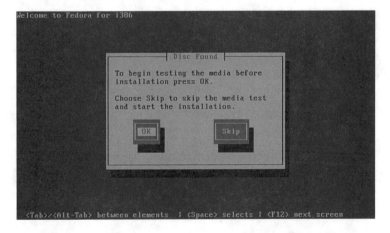

FIGURE 1.7   You can check your CD-ROM or DVD media before installing Fedora.

This check can take quite some time (depending on the speed of your optical drive), but can ensure the integrity of the CD-ROM/DVD's contents, as an md5sum value is embedded on each CD-ROM and DVD. This check can help foil installation of malicious software from CD-ROMs and DVDs with tampered contents. The check can also be helpful to make sure that the CD-ROM or DVD you are using works on your PC and in your optical drive. To perform the check, choose OK; otherwise, use the Tab key to navigate to the Skip button and press Enter to choose it.

After you check your CD-ROM or DVD or even skip the check, the display clears. The Fedora installer, Anaconda, loads, and you are presented with a graphical welcome screen, as shown in Figure 1.8. The installer should recognize your PC's graphics hardware and mouse. You can then click the Release Notes button to get detailed information about Fedora, along with tips on hardware requirements and how to perform various installs.

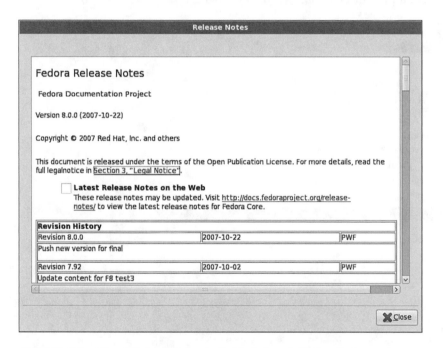

FIGURE 1.8   Read Help or Release Notes before installing Fedora.

NOTE

Fedora's installer supports the capability to monitor background and install processes running during an installation. You can watch the progress of an install and hardware information reported by the Linux install kernel by navigating to a different console display or virtual console. To do so, simultaneously press the Ctrl, Alt, and the appropriate function key (such as F1–F5).

Use this approach to watch for kernel messages, monitor hardware detection, gain access to a single-user shell, and view the progress of the installer script.

When using a graphical installer, press Ctrl+Alt+F4 (then Alt+F2 or Alt+F3) to navigate to the various screens. Press Alt+F7 to jump back to the installer. When performing a text-based installation, use Alt+F2 (then Alt+F3 or Alt+F4). Use Alt+F1 to jump back to a text-based install.

If your pointing device (mouse) is not recognized, you can press Alt+R to "press" the Release Notes button. Similarly, you can press Alt+H to hide text shown on the left side of the screen, but you should take a minute to read the frame's contents.

Click Next (or press Alt+N) to continue, and the installer asks you to select one of 31 different languages for the installation, as shown in Figure 1.9.

FIGURE 1.9   Select a language to use when installing Fedora.

You can navigate the installer's dialogs (during a text-based or graphical install) by using the Tab key. You can scroll through lists by using your cursor keys. Note that you can now step backward through the install by using a Back button. Select a language and click the Next button.

You'll then be asked to select a keyboard for the install, as shown in Figure 1.10.

FIGURE 1.10   Select a default keyboard to use when installing and using Fedora.

Scroll to the appropriate keyboard option. You use this option to configure the install to support one of 53 different language keyboards. Click Next after making your selection.

At this point, if you are installing Fedora to a brand new hard drive, you will get a warning that Fedora was unable to read the partition table. By clicking Yes, you are giving Fedora permission to initialize the disk and use it for installation. If you are happy that it is a totally blank drive, feel free to proceed; otherwise, we recommend using the Live CD to install Fedora.

If an existing Linux install is detected, you are asked whether you want to upgrade and reinstall; otherwise, you are asked to partition your disk to make room for Fedora, as shown in Figure 1.11.

Partitioning Your Hard Drive

For the moment, select Create Custom Layout and click Next to move to the screen shown in Figure 1.12. You could, however, opt to delete all partitions (including Windows partitions) on the drive, remove only Linux partitions on the drive, or use only unallocated space.

NOTE

If you followed the earlier partitioning instructions, choose to Use Free Space on Selected Drives and Create Default Layout.

FIGURE 1.11   Select how you want to partition your drive.

If you choose one of these three, you get a default layout that uses logical volume management. This is a special type of partitioning that makes disk partitions much easier to work with.

Logical Volume Management for Beginners

Logical volume management sounds a lot more difficult than it is. In effect, what it does is allow you to produce single logical partitions that can be made up of multiple physical drives. Logical volumes can also be resized as required, something that is usually difficult when dealing with ext3 partitions (Fedora's native partition type). There is one thing that you need to remember: Create a separate /boot partition independent of the logical volumes; otherwise, your system will not boot!

This example looks at creating a partition table on one hard drive. To get started, click the New button to bring up the screen shown in Figure 1.13. First of all, you need to create a small partition that has the mount point /boot. This is to enable Fedora to actually boot and needs to be a maximum of only about 100MB in size. Make sure that only the first disk is checked (sda in the example) and select /boot from the drop-down mount point menu. Finally, change the size of the partition to 100MB and click the OK button to create the first partition.

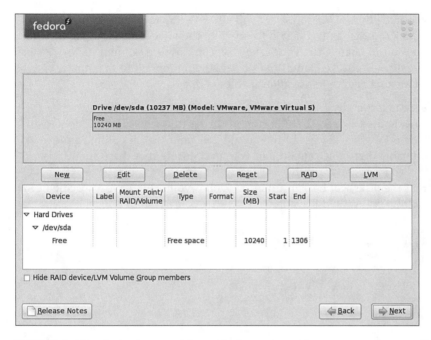

FIGURE 1.12   Fedora's powerful partitioning tool enables you to create a partition scheme unique to your requirements.

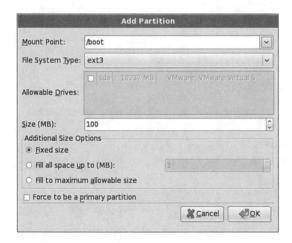

FIGURE 1.13   Make sure to create your boot partition; otherwise, all your good work will be in vain!

Now we need to create physical volumes that will allow Fedora to combine them into a logical volume. Click the New button again to bring up the same window as Figure 1.13, but this time you want to change the File System Type to physical volume (LVM). Make sure that only one drive is checked, and finally select the option Fill to Maximum Allowable Size to instruct Fedora to use all available space.

When you have created the physical volumes, you now need to bind them together through a logical volume. Click the LVM button in the partitioner's main window to bring up the LVM options (see Figure 1.14). You can give your logical volume group a more meaningful name than VolGroup00, but you must ensure that there are no spaces in the name. Next you can choose a physical extent size for your volumes, or rather the size of chunks that the disks will be "cut up into." Unless you really have a specific need to change this setting, you should leave it at 32.

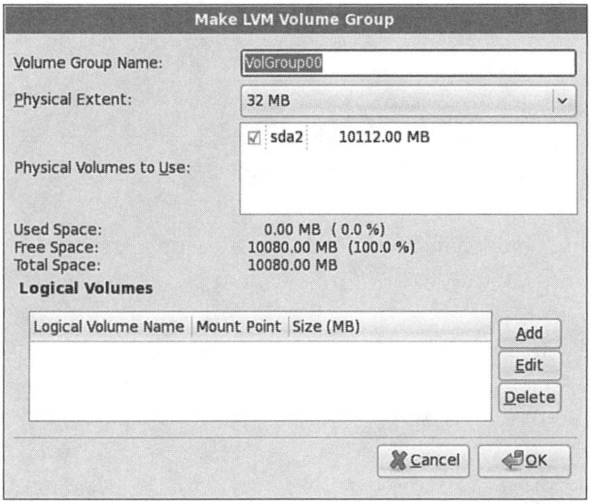

FIGURE 1.14   Harness the flexibility of logical volumes through Fedora's easy-to-use utility.

Now you need to create your partitions within your logical volume group, and you do this as you would any other Linux distribution, making sure that you at least have a / partition and a swap partition. In the example, click the Add button to be taken to the Make Logical Volume screen (see Figure 1.15) where you can specify a mount point, file system type, volume name (again no spaces), and finally the size of the partition.

You have to create at least two partitions: the / partition and the swap partition. However, you can add several mount points, depending on your specific requirements. Some users find it helpful to create a separate /home partition, which we do in the example. As you add each logical volume, it appears in the main LVM Group options screen (refer to Figure 1.14). When you are finished, click the OK button to return to the main partition screen, which should look similar to Figure 1.16.

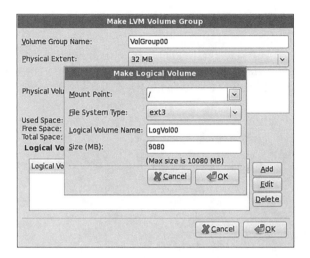

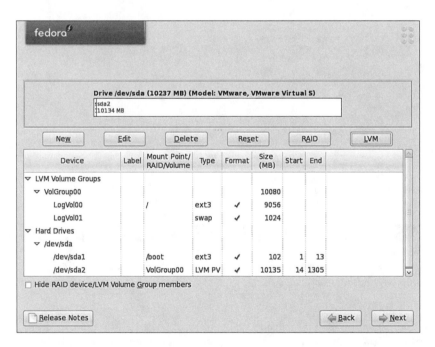

FIGURE 1.15   Use this screen to define the logical volumes that make up your logical group.

FIGURE 1.16   The completed masterpiece. It is worthwhile spending extra time to get the best partition layout for your requirements.

Now you are ready to proceed to the next screen by clicking the Next button.

Choosing, Configuring, and Installing the Boot Loader

After you accept the partitioning scheme, a screen appears asking you to select a boot loader for booting Fedora (see Figure 1.17). This screen also enables you to choose not to use a boot loader (when booting from removable media, a commercial boot utility, a DOS partition, or over a network), and to boot other operating systems if you have configured a dual-boot system.

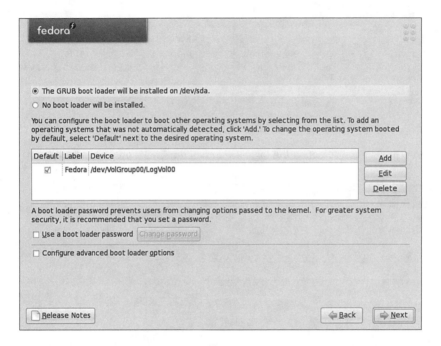

FIGURE 1.17   Select whether you want to use a boot loader and configure other boot options.

<table>
<tr><td>TIP</td></tr>
</table>

Fedora works well with other operating systems, but the reverse is not always true. If you need specialized help with configuring a dual-boot system, check various HOWTOs at http://www.tldp.org for hints and tips.

Select the GRUB boot loader. GRUB is typically installed in the MBR of the first IDE hard drive in a PC. However, the boot loader can also be installed in the first sector of the Linux boot partition, or even not installed on the hard drive. Note that you can also backtrack through the install process to change any settings.

Note that you can assign a password for the boot loader. If you choose to use this option, you have to enter a password at the GRUB boot screen (see the section "Logging In and

Shutting Down" at the end of this chapter for information on graphical logins). Carefully note the password! It does not have to be the same password used to log in, but if you password protect booting through your computer's BIOS and use a boot loader password here, you will subsequently need to enter three passwords (BIOS, boot loader, and login) to access Linux. Type in a password of at least eight characters twice (once on each line); then click OK or Cancel to exit the dialog.

> **NOTE**
>
> If you are planning to dual boot your PC with Windows, it appears in the list of boot options as Other. You can click the Edit button to access options that enable you to rename it something a little more informative, or even set Windows as the default option for GRUB.

If you click the Configure Advanced Boot Loader Options button, you are asked for arguments to pass to the Linux kernel before booting. Kernel arguments are used to enable or disable various features of Linux at boot time. If you install the source to the Linux kernel, you can find documentation about the more than 200 different kernel arguments in the file `kernel-parameters.txt` under the `/usr/src/linux/Documentation` directory.

Click Next to set your boot loader configuration. You then proceed to the network interface configuration, as shown in Figure 1.18.

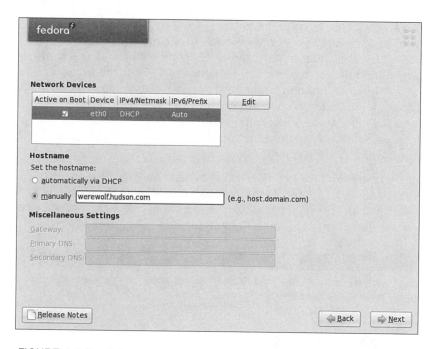

FIGURE 1.18   Select or enter networking configuration information.

Network Configuration

If you have an installed network adapter, you are asked for network configuration details, as already shown in Figure 1.18. Fedora can be set to automatically configure networking upon booting. Note that you can also configure networking following installation, using Fedora's system-config-network graphical network administration tool (see Chapter 10, "Managing Users," for details about using these tools).

> **NOTE**
>
> If the Linux kernel finds more than one network interface installed on your computer, you might be asked to configure a second ethernet device. This might be the case, for example, if you are installing Fedora on a computer that serves as a gateway or firewall. If you configure more than one ethernet device, the device named eth0 is the first active interface when you start Fedora.

You can choose to have your interface information automatically set with DHCP. Otherwise, especially if you are configuring a DHCP server, manually enter an IP address, hostname, or gateway address (such as for a router), along with DNS information if you click the Edit button listed by the interface (such as eth0 in the example). After making your selection, click Next to continue.

Setting the Time Zone

You are next shown a Time Zone Selection dialog (see Figure 1.19). There are two "clocks," or times, when using a PC: the hardware clock, maintained by hardware in the computer and a backup battery; and the system time, set upon booting and used by the Linux kernel. It is important to keep the two times accurate and in synchronization because automated system administration might need to take place at critical times. Many computer installations use computers with hardware clocks set to GMT, which stands for *Greenwich mean time*. The more modern designation is UTC or *coordinated universal time*. The Linux system time is set relative to this time and the default time zone, such as eastern standard time, which is –5 hours of UTC.

Setting the computer's hardware clock to UTC (GMT) has the advantage of allowing the Linux system time to be easily set relative to the geographic position of the computer and resident time zone (such as a Linux laptop user who would like to create files or send electronic mail with correct time stamps, and who has traveled from New York to Tokyo).

> **TIP**
>
> Read the man page for the hwclock command to learn how to keep a running Linux system synchronized with a PC's hardware clock.

Choose your time configuration, and then click Next.

FIGURE 1.19   Select your time zone.

Creating a Root Password and User Accounts

You are next asked to enter a root operator password, as shown in Figure 1.20. Type in a password, press Tab or Enter, and then type it again to make sure that it is verified. The password, which is case sensitive, should be at least eight characters (or more) and consist of letters and numbers. Note that the password is not echoed back to the display. Your root password is important because you need it to perform any system administration or user management with Fedora.

> **CAUTION**
>
> Do not forget your system's BIOS, boot loader, or root passwords! Some equipment, such as notebook computers, might require factory replacement of motherboard components if the owner forgets the BIOS password. The BIOS settings on most desktop PCs can usually be reset via a jumper or removal and insertion of the mother-board battery. If you forget your boot loader password, use a boot disk (perhaps created during installation as shown later on in this chapter) or boot to a rescue mode by using your Fedora disc and reset the root password, using the passwd command.

When finished, click Next to continue with software package selection for your new server.

FIGURE 1.20   Type in, and do not forget, your root password.

NOTE

You can create a root account only during a Fedora install. You will have to create user accounts after booting, using a command-line program (such as adduser) or the graphical system-config-users client. Create an account for yourself and any additional users. Usernames traditionally consist of the first letter of a person's first name and then the last name. For example, Tom Denning would have a username of tdenning. Do not forget to enter a password for any new user! If you create a user without a creating a password, the new user will not be able to log in.

You should create at least one user for your server in addition to the root operator. This is for security purposes and to avoid logging in as root, either through the keyboard at the server or remotely over the network. The default shell and home directory settings should remain set at the defaults, which are the *Bourne Again SHell* (bash) and the /home directory.

See Chapter 4, "Command-Line Quick Start," for how to become the root user or run root commands as a regular user. See Chapter 10 for details on managing users.

TIP

Good passwords are essential for system security. However, some people still rely on passwords as simple as admin. This is asking for trouble, and we would encourage you to create a strong password made up of letters, numbers, and even punctuation. It can be difficult to create a password that is easily memorable and that includes punctuation, but it can be simpler than you think. For instance, George Nedeff may want to use his full name as a password, but that would be easy to crack. What he could do is use punctuation and numbers to replace similar letters in his name, such as G30rg3n3defF. This is a very strong password, and not easily broken, but at the same time it is very easy to remember.

Software Selection and Installation

Fedora enables you to select three predefined options for the installation package manifest. For this example, we're just going to use Office and Productivity, but if you are going to explore the chapters in the latter third of this book, you will need Software Development, and you will definitely need Web Server if you are going to use what you learn in Chapter 17. This screen is shown in Figure 1.21.

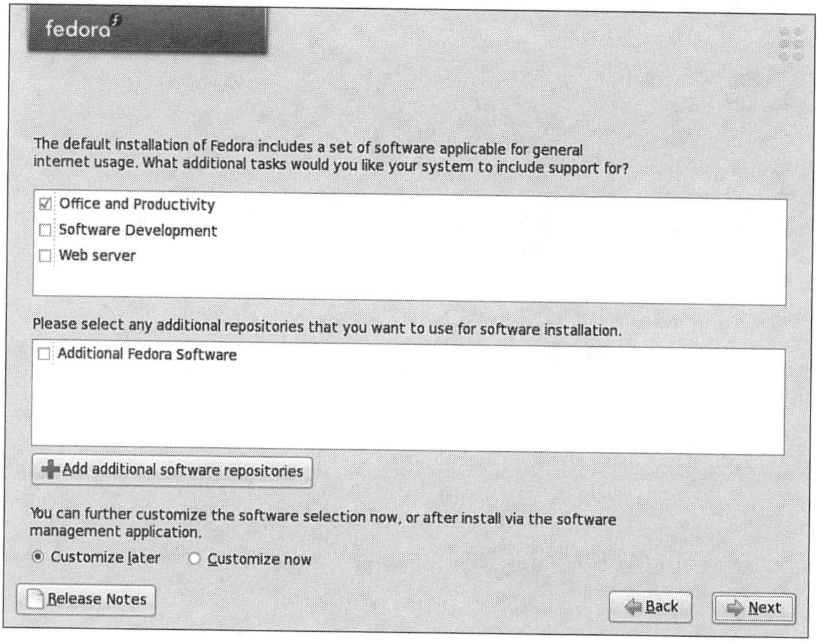

FIGURE 1.21   Fedora's new and simplified package selection screen.

What Happened to Install Everything?

In previous versions of Fedora and Red Hat Linux, there was an option to install everything available. This has now been removed from Fedora for a number of reasons. First of all, installing all the packages can create dependency nightmares when upgrading and installing new packages. Second, there can be too many packages for new users to handle. Third, and perhaps most important, it can pose a huge security risk to your system. The more software you have installed, the greater the risk that someone could find a vulnerable entry point into your system.

NOTE

Fedora can enter your own repositories at install time. Fedora takes these new repositories into account when you go through the Customize Packages screens. All you have to do is provide a name for the repository, as well as the FTP or HTTP server and path details to the `repomd.xml` file. Just click the Add Repository button to do this.

You are also able to specify whether you want to customize your package selection further by selecting the Customize Now button and clicking Next to go to Figure 1.22. Otherwise, just click Next to land at the final screen.

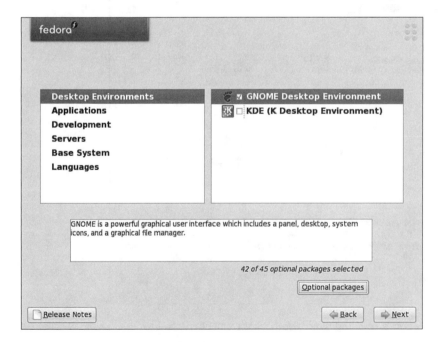

FIGURE 1.22   Specify the exact packages you want for your installation.

If you decided to customize your package choice, you will see a screen similar to Figure 1.22. On the left side are the generic categories that contain software. As you click each category, a new set of package groups appears on the right side. Mark the check box against each package group to install the default packages associated with that group. If you want to specify additional packages within the group, click the optional packages button to see all the other packages available for the group, shown in Figure 1.23. Select the ones that you require and click close to add them to your package list. After you finish selecting your packages, click Next to allow Fedora to scan for any dependency problems.

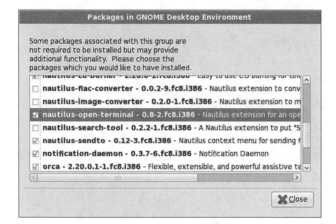

FIGURE 1.23   Fine-tune your installation by selecting only the packages that you really need.

You finally arrive at the last screen before Fedora actually starts to install anything, so it is a good idea to take a deep breath and think about anything you might have forgotten. It is easy to go back to any stage of the installation process by clicking the Back button until you reach where you want to go.

When you are happy, click Next to allow Fedora to install the system. Now is a good time to make a cup of coffee because it can take up to an hour to install Fedora, depending on the options that you have chosen. As Fedora is installed, it tells you which package it is currently working on, as shown in Figure 1.24.

If you are installing over a network or by DVD, take a break; the install proceeds unattended through the software installation.

Finishing the Install

You are finished! Click the Exit button, and the installer ejects any inserted media and reboots. The GRUB boot loader presents a boot prompt, as shown in Figure 1.25.

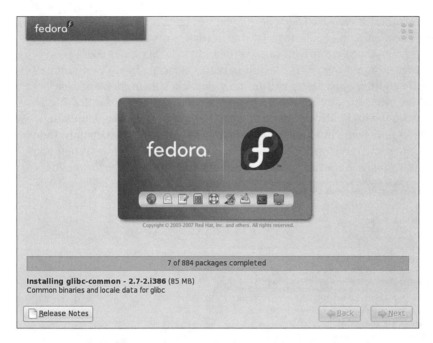

FIGURE 1.24   The Fedora installer formats your drive, and then installs selected software package groups.

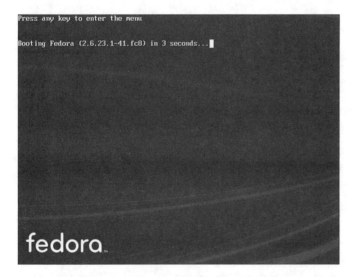

FIGURE 1.25   Boot Fedora with GRUB by pressing the Enter key or waiting 5 seconds.

If you have set a GRUB password, press **P**, type your password, and press Enter. If you do nothing for five seconds, or press Enter, either boot loader boots Linux.

NOTE

After installation, you can edit the file `/boot/grub/grub.conf` and change the `timeout=` setting to change the boot time to a value other than 5 seconds.

Firstboot Configuration

Although the vast majority of configuration is done during the actual installation, Fedora allows you to choose some more options before you log in for the first time. When you boot Fedora, it loads `firstboot`, which is the utility responsible for personalizing your computer. It asks you a few straightforward questions and the end result is that you are able to log in to Fedora.

The first screen welcomes you to `firstboot` and you should click Next to start. The next screen asks whether you accept the conditions under which Fedora is released. If you agree with what is said, click the Yes button and then click Next.

NOTE

To read the end-user licensing agreement for Fedora, go to http://fedoraproject.org/wiki/Legal/Licenses/EULA.

Firewall configuration is up next (see Figure 1.26), and you should always have your firewall enabled. Sensibly, Fedora defaults to this, but it also asks you whether you want to allow access to specific ports to allow services to run. Depending on your requirements, you might want to select one or more of the boxes. You can also enter in specific ports and the protocol (TCP or UDP), although you should be aware that the more services or ports you allow access to, the less secure your system becomes as it opens up more opportunities for attack.

SELinux allows a much more detailed security policy, and is still in development. Introduced in Fedora Core 2, *SELinux* is an NSA initiative to provide Linux with an in-depth mandatory access control system that compartmentalizes the system. Basically, if an intruder gets onto the system, SELinux limits the amount of damage that the intruder can cause.

SELinux

As mentioned earlier, SELinux came from the NSA *(National Security Agency)*, one of the most secret organizations in the United States. The community's shock at having this technology released to them can be summed up by Larry Loeb when he said, "Let me assure you that this action by the NSA was the crypto-equivalent of the pope coming down off the balcony in Rome, working the crowd with a few loaves of bread and some fish, and then inviting everyone to come over to his place to watch the soccer game and have a few beers. There are some things that one just never expects to see, and the NSA handing out source code along with details of the security mechanism behind it was right up there on that list."

FIGURE 1.26   The firewall is a key part of your defense against would-be crackers. When you are happy with your selection, click the Next button to start configuring SELinux.

You are able to choose how SELinux is implemented on your system, but unless you have a specific reason to change any of the default settings, just click the Next button to continue. The default settings provide a very secure system.

Following on from SELinux, Fedora gives you a chance to set up your Time and Date settings. You already gave Fedora your location in the world, but this screen (see Figure 1.27) enables you to fine-tune your time and date and to opt to use the Network Time Protocol and get an accurate time from one of the many hundreds of time servers across the world.

After the Time and Date settings comes your chance to actively contribute to Fedora's development. Smolt (see Figure 1.28) was designed to gather information about your hardware configuration so that the Fedora Project could build up a database of known working hardware configurations. It enables the Fedora Project to analyze on what kinds of systems Fedora is being used, and also enables them to prioritize development on specific platforms. If you have a network connection, we recommend that you take part. No personal details will be sent as part of Smolt's submission, and you will be helping in the future development of Fedora.

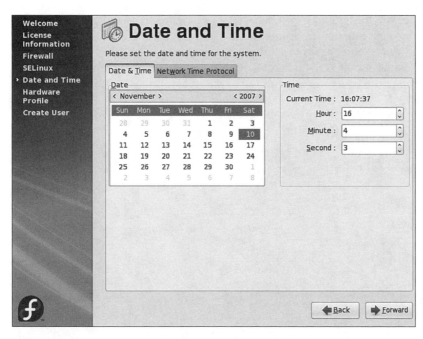

FIGURE 1.27   Never be late again by setting your system clock correctly.

FIGURE 1.28   Help Fedora by submitting information about your hardware.

Clicking Next takes you to the Add New User screen (see Figure 1.29) and allows you to enter details for one user initially. You can enter the user's full name, username, and password (which you need to enter again to confirm), and you can choose any other authentication settings such as use of Kerberos or NIS services. When you have completed firstboot, you can create other users, using the system-config-users utility.

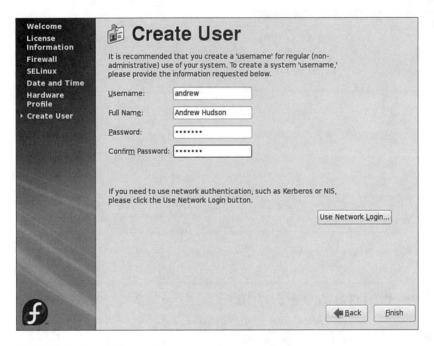

FIGURE 1.29   Add your first user in this screen.

Finally, click the Finish button to go straight to the login prompt, as shown in Figure 1.30. Here you should log in as the user you created during firstboot; do not log in as root because you can cause some serious damage if you do not know what you are doing.

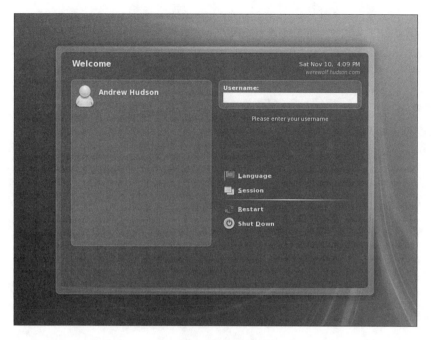

FIGURE 1.30   Enter your username and password to log in to Fedora.

Logging In and Shutting Down

If you chose to use the text-based installer during the installation, you normally log in at a text-based login prompt. If you used the graphical install and didn't remove X from the package manifest, you log in using a graphical login prompt, the screen clears after your system boots, and you are presented with a graphical login screen, as shown previously in Figure 1.30.

To log in at the text-based prompt, type your username and press Enter. You are then prompted for your password. After you press Enter, you are at the Linux command line. If you use a graphical login, you can use the shutdown or reboot menus in the screen's dialog to shut down or reboot your system. To immediately shut down your system from the command line of a text-based session, use the su command and its -c option to run the halt command, like this:

```
$ su -c '/sbin/shutdown -h now'
```

You can also use the reboot command to restart your computer, as follows:

```
$ su -c '/sbin/reboot'
```

For new users, installing Fedora is just the beginning of a new and highly rewarding journey on the path to learning Linux. See Chapter 4 for additional information about using Linux commands. For Fedora system administrators, the task ahead is to fine-tune the installation and to customize the server or user environment.

Reference

▶ **http://fedoraproject.org**—The place to start when looking for news, information, and documentation about installing, configuring, and using Fedora.

▶ **http://tinyurl.com/c2x5u**—Symantec's PartitionMagic utility includes BootMagic, which can be used to support booting of Linux or, regrettably, other less-capable operating systems, such as Windows XP.

▶ **http://www.v-com.com/product/System_Commander_Home.html**—V Communications, Inc.'s System Commander, a commercial 4.2MB download that can be used to support booting of any operating system capable of running on today's PCs. An intelligent partitioning utility, Partition Commander, is included.

▶ **http://www.nwc.com/columnists/1101colron.html**—How to use Intel's Pre-execution Environment (PXE) protocol to remote boot workstations.

▶ **http://www.gnu.org/software/grub/**—Home page for the GRUB boot loader.

# CHAPTER 2

Fedora Quick Start

Part of the challenge of moving to a new operating system is moving beyond any preconceived ideas about how things should work. If you have been locked into a Windows environment and this is your first move to Linux, you might start out by hunting for the My Documents and My Computer icons on your desktop, but without much success because you won't find them there. Likewise, if you are used to a Mac OS X desktop, you might feel somewhat lost without the presence of the Dock to help launch applications. No matter, though; in this chapter, you will learn the fundamentals of working with Fedora so that you can comfortably progress through the rest of the book.

In this chapter, we look at how to find your way around your new desktop, what each of the menu options contain, and we take you through the preinstalled software. We also look at how to install new software, and more important, we ensure that your installed software is kept up-to-date with relevant patches and security updates. Connecting to a network, either wirelessly or through a physical connection, is something that is common to almost everyone, so we look at this later on in the chapter.

The Fedora Desktop

After you have logged in to Fedora for the first time, you will be greeted with the default desktop. It resembles something like that shown in Figure 2.1.

Along the top and bottom are panels, which can contain items such as menu options (like on the top panel) or other shortcuts such as the Web Browser icon to the right of the System menu. The main window contains three icons: Computer, Home, and Trash.

FIGURE 2.1   The Fedora desktop, your gateway to a better computing life.

> **TIP**
>
> In Linux-speak, the tilde character (~) represents Home, or the folder that contains information that is specific to your login. So my home directory is called andrew's home, as this matches my login name. Your login name will differ, unless of course your name is Andrew, too!
>
> It's useful to remember the tilde, especially when you come to the "Command-Line Quick Start" (Chapter 4) or the "Command-Line Master Class" (Chapter 32) because it will help you with navigating via the terminal.

Apart from these three icons, a set of shortcut icons is immediately to the right of the System menu; these represent five useful applications you may want to access quickly. You'll also see the clock farther along the top panel, as well as a Speaker icon representing the sound options. You may also see an icon denoting your network connection status; more on this as part of the "Configuring Wireless Networks" section.

At the bottom left of the screen is another small icon that is used to show your desktop. When you have many different windows open and you need to quickly access something on your desktop, you can click this icon and all the windows minimize, leaving you with your desktop. If you want, you can then click again on this icon and the windows all reappear.

The bottom-right side of the screen holds something that until recently was exclusive to UNIX/Linux platforms: the Workspace Switcher. You can click any of the four screens to access that screen.

Workspace Switcher—A Quick Primer

Workspaces are something that you probably haven't come across in other operating systems, but you will see them a lot in Fedora and other Linux, FreeBSD, and UNIX systems. Essentially, Fedora creates four workspaces across which you can run several applications, depending on how you work. For instance, you could use workspace one for your word processor, workspace two for your spreadsheet, workspace three for your email, and workspace four for your configuration tools.

Accessing each workspace is as simple as clicking it in the Workspace Switcher. Fedora immediately switches to that workspace and displays whatever applications are present. Your desktop and any icons on it remain on the workspace, ready for your use.

Alternatively, if you want to use the keyboard to switch between workspaces, you need to press Ctrl+Alt and either the left or right cursor key to move left a workspace or right a workspace. Fedora keeps you in the loop as to which workspace is currently active by highlighting it in the Workspace Switcher. You can also see small windows open within the workspaces that have active applications.

Finally, in the bottom-right corner is the trash can, to which you can drag files to be deleted when you are ready. By default it is empty, but as you delete things, the trash can becomes full, indicating that there is something there.

Getting Around Fedora

As mentioned earlier, Fedora is the gateway to a better computing life. But getting to that better computing life means that you need to understand where Fedora stores things on its desktop. We have already covered the basics of what the desktop looks like, but in this section we go a little deeper and explore some of the menu options, as well as some of the tips and tricks you can use to get around Fedora.

The Menu Options

Fedora automatically creates three menu options for you along the top panel. These are Applications, Places, and System. Don't be confused into thinking that the Fedora logo is a menu in itself; it is just part of the Applications menu.

The three menus hold different things, and it is important for you to understand where you can find specific applications, utilities, and shortcuts that you will use to interact with your system.

The Applications menu holds all the GUI applications that are currently installed on your system, arranged into predefined groups such as Accessories, Office, Internet, and so on. At the bottom of this menu is an entry that enables you to add or remove additional applications.

The Places menu enables you to quickly navigate to certain locations that are either local to your computer or, in the case of network server, that are on remote machines. You will also find options for searching as well as accessing recent documents in the Places menu.

The final entry is the System menu, which holds all the associated utilities that you need to administer your system, including options to log out and shut down your system. Two submenus under the System menu neatly separate systemwide changes from user-based changes. The Preferences submenu enables you to change settings that are specific to your user login, so they affect only you and not any other users. Administration, on the other hand, enables you to make systemwide changes such as adding printers, working with logical volumes, and modifying system services, to name but a few.

Window Selector

An important part of the Fedora desktop is the Window Selector (shown in Figure 2.2), which appears on the bottom panel by default. As you launch applications, they appear in the main desktop, and an icon and associated application name appear in the bottom panel. Each application appears in the panel for that specific workspace, enabling you to easily organize your applications. The Window Selector also enables you to quickly switch between windows by clicking each entry. By clicking each entry, you bring the associated window to the front of the screen. If you then click again on the entry, you minimize that application, and maximize it if you click it once more.

FIGURE 2.2   Use the Window Selector to switch between open applications.

The Computer Icon

As an entry point to your system, the Computer icon is one tool for navigating through your system with the GUI interface. The interface itself is called Nautilus, and is the default file manager for Fedora. You will see a screen similar to that in Figure 2.3, although it may vary depending on whether you have additional drives and storage devices attached to your computer. You navigate through the file system by double-clicking each icon, opening the contents of the folder into a new window.

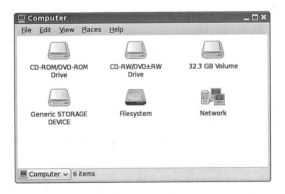

FIGURE 2.3   Use Nautilus, Fedora's GUI file manager, to navigate through the directories on your file system.

The Home Icon

Fedora uses the UNIX method of assigning a home directory to every end user. The directories are collectively stored under the /home directory, so you may see entries for /home/andrew or /home/bernice. However, Fedora also creates a shortcut icon for each user that appears on her desktop when she logs in. This shortcut icon takes the user directly to her home directory, where she can store documents and files that are specific to her. All your personalized settings are stored under the home directory because they are specific to you.

> **NOTE**
>
> So we said that all your personalized settings are stored in your home directory, but when you open it up you find that you can't see anything but the default directories. This is because all your personalized settings are stored in hidden folders, commonly prefixed with a period. Simply go to the View menu and select Show Hidden Files and suddenly you'll see all the folders related to your settings.

In older releases, Fedora left the home directory pretty much empty (with the exception of the personalized settings, which are hidden), but now there are seven folders to help you organize your files. You don't have to keep any of them, but they are there as a helping hand in your move to Fedora.

When you double-click a folder, the icon changes to denote that the folder's contents are open in another window, as shown in Figure 2.4.

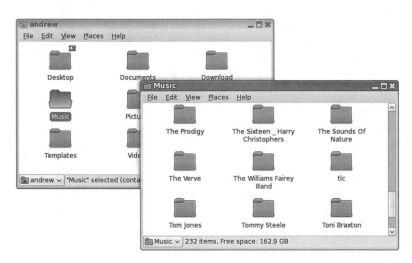

FIGURE 2.4   Keep track of which folders are open by looking at the folder icons.

If you find that you are working with a lot of folders, Nautilus has a handy feature that lets you close all folders, or just the parents of the folder with which you are currently working. Just select the File menu within the Nautilus window and select your desired option.

Accessing the Command Line

Throughout this book, you will see references to the command line, also known as the terminal. This is your way to execute commands directly, using a text-based input rather than a GUI utility.

Earlier versions of Fedora kept the Terminal application in the Applications, Accessories menu. Fedora 8 has changed this so that the Terminal now appears under Applications, System Tools, reflecting its status as a tool for accessing system settings and carrying out administration. You can use several terminal applications, but Fedora defaults to gnome-terminal, and unless you have a really good reason for switching, you should find it does everything you need.

Available Applications

If you have installed Fedora using the DVD supplied with this book, and used the default selection of packages (Productivity), congratulations; you now have a fully functional operating system, complete with word processor, spreadsheet, email client, calendar, instant messaging client, and other programs that will enable you to work with Fedora.

This section touches briefly on the different applications installed when you use the Productivity package set that is defined during the installation.

Office Suite

The office suite of choice for Fedora is OpenOffice.org. If you have hung around any Linux geeks for long enough, you are bound to have heard of this increasingly popular open source office suite. It comprises several components, but Fedora delivers word processing (Writer), spreadsheet analysis (Calc), and presentation delivery (Impress) out of the box. Chapter 6, "Productivity Applications," looks at OpenOffice.org in more depth. You can access Writer, Impress, and Calc by clicking the shortcut icons in the top panel.

Internet Workstation

Linux was designed with communication in mind, and it is fitting that Fedora comes with a suite of Internet tools, including the popular Firefox web browser, Evolution PIM (*Personal Information Management*) software, Pidgin (instant messaging client formerly known as GAIM), and Ekiga (videoconferencing). You can launch Firefox by clicking the Firefox icon in the top panel bar, and can launch Evolution by clicking the Envelope icon, again in the top panel bar. Chapter 5, "On the Internet," covers Internet applications.

Multimedia

Multimedia is a big thing these days, with many different people carrying USB flash drives full of music, photos, and other media types. Fedora itself includes the GIMP, a powerful graphic manipulation package, along with gThumb for managing your photo collections. It is also well served in the music department, offering a CD player, CD ripper, and media player to handle various free codec-based files. You are also able to obtain software to watch DVDs and other proprietary video formats, although this may be illegal in your country.

NOTE

Fedora doesn't ship with MP3 support as standard, nor does it include support for many of the standard formats found within Windows or Mac OS X. This is down to the patents that are used in the development of these formats, more commonly known as *codecs*. Inclusion of these codecs in Fedora is prevented due to the legality of the licenses and patents involved. However, all is not lost. Some third-party repositories offer plug-ins for the multimedia applications bundled with Fedora, which allow them to use additional codecs.

Games

Because Windows 386 included Reversi, it's kind of been a given that most operating systems include some simple games. Fedora follows in this tradition with a selection of games and puzzles to provide a momentary distraction. We don't actually cover the default selection of games because they're pretty straightforward, but Chapter 9, "Games," takes a look at some of the better known games available for Fedora.

Keeping Your Software Up-to-Date

With any operating system, it is important to ensure that you have the most recent bug fixes and patches, which are designed to make your applications even more stable.

Fedora makes updating your software extremely easy and relies on an application called pup, which can be found under Applications, System Tools as the Software Updater entry. In fact, when you log in to Fedora, pup automatically checks the configured software repositories to see whether any updates are available and then asks whether you want to download them. This is shown in Figure 2.5.

FIGURE 2.5   *pup* keeps an eye out for any updates and notifies you through an alert in the top panel.

The nice thing about updating with pup is that it updates all the software installed through Fedora at one time, as shown in Figure 2.6, instead of updating only the core operating system or certain parts of it.

FIGURE 2.6   Use *pup* to manually update your entire system.

The partner to pup is pirut, or the Add/Remove Software item under the Applications menu. This is Fedora's default software management tool and allows you to install further software packages or remove them as necessary. pirut (shown in Figure 2.7) enables you to select using groups of packages (for example, Window Managers, Software Development), individual packages from a list, or by searching for specific packages.

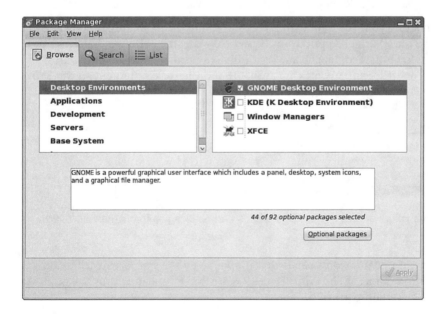

FIGURE 2.7   *pirut* helps you manage your selection of software.

Configuring Wireless Networks

Wireless networking used to be a pig to configure for Linux, requiring a lot of complicated steps to connect to a wireless network. However, Fedora includes a great utility
called NetworkManager that makes connecting to and managing wireless networks
extremely easy. Thanks to the inclusion of several wireless chipset drivers in the Fedora
Linux kernel, it is now very easy to connect to WEP-and WPA-encrypted wireless
networks.

Fedora now includes support for Intel wireless chipsets out of the box, so if you have a
Centrino notebook, you should have no problem connecting to a wireless network. This
also extends to anyone who uses a device based upon the zd1211 chipset, which includes
some USB adaptors. However, for Broadcom-based wireless systems, you need to retrieve
the bcm43xx-fwcutter program to extract the firmware from the relevant driver file. Head
on over to http://tinyurl.com/32tv5r to download drivers for earlier Broadcom chips, or
go to http://tinyurl.com/36mbr5 to download firmware for later Broadcom chips. You are
interested in the files that begin with WL, so copy them to a folder in your home directory.

> **NOTE**
>
> For the broadcom-wl-4.80.53.0.tar.bz2 file, you will need to double-click it because
> it is a compressed file. When Archive Manager opens, browse to broadcom-wl-
> 4.80.53.0/kmod/ and copy both wl_apsta.o and wl_apsta.mimo.o to your home
> directory, either by dragging both files onto your Home icon, or by clicking Extract in the
> toolbar and browsing to your home directory.

Unfortunately it's trial and error from here in, so you will have to try each file in turn to
see if it enables your hardware. For the files wl_apsta.o and wl_apsta-3.130.20.0.o, you
need to use the command bcm43xx-fwcutter; for the wl_apsta_mimo.o file, you need to
use b43-fwcutter. Either way, the syntax is *command file*. So, for example, you might
enter the following:

```
$ bcm43xx-fwcutter wl_apsta.o
```

You then press Enter to extract the firmware. After you have done this, you need to
switch to root to move the extracted files to the location that Fedora requires them to be
in. You change to root by issuing the command su and entering the root password when
requested.

At the root prompt, enter the following command when you have used the bcm43xx-
fwcutter command:

```
# mv *.fw /lib/firmware/
```

Or, if you used the b43-fwcutter command earlier, enter this command:

```
# mv b43 /lib/firmware/
```

At this point, you must restart your system to ensure that Fedora recognizes the new firmware Go to System, Shutdown, and choose Restart.

When your system comes back up, it's best to open a new terminal window (Applications, System Tools, Terminal) and enter the command dmesg ¦ grep bcm or dmesg ¦ grep b43 depending on which tool you used to extract the firmware. You should see something similar to this:

```
b43-phy0: Broadcom 4306 WLAN found
b43-phy0 debug: Found PHY: Analog 2, Type 2, Revision 2
b43-phy0 debug: Found Radio: Manuf 0x17F, Version 0x2050, Revision 2
b43-phy0 debug: Adding Interface type 2
b43-phy0 debug: Loading firmware version 351.126 (2006-07-29 05:54:02)
b43-phy0 debug: Chip initialized
b43-phy0 debug: 30-bit DMA initialized
b43-phy0 debug: Wireless interface started
```

This means that Fedora has successfully recognized your Broadcom-based wireless card.

Now all you have to do is start NetworkManager to help you manage your wireless network. To do this, go to System, Administration and choose Services to see the Service Configuration tool shown in Figure 2.8.

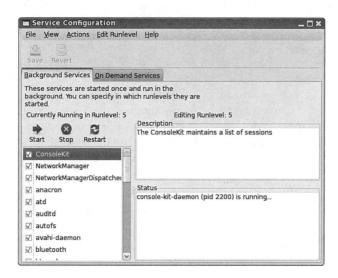

FIGURE 2.8   Control the services that are loaded in Fedora using the Service Configuration tool.

You need to make sure that the check box is marked next to both NetworkManager and NetworkManagerDispatcher; as you check the boxes, click the Start button directly above them to start the services immediately. Finally, click the Save button in the toolbar, and close the Service Configuration tool by going to File, Quit. When you've done this, the NetworkManager icon appears in the notification area of your top panel (see Figure 2.9). This is the applet that handles and monitors network connections.

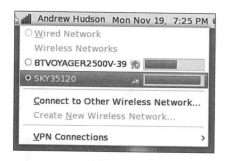

FIGURE 2.9   The NetworkManager notification applet, shown here already connected to a wireless network.

When you are ready, click the NetworkManager icon in the toolbar to connect to a wireless network. If your wireless access point broadcasts its SSID, it should appear in the list under wireless networks (similar to Figure 2.9). Simply click the required network and NetworkManager detects what encryption (if any) is in use and asks you for the passkey. Enter this and NetworkManager starts the wireless connection. The passkey is then stored in the default keyring (essentially a central way of managing security in Fedora); so if you have not yet used the keyring, you are asked to create a password. From now on, whenever you log in to Fedora, you will be asked for the key to unlock the keyring.

If for some reason your wireless network does not appear (you might have your SSID hidden), you have to use the Connect to Other Wireless Network option, which brings up the screen shown in Figure 2.10.

NetworkManager can handle WEP and WPA encryption, as well as enterprise variations of WPA. You are advised to use WPA encryption as it is the stronger of the two.

NetworkManager can also connect to Cisco VPN connections. You are able to specify connection settings as appropriate, or if you have access to a predefined configuration (PCF file) you can import it directly into NetworkManager.

FIGURE 2.10   Use NetworkManager to configure your wireless network connection settings.

CHAPTER 3

Working with GNOME

Imagine a world of black screens with white text, or for those of you who remember, black screens with green text. That used to be the primary interface for users accessing computers. Computing has moved on significantly since then and has adopted the graphical user interface, or GUI, as standard on most desktop and workstation platforms.

Fedora is no different, and its primary window manager is called *GNOME (the Gnu Network Object Model Environment)*. Based on the ethos of simplicity by design, GNOME offers a rich and full interface that you can use easily to be productive. The principle design objectives include an intuitive system, meaning that it should be easy to pick up and use, as well as good localization/internationalization support and accessibility.

GNOME is founded upon the X Window System, the graphical networking interface found on many Linux distributions, which provides the basis for a wide range of graphical tools and window managers. More commonly known as just *X*, it can also be referred to as X11R7 and X11 (such as that found on Mac OS X). Coming from the world-renowned Massachusetts Institute of Technology, X has gone through several versions, each of which has extended and enhanced the technology. The open source implementation is managed by the X.Org foundation, the board of which is made up of several key figures from the open source world.

The best way to think about how X works is to see it as a client/server system. The X server provides services to programs that have been developed to make the most of the graphical and networking capabilities that are available under the server and in the supported libraries. X.Org provides versions for many different platforms, including Linux and Mac OS X. Originally implemented as XFree86,

X.Org was forked when a disagreement broke out over certain restrictions that were going to be included in the XFree86 license. Taking a snapshot of code that was licensed under the previous version of the license, X.Org drove forward with its own implementation based on the code. Almost in unison, most Linux distributions turned their back on XFree86 and switched their development and efforts to X.Org.

In this chapter, you learn how to work with GNOME and also the version of X that is included with Fedora. We look at the fundamentals of X and how to get X to work with any upgrades that might affect it, such as a new graphics card or that new flat-panel display you just bought. We also take a look at some of the other Window Managers that are included with Fedora, including KDE and Xfce.

The Red Hat and Fedora Desktop

If you have used earlier versions of Fedora and indeed Red Hat Linux, you will be more than aware of Bluecurve and perhaps also Clearlooks. Fedora has now settled on a consistent style throughout the whole distribution and has finally done away with the slightly older-looking Bluecurve icon set in favor of the Nodoka theme. KDE, another window manager you'll learn about later, has also received some polish, and the two window managers have a consistent look and feel.

The GNOME Desktop Environment

A desktop environment for X provides one or more window managers and a suite of clients that conform to a standard graphical interface, based on a common set of software libraries. When they are used to develop associated clients, these libraries provide graphical consistency for the client windows, menus, buttons, and other onscreen components, along with some common keyboard controls and client dialogs. The following sections discuss the primary desktop environment that is included with Fedora: GNOME.

The GNOME project, which was started in 1997, is the brainchild of programmer whiz Miguel de Icaza. GNOME provides a complete set of software libraries and clients. GNOME depends on a window manager that is GNOME-aware. This means that to provide a graphical desktop with GNOME elements, the window manager must be written to recognize and use GNOME. Some compliant window managers that are GNOME-aware include Havoc Pennington's `metacity` (the default GNOME window manager), Enlightenment, Compiz, Window Maker, and IceWM.

Fedora uses GNOME's user-friendly suite of clients to provide a consistent and user-friendly desktop. GNOME is a staple feature of Red Hat Enterprise Linux distribution and Fedora because Red Hat actively supports its development. GNOME clients are found under the `/usr/bin` directory, and GNOME configuration files are stored under the `/etc/GNOME` and `/usr/share/GNOME` directories, with user settings stored in the home directory under `.GNOME` and `GNOME2`.

A representative GNOME desktop, running the removable media preferences tool used for setting actions to events, is shown in Figure 3.1.

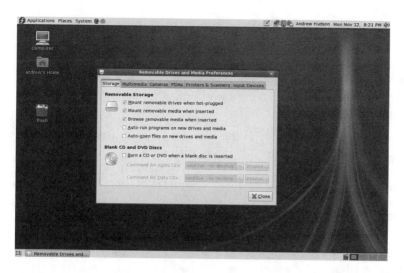

FIGURE 3.1   Fedora's GNOME desktop uses the *metacity* window manager and offers a selection of GNOME themes.

You can configure your desktop in various ways and by using different menu items under the Preferences menu, which can be found as part of the main Desktop menu. With the myriad configuration options, you can tailor every aspect of your system's look and feel. Figure 3.2 shows a selection of the Preferences options available to you.

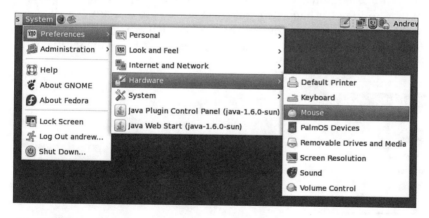

FIGURE 3.2   You can customize your Fedora desktop by using the Preferences settings that are available in the System, Preferences menu.

AIGLX—Eye Candy for the Masses

Recent development work carried out on X has allowed the introduction of a number of hardware-accelerated effects within Fedora and its window managers. No longer do you have to drool at your Mac OS X–using colleagues when they work; now Fedora has a whole load of "wow" effects designed to add that professional touch to Linux.

Up until recently, enabling these desktop effects has required a lot of work, including downloading specific packages and using the console to configure some of them. However, with Fedora 8, all of this has been done away with, and there is very little that you need to do to get access to the effects.

If you want the flashy effects, Fedora relies upon the alternate Compiz window manager, which to most end users does not appear any differently than `metacity`, the standard window manager in use by Fedora. You need to make sure you have the latest version of drivers for your graphics card/chipset; we cover this in Chapter 9, "Games."

> **NOTE**
>
> You might wonder why installation of graphics drivers is placed alongside information on games. For the most part, 3D acceleration is not a necessity if you are using Fedora for productivity only. However, if you are intending to work off a bit of aggression by blowing away some opponents in Unreal Tournament, you are going to need 3D acceleration enabled, and you need the specific graphics drivers for that.

After you have verified your graphic driver situation, you will find a menu option under System, Preferences, Look and Feel, called Desktop Effects (see Figure 3.3). Open it and select the option to Enable Desktop Effects. After a couple of seconds, you may see your window decorations (title bar, minimize and maximize buttons) disappear and then reappear. It may seem that nothing has happened, but check the box to activate Wobbly Windows and then grab hold of the window title bar and move it around. If everything has gone according to plan, it should wobble! Click Keep Settings to save the settings, and welcome to a world of fancy effects.

FIGURE 3.3   Use the Desktop Effects tool to set the scene for some snazzy 3D effects.

The "wobbly windows" are the most obvious effect, and it provides a fluid effect when you move your windows around the desktop area. Or if you hold down the Ctrl and Alt keys and press either the left or right cursor button, your desktop should move as if it is part of a cube, taking you from one virtual desktop to another.

This technology is still very much in its infancy, so expect great things in future versions!

Basic X Concepts

The underlying engine of X11 is the X protocol, which provides a system of managing displays on local and remote desktops. The protocol uses a client/server model that allows an abstraction of the drawing of client windows and other decorations locally and over a network. An X server draws client windows, dialog boxes, and buttons that are specific to the local hardware and in response to client requests. The client, however, does not have to be specific to the local hardware. This means that system administrators can set up a network with a large server and clients and enable users to view and use those clients on workstations with totally different CPUs and graphics displays.

> **NOTE**
>
> We couldn't think of a better way to demonstrate the capability of X to handle remote clients than by using its capabilities to produce this chapter. Although the OpenOffice.org file for this chapter resided on a Mac mini (running Fedora), the display and keyboard used were actually part of an Acer Ferrari notebook running Ubuntu 6.06 LTS, via an ethernet connection. Revisions were done with the Logitech keyboard and mouse of a desktop machine running Fedora 8, again connected to the Mac mini via X, but this time using a wireless connection.

Because X offers users a form of distributed processing, this means that Fedora can be used as a very cheap desktop platform for clients that connect to a powerful X server. The more powerful the X server, the larger the number of X-based clients that can be accommodated. This functionality can breathe new life into older hardware, pushing most of the graphical processing on to the server. A fast network is a must if you intend to run many X clients because X can become bandwidth-hungry.

X is hugely popular in the UNIX and Linux world for a variety of reasons. It supports nearly every hardware graphics system, and strong multiplatform programming standards give it a solid foundation of developers committed to X. Another key benefit of X is its networking capability, which plays a central point in administration of many desktops and can also assist in the deployment of a thin-client computing environment. The capability to launch applications on remote desktops and also standardize installations highlight the versatility of this powerful application.

More recent versions of X have also included support for shaped windows (that is, nonrectangular), graphical login managers (also known as *display managers*), and compressed fonts. Each release of X brings more features designed to enhance the user experience, including being able to customize how X client applications appear, right down to buttons and windows. Most office and home environments run Linux and X on their local machines. The more-enlightened companies and users harness the power of the networking features of X, enabling thin-client environments and allowing the use of customized desktops designed specifically for that company. Having applications launch from a single location makes the lives of system administrators a lot easier because they have to work on only one machine, not several.

Using X

X.Org 7.3 is the X server that is used with Fedora. The base Xorg distribution consists of 30 RPM packages (almost 120MB), which contain the server, along with support and development libraries, fonts, various clients, and documentation. An additional 1,000 or more X clients, fonts, and documentation are also included with Fedora.

> **NOTE**
>
> A full installation of X and related X.Org 7.3 files can consume more—usually much more—than 170MB of hard drive space. This happens because additional clients, configuration files, and graphics (such as icons) are under the /usr/bin and /usr/share directory trees. You can pare excessive disk requirements by judiciously choosing which X-related packages (such as games) to install on workstations. However, with the increased capacity of most desktop PC hard drives today, the size requirements are rarely a problem, except in configuring thin-client desktops or embedded systems.

The /usr directory and its subdirectories contain the majority of Xorg's software. Some important subdirectories are

- ► **/usr/bin**—This is the location of the X server and various X clients. (Note that not all X clients require active X sessions.)

- ► **/usr/include**—This is the path to the files necessary for developing X clients and graphics such as icons.

- ► **/usr/lib**—This directory contains required software libraries to support the X server and clients.

- ► **/usr/lib/X11**—This directory contains fonts, default client resources, system resources, documentation, and other files that are used during X sessions and for various X clients. You can also find a symbolic link to this directory, named X11, under the /usr/lib directory.

- ► **/usr/lib/modules**—This path to drivers and the X server modules used by the X server enables use of various graphics cards.

The main components required for an active local X session are installed on your system if you choose to use a graphical desktop. These components are the X server, miscellaneous fonts, a *terminal client* (that is, a program that provides access to a shell prompt), and a client known as a *window manager*. Window managers administer onscreen displays, including overlapping and tiling windows, command buttons, title bars, and other onscreen decorations and features.

Elements of the `xorg.conf` File

The most important file for Xorg is the `xorg.conf` configuration file, which can be located in the `/etc/X11` directory. This file contains configuration information that is vital for X to function correctly, and is usually created during the installation of Fedora. Should you need to change anything post-install, you should use the `system-config-display` application, which is covered later in this chapter. Information relating to hardware, monitors, graphics cards, and input devices is stored in the `xorg.conf` file, so be careful if you decide to tinker with it in a text editor!

Of course, we would not send you in blindly to edit such an important file. Let's take a look at the contents of the file so that you can get an idea of what X is looking for. The components, or sections, of the `xorg.conf` file specify the X session or *server layout*, along with pathnames for files that are used by the server, any options relating directly to the server, any optional support modules needed, information relating to the mouse and keyboard attached to the system, the graphics card installed, the monitor in use, and of course the resolution and color depth that Fedora uses. Of the 12 sections of the file, these are the essential components:

- ▶ **ServerLayout**—Defines the display, defines one or more screen layouts, and names input devices.

- ▶ **Files**—Defines the location of colors, fonts, or port number of the font server.

- ▶ **Module**—Tells the X server what graphics display support code modules to load.

- ▶ **InputDevice**—Defines the input devices, such as the keyboard and mouse; multiple devices can be used.

- ▶ **Monitor**—Defines the capabilities of any attached display; multiple monitors can be used.

- ▶ **Device**—Defines one or more graphics cards and specifies what optional features (if any) to enable or disable.

- ▶ **Screen**—Defines one or more resolutions, color depths, perhaps a default color depth, and other settings.

The following sections provide short descriptions of these elements; the `xorg.conf` man page contains full documentation of all the options and other keywords you can use to customize your desktop settings.

The `ServerLayout` Section

As noted previously, the `ServerLayout` section of the `xorg.conf` file defines the display and screen layouts, and it names the input devices. A typical `ServerLayout` section from an automatically configured `xorg.conf` file might look like this:

```
Section "ServerLayout"
        Identifier      "single head configuration"
        Screen      0   "Screen0" 0 0
```

```
        InputDevice     "Mouse0" "CorePointer"
        InputDevice     "Keyboard0" "CoreKeyboard"
        InputDevice     "DevInputMice" "AlwaysCore"
EndSection
```

In this example, a single display is used (the numbers designate the position of a screen), and two default input devices, Mouse0 and Keyboard0, are used for the session.

The Files Section

The Files section of the xorg.conf file might look like this:

```
Section "Files"
    RgbPath     "/usr/lib/X11/rgb"
    FontPath   "unix/:7100"
EndSection
```

This section lists available session colors (by name, in the text file rgb.txt) and the port number to the X font server. The font server, xfs, is started at boot time and does not require an active X session. If a font server is not used, the FontPath entry could instead list each font directory under the /usr/lib/X11/fonts directory, as in this example:

```
FontPath "/usr/lib/X11/fonts/100dpi"
FontPath "/usr/lib/X11/fonts/misc"
FontPath "/usr/lib/X11/fonts/75dpi"
FontPath "/usr/lib/X11/fonts/type1"
FontPath "/usr/lib/X11/fonts/Speedo"
...
```

These directories contain the default compressed fonts that are available for use during the X session. You configure the font server by using the file named config under the /etc/X11/fs directory. This file contains a listing, or catalog, of fonts for use by the font server. By adding an alternate-server entry in this file and restarting the font server, you can specify remote font servers for use during X sessions. This can help centralize font support and reduce local storage requirements (even though only 25MB is required for the almost 5,000 fonts installed with Fedora and X).

The Module Section

The Module section of the xorg.conf file specifies loadable modules or drivers to load for the X session. This section might look like this:

```
Section "Module"
        Load   "dbe"
        Load   "extmod"
        Load   "fbdevhw"
        Load "glx"
        Load "record"
```

```
        Load  "freetype"
        Load  "type1"
        Load  "dri"
EndSection
```

These modules can range from special video card support to font rasterizers. The modules are located in subdirectories under the /usr/lib/modules directory.

The InputDevice Section

The InputDevice section configures a specific device, such as a keyboard or mouse, as in this example:

```
Section "InputDevice"
        Identifier  "Keyboard0"
        Driver      "kbd"

        Option  "XkbModel"    "pc105"
        Option  "XkbLayout"   "us"
EndSection
Section "InputDevice"
        Identifier  "Mouse0"
        Driver      "mouse"
        Option      "Protocol" "IMPS/2"
        Option      "Device" "/dev/input/mice"
        Option      "ZAxisMapping" "4 5"
        Option      "Emulate3Buttons" "yes"
EndSection
```

You can configure multiple devices, and there might be multiple InputDevice sections. The preceding example specifies a basic keyboard and a two-button PS/2 mouse (actually, a Dell touchpad pointer). An InputDevice section that specifies use of a USB device could be used at the same time (to enable mousing with PS/2 and USB pointers) and might look like this:

```
Section "InputDevice"
        Identifier  "Mouse0"
        Driver      "mouse"
        Option      "Device" "/dev/input/mice"
        Option      "Protocol" "IMPS/2"
        Option      "Emulate3Buttons" "off"
        Option      "ZAxisMapping" "4 5"
EndSection
```

NOTE

If you change your computer's pointing device, you should then run Fedora's system-config-mouse client, which automatically updates your system's xorg.conf file.

CAUTION

From Fedora Core 3 onward, the location for the mouse device changed from /dev/mouse to /dev/input/mice. Unfortunately, when system-config-display writes the xorg.conf file, it sometimes gets a little confused and still maps the mouse to /dev/mouse rather than /dev/input/mice. This is where a little knowledge of vi comes in handy!

The Monitor Section

The Monitor section configures the designated display device as declared in the ServerLayout section, as shown in this example:

```
Section "Monitor"
        Identifier    "Monitor0"
        VendorName    "Monitor Vendor"
        ModelName     "Monitor Model"
        DisplaySize  300     220
        HorizSync    31.5-48.5
        VertRefresh 50-70
        Option "dpms"
EndSection
```

Note that the X server automatically determines the best video timings according to the horizontal and vertical sync and refresh values in this section. If required, old-style mode-line entries (used by distributions and servers prior to XFree86 4.0) might still be used. If the monitor is automatically detected when you configure X (see the "Configuring X" section later in this chapter), its definition and capabilities are inserted in your xorg.conf file from the MonitorsDB database. This database contains more than 600 monitors and is located in the /usr/share/hwdata directory.

The Device Section

The Device section provides details about the video graphics chipset used by the computer, as in this example:

```
Section "Device"
        Identifier    "Videocard0"
        Driver        "radeon"
        VendorName    "Videocard vendor"
        BoardName     "ATI Radeon Mobility M6"
EndSection
```

This example identifies an installed video card as using an ATI Mobility M6 graphics chipset. The Driver entry tells the Xorg server to load the radeon_drv.o module from the /usr/lib/modules/drivers directory. Different chipsets have different options. For example, here's the entry for a NeoMagic video chipset:

```
Section "Device"
        Identifier    "NeoMagic (laptop/notebook)"
        Driver        "neomagic"
        VendorName    "NeoMagic (laptop/notebook)"
        BoardName     "NeoMagic (laptop/notebook)"
    Option    "externDisp"
    Option    "internDisp"
EndSection
```

In this example, the Device section specifies the driver for the graphics card (neomagic_drv.o) and enables two chipset options (externDisp and internDisp) to allow display on the laptop's LCD screen and an attached monitor.

The Xorg server supports hundreds of different video chipsets. If you configure X11 but subsequently change the installed video card, you need to edit the existing Device section or generate a new xorg.conf file, using one of the X configuration tools discussed in this chapter, to reflect the new card's capabilities. You can find details about options for some chipsets in a companion man page. You should look at these sources for hints about optimizations and troubleshooting.

The Screen Section

The Screen section ties together the information from the previous sections (using the Screen0, Device, and Monitor Identifier entries). It can also specify one or more color depths and resolutions for the session. Here's an example:

```
Section "Screen"
        Identifier "Screen0"
        Device     "Videocard0"
        Monitor    "Monitor0"
        DefaultDepth    24
        SubSection "Display"
                Viewport   0 0
                Depth    16
                Modes    "1024x768" "800x600" "640x480"
        EndSubSection
EndSection
```

In this example, a color depth of thousands of colors and a resolution of 1024×768 is the default, with optional resolutions of 800×600 and 640×480. Multiple Display subsection entries with different color depths and resolutions (with settings such as Depth 24 for millions of colors) can be used if supported by the graphics card and monitor combination. You can also use a DefaultDepth entry (which is 24, or thousands of colors, in the example), along with a specific color depth to standardize display depths in installations.

You can also specify a desktop resolution larger than that supported by the hardware in your monitor or notebook display. This setting is known as a *virtual resolution* in the Display subsection. This allows, for example, an 800×600 display to pan (that is, slide around inside) a virtual window of 1024×768.

NOTE

If your monitor and graphics card support multiple resolutions and the settings are properly configured, you can use the key combination of Ctrl+Alt+Keypad+ or Ctrl+Alt+Keypad to change resolutions on-the-fly during your X session.

Configuring X

Although the Fedora installer can be used to configure X during installation, problems can arise if the PC's video card is not recognized. If you are unable to configure X during installation (refer to Chapter 1, "Installing Fedora"), do not specify booting to a graphical configuration and skip the X configuration portion of the installation. Note that some installs, such as for servers, don't require that X be configured for use to support active X sessions, but might require installation of X and related software to support remote users and clients.

You can use the following configuration tools, among others, to create a working xorg.conf file:

▶ **system-config-display**—This is Fedora's graphical configuration tool, which launches an X session to create an xorg.conf file.

▶ **Xorg**—The X server itself can create a skeletal working configuration.

The following sections discuss how to use each of these software tools to create a working xorg.conf file.

Configuring X with the system-config-display Client

You can use the system-config-display client to create or update an xorg.conf file. You can start by clicking the Display menu item found under System, Administration if you are already running X, but you can also begin, as root, by starting the client from the command line during a console session, like this:

```
# system-config-display
```

The screen clears, and system-config-display attempts to start an X session. If you start this client during an X session, its main window appears, as shown in Figure 3.4.

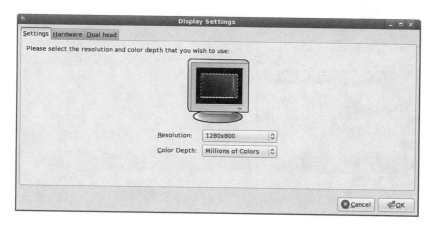

FIGURE 3.4   The `system-config-display` client provides a graphical configuration interface for creating or updating a system's `xorg.conf` file. Here you see the Display Settings main screen, offering resolution and color-depth settings.

The Display Settings main screen is a dialog showing the current monitor and video card settings (if configured). You can change the resolution (horizontal and vertical pixels) and color depth (number of supported colors) by clicking the specific drop-down menu that you want to alter. Click the OK or Cancel button to save or cancel any change.

If you click the Hardware tab, other configuration options become available, as shown in Figure 3.5.

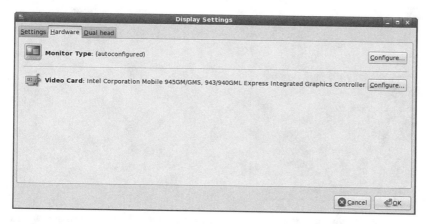

FIGURE 3.5   `system-config-display`'s Hardware settings are used to configure a monitor and video card (and multihead video card) for X11R7.

Click the Configure button in the Monitor Type area of the Hardware tab dialog to change your Monitor settings, as shown in Figure 3.6. You can use this dialog to configure a different monitor or to change current monitor settings.

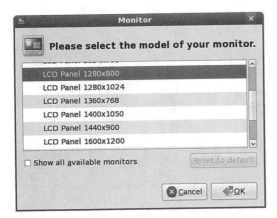

FIGURE 3.6   You can scroll to select a new monitor to use for your X sessions.

First, scroll through the list of monitor brands (from the MonitorDB database), and then click the small triangle to the left of the name of the manufacturer or type. You then see a list of model names. Click to select one, and when you have finished, click the OK button to use the new settings or click the Cancel button to abort changes.

To configure a video card, you can click the Video Card area's Configure button in the Hardware tab dialog. The Video Card dialog appears, as shown in Figure 3.7.

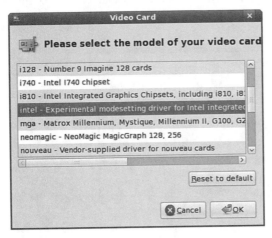

FIGURE 3.7   Use the Hardware tab's Video Card Configure button to choose a new video card for your X sessions.

You can scroll through the list of video cards. You can click one to select it, and when you have finished, click the OK button to finalize your selection.

If your video card supports the use of two or more monitors, you can use the Dual head tab to configure multiple monitor support. Xorg supports multiple displays, using a feature named Xinerama. This feature enables multiple monitors to appear as a single display, and each display can be located in any quadrant of a screen's layout.

To use Xinerama for your desktop sessions, you must start the Xorg server with its +xinerama option. Your xorg.conf file must also have proper settings, and each display must be capable of supporting identical color depth (usually 16bpp or thousands of colors). You can find details about using Xinerama with Xorg in the Xorg man page and in the Xinerama HOWTO at http://www.tldp.org/HOWTO/Xinerama-HOWTO/.

When you have finished your changes to your X server settings, click the OK button. You will then see a dialog advising that you have to log out and then log back in (or exit your X session and restart X) to use the new settings.

The new settings are stored in a new xorg.conf file under the /etc/X11 directory. If you find that the new settings do not work, you can simply copy the backup xorg.conf file named xorg.conf.backup to xorg-conf in the same directory to revert to your original settings.

Using Xorg to Configure X

You can create the xorg.conf file manually by typing one from scratch in a text editor, but you can also create one automatically by using the Xorg server or configuration utilities (as discussed in the previous sections). As the root operator, you can use the following on the server to create a test configuration file:

```
# X -configure
```

After you press Enter, a file named xorg.conf.new is created in root's home directory, the /root directory. You can then use this file for a test session, like this:

```
# X -config /root/xorg.conf.new
```

Starting X

You can start X sessions in a variety of ways. The Fedora installer sets up the system initialization table /etc/inittab to have Linux boot directly to an X session, using a *display manager* (that is, an X client that provides a graphical login). After you log in, you use a local session (running on your computer) or, if the system is properly configured, an X session running on a remote computer on the network. Logging in via a display manager requires you to enter a username and password. You can also start X sessions from the command line. The following sections describe these two methods.

Using a Display Manager

An X display manager presents a graphical login that requires a username and password to be entered before access is granted to the X desktop. It also allows you to choose a different desktop for your X session. Whether an X display manager is presented after you boot Linux is controlled by a *runlevel*—a system state entry in /etc/inittab. The following runlevels are defined in the file:

```
# 0 - halt (Do NOT set initdefault to this)
# 1 - Single user mode
# 2 - Multiuser, without NFS (The same as 3, if you do not have networking)
# 3 - Full multiuser mode
# 4 - unused
# 5 - X11
# 6 - reboot (Do NOT set initdefault to this)
```

Runlevel 5 is used for multiuser mode with a graphical X login via a display manager; booting to runlevel 3 provides a console, or text-based, login. The initdefault setting in the /etc/inittab file determines the default runlevel:

```
id:5:initdefault:
```

In this example, Linux boots and then runs X.

The default display manager might also be specified in /etc/inittab, as follows:

```
x:5:respawn:/usr/bin/xdm -nodaemon
```

However, Fedora uses a shell script named prefdm, found under the /etc/X11 directory, to set the display manager:

```
x:5:respawn:/etc/X11/prefdm -nodaemon
```

According to this script, the display manager is based on the file named desktop under the /etc/sysconfig directory. The words GNOME, KDE, and XDM following a DESKTOP= entry determine what display manager is used for login. The following sections describe how to configure the three most commonly used display managers: gdm, kdm, and xdm.

Configuring gdm

The gdm display manager is part of the GNOME library and client distribution included with Fedora, and it provides a graphical login when a system boots directly to X. Its login (which is actually displayed by the gdmlogin client) hosts pop-up menus of window managers, languages, and system options for shutting down (halting) or rebooting the workstation. Although you can edit (as root) gdm.conf under the /etc/X11/gdm directory to configure gdm, a much better way to configure GNOME's display manager is to use the gdmsetup client.

You can use the gdmsetup client to configure many aspects of how GDM appears and behaves. You launch this client from the GNOME System menu, under Administration, Login Window.

When gdmsetup loads, you'll see the GDM Setup window, as shown in Figure 3.8.

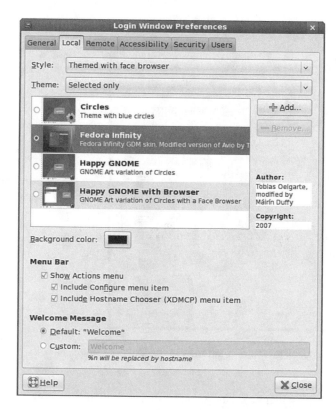

FIGURE 3.8   You use *gdmsetup* to configure the *gdmlogin* screen when using *gdm* as a display manager.

You can specify settings for security, remote network logins, the X server, and session and session chooser setup by clicking the tabs in the GDM Setup dialog.

Configuring kdm

The kdm client, which is part of KDE (which is covered later in this chapter), offers a graphical login similar to gdm. You configure kdm by running the KDE Control Center client kcontrol, as the root operator, which you do by clicking the Control Center menu item from the KDE kicker or desktop panel menu.

In the Index tab of the left pane of the KDE Control Center window, you click the System Administration menu item to open its contents, and then you click the Login Manager menu item. The right pane of the Control Center window displays the tabs and configuration options for the kdm Login Manager, as shown in Figure 3.9.

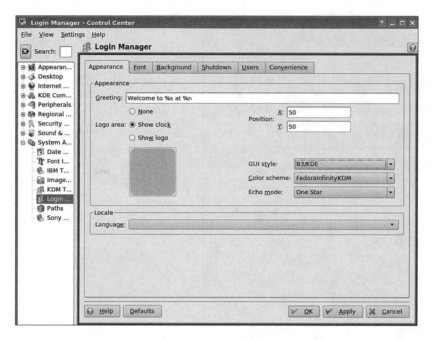

FIGURE 3.9   You configure *kdm* by choosing tabs and settings in the Control Center dialog box.

To make any changes to the KDE display manager while logged in as a regular user, you must first click the Administrator Mode button, and then enter the root operator password. You can click a tab in the Control Center dialog to set configuration options. Options in these tabs enable you to control the login display, prompts, user icons, session management, and configuration of system options (for shutting down or rebooting). After you make your configuration choices in each tab, click the Apply button to apply the changes immediately; otherwise, the changes are applied when the X server restarts.

Using the xdm Display Manager

The xdm display manager is part of the Xorg distribution and offers a bare-bones login for using X. Although it is possible to configure xdm by editing various files under the /etc/X11/xdm directory, GNOME and KDE offer a greater variety of options in display manager settings. The default xdm login screen's display is handled by the xsetroot client, which is included with Xorg, and Owen Taylor's xsri client, as specified in the file Xsetup_0 in the xdm directory under /etc/X11. The xsri client can be used to set the background color of the login display's desktop and to place an image in the initial display.

Starting X from the Console by Using startx

If you have Fedora set to boot to runlevel 3, a text-based console login, you can start an X session from the command line. You use the startx command (which is actually a shell script) to do so. You launch the X server and an X session by using startx, like this:

```
$ startx
```

startx first looks in your home directory for a file named .xinitrc. This file can contain settings that will launch an alternative desktop and X clients for your X session. The default system .xinitrc is found in the /etc/X11/xinit directory, but a local file can be used instead to customize an X session and launch default clients.

Using a custom .xinitrc is not necessary if you're using Fedora's desktop, which runs X and either a GNOME-aware window manager or KDE as a desktop environment.

You can also use the startx command with one or more command-line options. These options are passed to the X server before it launches an X session. For example, you can use startx to specify a color depth for an X session by using the -depth option, followed by a number such as 8, 16, 24, or 32 for 256, thousands, or millions of colors (as defined in the X configuration file and if supported). Using different color depths can be useful during development for testing how X clients look on different displays, or to conserve use of video memory, such as when trying to get the highest resolution (increased color depth can sometimes affect the maximum resolution of older video cards).

For example, to start a session with thousands of colors, you use the startx command like this:

```
$ startx -- -depth 16
```

Another option that can be passed is a specific *dots per inch (dpi)* resolution that is to be used for the X session. For example, to use 100dpi, you use the -dpi option followed by 100, like this:

```
$ startx -- -dpi 100
```

You can also use startx to launch multiple X sessions. This feature comes as a result of Fedora's support for *virtual consoles*, or multiple text-based displays. To start the first X session, you use the startx command followed by a *display number*, or an X server instance (the first is 0, using screen 0) and a number that represents a virtual console. The default console used for X is number 7, so you can start the session like this:

```
$ startx -- :0 vt7
```

After X starts and the window manager appears, you press Ctrl+Alt+F2 and then log in again at the prompt. Next, you start another X session like this, specifying a different display number and virtual console:

```
$ startx -- :1 vt8
```

Another X session starts. To jump to the first X session, press Ctrl+Alt+F7. You use Ctrl+Alt+F8 to return to the second session. If you exit the current session and go to another text-based login or shell, you use Alt+F7 or Alt+F8 to jump to the desired session.

Using startx is a flexible way to launch X sessions, but multiple sessions can be confusing, especially to new users, and are a horrific resource drain on a system that does not have enough CPU horsepower and memory. A better approach is to use multiple workspaces, also known as *virtual desktops*, as discussed in the following section.

Using Fedora's switchdesk Client

You can use Fedora's switchdesk client to change the default window manager or desktop environment such as GNOME or KDE. Most desktop environments also include the capability to save a session *state* (such as running applications, the applications' window sizes and positions, and so on), using a feature known as *session management.*

You can also use the switchdesk utility when running X or at a text-based console, along with a keyword (such as GNOME or KDE), to set the default X desktop before launching X. For example, to specify that you want to use the KDE desktop environment as the default, you use switchdesk like this:

```
$ switchdesk KDE
Red Hat Linux switchdesk 4.0
Copyright (C) 1999-2004 Red Hat, Inc
Redistributable under the terms of the GNU General Public License
Desktop now set up to run KDE.
For system defaults, remove /home/andrew/.Xclients
```

This example shows that the default X session will now use KDE. Settings are saving in the file named .Xclients in the home directory. You can launch switchdesk during an X session by clicking the Desktop Switching Tool menu item from the System, Preferences menu. You get a graphical dialog offering a choice of window managers for X sessions (depending on the window managers that are installed on the system), as shown in Figure 3.10.

FIGURE 3.10   You use *switchdesk* to set the default window manager for X sessions.

Choosing a window manager is a matter of preference, necessity, or policy. You might prefer to use one of the other window managers—such as the *Tab Window Manager* (twm) or Xfce—on legacy PCs because they have lower system resource requirements (that is, they require less hard drive space, CPU horsepower, and system memory). Newer desktop environments require 256MB or even more memory for good performance. The following sections describe some of the most popular window managers and their uses.

KDE—The Other Environment

One of the great things about Fedora is the choice it gives you. For many years, GNOME has been the desktop environment of choice for Fedora. However, with Fedora 8 you can now download a Live CD variant of Fedora that allows you to use the K Desktop Environment, or KDE for short.

KDE is somewhat different from GNOME in that it uses the QT libraries rather than GTK libraries, so the windows and other elements look different. Linus Torvalds himself expressed a distinct preference for KDE, and it also helps that KDE allows you to customize your working environment in pretty much any way imaginable.

If you used the DVD supplied with this book to install Fedora and did not choose to customize your installation, you need to use Applications, Add/Remove Software to select the base packages for KDE.

Figure 3.11 shows a standard KDE desktop.

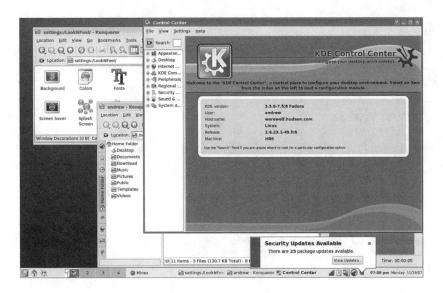

FIGURE 3.11   Unlimited customization options abound within KDE; just be prepared to switch!

Fedora uses GNOME by default, but you can use the `switchdesk` utility as described in the previous section to move to KDE. Alternatively, you can use the Options button on the login screen, click Select Session, and choose KDE. When you log in, you are prompted whether you want to use KDE as your default environment or just for this session. If you are dipping your toes into the water, we suggest using the one-time-only option.

Xfce

Xfce is another desktop environment, suitable for computers with not much memory or processing power. It's based on the same GTK libraries that are in use by GNOME, so it shares some of the look and feel of the GNOME desktop. That said, it comes bundled with a number of Xfce-specific applications to replace GNOME tools such as nautilus.

Some people just prefer the simplicity of Xfce, so we leave it up to you if you want to use it. You can access it in the same way as KDE (described previously) and a sample desktop is shown in Figure 3.12.

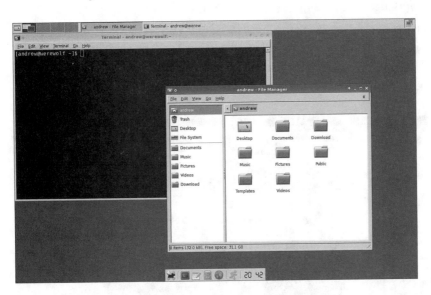

FIGURE 3.12   Xfce—lightweight and simplicity, molded together in a great package.

Related Fedora and Linux Commands

You can use these commands to create and configure the X Window System in Fedora:

▶ **Xorg**—The X server that is provided with the X Window System distribution from The X.Org Foundation

▶ **mouseconfig**—Fedora's text-based GUI pointing-device configuration program

▶ **kcontrol**—The KDE Control Center client

▶ **system-config-display**—Fedora's graphical X11R7 configuration tool

▶ **system-config-mouse**—Fedora's graphical mouse configuration tool

▶ **gdmsetup**—The GNOME display manager configuration client

▶ **startx**—A shell script used to start one or more X sessions from the shell command line

▶ **xsri**—A display manager root desktop decoration client

Reference

▶ http://www.x.org/—Curators of the X Window System.

▶ http://www.x.org/Downloads_mirror.html—Want to download the source to the latest revision of X? Start at this list of mirror sites.

▶ http://www.xfree86.org/—Home of the XFree86 Project, Inc., which has provided a graphical interface for Linux for nearly 10 years.

▶ http://www.kde.org/—The place to get started when learning about KDE and the latest developments.

▶ http://www.gnome.org/—The launch point for more information about GNOME, links to new clients, and GNOME development projects.

▶ http://people.redhat.com/~hp/metacity/—Havoc Pennington's metacity download page, where you can get the latest full-source version of this window manager.

▶ http://sawmill.sourceforge.net/—The home page for the sawfish window manager (formerly called sawmill).

▶ http://www.windowmaker.org/—The source for the latest version of Window Maker.

▶ http://www.icewm.org/—IceWM's home page.

▶ http://www.lesstif.org/—The home page of the LessTif project, which aims to provide GNU GPL versions of OSF/Motif-compatible software libraries.

▶ http://scwm.sourceforge.net/—The home page of a lightweight, yet virtual desktop-enabled window manager.

▶ http://www.fvwm.org/—The home page for FVWM2, where you can download the latest version.

▶ http://www.novell.com/products/desktop/—The place to get started with Ximian GNOME.

CHAPTER 4

Command-Line Quick Start

The command line is one of the most powerful tools available for use with Fedora, and indeed Linux. Knowledge of the commands associated with it and how to string them together will make working with Fedora that much easier, particularly if you are having a problem getting X to work.

This chapter looks at some of the basic commands that you need to know to be productive at the command line. You will find out how to get to the command line, and also get to grips with some of the commands used to navigate around the file system. Later on in this book is the "Command-Line Master Class" (Chapter 32), which explores the subject in more depth.

Understanding the Command Line

Hang around Linux users for any length of time and it won't be long before you hear them speak in hushed tones about the command line or the terminal. Quite rightly, too, because the command line offers a unique and powerful way to interact with Linux. However, for the most part, you may never need to access the command line because Fedora offers a variety of graphical tools that enable you to configure most things on your system.

But this is the real world, and sometimes things go wrong, meaning that you might not always have the luxury of a graphical interface to work with. It is in these situations that a fundamental understanding of the command line and its uses can be a real life saver.

It's tempting to think of the command line as the product of some sort of black and arcane art, and in some ways it can appear to be extremely difficult to use. By the end of this chapter, you should at least be comfortable with using the command line and ready to move on to Chapter 32.

More important, however, you will be able to make your way around a command line–based system, which you are likely to encounter if you work within a server environment.

This chapter introduces you to a number of commands, including commands that enable you to do the following tasks:

- ▶ **Perform routine tasks**—Logging in and out, using the text console, changing passwords, listing and navigating directories

- ▶ **Carry out basic file management**—Creating files and folders, copying or moving them around the file system, renaming and ultimately deleting them (if necessary)

- ▶ **Execute basic system management**—Shutting down or rebooting, reading man pages, and using text-based tools to edit system configuration files

The information in this chapter is valuable for individual users or system administrators who are new to Linux and are learning to use the command line for the first time.

TIP

Those of you who have used a computer for many years will probably have come into contact with MS-DOS, in which case being presented with a black screen will fill you with a sense of nostalgia. Do not get too comfy; the command line in Linux is far superior to its distant MS-DOS cousin. Whereas MS-DOS skills are transferable only to other MS-DOS environments, the skills that you learn at the Linux command line can be transferred easily to other UNIX-like operating systems, such as Solaris, OpenBSD, FreeBSD, and even Mac OS X (because it allows you access to a terminal).

Security

One concept you will have to get used to is that of user-based security. By and large, only two types of users will access the system as actual users. The first type is the regular user, of which you created one when you started Fedora for the first time (see Chapter 1, "Installing Fedora"). These users can change anything that is specific to them, such as the wallpaper on the desktop, their personal preferences, and so on. These users are prevented from making changes that will affect other users than themselves, sometimes called systemwide changes.

To make systemwide changes, you need to use the super-user or root account. This is a special-access privilege that gives you complete control over the entire system, with the ability to destroy everything should you so want. If you have installed Linux on your own PC, you automatically have access to the root account as you set it up during the installation. However, it is not unusual for users to not have any access to the root user, especially in corporate environments where security and system stability are of paramount importance.

An example of the destructive nature of root can be found in the age-old example of #rm -rf /, which erases all the data on your hard drive. You need to be especially careful when working as root; otherwise, you might irreparably damage your system.

Don't let this worry you, however, because the root user is fundamental to a healthy Linux system. Without it you would not be able to install new software, edit system configuration files, or do any number of administration tasks. By the end of this chapter, you will feel comfortable working as root and be able to adequately administer your system.

As with most things, Fedora offers you a number of ways to access the command line. You can use the terminal entry in Applications, System Tools, but by far the simplest way is to press Ctrl+Alt+F1. Fedora switches to a black screen and a traditional login prompt that resembles the following:

```
Fedora Release 8 (Werewolf)
Kernel 2.6.23-0.217.fc8 on an i686
fedora login:
```

TIP

This is actually one of six virtual consoles that Fedora provides for your use. After you have accessed a virtual console, you can use the Alt key and F1 through F6 to switch to a different console. If you want to get back to the graphical interface, press Alt+F7. You can also switch between consoles by holding the Alt key and pressing either the left or the right cursor key to move down or up a console, such as vt1 to vt2.

Fedora is waiting for you to log in as a user, so go ahead and enter your username and press the Return key. Fedora then prompts you for your password, which you should enter. Note that Fedora does not show any characters while you are typing your password in. This is a good thing because it prevents any shoulder surfers from seeing what you've typed or the length of the password.

Pressing the Return key drops you to a shell prompt, signified by the dollar sign:

```
andrew@fedora ~]$
```

This particular prompt tells me that I am logged in as the user andrew on the system fedora and I am currently in my home directory. (Linux uses the tilde as shorthand for the home directory.)

TIP

Navigating through the system at the command line can get confusing at times, especially when a directory name occurs in several different places. Fortunately, Linux includes a simple command that tells you exactly where you are in the file system. It's easy to remember because the command is just an abbreviation of present working directory, so type **pwd** at any point to get the full path of your location. For example, typing pwd after following these instructions shows /home/yourusername, meaning that you are currently in your home directory.

Using the pwd command can save you a lot of frustration when you have changed directory half a dozen times and have lost track.

Another way to quickly access the terminal is to go to Applications, Accessories and choose the Terminal entry. Fedora opens up gnome-terminal, which allows you to access the terminal while remaining in Gnome. This time, the terminal appears as black text on a white background. You can choose to access the terminal this way, or by using the Ctrl+Alt+F1 route; either way you will get to the same place.

Navigating Through the File System

Use the cd command to navigate through the Fedora file system. This command is generally used with a specific directory location or pathname, like this:

```
$ cd /usr/share/doc
```

Under Fedora, the cd command can also be used with several shortcuts. For example, to quickly move up to the *parent* (higher-level) directory, use the cd command like this:

```
$ cd ..
```

To return to one's home directory from anywhere in the Linux file system, use the cd command like this:

```
$ cd
```

You can also use the $HOME shell environment variable to accomplish the same thing. Type this command and press Enter to return to your home directory:

```
$ cd $HOME
```

You can accomplish the same thing by using the tilde (~) like this:

```
$ cd ~
```

CAUTION

Don't forget the pwd command to remind you where you are within the file system!

Another important command to use is the `ls` command, which lists the contents of the current directory. It's commonly used by itself, but a number of options (or switches) available for `ls` give you more information. For instance, the following command returns a listing of all the files and directories within the current directory, including any hidden files (denoted by a . prefix) as well as a full listing, so it will include details such as the permissions, owner and group, size, and last modified time and date:

```
$ ls -al
```

You can also issue the following command:

```
$ ls -R
```

This command scans and lists all the contents of the subdirectories of the current directory. This might be a lot of information, so you might want to redirect the output to a text file so that you can browse through it at your leisure by using the following:

```
$ ls alR > listing.txt
```

Table 4.1 shows some of the standard directories found in Fedora.

TABLE 4.1   Basic Linux Directories

Name	Description
/	The root directory
/bin	Essential commands
/boot	Boot loader files, Linux kernel
/dev	Device files
/etc	System configuration files
/home	User home directories
/initrd	Initial RAM disk boot support (used during boot time)
/lib	Shared libraries, kernel modules
/lost+found	Directory for recovered files (if found after a file system check)
/media	Mount point for removable media, such as DVDs and floppy disks
/mnt	Usual mount point for local, remote file systems
/opt	Add-on software packages
/proc	Kernel information, process control
/root	Super user (root home)
/sbin	System commands (mostly root only)
/selinux	Holds the data for SELinux, the security component of Fedora
/sys	Real-time information on devices used by the kernel
/tmp	Temporary files
/usr	Secondary software file hierarchy
/var	Variable data (such as logs); spooled files

Some of the important directories in Table 4.1, such as those containing user and root commands or system configuration files, are discussed in the following sections. You use and edit files under these directories when you use Fedora.

Linux also includes a number of GNU commands you can use to search the file system. These include the following:

▶ **whereis command**—Returns the location of the command and its man page.

▶ **whatis command**—Returns a one-line synopsis from the command's man page.

▶ **locate file command**—Returns locations of all matching file(s); an extremely fast method of searching your system because locate searches a database containing an index of all files on your system. However, this database (about 4MB in size and named slocate.db, under the /var/lib/slocate directory) is built daily at 4:20 a.m. by default, and does not contain pathnames to files created during the workday or in the evening. If you do not keep your machine on constantly, you can run the updatedb command as the super user to manually start the building of the database.

▶ **apropos subject command**—Returns a list of commands related to subject.

Managing Files with the Shell

Managing files in your home directory involves using one or more easily remembered commands. If you have any familiarity with the now-ancient DOS, you recognize some of these commands (although their names differ from those you remember). Basic file management operations include paging (reading), moving, renaming, copying, searching, and deleting files and directories. These commands include the following:

▶ **cat *filename***—Outputs contents of filename to display

▶ **less *filename***—Allows scrolling while reading contents of filename

▶ **mv *file1 file2***—Renames *file1* to *file2*

▶ **mv *file dir***—Moves file to specified directory

▶ **cp *file1 file2***—Copies *file1* and creates *file2*

▶ **rm *file***—Deletes file

▶ **rmdir *dir***—Deletes directory (if empty)

▶ **grep *string file(s)***—Searches through files(s) and displays lines containing matching string

Note that each of these commands can be used with pattern-matching strings known as *wildcards* or *expressions*. For example, to delete all files in the current directory beginning with the letters abc, you can use an expression beginning with the first three letters of the desired filenames. An asterisk (*) is then appended to match all these files. Use a command line with the rm command like this:

```
$ rm abc*
```

Linux shells recognize many types of filenaming wildcards, but this is different from the capabilities of Linux commands supporting the use of more complex expressions. You learn more about using wildcards in Chapter 11, "Automating Tasks."

> **NOTE**
>
> Learn more about using expressions by reading the ex or grep manual pages.

Working with Compressed Files

Another file management operation is compression and decompression of files, or the creation, listing, and expansion of file and directory archives. Linux distributions usually include several compression utilities you can use to create, compress, expand, or list the contents of compressed files and archives. These commands include the following:

- ▶ **bunzip2**—Expands a compressed file
- ▶ **bzip2**—Compresses or expands files and directories
- ▶ **gunzip**—Expands a compressed file
- ▶ **gzip**—Compresses or expands files and directories
- ▶ **shar file**—Creates a shell archive of files
- ▶ **tar**—Creates, expands, or lists the contents of compressed or uncompressed file or directory archives known as *tape archives* or *tarballs*

Most of these commands are easy to use. The tar command, however, has a somewhat complex (although capable) set of command-line options and syntax. Even so, you can quickly learn to use tar by remembering a few simple invocations on the command line. For example, to create a compressed archive of a directory, use tar's czf options like this:

```
$ tar czf dirname.tgz dirname
```

The result is a compressed archive (a file ending in .tgz) of the specified directory (and all files and directories under it). Add the letter v to the preceding options to view the list of files added during compression and archiving. To list the contents of the compressed archive, substitute the c option with the letter t, as follows:

```
$ tar tzf archive
```

Of course, if many files are in the archive, a better invocation (to easily read or scroll through the output) is the following:

```
$ tar tzf archive ¦ less
```

To expand the contents of a compressed archive, use tar's zxf options, like so:

```
$ tar zxf archive
```

The tar utility decompresses the specified archive and extracts the contents in the current directory.

Use Essential Commands from the /bin and /sbin Directories

The /bin directory (about 5MB if you do a full install) contains essential commands used by the system for running and booting Linux. In general, only the root operator uses the commands in the /sbin directory. Many (though not all) of these commands are *statically* linked; which means that these commands do not depend on software libraries residing under the /lib or /usr/lib directories. Nearly all the other applications on your system are *dynamically* linked—meaning that they require external software libraries (also known as *shared* libraries) to run.

Use and Edit Files in the /etc Directory

More than 90MB of system configuration files and directories reside under the /etc directory if you install all the software included with this book. Some major software packages, such as Apache, OpenSSH, and xinetd, have directories of configuration files under /etc. Other important system-related configuration files in /etc include the following:

▶ **fstab**—The file system table is a text file listing each hard drive, CD-ROM, floppy, or other storage device attached to your PC. The table indexes each device's partition information with a place in your Linux file system (directory layout) and lists other options for each device when used with Linux (see Chapter 35, "Managing the File System"). Nearly all entries in fstab can be manipulated by root using the mount command.)

▶ **inittab**—The system initialization table defines the default runlevel, also known as *run-control* level or *system state*. Changes to this file can determine whether your system boots to a graphical or text login, as well as whether dialup remote access is enabled. (You learn about default runlevels in the section "System Services and Runlevels" located in Chapter 11. See the section "Starting X" located in Chapter 3, "Working with GNOME," to learn more about changing inittab to boot to a graphical interface.)

▶ **modprobe.conf**—This configuration file contains directions and options used when loading kernel modules to enable various types of hardware, such as sound, USB, networking, and so on (discussed in the section "Managing Modules" in Chapter 36, "Kernel and Module Management"). The contents of this file are used during boot time, and the file can be manually edited or automatically updated by Fedora's kudzu hardware management tool.

▶ **passwd**—The list of users for the system, along with user account information. The contents of this file can be changed by various programs, such as useradd or chsh.

▶ **printcap**—The system's printer capabilities database (discussed in the section "Overview of Fedora Printing" in Chapter 8, "Printing with Fedora").

▶ **shells**—A list of approved shells (command-line interfaces).

The /etc/sysconfig directory contains many different hardware and software settings critical to the operation of your Fedora system. Knowing the location and contents of these files can prove helpful if you need to troubleshoot new hardware configurations. The best way to list the contents of /etc/sysconfig is to use the tree command, like so:

```
$ tree -afx /etc/sysconfig
```

The settings in various files under /etc/sysconfig (such as firstboot, keyboard, clock, and so on) are usually created automatically by a related Fedora graphical or console-based configuration utility.

These contents might change dynamically if you use the kudzu hardware configuration service. The kudzu service also prompts you at boot time to remove, configure, or ignore a related setting if kudzu detects new or different hardware (such as a new USB keyboard, network card, or monitor). The kudzu service creates a file called hwconf that contains a hardware profile of your PC's current state. Note that if kudzu is not enabled or running, you can use device-specific configuration utilities such as system-config-keyboard, or you can manually edit configuration files.

Information about the type of keyboard attached to the PC, for example, is contained in the file /etc/sysconfig/keyboard:

```
KEYBOARDTYPE="pc"
KEYTABLE="uk"
```

Here the keyboard in use is the U.K. layout, but if you are in the United States, you will likely see this:

```
KEYBOARDTYPE="pc"
KEYTABLE="us"
```

CAUTION

If you are new to Linux, the system-config-keyboard client is the best tool to use to configure a keyboard. You should manually edit system hardware configuration files used by graphical management clients only as a last resort.

Protect the Contents of User Directories—/home

The most important data on a Linux system resides in the user's directories, found under the /home directory. Segregating the system and user data can be helpful in preventing data loss and making the process of backing up easier. For example, having user data reside on a separate file system or mounted from a remote computer on the network might help shield users from data loss in the event of a system hardware failure.

Use the Contents of the /proc Directory to Interact with the Kernel

The content of the /proc directory is created from memory and exists only while Linux is running. This directory contains special "files" that either extract information from or send information to the kernel. Many Linux utilities extract information from dynamically created directories and files under this directory, also known as a *virtual file system*. For example, the free command obtains its information from a file named meminfo:

```
$ free
             total       used       free     shared    buffers     cached
Mem:        1026320     822112     204208          0      41232     481412
-/+ buffers/cache:      299468     726852
Swap:       2031608          0    2031608
```

This information constantly changes as the system is used. You can get the same information by using the cat command to see the contents of the meminfo file:

$ cat /proc/meminfo

```
MemTotal:      1026320 kB
MemFree:        204200 kB
Buffers:         41252 kB
Cached:         481412 kB
SwapCached:          0 kB
Active:         307232 kB
Inactive:       418224 kB
HighTotal:      122692 kB
HighFree:          244 kB
LowTotal:       903628 kB
LowFree:        203956 kB
SwapTotal:     2031608 kB
SwapFree:      2031608 kB
Dirty:               0 kB
Writeback:           0 kB
AnonPages:      202804 kB
Mapped:          87864 kB
Slab:            21736 kB
SReclaimable:    12484 kB
```

```
SUnreclaim:         9252 kB
PageTables:         5060 kB
NFS_Unstable:          0 kB
Bounce:                0 kB
CommitLimit:     2544768 kB
Committed_AS:     712024 kB
VmallocTotal:     114680 kB
VmallocUsed:        6016 kB
VmallocChunk:     108148 kB
HugePages_Total:       0
HugePages_Free:        0
HugePages_Rsvd:        0
Hugepagesize:       4096 kB
```

The /proc directory can also be used to dynamically alter the behavior of a running Linux kernel by "echoing" numeric values to specific files under the /proc/sys directory. For example, to "turn on" kernel protection against one type of *denial-of-service (DoS)* attack known as *SYN flooding*, use the echo command to send the number 1 (one) to the following /proc path:

```
# echo 1 >/proc/sys/net/ipv4/tcp_syncookies
```

> **NOTE**
>
> The Linux kernel has a number of built-in protections, but good system administration security policies and a secure firewall protecting your gateway, router, or Internet-connected system are the best protection you can use. See Chapter 30, "Securing Your Machines," for an overview of firewalling and examples of how to implement network security tools included with Fedora.

Other ways to use the /proc directory include

▶ Getting CPU information, such as the family, type, and speed from /proc/cpuinfo.

▶ Viewing important networking information under /proc/net, such as active interfaces information under /proc/net/dev, routing information in /proc/net/route, and network statistics in /proc/net/netstat.

▶ Retrieving file system information.

▶ Reporting media mount point information via USB; for example, the Linux kernel reports what device to use to access files (such as /dev/sda) if a USB camera or hard drive is detected on the system. You can use the dmesg command to see this information.

▶ Getting the kernel version in /proc/version, performance information such as uptime in /proc/uptime, or other statistics such as CPU load, swap file usage, and processes in /proc/stat.

Work with Shared Data in the /usr Directory

The /usr directory (nearly 3GB in size if you do a default install) contains software applications, libraries, and other types of shared data for use by anyone on the system. Many Linux system administrators give /usr its own partition. A number of subdirectories under /usr contain the X Window System (/usr/bin), manual pages (/usr/share/man), software package shared files (/usr/share/*name_of_package*, such as /usr/share/emacs), additional application or software package documentation (/usr/share/doc), and an entire subdirectory tree of locally built and installed software, /usr/local.

Temporary File Storage in the /tmp Directory

As its name implies, the /tmp directory is used for temporary file storage; as you use Linux, various programs create files in this directory. The /tmp directory is cleaned of stale files each day by the tmpwatch command. (A stale file is any file not used after 10 days.) Settings in your system's scheduling table, /etc/crontab, configure Fedora by default to use tmpwatch to check /tmp each day.

Access Variable Data Files in the /var Directory

The /var directory contains subdirectories used by various system services for spooling and logging. Many of these variable data files, such as print spooler queues, are temporary, whereas others, such as system and kernel logs, are renamed and rotated in use. Incoming electronic mail is usually directed to files under /var/spool/mail.

Linux also uses /var for other important system services. These include the topmost *File Transfer Protocol (FTP)* directory under /var/ftp (see Chapter 20, "Remote File Serving with FTP"), and the Apache web server's initial home page directory for the system, /var/www/html. (See Chapter 17, "Apache Web Server Management," for more information on using Apache.)

Logging In to and Working with Linux

You can access and use a Linux system in a number of ways. One way is at the console with a monitor, keyboard, and mouse attached to the PC. Another way is via a serial console, either by dialup via a modem or a PC running a terminal emulator and connected to the Linux PC via a null modem cable. You can also connect to your system through a wired or wireless network, using the telnet or ssh commands. The information in this section shows you how to access and use the Linux system, using physical and remote text-based logins.

> **NOTE**
>
> This chapter focuses on text-based logins and use of Linux. Graphical logins and using a graphical desktop are described in Chapter 3.

Text-Based Console Login

If you sit down at your PC and log in to a Linux system that has not been booted to a graphical login, you see a prompt similar to this one:

```
Fedora release 8 (Werewolf)
Kernel 2.6.23-1.217_fc8 on an i686

login:
```

Your prompt might vary, depending on the version of Fedora you are using. In any event, at this prompt, type in your username and press Enter. When you are prompted for your password, type it in and press Enter.

> **NOTE**
>
> Note that your password is not echoed back to you, which is a good idea. Why is it a good idea? Well, people are prevented from looking over your shoulder and seeing how many characters are on your screen. It is not difficult to guess that a five-letter password might correspond to the user's spouse's first name!

Logging Out

Use the `exit` or `logout` commands to exit your session. Type the command and press Enter. You are then returned to the login prompt. If you use virtual consoles, remember to exit each console before leaving your PC. (Otherwise, someone could easily sit down and use your account.)

Logging In and Out from a Remote Computer

Although you can happily log in on your computer, an act known as a *local* login, you can also log in to your computer via a network connection from a remote computer. Linux-based operating systems provide a number of remote access commands you can use to log in to other computers on your *local area network (LAN)*, *wide area network (WAN)*, or the Internet. Note that not only must you have an account on the remote computer, but the remote computer must be configured to support remote logins—otherwise, you won't be able to log in.

> **NOTE**
>
> See Chapter 14, "Networking," to see how to set up network interfaces with Linux to support remote network logins and Chapter 11 to see how to start remote access services (such as sshd).

The best and most secure way (barring future exploits) to log in to a remote Linux computer is to use the ssh or *Secure Shell* client. Your login and session are encrypted while you work on the remote computer. The ssh client features many different command-line options, but can be simply used with the name or IP address of the remote computer, like this:

```
[andrew@teletran ~]$ ssh 192.168.0.10
The authenticity of host '192.168.0.10 (192.168.0.10)' can't be established.
RSA key fingerprint is 32:90:31:1e:31:1c:a8:d4:9a:0b:07:78:93:9d:65:df.
Are you sure you want to continue connecting (yes/no)? yes
```

The first time you connect with a remote computer using ssh, Linux displays the remote computer's encrypted identity key and asks you to verify the connection. After you type **yes** and press Enter, you are warned that the remote computer's identity (key) has been entered in a file named known_hosts under the .ssh directory in your home directory. You are also prompted to enter your password:

```
Warning: Permanently added '192.168.0.10' (RSA) \
to the list of known hosts.
andrew@192.168.0.41's password:
andrew@fedora:~$
```

After entering your password, you can then work on the remote computer. Again, everything you enter on the keyboard in communication with the remote computer is encrypted. Use the exit or logout commands to exit your session and return to the shell on your computer.

Using Environment Variables

A number of in-memory variables are assigned and loaded by default when the user logs in. These variables are known as shell *environment variables*, which can be used by various commands to get information about your environment, such as the type of system you are running, your home directory, and the shell in use. Environment variables are used by Linux operating systems to help tailor the computing environment of your system, and include helpful specifications and setup, such as default locations of executable files and software libraries. If you begin writing shell scripts, you might use environment variables in your scripts. Until then, you only need to be aware of what environment variables are and do.

The following list includes a number of environment variables, along with descriptions of how the shell uses them:

▶ **PWD**—To provide the name of the current working directory, used by the pwd command (such as /home/andrew/foo)

▶ **USER**—To declare the user's name, such as andrew

▶ **LANG**—To set language defaults, such as English

▶ **SHELL**—To declare the name and location of the current shell, such as /bin/bash

▶ **PATH**—To set the default location of executable files, such as /bin, /usr/bin, and so on

▶ **LD_LIBRARY_PATH**—To declare the location of important software libraries (because most, but not all, Linux commands use shared resources)

▶ **TERM**—To set the type of terminal in use, such as vt100, which can be important when using screen-oriented programs, such as text editors

▶ **MACHINE**—To declare system type, system architecture, and so on

> **NOTE**
>
> Each shell can have its own feature set and language syntax, as well as a unique set of default environment variables. See Chapter 15, "Remote Access with SSH," for more information about using the different shells included with Fedora.

At the command line, you can use the env or printenv commands to display these environment variables, like so:

```
$ env
SSH_AGENT_PID=2881
HOSTNAME=teletran.hudson.com
SHELL=/bin/bash
TERM=xterm
DESKTOP_STARTUP_ID=
USERNAME=andrew
MAIL=/var/spool/mail/andrew
PATH=/usr/kerberos/bin:/usr/lib/ccache:/usr/local/bin:\
/usr/bin:/bin:/home/andrew/bin
DESKTOP_SESSION=default
INPUTRC=/etc/inputrc
PWD=/home/andrew
KDEDIRS=/usr
SSH_ASKPASS=/usr/libexec/openssh/gnome-ssh-askpass
SHLVL=2
HOME=/home/andrew
DISPLAY=:0.0
```

This abbreviated list shows a few common variables. These variables are set by configuration or *resource* files contained in the /etc, /etc/skel, or user /home directory. You can find default settings for bash, for example, in /etc/profile, /etc/bashrc, .bashrc, or .bash_profile files installed in your home directory. Read the man page for bash for details about using these configuration files.

One of the most important environment variables is $PATH, which defines the location of executable files. For example, if, as a regular user, you try to use a command that is not located in your $PATH (such as the ifconfig command), you will see something like this:

```
$ ifconfig
-bash: ifconfig: command not found
```

However, you might know that ifconfig is definitely installed on your system, and you can verify this by using the whereis command, like so:

```
$ whereis ifconfig
ifconfig: /sbin/ifconfig /usr/share/man/man8/ifconfig.8.gz
```

You can also run the command by typing its full pathname, or complete directory specification like this:

```
$ /sbin/ifconfig
```

As you can see in this example, the ifconfig command is indeed installed. What happened is that by default, the /sbin directory is not in your $PATH. One of the reasons for this is that commands under the /sbin directory are normally intended to be run only by root. You can add /sbin to your $PATH by editing the file .bash_profile in your home directory (if you use the bash shell by default, like most Linux users). Look for the following line:

```
PATH=$PATH:$HOME/bin
```

You can then edit this file, perhaps using the vi editor (discussed in this chapter), to add the /sbin directory like so:

```
PATH=$PATH:/sbin:$HOME/bin
```

Save the file. The next time you log in, the /sbin directory is in your $PATH. One way to use this change right away is to read in the new settings in .bash_profile by using the bash shell's source command as follows:

```
$ source .bash_profile
```

You can now run ifconfig without the need to explicitly type its full pathname.

Some Linux commands also use environment variables—for example, to acquire configuration information (such as a communications program looking for a variable such as BAUD_RATE, which might denote a default modem speed).

To experiment with the environment variables, you can modify the PS1 variable to manipulate the appearance of your shell prompt. If you are working with bash, you can use its built-in export command to change the shell prompt. For example, if your default shell prompt looks like

```
[andrew@teletran ~]$
```

you can change its appearance by using the PS1 variable like this:

```
$  PS1='$OSTYPE r00lz ->'
```

After you press Enter, you see the following:

```
linux-gnu r00lz ->
```

> **NOTE**
>
> See the bash man page for other variables you can use for prompt settings.

Using the Text Editors

Linux distributions include a number of applications known as *text editors* that you can use to create text files or edit system configuration files. Text editors are similar to word processing programs, but generally have fewer features, work only with text files, and might or might not support spell checking or formatting. The text editors range in features and ease of use, but are found on nearly every Linux distribution. The number of editors installed on your system depends on what software packages you've installed on the system.

Some of the console-based text editors are as follows:

▶ **emacs**—The comprehensive GNU emacs editing environment, which is much more than an editor; see the section "Working with emacs" later in this chapter

▶ **joe**—Joe's Own Editor, a text editor, which can be used to emulate other editors

▶ **nano**—A simple text editor similar to the pico text editor included with the pine email program

▶ **vim**—An improved, compatible version of the vi text editor (which we call vi in the rest of this chapter because it has a symbolic link named vi and a symbolically linked manual page)

Note that not all text editors described here are *screen oriented*. Some of the text editors for the X Window System, which provide a graphical interface, such as menu bars, buttons, scrollbars and so on, are the following:

▶ **gedit**—A GUI text editor for GNOME

▶ **kate**—A simple KDE text editor

▶ **kedit**—Another simple KDE text editor

A good reason to learn how to use a text-based editor, such as vi, is that system maintenance and recovery operations generally never take place during X Window sessions (negating the use of a GUI editor). Many larger, more complex and capable editors do not work when Linux is booted to its single-user or maintenance mode. See Chapter 11 for more information about how Fedora boots. If anything does go wrong with your system, you probably won't be able to get into the X Window System, making knowledge and experience of using both the command line and text editors such as vi important. Make a point of opening some of the editors and playing around with them; you never know— you might just thank me someday!

Another reason to learn how to use a text-based editor under the Linux console mode is so that you can edit text files through dialup or network shell sessions because many servers do not host graphical desktops.

Working with vi

The editor found on nearly every UNIX and Linux system is, without a doubt, the vi editor, originally written by Bill Joy. This simple-to-use but incredibly capable editor features a somewhat cryptic command set, but you can put it to use with only a few commands. Although more experienced UNIX and Linux users continue to use vi extensively during computing sessions, many newer users might prefer learning an easier-to-use text editor such as pico or GNU nano. Diehard GNU fans and programmers definitely use emacs.

That said, learning how to use vi is a good idea. You might need to edit files on a Linux system with a minimal install, or a remote server without a more extensive offering of installed text editors. Chances are better than good that vi will be available.

You can start an editing session by using the vi command like this:

```
$ vi file.txt
```

The vi command works by using an insert (or editing) mode, and a viewing (or command) mode.

When you first start editing, you are in the viewing mode. You can use your cursor or other navigation keys (as shown later) to scroll through the text. To start editing, press the **i** key to insert text or the **a** key to append text. When finished, use the Esc key to toggle out of the insert or append modes and into the viewing (or command) mode. To enter a command, type a colon (:), followed by the command, such as **w** to write the file, and press Enter.

Although vi supports many complex editing operations and numerous commands, you can accomplish work by using a few basic commands. These basic vi commands are the following:

▶ **Cursor movement**—h, j, k, l (left, down, up, and right)

▶ **Delete character**—x

▶ **Delete line**—dd

▶ **Mode toggle**—Esc, Insert (or i)

▶ Quit—`:q`

▶ Quit without saving—`:q!`

▶ Run a shell command—`:sh` (use `'exit'` to return)

▶ Save file—`:w`

▶ Text search—`/`

NOTE

Use the `vimtutor` command to quickly learn how to use vi's keyboard commands. The tutorial takes less than 30 minutes, and it teaches new users how to start or stop the editor; navigate files; insert and delete text; and perform search, replace, and insert operations.

Working with `emacs`

Richard M. Stallman's GNU `emacs` editor, like `vi`, is included with Linux and nearly every other Linux distribution. Unlike other UNIX and Linux text editors, `emacs` is much more than a simple text editor—it is an editing environment and can be used to compile and build programs, act as an electronic diary, appointment book and calendar, compose and send electronic mail, read Usenet news, and even play games. The reason for this capability is that `emacs` contains a built-in language interpreter that uses the *Elisp* (emacs LISP) programming language.

The GNU version of this editor requires more than 30MB of hard drive space. However, there are versions with fewer resource requirements, and at least one other text editor included with Linux, named `joe`, can be used as an `emacs` clone (albeit with fewer features).

You can start an `emacs` editing session like this:

```
$ emacs file.txt
```

TIP

If you start `emacs` when using X11, the editor launches in its own floating window. To force `emacs` to display inside a terminal window rather than its own window (which can be useful if the window is a login at a remote computer), use the `-nw` command-line option like this: **`emacs -nw file.txt`**.

The `emacs` editor uses an extensive set of keystroke and named commands, but you can work with it by using a basic command subset. Many of these basic commands require you to hold down the Ctrl key, or to first press a *meta* key (generally mapped to the Alt key). The basic commands are listed in Table 4.2.

TABLE 4.2   Emacs Editing Commands

Action	Command
Abort	Ctrl+G
Cursor left	Ctrl+B
Cursor down	Ctrl+N
Cursor right	Ctrl+F
Cursor up	Ctrl+P
Delete character	Ctrl+D
Delete line	Ctrl+K
Go to start of line	Ctrl+A
Go to end of line	Ctrl+E
Help	Ctrl+H
Quit	Ctrl+X, Ctrl+C
Save As	Ctrl+X, Ctrl+W
Save file	Ctrl+X, Ctrl+S
Search backward	Ctrl+R
Search forward	Ctrl+S
Start tutorial	Ctrl+H, T
Undo	Ctrl+X, U

TIP

One of the best reasons to learn how to use emacs is that you can use nearly all the same keystrokes to edit commands on the bash shell command line. Another reason is that like vi, emacs is universally available on nearly every UNIX and Linux system, including Apple's Mac OS X.

Working As Root

The root, or super-user account, is a special account and user on UNIX and Linux systems. Super-user permissions are required in part because of the restrictive file permissions assigned to important system configuration files. You must have root permission to edit these files or to access or modify certain devices (such as hard drives). When logged in as root, you have total control over your system, which can be dangerous.

When you work in root, you can destroy a running system with a simple invocation of the rm command like this:

```
# rm -fr /
```

This command line not only deletes files and directories, but also could wipe out file systems on other partitions and even remote computers. This alone is reason enough to take precautions when using root access.

The only time you should run Linux as the super-user is when booting to runlevel 1, or system maintenance mode, to configure the file system, for example, or to repair or maintain the system. Logging in and using Linux as the root operator isn't a good idea because it defeats the entire concept of file permissions.

Knowing how to run commands as root without logging in as root can help avoid serious missteps when configuring your system. Linux comes with a command named su that enables you to run one or more commands as root and then quickly returns you to normal user status. For example, if you would like to edit your system's file system table (a simple text file that describes local or remote storage devices, their type, and location), you can use the su command like this:

```
$ su -c "nano -w /etc/fstab"
Password:
```

After you press Enter, you are prompted for a password that gives you access to root. This extra step can also help you "think before you leap" into the command. Enter the root password, and you are then editing /etc/fstab, using the nano editor with line wrapping disabled.

> **CAUTION**
>
> Before editing any important system or software service configuration file, make a backup copy. Then make sure to launch your text editor with line wrapping disabled. If you edit a configuration file without disabling line wrapping, you could insert spurious carriage returns and line feeds into its contents, causing the configured service to fail when restarting. By convention, nearly all configuration files are formatted for 80-character text width, but this is not always the case. By default, the vi and emacs editors don't use line wrap.

You can use sudo to assign specific users or groups permission to perform specific tasks (similar to BSD UNIX and its "wheel" group of users). The sudo command works by first examining the file named sudoers under the /etc directory; you modify this file with the visudo command. See the section "Granting Root Privileges on Occasion—The sudo Command" in Chapter 10, "Managing Users," for details on how to configure and use sudo.

Creating Users

When a Linux system administrator creates a user, an entry in /etc/passwd for the user is created. The system also creates a directory, labeled with the user's username, in the /home directory. For example, if you create a user named bernice, the user's home directory is /home/bernice.

> **NOTE**
>
> In this chapter, you learn how to manage users from the command line. See Chapter 10 for more information on user administration with Fedora using graphical administration utilities, such as the `system-config-users` client.

Use the useradd command, along with a user's name, to quickly create a user:

```
# useradd andrew
```

After creating the user, you must also create the user's initial password with the passwd command:

```
# passwd andrew
Changing password for user andrew.
New password:
Retype new password:
passwd: all authentication tokens updated successfully.
```

Enter the new password twice. If you do not create an initial password for a new user, the user cannot log in.

You can view useradd's default new user settings by using the command and its -D option, like this:

```
# useradd -D
GROUP=100
HOME=/home
INACTIVE=-1
EXPIRE=
SHELL=/bin/bash
SKEL=/etc/skel
CREATE_MAIL_SPOOL=yes
```

These options display the default group ID, home directory, account and password policy (active forever with no password expiration), the default shell, and the directory containing defaults for the shell.

The useradd command has many different command-line options. The command can be used to set policies and dates for the new user's password, assign a login shell, assign group membership, and manage other aspects of a user's account.

Deleting Users

Use the userdel command to delete users from your system. This command removes a user's entry in the system's /etc/passwd file. You should also use the command's -r option to remove all the user's files and directories (such as the user's mail spool file under /var/spool/mail):

```
# userdel -r andrew
```

If you do not use the `-r` option, you have to manually delete the user's directory under `/home`, along with the user's `/var/spool/mail` queue.

Shutting Down the System

Use the `shutdown` command to shut down your system. The `shutdown` command has a number of different command-line options (such as shutting down at a predetermined time), but the fastest way to cleanly shut down Linux is to use the `-h` or halt option, followed by the word now or the numeral zero (0), like this:

```
# shutdown -h now
```

or

```
# shutdown -h 0
```

To incorporate a timed shutdown and a pertinent message to all active users, use shut-down's time and message options, like so:

```
# shutdown -h 18:30 "System is going down for maintenance this evening"
```

This example shuts down your system and provides a warning to all active users 15 minutes before the shutdown (or reboot). Shutting down a running server can be considered drastic, especially if there are active users or exchanges of important data occurring (such as a backup in progress). One good approach is to warn users ahead of time. This can be done by editing the system *Message of the Day (MOTD)* motd file, which displays a message to users after login. To create your custom MOTD, use a text editor and change the contents of `/etc/motd`. You can also make downtimes part of a regular schedule, perhaps to coincide with security audits, software updates, or hardware maintenance.

You should shut down Fedora for only a few very specific reasons:

▶ You are not using the computer and want to conserve electrical power.

▶ You need to perform system maintenance that requires any or all system services to be stopped.

▶ You want to replaceintegral hardware.

TIP

Do not shut down your computer if you suspect that one or more intruders has infiltrated your system; instead, disconnect the machine from any or all networks and make a backup copy of your hard drives. You might want to also keep the machine running to examine the contents of memory and to examine system logs. See Chapter 14 and Chapter 30, "Securing Your Machines," for how to protect and monitor a network-connected system.

Rebooting the System

You should also use the shutdown command to reboot your system. The fastest way to cleanly reboot Linux is to use the -r option and the word now or the numeral zero (0):

```
# shutdown -r now
```

or

```
# shutdown -r 0
```

Both rebooting and shutting down can have dire consequences if performed at the wrong time (such as during backups or critical file transfers, which arouses the ire of your system's users). However, Linux-based operating systems are designed to properly stop active system services in an orderly fashion. Other commands you can use to shut down and reboot Linux are the halt and reboot commands, but the shutdown command is more flexible.

Reading Documentation

Although you learn the basics of using Fedora in this book, you need time and practice to master and troubleshoot more complex aspects of the Linux operating system and your distribution. As with any operating system, you can expect to encounter some problems or perplexing questions as you continue to work with Linux. The first place to turn for help with these issues is the documentation included with your system; if you cannot find the information you need there, check Fedora's website.

> **NOTE**
>
> Checking Fedora's website for security updates and bug fixes is a good idea. Browse to http://fedoraproject.org/wiki/. Alternatively, you can always do a quick yum update to make sure that your system has the most up-to-date software available.

Linux, like UNIX, is a self-documenting system, with man pages accessible through the man command. Linux offers many other helpful commands for accessing its documentation. You can use the apropos command—for example, with a keyword such as partition—to find commands related to partitioning, like this:

```
$ apropos partition
diskdumpfmt          (8)  - format a dump device or a partition
fdisk                (8)  - Partition table manipulator for Linux
GNU Parted [parted]  (8)  - a partition manipulation program
mpartition           (1)  - partition an MSDOS hard disk
MPI_Cart_sub         (3)  - Partitions a communicator into subgroups which form
                            lower-dimensional cartesian subgrids
partprobe            (8)  - inform the OS of partition table changes
pvcreate             (8)  - initialize a disk or partition for use by LVM
sfdisk               (8)  - Partition table manipulator for Linux
```

To find a command and its documentation, you can use the whereis command. For example, if you are looking for the fdisk command, you can do this:

```
$ whereis fdisk
fdisk: /sbin/fdisk /usr/share/man/man8/fdisk.8.gz
```

Using Man Pages

To learn more about a command or program, use the man command, followed by the name of the command. Man pages for Linux and X Window commands are within the /usr/share/man, /usr/local/share/man, and /usr/X11R6/man directories. So, for example, to read the rm command's man page, use the man command like this:

```
$ man rm
```

After you press Enter, the less command (a Linux command known as a *pager*) displays the man page. The less command is a text browser you can use to scroll forward and backward (even sideways) through the document to learn more about the command. Type the letter **h** to get help, use the forward slash to enter a search string, or press **q** to quit.

> **NOTE**
>
> Although nearly all the hundreds of GNU commands included with Linux each have a man page, you must use the info command to read detailed information about using a GNU command. For example, to learn even more about bash (which has a rather extensive manual page), use the info command like this:
>
> ```
> $ info bash
> ```
>
> Press the **n** and **p** keys to navigate through the document, or scroll down to a menu item on the screen and press Enter to read about a specific feature. Press **q** to quit reading.

> **Related Fedora and Linux Commands**
>
> The following programs and built-in shell commands are commonly used when working at the command line. These commands are organized by category to help you understand the command's purpose. If you need to find full information for using the command, you can find that information under the command's man page.
>
> ▶ **Managing users and groups**—chage, chfn, chsh, edquota, gpasswd, groupadd, groupdel, groupmod, groups, mkpasswd, newgrp, newusers, passwd, umask, useradd, userdel, usermod
>
> ▶ **Managing files and file systems**—cat, cd, chattr, chmod, chown, compress, cp, dd, fdisk, find, gzip, ln, mkdir, mksfs, mount, mv, rm, rmdir, rpm, sort, swapon, swapoff, tar, touch, umount, uncompress, uniq, unzip, zip
>
> ▶ **Managing running programs**—bg, fg, kill, killall, nice, ps, pstree, renice, top, watch

▶ **Getting information**—apropos, cal, cat, cmp, date, diff, df, dir, dmesg, du, env, file, free, grep, head, info, last, less, locate, ls, lsattr, man, more, pinfo, ps, pwd, stat, strings, tac, tail, top, uname, uptime, vdir, vmstat, w, wc, whatis, whereis, which, who, whoami

▶ **Console text editors**—ed, jed, joe, mcedit, nano, red, sed, vim

▶ **Console Internet and network commands**—bing, elm, ftp, host, hostname, ifconfig, links, lynx, mail, mutt, ncftp, netconfig, netstat, pine, ping, pump, rdate, route, scp, sftp, ssh, tcpdump, traceroute, whois, wire-test

Reference

This section lists some additional points of reference with background information on the standards and commands discussed in this chapter. Browse these links to learn more about some of the concepts discussed in this chapter and to expand your knowledge of your new Linux community:

▶ **http://www.winntmag.com/Articles/Index.cfm?ArticleID=7420**—An article by a Windows NT user who, when experimenting with Linux, blithely confesses to rebooting the system after not knowing how to read a text file at the Linux console.

▶ **http://standards.ieee.org/regauth/posix/**—IEEE's POSIX information page.

▶ **http://www.itworld.com/Comp/2362/lw-01-government/#sidebar**—Discussion of Linux and POSIX compliance.

▶ **http://www.pathname.com/fhs/**—Home page for the Linux FHS, Linux Filesystem Hierarchy Standard.

▶ **http://www.tldp.org/**—Browse the HOWTO section to find and read The Linux Keyboard and Console HOWTO—Andries Brouwer's somewhat dated but eminently useful guide to using the Linux keyboard and console.

▶ **http://www.gnu.org/software/emacs/emacs.html**—Home page for the FSF's GNU emacs editing environment; you can find additional documentation and links to the source code for the latest version here.

▶ **http://www.vim.org/**—Home page for the vim (vi clone) editor included with Linux distributions. Check here for updates, bug fixes, and news about this editor.

▶ **http://www.courtesan.com/sudo/**—Home page for the sudo command. Check here for the latest updates, security features, and bug fixes.

PART II

Desktop Fedora

On the Internet

The Internet has revolutionized our modern civilization within a very short time. Not all that long ago, it was unheard of to be communicating through the Internet, and computer networks were viewed with some suspicion thanks to various Hollywood blockbusters such as *WarGames* and *The Terminator*; nowadays you are deemed backward if you do not have an email account or an instant messenger "nick." This chapter introduces you to some of the more popular software that you can use to access the Internet, send and receive email, read the news, and talk in real time using instant messaging and even videoconferencing. You will find out how to set up each piece of software to access the resources you need.

Browsing the Internet

The Internet has forever changed how we access and share information. The ways in which we view the Internet have also changed and are continually improving to give better and richer experiences.

A Brief Introduction to the Internet

The Internet itself was first brought to life by the U.S. Department of Defense in 1969. It was called ARPANet after the Department of Defense's Advanced Research Projects Agency. Designed to build a network that would withstand major catastrophe (this was the peak of the Cold War), it soon grew to encompass more and more networks to build the Internet. Then, in 1991, Tim Berners-Lee of CERN developed the idea of the World Wide Web, including *Hypertext Transfer Protocol (HTTP)* and *Hypertext Markup Language (HTML)*. This gave us what we now know to be the Internet.

Mozilla Firefox

One of the most popular web browsers, and in fact the default web browser in Fedora, is Mozilla Firefox (see Figure 5.1). Built on a solid code base that is derived from the original Mozilla Suite, which itself comes from Netscape, Firefox offers a breath of fresh air to surfing the Internet, compared to the dominant Internet Explorer (which is only available on Windows). Firefox offers a secure browsing environment, coupled by the ability to extend the browsing experience by using plug-ins and extensions, which we cover briefly later in this section. There have been more than 416 million downloads of Firefox since its release in the middle of 2005, and it has grabbed significant market share from Internet Explorer.

In Fedora, you can find Firefox under the Applications, Internet menu at the top of your screen. An even simpler way to start Firefox is to click the small World icon next to the Actions menu. Either way, Firefox opens.

FIGURE 5.1   Mozilla Firefox—rediscover the Web. Firefox enables you to add on numerous upgrades, further enhancing your experience.

Beyond the basic program is a wealth of plug-ins and extensions that can increase the capabilities of Firefox beyond simple web browsing. Plug-ins such as Shockwave Flash and Java are available instantly, as are multimedia codecs for viewing video content, whereas extensions provide useful and sometimes humorous additions to the browsing experience. For example, ForecastFox is an extension that gives you your local weather conditions, and Bandwidth Tester is a tool that calculates your current bandwidth. Perhaps the best way to while away a lazy afternoon is to download the StumbleUpon extension, which provides you with the proverbial big red button that you can click to be taken to a web page based on certain predefined conditions that you select. More often than not you'll come across some Calvin and Hobbes strip that will make you smile just when you need it. However, you can find some real gems by using StumbleUpon. As Firefox grows, there will be more and more extensions and plug-ins that you can use to enhance your browsing pleasure.

Finding and obtaining these plug-ins and extensions is made very easy because Mozilla developers have helpfully created a site dedicated to helping you get more from Firefox. Particular favorites are the Adblock Plus and the StumbleUpon plug-ins. Adblock Plus allows you to nuke all those annoying banners and animations that take up so much bandwidth while you are browsing.

Another plug-in that we make a lot of use of is Google BrowserSync. If, like us, you work across multiple computers, you will no doubt have had to re-create bookmarks at every different computer and try to keep them the same. Google makes this whole process much easier by allowing you to synchronize not only your bookmarks, but also your cookies, browser history, and finally any saved passwords across multiple browsers. Bear in mind that you can choose what you want to synchronize, making it easy just to replicate your bookmarks.

Konqueror

KDE users have the option to use Konqueror, which is the default browser for KDE (see Figure 5.2). As well as handling file system navigation, Konqueror can be used to surf the web. It, too, is based on the Gecko rendering engine as found in Firefox.

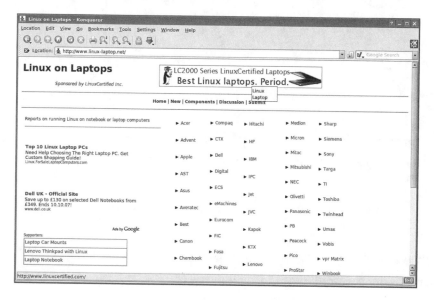

FIGURE 5.2   Konqueror, the standard KDE web and file system browser.

Choosing an Email Client

Back in the days of UNIX, there were various text-based email clients such as elm and pine (*Pine Is Not Elm*). Although they looked basic, they allowed the average user to inter-act with his email, both for composing and reading correspondence. With the advent of mainstream computing and the realization that people needed friendly GUI interfaces to be productive came a plethora of email clients, with some of them being cross-platform and compatible among Linux, Windows, and Mac OS X, not to mention UNIX.

Evolution

Evolution is the standard email client that comes with Fedora, and to call it an email client would be to sincerely underestimate its usefulness as an application. Not only does it handle email, it can also look after contacts and calendaring and can manage your tasks (see Figure 5.3). The next section demonstrates how to configure Evolution to handle email.

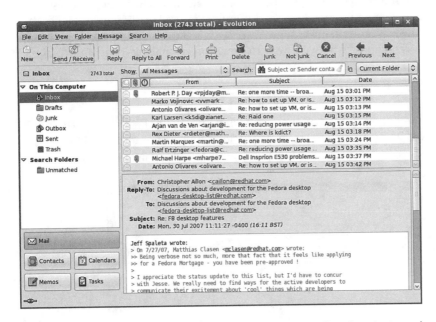

FIGURE 5.3   With Evolution, you can handle all your email and contacts and make appoint-ments and track tasks.

You need to have the following information to successfully configure Evolution:

▶ Your email address

▶ Your incoming email server name and type (that is, pop.email.com, POP, and IMAP)

▶ Your username and password for the incoming server

▶ Your outgoing email server name (that is, smtp.email.com)

After you have all the information, you can start Evolution. The first screen you are presented with is the Identity screen as part of the Account Setup Assistance Wizard (see Figure 5.4).

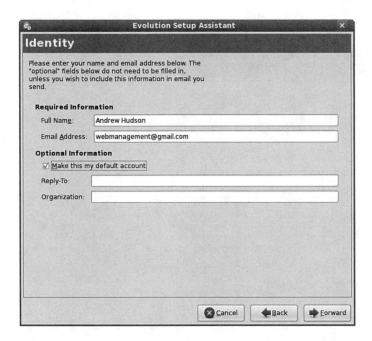

FIGURE 5.4   You can launch and configure Evolution with just a few simple commands. The Identity screen, the first of several screens, asks you to enter your information. Click Forward to proceed.

The next screen permits you to configure Evolution to use your *mail transfer agent* (*MAT*; the software used to transfer your mail from your computer to the wider network or Internet). You can choose POP, IMAP, the local spools found in /var/mail in either mbox or maildir format, a local MTA, or None if you simply want to use the other features of Evolution. As shown in Figure 5.5, you can also set your password.

Now you can select options that govern how Evolution handles incoming email. Here you can choose the frequency at which Evolution checks for email (check the box to get Evolution to check for emails every 10 minutes), as well as what Evolution should do with message storage; but, to be honest, we'd keep these specific settings unchecked. Click the Forward box to proceed.

TIP

If you connect to the Internet using a dialup modem, make sure you don't check the Checking for New Mail option; otherwise, you might find that you will be connecting every 10 minutes.

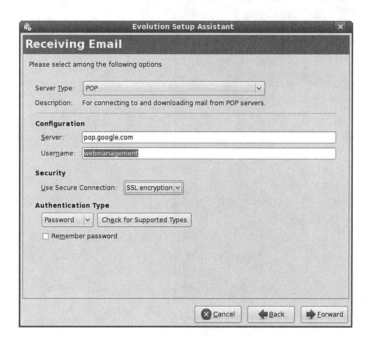

FIGURE 5.5   The Receiving Mail screen requires information from your ISP or system administrator.

You must also choose between SMTP or Sendmail for sending your mail; enter your email address, and choose a time zone (very important for your calendar). Finally, you will see the opening Evolution window in Figure 5.6.

Each icon in the left pane of the main Evolution window opens a different window when selected. Each view has options that can be configured to suit your needs; you'll find access to the preferences dialog box under the Edit menu, which is shown in Figure 5.7.

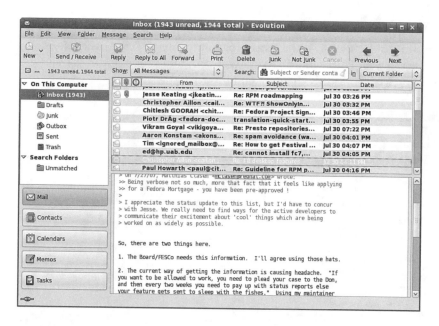

FIGURE 5.6   The standard Evolution display. On the left, you can see buttons to choose Mail, Contacts, Calendars, and Tasks windows.

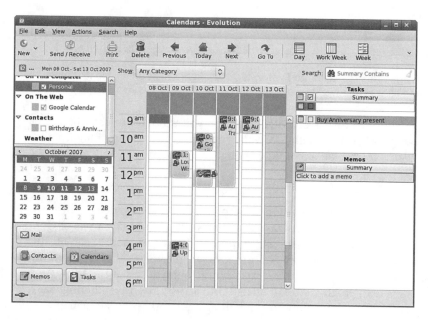

FIGURE 5.7   The calendar application Tools screen is where the information can be shared with others. Here you can configure the times and dates.

Mozilla Thunderbird

Mozilla Thunderbird (see Figure 5.8) is the sister program to Firefox. Whereas Firefox is designed to browse the web, Thunderbird's specialty is communication. It can handle email, network news (see later in this chapter), and RSS feeds.

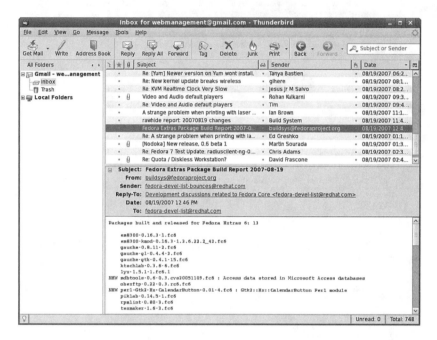

FIGURE 5.8   The natural companion to Firefox, Mozilla's lightweight email client Thunderbird can be found in use all over the world.

Thunderbird is not installed by default with Fedora, so you will have to use either Add/Remove Packages or yum to install it. As with Firefox, there are many plug-ins and extensions to enhance your email and news reading.

KMail

If you are using the KDE Desktop Environment rather than the Fedora default GNOME desktop, you will also have KMail installed. As with Balsa, it will not take users of Outlook Express or Mozilla Mail very long to get used to the KMail interface. Some useful features found in KMail are the choice of mbox or maildir formats, improved filter creation, the capability to sort mail into threads, and the capability to apply filters at the MTA. Figure 5.9 shows the KMail email program. KMail offers IMAP access, extensive filtering, mbox and maildir formats, and the capability to easily integrate MTAs such as Procmail, Spamassassin, or custom processing scripts.

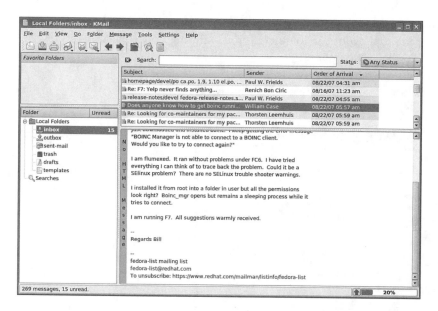

FIGURE 5.9   The KMail email client, part of the KDE Desktop Environment.

Other Mail Clients

The mail clients included by Fedora are only a few of those available. Claws Mail (not included) is very popular because it offers spell checking while typing and is well suited for use in large network environments in which network overhead and RAM usage are important considerations. You can find other mail clients and applications suitable for use with Fedora by searching http://freshmeat.net/.

RSS Readers

RSS is one of the protocols of Web 2.0, the next generation of Internet content. Although RSS has been in use for a couple of years now, it has only recently started to really take off, thanks to adoption across a large number of websites and portals.

The key advantage of RSS is that you can quickly read news from your specific choice of websites at a time that suits you. Some services offer just the articles' headlines, whereas others offer full articles for you to view. RSS feeds can be accessed in various ways, even through your web browser!

Firefox

Firefox implements RSS feeds as what it calls Live Bookmarks (shown in Figure 5.10), which are essentially bookmarks with subbookmarks, each linking to a new page from your chosen website. I like to have several news sites grouped together under a folder on my toolbar called News, allowing me to quickly browse through my collection of sites and pick out articles that really interest me.

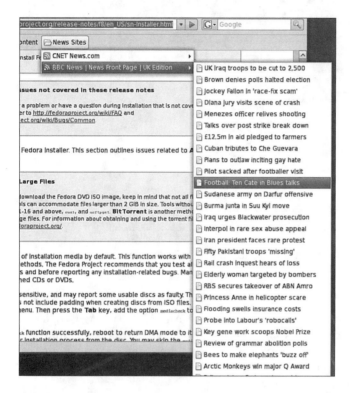

FIGURE 5.10   Live Bookmarks for Firefox, making all your news fixes just a mouse click away.

Liferea

Of course, not everyone wants to read RSS feeds with the browser. The main problem with reading RSS feeds with Firefox is that you get to see only the headline rather than any actual text. This is where a dedicated RSS reader comes in handy, and Liferea (see Figure 5.11) is one of the best.

It is not installed by default, so you have to retrieve it by going to Applications, Add/Remove Software. After it is installed, you can find it under the Applications, Internet menu labeled simply Liferea.

By default, Liferea offers a number of RSS feeds, including Fedora People, Red Hat Magazine, and Fedoranews.org. Adding a new feed is straightforward. All you need to do is select New Subscription under the Feeds menu and paste the URL of the RSS feed into the box. Liferea then retrieves all the current items available through that field, and displays the feed name on the left side for you to select and start reading.

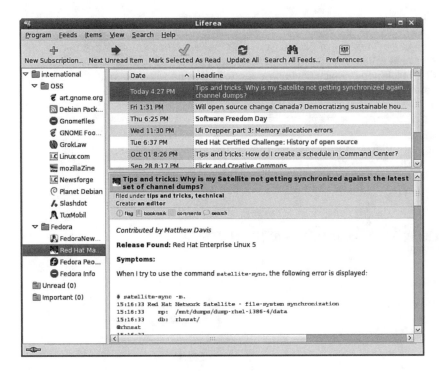

FIGURE 5.11   Read your daily news feeds with Liferea, a fantastic and easy-to-use RSS feed reader.

Instant Messaging with Pidgin

Instant messaging is one of the biggest ways for people to interact on the web. AOL was the primary force behind this, especially in America, but other networks and systems soon came onto the market providing users with a wealth of choice.

No longer just a consumer tool, instant messaging is now a part of the corporate world, with many different companies deploying internal instant messaging software for collaboration.

One of the biggest hurdles that Fedora had to overcome was the fact that with the exception of Jabber, there was no client software to access networks such as AIM or MSN. Fortunately, where there is a will there is a way, and Pidgin was created as a multiprotocol instant messaging client enabling you to connect to several different networks that use differing protocols.

NOTE

If you have used earlier versions of Fedora, you might be wondering why we are covering Pidgin rather than GAIM. Well, GAIM had a few legal problems surrounding their use of AIM within their name, which could have led to confusion with AOL Instant Messenger. As a result, GAIM rebranded itself Pidgin instead and is included within Fedora.

You can find Pidgin under Applications, Internet, listed as Internet Messenger, and it is shown in Figure 5.12.

FIGURE 5.12   Pidgin, the new name for GAIM, allows you to send instant messages to pretty much any IM network.

When you launch Pidgin for the first time, you are prompted to create an account. Just select an option from the protocol list, enter your screen name and password for that protocol/service (as shown in Figure 5.13), and click the Save button. Pidgin automatically tries to log in to that network using the credentials you have supplied. If successful, and if you have previously assigned contacts to your IM service, you should see them pop up in the Buddy List window.

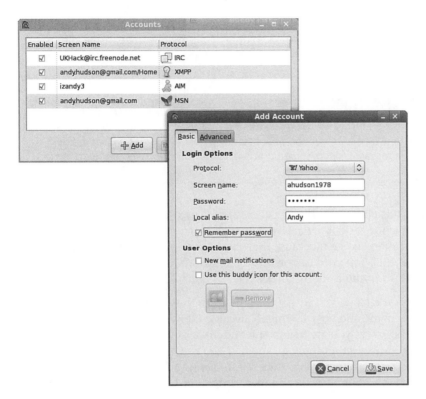

FIGURE 5.13   Pidgin offers a neat solution to keeping in touch with people, regardless of the IM network they use.

NOTE

Pidgin supports Jabber, an open XML-based IM protocol that can be used to set up a corporate IM server. Jabber is not supplied with Fedora, but you can obtain additional information about it from the Jabber home page at http://www.jabber.com/. You can obtain the Jabber server, Jabberd, from http://jabberd.jabberstudio.org/. If you want to use Pidgin locally for collaboration, Jabber would be an excellent choice for a private local server.

Internet Relay Chat

As documented in RFC 2812 and RFC 2813, the *Internet Relay Chat (IRC)* protocol is used for text conferencing. Like mail and news, IRC uses a client/server model. Although it is rare for an individual to establish an IRC server, it can be done. Most people use public IRC servers and access them with IRC clients.

Fedora provides a number of graphical IRC clients, including X-Chat, licq, and Chatzilla, but there is no default chat client for Fedora. Fedora also provides the console clients epic and licq for those who eschew X. If you don't already have a favorite, you should try them all.

CAUTION

You should never use an IRC client while you are the root user. It is better to create a special user just for IRC because of potential security problems. To use X-Chat in this manner, you open a terminal window, use su to change to your IRC user, and start the X-Chat client.

X-Chat is a popular IRC client, and it is the client that is used in this chapter's example. The HTML documents for X-Chat are available in /usr/share/docs/xchat. It is a good idea to read them before you begin because they include an introduction to and cover some of the basics of IRC. You need to download and install X-Chat to launch the X-Chat client, select X-Chat from Applications, Internet.

The X-Chat application enables you to assign yourself up to three nicknames. You can also specify your real name and your username. Because many people choose not to use their real names in IRC chat, you are free to enter any names you desire in any of the spaces provided. You can select multiple nicknames; you might be banned from an IRC channel under one name, and you could then rejoin using another. If this seems slightly juvenile to you, you are beginning to get an idea of the type of behavior on many IRC channels.

When you open the main X-Chat screen, a list of IRC servers appears, as shown in Figure 5.14. After you choose a server by double-clicking it, you can view a list of channels available on that server by choosing Window, List Window. The X-Chat Channel List window appears. In that window, you can choose to join channels featuring topics that interest you. To join a channel, you double-click it.

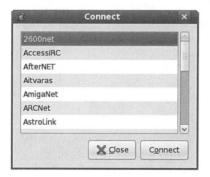

FIGURE 5.14   The main X-Chat screen presents a list of available public servers from which to select.

The Wild Side of IRC

Do not be surprised at the number of lewd topics and the use of crude language on public IRC servers. For a humorous look at the topic of IRC cursing, see http://www.irc.org/fun_docs/nocuss.html. This site also offers some tips for maintaining IRC etiquette, which is essential if you do not want to be the object of any of that profanity! Here are some of the most important IRC etiquette rules:

▶ Do not use colored text, all-capitalized text, blinking text, or "bells" (beeps caused by sending ^G to a terminal).

▶ Show respect for others.

▶ Ignore people who act inappropriately.

After you select a channel, you can join in the conversation, which appears as onscreen text. The messages scroll down the screen as new messages appear.

TIP

You can establish your own IRC server even though Fedora does not provide one. Setting up a server is not a task for anyone who is not well versed in Linux or IRC.

A popular server is IRCd, which you can obtain from ftp://ftp.irc.org/irc/server/. Before you download IRCd, look at the Read Me file to determine what files you need to download and read the information at http://www.irchelp.org/irchelp/ircd/.

Usenet Network Newsgroups

The concept of newsgroups revolutionized the way information was exchanged between people across a network. The Usenet network news system created a method for people to electronically communicate with large groups of people with similar interests. As you will see, many of the concepts of Usenet news are embodied in other forms of collaborative communication.

Usenet newsgroups act as a form of public bulletin board system. Any user can subscribe to individual newsgroups and send (or *post*) messages (called *articles*) to the newsgroup so that all the other subscribers of the newsgroup can read them. Some newsgroups include an administrator, who must approve each message before it is posted. These are called *moderated* newsgroups. Other newsgroups are *open*, allowing any subscribed member to post a message. When an article is posted to the newsgroup, it is transferred to all the other hosts in the news network.

Usenet newsgroups are divided into a hierarchy to make it easier to find individual newsgroups. The hierarchy levels are based on topics, such as computers, science, recreation, and social issues. Each newsgroup is named as a subset of the higher-level topic. For example, the newsgroup comp relates to all computer topics. The newsgroup comp.laptops relates to laptop computer issues. Often the hierarchy goes several layers deep. For example, the newsgroup comp.databases.oracle.server relates to Oracle server database issues.

NOTE

The format of newsgroup articles follows the strict guidelines defined in the Internet standards document *Request For Comments (RFC)* 1036. Each article must contain two distinct parts: header lines and a message body.

The header lines identify information about when and by whom the article was posted. The body of the message should contain only standard ASCII text characters. No binary characters or files should be posted within news articles. To get around this restriction, binary files are converted to text data, through use of either the standard UNIX uuencode program or the newer *Multipurpose Internet Mail Extensions (MIME)* protocol. The resulting text file is then posted to the newsgroup. Newsgroup readers can then decode the posted text file back into its original binary form.

A collection of articles posted in response to a common topic is called a *thread*. A thread can contain many articles as users post messages in response to other posted messages. Some newsreader programs allow users to track articles based on the threads to which they belong. This helps simplify the organization of articles in the newsgroup.

TIP

The free news server news.gmane.org makes the Red Hat and Fedora mail lists available via newsgroups. It is a handy way to read threaded discussions and easier than using the Fedora mail list archives.

The protocol used to transfer newsgroup articles from one host to another is *Network News Transfer Protocol (NNTP)*, defined in RFC 975. (You can search RFCs at ftp://metalab.unc.edu/pub/docs/rfc/; look at the file `rfc-index.txt`.) NNTP was designed as a simple client/server protocol that enables two hosts to exchange newsgroup articles in an efficient manner.

The Pan News Client Newsreader

Whether or not your Fedora server is set up as a news server, you can use a newsreader program to read newsgroup articles. The newsreader programs require just a connection to a news server. It does not matter whether the news server is on the same machine or is a remote news server on the other side of the world.

Several programs are available for UNIX systems to connect to news servers to read and post articles in newsgroups. Here we discuss the Pan news client.

Pan is a graphical newsreader client that works with GNOME and is the default newsreader for Fedora. If you have the GNOME libraries installed (and they usually are installed by default), you can also use Pan with the *K Desktop Environment (KDE)*. Pan can download and display all the newsgroups and display posted news articles. You can launch it by using the GNOME or KDE desktop panel or from the command line of an X terminal window with the command pan &. Pan supports combining multipart messages and the yenc encoding/decoding protocol. Figure 5.15 shows a sample Pan display.

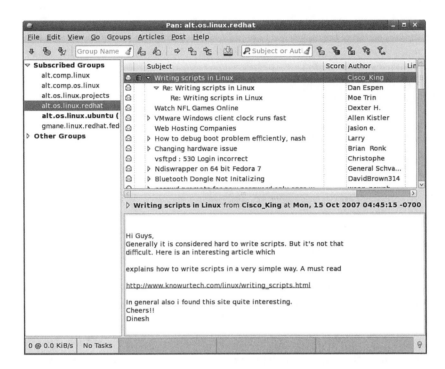

FIGURE 5.15   The Pan graphical newsreader is one of the nicest available for Linux, shown here browsing through a Red Hat usergroup.

The first time you run Pan, a configuration wizard appears and prompts you for your name, the SMTP server name, the NNTP server name, and the name you want to use to identify the connection. (In the example shown in Figure 5.16, we use a custom news server.) After the wizard has finished, you are prompted to download a list of the newsgroups the server provides; this might take a while. If you need to change the news server or add an additional server, you can access the Preferences item under the Edit menu to bring up the list of servers. Then, you highlight the appropriate one and click Edit to change it or just click the New button to add a new news server.

FIGURE 5.16   The Pan news server configuration window.

Videoconferencing with Ekiga

Ekiga is an Internet videoconferencing application that provides two-way voice and picture transmission over the Internet by using the H.323 protocol for IP telephony (also known as *Voice over IP [VoIP]*). It is an application similar to Microsoft NetMeeting and is provided with Fedora as the default videoconferencing client.

Before you can take full advantage of the phone and videoconferencing capabilities of Ekiga, you must configure a full-duplex-capable sound card and video device (see Chapter 7, "Multimedia") and a camera.

Ekiga is found in the Internet menu as Videoconferencing; you click the icon to launch it. When you start the Ekiga application for the first time, a configuration wizard (called a *druid*) runs and you are greeted by the first of four configuration screens. You simply enter your name, email address, and location and select your connection type. The settings for your audio and video devices are automatically detected; you can view them by selecting the Preferences item from the Edit menu. Figure 5.17 shows Ekiga in action, ready to dial another user.

When you have Ekiga running, you must register (from within Ekiga) with the server at http://ekiga.net/ to enable conferencing; Ekiga does this automatically for you if you told it to do so during the initial configuration.

You can find an informative FAQ at the Ekiga home page at http://www.Ekiga.org/ that you should read in full before using Ekiga. Also, an excellent article about VoIP is at http://freshmeat.net/articles/view/430/.

FIGURE 5.17   Ekiga is surprisingly simple to use. A video source is not necessary; a static picture can be used, too.

NOTE

If you frequently use VoIP applications such as Ekiga, you will tire of repetitively typing in long IP addresses to make connections. To avoid this hassle, you can use a *gatekeeper*—similar in purpose to a DNS server—to translate names into IP addresses. OpenH323 Gatekeeper is one such popular gatekeeper application. It is not provided with Fedora, but you can obtain it from http://www.gnugk.org/.

Reference

- ▶ http://www.novell.com/—The home of Ximian Evolution, the standard email client for Fedora.

- ▶ http://www.mozilla.org/—The home page for Mozilla Firefox, Thunderbird, and the Mozilla Suite.

- ▶ http://www.spreadfirefox.com/—The Firefox advocacy home page is useful for converting those Internet Explorer types.

- ▶ http://ekiga.net/—Sign up here for a free SIP account for use with Ekiga.

# CHAPTER 6

Productivity Applications

With the rapid growth of open source software, businesses have directly benefited from developments in office productivity suites. Many businesses already use OpenOffice.org and its commercial counterpart, StarOffice, and they are already enjoying the cost benefits of not having to pay license fees or support costs. Of course, more suites are available than just OpenOffice.org, and in this chapter we explore the options available.

> **NOTE**
>
> OpenOffice.org is not 100% compatible with Microsoft Office. Why is this? Well, Microsoft is notoriously secretive about its proprietary file formats, and the only way that OpenOffice.org could ensure compatibility would be to reverse-engineer each file format, an exercise akin to taking apart a telephone to see how it works. This reverse-engineering could be classed as illegal under U.S. law, which would make OpenOffice.org somewhat of a potential hot potato if they chose this path. However, OpenOffice.org manages to maintain a very high standard of importing and exporting, so you should not experience too many problems.

A productivity suite could be classed as containing two or more applications that could be used for creating documents, presentations, spreadsheets, and databases. Other applications could include email clients, calculators/formula editors, and even illustration packages. Commonly they are all tied together by a default look and feel, which makes sticking to one particular suite much easier. Because Fedora uses OpenOffice.org as its standard office suite, we introduce you to Writer and Calc, the two most popular OpenOffice.org components. We also take a brief look at some of the other Linux-based office suites that are available.

Working with OpenOffice.org

For the majority of users of productivity suites, OpenOffice.org should fulfill most, if not all, of your requirements. However, the first hurdle you need to get over is not whether it can do what you require of it, but rather whether it can successfully import and export to proprietary Microsoft formats. In the main, OpenOffice.org should import and export with minimal hassle, perhaps getting a bit stuck with some of the more esoteric Office formatting. Given that most users do not go much beyond tabs, columns, and tables, this level of compatibility should suffice.

However, you are strongly advised to round up a selection of documents that could potentially fall foul of the import/export filter and test them thoroughly (of course, keeping a backup of the originals!). There is nothing worse than for a system administrator who has deployed a new productivity suite than to suddenly get users complaining that they cannot read their files. This would quickly destroy any benefits felt from the other useful functions within OpenOffice.org, and could even spell the return of proprietary formats and expensive office suites. Many users do not mind switching to OpenOffice.org, largely because the user interface closely resembles that of similar Microsoft applications. This helps to settle users into their environment and should dispel any fears they have over switching. Such similarity makes the transition to OpenOffice.org a lot easier.

Of course, just looking similar to Microsoft applications is not the only direct benefit. OpenOffice.org supports a huge array of file formats, and is capable of exporting to nearly 70 different types of documents. Such a wide variety of file formats means that you should be able to successfully use OpenOffice.org in nearly any environment.

What Is in OpenOffice.org?

OpenOffice.org contains a number of productivity applications for use in creating text documents, preparing spreadsheets, organizing presentations, managing projects, and more. The following components of the OpenOffice.org package are included with Fedora:

▶ **Writer**—This word processing program enables you to compose, format, and organize text documents. If you are accustomed to using Microsoft Word, the functionality of OpenOffice.org Writer will be familiar to you. You will learn how to get up and running with Writer later in this chapter. Writer is found under Applications, Office, Word Processor.

▶ **Calc**—This spreadsheet program enables you to manipulate numbers in a spreadsheet format. Support for all but the most esoteric Microsoft Excel functions means that trading spreadsheets with Excel users should be successful. Calc offers some limited compatibility with Excel macros, but those macros generally have to be rewritten. We walk through setting up a basic spreadsheet with some formulas and show you how to build a basic Data Pilot later in this chapter. Calc is found under Applications, Office, Spreadsheet.

- **Impress**—This presentation program is similar to Microsoft PowerPoint and enables you to create slide show presentations that include graphs, diagrams, and other graphics. Impress also works well with PowerPoint files. Impress is found under Applications, Office, Presentation.

- **Math**—This math formula editor enables you to write mathematical formulas with a number of math fonts and symbols for inclusion in a word processing document. Such symbols are highly specialized and not easily included in the basic functionality of a word processor. This is of interest primarily to math and science writers, but Math can be useful to anyone who needs to include a complex formula in text. You download Math using Add/Remove Software.

- **Base**—This database was introduced with the OpenOffice.org 2.3 suite, which is provided with Fedora. It provides a fully functional database application. You download Base using Add/Remove Software.

- **Draw**—This graphics application enables you to create images for inclusion in the documents produced with OpenOffice.org. It saves files only in OpenOffice.org format, but it can import most common image formats. You download Draw using Add/Remove Software.

- **Dia**—This technical drawing editor from the GNOME Office suite enables you to create measured drawings, such as those used by architects and engineers. Its functionality is similar to that of Microsoft Visio. You download Dia using Add/Remove Software.

- **Planner**—You can use this project management application for project planning, scheduling, and tracking; this application is similar to, but not compatible with, Microsoft Project. It is found in the Office menu as the Project Management item.

A Brief History of OpenOffice.org

The OpenOffice.org office suite is based on a commercial suite called StarOffice. Originally developed by a German company, StarOffice was purchased by Sun Microsystems in the United States. One of the biggest complaints about the old StarOffice was that all the component applications were integrated under a StarOffice "desktop" that looked very much like a Microsoft Windows desktop, including a Start button and menus. This meant that to edit a simple document, unneeded applications had to be loaded, making the office suite slow to load, slow to run, and quite demanding on system resources.

After the purchase of StarOffice, Sun Microsystems released a large part of the StarOffice code under the *GPL (GNU Public License)*, and development began on what has become OpenOffice.org, which is freely available under the GPL. Sun continued development on StarOffice and released a commercial version as StarOffice 6.0. The significant differences between the free and commercial versions of the software are that StarOffice provides more fonts and even more import/export file filters than OpenOffice.org (these filters cannot be provided in the GPL version because of licensing restrictions) and StarOffice provides its own relational database, Software AG's Adabas D database. The StarOffice counterpart to OpenOffice.org 2.3 is StarOffice 8.

Installing and Configuring OpenOffice.org

Fedora provides an RPM package for OpenOffice.org. If you do not install the RPM package during your initial Fedora installation, you can install it later, using the Add/Remove Software tool or by using yum `install openoffice.org` from the command line.

TIP

OpenOffice.org is constantly improving its productivity applications. You can check the OpenOffice.org website (http://www.openoffice.org/) for the latest version. The website provides a link to download the source or a precompiled version of the most current working installation files. A more current version might offer file format support that you need. Should you need a Windows-compatible version, you will also find it at the website.

The installation of OpenOffice.org is done on a systemwide basis, meaning that all users have access to it. However, users have to go into OpenOffice.org to configure it for their individual needs. This initial configuration happens transparently the first time you load any of the OpenOffice.org components, and might mean the application takes a little longer to load as a result. Be patient, and your desired application will appear.

Shown in Figure 6.1 is OpenOffice.org Writer, with a blank document ready for you to compose your masterpiece. OpenOffice.org shares common preferences across all its associated applications, meaning that you only have to define once some of your personal details or paths to save documents.

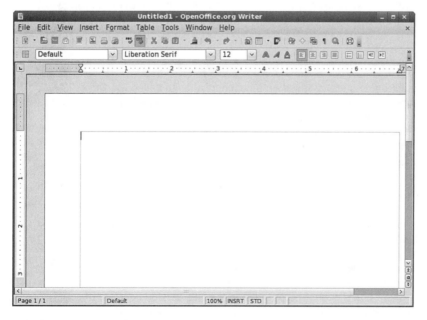

FIGURE 6.1   OpenOffice.org Writer, awaiting your input.

As is the case with many Linux applications, you might be somewhat overwhelmed by the sheer number of configuration options available to you in OpenOffice.org. Mercifully, a lot of thought has gone into organizing these options, which are available if you click the Tools menu and select Options. It does not matter which program you use to get to this dialog box; it appears the same if summoned from Writer, Impress, or Calc. It acts as a central configuration management tool for all OpenOffice.org applications. You can use it to set global options for all OpenOffice.org applications, or specific options for each individual component. For instance, in Figure 6.2, you can change the user details and information, and this is reflected across all OpenOffice.org applications.

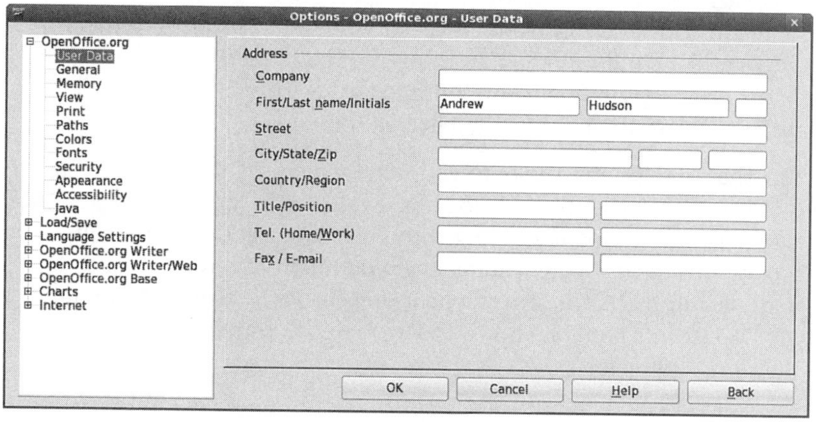

FIGURE 6.2   You can set user details for all OpenOffice.org applications from this dialog.

TIP

Two websites provide additional information on the functionality of OpenOffice.org:

▶ **http://lingucomponent.openoffice.org/download_dictionary.html**—This site provides instructions and files for installing spelling and hyphenation dictionaries, which are not included with OpenOffice.org.

▶ **http://sourceforge.net/projects/ooextras/**—This site provides templates, macros, and clip art, which are not provided with OpenOffice.org.

OpenOffice.org is a constant work in progress, but the current release is on par with the Sun version of StarOffice 8.0. You can browse to the OpenOffice.org website to get documentation and answers to frequently asked questions and to offer feedback.

Working with OpenOffice.org Writer

Out of all the applications that make up OpenOffice.org, the one that you are most likely to use on a regular basis is Writer, the OpenOffice.org word processor. With a visual style similar to Microsoft's Word, Writer has a number of strengths over its commercial and vastly more expensive rival. In this section, you learn how to get started with Writer and make use of some of its powerful formatting and layout tools.

> **NOTE**
>
> You might be interested to know that Writer was the primary word processor chosen to write and edit this book.

Getting Started

You can access Writer either through its shortcut on the panel or by going to the Applications, Office menu and selecting Word Processor. After a few seconds, Writer opens with a blank document and a blinking cursor awaiting your command. It can be tempting to just dive in and start typing your document, but it can be worthwhile to do some initial configuration before, so you are properly prepared for work.

First of all, make sure that the options are set to your requirements. Click the Tools menu and select Options to bring up the Options dialog box, as shown in Figure 6.2. The initial screen enables you to personalize OpenOffice.org with your name, address, and contact details, but there are options to configure features that you might also want to alter. First of all, check that your default paths are correct by clicking the Paths option. You might want to alter the My Documents path, as shown in Figure 6.3, to something a little more specific than just your home directory.

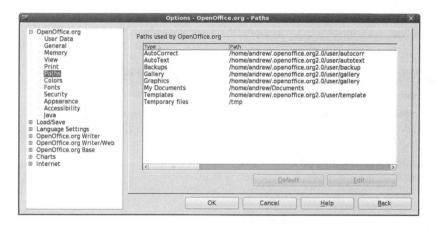

FIGURE 6.3   Click the Edit button to choose your default documents directory.

You might also want to change OpenOffice.org so that it saves in Microsoft Word format by default, should you so require. This can be done under the Load/Save General options shown in Figure 6.4, and it is a good idea if you value your work to change the Autorecovery settings so that it saves every couple of minutes.

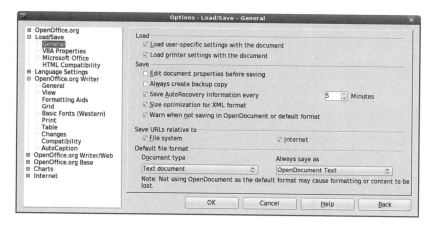

FIGURE 6.4   Make sure that you are working with most appropriate file formats for you.

Also shown in Figure 6.4 is a set of options that are specific to Writer. From top to bottom, they are

▶ **General**—Specify options that affect the general use of Writer.

▶ **View**—Specify what you want Writer to display.

▶ **Formatting Aids**—Specify whether you want to see nonprinting characters.

▶ **Grid**—Create a grid that you can use to snap frames and images in place.

▶ **Basic Fonts**—Select your default fonts for your document here.

▶ **Print**—Specify exactly what you want Writer to output when you print your document.

▶ **Table**—Set options for drawing tables within Writer.

▶ **Changes**—Define how Writer handles changes to documents.

▶ **Compatibility**—A set of rules that Writer uses to ensure close compatibility with earlier versions of Writer

▶ **AutoCaption**—Create automatic captions for images, charts, and other objects.

A little bit of time working through these options can give you a highly personalized and extremely productive environment.

Working with Styles and Formatting

One of the significant benefits of using Writer is the ability you have to easily apply formatting and styles to extremely complex documents. Depending on the types of documents you work with, you might want to consider creating your own styles beyond the 20 included by default. You can access styles through either the Style drop-down box in the toolbar or the Styles and Formatting window shown in Figure 6.5. If you cannot see the window, press the F11 key to display it.

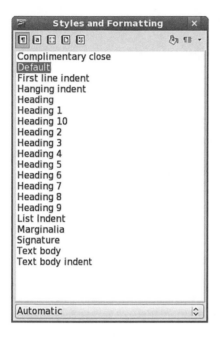

FIGURE 6.5   Writer's quick and easy-to-use Styles and Formatting tool.

The easiest way to work with the Styles and Formatting tool is to highlight the text you want to style and double-click the required style in the window. There are quite a few to choose from, but you might find them restrictive if you have more specialized needs. To start defining your own styles, press Ctrl+F11 to bring up the Style Catalog, shown in Figure 6.6, where you add, modify, and delete styles for pages, paragraphs, lists, characters, and frames.

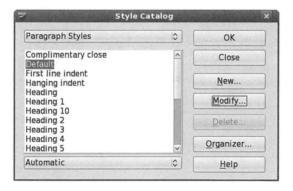

FIGURE 6.6   Writer's powerful Style Catalog gives you control over every aspect of styling.

Working with OpenOffice.org Calc

The spreadsheet component of OpenOffice.org is named Calc, and is a very capable Excel alternative.

Calc is used for storing numeric information that you need to analyze in some way. So, for instance, you could use it to help you budget month by month. It can take care of the calculations for you, as long as you tell Calc what you want it to do. Anyone with experience in Excel will feel right at home with Calc.

In this section, we show you how to get started with Calc, including entering formulas and formatting. We also take a look at some of the more advanced features of Calc, including the Data Pilot feature, which allows you to easily summarize information.

Getting Started

You can either click the shortcut icon that is located on the top GNOME panel, or select Spreadsheet from the Office menu under the Applications main menu. Whichever route you take, the result is the same and Calc starts to load.

By default, Calc loads with a blank spreadsheet just waiting for you to enter information into it. In Figure 6.7, you can see that we have already started to enter some basic information into Calc.

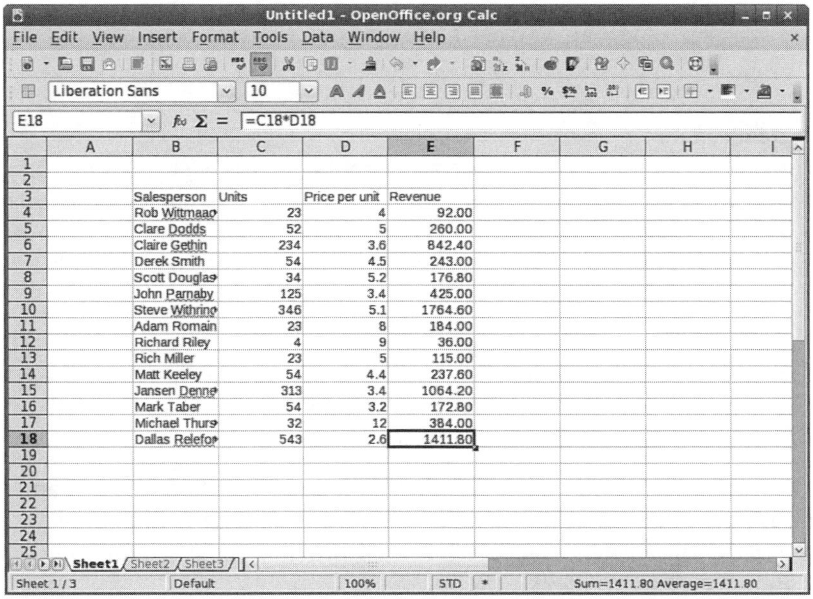

FIGURE 6.7   Use Calc to store numeric and statistical information.

Calc's layout makes it easy to organize information into rows and columns. As you can see in the example, we have salespeople listed in the left column, customers in the second column, invoice date in the third column, and finally revenue in the fourth column. At the moment, no formulas are entered to help you interpret the data. Clicking the E43 cell selects it and enables you to enter in a formula in the top formula bar. If you enter in the equal sign, Calc knows that you are entering a formula and works accordingly.

In this example, we want to know the total revenue brought in up to now, so the formula to enter is =sum(E4:E42), followed by Return. Calc automatically enters the result into cell E43 for you to see. Now you want to see what the average order value was. To do this, you have to obtain the number orders made. For this, you can use the counta function to count the number of entries in a given list. This is usually used when you need to find out how many entries there are in a text list. So, in cell B43, enter **=counta(B4:B42)** and press Enter. Calc now counts the number of entries in the range and returns the total in B43. All that remains for you to do is divide the total revenue by the number of orders to find the average order value. So, in cell E44, enter the formula **=E43/B43** to get the average order value.

TIP

Calc offers some nifty little features that you can use quickly if you need to. The handiest one in our opinion is the capability to select multiple cells and see immediately the total and average of the range. You will find these figures in the bottom-right status bar. This has saved us numerous times when we have needed to get this information quickly!

Formatting Your Spreadsheets

Getting back to our example, it looks a little basic at the moment as there is no formatting involved. For instance, what's the billing currency? You can also see that some of the cells have text that does not fit, which is highlighted by a small right arrow in the cell. We should also add some labels and titles to our spreadsheet to make it a bit more visually appealing.

To start off, all the revenue figures can be changed into currency figures. To do this, select all the cells containing revenue information and click the small icon shown in Figure 6.8. This immediately formats the cells so that they display the dollar sign and also puts in a thousands separator to make the numbers easier to read.

Now you need to space all the cells so that you can read all the information. A quick and easy way to do this is to click the area immediately to the left of column A and immediately above row 1 to select the entire spreadsheet. Now all you have to do is double-click the dividing lines and each column resizes according to its longest entry.

Next you can add a little color to the worksheet by using the Paint Can icon in the toolbar. Select the range B3 to E3 with the mouse cursor and click the background fill icon to bring up the color window shown in Figure 6.9. Now select the color you want to use and Calc fills the cells with that color. You can also change the font color by using the icon immediately to the right in the same way.

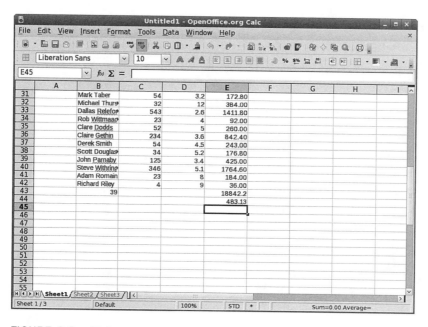

FIGURE 6.8   Make numbers more meaningful with the currency and percentage icons.

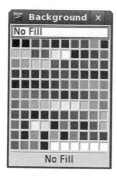

FIGURE 6.9   Add a touch of color to an otherwise dull spreadsheet with the Fill Background icon.

Finally, you need a couple more finishing touches. The first one is to enlarge the font for the column headers. Select the range B3 to E3 again and click the font size in the toolbar to change it to something a little larger. You might also want to use the bold and italic options to emphasize the headers and also the totals some more.

If you have followed the steps as described, you should end up with a spreadsheet similar to the one in Figure 6.10.

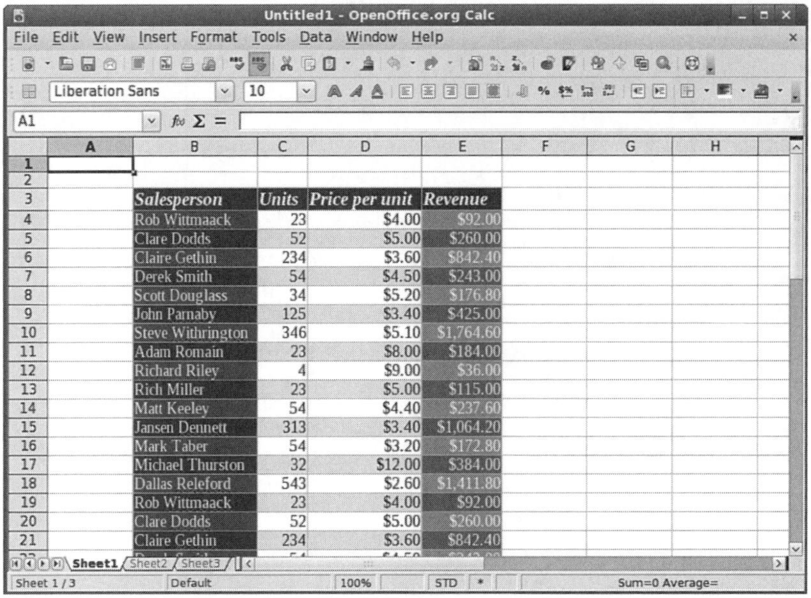

FIGURE 6.10   The finished article, looking a lot better than before!

Summarizing Data with Calc

Calc includes a powerful tool that lets you summarize large groups of data to help you when you need to carry out any analysis. This tool is called a *Data Pilot*, and you can use it to quickly summarize data that might normally take a long time if you did the calculations manually. Using the sample spreadsheet from earlier, we take you through how to build a simple Data Pilot, showing you how to analyze and manipulate long lists of data.

The previous section featured a spreadsheet that showed salespeople, customers, date of invoice, and revenue. At the foot of the spreadsheet were a couple of formulas that enabled you to quickly see the total revenue earned and the average order value.

Now you want to find out how much sales people have earned individually. Of course, you could add this up manually with a calculator, but that would defeat the point of using Calc. So, you need to create a Data Pilot to summarize the information.

First, you need to select all the cells from B3 to E42 as they contain the data you want to analyze. After these are selected, click the Data menu and select Data Pilot, Start to open the Data Pilot Wizard. The first screen is shown in Figure 6.11 and is defaulted to current selection. Make sure that you choose this one to use the data in the selected range and click OK to continue.

FIGURE 6.11   Use either the current selection or an external data source to provide the Data Pilot with information.

The next screen enables you to lay out your Data Pilot as you want it. In this example, you want to have Salesperson in the left column marked Row Fields, so click and drag the Salesperson option from the list on the right and drop it onto the Row Fields area. Next, drag out Revenue and drop it into the Data Fields area; it will automatically know to give you a sum of the revenue. We also want to know the average or mean price per unit, so drag Price per Unit onto the Data Fields area and double-click it. Select Average in the dialog box that appears and click OK. You should end up with something like Figure 6.12, and you are almost ready to display your Data Pilot.

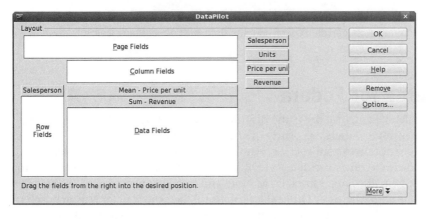

FIGURE 6.12   Lay out your Data Pilot as you want it.

The final piece in the puzzle is to tell Calc where you want it to place the finished Data Pilot. To do this, click the More button to drop down some extra options and then, to choose a new sheet, select the drop-down box next to Results To. When you click OK now, Calc builds the Data Pilot and displays it on a new sheet in your workbook. Figure 6.13 shows the new Data Pilot.

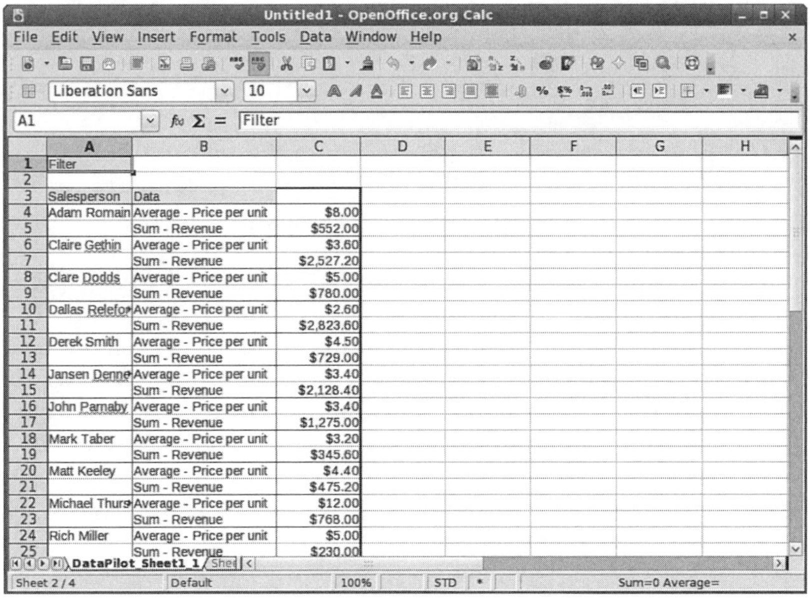

FIGURE 6.13   Summarize large volumes of numeric data with ease, using Calc's Data Pilot function.

Office Suites for Fedora

As mentioned earlier, OpenOffice.org is the default application suite for Fedora. However, with all things open source, there are plenty of alternatives should you find that OpenOffice.org does not meet your specific requirements. These include the popular Gnome Office and also KOffice, the default KDE productivity suite. You are more likely to hear more about OpenOffice.org, especially as more and more people wake up to the fact that it is compatible with Microsoft Office file formats. In fact, the state of Massachusetts recently elected to standardize on two file formats for use in government: the Adobe Acrobat PDF format and the OASIS OpenDocument format, both of which are supported natively in OpenOffice.org.

> **NOTE**
>
> The decision by the state of Massachusetts to standardize on PDF and OpenDocument has huge ramifications for the open source world. It is the first time that OpenDocument, an already-agreed open standard, has been specified in this way. What it means is that anyone who wants to do business with the state government must use OpenDocument-based file formats, and not the proprietary formats in use by Microsoft. Unfortunately for Microsoft, it does not have support for OpenDocument in any of its applications, making them useless to anyone wanting to work with the state government. This is despite Microsoft being a founding member of OASIS, who developed and ratified the OpenDocument standard!

Working with Gnome Office

The other office suite available for GNOME is Gnome Office, which is a collection of individual applications. Unlike OpenOffice.org, Gnome Office does not have a coherent suite of applications, meaning that you have to get used to using a word processor that offers no integration with a spreadsheet, and that cannot work directly with a presentation package. However, if you need only one or two components, it is worthwhile investigating Gnome Office.

The GTK Widget Set

Open source developers are always trying to make it easier for people to build applications and help in development. To this end, there are a number of widgets or toolkits that other developers can use to rapidly create and deploy GUI applications. These widgets control things such as drop-down lists, Save As dialogs, window buttons, and general look and feel. Unfortunately, whereas Windows and Apple developers have to worry about only one set of widgets each, Linux has a plethora of different widgets, including GTK+, QT, and Motif. What is worse is that these widgets are incompatible with one another, making it difficult to easily move a finished application from one widget set to another.

GTK is an acronym for *GIMP Tool Kit*. The *GIMP (The GNU Image Manipulation Program)* is a graphics application very similar to Adobe Photoshop. By using the GTK-based jargon, we save ourselves several hundred words of typing and help move along our discussion of GNOME Office. You might also see similar references to QT and Motif, as well as to other widget sets, in these chapters.

Here are some of the primary components of the Gnome Office suite that are available in Fedora:

▶ **AbiWord**—This word processing program enables you to compose, format, and organize text documents and has some compatibility with the Microsoft Word file format. It uses plug-ins (programs that add functionality such as language translation) to enhance its functionality.

▶ **Gnumeric**—This spreadsheet program enables you to manipulate numbers in a spreadsheet format. Support for all but the most esoteric Microsoft Excel functions means that users should have little trouble trading spreadsheets with Excel users.

▶ **The GIMP**—This graphics application enables you to create images for general use. It can import and export all common graphic file formats. The GIMP is analogous to Adobe's Photoshop application and is described in Chapter 7, "Multimedia."

▶ **Evolution**—Evolution is a mail client with an interface similar to Microsoft Outlook, providing email, scheduling, and calendaring. It is described in Chapter 5, "On the Internet."

The loose association of applications known as Gnome Office includes several additional applications that duplicate the functionality of applications already provided by Fedora. Those extra GNOME applications are not included in a default installation of Fedora to eliminate redundancy. They are all available from the Gnome Office website, at http://www.gnome.org/projects/ooo/. Both The GIMP and Evolution are available with Fedora by default. You have to use yum or pirut to retrieve the remaining components.

Fedora provides the AbiWord editor as part of its Extras, shown in Figure 6.14. AbiWord can import XML, Microsoft Word, RTF, UTF8, plain text, WordPerfect, KWord, and a few other formats. AbiWord is notable for its use of plug-ins, or integrated helper applications, that extend its capabilities. These plug-ins add language translation, HTML editing, a thesaurus, a Linux command shell, and an online dictionary, among other functions and features. If you just need a straightforward but powerful word processing application, you should examine AbiWord.

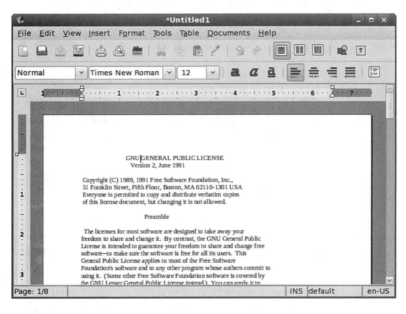

FIGURE 6.14   AbiWord is a word processing program for Fedora, GNOME, and X11. It handles some formats that OpenOffice.org cannot, but does not yet do well with Microsoft Word formats.

AbiWord is not installed by default in Fedora; instead, you need to use Add/Remove Programs to retrieve it. Just search for AbiWord, and install the package.

After you've installed AbiWord, it becomes available under Applications, Office, Abiword. If you are familiar with Microsoft Works, the AbiWord interface will be familiar to you because its designers based the interface upon Works.

You can use the Gnumeric spreadsheet application to perform financial calculations and to graph data, as shown in Figure 6.15. It can import comma- or tab-separated files, text, or files in the Gnumeric XML format, saving files only as XML or text. You need to install Gnumeric using either Add/Remove Software or the following command:

```
# yum install gnumeric
```

To launch Gnumeric from the menu, choose Applications, Office, Gnumeric Spreadsheet.

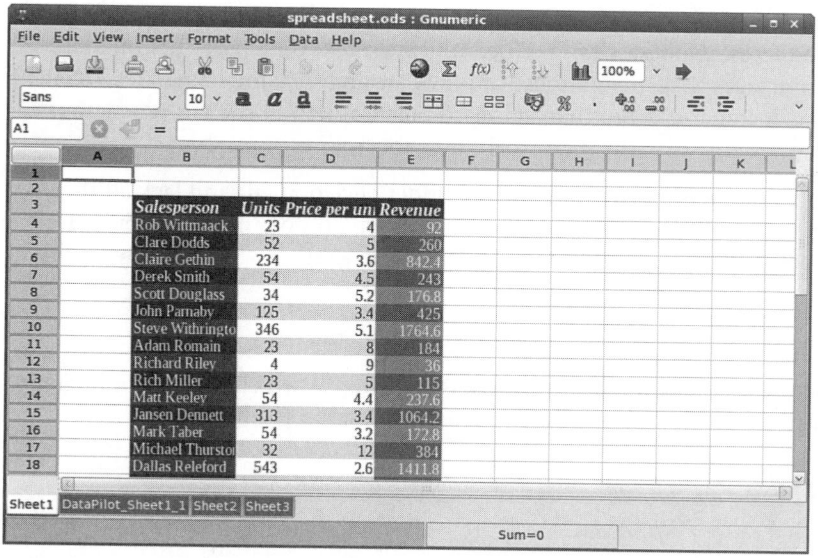

FIGURE 6.15   GNOME's Gnumeric is a capable financial data editor—here working with the same spreadsheet used earlier. OpenOffice.org also provides a spreadsheet application, as does KOffice.

After you press Enter, the main Gnumeric window appears. You enter data in the spreadsheet by clicking a cell and then typing in the text box. To create a graph, you click and drag over the spreadsheet cells to highlight the desired data, and then you click the Graph Wizard icon in Gnumeric's toolbar. Gnumeric's graphing component launches, and you are guided through a series of dialogs to create a graph. When you have finished, you can click and drag a blank area of your spreadsheet, and the graph appears.

The Project Planner application is useful for tracking the progress of projects, much like its Windows counterpart, Microsoft Project. When the main window is displayed, you can start a new project or import an existing project. The application provides three views: Resources, Gantt Charts, and Tasks.

Working with KOffice

The KDE office suite KOffice was developed to provide tight integration with the KDE desktop. Integration enables objects in one application to be inserted in other applications via drag-and-drop, and all the applications can communicate with each other, so a change in an object is instantly communicated to other applications. The application integration provided by KDE is a significant enhancement to productivity. (Some GNOME desktop applications share a similar communication facility with each other.) If you use the KDE desktop rather than the default GNOME desktop, you can enjoy the benefits of this integration, along with the Konqueror web and file browser.

The word processor for KOffice is KWord. KWord is a frames-based word processor, meaning that document pages can be formatted in framesets that hold text, graphics, and objects in enclosed areas. Framesets can be used to format text on a page that includes columnar text and images that the text needs to flow around, making KWord an excellent choice for creating documents other than standard business letters, such as newsletters and brochures.

KWord and other components of KOffice are still under development and lack all the polished features of OpenOffice.org and AbiWord. However, it does have the ability to work with the OpenDocument format found in OpenOffice.org, as well as limited compatibility with Microsoft file formats.

You can access the KOffice components from the Office menu.

KWord asks you to select a document for your session. The KWord client, shown in Figure 6.16, offers sophisticated editing capabilities, including desktop publishing.

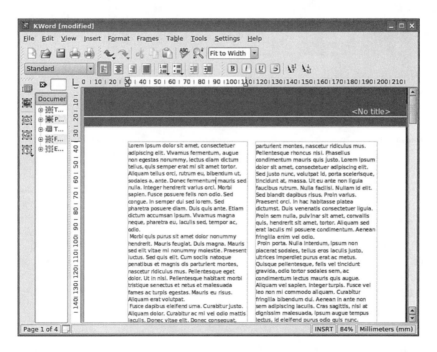

FIGURE 6.16   The KOffice KWord word processing component is a sophisticated frames-based WYSIWYG editor that is suitable for light desktop publishing, supporting several formats, including WordPerfect.

The KOffice KSpread client is a functional spreadsheet program that offers graphing capabilities. Like KWord, you can access KSpread from the Office menu.

KDE includes other productivity clients in its collection of KOffice and related applications. These clients include an address book, time tracker, calculator, notepad, and scheduler. One popular client is KOrganizer, which provides daily, weekly, work week, and monthly views of tasks, to-do lists, and scheduled appointments with background alarms. A journal, or diary, function is also supported within it, and you can synchronize information with your Palm Pilot. You can launch this client from the Office menu.

Figure 6.17 shows a typical KOrganizer window.

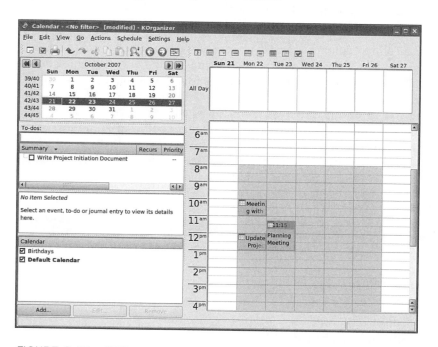

FIGURE 6.17   KDE's KOrganizer client supports editing of tasks and schedules that you can sync with your PDA.

Commercial Office Suites for Linux

Several commercial office suites are available for Fedora in addition to StarOffice, already mentioned. None of these commercial suites are provided with Fedora. Of note is Hancom Office. Using the same QT widget set found in the KDE desktop, Hancom Office scores well on Microsoft file format compatibility. The suite includes a word processor, a spreadsheet presentation tool, and a graphics application. Corel produced a version of its WordPerfect Office 2000 for Linux before it discontinued the release of any new Linux products. It still offers a support page, but the software is no longer available, nor is the excellent—but whiskered—WordPerfect 8 for Linux.

Productivity Applications Written for Microsoft Windows

Microsoft Windows is fundamentally different from Linux, but you can install and run some Microsoft Windows applications in Linux by using an application named Wine. Wine enables you to use Microsoft Windows and DOS programs on UNIX-based systems. Wine includes a program loader that you can use to execute a Windows binary, along with a DLL that implements Windows command calls, translating them to the equivalent UNIX and X11 command calls. Because of frequent updates to the Wine code base, Wine is not included with Fedora. Download a current version of Wine from http://www. winehq.org/. To see whether your favorite application is supported by Wine, you can look at the Wine application database at http://appdb.winehq.org/appbrowse.php.

In addition, there are other solutions to enable use of Microsoft productivity applications, primarily CodeWeavers' CrossOver Office. If you are after a painless way of running not only Microsoft Office, but also Apple iTunes and other software, you should really pay CodeWeavers a visit. CrossOver Office is one of the simplest programs you can use to get Windows-based programs to work. Check out http://www.codeweavers.com to download a trial version of the latest software. It requires registration, but don't worry—the guys at CodeWeavers are great and will not misuse your details. The big plus is that you get a whole month to play around with the trial before you decide whether to buy it. Of course, you might get to the end of the 30 days and realize that Linux does what you want it to do and you don't want to go back to Windows. Don't be afraid; take the plunge!

Relevant Fedora Commands

The following commands give you access to productivity applications, tools, and processes in Fedora:

- **oowriter**—OpenOffice.org's Writer
- **oocalc**—OpenOffice.org's Calc
- **ooimpress**—OpenOffice.org's Impress
- **koshell**—KDE's KOffice office suite shell
- **kspread**—KDE's KSpread spreadsheet
- **gimp**—The *GIMP (GNU Image Manipulation Package)*
- **gnumeric**—A spreadsheet editor for GNOME
- **planner**—A project management client for GNOME
- **abiword**—A graphical word processor for GNOME

Reference

- ▶ **http://www.openoffice.org**—The home page for the OpenOffice.org office suite

- ▶ **http://www.gnome.org/projects/ooo**—The GNOME Office site

- ▶ **http://www.koffice.org**—The home page for the KOffice suite

- ▶ **http://en.hancom.com**—The home page for the Hancom Office suite

- ▶ **http://bulldog.tzo.org/webcal/webcal.html**—The home page of the excellent WebCal web-based calendar and scheduling program

- ▶ **http://www.codeweavers.com**—Website of the hugely popular CrossOver Office from CodeWeavers that allows you to run Windows programs under Linux

Multimedia

The twenty-first century has become the century of the digital lifestyle, with millions of computer users around the world embracing new technologies, such as digital cameras, MP3 players, and other assorted multimedia gadgets. Whereas 10 years ago you might have had a collection of WAV files littering your Windows installation, nowadays you are more likely to have hundreds, if not thousands, of MP3 files scattered across various computers. Along with video clips, animations, and other graphics, the demand for organizing and maintaining these vast libraries is driving development of applications. Popular proprietary applications such as iTunes and Google's Picasa are coveted by Linux users, but open source applications are starting to appear that provide real alternatives, and for some the final reasons they need to move to Linux full time.

This chapter provides an overview of some of the basic multimedia tools included with Fedora. You will see how to create your own CDs, watch TV, rip audio CDs into the open source Ogg audio format for playback, as well as manage your media library. You will also learn about how Fedora handles graphics and pictures.

Listening to Music

Perhaps the most basic multimedia application you will need is a CD Player. Pretty much everyone knows what a CD is, and the vast majority of people own CDs. Fedora can easily handle CD Audio through the default CD Player under Applications, Sound & Video, as shown in Figure 7.1.

If all you are after is a basic CD playing application, then you can't really go wrong with CD Player.

FIGURE 7.1   Basic, but functional, is the order of the day for Fedora's CD Player.

The default music player is Rhythmbox, which is designed to play music files in a selection of different formats, such as locally stored Ogg files, Internet Radio Stations, or CDs (as shown in Figure 7.2). It is found in Applications, Sound & Video as Rhythmbox Music Player. You can also use it to subscribe to podcasts available through the Internet.

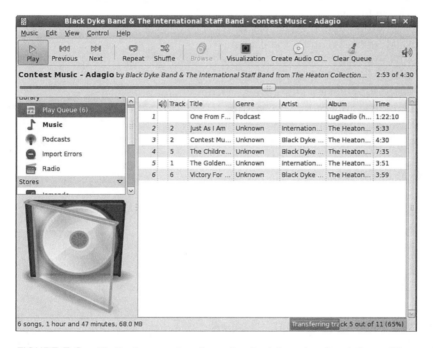

FIGURE 7.2   Rhythmbox can handle podcasts, Internet radio stations, CDs, and local sound files.

Another popular music player is Xmms, a Winamp clone, which in the full version can play not only music, but MPEG1/2/3 video as well. Xmms (see Figure 7.3) supports a number of plug-ins that can add dancing, lighted oscilloscope-like displays, redirect its output to other devices, support unusual file formats, sync animations to the music, and otherwise increase its geek appeal exponentially. You will have to use yum to install it with the following command:

```
#yum install xmms
```

after which it will be located under Applications, Sound & Video as the Audio Player entry.

FIGURE 7.3   The very popular Xmms music player, seen here playing a local Ogg-Vorbis file.

Other music and sound-related applications can be found in the Sound & Video menu, and, of course, you are free to install your own selection of applications as well.

Getting Music into Fedora with Sound Juicer

A handy utility that is included with Fedora is Sound Juicer, found under Applications, Sound and Video. Sound Juicer automatically detects when you install a CD and attempt to retrieve the track details from the Internet. From there it will rip the CD tracks into Ogg files for storage on your filesystem. You can see Sound Juicer in action in Figure 7.4.

FIGURE 7.4   Create your own digital music collection with Sound Juicer.

Streaming Audio

Streaming audio is for playing games, listening to Internet radio, and other online audio content. Streaming audio is designed to produce an uninterrupted sound output, but it requires the system to perform a content juggling act. Essentially, the system's audio buffer is continually filled with audio information, which is fed to the buffer through the system's Internet connection. Because of server and connection capabilities, the rate of input might vary. Because audio is used at a constant rate, the trick to managing streaming audio is to always keep the buffer full, although you might not be able to fill it at a constant rate.

Streaming audio is handled in Fedora in the .m3u format. The MPEG formats are also used for streaming audio. Although Xmms supports streaming audio, another popular application is the Real Player, available from http://www.real.com/linux/. An excellent resource for music and sound in Linux is http://linux-sound.org/. The Network Audio section of that website contains an extensive list of streaming audio applications.

> **NOTE**
>
> The Icecast application, not provided with Fedora, is a popular streaming audio server. You can use Icecast to serve your MP3 music collection over your home LAN. You can learn more about Icecast at http://www.icecast.org/. A nice tutorial on Icecast is available at http://www.linuxnetmag.com/en/issue4/m4icecast1.html.

Graphics Manipulation

Over a very short space of time, digital cameras and digital imagery have become extremely popular, to the point where some traditional film camera manufacturers are switching solely to digital. This meteoric rise has led to an increase in the number of applications that can handle digital imagery. Linux, thanks to its rapid pace of development, is now highly regarded as a multimedia platform of choice for editing digital images. Did you know that CGI effects for the film *The Lord of the Rings* were produced on Linux workstations and hundreds of Linux servers, all running Fedora?

This section of the chapter discusses The GIMP, a powerful graphics manipulation tool. You also learn about graphic file formats supported by Fedora, as well as some tools you can use to convert them if the application you want to use requires a different format.

The GNU Image Manipulation Program

One of the best graphics clients available is The GIMP. The GIMP is a free, GPLed image editor with sophisticated capabilities that can import and export more than 30 different graphics formats, including files created with Adobe Photoshop. It is often compared with Photoshop, and The GIMP represents one of the GNU Projects' first significant successes. Many images in Linux were prepared with The GIMP.

The GIMP can be found under the Applications, Graphics menu as simply The GIMP.

You see an installation dialog box when The GIMP is started for the first time, and then a series of dialog boxes that display information regarding the creation and contents of a local GIMP directory. This directory can contain personal settings, preferences, external application resource files, temporary files, and symbolic links to external software tools used by the editor.

What Does Photoshop Have That Isn't in The GIMP?

Although The GIMP is powerful, it does lack two features Adobe Photoshop offers that are important to some graphics professionals.

The first of these is the capability to generate color separations for commercial press printers (CMYK for the colors cyan, magenta, yellow, and key [or black]). The GIMP uses RGB (red, green, and blue), which is great for video display, but not so great for printing presses. The second feature The GIMP lacks is the use of Pantone colors (a patented color specification) to ensure accurate color matching.

If these features are unimportant to you, The GIMP is an excellent tool. If you must use Adobe Photoshop, the current version of CodeWeavers' CrossOver Office will run Photoshop in Linux.

These deficiencies might not last long. A CMYK plug-in is in the works, and the Pantone issues are likely to be addressed in the near future as well.

After the initial configuration has finished, The GIMP's main windows and toolboxes appear. The GIMP's main window contains tools used for selecting, drawing, moving, view enlarging or reducing, airbrushing, painting, smudging, copying, filling, and selecting color. Depending on the version installed on your system, the toolbox can host more than 25 different tools.

The toolbox's File, Xtns, and Help menus are used for file operations (including sending the current image by electronic mail), image acquisition or manipulation, and documentation, respectively. If you right-click an open image window, you see the wealth of The GIMP's menus, as shown in Figure 7.5.

Using Scanners in Fedora

With the rise of digital photography, there has been an equal decline in the need for image scanners. However, there are still times that you want to use a scanner, and Fedora makes it easy.

You can also use many types of image scanners with The GIMP. In the past, the most capable scanners required a SCSI port. Today, however, most scanners work through a USB port. You must have scanner support enabled for Linux (usually through a loaded kernel module, scanner.o) before using a scanner with The GIMP.

Although some scanners can work via the command line, you will enjoy more productive scanning sessions if you use a graphical interface because GUI features, such as previewing and cropping, can save time before actually scanning an image. Most scanners in use with Linux use the Scanner Access Now Easy (*SANE*) package, which supports and enables graphical scanning sessions.

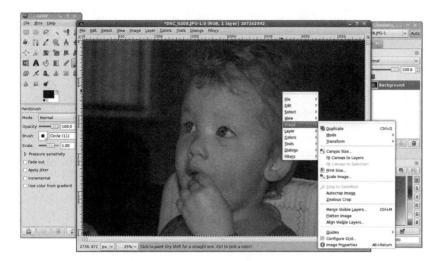

FIGURE 7.5   Right-click on an image window to access The GIMP's cascading menus.

SANE consists of two software components. A low-level driver enables the hardware support and is specific to each scanner. Next, a graphical scanner interface X client known as xsane is used as a plug-in or ancillary program (or script) that adds features to The GIMP.

NOTE

Although xsane is commonly used as a GIMP plug-in, it can also be used as a standalone program. Another useful program is Joerg Schulenburg's gocr client, used for optical character recognition (*OCR*). Although not a standalone application, it is included in the Kooka scanning application. This program works best with 300 dots per inch (*dpi*) scans in several different graphics formats. OCR is a resource-intensive task and can require hundreds of megabytes of disk storage!

A list of currently supported scanners can be found at http://www.sane-project.org/sane-supported-devices.html. Unfortunately, if your scanner doesn't appear on the list, you should not expect it to work with the SANE software. There is also a list on that same page for drivers not yet included, but you must be able to compile the application from source to use them.

Supported USB scanners are automatically detected and the appropriate driver is loaded automatically. The USB devices tell the USB system several pieces of information when they are connected—the most important of which are the vendor ID and the device ID. This identification is used to look up the device in a table and load the appropriate driver.

You will find that Fedora successfully identifies and configures most modern USB-based scanners.

Many scanners are supported in Linux. If yours is not, it still might be possible to use it. The Kooka and Xsane scanner applications are included with Fedora and are fairly straightforward to use. They can both be found in the Graphics menu as the Scanner Tool.

Working with Graphics Formats

Image file formats are developed to serve a specific technical purpose (lossless compression, for example, where the file size is reduced without sacrificing image quality) or to meet a need for a proprietary format for competitive reasons. Many file formats are covered by one or more patents. For example, the GIF format had fallen into disfavor with the open-source crowd because the patent holder waited a while before deciding to enforce his patent rights.

If you want to view or manipulate an image, you need to identify the file format to choose the proper tool for working with the image. The file's extension is your first indicator of the file's format. The graphics image formats supported by the applications included with Fedora include the following:

- ▶ **.bmp**—Bitmapped graphics, commonly used in Microsoft Windows
- ▶ **.gif**—CompuServe Graphics Interchange Format
- ▶ **.jpg**—Joint Photographic Experts Group
- ▶ **.pcx**—IBM Paintbrush
- ▶ **.png**—Portable Network Graphics
- ▶ **.svg**—Scalable Vector Graphics
- ▶ **.tif**—Tagged Image File format

An extensive list of image file extensions can be found in the man page for ImageMagick, an excellent application included with Fedora, which you learn more about in upcoming sections of this chapter.

> **TIP**
>
> Fedora includes dozens of graphics conversion programs that are accessible through the command line, and there are few, if any, graphics file formats that cannot be manipulated when using Linux. These programs can be called in Perl scripts, shell scripts, or command-line pipes to support many types of complex format conversion and image manipulation tasks. See the man pages for the ppm, pbm, pnm, and pgm families of commands. Also see the man page for the convert command, which is part of a suite of extremely capable programs included with the ImageMagick suite.

Often, a file you want to manipulate in some way is in a format that cannot be used by either your graphics application or the final application. The solution is to convert the image file—sometimes through several formats. The `convert` utility from ImageMagick is useful, as is the `netpbm` family of utilities. If it is not already installed, ImageMagick can be installed with the Add Remove Software GUI found in the System Settings menu; the `netpbm` tools are always installed by default.

The `convert` utility converts between image formats recognized by ImageMagick. Color depth and size also can be manipulated during the conversion process. You can use ImageMagick to append images, surround them with borders, add labels, rotate and shade them, and perform other manipulations well suited to scripting. Commands associated with ImageMagick include `display`, `animate`, `identify`, and `import`. The application supports more than 130 different image formats (all listed in the man page for ImageMagick).

Fun with ImageMagick's `identify`

You can use ImageMagick's `identify` command to identify details about image files. The welcoming splash image used for the GRUB bootloader is located in `/boot/grub` and is a `gzipped` `.xpm` image. If you run `identify` on the image, you'll discover that it's a 640×480 `xpm` image with 16-bit color depth. That's all you need to know to construct a replacement image of your own. Using The GIMP or another graphics tool, crop or resize your chosen image to 640×480 and change the color depth to 16 bits. Save the image as `splash.xpm` and then `gzip` the resulting file. Replace the original Fedora file, and you now have a custom boot image. The use of `identify` helped you duplicate the parameters of the original image to comply with the requirements of GRUB.

The `identify` command is also useful to identify unknown image files and to determine whether they're corrupt.

The `netpbm` tools are installed by default because they compose the underpinnings of graphics format manipulation. The man page for each image format lists related conversion utilities; the number of those utilities gives you some indication of the way that format is used and shows how one is built on another:

▶ The man page for ppm, the portable pixmap file format, lists 47 conversion utilities related to ppm. This makes sense because ppm, or *portable pixmap*, is considered the lowest common denominator for color image files. It is therefore often used as an intermediate format.

▶ The man page for pgm, the portable graymap file format, lists 22 conversion utilities. This makes sense because pgm is the lowest common denominator for grayscale image files.

▶ The man page for pnm, the portable anymap file format, lists 31 conversion utilities related to it. However, there is no format associated with PNM because it operates in concert with ppm, pgm, and pbm.

▶ An examination of the man page for pbm, the portable bitmap file format, reveals no conversion utilities. It's a monochrome format and serves as the foundation of the other related formats.

Capturing Screen Images

You can use graphics manipulation tools to capture images that are displayed on your computer screen. Although this technique was used for the production of this book, it has broader uses; there is truth to the cliché that a picture is worth a thousand words. Sometimes it is easier to show an example than it is to describe it.

A captured screen image (also called a *screen grab* or a *screenshot*) can be used to illustrate an error in the display of an application (a font problem, for example) or an error dialog that is too complex to copy down by hand. You might just want to share an image of your beautifully crafted custom desktop configuration with your friends or illustrate your written documents.

When using the GNOME desktop, you can take advantage of the built-in screenshot mechanism (gnome-panel-screenshot). Access this tool by pressing the Print Screen key. (Alt+Print Screen takes a screenshot of only the window that has focus on a desktop.) Captured images are saved in .png format.

Using Digital Cameras with Fedora

Most digital cameras used in connection with Fedora fall into one of two categories: webcams (small, low-resolution cameras connected to the computer's interface) or hand-held digital cameras that record image data on disks or memory cards for downloading and viewing on a PC. Fedora supports both types. Other types of cameras, such as surveillance cameras that connect directly to a network via wire or wireless connections, need no special support (other than a network connection and viewing software) to be used with a Linux computer.

Fedora supports hundreds of different digital cameras, from early parallel-port (CPiA chipset-based) cameras to today's USB-based cameras. You can even use Intel's QX3 USB microscope with Fedora. If you prefer a standalone network-based webcam, explore the capabilities of Linux-based cameras from Axis (at http://www.axis.com/products/video/camera/productguide.htm). The following sections describe some of the more commonly used still camera hardware and software supported by Fedora.

Handheld Digital Cameras

Digital cameras are one of the major success stories of the last few years. Now you can take pictures and see previews of your pictures immediately. The pictures themselves are stored on discs or memory cards that can be easily plugged into Fedora for further manipulation, using The GIMP or other software. Unfortunately, most of the supplied software that comes with the cameras tend to be for Windows users only, making you reliant on the packages supplied with Fedora.

The good news, though, is that because of the good development carried out in Fedora and GNOME, you are now able to plug pretty much any camera into your computer through a USB interface and Fedora automatically recognizes the camera as a USB mass storage device. You can even set Fedora to recognize when a camera is plugged in so that it automatically imports your photographs for you.

To do this, you need to set up your settings for removable drives and media. You can find this in the System, Preferences, Hardware menu. Click the Cameras tab and select the option to import digital photographs when connected (see Figure 7.6).

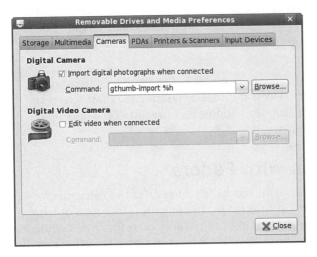

FIGURE 7.6   Use GNOME's intelligent handling of removable media by setting it to import your photographs automatically.

Now whenever you connect a digital camera to your computer GNOME automatically detects it (see Figure 7.7), and asks whether you want to import the photographs.

FIGURE 7.7   GNOME detects the presence of a digital camera and asks whether the photos should be imported.

By default GNOME uses the excellent gThumb package (see Figure 7.8), which, although basic-looking, offers an easy-to-use interface and powerful cataloging capabilities.

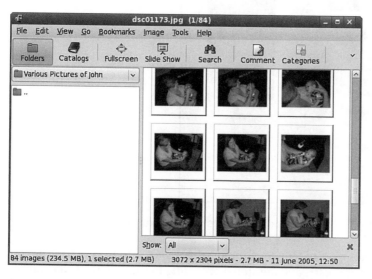

FIGURE 7.8   Make use of gThumb to manage your extensive photo collection.

Using F-Spot

With the inclusion of Mono into Fedora Extras, Fedora now has access to the superb F-Spot photo management application. You can find F-Spot under the Applications, Graphics menu listed as F-Spot Photo Manager. If you have used the popular Google Picasa application, you will feel instantly at home with F-Spot because it is similar in many ways.

The first time you open F-Spot, you are asked to import your first batch of photographs, as shown in Figure 7.9. You can also assign a tag to them, if you want to track particular types of photographs. You might want to allow F-Spot to copy the photograph to a new directory, Photos—something that may help you organize your photos on the system.

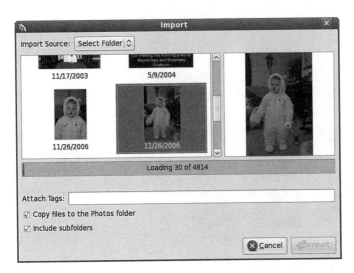

FIGURE 7.9   The versatile F-Spot makes adding photos to your library easy.

When you are ready, click Import to let F-Spot import the photos into the library. The pictures appear in the F-Spot library, and are stored according to the date they were taken. This information is given to F-Spot by the EXIF information that your camera stores each time you take a picture. In Figure 7.10, you can see the standard F-Spot window.

FIGURE 7.10   Browse through your extensive photo collection and correct minor problems using F-Spot.

Use the timeline across the top of the window to browse through your photographs, and you can do some minor editing by double-clicking on any photograph. F-Spot is still in its infancy, but development is ongoing, so keep a eye open for any major updates.

Burning CDs and DVDs in Fedora

Linux is distributed across the Internet through the use of ISOs that are waiting to be written to CDs or DVDs. Therefore, learning how to burn discs is essential if you have to download and install a Linux distribution. Not only that, but you are likely to want to use CDs and, more commonly, DVDs to back up your music, family pictures, or other important files. With DVD writers being so cheap, the format is now pervasive and more and more people use cheap DVDs as way of archiving simply due to the larger storage size available. Of course, you can use blank CD media, but they don't have anywhere near the capacity offered by DVDs. Today's high-resolution digital cameras can occupy upward of 3MB per shot, and music files can be anything from 1MB to 10MB+ in size. These file sizes make DVD the obvious choice, but there are still occasions when you need to write to a CD. You can use CDs and DVDs to

► Record and store multimedia data, such as backup files, graphics images, and music.

► Rip audio tracks from music CDs (*ripping* refers to extracting music tracks from a music CD) and compile your own music CDs for your personal use.

Linux audio clients and programs support the creation and use of many different types of audio formats. Later sections of this chapter discuss sound formats, sound cards, music players, and much more. Because CD burning is used for many other purposes in Fedora, we cover the essentials of that process first in this chapter. To record multimedia data on a CD, you must have installed a drive with CD writing capabilities on your system. To make certain that your CD writer is working, use wodim -scanbus to get the information for using the CD drive under SCSI (small computer system interface) emulation:

```
# wodim -scanbus
Cdrecord-Clone 2.01a32-dvd (i686-pc-linux-gnu) Copyright (C) 1995-2001 Jörg
Schilling
Linux sg driver version: 3.5.27
Using libscg version 'schily-0.8'
scsibus0:
        0,0,0     0) 'HL-DT-ST' 'RW/DVD GCC-4120B' '2.01' Removable CD-ROM
        0,1,0     1) *
        0,2,0     2) *
        0,3,0     3) *
        0,4,0     4) *
        0,5,0     5) *
        0,6,0     6) *
        0,7,0     7) *
```

Here, you can see that the CD writer (in this example, a CD writer/DVD reader) is present and is known by the system as device `0,0,0`. The numbers represent the `scsibus/target/lun` (logical unit number) of the device. You need to know this device number when you burn the CD, so write it down or remember it.

Creating CDs and DVDs with Fedora's Graphical Clients

Although adequate for quick burns and use in shell scripting, the command-line technique for burning CDs and DVDs is an awkward choice for many people until they become proficient at it and learn all the arcane commands. Fortunately, Fedora provides several graphical clients.

Nautilus

With Fedora, enhanced functionality has been included in the default file browser Nautilus. Under the Places menu item is a CD/DVD Creator selection. To use it, insert a blank CD or DVD into your CD-R/DVD-R drive. You must have two Nautilus windows open: one that shows the files you want to save to the CD, and a second one open to the CD/DVD Creator Folder (accessed in Nautilus by the Places menu, CD/DVD Creator) location. Click on the Write to Disc button as shown in Figure 7.11 to bring up the Write dialog; at the next dialog box, choose the format to which you want to write the disc. Nautilus CD/DVD Creator supports writing to a disc image file, commonly known as *ISO*. You can also give your new disc a label and tell Nautilus at what speed you want to write the disc. Finally, click the Write button to start the burning process—it is that simple!

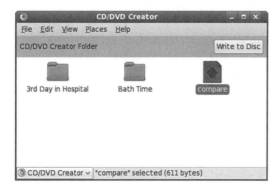

FIGURE 7.11   Creating a CD or DVD using the Nautilus browser is made easy with the drag-and-drop features it provides.

GnomeBaker

If you require a bit more flexibility than just dragging and dropping files into a CD folder, then you should consider GnomeBaker, which enables you to burn Data CDs and DVDs, and also master Audio CDs. It's not installed by default, so make sure you use the command

```
#yum install gnomebaker
```

to retrieve and install the application.

GnomeBaker itself is very easy to use, and can be found under the Applications, Sound and Video menu. When you start GnomeBaker, you are immediately prompted to choose what it is you want to create, as shown in Figure 7.12.

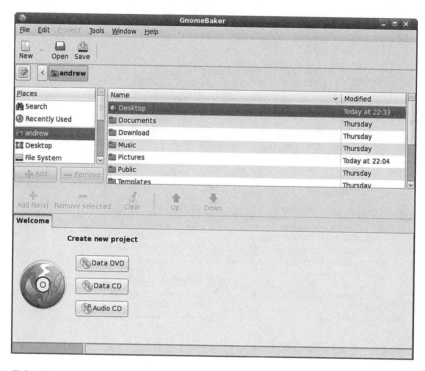

FIGURE 7.12   GnomeBaker offers a task-based approach to burning optical media.

After you've chosen what you want to create, you can then navigate to the files you want to burn in the top half of the GnomeBaker window and drag them to the bottom project area. In Figure 7.13, I am backing up an audio CD that was ripped to my hard drive by Sound Juicer.

TIP

An excellent Internet site for CD-related information is http://www.cdmediaworld.com/. The Gracenote CDDB Music Recognition Service licenses a database service to soft-ware developers so that they can include additional functionality in their applications by accessing the database and having their applications display information about the music CD, including the artist and song title, the CD's track list, and so on. The database server at cddb.cddb.org, when contacted by the appropriate software, identifies the appropriate CD and sends the information to be displayed locally. Many CD player applications provide this functionality. The service is interactive: If you have a CD that is not in the CDDB database, the website tells you how you can add the information to the database.

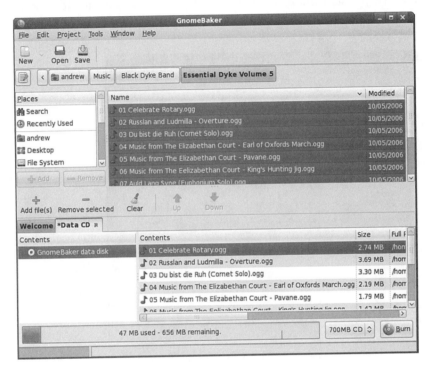

FIGURE 7.13   Use GnomeBaker to back up your CD or photo collection.

Creating CDs from the Command Line

In Linux, creating a CD at the command line is a two-step process. You first create the iso9660-formatted image, and you then burn or write the image onto the CD. The iso9660, as you will learn in Chapter 35, "Managing the File System," is the default file system for CD-ROMs.

Use the mkisofs command to create the ISO image. The mkisofs command has many options (see the man page for a full listing), but use the following for quick burns:

```
$ mkisofs -r -v -J -l -o /tmp/our_special_cd.iso /source_directory
```

The options used in this example are as follows:

- ▶ -r—Sets the permission of the files to more useful values. UID and GID (individual and group user ID requirements) are set to zero, all files are globally readable and searchable, and all files are set as executable (for Windows systems).

- ▶ -v—Displays verbose messages (rather than terse messages) so that you can see what is occurring during the process; these messages can help you resolve problems if they occur.

- ▶ -J—Uses the Joliet extensions to ISO9660 so that your Windows-using buddies can more easily read the CD. The Joliet (for Windows), Rock Ridge (for Unix), and HSF (for Mac) extensions to the iso9660 standard are used to accommodate long file-names rather than the eight-character DOS filenames that the iso9660 standard supports.

- ▶ -l—Allows 31-character filenames; DOS does not like it, but everyone else does.

- ▶ -o—Defines the directory where the image will be written (that is, the output) and its name. The /tmp directory is convenient for this purpose, but the image could go anywhere you have write permissions.

- ▶ /source_directory—Indicates the path to the source directory; that is, the directory containing the files you want to include. There are ways to append additional paths and exclude directories (and files) under the specified path—it is all explained in the man page, if you need that level of complexity. The simple solution is to construct a new directory tree and populate it with the files you want to copy, and then make the image using that directory as the source.

Many more options are available, including options to make the CD bootable.

After you have created the ISO image, you can write it to the CD with the cdrecord command:

```
$ cdrecord -eject -v speed=12 dev=0,0,0 /tmp/our_special_cd.iso
```

The options used in this example are as follows:

- ▶ -eject—Ejects the CD when the write operation is finished.

- ▶ -v—Displays verbose messages.

- ▶ speed=—Sets the speed; the rate depends on the individual drive's capabilities. If the drive or the recordable medium is poor, you can use lower speeds to get a good burn.

- ▶ dev=—Specifies the device number of the CD writer (the number I told you to write down earlier).

NOTE

You can also use the `blank=` option with the `cdrecord` command to erase CD-RW disks. The `cdrecord` command has fewer options than `mkisofs` does, but it offers the `-multi` option, which enables you to make multisession CDs. A multisession CD enables you to write a data track, quit, and then add more data to the CD later. A single-session CD can be written to only once; any leftover CD capacity is wasted. Read about other options in the `cdrecord` man page.

Current capacity for CD media is 700MB of data or 80 minutes of music. (There are 800MB/90 minute CDs, but they are rare.) Some CDs can be overburned; that is, recorded to a capacity in excess of the standard. The `cdrecord` command is capable of overburning if your CD-RW drive supports it. You can learn more about overburning CDs at http://www.cdmediaworld.com/hardware/cdrom/cd_oversize.shtml/.

Creating DVDs from the Command Line

There are several competing formats for DVD, and with prices rapidly falling, it is more likely that DVD-writing drives will become commonplace. The formats are as follows:

- ▶ DVD+R
- ▶ DVD-R
- ▶ DVD+RW
- ▶ DVD-RW

Differences in the + and – formats have mostly to do with how the data is modulated onto the DVD itself, with the + format having an edge in buffer underrun recovery. How this is achieved impacts the playability of the newly created DVD on any DVD player. The DVD+ format also has some advantages in recording on scratched or dirty media. Most drives support the DVD+ format. As with any relatively new technology, your mileage may vary.

We focus on the DVD+RW drives because most drives support that standard. The software supplied with Fedora has support for writing to DVD-R/W (rewritable) media as well. It will be useful for you to review the DVD+RW/+R/-R[W] for Linux HOWTO at http://fy.chalmers.se/~appro/linux/DVD+RW/ before you attempt to use `dvd+rw-tools`, which you need to install to enable DVD creation (also known as *mastering*) as well as the `cdrtools` package. You can ignore the discussion in the HOWTO about kernel patches and compiling the tools.

TIP

The 4.7GB size of DVD media is measured as 1000 megabytes per gigabyte, instead of the more commonly used 1024 megabytes per gigabyte, so do not be surprised when the actual formatted capacity, about 4.4GB, is less than you anticipated. `dvd+rw-tools` does not allow you to exceed the capacity of the disk.

You need to have the `dvd+rw-tools` package installed (as well as the `cdrtools` package). The `dvd+rw-tools` package contains the `growisofs` application (that acts as a front end to `mkisofs`) as well as the DVD formatting utility.

You can use DVD media to record data in two ways. The first way is much the same as that used to record CDs in a session, and the second way is to record the data as a true file system, using packet writing.

Session Writing

To record data in a session, you use a two-phase process:

1. Format the disk with `dvd+rw-format /dev/scd0` (only necessary the first time you use a disk).

2. Write your data to the disk with `growisofs -Z /dev/scd0 -R -J /your_files`.

The `growisofs` command simply streams the data to the disk. For subsequent sessions, use the `-M` argument instead of `-Z`. The `-Z` argument is used only for the initial session recording; if you use the `-Z` argument on an already used disk, it erases the existing files.

> **CAUTION**
>
> Some DVDs come preformatted; formatting them again when you use them for the first time can make the DVD useless. Always be sure to carefully read the packaging your DVD comes in to ensure that you are not about to create another coaster!

> **TIP**
>
> Writing a first session of at least 1GB helps maintain compatibility of your recorded data with other optical drives. DVD players calibrate themselves by attempting to read from specific locations on the disk; you need data there for the drive to read it and calibrate itself.
>
> Also, because of limitations to the ISO9660 file system in Linux, do not start new sessions of a multisession DVD that would create a directory past the 4GB boundary. If you do so, it causes the offsets used to point to the files to "wrap around" and point to the wrong files.

Packet Writing

Packet writing treats the CD or DVD disk like a hard drive in which you create a file system (like ext3) and format the disk, and then write to it randomly as you would to a conventional hard drive. This method, although commonly available on Windows-based computers, is still experimental for Linux and is not yet covered in detail here.

> **TIP**
>
> DVD+RW media are capable of only about 1,000 writes, so it is very useful to mount them with the `noatime` option to eliminate any writing to update their inodes or simply mount them read-only when it's not necessary to write to them.

It is possible to pipe data to the `growisofs` command:

```
# your_application ¦ growisofs -Z /dev/scd0=/dev/fd/0
```

It is also possible to burn from an existing image (or file, named pipe, or device):

```
# growisofs -Z /dev/scd0=image
```

The `dvd+rw-tools` documentation, found at `/usr/share/doc/dvd+rw-tools-*/index.html`, is required reading before your first use of the program. We also suggest that you experiment with DVD-RW (rewritable) media first, as if you make mistakes then you will still be able to reuse the disk, rather than creating several new coasters for your coffee mug.

Sound and Music

Linux historically had a reputation of lacking good support for sound and multimedia applications in general. However, great strides have been made in recent years to correct this, and support is now a lot better than it used to be. (It might make you smile to know that Microsoft no longer supports the Microsoft Sound Card, but Linux users still enjoy support for it, no doubt just to annoy the folks in Redmond.) Unix, however, has always had good multimedia support as David Taylor, Unix author and guru, points out:

> "The original graphics work for computers was done by Evans & Sutherland on Unix systems. The innovations at MIT's Media Lab were done on Unix workstations. In 1985, we at HP Labs were creating sophisticated multimedia immersive work environments on Unix workstations, so maybe Unix is more multimedia than suggested. Limitations in Linux support doesn't mean Unix had the same limitations. I think it was more a matter of logistics, with hundreds of sound cards and thousands of different possible PC configurations."

That last sentence sums it up quite well. Unix had a limited range of hardware to support; Linux has hundreds of sound cards. Sound card device driver support has been long lacking from manufacturers, and there is still no single standard for the sound subsystem in Linux.

In this section, you learn about sound cards, sound file formats, and the sound applications provided with Fedora.

Sound Cards

Fedora supports a wide variety of sound hardware and software. Two models of sound card drivers compete for prominence in today's market:

- ALSA, the Advanced Linux Sound Architecture, which is entirely open source

- OSS, the Open Sound System, which offers free and commercial drivers

Fedora uses ALSA because ALSA is the sound architecture for the 2.6 series kernels.

ALSA supports a long list of sound cards. You can review the list at http://www. alsa-project.org/alsa-doc/. If your sound card is not supported, it might be supported in the commercial version of OSS. You can download a trial version of commercial software and test your sound card at http://www.opensound.com/download.cgi.

Fedora detects most sound cards during the original installation. If you add or replace a sound card after the initial install, the Kudzu New Hardware Configuration utility automatically detects and configures it at the next reboot. To configure the sound card at any other time, use the `system-config-soundcard` graphical tool. The graphical tool can be found under the System, Administration menu as the Soundcard Detection menu item.

Adjusting Volume

Fedora now benefits from the inclusion of PulseAudio, a new way of controlling sound across Fedora. Instead of having a single global volume level, PulseAudio allows you to tailor each program to your specific needs. You may want to have music played at a louder volume than video; this is easy to do with PulseAudio, which is found under Applications, Sound and Video, as seen in Figure 7.14.

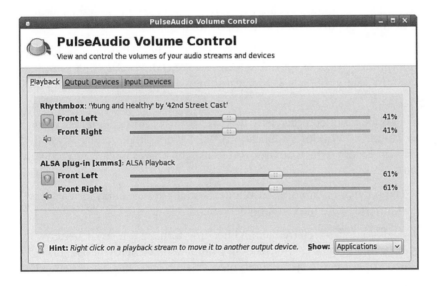

FIGURE 7.14   Control the volume level for each application that is currently handling sound with the volume slider.

You can also set the global output volume by using the slider found under the Output tab.

Alternatively you can control all the output volumes for the system to make sure that you have set everything to your taste, as shown in Figure 7.15. To access the volume control, right-click on the speaker icon and select Open Volume Control.

FIGURE 7.15   Use the volume control to manage volume settings for all your sound output devices.

Sound Formats

A number of formats exist for storing sound recordings. Some of these formats are associated with specific technologies, and others are used strictly for proprietary reasons. Fedora supports several of the most popular sound formats, including

- **raw (.raw)**—More properly known as *headerless format*, audio files using this format contain an amorphous variety of specific settings and encodings. All other sound files contain a short section of code at the beginning—a header—that identifies the format type.

- **MP3 (.mp3)**—A popular, but commercially licensed, format for the digital encoding used by many Linux and Windows applications. MP3 is not supported by any software included with Fedora (which advises you to use the open source Ogg-Vorbis format instead).

- **WAV (.wav)**—The popular uncompressed Windows audio-visual sound format. It is often used as an intermediate file format when encoding audio.

- **Ogg-Vorbis (.ogg)**—Fedora's preferred audio encoding format. You enjoy better compression and audio playback, and freedom from lawsuits when you use this open-source encoding format for your audio files.

> **NOTE**
>
> Because of patent and licensing issues, Fedora has removed support for the MPEG, MPEG2, and MPEG3 (MP3) file formats in Fedora Linux. Although we cannot offer any legal advice, it appears that individuals using MP3 software are okay; it is just that Fedora cannot distribute the code because it sells its distribution. It seems—at this point—perfectly all right for you to obtain an MP3-capable version of Xmms (for example), which is a Winamp clone that plays MPEG1/2/3 files. You can get Xmms directly from http://www.xmms.org/ because that group has permission to distribute the MP3 code.

You can also enable the MP3 codec within Fedora by using the livna.org `yum` repository. You do this by installing the `gstreamer-plugins-mp3` package, which enables the MP3 codec in all the GNOME applications.

Another alternative is to use the Ogg-Vorbis format; it is completely free of restrictions. A ripper for CD music is available from http://www.thekompany.com/projects/tkcoggripper/ and an MP3-to-Ogg converter is available from http://faceprint.com/code/. Or, you could download and install the non-crippled versions of multimedia applications from FreshRPMs at http://www.freshrpms.net/.

Fedora includes software (such as the `sox` command used to convert between sound formats) so that you can more easily listen to audio files provided in a wide variety of formats, such as AU (from NeXT and Sun), AIFF (from Apple and SGI), IFF (originally from Commodore's Amiga), RA (from Real Audio), and VOC (from Creative Labs).

TIP

To learn more about the technical details of audio formats, read Chris Bagwell's Audio Format FAQ at http://www.cnpbagwell.com/audio.html.

Fedora also offers utilities for converting sound files from one format to another. Conversion utilities come in handy when you want to use a sound in a format not accepted by your current application of choice. A repository of conversion utilities resides at http://ibiblio.org/pub/linux/apps/sound/convert/!INDEX.html and includes MP3 and music CD–oriented utilities not found in Fedora. You have to know how to compile and install from source, however. If you see something useful, have a look at http://www.rpmfind.net/ to locate a binary RPM if you don't feel up to the task.

Fedora does provide `sox`, a self-described sound translator that converts music among the AIFF, AU, VAR, DAT, Ogg, WAV, and other formats. It also can be used to change many other parameters of the sound files.

Timidity is a MIDI-to-WAV converter and player. If you are interested in MIDI and musical instruments, Timidity is a handy application; it handles karaoke files as well, displaying the words to accompany your efforts at singing.

Viewing Video

You can use Fedora tools and applications to view movies and other video presentations on your PC. This section presents some TV and motion picture video software tools included with the Fedora distribution you received with this book.

TV and Video Hardware

To watch TV and video content on your PC, you must install a supported TV card or have a video/TV combo card installed. A complete list of TV and video cards supported by Fedora is at http://www.exploits.org/v4l/.

Freely available Linux support for TV display from video cards that have a TV-out jack is poor. That support must come from the X driver, not from a video device that Video4Linux supports with a device driver. Some of the combo TV-tuner/video display cards have support, including the Matrox Marvel, the Matrox Rainbow Runner G-Series, and the RivaTV cards. Many other combo cards lack support, although an independent developer might have hacked something together to support his own card. Your best course of action is to perform a thorough Internet search with Google.

Many of the TV-only PCI cards are supported. In Linux, however, they are supported by the video chipset they use, and not by the name some manufacturer has slapped on a generic board (the same board is typically sold by different manufacturers under different names). The most common chipset is the Brooktree Bt*** series of chips; they are supported by the bttv device driver.

If you have a supported card in your computer, it should be detected during installation. If you add it later, the Kudzu hardware detection utility should detect it and configure it. You can always configure it by hand.

To determine what chipset your card has, use the lspci command to list the PCI device information, find the TV card listing, and look for the chipset that the card uses. For example, the lspci output for my computer shows the following:

```
# lspci
00:00.0 Host bridge: Advanced Micro Devices [AMD] AMD-760 [IGD4-1P]
➥System Controller (rev 13)
00:01.0 PCI bridge: Advanced Micro Devices [AMD] AMD-760 [IGD4-1P] AGP Bridge
00:07.0 ISA bridge: VIA Technologies, Inc. VT82C686 [Apollo Super South] (rev 40)
00:07.1 IDE interface: VIA Technologies, Inc. VT82C586B PIPC Bus Master IDE
➥ (rev 06)
00:07.2 USB Controller: VIA Technologies, Inc. USB (rev 1a)
00:07.3 USB Controller: VIA Technologies, Inc. USB (rev 1a)
00:07.4 SMBus: VIA Technologies, Inc. VT82C686 [Apollo Super ACPI] (rev 40)
00:09.0 Multimedia audio controller: Ensoniq 5880 AudioPCI (rev 02)
00:0b.0 Multimedia video controller: Brooktree Corporation Bt878 Video Capture
➥ (rev 02)
00:0b.1 Multimedia controller: Brooktree Corporation Bt878 Audio Capture (rev 02)
00:0d.0 Ethernet controller: Realtek Semiconductor Co., Ltd. RTL-8029(AS)
00:0f.0 FireWire (IEEE 1394): Texas Instruments TSB12LV23 IEEE-1394 Controller
00:11.0 Network controller: Standard Microsystems Corp [SMC] SMC2602W EZConnect
01:05.0 VGA compatible controller: nVidia Corporation NV15 [GeForce2 Ti] (rev a4)
```

Here, the lines listing the multimedia video controller and multimedia controller say that this TV board uses a Brooktree Bt878 Video Capture chip and a Brooktree Bt878 Audio Capture chip. This card uses the Bt878 chipset. Your results will be different, depending on what card and chipset your computer has. This card happened to be an ATI All-in-Wonder VE (also known as ATI TV-Wonder). (The VE means *Value Edition*; hence, there is no TV-out connector and no radio chip on the card; what a value!) The name of the chipset says that the card uses the `bttv` driver.

In the documentation directory is a file named CARDLIST, and in that file is the following entry, among others:

```
card=64 - ATI TV-Wonder VE
```

There are 105 cards listed, as well as 41 radio cards, including

```
card=0 -  *** UNKNOWN/GENERIC ***
```

which is what you could have used had you not known the manufacturer's name for the card.

The file named Modules.conf, located in the same directory, offers the following example of information to place in the /etc/modules.conf file:

```
# i2c
alias char-major-89    i2c-dev
options i2c-core       i2c_debug=1
options i2c-algo-bit   bit_test=1

# bttv
alias char-major-81    videodev
alias char-major-81-0  bttv
options bttv           card=2 radio=1
options tuner          debug=1
```

All you need do is enter this information into /etc/modules.conf and change the value for card=2 to card=64 to match your hardware. You can delete the reference to the radio card (radio=2) because there isn't one and leave the other values alone. Then you must execute

```
# depmod -a
```

to rebuild the modules dependency list so that all the modules are loaded automatically. When finished, all you need do is execute

```
# modprobe bttv
```

and your TV card should be fully functional. All the correct modules will be automatically loaded every time you reboot. Fedora is clever enough to detect and configure a supported TV card that is present during installation.

TIP

Other useful documentation can be found in `/usr/src/linux-2.6/Documentation/` `_video4linux`. After you have identified a driver for a device, it does not hurt to look at the source code for it because so little formal documentation exists for many drivers; much of it is in the source code comments.

The development of support for TV cards in Linux has coalesced under the Video4Linux project. The Video4Linux software provides support for video capture, radio, and teletext devices in Fedora.

Video Formats

Fedora recognizes a variety of video formats. The formats created by the MPEG group, Apple, and Microsoft dominate, however. At the heart of video formats are the *codecs*—the encoders and decoders of the video and audio information. These codecs are typically proprietary, but free codecs do exist. Here is a list of the most common video formats and their associated file extensions:

▶ `.mpeg`—The MPEG video format; also known as `.mpg`

▶ `.qt`—The QuickTime video format from Apple

▶ `.mov`—Another QuickTime video format

▶ `.avi`—The Windows audio visual format

TIP

An RPM that provides a Divx codec for Linux can be found at http://www.freshrpms. net/. Divx is a patented MPEG-4 video codec that is the most widely used codec of its type. It allows for compression of MPEG-2 video by a factor of 8. See http://www.divx. com/ for more information.

The GetCodecs application is a Python script with a GUI interface that downloads, installs, and configures your Fedora system with multimedia codecs not provided by Fedora, such as MP3, Divx, and DVD codecs. The script can be obtained from http://sourceforge.net/projects/getcodecs/.

If you need to convert video from one format to another, you use encoder applications called *grabbers*. These applications take raw video data from a video device such as a camera or TV card, and convert it to one of the standard MPEG formats or to a still image format, such as JPEG or GIF. Fedora does not supply any encoder applications (other than ppmtompeg, which encodes MPEG-1 video), but you can find them at http://www. freshrpms.net/ or another online source (see the "Reference" section at the end of this chapter).

Viewing Video in Linux

Because of the patent and licensing issues mentioned earlier, the capability to play video files has been removed from Fedora. This functionality can be restored if you install the full version of the applications described in this section from FreshRPMs at http://www. freshrpms.net/. There you can find multimedia applications such as Ogle, Xine, AlsaPlayer, Gstreamer, Grip, Mplayer, VCDImager, VideoLAN-client, Xmms, and Zapping.

You can use Linux software to watch TV, save individual images (take snapshots) from a televised broadcast, save a series of snapshots to build animation sequences, or capture video, audio, or both. The following sections describe some of the ways in which you can put Linux multimedia software to work for you.

The noatun viewer is provided with Fedora to use as an embedded viewer in the Konqueror browser. noatun is set up as the default association for the video file formats it plays. Open a video file in Konqueror or Nautilus, and the video is shown in the viewer if it is supported. The viewer provides basic Start, Stop, and Fast-Forward VCR-type functions.

You can watch MPEG and DVD video with Xine. Xine is a versatile and popular media player that is not included with Fedora. Xine is used to watch AVI, QuickTime, Ogg, and MP3 files (the latter is disabled in Fedora).

Macromedia Flash

The Macromedia Flash plug-in for the Mozilla browser is a commercial multimedia application that isn't provided with Fedora, but many people find it useful. Macromedia Flash enables you to view Flash content at websites that support it. The Mozilla plug-in can be obtained from http://macromedia.mplug.org/. Both `.rpm` and `.tar.gz` files are provided.

Having trouble with the Macromedia Flash plug-in for Mozilla? Just manually copy the files `flashplayer.xpt` and `libflashplayer.so` to `/usr/lib/firefox-2.0.0.x/plugins`, where x is the latest point release for Firefox (2.0.0.4 at the time of writing). An `.rpm` file for Flash that should install without problems is available from http://macromedia. mplug.org/.

Another interesting video viewer application is MPlayer (not provided by Fedora), a movie player for Linux. MPlayer can use Win32 codecs and it supports a wider range of video formats than Xine, including Divx and some RealMedia files. MPlayer also uses some special display drivers that support Matrox, 3Dfx, and Radeon cards and can make use of some hardware MPEG decoder boards for better MPEG decoding. Look for Fedora packages at http://www.mplayerhq.hu; a Win32 codec package is also available, as well as other codec packages and a GUI interface.

Personal Video Recorders

The best reason to attach a television antenna to your computer, however, is to use the video card and the computer as a personal video recorder.

The commercial personal video recorder, TiVo, uses Linux running on a PowerPC processor to record television programming with a variety of customizations. TiVo has a clever interface and wonderful features, including a record/playback buffer, programmed recording and pause, slow motion, and reverse effects. Fedora does not provide any of the many applications that attempt to mimic the TiVo functionality on a desktop PC running Linux. However, several such applications, including DVR, The Linux TV Project, and OpenPVR, are listed at http://www.exploits.org/v4l/. These projects are in development and do not provide .rpm files, so you have to know how to download from CVS and compile your own binaries. For something a little easier, check out MythTV at http://www.mythtv.org/; a Fedora .rpm file should be available from ATrpms.

Linux, TiVo, and PVRs

Some TiVo users say that using this Linux-based device has changed their lives. Indeed, the convenience of using a personal video recorder (*PVR*) can make life a lot easier for inveterate channel surfers. Although PVR applications are not included with Fedora, open source developers are working on newer and better versions of easy-to-install and easy-to-use PVR software for Linux. For more information about TiVo, which requires a monthly charge and a phone line (or broadband connection with a newer TiVo2), browse to http://www.tivo.com/. Unrepentant Linux hardware hackers aiming to disembowel or upgrade a TiVo can browse to http://www.9thtee.com/tivoupgrades.htm or read the TiVo Hack FAQ at http://www.tivofaq.com/. A PVR makes viewing television a lot more fun!

A number of Linux sites are devoted to PVR software development. Browse to the DVR project page at http://www.pierrox.net/dvr/.

DVD and Video Players

You can now easily play DVDs with Fedora as long as you install the appropriate software. (Fedora doesn't provide any.) Browse to http://www.videolan.org/, and then download, build, and install the vlc client.

You must have a CPU of at least 450MHz and a working sound card to use a DVD player. The default Fedora kernel supports the DVD CD-ROM file system. As mentioned earlier, Xine and MPlayer do a great job of playing DVD files.

NOTE

The VideoLAN HOWTO found at http://videolan.org/ discusses the construction of a network for streaming video. Although you might not want to create a network, a great deal of useful information about the software and hardware involved in the enterprise can be generalized for use elsewhere, so it is worth a look. The site also contains a link to a HOWTO about cross-compiling on Linux to produce a Windows binary.

Reference

▶ **http://www.cdcopyworld.com/**—A resource for technical information about CD media and CD writers.

▶ **http://hardware.redhat.com/hcl/**—A database of supported hardware.

▶ **http://www.opensound.com/download.cgi**—The commercial OSS sound driver trial version download.

▶ **http:/www.xmms.org/**—Home to the Xmms audio player.

▶ **http://www.thekompany.com/projects/tkcoggripper/**—A free (but not GPL) Ogg CD ripper.

▶ **http://faceprint.com/code/**—An MP3 to Ogg converter named mp32ogg.

▶ **http://www.ibiblio.org/pub/linux/apps/sound/convert/!INDEX.html**—Home to several sound conversion utilities.

▶ **http://linux-sound.org/**—An excellent resource for Linux music and sound.

▶ **http://www.cnpbagwell.com/audio.html**—The Audio Format FAQ.

▶ **http://www.icecast.org/**—A streaming audio server.

▶ **http://www.linuxnetmag.com/en/issue4/m4icecast1.html**—An Icecast tutorial.

▶ **http://linuxselfhelp.com/HOWTO/MP3-HOWTO-7.html**—The MP3 HOWTO contains brief descriptions of many audio applications and, although it focuses on the MP3 format, the information is easily generalized to other music formats.

▶ **http://www.exploits.org/v4l/**—Video for Linux resources.

▶ **http://fame.sourceforge.net/**—Video encoding tools.

▶ **http://teletext.mb21.co.uk/faq.shtml**—The Teletext FAQ.

▶ **http://xine.sourceforge.net/**—Home of the Xine DVD/video player.

▶ **http://www.MPlayerHQ.hu/homepage/**—Home to the MPlayer video player.

▶ **http://www.videolan.org/**—A VideoLAN project with good documentation.

▶ **http://fy.chalmers.se/~appro/linux/DVD+RW/**—The DVD+RW/+R/-R[W] for Linux, a HOWTO for creating DVDs under Linux.

▶ **http://www.gimp.org**—Home page of The GIMP (Gnu Image Manipulation Program).

▶ **http://f-spot.org**—Home page of the F-Spot project.

▶ **http://www.linuxformat.co.uk**—Website of Linux Format, home of a long-running GIMP tutorial by Michael J Hammel.

7

▶ **http://www.exif.org**—More information on EXIF and how it is used in digital cameras.

▶ **http://www.sane-project.org**—Home page of the SANE (*Scanner Access Now Easy*) project.

▶ **http://www.imagemagick.org**—Home page for ImageMagick.

▶ **http://www.codeweavers.com**—Home of the popular crossover office; required if you want to try to run Photoshop under Linux.

▶ **http://gimp.net/tutorials/**—Official tutorials for The GIMP.

CHAPTER **8**

Printing with Fedora

From the word *go*, Fedora provides support for a huge range of printers from many different manufacturers. This chapter looks at how to get your printer connected and talking to Fedora, as well as at the software that Fedora uses to manage printers and print jobs.

In keeping with most of the other Linux distributions, Fedora uses CUPS (*Common Unix Printing System*) to handle printers. Other systems are supported, such as LPRng, but you do not have access to some of the graphical management tools from within Fedora.

The Internet Printing Protocol

CUPS supports the Internet Printing Protocol, known as *IPP*, and offers a number of unique features, such as network printer directory (printer browsing) services, support for encryption, and support for PostScript Printer Description (.ppd) files.

According to the Internet Engineering Task Force (*IETF*), IPP grew out of a 1996 proposal by Novell to create a printing protocol for use over the Internet. Since then, the system has been developed and has matured into a stable print system for use on a variety of Linux and Unix-like operating platforms.

Overview of Fedora Printing

Fedora's print filter system is the main engine that enables the printing of many types of documents. The heart of that engine is the GNU GPL version of Aladdin's Ghostscript interpreter, the gs client. The system administrator's printer configuration tool is the system-config-printer client.

NOTE

Fedora's print system can be used to print to local (attached) or remote (network) printers. If you use a local printer, it is represented by a printer device, such as `/dev/lp0` or `/dev/usb/lp0` (if you have a USB printer). Local and remote printers use print *queues* defined in your system's printer capabilities database, `/etc/printcap`. A document being printed is known as a print *job*, and you can view and control your list, or queue, of current print jobs in the spool directory, which is `/var/spool/cups`. Note that you may control only your print jobs; only the root operator can control print jobs of any user on the system.

To add a printer to your system, you use the `system-config-printer` client to create, configure, and save the printer's definition. The client saves the definition as an entry in your system's printer capabilities database, `/etc/printcap`. Each definition contains a text field with the name of the printer, its host, and name of the print queue. Printed documents are spooled to the `/var/spool/cups` directory. A sample `printcap` definition might look like the following:

```
# This file was automatically generated by cupsd(8) from the
# /etc/cups/printers.conf file.  All changes to this file
# will be lost.
Officejet¦Officejet Pro K5400:rm=teletran.hudson.com:rp=Officejet:
```

CUPS maintains its own database of defined printers under the `/etc/cups` directory in a file named `printers.conf`. For example, an associated printer defined in `/etc/printcap` previously might have the following entry in `/etc/cups/printers.conf`:

```
# Printer configuration file for CUPS v1.3.3
# Written by cupsd on 2007-10-28 19:30
<DefaultPrinter Officejet>
Info Officejet Pro K5400
Location Office
DeviceURI socket://192.168.0.100:9100
State Idle
StateTime 1193599791
Accepting Yes
Shared Yes
JobSheets none none
QuotaPeriod 0
PageLimit 0
KLimit 0
OpPolicy default
ErrorPolicy stop-printer
</Printer>
```

This example shows the definition for the printer named `lp`, along with its associated device, description, state, and other information. The various possible fields and entries in this file are documented in the `printer.conf` man page.

CUPS uses a print server (daemon) named cupsd, also called a *scheduler* in the CUPS documentation. The server can be controlled, like other Fedora services, by the service command or system-config-services client. How the server works on a system is determined by settings in its configuration file, cupsd.conf, found under the /etc/cups directory. CUPS executables are found under the /usr/lib/cups directory.

The cupsd.conf man page documents more than 80 different settings for the server, which you can configure to match your system, network, or printing environment. Default CUPS-related files and directories are stored under the /usr/share/cups directory. Logging can be set to seven different levels, with information about access and errors stored in log files under the /var/log/cups directory.

Resource requirements can be tailored through other settings, such as MaxCopies to set the maximum number of copies of a print job by a user, MaxJobs to set a limit on the number of active print jobs, and MaxJobsPerUser to set a limit on the number of active jobs per user. The RIPCache setting (8MB by default) controls the amount of memory used for graphics cache during printing.

For example, if you want to limit printing to 20 copies of a document or page at a time and only 10 simultaneous print jobs per user, use settings such as the following:

```
MaxCopies 20
MaxJobsPerUser 10
```

> **TIP**
>
> Do not forget to restart the CUPS server after making any changes to its configuration file. Changes are activated only when the service is restarted (when the daemon rereads its configuration file). See the "GUI-Based Printer Configuration Quick Start" section later in this chapter.

Because CUPS does not use the traditional Berkeley-style print spooling system, lpd, you can change the name of the printer capabilities database from the default /etc/printcap. Encryption can be used for printing, with secure access behavior determined by settings in /etc/cups/client.conf. Network access settings include port, connection, IP address, domains, and limits to the number and size of client requests.

Configuring and Managing Print Services

Your task as a system administrator (or root operator of your workstation) is to properly define local or remote printers and to ensure that printing services are enabled and running properly. Fortunately, Fedora includes a graphical print service configuration tool that makes this job easy. You should use these tools to configure printing, as you learn in this section of the chapter. But first, take a moment to read through a quick overview of the configuration process.

CAUTION

Do not manually edit your /etc/printcap. Any changes will be lost when the printing service is restarted or if your system is rebooted. If you need to create customized printer entries, save the entries in /etc/printcap.local and then restart the printing service.

You can configure printing services using either the command line `system-config-printer-tui` program or the `system-config-printer-gui` graphical interface. Most of the detailed information in this chapter refers to the use of the GUI. The overview sections that follow, however, give you a solid foundation in both configuration approaches. You learn the details of these processes in later sections of the chapter.

GUI-Based Printer Configuration Quick Start

Configuring a printer for Fedora is easy but you must use root permission to do it. Make sure that the `cupsd` daemon is installed and running. If you elect to use printing support when you install Fedora, the daemon and related software will be installed. If you're not sure whether `cupsd` is running, you can quickly drop to a terminal and use the `service` command with the name of the service and the `status` keyword like so:

```
# service cups status
```

You will see either

```
cupsd is stopped
```

or, if `cupsd` is running, an acknowledgement, along with its process ID, such as

```
cupsd (pid 2378) is running...
```

If `cupsd` is installed but not running, start the daemon like so:

```
# /etc/rc.d/init.d/cups start
```

You can also use the `service` command to start the daemon, like so:

```
# service cups start
```

If you are using the desktop, select System, Administration, Printing. You will be asked to enter the root password. If not, you are using X as root, which is a bad idea. Log out, and then log back in as a regular user! After you enter the root password, the printer configuration dialog appears.

You then simply follow the prompts to define your printer and add local or remote printing services. You should print a test page before saving your changes. Use the printer configuration client or the File menu's Print menu item from a GNOME or KDE client.

NOTE

The `system-config-printer` utility is an update to the now-legacy `printtool` client included with previous Red Hat Linux distributions. Although you might also find related tools (or symbolic links), such as `printtool`, `printconf-tui`, and `/usr/sbin/printconf-gui` installed on your system, you should use the `system-config-printer` client to manage printers under Fedora.

Managing Printing Services

After defining a printer, you can use the command line to view and control your print jobs, or if root, all print jobs and printers on your system. Table 12.1 contains a partial list of CUPS and related printing commands and drivers included with Fedora.

TABLE 12.1   Print-Related Commands and Drivers

Name	Description
a2ps	Formats text files for PostScript printing
accept	Controls CUPS print job destinations
cancel	Cancels a CUPS print job
disable	Controls CUPS printers
dvi[lj, lj4l, lj2p, lj4]	Converts TeX DVI files to specific PCL format
enable	Controls CUPS printers
encscript	Converts text files to PostScript
escputil	Epson Stylus inkjet printer utility
grolbp	`groff` driver for Canon LBP-4 and LBP-8 laser printers
gs	The Ghostscript interpreter
gsbj[dj500, lp]	Ghostscript BubbleJet printer drivers
gsdj[dj500, lj, lp]	Ghostscript DeskJet printer drivers
lpadmin	CUPS command-line–based printer utility
lp	Starts a CUPS print job
lpc	A Berkeley-subset CUPS printer control client
lpf	General printer filter
lprm	A Berkeley-compatible CUPS job queue utility
lpstat	Displays CUPS print jobs and printer status
mpage	PostScript text formatting utility
pbm[2ppa, page, to10x, toepson, toppa, toptx]	Portable bitmap conversion utilities
pr	Text formatting command
psmandup	Duplex printing utility for nonduplex printers
reject	Controls CUPS print job destinations
setup	Launches printer configuration tool
smbclient	SMB print spooler
smbprint	SMB print shell script
smbspool	SMB printer spooler
thinkjettopbm	Portable bitmap to ThinkJet printer conversion utility

8

Most Linux systems use PostScript as the default document format for printing. Fedora uses the gs command along with CUPS to manage local and remote print jobs and the type of data transferred during a print job. The gs command is used to translate the document stream into a format accepted by the destination printer (which most likely uses HPCL).

You can use the Ghostscript interpreter gs to display its built-in printer devices by using the gs interpreter with its --help command-line option like this:

```
# gs --help
```

The gs command outputs many lines of help text on command-line usage and then lists built-in printer and graphics devices. Another way to get this information is to start gs and then use the devicenames == command like this:

```
# gs
GPL Ghostscript 8.60 (2007-08-01)
Copyright (C) 2007 Artifex Software, Inc.  All rights reserved.
...Input formats: PostScript PostScriptLevel1 PostScriptLevel2 PostScriptLevel3 PDF
Default output device: display
Available devices:
   alc1900 alc2000 alc4000 alc4100 alc8500 alc8600 alc9100 ap3250 appledmp
   atx23 atx24 atx38 bbox bit bitcmyk bitrgb bj10e bj10v bj10vh bj200 bjc600
   bjc800 bjc880j bjccmyk bjccolor bjcgray bjcmono bmp16 bmp16m bmp256
   bmp32b bmpa16 bmpa16m bmpa256 bmpa32b bmpamono bmpasep1 bmpasep8 bmpgray
   bmpmono bmpsep1 bmpsep8 ccr cdeskjet cdj1600 cdj500 cdj550 cdj670 cdj850
   cdj880 cdj890 cdj970 cdjcolor cdjmono cfax cgm24 cgm8 cgmmono chp2200 cif
   cljet5 cljet5c cljet5pr coslw2p coslwxl cp50 cups declj250 deskjet
   devicen dfaxhigh dfaxlow display dj505j djet500 djet500c dl2100 dnj650c
   epl2050 epl2050p epl2120 epl2500 epl2750 epl5800 epl5900 epl6100 epl6200
   eps9high eps9mid epson epsonc epswrite escp escpage faxg3 faxg32d faxg4
...
Search path:
   . : /usr/share/ghostscript/8.15/lib :
   /usr/share/ghostscript/8.15/Resource : /usr/share/ghostscript/fonts :
   /usr/share/fonts/default/ghostscript : /usr/share/fonts/default/Type1 :
   /usr/share/fonts/default/amspsfnt/pfb :
   /usr/share/fonts/default/cmpsfont/pfb : /usr/share/fonts/japanese :
   /etc/ghostscript
```

Not all the devices are listed in this example.

> **Aladdin or GNU?**
>
> At least two versions of Ghostscript are available for Linux. One version is named AFPL Ghostscript, which formerly went by the name Aladdin Ghostscript. This version is licensed under the Aladdin Free Public License, which disallows commercial distribution. The other version is called GNU Ghostscript, which is distributed under the GNU General Public License. For details about the different versions or for answers to questions regarding licensing, see the Ghostscript home page at http://www.cs.wisc.edu/ ~ghost/.

Creating and Configuring Local Printers

Creating a local printer for your Fedora system can be accomplished in six easy steps. You must have root permission to use the system-config-printer client. The cupsd daemon should also be running before you begin (start the daemon manually as shown earlier in this chapter, or use the ntsysv, chkconfig, or system-config-services commands to ensure that lpd is started at boot time).

To launch system-config-printer, go to System, Administration and choose the Printing menu option or use the command line of an X terminal window like this:

```
# system-config-printer &
```

Creating the Print Queue

The Fedora system-config-printer tool walks you through a process to create a new print queue, which effectively defines a new printer on your system. To begin configuration of a local (attached) printer, click the New Printer toolbar button in system-config-printer's main window. The New Printer configuration dialog appears, as shown in Figure 8.1.

Select the connection type that is appropriate for you. You can select a number of different connection types, depending on your specific requirements. Normally you will use the LPT#1 option if your printer is connected by a standard Parallel (or what used to be called Centronics) cable. Alternatively, if you are connecting to a printer that has a JetDirect port (most HP network-capable printers fit in this category), then select the appropriate option and enter the network address for the printer.

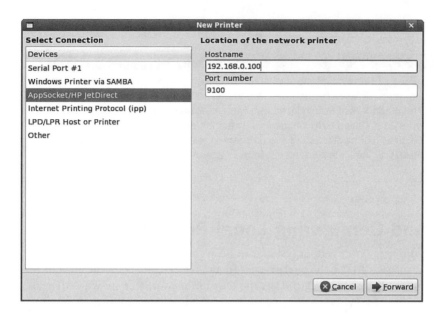

FIGURE 8.1   Select the appropriate connection method for your printer and enter the relevant details.

Next up you need to select the make/manufacturer of the printer that you are setting up, shown in Figure 8.2.

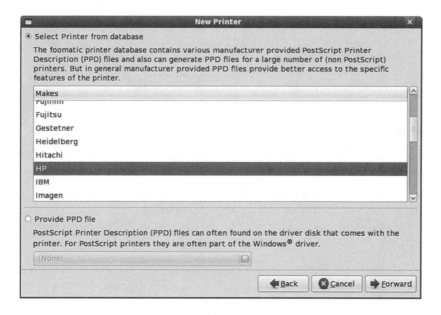

FIGURE 8.2   Select the make or manufacturer of your printer from this dialog box to help Fedora narrow down the driver options.

Note that you can configure a printer for Fedora even if it is not attached to your computer. After you select your printer's manufacturer, a list of printers from that manufacturer (such as HP, as shown in Figure 8.3) appears. Select your printer from the list, and then click the Forward button.

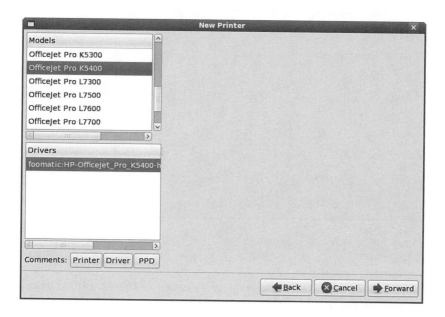

FIGURE 8.3   Select your printer from the list and click the Forward button to finish the configuration of a locally connected printer.

Do not worry if you do not see your printer listed in the selection; it is possible to select a related, although different, printer model and still be able to print to your printer. For example, many HP printers can be used by selecting the DeskJet 500 for monochrome or 500C model for color printing.

> **NOTE**
>
> You can also browse to http://www.linuxprinting.org/ to find out what drivers to use with your printer or to see a cross-referenced listing of printers supported by each driver. You might also find new and improved drivers for the latest printers on the market.

You can experiment to see which printer selection works best for your printer if its model is not listed. You might not be able to use all the features of your printer, but you will be able to set up printing service. Click Forward when you have made your choice.

The final screen allows you to name your printer and also provide more detailed information to help you identify and manage it (useful if you have a few dozen printers dotted around an office). This screen is shown in Figure 8.4.

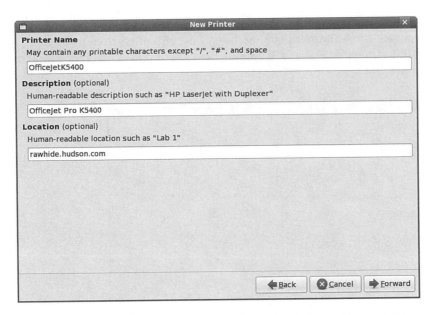

FIGURE 8.4   Help yourself by providing information that could be useful if you need to track down the printer for any reason.

The final screen (shown in Figure 8.5) summarizes what `system-config-printer` is about to do. If you are happy with the details, click the Apply button to commit your changes to the system.

FIGURE 8.5   Double-check the details shown before you commit to creating a new printer entry in `/etc/printcap`; when you are happy, click Apply to create the new print queue.

When the print queue has been created, you are asked whether you would like to print a test page. Click Yes to save your new printer setup and to print a test page. If you click No, a test page is not printed, and you have to delete the new printer entry or save or cancel your changes before you quit `system-config-printer`.

You can see the new printer defined in the `system-config-printer` main window as shown in Figure 8.6.

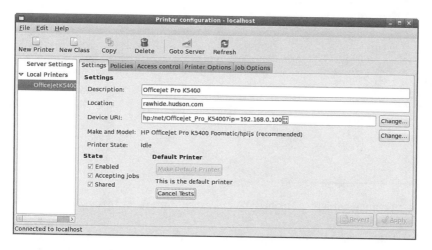

FIGURE 8.6   New printer entries created in `/etc/printcap` displayed in `system-config-printer`'s main window.

> **TIP**
>
> You can also configure multiple print queues for the same printer. Use this technique to test printing using different print drivers with the same printer. Create a new queue, give it a specific name (such as `testpcl3`), and select a different printer. Finish the configuration and print a test page to compare the results against other entries to find the best output. You can also use this technique to define a monochrome or color printer entry for the same printer or to use different drivers for different types of media (such as regular or photo paper).

Editing Printer Settings

You also use the `system-config-printer` tool to edit the newly defined printers. To edit the printer settings, highlight the printer's listing in the printer browser window. You can then select specific settings related to that printer by using the tabs that appear in the right side of the dialog box. The Printer Options dialog, part of the printer settings, is shown in Figure 8.7.

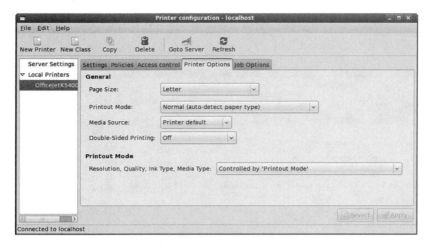

FIGURE 8.7   Edit a printer's settings by using tabs in system-config-printer.

The first tab in this dialog enables you to assign a new description for the printer. In this example, the printer has the description OfficeJet Pro K5400. Other tabs in this dialog enable you to change the queue type or queue options (such as whether to print a banner page or set the image area of a page), to select or update the driver, or to set print job options (shown in Figure 8.8).

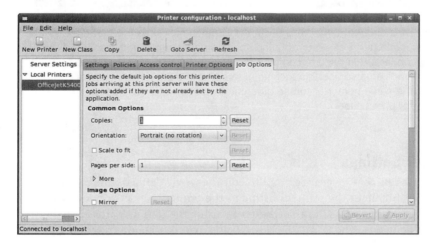

FIGURE 8.8   Configure how system-config-printer handles print jobs that are submitted to it using the Job Options tab.

When you make changes, make sure to click the Apply button in the bottom right-hand corner of system-config-printer in order to restart CUPS and for the changes to take effect. Click Quit from the Action menu when you're finished.

Related Fedora and Linux Commands

The following commands help you manage printing services:

- ▶ **accept**—Controls print job access to the CUPS server via the command line
- ▶ **cancel**—Cancels a print job from the command line
- ▶ **cancel**—Command-line control of print queues
- ▶ **disable**—Controls printing from the command line
- ▶ **enable**—Command-line control CUPS printers
- ▶ **lp**—Command-line control of printers and print service
- ▶ **lpc**—Displays status of printers and print service at the console
- ▶ **lpq**—Views print queues (pending print jobs) at the console
- ▶ **lprm**—Removes print jobs from the print queue via the command line
- ▶ **lpstat**—Displays printer and server status
- ▶ **system-config-printer**—Fedora's graphical printer configuration tool

Reference

- ▶ **http://www.linuxprinting.org/**—Browse here for specific drivers and information about USB and other types of printers.

- ▶ **http://www.hp.com/wwsolutions/linux/products/printing_imaging/ index.html**—Short but definitive information from HP regarding printing product support under Linux.

- ▶ **http://www.cups.org/**—A comprehensive repository of CUPS software, including versions for Fedora.

- ▶ **http://www.pwg.org/ipp/**—Home page for the Internet Printing Protocol standards.

- ▶ **http://www.linuxprinting.org/cups-doc.html**—Information about the Common UNIX Printing System (CUPS).

- ▶ **http://www.cs.wisc.edu/~ghost/**—Home page for the Ghostscript interpreter.

8

CHAPTER 9

Games

For any operating system to have mass-market appeal, it has to have a number of games that are compatible with it. Let's face it, no one wants to use computers just for word processing or databases—they want to be able to use them as a source of relaxation and even fun! This chapter looks at the state of Linux gaming and tells you how to get some of the current blockbusters up and running in a Linux environment. We even show you how to run Windows-based games under Linux.

Linux Gaming

A number of games come as part of the Fedora distribution, and they are divided into three distinct camps: KDE games, GNOME games, and X games. Our favorites are Planet Penguin Racer and Frozen Bubble (see Figure 9.1), but there are a few others for you to choose from. The best part, of course, is trying each one and seeing what you think. Many other free games are available across the web, so go to Google and see what you come up with.

However, games for Linux do not stop there—a few versions of popular Windows-based games are being ported across to the Linux platform, including Doom 3, Unreal Tournament 2004, and Quake 4. These three popular games have native Linux support and in some cases can run at similar, if not better, speeds than their Windows counterparts.

Finally, an implementation of the Wine code, called Cedega, is optimized especially for games. This uses application interfaces to make Windows games believe they are running on a Windows platform and not a Linux platform. Bear in mind that Wine stands for "Wine is not an emulator," so do not start thinking of it as such—the community can get quite touchy about it!

FIGURE 9.1   Be very careful; Frozen Bubble can become extremely addictive!

A historical gripe of Linux users has been the difficulty involved in getting modern 3D graphics cards working under Linux. Thankfully, since ATI (one of the major graphics card vendors) was bought up by AMD, they have released a true open source driver that is available to install under Fedora. NVIDIA also supports Linux, albeit by using closed source drivers. This means that Fedora does not ship with native 3D drivers for NVIDIA cards. It is fairly easy to get hold of the driver and install it; the Livna.org site has RPMs that are ready and waiting to be installed using yum.

Installing Proprietary Video Drivers

Fedora does not provide the official NVIDIA or ATI display drivers because they are closed source and Fedora is committed to delivering a totally free (as in speech) distribution. You can download the latest official drivers from http://www.nvidia.com/object/linux.html or from http://www.ati.com/. If you encounter problems with the NVIDIA drivers in particular, check out http://www.nvnews.net/vbulletin/forumdisplay.php?f=14 for more help. The NVIDIA staff do contribute to that forum, so you should be able to find expert help when you need it.

Bear in mind that if you go down the "official" route, you will have to take certain steps. It would be great to be able to access the drivers through yum, so much so that the Livna repository now has prepackaged the drivers into an RPM that is easily downloaded as long as you have the Livna repository enabled for yum.

> **CAUTION**
>
> The Livna repository is home to not only a wide range of kernel modules and drivers for many popular items of hardware, but also contains a number of legally questionable packages that are not enabled in Fedora by default, including native MP3 support. If you are using Fedora for personal use, you should not have any real problems, but make sure to check before you start installing packages from Livna onto a corporate workstation or server!

To get the NVIDIA driver using yum, you need to have enabled the Livna repository (see Chapter 34, "Advanced Software Management," for more information on setting up repositories). At the command line, type

```
#yum install kmod-nvidia
```

and press Enter. After a few seconds, yum retrieves and downloads the latest NVIDIA driver that is appropriate for your current kernel version. After it finishes installing the packages, you have to restart your machine to take advantage of the improvements.

Installing the ATI driver is much the same because Livna.org also has a set of drivers available for ATI hardware. As with the NVIDIA driver, you need to be a super user and enter the following command:

```
#yum install kmod-fglrx
```

A restart of the system is necessary before you can make full use of the 3D capabilities of your card.

> **CAUTION**
>
> Both sets of graphics card drivers are very dependent on the kernel version you are running. Every time you update your kernel, you also have to update your driver. If you have used the kmod-* package from Livna, it should automatically update when you run yum upgrade.

Installing Popular Games in Fedora

6

It's a common misconception that Linux doesn't do games. In fact, that assumption is very wrong, as you are about to see. In this section, we walk through how to install five popular games that you can play within Fedora. Make sure that you have followed the earlier instructions on how to install graphics drivers for your graphics card; otherwise, you are likely to struggle with the likes of Doom 3, Unreal Tournament 2004, and Quake 4.

DOOM 3

The follow-up to the infamous Doom and Doom II was released in the second half of 2004 (see Figure 9.2), and it provides a way to run it under Linux. You still have to purchase the Windows version because you need some of the files that are on the CDs. The rest of the files are available from id Software at http://zerowing.idsoftware.com/linux/doom.

FIGURE 9.2   Descending into the pits of hell. Doom 3 is one of the most graphic computer games available.

You can download the file doom3-linux-1.1.1282.x86.run from the id Software FTP server or by using BitTorrent. When that's finished, open a terminal and change to the directory in which you saved the file. Type the following command:

```
# sh doom3-linux-1.1.1282.x86.run
```

This begins the installation of the demo. As with other commercial games, you must agree to a EULA before you can install. Follow the installation procedure, and when it finishes you need to get the Windows CDs ready.

You need to copy across the following files:

▶ pak000.pk4

▶ pak001.pk4

- ▶ pak002.pk4

- ▶ pak003.pk4

- ▶ pak004.pk4

They must be saved in the /usr/local/games/doom3/base/ directory. After you copy the files, you can start the game by typing **doom3** or start the dedicated server for multiplayer games by typing **doom3-dedicated**.

Unreal Tournament 2004

Unreal Tournament 2004 (or *UT2004*, as it is affectionately known) from Epic natively supports Linux in both its 32-bit and 64-bit incarnations (see Figure 9.3). Be aware that if you run the 64-bit version, you need to ensure that your graphics drivers are supported under 64-bit mode.

FIGURE 9.3   Unreal Tournament 2004 builds on the classic death-match scenario with more enemies and more combatants.

Installation is easy, and there are two ways to do it. You can insert the DVD and mount it, or you can open the DVD in GNOME and double-click the linux-installer.sh icon. When you are asked whether you want to run it or display its contents, click Run in

Terminal to launch the graphical installer. As with Doom 3, you must read and accept the terms of the EULA before you are allowed to install UT2004. You are given the option of where you want to install the software; the default is in your home directory. After you select the destination directory, click Begin Install; UT2004 does the rest.

The alternative way of accessing the graphical installer is via the command line. Change directory to /media/cdrom/ and enter the following:

```
$ sh linux-install.sh
```

This brings up the graphical installer. Continue through this and, when finished, you should find Unreal Tournament 2004 in /home/username/ut2004.

If you want to uninstall UT2004, you can use the uninstall script in the ut2004 directory. Enter the following:

```
$ sh uninstall.sh
```

After confirmation, Unreal Tournament removes itself from your system.

Quake 4

Being based on the Doom 3 engine, you could almost expect Quake 4 (see Figure 9.4) to ship with a good deal of support for Linux. To get started, you must have the Windows version of the software because you need several files as well as the CD key to be able to play the game. First things first, though. Head on over to http://zerowing.idsoftware.com/linux/quake4/ to download the required Linux installer (quake4-linux-1.0*.run) by either direct FTP or the more bandwidth-friendly BitTorrent.

After you download the file, drop down to a command line and type in

```
#sh quake4-linux-1.0*.run
```

and then press Enter. The installer starts up and asks you a couple of questions. After you answer these, the installer creates the necessary files and folders. All you need to do is to copy several files from the /quake4/qbase directory on the DVD to /usr/local/bin/quake4/qbase. You can start the game by typing **quake4** at a command prompt.

Wolfenstein: Enemy Territory

Whereas the earlier Return to Castle Wolfenstein was both single- and multiplayer, the freely available Wolfenstein: Enemy Territory is multiplayer only (see Figure 9.5).

Available in Win32 and Linux native versions, you can download it via http://www.SplashDamage.com/. After you download the 260MB file named et-linux-2.55.x86.run, install the game by entering the following:

```
# sh et-linux-2.55.x86.run
```

FIGURE 9.4   Based on the popular Doom 3 engine, Quake 4 pits you against the evil Strogg. Get out there and frag 'em!

FIGURE 9.5   Teamwork is the key to victory in this lush but hostile graphical environment.

Then accept the defaults. A symlink exists in /usr/local/bin to the script that loads the game. When using the KDE desktop, we had difficulty with sound because of a conflict with the KDE sound daemon artsd. The fix prepended a line to the et script that read killall artsd.

Battle for Wesnoth

Of course, games for Fedora are not all first-person shooters like those described in the previous sections. For the more cunning among you, there exists a strategy game called Battle for Wesnoth (see Figure 9.6). In this classic turn-based strategy game, you set out to conquer your foes through a set of increasingly complex scenarios. If you have played the Windows game Age of Empires, you will feel instantly at home with Wesnoth.

Battle for Wesnoth is simple to install. All you have to do is enter the following command:

```
# yum install wesnoth
```

Fedora takes care of the rest. A new entry will appear in Applications, Games that will enable you to launch Battle for Wesnoth.

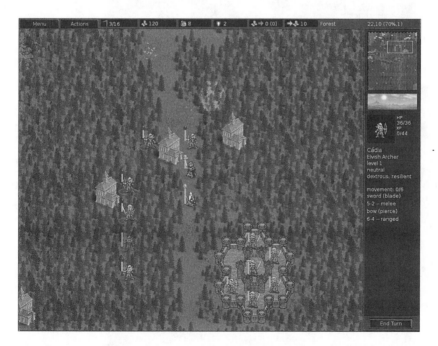

FIGURE 9.6   Flex your strategic brain by playing Battle for Wesnoth, a rich and bountiful land of fantasy and adventure.

KDEedu

There are other games available for Fedora that fall under the term "edutainment." These types of games attempt to aid learning with often simple games. All of them are available through the meta-package kdeedu, so all you have to do is use yum to retrieve this package.

> **NOTE**
>
> You can probably tell by the name that KDEedu is a KDE-based package. As a result, when you install KDEedu, you also need to install several KDE components, enough in fact to allow you to run KDE. See Chapter 3, "Working with GNOME," for more information about KDE and how to access it.

Among the games are hangman (see Figure 9.7), an anagram game, a tool to learn about the periodic table of elements, and a great stargazing tool called Kstars. There are others for you to explore and that can provide hours of learning and fun for your children.

FIGURE 9.7   Enjoy a game of hangman with your kids and learn some language in this colorful part of KDEedu.

Playing Windows Games with Cedega

As mentioned earlier, the key to mass-market appeal of an operating system is in the applications available for it. A group of developers saw that the vast majority of the computing world was using Windows-based productivity and gaming software and decided to develop a way to run this software on Linux, thereby giving Linux users access to this large application base. The developers came up with a program called Wine, which has been updated regularly and forms the basis of the gaming variant called Cedega. This is a commercial product available from developers TransGaming Technologies (http://www.transgaming.com/), so you cannot retrieve it by using yum.

However, Cedega is a very popular and up-to-date product with support for recent releases such as Elder Scrolls IV and Command & Conquer 3: Tiberium Wars. Because the state of Cedega is constantly changing, TransGaming Technologies has a subscription service which means that you get updates for the code when they are released—ensuring that you are able to enjoy not only the games of today, but also those of tomorrow.

So, if you can't wait for Linux to become more popular with game developers, use Cedega as a stop-gap until they can be persuaded to support Linux directly.

TIP

The keys to successful gaming in Linux are to always read the documentation thoroughly, always investigate the Internet resources thoroughly, and always understand your system. Installing games is a great way to learn about your system because the reward of success is so much fun.

Reference

▶ **http://www.transgaming.com/**—The official TransGaming Technologies website provides details of games that are directly supported under Cedega.

▶ **http://www.linuxgames.com/**—A good source of up-to-date information about the state of Linux gaming.

▶ **http://zerowing.idsoftware.com/linux/doom/**—Includes a complete how-to and troubleshooting guide for running Doom 3 under Linux.

▶ **http://www.unrealtournament.com/**—The official site of Unreal Tournament.

▶ **http://www.nvnews.net/vbulletin/forumdisplay.php?f=14**—The Official NVIDIA Linux driver support forum.

▶ **http://www.nvidia.com/object/linux.html**—Home page for the NVIDIA Linux drivers.

▶ **http://tinyurl.com/3pm2v**—Home page for the ATI Linux drivers (courtesy of tinyurl.com).

PART III

System Administration

Managing Users

One of the most important things you need to learn while using Fedora is effective user administration. Whether you are setting up a system for use just by yourself, sharing it among a family of five, or even working with a machine that has to handle several thousand different users, it is important that you understand how to effectively assign user permissions and lock down the areas you want to protect. Equally important is the ability to fine-tune user access rights, to enable people to do what they need to do, and not necessarily what they want to!

Managing users includes managing home directories and settings that are unique to each user. You also have to examine how much of the overall system to which you want to give the users access, as well as establish good password practice. This chapter covers all these tasks, as well as others that teach you how to effectively manage the users of your system. It also takes a look at the super-user account so that you can understand why it is so important and also how to let others access some, if not all, of the super-user's power.

User Accounts

Every Fedora installation typically contains three types of accounts: the super user, the day-to-day user, and the system user. Each type is important in its own right, and you must know what each is responsible for. If they didn't work together, Fedora would have a hard time doing anything!

All users must have accounts on the system. Fedora uses the /etc/passwd file to hold information on user accounts. Each user, regardless of type, has a one-line entry of account information stored in the /etc/passwd text file.

Each account entry contains a username (used for logging in), a password field containing an x (as passwords are actually contained in /etc/shadow), a *user ID (UID)*, and a *group ID (GID)*. The fifth field contains optional human ID information, such as real name, office location, phone number, and so on. The last two fields are the location of the user's home directory and the user's default login shell. See the section "The Password File" later in this chapter for more information.

Like other Linux distributions, Fedora makes use of the established UNIX file ownership and permission system. Each file (which can include directories and even devices) can be assigned one or more of read, write, and/or execute permissions. These can be assigned further to the owner, a member of a group, or anyone on the system. File security is drawn from combining ownership and permissions. The system administrator (most commonly referred to as the *super user*) has total responsibility to make sure that users have proper UIDs and GIDs, and to ensure that sensitive files (which can include important system files) are locked down using file permissions. You'll learn more about permissions in the section "Managing Permissions."

Regardless of how many system administrators are present on the system, there can only be one root user. This is the user who has access to everything, and can grant or take away any privileges on the system. The root user has a UID of 0 and a GID of 0, making it unique among all other users on the system. The root user can use any program, manipulate any file, go anywhere in the file system, and do anything within the Fedora system. For reasons of security, that kind of raw power should be given to only a single trusted individual.

It is often practical for that power to be delegated by the root user to other users. This delegation is referred to as an elevation of privileges, and these individuals are known as *super users* because they enjoy the same powers that root enjoys. This approach is normally used only on large systems in which one person cannot effectively act as the sole system administrator.

> **NOTE**
>
> On your Fedora system, when you log in as root, you are root or the super user. In this chapter, the terms *root*, *super user*, *system administrator*, and *sysadmin* are used interchangeably, although they need not all refer to a single person.

A regular user is someone who logs on to the system to make use of it for nonadministrative tasks such as word processing or email. These users do not need to make systemwide changes, nor do they have to manage any other users. However, they might want to be able to change settings that are specific to them (for instance, a desktop background). Of course, depending on how draconian the root user is, regular users might not even be able to do that!

The super user grants privileges to regular users by means of file and directory permissions. (Those are covered in the section entitled "Managing Permissions.") For example, if the super user does not want you to change your settings in ~/.profile (the ~ is a shell shortcut representing your home directory), root can alter the permissions so that you may read from, but not write to, that file.

CAUTION

Because of the potential for making a catastrophic error as the super user (using the command rm -rf /* is the classic example, but do not ever try it!), always use your system as a regular user and become root only temporarily to do sysadmin duties. While you are on a multiuser system, consider this advice an absolute rule; if root were to delete the wrong file or kill the wrong process, the results could be disastrous for the business. On your home system, you can do as you please and running as root makes many things easier, but less safe. In any setting, however, the risks of running as root full time are significant. (In case you're wondering, the above command would completely wipe your entire file system, leaving you with nothing but a red face!)

The third type of user is the system user. The system user is not a person, but rather an administrative account that the system uses during day-to-day running of various services. For example, the system user named apache owns the Apache Web Server and all the associated files. Only it and root can have access to these files—no one else can access or make changes to these files. System users do not have a home directory or password, nor do they permit access to the system through a login prompt.

You will find a list of all the users on a system in the /etc/passwd file. Fedora refers to these users as the *standard users* because they are found on every Fedora computer as the default set of system (or logical) users provided during the initial installation. This "standard" set differs among Linux distributions.

Adding New Users

The command-line approach to adding any user is actually quite simple and can be accomplished on a single line. In the example shown here, the sysadmin uses the useradd command to add the new user bernice. The command adduser (a variant found on some UNIX systems) is a symbolic link to useradd, so both commands work the same. In this example, we use the -p option to set the password the user requested; we use the -s option to set his special shell, and the -u option to specify his UID. (If we created a user with the default settings, we would not need to use these options.) All we want to do can be accomplished on one line:

```
# useradd bernice -p sTitcher -s /bin/bash -u 507
```

The sysadmin can also use the graphical interface that Fedora provides, as shown in Figure 10.1. It is accessed as the Users and Groups item from the System Settings menu item. Here, the sysadmin is adding a new user to the system where user bernice uses the bash command shell.

These are the steps we used to add the same account as shown in the preceding command, but using the graphical User Manager graphical interface:

1. Launch the Fedora User Manager graphical interface by clicking the Users and Groups menu item found in the System, Administration.

2. Click the Add User button to bring up the Add User dialog window.

3. Fill in the form with the appropriate information, as described in the first paragraph in this section.

4. Click the drop-down Login Shell menu to select the bash shell.

5. Check the Specify User ID box to permit access to the UID dialog.

6. Using the arrows found in the UID dialog, increment the UID to 5413.

7. Click OK to save the settings.

FIGURE 10.1   Adding a new user is simple. The GUI provides a more complete set of commands for user management than for group management.

Note that the user is being manually assigned the UID of 549 because that is her UID on another system machine that will be connected to this machine. Because the system only knows her as 549 and not as bernice, the two machines would not recognize bernice as the same user if two different UIDs were assigned.

A Linux username can be any alphanumeric combination that does not begin with a special character reserved for shell script use (see Chapter 11, "Automating Tasks," for disallowed characters, mostly punctuation characters). Usernames are typically the user's first name plus the first initial of her last name, something that is a common practice on larger systems with many users because it makes life simpler for the sysadmin, but is neither a rule nor a requirement.

User IDs and Group IDs

A computer is, by its very nature, a number-oriented machine. It identifies users and groups by numbers known as the *user ID (UID)* and *group ID (GID)*. The alphabetic names displayed on your screen are there exclusively for your ease of use.

As was already mentioned, the root user is UID 0. Numbers from 1 through 499 and 65,534 are the system, or logical, users. Regular users have UIDs beginning with 500; Fedora assigns them sequentially beginning with this number.

With only a few exceptions, the GID is the same as the UID. Those exceptions are system users who need to act with root permissions: sync, shutdown, halt, and operator.

Fedora creates a private GID for every UID of 500 and greater. The system administrator can add other users to a GID or create a totally new group and add users to it. Unlike Windows NT and some UNIX variants, a group cannot be a member of another group in Linux.

If you intend to make use of NFS, it is extremely important that you use the same UID for the user on the host and guest machines; otherwise, you will not be able to connect!

User Stereotypes

As is the case in many professions, exaggerated characterizations (*stereotypes* or *caricatures*) have emerged for users and system administrators. Many stereotypes contain elements of truth mixed with generous amounts of hyperbole and humor and serve to assist us in understanding the characteristics of and differences in the stereotyped subjects. The stereotypes of the "luser" and the "BOFH" (users and administrators, respectively) also serve as cautionary tales describing what behavior is acceptable and unacceptable in the computing community.

Understanding these stereotypes allows you to better define the appropriate and inappropriate roles of system administrators, users, and others. The canonical reference to these terms is found in the alt.sysadmin.recovery FAQ found at http://www.ctrl-c.liu.se/~ingvar/asr/.

10

Managing Groups

Groups can make managing users a lot easier. Instead of having to assign individual permissions to every user, you can use groups to grant or revoke permissions to a large number of users quickly and easily. Setting group permissions allows you to set up workspaces for collaborative working and also to control what devices can be used, such as external drives or DVD writers. This approach also represents a secure method of limiting access to system resources to only those users who need them. As an example, the sysadmin could put the users andrew, paul, scott, derek, mark, and vanessa in a new group named unleashed. Those users could each create files intended for their group work and chgrp those files to unleashed.

Now, everyone in the unleashed group—but no one else except root—can work with those files. The sysadmin would probably create a directory owned by that group so its members could have an easily accessed place to store those files. The sysadmin could also add other users such as bernice and ildiko to the group and remove existing users when their part of the work is done. The sysadmin could make the user andrew the group administrator so that andrew could decide how group membership should be changed. You could also put restrictions on the DVD writer so that only andrew could burn DVDs, thus protecting sensitive material from falling into the wrong hands.

Different UNIX operating systems implement the group concept in various ways. Fedora uses a scheme called *UPG*, the *user private group*, in which all users are assigned to a group with their own name by default. (The user's username and group name are identical.) All the groups are listed in /etc/group file. Here is a partial list of a sample /etc/group file:

```
# cat /etc/group
root:x:0:root
bin:x:1:root,bin,daemon
daemon:x:2:root,bin,daemon
sys:x:3:root,bin,adm
adm:x:4:root,adm,daemon

dovecot:x:97:
...
postdrop:x:90:
postfix:x:89:
andrew:x:500:
```

In this example, there are a number of groups, mostly for services (mail, ssh, and so on) and devices (CD-ROM, disk, and so on). As previously mentioned, the system services groups enable those services to have ownership and control of their files. For example, adding postfix to the mail group, as shown previously, enables the postfix application to access mail's files in the manner that mail would decide for group access to its file. Adding a regular user to a device's group permits the regular user to use the device with permissions granted by the group owner. Adding user andrew to the group cdrom, for example, would allow andrew to use the CD drive. You learn how to add and remove users from groups in the next section.

Group Management Tools

Fedora provides several command-line tools for managing groups as well as graphical tools. Many experienced sysadmins prefer the command-line tools because they are quick and easy to use and they can be included in scripts if the sysadmin desires to script a repetitive task. Here are the most commonly used group management command-line tools:

- **groupadd**—This command creates and adds a new group.

- **groupdel**—This command removes an existing group.

- **groupmod**—This command creates a group name or GIDs, but doesn't add or delete members from a group.

- **gpasswd**—This command creates a group password. Every group can have a group password and an administrator. Use the -A argument to assign a user as group administrator.

- **useradd -G**—The -G argument adds a user to a group during the initial user creation. (More arguments are used to create a user.)

- **usermod -G**—This command enables you to add a user to a group as long as the user is not logged in at the time.

- **grpck**—A command for checking the /etc/group file for typos.

As an example, imagine that there is a DVD-RW device (/dev/scd0) computer to which the sysadmin wants a regular user named vanessa to have access. To grant vanessa that access, he would use these steps:

1. Add a new group with the groupadd command:

   # groupadd dvdrw

2. Change the group ownership of the device to the new group with the chgrp command:

   # chgrp dvdrw /dev/scd0

3. Add the approved user to the group with the usermod command:

   # usermod -G dvdrw vanessa

4. Make user vanessa the group administrator with the gpasswd command so that she can add new users to the group:

   # gpasswd -A vanessa

10

Now, the user vanessa has permission to use the DVD-RW drive, as would anyone else added to the group by the super user or vanessa because she is now also the group administrator and can add users to the group.

The sysadmin can also use the graphical interface that Fedora provides, as shown in Figure 10.2. It is accessed as the Users and Groups item from the System Settings menu item.

FIGURE 10.2   Just check the box to add a user to a group.

You will note that the full set of group commands and options are not available from the graphical interface, limiting the usefulness of the GUI to a subset of the most frequently used commands. You learn more about using the Fedora User Manager GUI in the next section.

Managing Users

You've read about users previously, but this section examines how the sysadmin can manage the users. Users must be created, assigned a UID, provided a home directory, provided an initial set of files for their home directory, and assigned to groups so that they can use the system resources securely and efficiently. The system administrator might elect to restrict a user's access not only to files, but to the amount of disk space they use as well. (You learn more about that in the "Disk Quotas" section later in this chapter.)

User Management Tools

Fedora provides several command-line tools for managing users, as well as graphical tools. Many experienced sysadmins prefer the command-line tools because they are quick and easy to use and they can be included in scripts if the sysadmin wants to script a repetitive task. Here are the most commonly used commands for managing users:

▶ **useradd**—This command is used to add a new user account to the system. Its options permit the sysadmin to specify the user's home directory and initial group or to create the user with the default home directory and group assignments.

▶ **useradd -D**—This command sets the system defaults for creating the user's home directory, account expiration date, default group, and command shell. See the specific options in man useradd. Used without any arguments, it displays the defaults for the system. The default set of files for a user are found in /etc/skel.

NOTE

The set of files initially used to populate a new user's home directory are kept in /etc/skel. This is convenient for the system administrator because any special files, links, or directories that need to be universally applied can be placed in /etc/skel and will be duplicated automatically with appropriate permissions for each new user.

```
# ls -al /etc/skel
total 60
drwxr-xr-x   4 root root  4096 2007-10-21 19:58 .
drwxr-xr-x 112 root root 12288 2007-10-22 20:40 ..
-rw-r--r--   1 root root    33 2007-08-31 15:20 .bash_logout
-rw-r--r--   1 root root   176 2007-08-31 15:20 .bash_profile
-rw-r--r--   1 root root   124 2007-08-31 15:20 .bashrc
drwxr-xr-x   2 root root  4096 2007-10-17 17:52 .gnome2
```

Each line provides the file permissions, the number of files housed under that file or directory name, the file owner, the file group, the file size, the creation date, and the filename.

As you can see, root owns every file here, but the adduser command (a symbolic link to the actual command named useradd) copies everything in /etc/skel to the new home directory and resets file ownership and permissions to the new user.

Certain user files might exist that the system administrator does not want the user to change; the permissions for those files in /home/username can be reset so that the user can read them but can't write to them.

▶ **userdel**—This command completely removes a user's account (thereby eliminating that user's home directory and all files it contains).

▶ **passwd**—This command updates the authentication tokens used by the password management system.

10

TIP

To lock a user out of his account, use the following command:

```
# passwd -l username
```

This prepends a double ! (exclamation point, also called a *bang*) to the user's encrypted password; the command to reverse the process uses the -u option. This is a more elegant and preferred solution to the problem than the traditional UNIX way of manually editing the file.

▶ **usermod**—This command changes several user attributes. The most commonly used arguments are -s to change the shell and -u to change the UID. No changes can be made while the user is logged in or running a process.

▶ **chsh**—This command changes the user's default shell. For Fedora, the default shell is /bin/bash, known as the *Bash*, or Bourne Again Shell.

Monitoring User Activity on the System

Monitoring user activity is part of the sysadmin's duties and an essential task in tracking how system resources are being used. The w command tells the sysadmin who is logged in, where he is logged in, and what he is doing. No one is able to hide from the super user. The w command can be followed by a specific user's name to show only that user.

The ac command provides information about the total connect time of a user measured in hours. It accesses the /var/log/wtmp file for the source of its information. The ac command is most useful in shell scripts to generate reports on operating system usage for management review.

TIP

Interestingly, a phenomenon known as *timewarp* can occur in which an entry in the wtmp files jumps back into the past and ac shows unusual amounts of connected time for users. Although this can be attributed to some innocuous factors having to do with the system clock, it is worthy of investigation by the sysadmin because it can also be the result of a security breach.

The last command searches through the /var/log/wtmp file and lists all the users logged in and out since that file was first created. The user reboot exists so that you might know who has logged in since the last reboot. A companion to last is the command lastb, which shows all failed, or bad, logins. It is useful for determining whether a legitimate user is having trouble or a hacker is attempting access.

NOTE

The accounting system on your computer keeps track of user usage statistics and is kept in the current /var/log/wtmp file. That file is managed by the init and login processes. If you want to explore the depths of the accounting system, use the GNU info system: info accounting.

Managing Permissions

Under Linux (and UNIX), everything in the file system, including directories and devices, is a file. And every file on your system has an accompanying set of permissions based on ownership. These permissions form the basis for security under Linux, and designate each file's read, write, and execute permission for you, members of your group, and all others on the system.

You can examine the default permissions for a file you create by using the umask command, or as a practical example, by using the touch command and then the ls command's long-format listing, like this:

```
$ touch file
$ ls -l file
-rw-rw-r-- 1 andrew andrew 0 2007-10-23 18:50 file
```

In this example, the touch command is used to quickly create a file. The ls command then reports on the file, displaying information (from left to right) in the first field of output (such as -rw-rw-r-- previously):

▶ **The first character of the field is the type of file created**—The common indicator of the type of file is a leading letter in the output. A blank (which is represented by a dash in the preceding example) designates a plain file, d designates a directory, c designates a character device (such as /dev/ttyS0), and b is used for a block device (such as /dev/hda).

▶ **Permissions**—Read, write, and execute permissions for the owner, group, and all others on the system. (You learn more about these permissions later in this section.)

▶ **Number of links to the file**—The number one (1) designates that there is only one file, whereas any other number indicates that there might be one or more hard-linked files. Links are created with the ln command. A hard-linked file is an exact copy of the file, but it might be located elsewhere on the system. Symbolic links of directories can also be created, but only the root operator can create a hard link of a directory.

▶ **The owner**—The account that created or owns the file; you can change this designation by using the chown command.

▶ **The group**—The group of users allowed to access the file; you can change this designation by using the chgrp command.

▶ **File size and creation/modification date**—The last two elements indicate the size of the file in bytes and the date the file was created or last modified.

Assigning Permissions

Under Linux, permissions are grouped by owner, group, and others, with read, write, and execute permission assigned to each, like so:

```
Owner    Group    Others
rwx      rwx      rwx
```

Permissions can be indicated by mnemonic or octal characters. You can use the following mnemonic characters:

▶ r indicates permission for an owner, member of the owner's group, or others to open and read the file.

▶ w indicates permission for an owner, member of the owner's group, or others to open and write to the file.

▶ x indicates permission for an owner, member of the owner's group, or others to execute the file (or read a directory).

In the previous example for the file named file, the owner, andrew, has read and write permission, as does any member of the group named andrew. All other users may only read the file. Also note that default permissions for files created by the root operator will differ! This happens because of umask settings assigned by the shell.

Many users prefer to represent permissions with numeric codes, based on octal (base 8) values. Here's what these values mean:

▶ 4 indicates read permission.

▶ 2 indicates write permission.

▶ 1 indicates execute permission.

In octal notation, the previous example file has a permission setting of 664 (read + write or 4 + 2, read + write or 4 + 2, read-only or 4). Although you can use either form of permissions notation, octal is easy to use quickly after you visualize and understand how permissions are numbered.

> **NOTE**
>
> In Linux, you can create groups to assign a number of users access to common directories and files based on permissions. You might assign everyone in accounting to a group named accounting, for example, and allow that group access to accounts payable files while disallowing access by other departments. Defined groups are maintained by the root operator, but you can use the newgrp command to temporarily join other groups to access files (as long as the root operator has added you to the other groups). You can also allow or deny access to your files by other groups by modifying the group permissions of your files.

Directory Permissions

Directories are also files under Linux. For example, again use the ls command to show permissions like this:

```
$ mkdir foo
$ ls -ld foo
drwxrwxr-x 2 andrew andrew 4096 2007-10-23 19:06 foo
```

In this example, the mkdir command is used to create a directory. The ls command and its -ld option is used to show the permissions and other information about the directory (not its contents). Here you can see that the directory has permission values of 775 (read + write + execute or 4 + 2 + 1, read + write + execute or 4 + 2 + 1, and read + execute or 4 + 1).

This shows that the owner and group members can read and write to the directory and, because of execute permission, also list the directory's contents. All other users can only list the directory contents. Note that directories require execute permission for anyone to be able to view their contents.

You should also notice that the ls command's output shows a leading d in the permissions field. This letter specifies that this file is a directory; normal files have a blank field in its place. Other files, such as those specifying a block or character device, have a different letter.

For example, if you examine the device file for a Linux serial port, you will see the following:

```
$ ls -l /dev/ttyS0
crw-rw---- 1 root uucp 4, 64 2007-10-23 18:11 /dev/ttyS0
```

Here, /dev/ttyS0 is a character device (such as a serial communications port and designated by a c) owned by root and available to anyone in the uucp group. The device has permissions of 660 (read + write, read + write, no permission).

On the other hand, if you examine the device file for a hard drive, you see the following:

```
$ ls -l /dev/sda
brw-r----- 1 root disk 8, 0 2007-10-23 18:11 /dev/sda
```

In this example, b designates a block device (a device that transfers and caches data in blocks) with similar permissions. Other device entries you will run across on your Linux system include symbolic links, designated by s.

You can use the chmod command to alter a file's permissions. This command uses various forms of command syntax, including octal or a mnemonic form (such as u, g, o, or a and

10

rwx, and so on) to specify a desired change. The chmod command can be used to add, remove, or modify file or directory permissions to protect, hide, or open up access to a file by other users (except for root, which can access any file or directory on a Linux system).

The mnemonic forms of chmod's options (when used with a plus character, +, to add, or a minus sign, -, to take away) designate the following:

- ▶ **u**—Adds or removes user (owner) read, write, or execute permission

- ▶ **g**—Adds or removes group read, write, or execute permission

- ▶ **o**—Adds or removes read, write, or execute permission for others not in a file's group

- ▶ **a**—Adds or removes read, write, or execute permission for all users

- ▶ **r**—Adds or removes read permission

- ▶ **w**—Adds or removes write permission

- ▶ **x**—Adds or removes execution permission

For example, if you create a file, such as a readme.txt, the file will have default permissions (set by the umask setting in /etc/bashrc) of the following:

```
-rw-rw-r-- 1 andrew andrew    0 2007-10-23 19:08 readme.txt
```

As you can see, you and members of your group can read and write the file. Anyone else can only read the file (and only if it is outside of your home directory, which will have read, write, and execute permission set only for you, the owner). You can remove all write permission for anyone by using chmod, the minus sign, and aw, as follows:

```
$ chmod a-w readme.txt
$ ls -l readme.txt
-r--r--r--    1 andrew    andrew        12 Jan  2 16:48 readme.txt
```

Now, no one can write to the file (except you, if the file is in your home or /tmp directory because of directory permissions). To restore read and write permission for only you as the owner, use the plus sign and the u and rw options, like this:

```
$ chmod u+rw readme.txt
$ ls -l readme.txt
-rw-------  1 andrew andrew    0 2007-10-23 19:08 readme.txt
```

You can also use the octal form of the chmod command (for example, to modify a file's permissions so that only you, the owner, can read and write a file). Use the chmod command and a file permission of 600, like this:

```
$ chmod 600 readme.txt
```

If you take away execution permission for a directory, files might be hidden inside and may not be listed or accessed by anyone else (except the root operator, of course, who has access to any file on your system). By using various combinations of permission settings, you can quickly and easily set up a more secure environment, even as a normal user in your home directory.

Other useful commands for assigning and managing permissions include the following:

▶ **chgrp**—Changes the group ownership of a file or directory

▶ **chown**—Changes the owner of a file or directory

These commands, which modify file ownerships and permissions, can be used to model organizational structures and permissions in the real world onto your Fedora system. For example, a human resources department can share health-benefit memos to all company employees by making the files readable (but not writable) by anyone in an accessible directory. On the other hand, programmers in the company's research and development section, although able to access each other's source code files, would not have read or write access to HR payscale or personnel files (and certainly would not want HR or Marketing poking around R&D).

These commands help you easily manage group and file ownerships and permissions from the command line. It is essential that you know these commands because some-times you might have only a command-line interface to work with; perhaps some idiot system administrator set incorrect permissions on X11, rendering the system incapable of working with a graphical interface.

Understanding Set User ID and Set Group ID Permissions

Another type of permission is "set user ID (*suid*) and "set group ID" (*sgid*) permissions. These settings, when used in a program, enable any user running that program to have program owner or group owner permissions for that program. These settings enable the program to be run effectively by anyone, without requiring that each user's permissions be altered to include specific permissions for that program.

One commonly used program with suid permissions is the passwd command:

```
$ ls -l /usr/bin/passwd
-rwsr-xr-x 1 root root 25604 2007-04-05 09:54 /usr/bin/passwd
```

This setting allows normal users to execute the command (as root) to make changes to a root-only accessible file, /etc/passwd.

You also can assign similar permission using the chfn command. This command allows users to update or change finger information in /etc/passwd. You accomplish this permission modification by using a leading 4 (or the mnemonic s) in front of the three octal values.

10

> **NOTE**
>
> Other files that might have suid or guid permissions include `at`, `rcp`, `rlogin`, `rsh`, `chage`, `chsh`, `ssh`, `crontab`, `sudo`, `sendmail`, `ping`, `mount`, and several UNIX-to-UNIX Copy (UUCP) utilities. Many programs (such as games) might also have this type of permission to access a sound device.

Files or programs that have suid or guid permissions can sometimes present security holes because they bypass normal permissions. This problem is especially compounded if the permission extends to an executable binary (a command) with an inherent security flaw because it could lead to any system user or intruder gaining root access. In past exploits, this typically happened when a user fed a vulnerable command with unexpected input (such as a long pathname or option); the command would bomb out, and the user would be presented a root prompt. Although Linux developers are constantly on the lookout for poor programming practices, new exploits are found all the time, and can crop up unexpectedly, especially in newer software packages that haven't had the benefit of peer developer review.

Savvy Linux system administrators keep the number of suid or guid files present on a system to a minimum. The `find` command can be used to display all such files on your system:

```
# find / -type f -perm +6000 -exec ls -l {} \;
```

> **NOTE**
>
> The `find` command is quite helpful and can be used for many purposes, such as before or during backup operations. See the section "Using Backup Software" in Chapter 13, "Backing Up."

Note that the programs do not necessarily have to be removed from your system. If your users really do not need to use the program, you can remove execute permission of the program for anyone. You have to decide, as the root operator, whether your users are allowed to, for example, mount and unmount CD-ROMs or other media on your system. Although Linux-based operating systems can be set up to accommodate ease of use and convenience, allowing programs such as `mount` to be suid might not be the best security policy. Other candidates for suid permission change could include the `chsh`, `at`, and `chage` commands.

Managing Passwords

Passwords are an integral part of Linux security, and they are the most visible part to the user. In this section, you learn how to establish a minimal password policy for your system, where the passwords are stored, and how to manage passwords for your users.

An effective password policy is a fundamental part of a good system administration plan. The policy should cover the following:

▶ Allowed and forbidden passwords

▶ Frequency of mandated password changes

▶ Retrieval or replacement of lost or forgotten passwords

▶ Password handling by users

The Password File

The password file is /etc/passwd, and it is the database file for all users on the system. The format of each line is as follows:

```
username:password:uid:gid:gecos:homedir:shell
```

The fields are self-explanatory except for the *gecos* field. This field is for miscellaneous information about the user, such as the user's full name, his office location, office and home phone numbers, and possibly a brief text message. For security and privacy reasons, this field is little used nowadays, but the system administrator should be aware of its existence because the *gecos* field is used by traditional UNIX programs such as finger and mail. For that reason, it is commonly referred to as the *finger information field*. The data in this field is comma delimited; the *gecos* field can be changed with the cgfn (change finger) command.

Note that a colon separates all fields in the /etc/passwd file. If no information is available for a field, that field is empty, but all the colons remain.

If an asterisk appears in the password field, that user is not permitted to log on. Why does this feature exist? So that a user can be easily disabled and (possibly) reinstated later without having to be created all over again. The system administrator manually edits this field, which is the traditional UNIX way of accomplishing this task. Fedora provides improved functionality with the passwd -l command mentioned earlier.

Several services run as pseudo-users, usually with root permissions. These are the system, or logical, users mentioned previously. You would not want these accounts available for general login for security reasons, so they are assigned /sbin/nologin as their shell, which prohibits any logins from those "users."

A list of /etc/passwd reveals the following:

```
# cat /etc/passwd
root:x:0:0:root:/root:/bin/bash
bin:x:1:1:bin:/bin:/sbin/nologin
daemon:x:2:2:daemon:/sbin:/sbin/nologin
adm:x:3:4:adm:/var/adm:/sbin/nologin
...
```

```
gdm:x:42:42::/var/gdm:/sbin/nologin
named:x:25:25:Named:/var/named:/sbin/nologin
dovecot:x:97:97:dovecot:/usr/libexec/dovecot:/sbin/nologin
postfix:x:89:89::/var/spool/postfix:/sbin/nologin
andrew:x:500:500:Andrew Hudson:/home/andrew:/bin/bash
```

Note that the password fields do not show a password, but contain an x because they are *shadow passwords*, a useful security enhancement to Linux, discussed in the following section.

Shadow Passwords

It is considered a security risk to keep any password in /etc/passwd because anyone with read access can run a cracking program on the file and obtain the passwords with little trouble. To avoid this risk, *shadow passwords* are used so that only an x appears in the password field of /etc/passwd; the real passwords are kept in /etc/shadow, a file that can be read by only the sysadmin (and *PAM*, the *Pluggable Authentication Modules* authentication manager; see the "PAM Explained" sidebar for an explanation of PAM).

Special versions of the traditional password and login programs must be used to enable shadow passwords. Shadow passwords are automatically enabled during the installation phase of the operating system on Fedora systems.

Let's examine a listing of the shadow companion to /etc/passwd, the /etc/shadow file:

```
# cat /etc/shadow
root:*:13121:0:99999:7:::
daemon:*:13121:0:99999:7:::
bin:*:13121:0:99999:7:::
sys:*:13121:0:99999:7:::
sync:*:13121:0:99999:7:::
games:*:13121:0:99999:7:::
man:*:13121:0:99999:7:::

...
andrew:$1$z/9LTBHL$omt7QdYk.KJL7rwBiM0511:13121:0:99999:7:::
```

The fields are separated by colons and are, in order, the following:

- ▶ The user's login name.
- ▶ The encrypted password for the user.

▶ When the password was last changed, measured in the number of days since January 1, 1970. This date is known in UNIX circles as the epoch. Just so you know, the billionth second since the epoch occurred was in September 2001; that was the UNIX version of Y2K—not much happened because of it.

▶ The number of days before the password can be changed (prevents changing a password and then changing it back to the old password right away—a dangerous security practice).

▶ The number of days after which the password must be changed. This can be set to force the change of a newly issued password known to the system administrator.

▶ The number of days before password expiration that the user is warned it will expire.

▶ The number of days after the password expires that the account is disabled (for security).

▶ The number of days since January 1, 1970 that the account has been disabled.

▶ The final field is a "reserved" field and is not currently allocated for any use.

Note that password expiration dates and warnings are disabled by default in Fedora. These features are not used on home systems and usually not used for small offices. It is the sysadmin's responsibility to establish and enforce password expiration policies.

The permissions on the /etc/shadow file should be set so that it is not writable or readable by regular users: The permissions should be 600.

PAM Explained

Pluggable Authentication Modules (PAM) is a system of libraries that handle the tasks of authentication on your computer. It uses four management groups: account management, authentication management, password management, and session management. This allows the system administrator to choose how individual applications will authenticate users. Fedora has preinstalled and preconfigured all the necessary PAM files for you.

The configuration files in Fedora are found in /etc/pam.d. These files are named for the service they control, and the format is as follows:

```
type control module-path module-arguments
```

The type field is the management group to which the rule corresponds. The control field tells PAM what to do if authentication fails. The final two items deal with the PAM module used and any arguments it needs. Programs that use PAM typically come packaged with appropriate entries for the /etc/pam.d directory. To achieve greater security, the system administrator can modify the default entries. Misconfiguration can have unpredictable results, so back up the configuration files before you modify them. The defaults provided by Fedora are adequate for home and small office users.

10

An example of a PAM configuration file with the formatted entries as described previously is shown next. Here are the contents of `/etc/pam.d/system-config-users`:

```
#%PAM-1.0
auth        include     config-util
account     include     config-util
session     include     config-util
```

Amusingly, even the PAM documents state that you do not really need (or want) to know a lot about PAM to use it effectively.

You will likely need only the PAM system administrator's guide. Look under the `/usr/share/doc/pam*` directory for additional documents in PostScript, text, and HTML formats.

Managing Password Security for Users

Selecting appropriate user passwords is always an exercise in trade-offs. A password such as *password* (don't laugh, it has been used too often before in the real world) is just too easy to guess by an intruder, as are simple words or number combinations (a street address, for example). A security auditor for one of my former employers used to take the cover sheet from an employee's personnel file (which contained the usual personal information of name, address, birth date, and so on) and then attempt to log on to a terminal with passwords constructed from that information—and often succeeded in logging on.

On the other hand, a password such as 2a56u'"F($84u&#^Hiu44Ik%$([#EJD is sure to present great difficulty to an intruder (or an auditor). However, that password is so difficult to remember that it would be likely that the password owner would write that password down and tape it next to her keyboard. I worked for a business in which the safe combination was written on the ceiling tile over the safe; the manager could not remember it and was told he should not keep it on a piece of paper in his wallet. This is but one of many examples of poor security in the field.

The sysadmin has control, with settings in the `/etc/shadow` file, over how often the password must be changed. The settings can be changed with a text editor, the `change` command, or a configuration tool such as Fedora's User Manager, as shown in Figure 10.1. Click the Password Info tab under that particular user's Properties to set individual password policies.

Changing Passwords in a Batch

On a large system, there might be times when a large number of users and their passwords need some attention. The super user can change passwords in a batch by using the `chpasswd` command, which accepts input as a name/password pair per line in the following form:

```
# chpasswd username:password
```

You can change passwords *en masse* by redirecting a list of name and password pairs to the command. An appropriate shell script can be constructed with the information gleaned from this chapter.

However, Fedora also provides the newusers command to add users in a batch from a text file. This command also allows a user to be added to a group, and a new directory can be added for the user, too.

Granting System Administrator Privileges to Regular Users

It may be necessary for regular users to run a command as if they were the root user. They usually do not need these powers, but they might on occasion—for example, to temporarily access certain devices or run a command for testing purposes.

There are two ways to run commands with root privileges: The first is useful if you are the super user and the user; the second if you are not the regular user (as on a large, multiuser network).

Temporarily Changing User Identity with the su Command

What if you are also root, but are logged on as a regular user because you are performing nonadministrative tasks and you need to do something that only the super user can do? The su command is available for this purpose.

> **NOTE**
>
> A popular misconception is that the su command is short for *super user*; it just means *substitute user*. An important but often overlooked distinction is that between su and su -. In the former instance, you become that user but keep your own environmental variables (such as paths). In the latter, you inherit the environment of that user. This is most noticeable when you use su to become the super user, root. Without appending the -, you do not inherit the path variable that includes /bin or /sbin, so you must always enter the full path to those commands when you just su to root.

Because almost all Linux file system security revolves around file permissions, it can be useful to occasionally become a different user with permission to access files belonging to other users or groups or to access special files (such as the communications port /dev/ttyS0 when using a modem, or the sound device /dev/audio when playing a game). You can use the su command to temporarily switch to another user identity, and then switch back.

10

> **TIP**
>
> It is never a good idea to use an *Internet Relay Chat (IRC)* client as the root user, and you might not want to run it using your regular user account. Just create a special new user just for IRC and su to that user in a terminal widow to launch your IRC client.

The su command spawns a new shell, changing both the UID and GID of the existing user and automatically changes the environmental variables associated with that user. This behavior is known as *inheriting the environment*. See Chapter 4, "Command-Line Quick Start," for more information on environmental variables.

The syntax for the su command is this:

```
$ su option   username   arguments
```

The man page for su gives more details, but some highlights of the su command are as follows:

```
-c, --command COMMAND
      pass a single COMMAND to the shell with -c

-m, --preserve-environment
      do not reset environment variables

-l    a full login simulation for the substituted user,
      the same as specifying the dash alone
```

You can invoke the su command in different ways that yield diverse results. By using su alone, you can become root, but you keep your regular user environment. You can verify this by using the printenv command before and after the change. Note that the working directory (you can execute pwd as a command line to print the current working directory) has not changed. By executing the following, you become root and inherit root's environment:

```
$ su -
```

By executing the following, you become that user and inherit the super user's environment—a pretty handy tool. (Remember: Inheriting the environment comes from using the dash in the command; omit that, and you keep your "old" environment.) To become another user, specify a different user's name on the command line:

```
$ su - other_user
```

When leaving an identity to return to your usual user identity, use the exit command. For example, while logged on as a regular user, use this:

```
$ su -
```

The system prompts for a password:

```
Password:
```

When the password is entered correctly, the root user's prompt appears:

```
#
```

To return to the regular user's identity, just enter the following:

```
# exit
```

This takes you to the regular user's prompt:

```
$
```

If you need to allow other users access to certain commands with root privileges, it is necessary to give them the root password so that they can use su—that definitely is not a secure solution. The next section describes a more flexible and secure method of allowing normal users to perform selected root tasks.

Granting Root Privileges on Occasion—The sudo Command

It is often necessary to delegate some of the authority that root wields on a system. For a large system, this makes sense because no single individual will always be available to perform super-user functions. The problem is that UNIX permissions come with an all-or-nothing authority. Enter sudo, an application that permits the assignment of one, several, or all of the root-only system commands.

After it is configured, using sudo is simple. An authorized user merely precedes the command that requires super-user authority with the sudo command, as follows:

```
$ sudo command
```

After getting the user's password, sudo checks the /etc/sudoers file to see whether that user is authorized to execute that particular command; if so, sudo generates a "ticket" for a specific length of time that authorizes the use of that command. The user is then prompted for his password (to preserve accountability and provide some measure of security), and then the command is run as if root had issued it. During the life of the ticket, the command can be used again without a password prompt. If an unauthorized user attempts to execute a sudo command, a record of the unauthorized attempt is kept in the system log and a mail message is sent to the super user.

Three man pages are associated with sudo: sudo, sudoers, and visudo. The first covers the command itself, the second the format of the /etc/sudoers file, and the third the use of the special editor for /etc/sudoers. You should use the special editing command because it checks the file for parse errors and locks the file to prevent others from editing it at the same time. The visudo command uses the vi editor, so you might need a quick review of

10

the vi editing commands found in Chapter 4 in the section "Working with vi." You
begin the editing by executing the visudo command with this:

visudo

The default /etc/sudoers file looks like this:

```
# sudoers file.
#
#
# This file MUST be edited with the 'visudo' command as root.
#
# See the sudoers man page for the details on how to write a sudoers file.
#

# Host alias specification

# User alias specification

# Cmnd alias specification

# Defaults specification

# User privilege specification
root    ALL=(ALL) ALL

# Uncomment to allow people in group wheel to run all commands
# %wheel        ALL=(ALL)        ALL

# Same thing without a password
# %wheel        ALL=(ALL)        NOPASSWD: ALL

# Samples
# %users  ALL=/sbin/mount /cdrom,/sbin/umount /cdrom
# %users  localhost=/sbin/shutdown -h now
```

The basic format of a sudoers line in the file is as follows:

```
user host_computer=command
```

The user can be an individual user or a group (prepended by a % to identify the name as a
group). The host_computer is normally ALL for all hosts on the network and localhost
for the local machine, but the host computer can be referenced as a subnet of any specific
host. The command in the sudoers line can be ALL, a list of specific commands, or a restriction on specific commands (formed by prepending a ! to the command). A number of

options are available for use with the `sudoers` line, and aliases can be used to simplify the assignment of privileges. Again, the `sudoers` man page gives the details, but here are a few examples:

If you uncomment the line, as follows

```
# %wheel        ALL=(ALL)        ALL
```

any user you add to the `wheel` group can execute any command after entering their specific password.

Suppose that you want to give user `vanessa` permission across the network to be able to add users with the graphical interface. You would add the following line:

```
vanessa ALL=/system-config-users
```

Or perhaps you would grant permission only on her local computer:

```
vanessa 192.168.1.87=/usr/bin/system-config-users
```

If you want to give the editor group systemwide permission with no password required to delete files, you use this:

```
%editors ALL=NOPASSWD: /bin/rm
```

If you want to give every user permission with no password required to mount the CD drive on the `localhost`, use the following:

```
ALL localhost=NOPASSWD:/sbin/mount /dev/scd0 /mnt/cdrom /sbin/umount /mnt/cdrom
```

It is also possible to use wildcards in the construction of the `sudoers` file. Aliases can be used, as well, to make it easier to define users and groups. Although the man page for `sudoers` contains some examples, http://www.komar.org/pres/sudo/toc.html provides illustrative notes and comments of `sudo` use at a large aerospace company. The `sudo` home page at http://www.sudo.ws/ is also a useful resource for additional explanations and examples.

The following command presents users with a list of the commands they are entitled to use:

```
$ sudo -l
```

Disk Quotas

On large systems with many users, you need to control the amount of disk space a user has access to. Disk quotas are designed for this purpose. Quotas, managed per each partition, can be set for both individual users and for groups; quotas for the group need not be as large as the aggregate quotas for the individuals in the groups.

When files are created, both a user and a group own them; ownership of the files is always part of the metadata about the files. This makes quotas based on both users and groups easy to manage.

To manage disk quotas, you must have the quota package installed on your system; it is usually installed by default. Quota management with Fedora is not enabled by default and has traditionally been enabled and configured manually by system administrators. Sysadmins use the family of quota commands, such as `quotacheck` to initialize the quota database files, `edquota` to set and edit user quotas, `setquota` to configure disk quotas, and `quotaon` or `quotaoff` to control the service. (Other utilities include `warnquota` for automatically sending mail to users over their disk-space usage limit.)

Implementing Quotas

To reiterate, quotas might not be enabled by default, even if the quota software package is installed on your system. When quotas are installed and enabled, you can see which partitions have user quotas, group quotas, or both by looking at the fourth field in the `/etc/fstab` file. For example, one line in `/etc/fstab` shows that quotas are enabled for the `/home` partition:

```
/dev/sda5    /home    ext3    defaults,usrquota,grpquota 1 1
```

The root of the partition with quotas enabled has the files `aquota.user` or `aquota.group` in them (or both files, if both types of quotas are enabled), and the files contain the actual quotas. The permissions of these files should be `600` so that users cannot read or write to them. (Otherwise, users would change them to allow ample space for their music files and Internet art collections.) To initialize disk quotas, the partitions must be remounted. This is easily accomplished with the following:

```
# mount -o ro,remount partition_to_be_remounted mount_point
```

The underlying console tools (complete with man pages) are as follows:

- **`quotaon`**, **`quotaoff`**—Toggles quotas on a partition.

- **`repquota`**—A summary status report on users and groups.

- **`quotacheck`**—Updates the status of quotas (compares new and old tables of disk usage); it is run after `fsck`.

- **`edquota`**—A basic quota management command.

Manually Configuring Quotas

Manual configuration of quotas involves changing entries in your system's file system table, `/etc/fstab`, to add the `usrquota` mount option to the desired portion of your file system. As an example in a simple file system, quota management can be enabled like this:

```
LABEL=/          /          ext3    defaults,usrquota    1 1
```

Group-level quotas can also be enabled by using the grpquota option. As the root operator, you must then create a file (using the example of creating user quotas) named aquota.user in the designated portion of the file system, like so:

```
# touch /quota.user
```

You should then turn on the use of quotas by using the quotaon command:

```
# quotaon -av
```

You can then edit user quotas with the edquota command to set hard and soft limits on file system use. The default system editor (vi unless you change your EDITOR environment variable) is launched when a user's quota is edited.

Any user can find out what her quotas are with the following:

```
$ quota -v
```

> **NOTE**
>
> No graphical tools supported by Fedora can be used to configure disk quotas. A Quota mini-HOWTO is maintained at http://www.tldp.org/HOWTO/Quota.html.

Related Fedora Commands

You will use these commands to manage user accounts in Fedora:

- ▶ **ac**—A user account-statistics command
- ▶ **change**—Sets or modifies user password expiration policies
- ▶ **chfn**—Creates or modifies user finger information in /etc/passwd
- ▶ **chgrp**—Modifies group memberships
- ▶ **chmod**—Changes file permissions
- ▶ **chown**—Changes file ownerships
- ▶ **chpasswd**—Batch command to modify user passwords
- ▶ **chsh**—Modifies a user's shell
- ▶ **groups**—Displays existing group memberships
- ▶ **logname**—Displays a user's login name
- ▶ **newusers**—Batches user management command
- ▶ **passwd**—Creates or modifies user passwords
- ▶ **su**—Executes shell or command as another user
- ▶ **sudo**—Manages selected user execution permissions
- ▶ **system-config-users**—Fedora's graphical user management tool
- ▶ **useradd**—Creates, modifies, or manages users
- ▶ **userinfo**—Fedora's graphical chfn command
- ▶ **usermod**—Edits a user's login profile
- ▶ **userpasswd**—Fedora's graphical user password command

10

Reference

▶ **http://howtos.linux.com/howtos/User-Authentication-HOWTO/index.shtml—** The User-Authentication HOWTO describes how user and group information is stored and used for authentication.

▶ **http://www.ibiblio.org/pub/Linux/docs/HOWTO/other-formats/html_single/ Shadow-Password-HOWTO.html—**The Shadow-Password HOWTO delves into the murky depths of shadow passwords and even discusses why you might not want to use them.

▶ **http://www.ibiblio.org/pub/Linux/docs/HOWTO/other-formats/html_single/ Security-HOWTO.html—**A must-read HOWTO, the Security HOWTO is a good overview of security issues. Especially applicable to this chapter are sections on creating accounts, file permissions, and password security.

▶ **http://www.secinf.net/unix_security/Linux_Administrators_Security_Guide/—**A general guide, the Linux System Administrator's Security Guide has interesting sections on limiting and monitoring users.

▶ **http://www.ibiblio.org/pub/Linux/docs/HOWTO/other-formats/html_single/ Path.html—**How can one know the true path? The Path HOWTO sheds light on this issue. You need to understand paths if you want to guide the users to their data and applications.

▶ **http://www.courtesan.com/sudo/—**The SUperuser DO command is a powerful and elegant way to delegate authority to regular users for specific commands.

▶ **http://www.kernel.org/pub/linux/libs/pam/index.html—**The Pluggable Authentication Modules suite contains complex and highly useful applications that provide additional security and logging for passwords. PAM is installed by default in Fedora. It is not necessary to understand the intricacies of PAM to use it effectively.

▶ **http://localhost/localdomain/—**Your Fedora system contains man and info pages on just about everything covered here. Use man -k to search on a keyword.

CHAPTER 11

Automating Tasks

In this chapter, you will learn about the three ways to automate tasks on your system: making them services that run as your system starts, making them services you start and stop by hand, and scheduling them to run at specific times.

After you turn on the power switch, the boot process begins with the computer executing code stored in a chip called the BIOS; this process occurs no matter what operating system you have installed. The Linux boot process begins when the code known as the boot loader starts loading the Linux kernel and ends only when the login prompt appears.

As a system administrator, you will use the skills you learn in this chapter to control your system's services and manage runlevels on your computer. Understanding the management of the system services and states is essential to understanding how Linux works (especially in a multi-user environment) and will help untangle the mysteries of a few of your Fedora system's configuration files. Furthermore, a good knowledge of the cron daemon that handles task scheduling is essential for administrators at all skill levels.

In this chapter, you'll take your first steps in shell scripting, but if you want to take it further, Chapter 33, "Writing and Executing a Shell Script," is dedicated exclusively to programming shell scripts. These are preset lists of commands that you want to execute all at once, so putting them in a shell script means you can just type the name of the script and all the commands run in sequence. For now, though, we're more interested in having things done automatically for us *without* much user intervention.

Running Services at Bootup

Although most people consider a computer to be either on or off, in Fedora there are a number of states in between. Known as *runlevels*, they control what system services are started at bootup. These services are simply applications running in the background that provide some needed function to your system, such as getting information from your mouse and sending it to the display; or a service could monitor the partitions to see whether they have enough free space left on them. Services are typically loaded and run (also referred to as *being started*) during the boot process, in the same way as Microsoft Windows services are.

You can manage nearly every aspect of your computer and how it behaves after booting via configuring and ordering boot scripts, as well as by using various system administration utilities included with Fedora. In this chapter, you learn how to work with these boot scripts and system administration utilities. This chapter also offers advice for troubleshooting and fixing problems that might arise with software configuration or the introduction or removal of various types of hardware from your system.

Beginning the Boot Loading Process

Although the actual boot loading mechanism for Linux varies on different hardware platforms (such as the SPARC, Alpha, or PowerPC systems), Intel-based PCs running Fedora most often use the same mechanism throughout product lines. This process is accomplished through a Basic Input Output System, or BIOS. The BIOS is an application stored in a chip on the motherboard that initializes the hardware on the motherboard (and often the hardware that's attached to the motherboard). The BIOS gets the system ready to load and run the software that we recognize as the operating system.

As a last step, the BIOS code looks for a special program known as the *boot loader* or *boot code*. The instructions in this little bit of code tell the BIOS where the Linux kernel is located, how it should be loaded into memory, and how it should be started.

If all goes well, the BIOS looks for a bootable volume such as a floppy disk, CD-ROM, hard drive, RAM disk, or other media. The bootable volume contains a special hexadecimal value written to the volume by the boot loader application (likely either GRUB or LILO, although LILO is not provided with Fedora) when the boot loader code was first installed in the system's drives. The BIOS searches volumes in the order established by the BIOS settings (for example, the floppy first, followed by a CD-ROM, and then a hard drive) and then boots from the first bootable volume it finds. Modern BIOSs allow considerable flexibility in choosing the device used for booting the system.

> **NOTE**
>
> If the BIOS detects a hardware problem, the boot process fails and the BIOS generates a few beeps from the system speaker. These "beep codes" indicate the nature of the problem the BIOS has encountered. The codes vary among manufacturers, and the diagnosis of problems occurring during this phase of the boot process is beyond the scope of this book and does not involve Linux. If you encounter a problem, you should consult the motherboard manual or contact the motherboard's manufacturer.

Next, the BIOS looks on the bootable volume for boot code in the partition boot sector also known as the Master Boot Record (*MBR*) of the first hard disk. The MBR contains the boot loader code and the partition table—think of it as an index for a book, plus a few comments on how to start reading the book. (We cover the MBR in more detail in Chapter 35, "Managing the File System.") If the BIOS finds a boot loader, it loads the boot loader code into memory. At that point, the BIOS's job is completed, and it passes control of the system to the boot loader.

The boot loader locates the Linux kernel on the disk and loads it into memory. After that task is completed, the boot loader passes control of the system to the Linux kernel. You can see how one process builds on another in an approach that enables many different operating systems to work with the same hardware.

Fedora can use a variety of boot loaders, including GRUB (the default for Fedora), LILO (a long-time standard but not available with Fedora), BootMagic (a commercial program), and others.

> **NOTE**
>
> Linux is very flexible and can be booted from multiple images on a CD-ROM, over a network using PXE (pronounced "pixie") or NetBoot, or on a headless server with the console display sent over a serial or network connection. Work is even underway to create a special Linux BIOS at http://www.linuxbios.org/ that expedites the boot process because Linux does not need many of the services offered by the typical BIOS.
>
> This kind of flexibility enables Linux to be used in a variety of ways, such as remote servers or diskless workstations, which are not generally seen in personal home use.

Loading the Linux Kernel

In a general sense, the kernel manages the system resources. As the user, you do not often interact with the kernel, but instead just the applications that you are using. Unix refers to each application as a process, and the kernel assigns each process a number called a *process ID* (*PID*). First, the Linux kernel loads and runs a process named init, which is also known as the "father of all processes" because it starts every subsequent process. The init process looks for a list of instructions in a file named /etc/rc.d/rc.sysinit. That script issues a number of commands that are run only once—each time the system is turned on.

> **NOTE**
>
> Details about the sequence of events that occur when the Linux kernel is loaded can be found in the file /usr/src/linux-2.6/init/main.c if you installed the Linux kernel documentation.

This next step of the boot process begins with a message that the Linux kernel is loading, and a series of messages is printed to the screen, giving you the status of each command in rc.sysinit script language. A failure should display an error message. The -quiet option may be passed to the kernel at boot time to suppress many of these messages.

Although it is not intended that you modify the rc.sysinit script, knowledge of the contents of the file might aid you in diagnosing a problem if the boot process fails during this step. Look at /etc/rc.d/rc.sysinit, and you will discover that it's just a text file filled with shell script language.

After the rc.sysinit script has run, the basic system is configured and the kernel is in control of the system. If the boot process were halted at this point, the system would just sit idle and the screen would be blank. To make the system useful for users, you need to start the system services. Those services are some of the applications that enable you to interact with the system.

System Services and Runlevels

After finishing with rc.sysinit script during the bootloading process, the init command uses the Linux system initialization table found in /etc/inittab to boot Fedora to a specific system state. The state of the system is commonly referred to as its *runlevel*.

Several different ways of starting and stopping system services exist, and Fedora uses a method derived from System V Unix. The System V (pronounced "System Five") method uses runlevels and different combinations of services to define different states of operation. Runlevels determine which of the many available system services are started, as well as in which order they start. A special runlevel is used to stop the system, and a special runlevel is used for system maintenance. As you will see, there are other runlevels for special purposes.

> **NOTE**
>
> The System V method makes extensive use of symbolic links, which are ways to reference a file in another location and make it appear as if it were in two or more places at once. The benefit is that you need to edit only one file to change them all. In addition, any reorganization to be done means that only links need to be changed, not the files themselves.

You use runlevels to manage the system services running on your computer. All these special files and scripts are set up during your installation of Fedora Linux, and they receive their initial values based on your choices during the installation—as described in Chapter 1, "Installing Fedora," You can change and control them manually, as you learn later in this chapter, using tools of varying sophistication.

Runlevel Definitions

The Fedora runlevels are defined for the Fedora system in /etc/inittab.

> **NOTE**
>
> Not all Linux distributions use the same runlevel configurations or runlevel definitions! For example, although Fedora uses runlevel 3 for a full, console-based multiuser mode, pre-7.1 versions of SUSE Linux defined this system state as runlevel 2. Red Hat, Fedora, and SUSE now use the same runlevels to conform to the Linux Standards Base, or *LSB*. As a system administrator, you should be aware of this issue, especially if you have devised any administrative scripts or tools that deal with system states.

Each runlevel tells the `init` command what services to start or stop. Although runlevels might all have custom definitions, Fedora has adopted some standards for runlevels:

▶ **Runlevel 0**—Known as "halt," this runlevel is used to shut down the system.

▶ **Runlevel 1**—This is a special runlevel, defined as "single," which boots Fedora to a root access shell prompt where only the root user may log in. Networking, X, and multiuser access are turned off. This is the maintenance or rescue mode. It allows the system administrator to perform work on the system, make backups, or repair configuration or other files.

▶ **Runlevel 2**—This runlevel dictates that Fedora be booted to a console, or text-based mode, with multiuser access.

▶ **Runlevel 3**—This runlevel is identical to runlevel 2, except that it also starts any networking services.

▶ **Runlevel 4**—This runlevel is undefined, and it can readily be configured to boot Fedora to a custom system state.

▶ **Runlevel 5**—This runlevel boots Fedora to a networking, multiuser state with an active X session. This is the most common runlevel for home users who want a graphical interface.

▶ **Runlevel 6**—This runlevel is used to reboot the system.

Runlevel 1 (also known as *single-user mode* or *maintenance mode*) is most commonly used to repair file systems and change the root password on a system when the password has been forgotten. Trespassers with physical access to the machine can also use runlevel 1 to access your system.

> **CAUTION**
>
> Never forget that uncontrolled physical access is virtually a guarantee of access to your data by an intruder.

Booting into the Default Runlevel

Entries in /etc/inittab use a field-based notation that determines the runlevel—when to execute the process, whether or not the process is executed when booting, whether or not to wait for the process to complete, and when to execute the process during booting. The default choices are adequate and need be changed only in unique circumstances that the average user is not likely to encounter.

The value of the default entry, or the `initdefault` line in `/etc/inittab`, determines the particular system state in which Fedora is when the login prompt is finally presented. For example,

```
id:5:initdefault:
```

In this example, Fedora boots to runlevel 5, a network-enabled, multiuser mode with an active X session and a graphical login. The value 5 is forwarded to the script named `rc` under the `/etc/rc.d` directory. This script is used when booting or changing runlevels; it also acts as an interpreter when you boot Fedora in "Interactive" mode when you press **i** during the boot.

After `/etc/rc.d/rc.sysinit` has finished, `init` uses the corresponding `/etc/inittab` entry that matches the designated default runlevel. Using the previous example, the line in `/etc/inittab` would then be:

```
l5:5:wait:/etc/rc.d/rc 5
```

Under the `/etc/rc.d` directory is a series of directories that correspond to each runlevel:

```
# ls /etc/rc.d
init.d  rc0.d  rc2.d  rc4.d  rc6.d     rc.sysinit
rc      rc1.d  rc3.d  rc5.d  rc.local
```

Assuming that the value is 5, the `rc` script executes all the scripts under the `/etc/rc.d/rc.5` directory and then launches the graphical login.

If Fedora is booted to runlevel 5, it executes scripts from the /etc/rc.d/rc5.d directory. Scripts beginning with the letter K are executed first, followed by scripts beginning with the letter S:

```
# ls /etc/rc.d/rc5.d/
K01yum        K20bootparamd    K28amd        K45named     K61ldap
K74ypxfrd       S05kudzu      S24pcmcia    S85gpm  K05innd
K20iscsi        K30sendmail    K46radvd      K65identd   K84bgpd
S08ip6tables  S25netfs      S90crond K05saslauthd   K20netdump-server
K34dhcrelay   K50netdump    K65kadmin   K84ospf6d      S08ipchains
S26apmd        S90FreeWnn   K10psacct    K20nfs         K34yppasswdd
K50snmpd       K65kprop     K84ospfd       S08iptables  S28autofs
S90xfs  K10radiusd    K20rstatd      K35atalk     K50snmptrapd
K65krb524  K84ripd          S10network   S40smartd   S92lisa
K12canna     K20rusersd        K35dhcpd     K50tux      K65krb5kdc
K84ripngd       S12syslog     S44acpid      S95anacron  K12mailman
```

```
K20rwalld        K35smb        K50vsftpd    K70aep1000  K85zebra
S13irqbalance  S55cups       S95atd K12mysqld     K20rwhod
K35vncserver  K54dovecot    K70bcm5820  K90isicom        S13portmap
S55sshd        S97messagebus K15httpd      K20spamassassin    K35winbind
K54pxe          K74ntpd       K91isdn        S14nfslock      S56rawdevices
S97rhnsd K15postgresql  K24irda        K40mars-nwe   K55routed
K74ups          K95firstboot  S17keytable   S56xinetd      S99local
K16rarpd        K25squid      K45arpwatch  K61hpoj      K74ypserv
S00microcode_ctl  S20random      S84privoxy    S99mdmonitor
```

These scripts are actually symbolic links to system service scripts under the /etc/rc.d/ init.d directory (yours might look different, depending on whether you are working with a workstation or server installation and the services or software packages installed on your system):

```
# ls /etc/rc.d/init.d/
acpid      bgpd        firstboot ip6tables  keytable    mars-nwe        nfs
postgresql ripd        smartd      vncserver  zebra  aep1000   bluetooth
FreeWnn    ipchains    killall    mdmonitor      nfslock  privoxy
ripngd    smb          vsftpd    amd        bootparamd functions iptables
kprop     messagebus   nscd      psacct      routed      snmpd       winbind
anacron   canna        gkrellmd   irda        krb524      microcode_ctl ntpd
pxe       rstatd       snmptrapd   xfs  apmd        cpqarrayd   gpm
irqbalance krb5kdc      mysqld        ospf6d   radiusd     rusersd
spamassassin xinetd   arpwatch  crond        halt        iscsi       kudzu
named          ospfd      radvd        rwalld   squid        ypbind
atalk     cups        hpoj      isdn        ldap        netdump       pand
random    rwhod       sshd        yppasswdd atd        dhcpd
httpd     isicom      lisa        netdump-server pcmcia  rarpd
saslauthd syslog       ypserv autofs   dhcrelay  identd       kadmin
lm_sensors netfs       portmap  rawdevices sendmail    tux
ypxfrd bcm5820   dovecot      innd        kdcrotate  mailman
network         postfix  rhnsd        single      ups          yum
```

The rc5.d links are prefaced with a letter and number, such as K15 or S10. The (K) or (S) in these prefixes indicates whether a particular service should be killed (K) or started (S), and passes a value of stop or start to the appropriate /etc/rc.d/init.d script. The number in the prefix executes the specific /etc/rc.d/init.d script in a particular order. The symlinks have numbers to delineate the order in which they are started. Nothing is sacred about a specific number, but some services need to be running before others are started. You would not want your Fedora system to attempt, for example, to mount a remote Network File System (NFS) volume without first starting networking and NFS services.

After all the system services are started for your runlevel, `init` starts the graphical login (because you are in runlevel 5). The graphical login's definition appears toward the end of /etc/inittab and looks like this:

```
# Run xdm in runlevel 5

x:5:respawn:/etc/X11/prefdm -nodaemon
```

This example shows that the shell script named `prefdm` executes the proper X11 display manager when Fedora is booted to runlevel 5.

Booting to a Nondefault Runlevel with GRUB

After you select a default runlevel, that runlevel is selected every time you restart the system from a power-off state. There might come a time when you do not want to boot into that runlevel. You might want to enter the maintenance mode or start the system without an active X server and graphical login to modify or repair the X server or desktop manager. You have to follow several specific steps to boot to a nondefault runlevel if you use GRUB, the default boot loader for Fedora.

> **NOTE**
>
> If you have enabled a GRUB password, you must first press **p**, type your password, and then press Enter before using this boot method.

The GRUB boot loader passes arguments, or commands, to the kernel at boot time. These arguments are used, among other things, to tell GRUB where the kernel is located and also to pass specific parameters to the kernel, such as how much memory is available or how special hardware should be configured.

To override the default runlevel, you can add an additional kernel argument to GRUB as follows:

1. At the graphical boot screen, press **e** (for edit), scroll down to select the kernel, and press **e** again.

2. Press the spacebar, type **single** or **1** (Fedora allows S and **s** as well), and press Enter.

3. Finally, press **b** to boot, and you'll boot into runlevel 1 instead of the default runlevel listed in /etc/inittab.

Fedora includes several command-line and graphical system administration utilities you can use to start, stop, reorder, or restart various services in different runlevels. These commands (discussed later in this chapter) work by renaming, removing, or creating symbolic links from /etc/rc.d/init.d to /etc/rc.d/rc.* as appropriate. Many administrators use these commands to change the symbolic links to the scripts under each /etc/rc.d/rc* directory rather than do it by hand.

The locations of symbolic links can also be confusing. Red Hat (and now Fedora) has traditionally kept them in one place, and the Linux Standards Base (*LSB*) requires that they now be located elsewhere. Because other scripts reference these files and it would be difficult to change them all, Fedora places symbolic links in the places specified by the LSB.

As you might surmise, symbolic links are very powerful tools in the system administrator's toolbox.

Understanding `init` Scripts and the Final Stage of Initialization

Each `/etc/rc.d/init.d` script, or `init` script, contains logic that determines what to do when receiving a start or stop value. The logic might be a simple switch statement for execution, as in this example:

```
case "$1" in
  start)
        start
        ;;
  stop)
        stop
        ;;
  restart)
        restart
        ;;
  reload)
        reload
        ;;
  status)
        rhstatus
        ;;
  condrestart)
        [ -f /var/lock/subsys/smb ] && restart ¦¦ :
        ;;
  *)
        echo $"Usage: $0 {start¦stop¦restart¦status¦condrestart}"
        exit 1
esac
```

Although the scripts can be used to customize the way that the system runs from power-on, absent the replacement of the kernel, this script approach also means that the system does not have to be halted in total to start, stop, upgrade, or install new services.

Note that not all scripts use this approach, and that other messages might be passed to the service script, such as `restart`, `reload`, or `status`. Also, not all scripts respond to the same set of messages (with the exception of `start` and `stop`, which they all have to accept by convention) because each service might require special commands.

> **TIP**
>
> You can write your own `init` scripts, using the existing scripts as examples. Sample scripts can also be found in `/usr/share/doc/initscripts/sysvinitfiles`, along with a brief tutorial written by Red Hat and a brief explanation of all the options available to use in `init` scripts.

After all the system scripts have been run, your system is configured and all the necessary system services have been started. If you are using a runlevel other than 5, the final act of the `init` process is to launch the user shell, which on Linux is nearly always `bash`. The shell launches and you see a login prompt on the screen.

Controlling Services at Boot with Administrative Tools

As the master control file for system startup, `/etc/inittab` and its corresponding system of symbolic links control system services. You can manage `/etc/inittab` and its symbolic links, using these graphical and nongraphical administrative tools:

- ▶ `chkconfig`—A small script that helps you configure system services.

- ▶ `ntsysv`—A graphical interface for the `chkconfig` configuration script.

- ▶ `system-config-services`—A full graphical services configuration client. This application is found in the System Services/Sever settings menu as the Services menu item.

The following sections explain how to use all these administrative tools to configure and manage services in Fedora.

Using the `chkconfig` Text-Based Command-Line Tool

Traditionally, the command-line tool `chkconfig` has been used to effect administration of the services and their associations in the different runlevels. `chkconfig` was a major improvement over the process of configuring the symbolic links by hand. It is an effective, text-based command-line tool that you can use to display, diagnose, or change the starting or stopping of system services (as available under `/etc/rc.d/init.d`) in each runlevel.

For example, to list all services that are turned on in runlevel 5, you can pipe the output of `chkconfig` through the `grep` command like this:

```
# /sbin/chkconfig --list ¦ grep '5:on' | sort
anacron        0:off   1:off   2:on    3:on    4:on    5:on    6:off
apmd           0:off   1:off   2:on    3:on    4:on    5:on    6:off
atd            0:off   1:off   2:off   3:on    4:on    5:on    6:off
autofs         0:off   1:off   2:off   3:on    4:on    5:on    6:off
canna          0:off   1:off   2:on    3:off   4:on    5:on    6:off
crond          0:off   1:off   2:on    3:on    4:on    5:on    6:off
```

Not all the output is shown here, but as you can see, chkconfig can display the value of off or on for each service and each runlevel. The sample output shows only those services that are started in runlevel 5. The chkconfig command can be used to reassign start or stop values for each runlevel and each service. As an example, to alter the scripts to start power management (controlled by the apmd script under /etc/rc.d/init.d) when using Fedora during runlevel 5, use chkconfig like this:

```
# chkconfig --level 5 apmd on
```

You can then verify this action by again using grep on chkconfig's output like this:

```
# chkconfig --list | grep apmd
apmd            0:off   1:off   2:on    3:on    4:on    5:on    6:off
```

The chkconfig command does not start or stop a service; instead, it alters the scripts that start or stop a service, or it can report on the status of a service. It affects only the current runlevel by default; you can modify other runlevels by using the -levels option. You would use the ntsysv or service commands or run the daemons directly to actually start or stop services (as described later in this chapter). All these tools have useful man pages to refresh your memory of all the available options.

ntsysv is a graphical interface you can use to access chkconfig and use a graphical interface. ntsysv is an ncurses-based interface, meaning that it offers crude, block graphics and elements you can tab through and select by pressing the spacebar (see Figure 11.1).

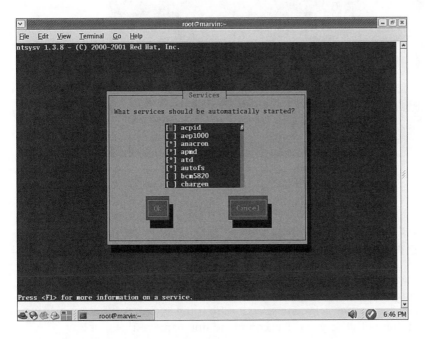

FIGURE 11.1   The ntsysv utility manages only which services are started in the current runlevel. Use the --level option to modify other runlevels.

When you have the ntsysv application open, you can scroll through the list of services and toggle a service on or off by pressing the spacebar on the keyboard. When finished, use the Tab key to highlight the OK or Cancel button. Your changes are saved and used the next time Fedora is booted.

> **NOTE**
>
> ntsysv is simple to use and it's an excellent tool for a system without X, but it works for only the runlevel in which you are currently. Use the --level option to modify other runlevels.

The Fedora tool setup is an ncurses-based menu for all the available ncurses-based command-line configuration tools (see Figure 11.2). It can be used to access ntsysv and all the other command-line configuration tools.

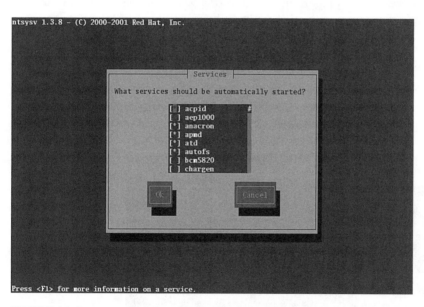

FIGURE 11.2   Use the setup command's System Services item to access the ntsysv command.

Using the GUI-Based Service Configuration Tool

Fedora's developers have added GUIs to many text-only, command-line–based system administration tools as Linux has matured. These tools provide an easier-to-use interface and don't require memorization or lookup of command-line options. Fedora provides its own Service Configuration tool for the control and administration of services (see Figure 11.3). You can access the GUI menu selection from the System Settings/Server Settings menu, and then select Services. The command-line name of this tool is system-config-services.

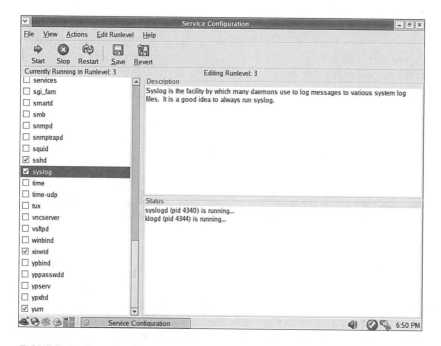

FIGURE 11.3   The new Service Configuration tool enables you to select runlevels to edit, displays all the available services, and provides an explanation of what the service does.

Running Services Through `xinetd`

The `xinetd` daemon is a replacement for `inetd`; it listens for requests for services on certain ports and starts those services as required. `xinetd` is called a super server because it controls other servers. Its purpose is to conserve resources by not running services when not needed. The `xinetd` daemon is more secure than the older `inetd`, offers better logging facilities than `inetd`, and can redirect service requests to another machine. It does not require the root user to start any services.

The configuration file for `xinetd` is found at `/etc/xinetd.conf`; configuration files for individual services are located in `/etc/xinet.d/`; the particulars of its format are covered in the man page for `xinetd.conf`, which also provides a sample file listing. Fedora provides the appropriate server RPM packages already configured to use `xinetd` if possible. If you are installing servers manually from source code, the included documentation describes the appropriate `xinetd` configuration. Services run under `xinetd` cannot be started and stopped in the same manner as the services run from scripts in `/etc/rc.d/init.d`; you must restart the `xinetd` service itself and let it control those services.

Here is a sample listing of the `rsync` file `/etc/xinet.d/rsync`:

```
# default: off
# description: The rsync server is a good addition to an ftp server, as it \
#        allows crc checksumming etc.
```

```
service rsync
{
        disable = yes
        socket_type     = stream
        wait            = no
        user            = root
        server          = /usr/bin/rsync
        server_args     = --daemon
        log_on_failure  += USERID
}
```

The items are straightforward and vary from service to service. Although you can edit this by hand, it can be configured via the command line or graphical service configuration clients.

Changing Runlevels

After making changes to system services and runlevels, you can use the `telinit` command to change runlevels on the fly on a running Fedora system. Changing runlevels this way enables system administrators to alter selected parts of a running system to make changes to the services or to put changes into effect that have already been made (such as reassignment of network addresses for a networking interface).

For example, a system administrator can quickly change the system to maintenance or single-user mode by using the `telinit` command with its **S** option, like this:

```
# telinit S
```

The `telinit` command uses the `init` command to change runlevels and shut down currently running services. The command then starts services for the specified runlevel; in this example, the single-user runlevel is the same as runlevel 2. The `init` command can be run only from a console, not from an `xterm` running in an X session.

After booting to single-user mode, you can then return to multiuser mode without X, like this:

```
# telinit 3
```

If you have made changes to the system initialization table itself, `/etc/inittab`, use the `telinit` command's **q** command-line option to force `init` to re-examine the table.

> **TIP**
>
> Linux is full of shortcuts: If you exit the single-user shell by typing **exit** at the prompt, you go back to the default runlevel without worrying about using `telinit`.

Troubleshooting Runlevel Problems

Reordering or changing system services during a particular runlevel is rarely necessary when using Fedora unless some disaster occurs. But system administrators should have a basic understanding of how Linux boots and how services are controlled to perform troubleshooting or to diagnose problems. By using additional utilities such as the `dmesg | less` command to read kernel output after booting or by examining system logging with `cat /var/log/messages | less`, it is possible to gain a bit more detail about what is going on when faced with troublesome drivers or service failure.

To better understand how to troubleshoot service problems in Fedora, look at the diagnosis and resolution of a typical service-related issue. In this example, X doesn't start: You don't see a desktop displayed, nor does the computer seem to respond to keyboard input. The X server might be hung in a loop, repeatedly failing, or might exit to a shell prompt with or without an error message.

The X server attempts to restart itself only in runlevel 5, so to determine whether the X server is hung in a loop, try switching to runlevel 3.

TIP

If you are working on a multiuser system and might inadvertently interrupt the work of other users, ask them to save their current work; then change to a safer runlevel, such as single-user mode.

Change to runlevel 3 by switching to another virtual console with Ctrl+Alt+F2, logging in as root, and running the command `telinit 3`. This switch to runlevel 3 stops the X server from attempting to restart. Now you can easily examine the error and attempt to fix it.

First, try to start the X server "naked" (without also launching the window manager). If you are successful, you get a gray screen with a large X in the middle. If so, kill X with the Ctrl+Alt+Backspace key combination and look at your window manager configuration. (This configuration varies according to which window manager you have chosen.)

Let's assume that X won't run "naked." If you look at the log file for Xorg (it's clearly identified in the `/var/log` directory), pay attention to any line that begins with (EE), the special error code. You can also examine the error log file, `.xsessions-error`, in the home directory if such a file exists.

If you find an error line, the cause of the error might or might not be apparent. One nice thing about the Linux community is that it is very unlikely that you are the first person to experience that error. Enter the error message (or better, a unique part of it) into http://www.google.com/linux and discover what others have had to say about the problem. You might need to adjust your search to yield usable results, but that level of detail is beyond the scope of this chapter. Make adjustments and retest as before until you achieve success. Fix the X configuration and start X with `startx`. Repeat as necessary.

> **CAUTION**
>
> Before making any changes to any configuration file, always make a backup copy of the original, unmodified file. Our practice is to append the extension `.original` to the copy because that is a unique and unambiguous identifier.
>
> If you need to restore the original configuration file, do not rename it, but copy it back to its original name.

Starting and Stopping Services Manually

If you change a configuration file for a system service, it is usually necessary to stop and restart the service to make it read the new configuration. If you are reconfiguring the X server, it is often convenient to change from runlevel 5 to runlevel 3 to make testing easier and then switch back to runlevel 5 to re-enable the graphical login. If a service is improperly configured, it is easier to stop and restart it until you have it configured correctly than it is to reboot the entire machine.

There are several ways to manually start or stop services or to change runlevels while using Fedora. The traditional way to manage a service (as root) is to call the service's `/etc/rc.d/init.d` name on the command line with an appropriate keyword, such as start, status, or stop. For example, to start the automated nightly update of the yum RPM package database, call the `/etc/rc.d/init.d/yum` script like this:

```
# /etc/rc.d/init.d/yum start
Enabling nightly yum update:                                    [  OK  ]
```

The script executes the proper programs and reports their status. Stopping services is equally easy, and in fact, you can also check the status of some services by using the status keyword like this:

```
# /etc/rc.d/init.d/yum status
Nightly yum update is enabled.
```

In this example, the yum script reports that the daemon is running. This information might be useful for other system management tasks.

A much easier way to manually start or stop a service is to use a script named `service`. Using `service`, you do not have to know the full pathname to the system service; you need know only the name of the system service you want to manipulate. Using this approach, the previous yum example looks like this:

```
# service yum start
Nightly yum update is enabled:                                  [  OK  ]
```

Of course, the GUI tools mentioned earlier also have the functionality to start and stop specific services in your current runlevel. The tool you choose is a matter of personal preference; a good system administrator is aware of them all.

Relevant Fedora Commands

Here are some of the commands you learned so far:

▶ **chkconfig**—Fedora's text-only command-line runlevel configuration utility

▶ **ntsysv**—Fedora's text-based system services configuration tool for the command line

▶ **setup**—Actually a bash script, it is a menu to all the individual ncurses-based configuration tools, including ntsysv

▶ **system-config-services**—Fedora's GUI runlevel configuration tool, named Configure Services

▶ **telinit**—Changes the current runlevel

Scheduling Tasks

There are three ways to schedule commands in Fedora, all of which work in different ways. The first is the at command, which specifies a command to run at a specific time and date relative to today. The second is the batch command, which is actually a script that redirects you to the at command with some extra options set so that your command runs when the system is quiet. The last option is the cron daemon, which is the Linux way of executing tasks at a given time.

Using at and batch to Schedule Tasks for Later

If there is a time-intensive task you want to run, but you do not want to do it while you are still logged in, you can tell Fedora to run it later with the at command. To use at, you need to tell it the time at which you want to run and then press Enter. You then see a new prompt that starts with at>, and everything you type there—until you press Ctrl+D—comprises the commands you want at to run.

When the designated time arrives, at performs each action individually and in order, which means later commands can rely on the results of earlier commands. In this next example, run at just after 5 p.m., at is used to download and extract the latest Linux kernel at a time when the network should be quiet:

```
[paul@caitlin ~]$ at now + 7 hours
at> wget http://www.kernel.org/pub/linux/kernel/v2.6/linux-2.6.10.tar.bz2
at> tar xvfjp linux-2.6.10.tar.bz2
at> <EOT>
job 2 at 2005-01-09 17:01
```

Specifying now + 7 hours as the time does what you would expect: at was run at 5 p.m., so the command runs just after midnight that night. When your job finishes, at sends you mail with a full log of your job's output; type **mail** at the console to bring up your mailbox and then press the relevant number to read at's mail.

If you have a more complex job, you can use the -f parameter to have at read its commands from a file, like this:

```
echo wget http://www.kernel.org/pub/linux/kernel/v2.6/linux-2.6.10.tar.bz2\;
tar xvfjp linux-2.6.10.tar.bz2 > myjob.job
at -f myjob.job tomorrow
```

As you can see, at is flexible about the time format it takes; you can specify it in three ways:

▸ Using the now parameter, you can specify a number of minutes, hours, days, or weeks relative to the current time—for example, now + 4 weeks would run the command one month from today.

▸ You can also specify several special times, including tomorrow, midnight, noon, or teatime (4 p.m.). If you do not specify a time with tomorrow, your job is set for precisely 24 hours from the current time.

▸ You can specify an exact date and time using HH:MM MM/DD/YY format—for example, 16:40 22/12/05 for 4:40 p.m. on the 22nd of December 2005.

When your job is submitted, at reports the job number, date, and time that the job will be executed; the queue identifier; plus the job owner (you). It also captures all your environment variables and stores them along with the job so that, when your job runs, it can restore the variables, preserving your execution environment.

The job number and job queue identifier are both important. When you schedule a job using at, it is placed into queue a by default, which means it runs at your specified time and takes up a normal amount of resources.

There is an alternative command, batch, which is really just a shell script that calls at with a few extra options. These options (-q b -m now, if you were interested) set at to run on queue b (-q b), mailing the user on completion (-m), and running immediately (now). The queue part is what is important: Jobs scheduled on queue b are executed only when the system load falls below 0.8—that is, when the system is not running at full load. Furthermore, they run with a lower niceness, meaning queue a jobs usually have a niceness of 2, whereas queue b jobs have a niceness of 4.

Because batch always specifies now as its time, you need not specify your own time; it simply runs as soon as the system is quiet. Having a default niceness of 4 means that batched commands get fewer system resources than queue jobs (at's default) and fewer system resources than most other programs. You can optionally specify other queues using at. Queue c runs at niceness 6, queue d runs at niceness 8, and so on. However, it is important to note that the system load is checked only before the command is run. If the load is lower than 0.8, your batch job is run. If the system load subsequently rises beyond 0.8, your batch job continues to run, albeit in the background, thanks to its niceness value.

When you submit a job for execution, you are also returned a job number. If you forget this or just want to see a list of other jobs you have scheduled to run later, use the atq command with no parameters. If you run this as a normal user, it prints only your jobs; running it as a super-user prints everyone's jobs. The output is in the same format as when you submit a job, so you get the ID number, execution time, queue ID, and owner of each job.

If you want to delete a job, use the `atrm` command followed by the ID number of the job you want to delete. The next example shows `atq` and `atrm` being used to list jobs and delete one:

```
[paul@caitlin ~]$ atq
14      2005-01-20 23:33 a paul
16      2005-02-03 22:34 a paul
17      2005-01-25 22:34 a paul
15      2005-01-22 04:34 a paul
18      2005-01-22 01:35 b paul
[paul@caitlin ~]$ atrm 16
[paul@caitlin ~]$ atq
14      2005-01-20 23:33 a paul
17      2005-01-25 22:34 a paul
15      2005-01-22 04:34 a paul
18      2005-01-22 01:35 b paul
```

In that example, job 16 is deleted by `atrm`, and so it does not show up in the second call to `atq`.

The default configuration for `at` and `batch` is to allow everyone to use it, which is not always the desired behavior. Access is controlled through two files: `/etc/at.allow`, and `/etc/at.deny`. By default, `at.deny` exists but is empty, which allows everyone to use `at` and `batch`. You can enter usernames into `at.deny`, one per line, to stop those users scheduling jobs.

Alternatively, you can use the `at.allow` file; this does not exist by default. If you have a blank `at.allow` file, no one except root is allowed to schedule jobs. As with `at.deny`, you can add usernames to `at.allow` one per line, and those users can schedule jobs. You should use either `at.deny` or `at.allow`: When someone tries to run `at` or `batch`, Fedora checks for the username in `at.allow`. If it is in there, or if `at.allow` does not exist, Fedora checks for the username in `at.deny`. If the username is in `at.deny` or `at.deny` does not exist, the user is not allowed to schedule jobs.

Using cron to Run Jobs Repeatedly

The `at` and `batch` commands work well if you want to execute a just single task at a later date, but they are less useful if you want to run a task frequently. Instead, there is the `crond` daemon for running tasks repeatedly based on system—and user—requests. `cron` has a similar permissions system to `at`: Users listed in the `cron.deny` file are not allowed to use `cron`, and users listed in the `cron.allow` file are. An empty `cron.deny` file—the default—means everyone can set jobs. An empty `cron.allow` file means that no one (except root) can set jobs.

There are two types of jobs: system jobs and user jobs. Only root can edit *system* jobs, whereas any user whose name appears in cron.allow or does not appear in cron.deny can run *user* jobs. System jobs are controlled through the /etc/crontab file, which by default looks like this:

```
SHELL=/bin/bash
PATH=/sbin:/bin:/usr/sbin:/usr/bin
MAILTO=root
HOME=/

# run-parts
01 * * * * root run-parts /etc/cron.hourly
02 4 * * * root run-parts /etc/cron.daily
22 4 * * 0 root run-parts /etc/cron.weekly
42 4 1 * * root run-parts /etc/cron.monthly
```

The first four lines are optional: SHELL specifies which shell should be used to execute the job (defaults to the shell of the user who owns the crontab file, usually /bin/bash), PATH specifies the search path for executables to use, and you should avoid using environment variables there. MAILTO defines to whom mail should be sent. If this is not set, it uses the owner of the crontab, but if you do not want to receive mail when your job runs, just set it to "". Finally, HOME specifies the home directory of the user; again, this defaults to the user's home directory if left unspecified.

The next line, # run-parts, starts with a pound sign (#) and so is treated as a comment and ignored. The next four lines are the important parts: They are the jobs themselves.

Each job is specified in seven fields that define the time to run, owner, and command. The first five commands specify the execution time in quite a quirky order: minute (0–59), hour (0–23), day of the month (1–31), month of the year (1–12), and day of the week (0–7). For day of the week, both 0 and 7 are Sunday, which means that 1 is Monday, 3 is Wednesday, and so on. If you want to specify "all values" (that is, every minute, every hour, every day, and so on), use an asterisk, *.

The next field specifies the username of the owner of the job. When a job is executed, it uses the username specified here. The last field is the command to execute.

So, the first job runs at minute 1, every hour of every day of every month and executes the command run-parts /etc/cron.hourly. The run-parts command is a simple script that runs all programs inside a given directory—in this case, /etc/cron.hourly. So, in this case, the job executes at 00:01 (1 minute past midnight), 01:01, 02:01, 03:01, and so on, and uses all the programs listed in the cron.hourly directory.

The next job runs at minute 2 and hour 4 of every day of every month, running run-parts /etc/cron.daily. Because of the hour limitation, this script runs only once per day, at 4:02 a.m. Note that it uses minute 2 rather than minute 1 so that daily jobs do not clash with hourly jobs. You should be able to guess what the next two jobs do, simply by looking at the commands they run!

Inside each of those four directories (cron.hourly, cron.daily, cron.weekly, and cron.monthly) is a collection of shell scripts that are run by run-parts. For example, in cron.daily are scripts such as rpm, which saves a list of your packages in /var/log/rpmpkgs every day; logrotate, which handles backing up of log files; and makewhatis, which updates the whatis database. You can add other system tasks to these directories if you want to, but you should be careful to ensure your scripts are correct.

> **CAUTION**
>
> The cron daemon reads all the system crontab files and all user crontab files once a minute (on the minute; that is, at 6:00:00, 6:01:00, and so on) to check for changes. However, any new jobs it finds are not executed until at least one minute has passed.
>
> For example, if it is 6:01:49 (that is, 49 seconds past one minute past 6 a.m.) and you set a cron job to run at 6:02, it does not execute. At 6:02, the cron daemon rereads its configuration files and sees the new job, but is not able to execute it. If you set the job to run at 6:02 a.m. every day, it is executed the following morning and every subsequent morning.
>
> This same situation exists when deleting jobs. If it is 6:01:49 and you have a job scheduled to run at 6:02, deleting the job makes no difference: cron runs it before it rereads the crontab files for changes. However, after it has reread the crontab file and noticed the job is no longer there, it is not executed on subsequent days.

There are alternative ways of specifying dates. For example, you can use sets of dates and times by using hyphens or commas, such as hours 9–15 would execute at 9, 10, 11, 12, 13, 14, and 15 (from 9 a.m. to 3 p.m.), whereas 9, 11, 13, 15 would miss out at the even hours. Note that it is important that you do not put spaces into these sets because the cron daemon would interpret them as the next field. You can define a step value with a slash (/) to show time division: */4 for hours means "every four hours all day," and 0-12/3 means "every three hours from midnight to noon." You can also specify day and month names rather than numbers, using three-character abbreviations: Sun, Mon, Tue, Fri, Sat for days, or Jan, Feb, Mar, Oct, Nov, Dec for months.

As well as system jobs, there are also user jobs for those users who have the correct permissions. User jobs are stored in the /var/spool/cron directory, with each user having his own file named after his username—for instance, /var/spool/cron/paul or /var/spool/cron/root. The contents of these files contain the jobs the user wants to run and take roughly the same format as the /etc/crontab file, with the exception that the owner of the job should not be specified because it is always the same as the filename.

To edit your own crontab file, type **crontab -e**. This brings up a text editor (vim by default, but you can set the EDITOR environment variable to change that) in which you can enter your entries. The format of this file is a little different from the format for the main crontab because this time there is no need to specify the owner of the job—it is always you.

So, this time each line is made up of six fields: minute (0–59), hour (0–23), day of the month (1–31), month of the year (1–12), day of the week (0–7), and then the command to run. If you are using vim and are new to it, press **i** to enter insert mode to edit your text; then press Esc to exit insert mode. To save and quit, type a colon followed by **wq** and press Enter.

When programming, we tend to use a sandbox subdirectory in our home directory where we keep all sorts of temporary files that we were just playing around with. We can use a personal job to empty that directory ever morning at 6 a.m. so that we get a fresh start each morning. Here is how that would look in our crontab file:

```
0 6 * * * rm -rf /home/paul/sandbox/*
```

If you are not allowed to schedule jobs, you will be stopped from editing your crontab file.

When your jobs are placed, you can use the command **crontab -l** to list your jobs. This just prints the contents of your crontab file, so its output is the same as the line you just entered.

If you want to remove just one job, the easiest thing to do is type **crontab -e** to edit your crontab file in vim; then, after having moved the cursor to the job you want to delete, type **dd** (two *d*s) to delete that line. If you want to delete all your jobs, you can use crontab -r to delete your crontab file.

Basic Shell Control

Fedora includes a rich assortment of capable, flexible, and powerful shells. Each shell is different but has numerous built-in commands and configurable command-line prompts and might include features such as command-line history, the capability to recall and use a previous command line, and command-line editing. As an example, the bash shell is so powerful that it is possible to write a minimal web server entirely in bash's language using 114 lines of script (see Chapter 33 for more information).

Although there are many shells to choose from, nearly everyone sticks with the default, bash. The bash shell does everything most people need to do, and more. Change your shell only if you really need to.

Table 11.1 lists each shell, along with its description and location, in your Fedora file system.

TABLE 11.1   Shells with Fedora

Name	Description	Location
ash	A small shell (sh-like)	/bin/ash
ash.static	A version of ash not dependent on software libraries	/bin/ash.static
bash	The Bourne Again SHell	/bin/bash
bsh	A symbolic link to ash	/bin/bsh

TABLE 11.1   Continued

Name	Description	Location
csh	The C shell, a symbolic link to tcsh	/bin/csh
ksh	The Korn shell	/bin/ksh, /usr/bin/ksh
pdksh	A symbolic link to ksh	/usr/bin/pdksh
rsh	The restricted shell (for network operation)	/usr/bin/rsh
sash	A standalone shell	/sbin/sash
sh	A symbolic link to bash	/bin/sh
tcsh	A csh-compatible shell	/bin/tcsh
zsh	A compatible csh, ksh, and sh shell	/bin/zsh

Learning More About Your Shell

All the shells listed in Table 11.1 have accompanying man pages, along with other documentation under the /usr/share/doc directory. Some of the documentation can be quite lengthy, but it is generally much better to have too much documentation than too little! The bash shell includes more than 100 pages in its manual, and the zsh shell documentation is so extensive that it includes the zshall meta man page (use man zshall to read this overview)!

The Shell Command Line

Having a basic understanding of the capabilities of the shell command line can help you write better shell scripts. If, after you have finished reading this short introduction, you want to learn more about the command line, check out Chapter 32, "Command-Line Master Class." You can use the shell command line to perform a number of different tasks, including

▶ Getting data from and sending data to a file or command, known as *input* and *output redirection.*

▶ Feeding or filtering a program's output to another command (called using *pipes*).

A shell can also have built-in *job-control* commands to launch the command line as a background process, suspend a running program, selectively retrieve or kill running or suspended programs, and perform other types of process control.

Multiple commands can be run on a single command line, with a semicolon to separate commands:

```
$ w ; free ; df
 6:02pm  up 4 days, 24 min,  1 user,  load average: 0.00, 0.00, 0.00
USER    TTY    FROM            LOGIN@  IDLE   JCPU   PCPU  WHAT
bball   pts/0  shuttle.home.org 1:14pm 0.00s  0.57s  0.01s  w
total       used       free      shared    buffers     cached
```

```
Mem:            190684      184420        6264          76        17620      142820
-/+ buffers/cache:          23980       166704
Swap:      1277156          2516      1274640
Filesystem                1k-blocks       Used  Available  Use%  Mounted on
/dev/hda1                 11788296    4478228    6711248   41%  /
none                         95340          0      95340    0%  /dev/shm
```

This example displays the output of the w, free, and df commands. You can extend long shell command lines inside shell scripts or at the command line if you use the backslash character (\). For example,

```
$ echo ""this is a long \
> command line and"" ; echo ""shows that multiple commands \
> may be strung out.""
this is a long command line and
shows that multiple commands may be strung out.
```

The first three lines of this example are a single command line. In that single line are two instances of the echo command. Note that when you use the backslash as a line-continuation character, it must be the last character on the command line (or in your shell script, as you will see later in this chapter).

Using the basic features of the shell command line is easy, but mastering use of all features can be difficult. Entire books have been devoted to using shells, writing shell scripts, and using pattern-matching expressions. The following sections provide an overview of some features of the shell command line relating to writing scripts.

Grokking grep

If you plan to develop shell scripts to expand the capabilities of pattern-matching commands such as grep, you will benefit from learning more about using expressions. One of the definitive guides to using the pattern-matching capabilities of Unix and Linux commands is *Mastering Regular Expressions* by Jeffrey E. F. Freidl (O'Reilly), ISBN: 0-596-00289-0.

Shell Pattern-Matching Support

The shell command line allows you to use strings of specially constructed character patterns for wildcard matches. This is a simpler capability than that supported by GNU utilities such as grep, which can use more complex patterns, known as *expressions*, to search through files or directories or to filter data input to or out of commands.

The shell's pattern strings can be simple or complex, but even using a small subset of the available characters in simple wildcards can yield constructive results at the command line. Some common characters used for shell pattern matching are the following:

▶ *—Matches any character. For example, to find all files in the current directory ending in .txt, you could use

```
$ ls *.txt
```

▶ ?—Matches a single character. For example, to find all files in the current directory ending in the extension .d?c (where ? could be 0–9, a–z, or A–Z),

```
$ ls *.d?c
```

▶ [*xxx*] or [*x-x*]—Matches a range of characters. For example, to list all files in a directory with names containing numbers,

```
$ ls *[0-9]*
```

▶ \x—Matches or escapes a character such as ? or a tab character. For example, to create a file with a name containing a question mark,

```
$ touch foo\?
```

Note that the shell might not interpret some characters or regular expressions in the same manner as a Linux command, and mixing wildcards and regular expressions in shell scripts can lead to problems unless you're careful. For example, finding patterns in text is best left to regular expressions used with commands such as grep; simple wildcards should be used for filtering or matching filenames on the command line. And although both Linux command expressions and shell scripts can recognize the backslash as an escape character in patterns, the dollar sign ($) has two wildly different meanings (single-character pattern matching in expressions and variable assignment in scripts).

CAUTION

Make sure that you read your command carefully when using wildcards; an all-too-common error is to type something like **rm -rf * .txt** with a space between the * and the .txt. By the time you wonder why the command is taking so long, bash will already have deleted most of your files. The problem is that it treats the * and the .txt separately. * matches everything, so bash deletes all your files.

Piping Data

Many Linux commands can be used in concert in a single, connected command line to transform data from one form to another. Stringing Linux commands together in this fashion is known as using or creating *pipes*. Pipes are created on the command line with the bar operator (¦). For example, a pipe can be used to perform a complex task from a single command line like this:

```
$ find /d2 -name '*.txt' -print ¦ xargs cat ¦ \
tr ' ' '\n' ¦ sort ¦ uniq >output.txt
```

This example takes the output of the find command to feed the cat command (via xargs) the name of all text files under the /d2 command. The content of all matching files is then fed through the tr command to change each space in the data stream into a carriage return. The stream of words is then sorted, and identical adjacent lines are removed with the uniq command. The output, a raw list of words, is then saved in the file named output.txt.

Background Processing

The shell enables you to start a command and then launch it into the background as a process by using an ampersand (&) at the end of a command line. This technique is often used at the command line of an X terminal window to start a client and return to the command line. For example, to launch another terminal window using the xterm client,

```
$ xterm &
[3] 1437
```

The numbers echoed back show a number (3 in this example), which is a *job* number, or reference number for a shell process, and a *Process ID* number, or PID (1437 in this example). You can kill the xterm window session by using the shell's built-in kill command, along with the job number like this:

```
$ kill %3
```

Or the process can be killed with the kill command, along with the PID, like so:

```
$ kill 1437
```

Background processing can be used in shell scripts to start commands that take a long time, such as backups:

```
# tar -czf /backup/home.tgz /home &
```

Related Fedora and Linux Commands

You can use these commands and tools when using the shell or writing shell scripts:

▶ **chsh**—Command used to change one's login shell

▶ **kibitz**—Allows two-person interaction with a single shell

▶ **mc**—A visual shell named the GNU Midnight Commander

▶ **nano**—An easy-to-use text editor for the console

▶ **system-config-users**—A graphical user-management utility that can be used to change one or more user login shells

▶ **shar**—Command used to create shell archives

▶ **vi**—The vi (actually vim) text editor

Reference

▶ http://www.linuxgazette.com/issue70/ghosh.html—A Linux Gazette article on "Bootstrapping Linux," which includes much detail on the BIOS and MBR aspects of the boot process.

▶ http://www.lostcircuits.com/advice/bios2/1.shtml—the LostCircuits BIOS guide; much detail on the meaning of all those BIOS settings.

▶ http://www.rojakpot.com/default.aspx?location=1—The BIOS Optimization Guide; details on tweaking those BIOS settings to your heart's content.

▶ http://www-106.ibm.com/developerworks/linux/library/l-slack.html—A link through IBM's website to an article on booting Slackware Linux, along with a sidebar about the history of System V versus BSD init scripts.

▶ /usr/src/linux/init/main.c—This file in the Linux source code is the best place to learn about how Linux boots. Fascinating reading, really. Get it from the source!

▶ http://sunsite.dk/linux-newbie/—Home page for the Linux Newbie Administrator Guide—a gentle introduction to Linux System Administration.

▶ http://www.gnu.org/software/grub/manual/—The still yet-to-be-completed GRUB Manual. On your Fedora system, info grub provides a plethora of information, and a sample grub.conf file (/boot/grub/menu.1st is a symbolic link to /boot/grub/grub.conf; use either name) can be found in /usr/doc/grub.

▶ *LILO User's Guide*—Werner Almesberger's definitive technical tome on the LInux LOader, or LILO, and how it works on Intel-based PCs. Look under the /usr/share/doc/lilo*/doc directory for the file User_Guide.ps, which can be viewed with the gv client. LILO has been dropped from Fedora; GRUB is now the default boot loader supported in the distribution.

▶ **"Managing Initscripts with Red Hat's chkconfig"**—by Jimmy Ball, *Linux Journal*, April 2001; pp. 128–132.

▶ **"Grub, Glorious Grub"**—Hoyt Duff, *Linux Format*, August 2001; pp. 58–61. A tutorial on the GRUB boot loader.

▶ http://www.redhat.com/docs/manuals/linux/RHL-9-Manual/custom-guide/s1-services-serviceconf.html—Red Hat's guide to use the system-config-service client (then called redhat-config-service).

▶ http://www.linuxbase.org/spec/refspecs/LSB_1.0.0/gLSB/sysinit.html—The Linux Standard Base description of system initialization; this is the standard.

System-Monitoring Tools

To keep your system in optimum shape, you need to keep a close eye on it. Such monitoring is imperative in a corporate environment where uptime is vital and any system failures can cost real money. Whether it is checking processes for any errant daemons or keeping a close eye on CPU and memory use, Fedora provides a wealth of utilities designed to give you as little or as much feedback as you want. This chapter looks at some of the basic monitoring tools, along with some tactics designed to keep your system up longer. Some of the monitoring tools cover network connectivity, memory, and hard drive use, but all should find a place in your sysadmin toolkit. Finally, you will learn how to manipulate active system processes, using a mixture of graphical and command-line tools.

Console-Based Monitoring

Those familiar with UNIX system administration already know about the ps or process display command commonly found on most flavors of UNIX. Because Linux is closely related to UNIX, it also benefits from this command and allows you to quickly see the current running processes on the system, as well as who owns them and how resource hungry they are.

Although the Linux kernel has its own distinct architecture and memory management, it also benefits from enhanced use of the /proc file system, the virtual file system found on many UNIX flavors. Through the /proc file system, you can communicate directly with the kernel to get a deep view of what is currently happening. Developers tend to use the /proc file system as a way of getting information out from the kernel and for their programs to manipulate it into more human-readable formats. The /proc file system is beyond the scope of this book, but if you want to get a better idea of what it contains you should head on over to http://en.tldp.org/LDP/ Linux-Filesystem-Hierarchy/html/proc.html for an excellent and in-depth guide.

Processes can also be controlled at the command line, which is important because you might sometimes have only a command-line interface. Whenever an application or command is launched, either from the command line or a clicked icon, the process that comes from the kernel is assigned an identification number called a *process ID* or *PID* for short. This number is shown in the shell if the program is launched via the command line:

```
# system-config-display &
```

```
[1] 4286
```

In this example, the system-config-display client has been launched in the background, and the (bash) shell reported a shell job number ([1] in this case). A job number or job control is a shell-specific feature that allows a different form of process control, such as sending or suspending programs to the background and retrieving background jobs to the foreground (see your shell's man pages for more information if you are not using bash).

The second number displayed (4286 in this example) represents the process ID. You can get a quick list of your processes by using the ps command like this:

```
# ps
  PID TTY          TIME CMD
 4242 pts/0    00:00:00 su
 4245 pts/0    00:00:00 bash
 4286 pts/0    00:00:00 consolehelper-g
 4287 pts/0    00:00:00 userhelper
 4290 pts/0    00:00:00 system-config-d
 4291 pts/0    00:00:00 python2
 4293 pts/0    00:00:00 ps
```

Note that not all output from the display is shown here. But as you can see, the output includes the process ID, abbreviated as PID, along with other information, such as the name of the running program. As with any UNIX command, many options are available; the proc man page has a full list. A most useful option is aux, which provides a much more detailed and helpful list of all the processes. You should also know that ps works not by polling memory, but through the interrogation of the Linux /proc or process file system. (ps is one of the interfaces mentioned at the beginning of this section.)

The /proc directory contains quite a few files—some of which include constantly updated hardware information (such as battery power levels and so on). Linux administrators often pipe the output of ps through a member of the grep family of commands to display information about a specific program, perhaps like this:

```
$ ps aux | grep system-config-display
root      4286  0.0  0.3  13056  3172 pts/0    S    11:57   0:00 system-config-
➥display
```

This example returns the owner (the user who launched the program) and the PID, along with other information, such as the percentage of CPU and memory use, size of the command (code, data, and stack), time (or date) the command was launched, and name of the command. Processes can also be queried by PID, as follows:

```
$ ps 4286
4286 pts/0    S      0:00 system-config-display
```

You can use the PID to stop a running process by using the shell's built-in `kill` command. This command asks the kernel to stop a running process and reclaim system memory. For example, to stop the `system-config-display` client in the example, use the kill command like this:

```
$ kill 4286
```

After you press Enter (or perhaps press Enter again), the shell might report the following:

```
[1]+  Terminated              system-config-display
```

Note that users can `kill` only their own processes, but `root` can kill them all. Controlling any other running process requires root permission, which should be used judiciously (especially when forcing a `kill` by using the -9 option); by inadvertently killing the wrong process through a typo in the command, you could bring down an active system.

Using the `kill` Command to Control Processes

The `kill` command is a basic UNIX system command. You can communicate with a running process by entering a command into its interface, such as when you type into a text editor. But some processes (usually system processes rather than application processes) run without such an interface, and you need a way to communicate with them, too, so we use a system of signals. The `kill` system accomplishes that by sending a signal to a process, and you can use it to communicate with any process. The general format of the `kill` command is as follows:

```
# kill option PID
```

A number of signal options can be sent as words or numbers, but most are of interest only to programmers. One of the most common is this:

```
# kill PID
```

This tells the process with PID to stop; you supply the actual PID.

```
# kill -9 PID
```

is the signal for `kill` (9 is the number of the SIGKILL signal); use this combination when the plain `kill` shown previously does not work.

```
# kill -SIGHUP PID
```

is the signal to "hang up"—stop—and then clean up all associated processes as well. (Its number is `-1`.)

As you become proficient at process control and job control, you will learn the utility of a number of `kill` options. You can find a full list of signal options in the `signal` man page.

Using Priority Scheduling and Control

No process can make use of the system's resources (CPU, memory, disk access, and so on) as it pleases. After all, the kernel's primary function is to manage the system resources equitably. It does this by assigning a priority to each process so that some processes get better access to system resources and some processes might have to wait longer until their turn arrives. Priority scheduling can be an important tool in managing a system supporting critical applications or in a situation in which CPU and RAM use must be reserved or allocated for a specific task. Two legacy applications included with Fedora include the nice and `renice` commands. (`nice` is part of the GNU `sh-utils` package, whereas `renice` is inherited from BSD UNIX.)

The `nice` command is used with its `-n` option, along with an argument in the range of `-20` to 19, in order from highest to lowest priority (the lower the number, the higher the priority). For example, to run the `gkrellm` client with a low priority, use the `nice` command like this:

```
$ nice -n 12 gkrellm &
```

The `nice` command is typically used for disk- or CPU-intensive tasks that might be obtrusive or cause system slowdown. The `renice` command can be used to reset the priority of running processes or control the priority and scheduling of all processes owned by a user. Regular users can only numerically increase process priorities (that is, make tasks less important) with this command, but the root operator can use the full `nice` range of scheduling (`-20` to 19).

System administrators can also use the `time` command to get an idea of how much time and what proportion of a system's resources are required for a task, such as a shell script. (Here, `time` is used to measure the duration of elapsed time; the command that deals with civil and sidereal time is the `date` command.) This command is used with the name of another command (or script) as an argument like this:

```
# time -p find / -name core -print
/dev/core
```

```
/proc/sys/net/core
```

```
real 1.20
user 0.14
sys 0.71
```

Output of the command displays the time from start to finish, along with the user and system time required. Other factors you can query include memory, CPU use, and file system *input/output (I/O)* statistics. See the time command's man page for more details.

Nearly all graphical process-monitoring tools include some form of process control or management. Many of the early tools ported to Linux were clones of legacy UNIX utilities. One familiar monitoring (and control) program is top. Based on the ps command, the top command provides a text-based display of constantly updated console-based output showing the most CPU-intensive processes currently running. It can be started like this:

```
# top
```

After you press Enter, you see a display as shown in Figure 12.1. The top command has a few interactive commands: Pressing **h** displays the help screen; pressing **k** prompts you to enter the PID of a process to kill; pressing **n** prompts you to enter the PID of a process to change its nice value. The top man page describes other commands and includes a detailed description of what all the columns of information top can display actually represent; have a look at top's well-written man page.

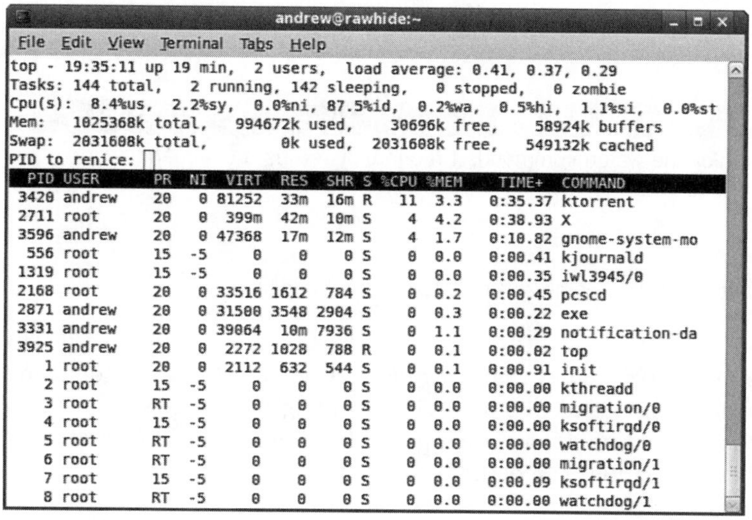

FIGURE 12.1   The *top* command can be used to monitor and control processes. Here, we are prompted to *renice* a process.

The top command displays quite a bit of information about your system. Processes can be sorted by PID, age, CPU or memory use, time, or user. This command also provides process management, and system administrators can use its k and r keypress commands to kill and reschedule running tasks, respectively.

The top command uses a fair amount of memory, so you might want to be judicious in its use and not leave it running all the time. When you've finished with it, simply press **q** to quit top.

Displaying Free and Used Memory with free

Although top includes some memory information, the free utility displays the amount of free and used memory in the system in kilobytes (the -m switch displays in megabytes). On one system, the output looks like this:

```
# free
                total      used       free     shared    buffers     cached
Mem:          1025368    995860      29508          0      56472     551464
-/+ buffers/cache:       387924     637444
Swap:         2031608         0    2031608


Swap:                    433712         0     433712
```

This output describes a machine with 1GB of RAM memory and a swap partition of 2GB. Note that no swap is being used, although the machine is heavily loaded. Linux is very good at memory management and "grabs" all the memory it can in anticipation of future work.

TIP

A useful trick is to employ the watch command; it repeatedly reruns a command every 2 seconds by default. If you use

```
#  watch free
```

you can see the output of the free command updated every 2 seconds.

Another useful system-monitoring tool is vmstat (*virtual memory statistics*). This command reports on processes, memory, I/O, and CPU, typically providing an average since the last reboot; or you can make it report use for a current period by telling it the time interval in seconds and the number of iterations you desire, as follows:

```
# vmstat 5 10
```

The preceding command runs vmstat every 5 seconds for 10 iterations.

Use the `uptime` command to see how long it has been since the last reboot and to get an idea of what the load average has been; higher numbers mean higher loads.

Disk Quotas

Disk quotas are a way to restrict the use of disk space either by user or by groups. Although rarely—if ever—used on a local or standalone workstation, quotas are definitely a way of life at the enterprise level of computing. Use limits on disk space not only conserve resources, but also provide a measure of operational safety by limiting the amount of disk space any user can consume.

Disk quotas are more fully covered in Chapter 10, "Managing Users."

Graphical Process and System Management Tools

The GNOME and KDE desktop environments offer a rich set of network and system-monitoring tools. Graphical interface elements, such as menus and buttons, and graphical output, including metering and real-time load charts, make these tools easy to use. These clients, which require an active X session and (in some cases) root permission, are included with Fedora.

If you view the graphical tools locally while they are being run on a server, you must have X properly installed and configured on your local machine. Although some tools can be used to remotely monitor systems or locally mounted remote file systems, you have to properly configure pertinent X11 environment variables, such as $DISPLAY, to use the software or use the `ssh` client's `-X` option when connecting to the remote host.

Fedora no longer includes the `xosview` client, which provided load, CPU, memory and swap use, disk I/O use and activity, page-swapping information, network activity, I/O activity, I/O rates, serial port status, and if APM is enabled, the battery level (such as for a laptop). However, a great replacement is GKrellM, which provides a much neater interface and a host of additional plug-ins. You have to use this command to retrieve GKrellM:

```
# yum install gkrellm
```

After you have installed GKrellM, you can find it under Applications, System Tools. Figure 12.2 shows GKrellM.

Graphical system- and process-monitoring tools that come with Fedora include the following:

- ▶ **vncviewer**—AT&T's open source remote session manager (part of the Xvnc package), which can be used to view and run a remote desktop session locally. This software (discussed in more detail in Chapter 15, "Remote Access with SSH") requires an active, background, X session on the remote computer.

- ▶ **gnome-nettool**—A GNOME-developed tool that enables system administrators to carry out a wide range of diagnostics on network interfaces, including port scanning and route tracing.

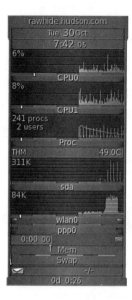

FIGURE 12.2   GKrellM allows you to monitor most system processes on Fedora.

- ► **ethereal**—This graphical network protocol analyzer can be used to save or display packet data in real time and has intelligent filtering to recognize data signatures or patterns from a variety of hardware and data captures from third-party data capture programs, including compressed files. Some protocols include AppleTalk, *Andrew File System (AFS)*, AOL's Instant Messenger, various Cisco protocols, and many more.

- ► **gnome-system-monitor**—This tool is a simple process monitor offering three views: a list view, a moving graph, and a storage status overview. To access it, choose Applications, System Tools, and select the System Monitor entry (see Figure 12.3).

From the Process Listing view (chosen via the Processes tab in the upper-left portion of the window), select a process and click More Info at the bottom left of the screen to display details on that process at the bottom of the display. You can select from three views to filter the display, available in the drop-down View list: All Processes, My Processes (those you alone own), or Active Processes (all processes that are active).

Choose Hidden Processes under the Edit command accessible from the top of the display to show any hidden processes (those that the kernel does not enable the normal monitoring tools to see). Select any process and kill it with End Process.

You can change the nice value of the processes by selecting Edit, Change Priority. The View selection from the menu bar also provides a memory map. In the Resources tab, you can view a moving graph representing CPU and memory use (see Figure 12.4).

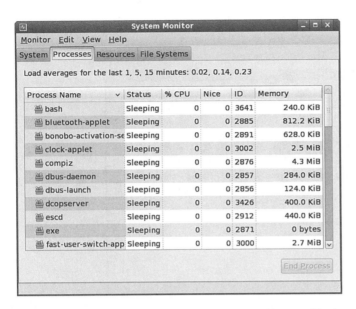

FIGURE 12.3   The Process Listing view of the System Monitor.

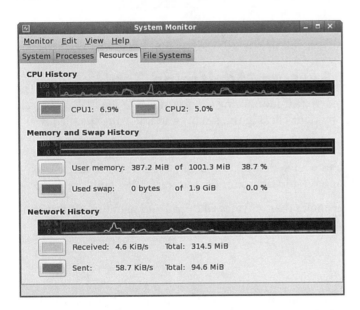

FIGURE 12.4   The Graph view of the System Monitor. It shows CPU use, memory/swap use, and disk use. To get this view, select the Resources tab.

Finally, you can see the status of your file system and storage devices by clicking the File Systems tab shown in Figure 12.5.

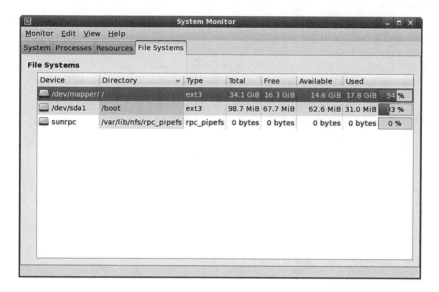

FIGURE 12.5   Keep a close eye on your free disk space.

KDE Process- and System-Monitoring Tools

KDE provides several process- and system-monitoring clients. Integrate the KDE graphical clients into the desktop taskbar by right-clicking the taskbar and following the menus.

These KDE monitoring clients include the following:

▶ **kdf**—A graphical interface to your system's file system table that displays free disk space and enables you to mount and unmount file systems with a pointing device

▶ **ksysguard**—Another panel applet that provides CPU load and memory use information in animated graphs

Reference

▶ **http://and.sourceforge.net/**—Home page of the AND auto-nice daemon, which can be used to prioritize and reschedule processes automatically.

▶ **http://sourceforge.net/projects/schedutils/**—Home page for various projects offering scheduling utilities for real-time scheduling.

▶ **http://freetype.sourceforge.net/patents.html**—A discussion of the FreeType byte-code interpreter patents.

▶ **http://www.ethereal.com/**—Home page for the Ethereal client.

▶ **http://www.realvnc.com/**—The home page for the Virtual Network Computing remote desktop software, available for a variety of platforms, including Fedora Core Linux. This software has become so popular that it is now included with nearly every Linux distribution.

12

CHAPTER 13

Backing Up

This chapter examines the practice of safeguarding data through backups, restoring that same data if necessary, and recovering data in case of a catastrophic hardware or software failure. After reading this chapter, you will have a full understanding of the reasons for sound backup practices. You can use the information in this chapter to make intelligent choices about which strategies are best for you. The chapter also shows you how to perform some types of data recovery and system restoration on your own and when to seek professional assistance.

Choosing a Backup Strategy

Backups are always trade-offs. Any backup consumes time, money, and effort on an ongoing basis; backups must be monitored, validated, indexed, stored, and new media continuously purchased. Sound expensive? The cost of not having backups is the loss of your critical data. Re-creating the data from scratch costs time and money, and if the cost of doing it all again is greater than the cost associated with backing up, you should be performing backups. At the where-the-rubber-meets-the-road level, backups are nothing more than insurance against financial loss for you or your business.

Your first step in formulating and learning to use an effective backup strategy is to choose the strategy that is right for you. First, you must understand some of the most common (and not so common) causes of data loss so that you are better able to understand the threats your system faces. Then you need to assess your own system, how it is used and by whom, your available hardware and software resources, and your budget constraints. The following sections describe each of these issues in detail, and also offer some sample backup systems and discuss their use.

Why Data Loss Occurs

Files disappear for any number of reasons: They can be lost because the hardware fails and causes data loss; your attention might wander and you accidentally delete or overwrite a file. Some data loss occurs as a result of natural disasters and other circumstances beyond your control. A tornado, flood, or earthquake could strike, the water pipes could burst, or the building could catch on fire. Your data, as well as the hardware, would likely be destroyed in such a disaster. A disgruntled employee might destroy files or hardware in an attempt at retribution. And any equipment might fail, and it all *will* fail at some time—most likely when it is extremely important for it not to fail.

A Case in Point

A recent Harris poll of Fortune 500 executives found that roughly two-thirds of them had problems with their backups and disaster-recovery plans. How about you?

Data can also be lost because of malfunctions that corrupt the data as it attempts to write to the disk. Other applications, utilities, and drivers might be poorly written, buggy (the phrase most often heard is "still beta quality"), or might suffer some corruption and fail to correctly write that all-important data you just created. If that happens, the contents of your data file would be indecipherable garbage, of no use to anyone.

All these accidents and disasters offer important reasons for having a good backup strategy; however, the most frequent cause of data loss is human error. Who among us has not overwritten a new file with an older version or unintentionally deleted a needed file? This applies not only to data files, but also to configuration files and binaries. Among users perusing the mail lists or the Usenet newsgroup postings, stories about deleting entire directories such as /home, /usr, or /lib seem all too common. Incorrectly changing a configuration file and not saving the original in case it has to be restored (which it does more often than not because the person reconfigured it incorrectly) is another common error.

TIP

To make a backup of a configuration file you are about to edit, use the `cp` command:

```
$ cp filename filename.original
```

And to restore it:

```
$ cp filename.original filename
```

Never edit or move the `*.original` file, or the original copy will be lost.

Proper backups can help you recover from these problems with a minimum of hassle, but you have to put in the effort to keep backups current, verify their intactness, and practice restoring the data in different disaster scenarios.

Assessing Your Backup Needs and Resources

By now you realize that some kind of plan is needed to safeguard your data, and, like most people, you are overwhelmed by the prospect. Entire books, as well as countless articles and whitepapers, have been written on the subject of backing up and restoring data. What makes the topic so complex is that each solution is truly individual.

Yet the proper approach to making the decision is very straightforward. You start the process by asking

- ▶ What data must be safeguarded?

- ▶ How often does the data change?

The answers to these two questions determine how important the data is, determine the volume of the data, and determine the frequency of the backups. This in turn determines the backup medium. Only then can the software that accommodates all these considerations be selected. (You learn about choosing backup software, hardware, and media later in this chapter.)

Available resources are another important consideration when selecting a backup strategy. Backups require time, money, and personnel. Begin your planning activities by determining what limitations you face for all these resources. Then construct your plan to fit those limitations, or be prepared to justify the need for more resources with a careful assessment of both backup needs and costs.

> **TIP**
>
> If you are not willing or capable of assessing your backup needs and choosing a backup solution, a legion of consultants, hardware vendors, and software vendors would love to assist you. The best way to choose one in your area is to query other Unix and Linux system administrators (located through user groups, discussion groups, or mail lists) that are willing to share their experiences and make recommendations. If you cannot get a referral, ask the consultant for references and check them out.

Many people also fail to consider the element of time when formulating their plan. Some backup devices are faster than others, and some recovery methods are faster than others. You need to consider that when making choices.

To formulate your backup plan, you need to determine the frequency of backups. The necessary frequency of backups should be determined by how quickly the important data on your system changes. On a home system, most files never change, a few change daily, and some change weekly. No elaborate strategy needs to be created to deal with that. A good strategy for home use is to back up (to any kind of removable media) critical data frequently and back up configuration and other files weekly.

At the enterprise level on a larger system with multiple users, a different approach is called for. Some critical data is changing constantly, and it could be expensive to re-create; this typically involves elaborate and expensive solutions. Most of us exist somewhere in between these extremes. Assess your system and its use to determine where you fall in this spectrum.

Backup schemes and hardware can be elaborate or simple, but they all require a workable plan and faithful follow-through. Even the best backup plan is useless if the process is not carried out, data is not verified, and data restoration is not practiced on a regular basis. Whatever backup scheme you choose, be sure to incorporate in it these three principles:

▶ **Have a plan**—Design a plan that is right for your needs and have equipment appropriate to the task. This involves assessing all the factors that affect the data you are backing up. We will get into more detail later in the chapter.

▶ **Follow the plan**—Faithfully complete each part of your backup strategy, and then verify the data stored in the backups. Backups with corrupt data are of no use to anyone. Even backup operations can go wrong.

▶ **Practice your skills**—Practice restoring data from your backup systems from time to time, so when disaster strikes, you are ready (and able) to benefit from the strength of your backup plan. (For more about restoring data, see the "Using Backup Software" section later in this chapter.) Keep in mind that it is entirely possible that the flaws in your backup plan will become apparent only when you try restoring!

Sound Practices

You have to create your own best-backup plan, but here are some building blocks that should be incorporated into the foundation of any sound backup program:

▶ Maintain more than one copy of critical data.

▶ Label the backups.

▶ Store the backups in a climate-controlled and secure area.

▶ Use secure, offsite storage of critical data. Many companies choose bank vaults for their offsite storage, and this is highly recommended.

▶ Establish a backup policy that makes sense and can be followed religiously. Try to back up your data when the system is consistent (that is, no data is being written), which is usually overnight.

▶ Keep track of who has access to your backup media, and keep the total number of people as low as possible. If you can, allow only trusted personnel near your backups.

▶ Routinely verify backups and practice restoring data from them.

▶ Routinely inspect backup media for defects and regularly replace them (after destroying the data on them, if it is sensitive).

Evaluating Backup Strategies

Now that you are convinced you need backups, you need a strategy. It is difficult to be specific about an ideal strategy because each user or administrator's strategy will be highly individualized, but here are a few general examples:

▶ **Home user**—At home, the user has the Fedora installation DVD that takes an hour or so to reinstall, so the time issue is not a major concern. The home user should back up any configuration files that have been altered, keep an archive of any files that have been downloaded, and keep an archive of any data files created while using any applications. Unless the home user has a special project in which constant backups are useful, a weekly backup is adequate. The home user is likely to use a DVD-RW drive or other removable media for backups.

▶ **Small office**—Many small offices tend to use the same strategy as home users, but are more likely to back up critical data daily and use manually changed tape drives. If they have a tape drive with adequate storage, they will likely have a full system backup as well because restoring from the tape is quicker than reinstalling from the CDs. They also might be using CD-RW or DVD writers for backups. Although they will use scripts to automate backups, most of it is probably done by hand.

▶ **Small enterprise**—Here is where backups begin to require higher-end equipment such as autoloading tape drives with fully automated backups. Commercial backup software usually makes an introduction at this level, but a skillful system adminis-trator on a budget can use one of the basic applications discussed in this chapter. Backups are highly structured and supervised by a dedicated system administrator.

▶ **Large enterprise**—These are the most likely settings for the use of expensive, pro-prietary, highly automated backup solutions. At this level, data means money, lost data means lost money, and delays in restoring data means money lost as well. These system administrators know that backups are necessary insurance and plan accordingly.

Does all this mean that enterprise-level backups are better than those done by a home user? Not at all. The "little guy" with Fedora can do just as well as the enterprise opera-tion at the expense of investing more time in the process. By examining the higher-end strategies, you can learn useful concepts that apply across the board.

> **NOTE**
>
> If you are a new sysadmin, you might be inheriting an existing backup strategy. Take some time to examine it and see whether it meets the current needs of the organiza-tion. Think about what backup protection your organization really needs, and determine whether the current strategy meets that need. If it does not, change the strategy. Consider whether users practice the current policy, and, if not, why it is not.

> **Backup Levels**
>
> Unix uses the concept of backup levels as a shorthand way of referring to how much data is backed up in relation to a previous backup. It works this way:
>
> A level 0 backup is a full backup. The next backup level would be 1. Backups at the other numbered levels back up everything that has changed since the last backup at that level or a numerically higher level (the `dump` command, for example, offers

10 different backup levels). For example, a level 3 backup followed by a level 4 generates an incremental backup from the full backup, whereas a level 4 followed by a level 3 generates a differential backup between the two.

The following sections examine a few of the many strategies in use today. Many strategies are based on these sample schemes; one of them can serve as a foundation for the strategy you construct for your own system.

Simple Strategy

If you need to back up just a few configuration files and some small data files, copy them to a USB stick, engage the write-protect tab, and keep it someplace safe. If you need just a bit more backup storage capacity, you can copy the important files to a Zip disk (100,250 and 750MB in size), CD-RW disk (up to 700MB in size), or DVD-RW disk (up to 8GB for data).

In addition to configuration and data files, you should archive each user's home directory, as well as the entire /etc directory. Between the two, that backup would contain most of the important files for a small system. Then you can easily restore this data from the backup media device you have chosen, after a complete reinstall of Fedora, if necessary.

Experts believe that if you have more data than can fit on a floppy disk, you really need a formal backup strategy. Some of those strategies are discussed in the following sections. We use a tape media backup as an example.

Full Backup on a Periodic Basis

This backup strategy involves a backup of the complete file system on a weekly, biweekly, or other periodic basis. The frequency of the backup depends on the amount of data being backed up, the frequency of changes to the data, and the cost of losing those changes.

This backup strategy is not complicated to perform, and it can be accomplished with the swappable disk drives discussed later in the chapter. If you are connected to a network, it is possible to mirror the data on another machine (preferably offsite); the rsync tool is particularly well suited to this task. Recognize that this does not address the need for archives of the recent state of files; it only presents a snapshot of the system at the time the update is done.

Full Backups with Incremental Backups

This scheme involves performing a full backup of the entire system once a week, along with a daily incremental backup of only those files that have changed in the previous day, and it begins to resemble what a sysadmin of a medium to large system would traditionally use.

This backup scheme can be advanced in two ways. In one way, each incremental backup can be made with reference to the original full backup. In other words, a level 0 backup is followed by a series of level 1 backups. The benefit of this backup scheme is that a restoration requires only two tapes (the full backup and the most recent incremental backup).

But because it references the full backup, each incremental backup might be large (and grow ever larger) on a heavily used system.

Alternatively, each incremental backup could reference the previous incremental backup. This would be a level 0 backup followed by a level 1, followed by a level 2, and so on. Incremental backups are quicker (less data each time), but require every tape to restore a full system. Again, it is a classic trade-off decision.

Modern commercial backup applications such as Amanda and BRU assist in organizing the process of managing complex backup schedules and tracking backup media. Doing it yourself using the classic dump or employing shell scripts to run tar requires that the system administrator handle all the organization herself. For this reason, complex backup situations are typically handled with commercial software and specialized hardware products that are packaged, sold, and supported by vendors.

Mirroring Data or RAID Arrays

Given adequate (and often expensive) hardware resources, you can always mirror the data somewhere else, essentially maintaining a real-time copy of your data on hand. This is often a cheap, workable solution if no large amounts of data are involved. The use of RAID arrays (in some of their incarnations—refer to Chapter 35, "Managing the File System," for more information on RAID) provides for a recovery if a disk fails.

Note that RAID arrays and mirroring systems are just as happy to write corrupt data as valid data. Moreover, if a file is deleted, a RAID array does not save it. RAID arrays are best suited for protecting the current state of a running system, not for providing backups.

Making the Choice

Only you can decide what is best for your situation. After reading about the backup options in this book, put together some sample backup plans; run through a few likely scenarios and assess the effectiveness of your choice.

In addition to all the other information you have learned about backup strategies, here are a couple of good rules of thumb to remember when making your choice:

▶ If the backup strategy and policy is too complicated (and this holds true for most security issues), it will eventually be disregarded and fall into disuse.

▶ The best scheme is often a combination of strategies; use what works.

Choosing Backup Hardware and Media

Any device that can store data can be used to back it up, but that is like saying that anything with wheels can take you on a cross-country trip. Trying to fit several gigabytes of data on a big stack of CD-RWs is an exercise in frustration, and using an expensive automated tape device to save a single copy of an email is a waste of resources.

Many people use what hardware they already have for their backup operations. Most consumer-grade workstations have a CD-RW drive, but they typically do not have the abundant free disk space necessary for performing and storing multiple full backups.

In this section, you learn about some of the most common backup hardware available and how to evaluate its appropriateness for your backup needs. With large storage devices becoming increasingly affordable (160GB IDE drives can be had for around $100) and prices falling on DVD recorders, decisions about backup hardware for the small business and home users have become more interesting.

Removable Storage Media

Choosing the right media for you isn't as easy as it used to be back when floppy drives were the only choice. Today, most machines have CD-ROM drives that can read, but not write, CDs, which rules them out for backup purposes. Instead, USB hard drives and solid-state "pen" drives have taken over the niche previously held by floppy drives: you can get a 256MB drive for under $10, and you can even get capacities up to 16GB for good prices if you shop around. If your machine supports them (or if you have purchased a card reader), you can also use Compact Flash devices, which come in sizes up to 8GB in the Flash memory versions and 4GB for Hitachi Microdrives. Both USB hard drives and solid-state drives are highly portable. Support for these drives under Fedora is very good, accommodating these drives by emulating them as SCSI drives—the system usually sees them as /dev/scd1. Watch for improved support and ever-falling prices in the future. A 500GB USB hard drive costs about $150. The biggest benefits of USB drives are data transfer speed and portability.

FireWire Drives

FireWire (IEEE-1394) hard drives are similar to USB drives; they just use a different inter-face to your computer. Many digital cameras and portable MP3 players use FireWire. Kernel support is available if you have this hardware. The cost of FireWire devices is now essentially zero, because many external drives come with both USB and FireWire as standard.

CD-RW and DVD+RW/-RW Drives

Compared to floppy drives and some removable drives, CD-RW drives and their cousins, DVD+RW/-RW drives, can store large amounts of data and are useful for a home or small business. Although very expensive in the past, CD writers and media are at commodity prices today, but automated CD changing machines, necessary for automatically backing up large amounts of data, are still quite costly. A benefit of CD and DVD storage over tape devices is that the archived uncompressed file system can be mounted and its files accessed randomly just like a hard drive (you do this when you create a data CD; refer to Chapter 7, "Multimedia"), making the recovery of individual files easier.

Each CD-RW disk can hold 650MB–700MB of data (the media comes in both capacities at roughly the same cost); larger chunks of data can be split to fit on multiple disks. Some backup programs support this method of storage. After it is burned and verified, the shelf life for the media is at least a decade or longer. Prices increase with writing speed, but a serviceable CD-RW drive can be purchased for less than $20.

DVD+RW/-RW is similar to CD-RW, but it is more expensive and can store up to 8GB of uncompressed data per disk. These drives sell for less than $50.

Network Storage

For network backup storage, remote arrays of hard drives provide one solution to data storage. With the declining cost of mass storage devices and the increasing need for larger storage space, network storage (NAS, or Network Attached Storage) is available and supported in Linux. These are cabinets full of hard drives and their associated controlling circuitry, as well as special software to manage all of it. These NAS systems are connected to the network and act as a huge (and expensive) mass storage device.

More modest and simple network storage can be done on a remote desktop-style machine that has adequate storage space (up to eight 250GB IDE drives is a lot of storage space, easily accomplished with off-the-shelf parts), but then that machine (and the local system administrator) has to deal with all the problems of backing up, preserving, and restoring its own data, doesn't it? Several hardware vendors offer such products in varying sizes.

Tape Drive Backup

Tape drives have been used in the computer industry from the beginning. Tape drive storage has been so prevalent in the industry that the tar command (the most commonly used command for archiving) is derived from the words Tape ARchive. Modern tape drives use tape cartridges that can hold 70GB of data (or more in compressed format). Capacities and durability of tapes vary from type to type and range from a few gigabytes to hundreds of gigabytes with commensurate increases in cost for the equipment and media. Autoloading tape-drive systems can accommodate archives that exceed the capacity of the file systems.

TIP

Older tape equipment is often available in the used equipment market and might be useful for smaller operations that have outgrown more limited backup device options.

Tape equipment is well supported in Linux and, when properly maintained, is extremely reliable. The tapes themselves are inexpensive, given their storage capacity and their opportunity for reuse. Be aware, however, that tapes do deteriorate over time and, being mechanical, tape drives can and will fail.

CAUTION

Neglecting to clean, align, and maintain tape drives puts your data at risk. The tapes themselves are also susceptible to mechanical wear and degradation. Hardware maintenance is part of a good backup policy. Do not ever forget that it is a question of when—not if—hardware will fail.

Using Backup Software

Because there are thousands of unique situations requiring as many unique backup solutions, it comes as no surprise that Linux offers many backup tools. Along with command-line tools such as tar and dd, Fedora also provides a graphical archiving tool, File Roller, that can create and extract files from archives. Finally, Fedora provides support for the Amanda backup application—a sophisticated backup application that works well over network connections and can be configured to automatically back up all the computers on your network. Amanda works with drives as well as tapes. The book *Unix Backup and Recovery* by W. Curtis Preston includes a whole chapter on setting up and using Amanda, and this chapter is available online at http://www.backupcentral.com/amanda.html.

> **NOTE**
>
> The software in a backup system must support the hardware, and this relationship can determine which hardware or software choices you make. Many sysadmins choose a particular backup software not because they prefer it to other options, but because it supports the hardware they own.
>
> The price seems right for free backup tools, but consider the software's ease of use and automation when assessing costs. If you must spend several hours implementing, debugging, documenting, and otherwise dealing with overly elaborate automation scripts, the real costs go up.

tar: The Most Basic Backup Tool

The tar tool, the bewhiskered old man of archiving utilities, is installed by default. It is an excellent tool for saving entire directories full of files. For example, here is the command used to back up the /etc directory:

```
# tar cvf etc.tar /etc
```

Here, the options use tar to create an archive, are verbose in the message output, and use the filename etc.tar as the archive name for the contents of the directory /etc.

Alternatively, if the output of tar is sent to the standard output and redirected to a file, the command appears as follows:

```
# tar cv /etc > etc.tar
```

The result is the same.

All files in the /etc directory will be saved to a file named etc.tar. With an impressive array of options (see the man page), tar is quite flexible and powerful in combination with shell scripts. With the -z option, it can even create and restore gzip compressed archives, whereas the -j option works with bzipped files.

Creating Full and Incremental Backups with tar

If you want to create a full backup,

```
# tar cjvf fullbackup.tar.bz2 /
```

creates a bzip2-compressed tarball (the j option) of the entire system.

To perform an incremental backup, you must locate all the files that have been changed since the last backup. For simplicity, assume that you do incremental backups on a daily basis. To locate the files, use the find command:

```
# find / -newer name_of_last_backup_file ! -a -type f -print
```

When run alone, find generates a list of files systemwide and prints it to the screen. The ! -a -type eliminates everything but regular files from the list; otherwise, the entire directory would be sent to tar even if the contents were not all changed.

Pipe the output of the find command to tar as follows:

```
# find / -newer name_of_last_backup_file ! -type d -print |\
 tar czT - backup_file_name_or_device_name
```

Here, the T - option gets the filenames from a buffer (where the - is the shorthand name for the buffer).

NOTE

The tar command can back up to a raw device (one with no file system) as well as a formatted partition. For example,

```
    # tar cvzf /dev/hdd  /boot  /etc /home
```

backs up those directories to device /dev/hdd (not /dev/hda1, but to the unformatted device itself).

The tar command can also back up over multiple floppy disks:

```
    # tar czvMf /dev/fd0 /home
```

backs up the contents of /home and spreads the file out over multiple floppies, prompting you with this message:

```
    Prepare volume #2 for '/dev/fd0' and hit return:
```

Restoring Files from an Archive with tar

The xp option in tar restores the files from a backup and preserves the file attributes as well, and tar creates any subdirectories it needs. Be careful when using this option because the backups might have been created with either relative or absolute paths. You should use the tvf option with tar to list the files in the archive before extracting them so that you know where they will be placed.

For example, to restore a tar archive compressed with bzip2,

```
# tar xjvf fedoratest.tar.bz2
```

To list the contents of a tar archive compressed with bzip2,

```
# tar tjvf fedoratest.tar.bz2
drwxrwxr-x paul/paul       0 2003-09-04 18:15:05 fedoratest/
-rw-rw-r-- paul/paul     163 2003-09-03 22:30:49
                             fedoratest/fedora_screenshots.txt
-rw-rw-r-- paul/paul     840 2003-09-01 19:27:59
                             fedoratest/fedora_guideline.txt
-rw-rw-r-- paul/paul    1485 2003-09-01 18:14:23 fedoratest/style-sheet.txt
-rw-rw-r-- paul/paul     931 2003-09-01 19:02:00 fedoratest/fedora_TOC.txt
```

Note that because the pathnames do not start with a backslash, they are relative pathnames and install in your current working directory. If they were absolute pathnames,
they would install exactly where the paths state.

The GNOME File Roller

The GNOME desktop file archiving graphical application File Roller (file-roller) views,
extracts, and creates archive files using tar, gzip, bzip, compress, zip, rar, lha, and
several other compression formats. Note that File Roller is only a front end to the
command-line utilities that actually provide these compression formats; if they are not
installed, File Roller cannot use that format.

CAUTION

File Roller does not complain if you select a compression format that is not supported
by installed software until after you attempt to create the archive. Install any needed
compression utilities first.

File Roller is well integrated with the GNOME desktop environment to provide convenient drag-and-drop functionality with the Nautilus file manager. To create a new archive,
select Archive, New to open the New Archive dialog box and navigate to the directory
where you want the archive to be kept. Type your archive's name in the Selection: /root
text box at the bottom of the New Archive dialog box. Use the Archive type drop-down
menu to select a compression method. Now, drag the files that you want to be included
from Nautilus into the empty space of the File Roller window, and the animated icons
will show that files are being included in the new archive. When you are finished, a list of
files will be shown in the previously blank File Roller window (see Figure 13.1). To save
the archive, simply select Archive, Close. Opening an archive is as easy as using the
Archive, Open dialog to select the appropriate archive file.

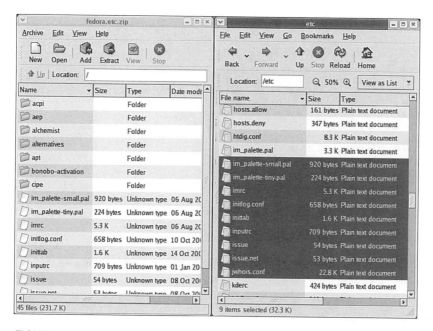

FIGURE 13.1   Drag and drop files to build an archive with the GNOME File Roller.

The KDE Archiving Tools (KDE ark and kdat)

Fedora provides you with the KDE ark and kdat GUI tools for backups; they are installed only if you select the KDE desktop during installation. Archiving has traditionally been a function of the system administrator and has not been seen as a task for the individual user, so no elaborate GUI was believed necessary. Backing up has also been seen as a script-driven, automated task in which a GUI is not as useful.

You launch ark from the command line. It is integrated with the KDE desktop (as File Roller is with GNOME), so it might be a better choice if you use KDE. This application provides a graphical interface to viewing, creating, adding to, and extracting from archived files as shown in Figure 13.2. Several configuration options are available with ark to ensure its compatibility with MS Windows. You can drag and drop from the KDE desktop or Konqueror file browser to add or extract files, or you can use the ark menus.

As long as the associated command-line programs are installed, ark can work with tar, gzip, bzip2, zip, and lha files (the latter four being compression methods used to save space by compaction of the archived files).

Existing archives are opened after the application itself has launched. You can add files and directories to the archive or delete them from the archive, as shown in Figure 13.3. After opening the archive, you can extract all its contents or individual files. You can also perform searches, using patterns (all *.jpg files, for example) to select files.

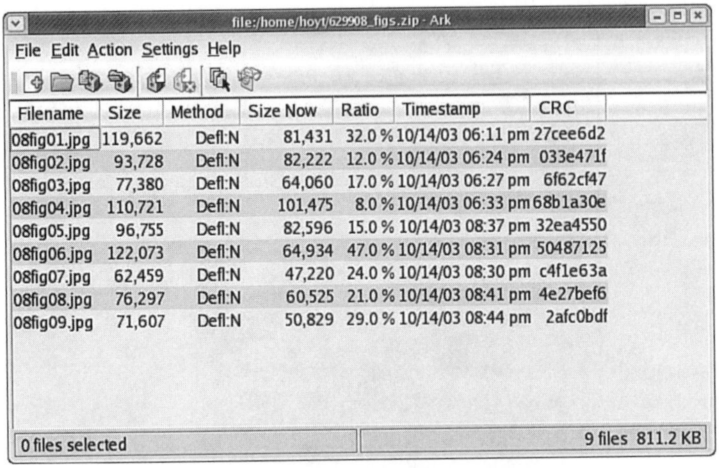

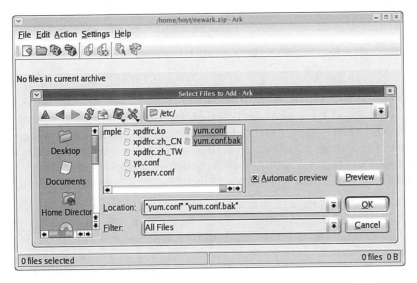

FIGURE 13.2   Here, the contents of a `.zip` file containing some JPEGs are displayed.

FIGURE 13.3   The opening view of `ark` presented as a simple GUI browser. Here, several files are being selected to add to the new archive.

Choosing New from the File menu creates new archives. You then type the name of the archive, providing the appropriate extension (`.tar`, `.gz`, and so on), and then proceed to add files and directories as you desire.

Using the Amanda Backup Application

Provided with Fedora, Amanda is a powerful network backup application created by the University of Maryland at College Park. Amanda is a robust backup and restore application best suited to unattended backups with an autoloading tape drive of adequate capacity. It benefits from good user support and documentation.

Amanda's features include compression and encryption. It is intended for use with high-capacity tape drives, optical, CD-R, and CD-RW devices.

Amanda uses GNU tar and dump; it is intended for unattended, automated tape backups, and is not well suited for interactive or ad hoc backups. The support for tape devices in Amanda is robust, and file restoration is relatively simple. Although Amanda does not support older Macintosh clients, it uses Samba to back up Microsoft Windows clients, as well as any Unix client that can use GNU tools (which includes Mac OS X). Because Amanda runs on top of standard GNU tools, you can restore files using those tools on a recovery disk even if the Amanda server is not available. File compression can be done on either the client or server, thus lightening the computational load on less powerful machines that need backing up.

> **CAUTION**
>
> Amanda does not support dump images larger than a single tape and requires a new tape for each run. If you forget to change a tape, Amanda continues to attempt backups until you insert a new tape, but those backups will not capture the data as you intended them to. Do not use too small a tape or forget to change a tape, or you will not be happy with the results.

There is no GUI interface for Amanda. Configuration is done in the time-honored Unix tradition of editing text configuration files located in /etc/amanda. The default installation in Fedora includes a sample cron file because it is expected that you will be using cron to run Amanda regularly. The client utilities are installed with the package am-utils; the Amanda server must be obtained from the Amanda website. As far as backup schemes are concerned, Amanda calculates an optimal scheme on the fly and schedules it accordingly. It can be forced to adhere to a traditional scheme, but other tools are possibly better suited for that job.

The man page for Amanda (the client is amdump) is well written and useful, explaining the configuration of Amanda as well as detailing the programs that actually make up Amanda. The configuration files found in /etc/amanda are well commented; they provide a number of examples to assist you in configuration.

The program's home page is http://www.amanda.org/. There, you will find information on subscribing to the mail list, as well as links to Amanda-related projects and a FAQ.

Alternative Backup Software

The free download version of Fedora does not provide any other sophisticated backup applications, but Red Enterprise Linux has a variety of third-party software available. Commercial and other freeware backup products do exist; BRU and Veritas are good examples of effective commercial backup products. Here are some useful free software backup tools that are not installed with Fedora:

▶ flexbackup—This backup tool is a large file of Perl scripts that makes dump and restore easier to use. You can access flexbackup's command syntax by using the command with the -help argument. You also can use afio, cpio, and tar to create and restore archives locally, or over a network by using rsh or ssh if security is a concern. Its home page is http://www.flexbackup.org/.

▶ afio—This tool creates cpio-formatted archives, but handles input data corruption better than cpio (which does not handle data input corruption very well at all). It supports multivolume archives during interactive operation and can make compressed archives. If you feel the need to use cpio, you might want to check out afio at http://freshmeat.net/projects/afio/.

▶ cdbackup—Designed for the home or small office user, cdbackup works with any backup and restores software that can read from stdin, write to stdout, and can handle linear devices such as tape drives. It makes it easier to use CD-Rs as the storage medium. Similar applications are available elsewhere as well; the home page for this application is at http://www.muempf.de/index.html.

Many other alternative backup tools exist, but covering all of them is beyond the scope of this book. Two good places to look for free backup software are Freshmeat (http://www.freshmeat.net/) and Google (http://www.google.com/linux).

Copying Files

Often, when you have only a few files that you need to protect from loss or corruption, it might make better sense to simply copy the individual files to another storage medium rather than to create an archive of them. You can use the tar, cp, rsync, or even the cpio commands to do this, as well as a handy file management tool known as mc. Using tar is the traditional choice because older versions of cp did not handle symbolic links and permissions well at times, causing those attributes (characteristics of the file) to be lost; tar handled those file attributes in a better manner. cp has been improved to fix those problems, but tar is still more widely used.

To illustrate how to use file copying as a backup technique, the examples here show how to copy (not archive) a directory tree. This tree includes symbolic links and files that have special file permissions that must be kept intact.

Copying Files Using tar

One choice for copying files into another location is to use the tar command where you would create a tar file that would be piped to tar to be uncompressed in the new location. To accomplish this, first change to the source directory. Then, the entire command resembles

```
# tar cvf - files | (cd target_directory ; tar xpf -)
```

where *files* are the filenames you want to include; use * to include the entire current directory.

Here is how the command shown works: You have already changed to the source directory and executed `tar` with the `cvf` - arguments that tell `tar` to

- ▶ c—Create an archive.

- ▶ v—Be Verbose; lists the files processed so we can see that it is working.

- ▶ f—Use the filename of the archive will be what follows. (In this case, it is -.)

- ▶ -—Use a buffer; a place to hold data temporarily.

The following `tar` commands can be useful for creating file copies for backup purposes:

- ▶ l—Stay in the local file system (so that you do not include remote volumes).

- ▶ atime-preserve—Do not change access times on files, even though you are accessing them now, to preserve the old access information for archival purposes.

The contents of the `tar` file (held temporarily in the buffer, which is named -) are then piped to the second expression, which extracts the files to the target directory. In shell programming (refer to Chapter 10, "Managing Users"), enclosing an expression in parentheses causes it to operate in a subshell and be executed first.

First we change to the target directory, and then

- ▶ x—Extract files from a `tar` archive.

- ▶ p—Preserve permissions.

- ▶ f—Read from -, the temporary buffer that holds the `tar`'ed files.

Compressing, Encrypting, and Sending tar Streams

The file copy techniques using the `tar` command in the previous section can also be used to quickly and securely copy a directory structure across a LAN or the Internet (using the `ssh` command). One way to make use of these techniques is to use the following command line to first compress the contents of a designated directory, and then decompress the compressed and encrypted archive stream into a designated directory on a remote host:

```
$ tar cvzf - data_folder | ssh remote_host `( cd ~/mybackup_dir; tar xvzf - )'
```

The `tar` command is used to create, list, and compress the files in the directory named `data_folder`. The output is piped through the `ssh` (secure shell) command and sent to the remote computer named `remote_host`. On the remote computer, the stream is then extracted and saved in the directory named `/mybackup_dir`. You are prompted for a password to send the stream.

Copying Files Using cp

To copy files, we could use the cp command. The general format of the command when used for simple copying is the following:

```
$ cp -a source_directory target_directory
```

The -a argument is the same as giving -dpR, which would be

▶ -d—Dereferences symbolic links (never follows symbolic links) and copies the files to which they point, instead of copying the links.

▶ -p—Preserves all file attributes if possible. (File ownership might interfere.)

▶ -R—Copies directories recursively.

You can also use the cp command to quickly replicate directories and retain permissions by using the -avR command-line options. Using these options preserves file and directory permissions, gives verbose output, and recursively copies and re-creates subdirectories. You can also create a log of the backup during the backup by redirecting the standard output like this:

```
# cp -avR directory_to_backup destination_vol_or_dir 1>/root/backup_log.txt
```

or

```
# cp -avR fedora /test2 1>/root/backup_log.txt
```

This example makes an exact copy of the directory named /fedora on the volume named /test2, and saves a backup report named backup_log.txt under /root.

Using mc to Copy Files

The Midnight Commander is a command-line file manager that is useful for copying, moving, and archiving files and directories. The Midnight Commander has a look and feel similar to the Norton Commander of DOS fame. When you execute mc at a shell prompt, a dual-pane view of the files is displayed. It contains drop-down menu choices and function keys to manipulate files. It also uses its own virtual file system, enabling it to mount FTP directories and display the contents of tar files, gzipped tar files (.tar.gz or .tgz), bzip files, DEB files, and RPM files, as well as extract individual files from them. As if that were not enough, mc contains a File Undelete virtual file system for ext2/3 partitions. By using cd to "change directories" to an FTP server's URL, you can transfer files with the FTP protocol. The default font chosen for Fedora makes the display of mc ugly when used in a tty console (as opposed to an xterm), but does not affect its performance.

Figure 13.4 shows the default dual-panel display. Pressing the F9 key drops down the menu, and pressing F1 displays the Help file. A "feature" in the default GNOME terminal intercepts the F10 key used to exit mc, so use F9 instead to access the menu item to quit, or simply click on the menu bar at the bottom with your mouse. The configuration files are well documented, and it would appear easy to extend the functionality of mc for your system if you understand shell scripting and regular expressions. It is an excellent choice for file management on servers not running X.

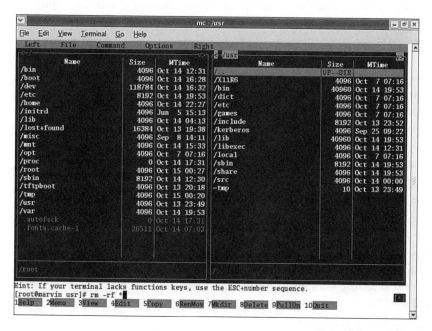

FIGURE 13.4   The Midnight Commander is a highly versatile file tool. If it does not display properly on your screen, launch it with the -a argument to force ASCII mode.

System Rescue

There will come a time when you need to engage in system rescue efforts. This need arises when the system will not even start Linux so that you can recover any files. This problem is most frequently associated with the boot loader program or partition table, but it could be that critical system files have been inadvertently deleted or corrupted. If you have been making backups properly, these kinds of system failures are easily, although not quickly, recoverable through a full restore. Still, valuable current data might not have been backed up since the last scheduled backup, and the backup archives could be found to be corrupt, incomplete, or missing. A full restore also takes time you might not have. If the problem causing the system failure is simply a damaged boot loader, a damaged partition table, a missing library, or misconfiguration, a quick fix can get the system up and running and the data can then be retrieved easily.

This section first examines a way to back up and restore the boot loader itself or, having failed to do that, restore it by hand. It then looks at a few alternatives to booting the damaged system so that you can inspect it, fix it, or retrieve data from it.

The Fedora Rescue Disc

Fedora provides a rescue disc hidden in the installation DVD. To use it, insert the disc and reboot the computer, booting from the DVD just as you did when you installed Fedora originally. At the intro screen, press the F1 key to see all the available choices, but simply enter **linux rescue** at the LILO boot prompt to enter rescue mode, like so:

```
boot: linux rescue
```

You will learn more about the rescue mode later in this section, but feel free to explore it at any time. A graphical interface is not available, so you need to bone up on your command-line skills. If necessary, you can perform all the operations discussed in this section from rescue mode.

Backing Up and Restoring the Master Boot Record

The Master Boot Record (MBR) is the first 512 bytes of a hard disk. It contains the boot loader code in the first 446 bytes and the partition table in the next 64 bytes; the last two bytes identify that sector as the MBR. The MBR can become corrupted, so it makes sense to back it up.

This example uses the dd command as root to back up the entire MBR. If the boot loader code changes from the time you make this image and restore the old code, the system will not boot when you restore it all; it is easy enough to keep a boot floppy disk handy and then rerun LILO if that is what you are using.

To copy the entire MBR to a file, use this:

```
# dd if=/dev/hda of=/tmp/hdambr bs=512 count=1
```

To restore the entire MBR, use this:

```
# dd if=/tmp/hdambr of=/dev/hda bs=512 count=1
```

To restore only the partition table, skipping the boot loader code, use this:

```
# dd if=/tmp/hdambr of=/dev/hda bs=1 skip=446 count=66
```

Of course, it would be prudent to move the copy of the MBR to a floppy disk or other appropriate storage device. (The file is only 512 bytes in size.) You will need to be able to run dd on the system to restore it (which means that you will be using the Fedora rescue disc, as described later, or any equivalent to it).

Manually Restoring the Partition Table

A different way of approaching the problem is to have a printed copy of the partition table that can then be used to restore the partition table by hand with the Fedora rescue disc and the fdisk program.

You can create a listing of the printout of the partition table with fdisk by using the -l option (for list), as follows:

```
# fdisk /dev/hda -l > /tmp/hdaconfig.txt
```

or send the listing of the partition table to the printer:

```
# fdisk /dev/hda -l ¦ kprinter
```

You could also copy the file /tmp/hdaconfig.txt to the same backup floppy disk as the MBR for safekeeping.

Now that you have a hard copy of the partition table (as well as having saved the file itself somewhere), it is possible to restore the MBR by hand at some future date.

Use the Fedora Rescue Disc for this process. After booting into rescue mode, you have the opportunity to use a menu to mount your system read/write, not to mount your system, or to mount any found Linux partitions as read-only. If you plan to make any changes, you need to have any desired partitions mounted with write permission.

After you are logged on (you are root by default), start fdisk on the first drive:

```
# fdisk /dev/had
```

Use the p command to display the partition information and compare it to the hard copy you have. If the entries are identical, you have a problem somewhere else; it is not the partition table. If there is a problem, use the d command to delete all the listed partitions.

Now use the n command to create new partitions that match the partition table from your hard copy. Make certain that the partition types (ext2, FAT, swap, and so on) are the same. If you have a FAT partition at /dev/hda1, make certain that you set the bootable flag for it; otherwise, Windows or DOS will not boot.

If you find that you have made an error somewhere along the way, just use the q command to quit fdisk without saving any changes and start over. If you don't specifically tell fdisk to write to the partition table, no changes are actually made to it.

When the partition table information shown on your screen matches your printed version, write the changes to the disk with the w command; you will be automatically exited from fdisk. Restart fdisk to verify your handiwork, and then remove the rescue disc and reboot.

It helps to practice manually restoring the partition table on an old drive before you have to do it in an emergency situation.

Booting the System from the Rescue Disc

For advanced Linux users, you can use the rescue disc to boot the system if the boot loader code on your computer is damaged or incorrect. To use the Rescue DVD to boot your system from /dev/hda1, for example, first boot the disc and press the F1 key. At the LILO prompt, enter something similar to this example. Note that you are simply telling the boot loader what your root partition is.

```
boot: linux rescue root=/dev/hda1
```

Using the Recovery Facility from the Installation Disc

Rescue mode runs a version of Fedora from the DVD that is independent of your system and permits you to mount your root partition for maintenance. This alternative is useful when your root partition is no longer bootable because something has gone wrong. Fedora is constantly improving the features of the Recovery Facility.

On beginning the rescue mode, you get your choice of language and keyboard layouts. You are given an opportunity to configure networking in rescue mode and are presented with a nice ncurses-based form to fill in the information. The application attempts to find your existing partitions and offers you a choice of mounting them read-write, read-only (always a wise choice the first time), or skip any mounting and drop to a command prompt. With multiple partitions, you must then indicate which is the root partition. That partition is then mounted at /mnt/sysimage. When you are finally presented with a command prompt, it is then possible to make your system the root file system with the following:

```
# chroot /mnt/sysimage
```

To get back to the rescue file system, type **exit** at the prompt. To reboot, type **exit** at the rescue system's prompt.

The rescue function does offer support for software RAID arrays (RAID 0, 1, and 5), as well as IDE or SCSI partitions formatted as ext2/3. After the recovery facility asks for input if it is unsure how to proceed, you eventually arrive at a command shell as root; there is no login or password. Depending on your configuration, you might or might not see prompts for additional information. If you get lost or confused, you can always reboot. (It helps to practice the use of the rescue mode.)

In rescue mode, a number of command-line tools are available for you, but no GUI tools are provided. For networking, you have the ifconfig, route, rcp, rlogin, rsh, and ftp commands. For archiving (and restoring archives), gzip, gunzip, dd, zcat, and md5sum commands are there. As for editors, vi is emulated by BusyBox, and pico, jmacs, and joe are provided by the joe editor. There are other useful system commands. A closer look at these commands reveals that they are all links to a program called BusyBox (home page at http://www.busybox.net/).

BusyBox provides a reasonably complete POSIX environment for any small or embedded system. The utilities in BusyBox generally have fewer options than their full-featured GNU cousins; however, the included options "provide the expected functionality and behave very much like their GNU counterparts." This means that you should test the rescue mode first to see whether it can restore your data and check which options are available to you because the BusyBox version will behave slightly differently than the full GNU version. (Some options are missing; some options do not work quite the same—you need to know whether this will affect you *before* you are in an emergency situation.)

There are a few useful tricks to know when using rescue mode. If your system is functional, you can use the chroot command to change the root file system from the CD to your system in this manner:

```
# chroot /mnt/sysimage
```

You will find yourself at a new command prompt with all your old files in—you hope—the right place. Your familiar tools—if intact—should be available to you. To exit the chrooted environment, use the exit command to return to the rescue system prompt. If you use the exit command again, the system reboots.

The rescue environment provides a nice set of networking commands and network-enabled tools such as scp, sftp, and some of the rtools. It also provides rpm, which can fetch packages over a network connection. Installing them is tricky because you want them installed in the file system mounted at /mnt/sysimage, not at /. To accomplish that, use the --root argument to set an alternative path to root:

```
# rpm -ivh --root /mnt/sysimage ftp://location/package.rpm
```

Alternatives to the Fedora Rescue Disc

The Fedora rescue disc might be inadequate for your system restoration needs; it might lack specific ethernet device support, file system support, or the kind of full utility functionality that you require for a successful recovery operation. An alternative exists in the SuperRescue CD created by H. Peter Anvin.

Essentially, the SuperRescue CD is a reasonably full and robust Red Hat distribution (based on Red Hat 7.2 and the 2.4.20-rc1 kernel) that runs completely from a bootable CD. The best thing about the SuperRescue CD is that it comes with build scripts, so it is incredibly easy to add new software (that special driver or application) and create a new CD. The home page is at http://freshmeat.net/projects/superrescue/, but you can grab a copy directly at http://www.kernel.org/pub/dist/superrescue/v2/.

Relevant Fedora Commands

The following commands are useful in performing backup, recovery, and restore operations in Fedora:

- ▶ **amdump**—Amanda is a network-based backup system, consisting of 18 separate commands, for use with Linux.
- ▶ **ark**—A KDE desktop GUI archiving utility.
- ▶ **cp**—The copy command.
- ▶ **scp**—The secure shell copy command.
- ▶ **cpio**—A data archive utility.
- ▶ **dd**—A data copy and conversion utility.
- ▶ **gzip**—The GNU compression utility.
- ▶ **tar**—The GNU tape archive utility.

Reference

- ▶ **http://www.tldp.org/LDP/solrhe/Securing-Optimizing-Linux-RH-Edition-v1.3/ whywhen.html**—A thorough discussion with examples of using dump and restore for backups.

- ▶ **http://en.tldp.org/LDP/solrhe/Securing-Optimizing-Linux-RH-Edition-v1.3/ chap29sec306.html**—Making automatic backups with tar using cron.

- ▶ **http://kmself.home.netcom.com/Linux/FAQs/backups.html**—The Linux Backups mini FAQ contains some useful, although brief, comments on backup media, compression, encryption, and security.

- ▶ **http://www.tldp.org/**—The Linux Documentation Project offers several useful HOWTO documents that discuss backups and disk recovery.

- ▶ **http://www.ibiblio.org/pub/Linux/docs/HOWTO/other-formats/html_single/ Ext2fs-Undeletion.html**—If you need to undelete a file from an ext2/3 file system, the Linux Ext2fs Undeletion mini HOWTO is the document for you. You will be more successful if you practice.

- ▶ **http://www.ibiblio.org/pub/Linux/docs/HOWTO/other-formats/html_single/ Ext2fs-Undeletion-Dir-Struct.html**—The Ext2fs Undeletion of Directory Structures is a companion HOWTO to the Linux Ext2fs Undeletion mini HOWTO, helping you cope with an errant rm -rf *.

- ▶ **http://www.ibiblio.org/pub/Linux/docs/HOWTO/other-formats/html_single/ Bootdisk-HOWTO.html#AEN1483**—Here is a list of LILO boot error codes to help you debug a cranky system that will not boot.

- ▶ **http://www.ibiblio.org/pub/Linux/docs/HOWTO/other-formats/html_single/ Ftape-HOWTO.html**—This is a HOWTO for the floppy tape device driver.

▶ **http://www.linux-usb.org/USB-guide/x498.html**—The USB Guide for mass storage devices. If you have a USB device and need to know whether it is supported, check here.

▶ **http://www.backupcentral.com/amanda.html**—This is the Amanda chapter of *Unix Backup and Recovery* (written by John R. Jackson and published by O'Reilly and Associates). The chapter is available online and covers every aspect of using Amanda. The site features a handy search tool for the chapter.

▶ **http://twiki.org/cgi-bin/view/Wikilearn/RsyncingALargeFileBeginner**—Rsyncing a large file to "repair" a local ISO image that does not pass the md5sum check.

▶ **http://www.lycoris.org/sections.php?op=viewarticle&artid=8**—Lycoris ISO rsync mini HOWTO. A step-by-step tutorial on using rsync to sync files.

▶ **http://www.mikerubel.org/computers/rsync_snapshots/**—Automated snapshot-style backups using rsync.

▶ **http://www.mondorescue.org/**—Mondo Rescue is a bare-metal backup/rescue tool independent of Fedora, using CD, DVD, tape, or NFS; it can produce bootable CDs to restore the system.

▶ **http://www.ccp14.ac.uk/ccp14admin/linux-server/mondorescue/ dvd_mondo.html**—A HOWTO for using MondoRescue to back up on a DVD.

▶ **http://www.linuxorbit.com/modules.php?op=modload&name=Sections&file= index&req=viewarticle&artid=222&page=1**—A HOWTO using split and mkisofs to manually back up large archives to CD.

13

One of the benefits of open source technology in general and Linux in particular is that it is now mature enough to be used effortlessly across several different networking environments as well as the Internet. With strong support for the standard Internet protocol TCP/IP, Linux can also talk to all the UNIX flavors, as well as Mac OS X, Windows (with the help of Samba), NetWare (IPX), and even older protocols such as DECnet and Banyan Vines. Many organizations use Linux as an Internet gateway, allowing many different clients to access the Internet through Linux, as well as communicate via email and instant messaging. This chapter covers network and Internet connectivity because most networks invariably end up connected to the Internet by one means or another. You will learn about how to get the basics right, including configuration and management of *network interface cards (NICs)* and other network services with Fedora. You will also find out how to manage network services from the command line—again an important lesson in case you are ever confined to a command prompt. We also look at connectivity options, both for inbound and outbound network traffic and the importance of *PPP (Point-to-Point Protocol)*. Also included is an overview of graphical management clients for Fedora, which are becoming more and more popular.

Using Network Configuration Tools

If you add or replace networking hardware after your initial installation, you must configure the new hardware. You can use either the command line or the graphical configuration tools to do so. To configure a network client host using the command line, you can use a combination of commands or edit specific files under the /etc/sysconfig directory. To configure the hardware through a graphical interface, you can use Fedora's graphical tool called system-config-network. This section introduces command-line and graphical software tools you can use to configure a network interface and network settings on your Fedora system. You'll see how to control your NIC and manage how your system interacts with your network.

Using the command-line configuration tools can seem difficult if you are new to Linux. For anyone new to networking, the system-config-network graphical tool is the way to go. Both manual and graphical methods require root access to work. If you do not have root access, get it before trying any of these actions. You should not edit any scripts or settings files used by graphical network administration tools on your system. Your changes will be lost the next time the tool, such as system-config-network, is run! Either use a manual approach and write your own network setup script, or stick to using graphical configuration utilities.

> **NOTE**
>
> The network configuration process described in this section is for client hosts. You cannot perform server network configuration, such as *Domain Name System (DNS)* and DHCP during installation. (See Chapter 23, "Managing DNS," for more information on configuring DNS; see the "DHCP" section later in this chapter for more information on that item.)

Using Graphical Configuration Tools

If you are new to networking or still becoming proficient with the command line, the graphical configuration tool is your best method for configuring new hardware in Fedora. Like most graphical tools, system-config-network enables you to fill in the blanks; press the proper buttons, and the tool modifies the required files and issues the proper commands. Remember, you must be root to run system-config-network.

You can access system-config-network by going to the System, Administration menu and selecting Network. You will be asked for the root password because you are able to make systemwide changes using this tool.

After it is started, system-config-network will display the screen shown in Figure 14.1.

Click the DNS tab to configure your system's DNS settings, hostname, or DNS search path. Click the Hosts tab, and then click either the New or Edit button (after selecting a host) to create or edit an entry in your system's /etc/hosts file—for example, to add the IP addresses, hostnames, and aliases of hosts on your network. See Figure 14.2 for an example of editing a host entry.

FIGURE 14.1   Use the initial *system-config-network* networking screen to begin configuring your network client host.

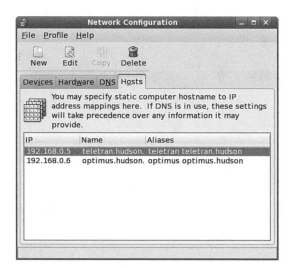

FIGURE 14.2   Highlight an existing entry, and then click the Edit button to change */etc/hosts* entries in the Hosts tab of the Network Configuration screen.

Click the Devices tab, and then either click New or select an existing setting and click Edit to automatically or manually set up an ethernet device. Figure 14.3 shows the Ethernet Device dialog box with all necessary information in place for a *static*, or fixed, IP address assignment. Choose how your card will get its configuration: manually from *Dynamic Host Control Protocol (DHCP)* (see the next section) or from Bootp. Just fill in the blanks as needed.

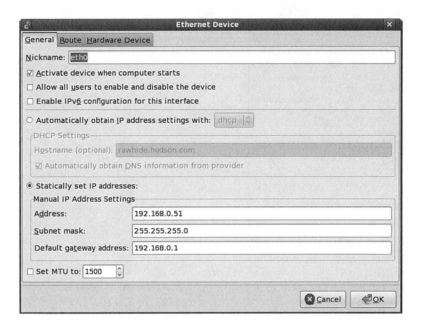

FIGURE 14.3   Configure an ethernet device to use a static IP address by double clicking the device.

When you finish configuring your NIC or editing an IP address or assignment scheme for a NIC, save your changes, using the File menu's Save menu item. Note that you can also use the Profile menu (as shown previously in Figure 14.1) to create different network configurations and IP address assignments for your installed NICs. This is handy if you want to create, for example, a different network setup for home or work on a laptop running Fedora.

Command-Line Network Interface Configuration

You can configure a network interface from the command line, using the basic Linux networking utilities. You configure your network client hosts with the command line by using commands to change your current settings or by editing a number of system files. Two commands, `ifconfig` and `route`, are used for network configuration. The `netstat` command displays information about the network connections.

/sbin/ifconfig

ifconfig is used to configure your network interface. You can use it to

- ► Activate or deactivate your NIC or change your NIC's mode.

- ► Change your machine's IP address, netmask, or broadcast address.

- ► Create an IP alias to allow more than one IP address on your NIC.

- ► Set a destination address for a point-to-point connection.

You can change as many or as few of these options as you'd like with a single command. The basic structure for the command is as follows:

```
# ifconfig [network device] options
```

Table 14.1 shows a subset of ifconfig options and examples of their uses.

TABLE 14.1   **ifconfig** Options

Use	Option	Example
Create alias	[*network device*] 10.10.10.10	ifconfig eth0:0_:[number]
Change IP address		ifconfig eth0 10.10.10.12
Change the netmask	netmask [*netmask*]	fconfig eth0 netmask 255.255.255.0
Change the broadcast	broadcast [*address*]	ifconfig eth0 broadcast 10.10.10.255
Take interface down	down	ifconfig eth0 down
Bring interface up	up (*add IP address*)	ifconfig eth0 up (ifconfig eth0 10.10.10.10)
Set NIC promiscuous	[-]promisc [ifconfig eth0 -promisc]	ifconfig eth0 promisc mode on [off]
Set multicasting mode	[-]allmulti	ifconfig eth0_on [off] allmulti [ifconfig eth0 - allmulti]
Enable [disable] [*address*]	[-]pointopoint eth0_pointopoint	ifconfig_point-to-point address 10.10.10.20 [ifconfig eth0 pointopoint_10.10.10.20]

The ifconfig man page shows other options that enable your machine to interface with a number of network types such as AppleTalk, Novell, IPv6, and others. Again, read the man page for details on these network types.

NOTE

Promiscuous mode causes the NIC to receive all packets on the network. It is often used to sniff a network. Multicasting mode enables the NIC to receive all multicast traffic on the network.

If no argument is given, ifconfig displays the status of active interfaces. For example, the output of ifconfig, without arguments and one active and configured NIC, looks similar to this:

ifconfig

```
eth0    Link encap:Ethernet HWaddr 00:30:1B:0B:07:0D
        inet addr:192.168.0.7 Bcast:192.168.0.255 Mask:255.255.255.0
        UP BROADCAST RUNNING MULTICAST MTU:1500 Metric:1
        RX packets:127948 errors:0 dropped:0 overruns:0 frame:0
        TX packets:172675 errors:0 dropped:0 overruns:0 carrier:0
        collisions:7874 txqueuelen:100
        RX bytes:19098389 (14.2 Mb) TX bytes:73768657 (70.3 Mb)
        Interrupt:11 Base address:0x2000

lo      Link encap:Local Loopback
        inet addr:127.0.0.1 Mask:255.0.0.0
        UP LOOPBACK RUNNING MTU:16436 Metric:1
        RX packets:215214 errors:0 dropped:0 overruns:0 frame:0
        TX packets:215214 errors:0 dropped:0 overruns:0 carrier:0
        collisions:0 txqueuelen:0
        RX bytes:68739080 (65.5 Mb) TX bytes:68739080 (65.5 Mb)
```

The output is easily understood. The inet entry displays the IP address for the interface. UP signifies that the interface is ready for use, BROADCAST denotes that the interface is connected to a network that supports broadcast messaging (ethernet), RUNNING means that the interface is operating, and LOOPBACK shows which device (lo) is the loopback address. The *maximum transmission unit (MTU)* on eth0 is 1500 bytes. This determines the size of the largest packet that can be transmitted over this interface (and is sometimes "tuned" to other values for performance enhancement). Metric is a number from 0 to 3 that describes how much information from the interface is placed in the routing table. The lower the number, the smaller the amount of information.

The ifconfig command can be used to display information about or control a specific interface using commands as listed in Table 14.1. For example, to deactivate the first ethernet device on a host, use the ifconfig command, the interface name, and the command down, as follows:

ifconfig eth0 down

You can also configure and activate the device by specifying a hostname or IP address and network information. For example, to configure and activate ("bring up") the eth0 interface with a specific IP address, use the ifconfig command like this:

ifconfig eth0 192.168.0.9 netmask 255.255.255.0 up

If you have a host defined in your system's /etc/hosts file (see the section "Network Configuration Files" later in this chapter), you can configure and activate the interface according to the defined hostname, like this:

```
# ifconfig eth0 dogdog.hudson.com up
```

Read the next section to see how to configure your system to work with your LAN.

/sbin/route

The second command used to configure your network is the route command. It is used to build the routing tables (in memory) implemented for routing packets as well as displaying the routing information. It is used after ifconfig has initialized the interface. The route command is normally used to set up static routes to other networks via the gateway or to other hosts. The command configuration is like this:

```
# route [options] [commands] [parameters]
```

To display the routing table, use the route command with no options. The display will look similar to this:

```
# route
Kernel IP routing table
Destination     Gateway         Genmask         Flags Metric Ref Use Iface
149.112.50.64   *               255.255.255.192 U     0      0   0   eth0
208.59.243.0    *               255.255.255.0   U     0      0   0   eth0
127.0.0.0       *               255.0.0.0       U     0      0   0   lo
default         149.112.50.65 0.0.0.0           UG    0      0   0   eth0
```

In the first column, Destination is the IP address (or, if the host is in /etc/hosts or /etc/networks, the hostname) of the receiving host. The default entry is the default gateway for this machine. The Gateway column lists the gateway through which the packets must go to reach their destination. An asterisk (*) means that packets go directly to the host. Genmask is the netmask. The Flags column can have several possible entries. In our example, U verifies that the route is enabled and G specifies that Destination requires the use of a gateway. The Metric column displays the distance to the Destination. Some daemons use this to figure the easiest route to the Destination. The Ref column is used by some UNIX flavors to convey the references to the route. It isn't used by Linux. The Use column indicates the number of times this entry has been looked up. Finally, the Iface column is the name of the interface for the corresponding entry.

Using the -n option to the route command gives the same information but substitutes IP addresses for any names and asterisks (*) and looks like this:

```
# route -n
Kernel IP routing table
Destination     Gateway         Genmask         Flags Metric Ref Use Iface
149.112.50.64   0.0.0.0         255.255.255.192 U     0      0   0   eth0
208.59.243.0    0.0.0.0         255.255.255.0   U     0      0   0   eth0
```

14

```
127.0.0.0      0.0.0.0         255.0.0.0     U    0    0  0  lo
0.0.0.0        149.112.50.65   0.0.0.0       UG   0    0  0  eth0
```

The route command can add to the table by using the add option. With the add option, you can specify a host (-host) or a network (-net) as the destination. If no option is used, the route command assumes that you are configuring the host issuing the command. The most common uses for the route command are to add the default gateway for a host, for a host that has lost its routing table, or if the gateway address has changed. For example, to add a gateway with a specific IP address, you could use the following:

 # route add default gw 149.112.50.65

Note that you could use a hostname rather than an IP address if desired. Another common use is to add the network to the routing table right after using the ifconfig command to configure the interface. Assuming that the 208.59.243.0 entry from the previous examples was missing, replace it using the following command:

 # route add -net 208.59.243.0 netmask 255.255.255.0 dev eth0

You also can use /sbin/route to configure a specific host for a direct (point-to-point) connection. For example, suppose that you have a home network of two computers. One of the computers has a modem through which it connects to your business network. You typically work at the other computer. You can use the route command to establish a connection through specific hosts by using the following command:

 # route add -host 198.135.62.25 gw 149.112.50.65

The preceding example makes the computer with the modem the gateway for the computer you are using. This type of command line is useful if you have a gateway or firewall connected to the Internet. There are many additional uses for the route command, such as manipulating the default packet size. See the man page for those uses.

/bin/netstat

The netstat command is used to display the status of your network. It has several parameters that can display as much or as little information as you prefer. The services are listed by *sockets* (application-to-application connections between two computers). You can use netstat to display the information in Table 14.2.

TABLE 14.2   **netstat** Options

Option	Output
-g	Displays the multicast groups configured
-i	Displays the interfaces configured by ifconfig
-s	Lists a summary of activity for each protocol
-v	Gives verbose output, listing both active and inactive sockets
-c	Updates output every second (good for testing and troubleshooting)
-e	Gives verbose output for active connections only
-C	Displays information from the route cache and is good for looking at past connections

Several other options are available for this command, but they are used less often. As with the /sbin/route command, the man page can give you details about all options and parameters.

Network Configuration Files

As previously stated, seven network configuration files can be modified to make changes to basic network interaction of your system. The files are as follows:

- ▶ /etc/hosts—A listing of addresses, hostnames, and aliases

- ▶ /etc/services—Network service and port connections

- ▶ /etc/nsswitch.conf—Linux network information service configuration

- ▶ /etc/resolv.conf—Domain name service domain (search) settings

- ▶ /etc/host.conf—Network information search order (by default, /etc/hosts and then DNS)

- ▶ /etc/sysconfig/network—The hostname, IP address, boot activation control, and gateway settings (along with optional IPv6 settings)

- ▶ /etc/sysconfig/network-scripts/ifcfg-eth0—Network settings for the eth0 network device; see the file sysconfig.txt under the /usr/share/doc/initscripts/ directory for details about optional settings

After the first six of these files have been modified, the changes are active. As with most configuration files, comments can be added with a hash mark (#) preceding the comment. The last file (/etc/sysconfig/network) requires the networking daemons to be restarted before the file is used. All seven of these files have a man page written about them for more information.

Adding Hosts to /etc/hosts

The /etc/hosts file is a map of IP to hostnames. If you are not using DNS or another naming service, and you are connected to a large network, this file can get quite large and can be a real headache to manage. A small /etc/hosts file can look something like this:

```
127.0.0.1       localhost.localdomain  localhost
128.112.50.69   myhost.mydomain.com    myhost
128.112.50.169  yourhost.mydomain.com  yourhost
```

The first entry is for the loopback entry. The second is for the name of the machine. The third is another machine on the network. If no naming service is in use on the network, the only host that myhost recognizes by name is yourhost. (IP addresses on the network can still be used.)

If your network is using a naming service, the last line is not needed and can be deleted. However, if myhost connects to yourhost frequently, it might be good to leave the entry so that myhost does not need to consult the naming service each time. This can save time and reduce the strain on the network or the name service server. Edit this file if you need to change your hostname or IP address or if you aren't using a naming service and a host has been added to your network.

Service Settings in /etc/services

The /etc/services file maps port numbers to services. The first few lines look similar to this (the /etc/services file can be quite long, more than 500 lines):

```
# Each line describes one service, and is of the form:
#
# service-name port/protocol [aliases ...]   [# comment]


tcpmux     1/tcp                # TCP port service multiplexer
tcpmux     1/udp                # TCP port service multiplexer
rje        5/tcp                # Remote Job Entry
rje        5/udp                # Remote Job Entry
echo       7/tcp
echo       7/udp
discard    9/tcp        sink null
discard    9/udp        sink null
systat     11/tcp       users
```

Typically, there are two entries for each service because most services can use either TCP or UDP for their transmissions. Usually after /etc/services is initially configured, you will not need to change it.

Using /etc/nsswitch.conf After Changing Naming Services

This file was initially developed by Sun Microsystems to specify the order in which services are accessed on the system. A number of services are listed in the /etc/nsswitch.conf file, but the most commonly modified entry is the hosts entry. A portion of the file can look like this:

```
passwd:    files
shadow:    files
group:     files

#hosts:    db files nisplus nis dns
hosts:     files dns
```

This tells services that they should consult standard UNIX/Linux files for passwd, shadow, and group (/etc/passwd, /etc/shadow, /etc/group, respectively) lookups. For host lookups, the system checks /etc/hosts and if there is no entry, it checks DNS. The commented hosts entry lists the possible values for hosts. Edit this file only if your naming service has changed.

Setting a Name Server with `/etc/resolv.conf`

`/etc/resolv.conf` is used by DNS, the domain name service. (DNS is covered in detail in Chapter 23.) The following is an example of `resolv.conf`:

```
nameserver 192.172.3.8
nameserver 192.172.3.9
search mydomain.com
```

This sets the nameservers and the order of domains for DNS to use. The contents of this file are set automatically if you use Dynamic Host Configuration Protocol, or DHCP (see the section on "DHCP" later in this chapter).

> **CAUTION**
>
> If you make use of NetworkManager to handle your network connections, don't make any changes to `/etc/resolv.conf`, because it will cause havoc for NetworkManager. Instead, let NetworkManager dynamically work with this file of its own accord.

14

Setting DNS Search Order with `/etc/host.conf`

The `/etc/host.conf` file lists the order in which your machine will search for hostname resolution. The following is the default `/etc/host.conf` file:

```
order hosts, bind
```

In this example, the host checks the `/etc/hosts` file first and then performs a DNS lookup. A couple more options control how the name service is used. The only reason to modify this file is if you use NIS for your name service or you want one of the optional services. The `nospoof` option can be a good option for system security. It compares a standard DNS lookup to a reverse lookup (host-to-IP then IP-to-host) and fails if the two don't match. The drawback is that often when proxy services are used, the lookup fails, so you want to use this with caution.

Examining Host Network Settings in `/etc/sysconfig/network`

Changes to `/etc/sysconfig/network` do take effect until you restart the networking daemons or reboot the system. If you use Fedora's graphical configuration network tools (described in the next section), you should not edit this file. The file might look like this:

```
NETWORKING=yes
HOSTNAME=myhost
GATEWAY=192.112.50.99
```

A `GATEWAYDEV` setting is also available to associate a specific network device (such as `eth0` or `eth1` and so on). An additional optional entry to `/etc/sysconfig/network` is for NIS domain machines and would look like this:

```
NISDOMAIN=rebel
```

The network file previously supported a FORWARD_IPV4 value, which determined whether the host forwarded IP packets (usually "yes" for routers). This setting is now saved in /etc/sysctl.conf as a net.ipv4.ip_forward setting, which can be modified if the forwarding changes are required. See the sysctl.conf man page for more information.

Laying the Foundation: The localhost Interface

The first thing that needs to happen before you can successfully connect to a network or even to the Internet is creating a localhost interface, sometimes also called a *loopback interface*, but more commonly referenced as *lo*. The TCP/IP protocol (see "Networking with TCP/IP" later in this chapter) uses this interface to assign an IP address to your computer and is needed for Fedora to establish a PPP interface.

Checking for the Availability of the Loopback Interface

You should not normally have to manually create a loopback interface because Fedora creates one automatically for you during installation. To check that one is set up, you can use the ifconfig command while working as root to show something similar to this:

```
# ifconfig
lo          Link encap:Local Loopback
            inet addr:127.0.0.1  Mask:255.0.0.0
            UP LOOPBACK RUNNING   MTU:16436  Metric:1
            RX packets:12 errors:0 dropped:0 overruns:0 frame:0
            TX packets:12 errors:0 dropped:0 overruns:0 carrier:0
            collisions:0 txqueuelen:0
            RX bytes:760 (760.0 b)  TX bytes:760 (760.0 b)
```

What you see in this example is evidence that the loopback interface is present and active. It shows that the inet addr is the IP number assigned to the localhost, typically 127.0.0.1 along with the broadcast mask of 255.255.255.0, and that there has been little activity on this interface (RX = receive and TX = transmit). If your output does not look like the preceding one, you must hand-configure the localhost interface after you finish the rest of this section.

Configuring the Loopback Interface Manually

The localhost interface's IP address is specified in a text configuration file that is used by Fedora to keep record of various networkwide IP addresses. The file is called /etc/hosts and usually exists on a system, even if it is empty. The file is used by the Linux kernel and other networking tools to enable them to access local IP addresses and hostnames. If you have not configured any other networking interfaces, you may find that the file only contains one line:

```
127.0.0.1       localhost.localdomain                   localhost
```

This line defines the special `localhost` interface and assigns it an IP address of 127.0.0.1. You might hear or read about terms such as *localhost*, *loopback*, and *dummy interface*; all these terms refer to the use of the IP address 127.0.0.1. The term loopback interface indicates that to Linux networking drivers, it looks as though the machine is talking to a network that consists of only one machine; the kernel sends network traffic to and from itself on the same computer. *Dummy interface* indicates that the interface doesn't really exist as far as the outside world is concerned; it exists only for the local machine.

Each networked Fedora machine on a LAN will use this same IP address for its `localhost`. If for some reason a Fedora computer does not have this interface, edit the `/etc/hosts` file to add the `localhost` entry, and then use the `ifconfig` and `route` commands as root to create the interface like this:

```
# ifconfig lo 127.0.0.1
# route add 127.0.0.1 lo
```

These commands create the `localhost` interface in memory (all interfaces, such as `eth0` or `ppp0`, are created in memory with Linux), and then add the IP address 127.0.0.1 to an internal (in-memory) table so that the Linux kernel's networking code can keep track of routes to different addresses.

Use the `ifconfig` command as shown previously to test the interface.

You should now be able to use `ping` to check that the interface is responding properly like this (using either `localhost` or its IP address):

```
$ ping -c 3 localhost
PING localhost.localdomain (127.0.0.1) from 127.0.0.1 : 56(84) bytes of data.
64 bytes from localhost.localdomain (127.0.0.1): icmp_seq=0 ttl=255 time=212 \
usec
64 bytes from localhost.localdomain (127.0.0.1): icmp_seq=1 ttl=255 time=80 usec
64 bytes from localhost.localdomain (127.0.0.1): icmp_seq=2 ttl=255 time=50 usec

--- localhost.localdomain ping statistics ---
3 packets transmitted, 3 packets received, 0% packet loss
round-trip min/avg/max/mdev = 0.050/0.114/0.212/0.070 ms
```

The `-c` option is used to set the number of pings, and the command, if successful (as it was previously), returns information regarding the round-trip speed of a test packet sent to the specified host.

Networking with TCP/IP

The basic building block for any network based on UNIX hosts is the *Transport Control Protocol/Internet Protocol (TCP/IP)* suite of three protocols. The suite consists of the *Internet Protocol (IP)*, *Transport Control Protocol (TCP)*, and *Universal Datagram Protocol (UDP)*. IP is the base protocol. The TCP/IP suite is *packet*-based, which means that data is broken into little chunks on the transmit end for transmission to the receiving end. Breaking data up into manageable packets allows for faster and more accurate transfers. In TCP/IP, all data travels via IP packets, which is why addresses are referred to as IP addresses. It is the lowest level of the suite.

TCP is a connection-based protocol. Before data is transmitted between two machines, a connection is established between them. When a connection is made, a stream of data is sent to the IP to be broken into the packets that are then transmitted. At the receiving end, the packets are put back in order and sent to the proper application port. TCP/IP forms the basis of the Internet; without it, the Internet would be a very different place indeed, if it even existed!

On the other hand, UDP is a connectionless protocol. Applications using this protocol just choose their destination and start sending. UDP is normally used for small amounts of data or on fast and reliable networks. If you are interested in the internals of TCP/IP, see the "Reference" section at the end of this chapter for places to look for more information.

Fedora and Networking

Chances are that your network card was configured during the installation of Fedora. You can, however, use the `ifconfig` command at the shell prompt or Fedora's graphical network configuration tools, such as `system-config-network`, to edit your system's network device information or to add or remove network devices on your system. Hundreds of networking commands and utilities are included with Fedora—far too many to cover in this chapter and more than enough for coverage in two or three volumes.

Nearly all ethernet cards can be used with Linux, along with many PCMCIA wired and wireless network cards. The great news is that many USB wireless network devices also work just fine with Linux, and more will be supported with upcoming versions of the Linux kernel. Check the Linux USB Project at http://www.linux-usb.org/ for the latest developments or to verify support for your device.

After reading this chapter, you might want to learn more about other graphical network clients for use with Linux. The GNOME `ethereal` client, for example, can be used to monitor all traffic on your LAN or specific types of traffic. Another client, NmapFE, can be used to scan a specific host for open ports and other running services.

Advanced Wireless Networking

As stated earlier, Linux has had support for wireless networking since the first standards were developed in the early 1990s. With computers getting smaller and smaller, the uses for wireless networking have increased; meanwhile, the transmission speeds also are increasing all the time. There are several different ways to create a wireless network. The following sections introduce you to several Linux commands you can use to initialize, configure, and manage wireless networking on your Fedora system.

Support for Wireless Networking in Fedora

The Linux kernel that ships with Fedora provides extensive support for wireless networking. Related wireless tools for configuring, managing, or displaying information about a wireless connection include the following:

- ▶ **iwconfig**—Sets the network name, encryption, transmission rate, and other features of a wireless network interface

- ▶ **iwlist**—Displays information about a wireless interface, such as rate, power level, or frequency used

- ▶ **iwpriv**—Uses i to set optional features, such as roaming, of a wireless network interface

- ▶ **iwspy**—Shows wireless statistics of a number of nodes

Support varies for wireless devices—most likely in the form of a PCMCIA adapter—although some USB wireless devices now work with Linux. In general, Linux wireless device software (usually in the form of a kernel module) supports the creation of an ethernet device that can be managed by traditional interface tools such as ifconfig—with wireless features of the device managed by the various wireless software tools.

For example, when a wireless networking device is first recognized and initialized for use, the driver will most likely report a new device:

```
wvlan_cs: WaveLAN/IEEE PCMCIA driver v1.0.6
wvlan_cs: (c) Andreas Neuhaus <andy@fasta.fh-dortmund.de>
wvlan_cs: index 0x01: Vcc 3.3, irq 3, io 0x0100-0x013f
wvlan_cs: Registered netdevice eth0
wvlan_cs: MAC address on eth0 is 00 05 5d f3 1d da
```

This output (from the dmesg command) shows that the eth0 device has been reported. If DHCP is in use, the device should automatically join the nearest wireless subnet and be automatically assigned an IP address. If not, the next step is to use a wireless tool such as iwconfig to set various parameters of the wireless device. The iwconfig command, along with the device name (eth0 in this example), shows the status:

```
# iwconfig eth0
eth0    IEEE 802.11-DS ESSID:"GreyUFO" Nickname:"Prism I"
        Mode:Managed Frequency:2.412GHz Access Point: 00:02:2D:2E:FA:3C
        Bit Rate:2Mb/s  Tx-Power=15 dBm  Sensitivity:1/3
        RTS thr:off  Fragment thr:off
        Encryption key:off
        Power Management:off
        Link Quality:92/92 Signal level:-11 dBm Noise level:-102 dBm
        Rx invalid nwid:0 Rx invalid crypt:0 Rx invalid frag:0
        Tx excessive retries:0 Invalid misc:4  Missed beacon:0
```

This example shows a 2Mbps connection to a network named GreyUFO. To change a parameter, such as the transmission rate, use a command-line option with the iwconfig command, like so:

```
# iwconfig eth0 rate 11M
```

Other options supported by the iwconfig command include essid, used to set the NIC to connect to a specific network by named; mode, used to enable the NIC to automatically retrieve settings from an access point or connect to another wireless host; or freq, to set a frequency to use for communication. Additional options include channel, frag, enc (for encryption), power, and txpower. Details and examples of these options are in the iwconfig manual page.

You can then use the ifconfig command or perhaps a graphical Fedora tool to set the device networking parameters, and the interface will work as on a hardwired LAN. One handy output of the iwconfig command is the link quality output, which can be used in shell scripts or other graphical utilities for signal monitoring purposes (refer to Chapter 15, "Remote Access with SSH," for an example).

TCP/IP Addressing

To understand networking with Linux, you need to know the basics of TCP/IP addressing. Internet IP addresses are assigned (for the United States and some other hosts) by the American Registry for Internet Numbers, available at http://www.arin.net/. The agency assigns *Internet service providers (ISPs)* one or more blocks of IP addresses, which the ISPs can then assign to their subscribers.

You will quickly recognize the current form of TCP/IP addressing, known as IPv4 (IP version 4). In this method, a TCP/IP address is expressed of a series of four decimal numbers—a 32-bit value expressed in a format known as dotted-decimal format, such as 192.168.120.135. Each set of numbers is known as an *octet* (eight ones and zeros, such as 10000000 to represent 128) and ranges from 0 to 255.

The first octet usually determines what *class* the network belongs to. There are three classes of networks, as follows:

> ▶ **Class A**—Consists of networks with the first octet ranging from 1 to 126. There are only 126 Class A networks—each composed of up to 16,777,214 hosts. (If you are doing the math, there are potentially 16,777,216 addresses, but no host portion of an address can be all zeros or 255s.) The "10." network is reserved for local network use, and the "127." network is reserved for the *loopback* address of 127.0.0.1.

NOTE

Notice that zero is not included in Class A. The zero address is used for network-to-network broadcasts. Also, note that there are two other classes of networks, Classes D and E. Class D networks are reserved for multicast addresses and are not for use by network hosts. Class E addresses are deemed experimental, and thus are not open for public addressing.

▶ **Class B**—Consists of networks defined by the first two octets, with the first ranging from 128 to 191. The "128." network is also reserved for local network use. There are 16,382 Class B networks—each with 65,534 possible hosts.

▶ **Class C**—Consists of a network defined by the first three octets, with the first ranging from 192 to 223. The "192." network is another that is reserved for local network use. There are a possible 2,097,150 Class C networks of up to 254 hosts each.

No host portion of an IP address can be all zeros or 255s. These addresses are reserved for local network broadcasts. Broadcast messages are not typically seen by users. IP addresses with all zeros in the host portion are reserved for network-to-network broadcast addresses.

These classes are the standard, but a *netmask* also determines in what class your network is. The netmask determines what part of an IP address represents the network and what part represents the host. Common netmasks for the different classes are as follows:

▶ **Class A**—255.0.0.0

▶ **Class B**—255.255.0.0

▶ **Class C**—255.255.255.0

Because of the allocation of IP addresses for Internet hosts, it is now impossible to get a Class A network. It is also nearly impossible to get a Class B network (all the addresses have been given out, but some companies are said to be willing to sell theirs), and Class C network availability is dropping rapidly with the current growth of Internet use world-wide. See the following sidebar.

Limits of Current IP Addressing

The current IPv4 address scheme is based on 32-bit numbering and limits the number of available IP addresses to about 4.1 billion. Many companies and organizations (particularly in the United States) were assigned very large blocks of IP addresses in the early stages of the growth of the Internet, which has left a shortage of "open" addresses. Even with careful allocation of Internet-connected host IP addresses and the use of *network address translation* (*NAT*) to provide communication to and from machines behind an Internet-connected computer, the Internet might run out of available addresses.

To solve this problem, a newer scheme named IPv6 (IP version 6) is being implemented. It uses a much larger addressing solution based on 128-bit addresses, with enough room to include much more information about a specific host or device, such as *global positioning server (GPS)* or serial numbering. Although the specific details about the entire contents of the an IPv6 address have yet to be finalized, all Internet-related organizations appear to agree that something must be done to provide more addresses. It's difficult to gauge just how big the Internet actually is, but according to Internet World Stats, some 1.224 billion people use the Internet as of September 2007. Multiply that by the number of mail servers, newsgroup servers and other web servers that are attached to the web and you will quickly find that the range of addresses supplied by IPv4 is quickly running out.

You can get a good overview of the differences between IPv4 and IPv6 policies regarding IP address assignments, and the registration process of obtaining IP addresses, by browsing to http://www.arin.net/library/index.html. Read the Linux IPv6 HOWTO by browsing to http://tldp.org/HOWTO/Linux+IPv6-HOWTO/.

Fedora supports the use of IPv6 and includes a number of networking tools conforming to IPv6 addressing. You can configure support for IPv6 by using settings and options in the file named network under the /etc/sysconfig directory, along with making changes to related network configuration files, such as /etc/hosts. Many IPv6-based tools, such as ipcalc6, ping6, and traceroute6, are available for Fedora. See various files under the /usr/share/doc/initscripts directory for more information specific to setting up IPv6 addressing with Linux and Fedora.

Migration to IPv6 is slow in coming, however, because the majority of computer operating systems, software, hardware, firmware, and users are still in the IPv4 mindset. Supporting IPv6 will require rewrites to many networking utilities, portions of operating systems currently in use, and firmware in routing and firewall hardware.

Dynamic Host Configuration Protocol

As its name implies, *Dynamic Host Configuration Protocol (DHCP)* configures hosts for connection to your network. DHCP allows a network administrator to configure all TCP/IP parameters for each host as he connects to the network after activation of a NIC. These parameters include automatically assigning an IP address to a NIC, setting name server entries in /etc/resolv.conf, and configuring default routing and gateway information for a host. This section first describes how to use DHCP to obtain IP address assignment for your NIC, and then how to quickly set up and start a DHCP server using Fedora.

> **NOTE**
>
> You can learn more about DHCP by reading RFC 2131, "Dynamic Host Configuration Protocol." Browse to http://www.ietf.org/rfc/rfc2131.txt.

How DHCP Works

DHCP provides persistent storage of network parameters by holding identifying information for each network client that might connect to the network. The three most common pairs of identifying information are the following:

- ▶ **Network subnet/host address**—Used by hosts to connect to the network at will
- ▶ **Subnet/hostname**—Enables the specified host to connect to the subnet
- ▶ **Subnet/hardware address**—Enables a specific client to connect to the network after getting the hostname from DHCP

DHCP also allocates to clients temporary or permanent network (IP) addresses. When a temporary assignment, known as a *lease*, elapses, the client can request to have the lease extended, or, if the address is no longer needed, the client can relinquish the address. For hosts that will be permanently connected to a network with adequate addresses available, DHCP allocates infinite leases.

DHCP offers your network some advantages. First, it shifts responsibility for assigning IP addresses from the network administrator (who can accidentally assign duplicate IP addresses) to the DHCP server. Second, DHCP makes better use of limited IP addresses. If a user is away from the office for whatever reason, the user's host can release its IP address for use by other hosts.

Like most things in life, DHCP is not perfect. Servers cannot be configured through DHCP alone because DNS does not know what addresses DHCP assigns to a host. This means that DNS lookups are not possible on machines configured through DHCP alone; there-fore, services cannot be provided. However, DHCP can make assignments based on DNS entries when using subnet/hostname or subnet/hardware address identifiers.

> **NOTE**
>
> The problem of using DHCP to configure servers that make use of registered host-names is being addressed by Dynamic DNS which, when fully developed, will enable DHCP to register IP addresses with DNS. This will allow you, for example, to register a domain name (such as imalinuxuser.com) and be able to easily access that domain's web server without needing to use static IP addressing of a specific host. The largest hurdle to overcome is the security implication of enabling each host connecting to the system to update DNS. A few companies, such as DynDNS (http://www.dyndns.com/), are already offering Dynamic DNS services and have clients for Linux.

DHCP Software Installation

Installation of the DHCP client and server might be easiest during the initial install of Fedora, but you can also use yum later. This section describes configuring the dhclient and setting up and running the dhpcd daemon.

DHCP dhclient

As previously mentioned, using DHCP for an installed NIC is easily accomplished when installing Fedora on your host (read more about installation in Chapter 1, "Installing Fedora"), and during the network step of installation, you can choose to have DHCP initi-ated at boot time. If you choose to do this (and choose to install the DHCP client package), the DHCP client, dhclient, sends a broadcast message to which the DHCP server replies with networking information for your host. That's it; you're finished.

If you choose to install from source, you will have to (as root) download and install the server packages that include dhclient. Unpack the source file, run ./configure from the root of the source directory, run make, and then run make install. This should put the DHCP client binaries where they will start at the correct time in the boot process.

You can however, fine-tune how `dhclient` works, and where and how it obtains or looks for DHCP information. You probably will not need to take this additional effort; but if you do, you can create and edit a file named `dhclient.conf`, and save it in the `/etc` directory with your settings. A few of the `dhclient.conf` options include the following:

- ▶ **timeout** *time* ;—How long to wait before giving up trying (60 seconds is the default)

- ▶ **retry** *time* ;—How long to wait before retrying (5 minutes is the default)

- ▶ **select-timeout** *time* ;—How long to wait before selecting a DHCP offer (0 seconds is the default)

- ▶ **reboot** *time* ;—How long to wait before trying to get a previously set IP (10 seconds is the default)

- ▶ **renew** *date* ;—When to renew an IP lease, where *date* is in the form of *<weekday> <year>/<month>/<day> <hour>:<minute>:<second>*, such as 4 2004/1/1 22:01:01 for Thursday, January 4, 2004 at 10:01 p.m.

See the `dhclient.conf` man page for more information on additional settings.

DHCP Server

Again, the easiest way to install the DHCP server on your computer is to include the RPMs at install time or to use `yum` if you have installed your machine without installing the DHCP server. If you are so inclined, you can go to the *Internet Software Consortium (ISC)* website and download and build the source code yourself (http://www.isc.org/).

If you decide to install from a source downloaded from the ISC website, the installation is straightforward. Just unpack your `tar` file, run `./configure` from the root of the source directory, run `make`, and finally, if there are no errors, run `make install`. This puts all the files used by the DHCP daemon in the correct places. It's best to leave the source files in place until you are sure that DHCP is running correctly; otherwise, you can delete the source tree.

> **NOTE**
>
> For whichever installation method you choose, be sure that a file called `/etc/dhcpd.leases` is created. The file can be empty, but it does need to exist for `dhcpd` to start properly.

Using DHCP to Configure Network Hosts

Configuring your network with DHCP can look difficult, but is actually easy if your needs are simple. The server configuration can take a bit more work if your network is more complex and depending on how much you want DHCP to do.

DHCP Server Configuration

Configuring the server takes some thought and a little bit of work. Luckily, the work involves editing only a single configuration file, /etc/dhcpd.conf. To start the server at boot time, use the service command or the GUI-based system-config-services.

The /etc/dhcpd.conf file contains all the information needed to run dhcpd. Fedora includes a sample dhcpd.conf in /usr/share/doc/dhcp*/dhcpd.conf.sample. The DHCP server source files also contain a sample dhcpd.conf file.

The /etc/dhcpd.conf file can be looked at as a three-part file. The first part contains configurations for DHCP itself. The configurations include

▶ **Setting the domain name**—option domain-name "example.org".

▶ **Setting DNS servers**—option domain-name-servers ns1.example.org, ns2.example.org (IP addresses can be substituted).

▶ **Setting the default and maximum lease times**—default-lease-time 3600 and max-lease-time 14400.

Other settings in the first part include whether the server is the primary (authoritative) server and what type of logging DHCP should use. These settings are considered defaults and can be overridden by the subnet and host portion of the configuration in more complex situations.

> **NOTE**
>
> The dhcpd.conf file requires semicolons (;) after each command statement. If your configuration file has errors or runs improperly, check for this.

The next part of the dhcpd.conf deals with the different subnets that your DHCP server serves; this section is quite straightforward. Each subnet is defined separately and can look like this:

```
subnet 10.5.5.0 netmask 255.255.255.224 {
 range 10.5.5.26 10.5.5.30;
 option domain-name-servers ns1.internal.example.org;
 option domain-name "internal.example.org";
 option routers 10.5.5.1;
 option broadcast-address 10.5.5.31;
 default-lease-time 600;
 max-lease-time 7200;
}
```

This defines the IP addressing for the 10.5.5.0 subnet. It defines the IP address ranging from 10.5.5.26 through 10.5.5.30 to be dynamically assigned to hosts that reside on that subnet. This example shows that any TCP/IP option can be set from the subnet portion of the configuration file. It shows to which DNS server the subnet will connect, which can be good for DNS server load balancing, or which can be used to limit the hosts that can be reached through DNS. It defines the domain name, so you can have more than one domain on your network. It can also change the default and maximum lease time.

If you want your server to ignore a specific subnet, the following entry can be used to accomplish this:

```
subnet 10.152.187.0 netmask 255.255.255.0 {
}
```

This defines no options for the 10.152.187.0 subnet; therefore, the DHCP server ignores it.

The last part of your dhcp.conf is for defining hosts. This can be good if you want a computer on your network to have a specific IP address or other information specific to that host. The key to completing the host section is to know the hardware address of the host. The hardware address is used to differentiate the host for configuration. You can obtain your hardware address by using the ifconfig command as described previously. The hardware address is on the eth0 line labeled "Hwaddr".

```
host fantasia {
  hardware ethernet 08:00:07:26:c0:a5;
  fixed-address fantasia.fugue.com;
}
```

This example takes the host with the hardware address 08:00:07:26:c0:a5 and does a DNS lookup to assign the IP address for fantasia.fugue.com to the host.

DHCP can also define and configure booting for diskless clients like this:

```
host passacaglia {
  hardware ethernet 0:0:c0:5d:bd:95;
  filename "vmunix.passacaglia";
  server-name "toccata.fugue.com";
}
```

The diskless host passacaglia gets its boot information from server toccata.fugue.com and uses the vmunix.passacaglia kernel. All other TCP/IP configuration can also be included.

> **CAUTION**
>
> Remember, only one DHCP server should exist on a local network to avoid problems. Your DHCP might not work correctly on a LAN with hosts running outdated legacy operating systems. Often Windows NT servers have the Windows DHCP server installed by default. Because there is no configuration file for NT to sort through, that DHCP server

configures your host before the Linux server if both machines are on the same LAN. Check your Windows NT servers for this situation and disable DHCP on the Windows NT server; afterward, your other DHCP-enabled hosts should configure correctly. Also, check to make sure that there are no conflicts if you use a cable or DSL modem, wireless access point (WAP), or other intelligent router on your LAN that can provide DHCP.

Other Uses for DHCP

A whole host of options can be used in dhcpd.conf; entire books are dedicated to DHCP. The most comprehensive book is *The DHCP Handbook*, available at http://www.dhcp-handbook.com/. You can define NIS domains, configure NETBIOS, set subnet masks, and define time servers or many other types of servers—to name a few of the DHCP options you can use. The preceding example will get your DHCP server and client up and running.

The DHCP server distribution contains an example of the dhcpd.conf file that you can use as a template for your network. The file shows a basic configuration that can get you started with explanations for the options used.

Using IP Masquerading in Fedora

Three blocks of IP addresses are reserved for use on internal networks and hosts not directly connected to the Internet. The address ranges are from 10.0.0.0 to 10.255.255.255, or 1 Class A network; from 172.16.0.0 to 172.31.255.255, or 16 Class B networks; and from 192.168.0.0 to 192.168.255.255, or 256 Class C networks. Use these IP addresses when building a LAN for your business or home. Which class you choose can depend on the number of hosts on your network.

Internet access for your internal network can be provided by a PC running Fedora or other broadband or dialup router. The host or device is connected to the Internet and is used as an Internet gateway to forward information to and from your LAN. The host should also be used as a firewall to protect your network from malicious data and users while functioning as an Internet gateway.

A PC used in this fashion typically has at least two network interfaces. One is connected to the Internet with the other connected to the computers on the LAN (via a hub or switch). Some broadband devices also incorporate four or more switching network interfaces. Data is then passed between the LAN and the Internet using *network address translation*, or *NAT*, better known in Linux circles as *IP masquerading*. See Chapter 30, "Securing Your Machines," for more information.

14

> **NOTE**
>
> Do not rely on a single point of protection for your LAN, especially if you use wireless networking, provide dial-in services, or allow mobile (laptop or PDA) users internal or external access to your network. Companies, institutions, and individuals relying on a "moat mentality" have often discovered to their dismay that such an approach to security is easily breached. Make sure that your network operation is accompanied by a security policy that stresses multiple levels of secure access, with protection built in to every server and workstation—something easily accomplished with Linux.

Ports

Most servers on your network have more than one task. For example, web servers have to serve both standard and secure pages. You might also be running an FTP server on the same host. For this reason, applications are provided *ports* to use to make "direct" connections for specific software services. These ports help TCP/IP distinguish services so that data can get to the correct application. If you check the file /etc/services, you will see the common ports and their usage. For example, for FTP, HTTP, and Post Office Protocol (email retrieval server), you will see the following:

```
ftp        21/tcp
http       80/tcp      www www-http  # WorldWideWeb HTTP
pop3       110/tcp     pop-3         # POP version 3
```

The ports defined in /etc/services in this example are 21 for FTP, 80 for HTTP, and 110 for POP3. Other common port assignments are 25 for *Simple Mail Transport Protocol (SMTP)* and 22 for *Secure Shell (SSH)* remote login. Note that these ports are not set in stone, and you can set up your server to respond to different ports. For example, although port 22 is listed in /etc/services as a common default for SSH, the sshd server can be configured to listen on a different port if you edit its configuration file /etc/ssh/sshd_config. The default setting (commented out with a pound sign) looks like this:

```
#Port 22
```

Edit the entry to use a different port, making sure to select an unused port number, such as this:

```
Port 2224
```

Save your changes, and then restart the sshd server. (Refer to Chapter 11, "Automating Tasks," to see how to restart a service.) Remote users must now access the host through port 2224, which can be done using ssh's -p (port) option like so:

```
$ ssh -p 2224 remote_host_name_or_IP
```

Beyond the Network and Onto the Internet

Fedora supports Internet connections and the use of Internet resources in many different ways. You will find a wealth of Internet-related software included with this book's version of Fedora, and you can download hundreds of additional free utilities from a variety of sources. To use them, you must have a working Internet connection.

In this section, you learn how to set up an Internet connection in Fedora, using a modem and *Point-to-Point Protocol (PPP)* as well as other connection methods, including *Digital Subscriber Line (DSL)* and cable modem services. Just a few years ago, getting a dialup connection working was difficult—hence, an entire chapter of this book was devoted to it. Nowadays, as long as you have a hardware modem, dialup configuration is simple. The Fedora developers and the wider Linux community have made great progress in making connectivity easier.

Although many experienced Linux users continue to use manual scripts to establish their Internet connectivity, new users and experienced system administrators alike will find Fedora's graphical network configuration interface, the Internet Connection Wizard, much easier to use. You learn how to use the Internet Connection Wizard in this chapter, as well as how to configure Fedora to provide dial-in PPP support. The chapter also describes how to use Roaring Penguin's DSL utilities for managing connectivity through a cable modem connection.

Common Configuration Information

Although Fedora enables great flexibility in configuring Internet connections, that flexibility comes at the price of an increase in complexity. To configure Internet connectivity in Fedora, you must know more about the details of the connection process than you can learn from the information typically provided by your ISP. In this section, you learn what to ask about and how to use the information.

Some ISPs are unaware of Linux or unwilling to support its use with their service. Fortunately, that attitude is rapidly changing, and the majority of ISPs offer services using standard protocols that are compatible with Linux, even if they (or their technical support people) aren't aware that their own ISPs are Linux-friendly. You just need to press a little for the information you require.

If you are using a dialup modem account (referred to in Linux as *PPP* for the Point-to-Point Protocol it uses), your ISP provides your computer with a static or dynamic IP (*Internet Protocol*) address. A dynamic IP address changes each time you dial in, whereas a static IP address remains the same. The ISP also might automatically provide your computer with the names of the *Domain Name Service (DNS)* servers. You need to know the telephone number that your computer dials in to for making the connection; your ISP supplies that number, too. You also need a working modem and need to know the device name of the modem (usually `/dev/modem`).

> **NOTE**
>
> Most IP addresses are dynamically assigned by ISPs; ISPs have a pool of addresses, and you get whatever address is available. From the ISP's viewpoint, a small number of addresses can serve a large number of people because not everyone will be online at the same time. For most Internet services, a dynamic IP works well because it is the ISP's job to route that information to you, and it sits in the middle—between you and the service you want to use. But a dynamic IP address changes, and if someone needs to find you at the same address (if you run a website or a file transfer site, for example), an IP that changes every time you log on will not work well. For that, you need a static IP. Because your ISP cannot reuse that IP with its other customers, it will likely charge you more for a static IP than a dynamic IP. The average consumer doesn't need the benefit of a static IP, so he is happy paying less for a dynamically assigned IP. Also, the DNS information can be provided automatically by the ISP by the DHCP.

If you are using DSL access or a cable modem, you might have a dynamic IP provided through DHCP, or you might be assigned a static IP. You might automatically be provided with the names of the DNS servers if you use DHCP, or you might have to set up DNS manually (in which case, you have to know the IP addresses of the DNS servers).

In all cases, you have to know your username, your password, and for the configuration of other services, the names of the mail servers and the news server. This information can be obtained from your ISP if you specifically ask for it.

> **NOTE**
>
> The information in this book will help you understand and avoid many connection issues, but you might experience connection problems. Keep the telephone number of the technical help service for your ISP on hand in case you are not able to establish a connection. But be aware that few ISPs offer Linux support, and you might need to seek help from a Linux-savvy friend or a Linux user's group if your special circumstances cannot be handled from the knowledge you gain from this book. Of course, the best place to look is on the Internet. Use Google's Linux page (http://www.google.com/linux) to research the problem and see whether any other users have found fixes or workarounds.

Configuring DSL Access

Fedora also supports the use of a DSL service. Although it refers to the different types of DSL available as xDSL, that name includes ADSL, IDSL, SDSL, and other flavors of DSL service; they can all be configured with the Internet Connection Wizard. DSL service generally provides 128Kbps to 24Mbps transfer speeds and transmits data over copper telephone lines from a central office to individual subscriber sites (such as your home). Many DSL services provide asymmetric speeds with download speed greater than upload speeds.

14

> **NOTE**
>
> DSL service is an "always-on" type of Internet service, although you can turn off the connection under Fedora by using the Network Device Control, found under System, Administration. An always-on connection exposes your computer to malicious abuse from crackers who trawl the Internet attempting to gain access to other computer systems. In addition to the capability to turn off such connections, Fedora provides a firewall to keep crackers out; you configured a simple firewall during the original installation. The firewall can also be configured from the Security Level Configuration tool found in the System Settings menu selection as Security Level.

A DSL connection requires that you have an ethernet network interface card (sometimes a USB interface that is not easily supported in Linux) in your computer or notebook. Many users also configure a gateway, firewall, or other computer with at least two network interface cards to share a connection with a LAN. We looked at the hardware and protocol issues earlier in this chapter. Advanced configuration of a firewall or router, other than what was addressed during your initial installation of Fedora, is beyond the scope of this book.

Understanding Point-to-Point Protocol over Ethernet

Establishing a DSL connection with an ISP providing a static IP address is easy. Unfortunately, many DSL providers use a type of PPP protocol named *Point-to-Point Protocol over Ethernet (PPPoE)* that provides dynamic IP address assignment and authentication by encapsulating PPP information inside ethernet frames. Roaring Penguin's rp-pppoe clients are included with Fedora, and these clients make the difficult-to-configure PPPoE connection much easier to deal with.

Configuring a PPPoE Connection Manually

The basic steps involved in manually setting up a DSL connection using Fedora involve connecting the proper hardware and then running a simple configuration script if you use rp-pppoe from Roaring Penguin.

First, connect your DSL modem to your telephone line, and then plug in your ethernet cable from the modem to your computer's network interface card. If you plan to share your DSL connection with the rest of your LAN, you need at least two network cards—designated eth0 (for your LAN) and eth1 (for the DSL connection).

The following example assumes that you have more than one computer and will share your DSL connection on a LAN.

First, log in as root and ensure that your first eth0 device is enabled and up (perhaps by using the ifconfig command). Next, bring up the other interface, but assign a null IP address like this:

```
# ifconfig eth1 0.0.0.0 up
```

Now use the `pppoe-setup` command to set up your system. Type the command like this:

```
# pppoe-setup
```

You are presented with a text script and are asked to enter your username and the ethernet interface used for the connection (such as `eth1`). You are then asked to use "on-demand" service or have the connection stay up all the time (until brought down by the root operator). You can also set a timeout in seconds, if desired. You're then asked to enter the IP addresses of your ISP's DNS servers if you haven't configured the system's `/etc/resolv.conf` file.

After that, you are prompted to enter your password two times, and have to choose the type of firewall and IP masquerading to use. (You learned about IP masquerading in the "Using IP Masquerading in Fedora" section, earlier in this chapter.) The actual configuration is done automatically. Using a firewall is essential nowadays, so you should choose this option unless you intend to craft your own set of firewall rules—a discussion of which is beyond the scope of this book. After you have chosen your firewall and IP masquerading setup, you are asked to confirm, save, and implement your settings. You are also given a choice to allow users to manage the connection, a handy option for home users.

Changes are then made to your system's `/etc/sysconfig/network-scripts/ifcfg-ppp0`, `/etc/resolv.conf`, `/etc/ppp/pap-secrets`, and `/etc/ppp/chap-secrets` files.

After configuration has finished, use the `adsl-start` command to start a connection and DSL session, like this:

```
# adsl-start
```

The DSL connection should be nearly instantaneous, but if problems occur, check to make sure that your DSL modem is communicating with the phone company's central office by examining the status LEDs on the modem. Because this varies from modem to modem, consult your modem user's manual.

Check to make certain that all cables are properly attached, that your interfaces are properly configured, and that you have entered the correct information to the setup script.

If IP masquerading is enabled, other computers on your LAN on the same subnet address (such as 192.168.1.*xxx*) can use the Internet, but must have the same `/etc/resolv.conf` name server entries and a routing entry with the DSL-connected computer as a gateway. For example, if the host computer with the DSL connection has an IP address of 192.168.1.1, and other computers on your LAN use addresses in the 192.168.1.*xxx* range, use the `route` command on each computer like this:

```
# route add default gw 192.168.1.1
```

Note that you can also use a hostname instead if each computer has an `/etc/hosts` file with hostname and IP address entries for your LAN. To stop your connection, use the `adsl-stop` command like this:

```
# adsl-stop
```

Configuring Dialup Internet Access

Most ISPs provide dialup connections supporting PPP because it is a fast and efficient protocol for using TCP/IP over serial lines. PPP is designed for two-way networking; TCP/IP provides the transport protocol for data. One hurdle faced by new Fedora users is how to set up PPP and connect to the Internet. It is not necessary to understand the details of the PPP protocol to use it, and setting up a PPP connection is easy. You can configure the PPP connections manually, using the command line, or graphically during an X session, using Fedora's Internet Configuration Wizard. Each approach produces the same results.

PPP uses several components on your system. The first is a daemon called pppd, which controls the use of PPP. The second is a driver called the *high-level data link control (HDLC)*, which controls the flow of information between two machines. A third component of PPP is a routine called chat that dials the other end of the connection for you when you want it to. Although PPP has many "tunable" parameters, the default settings work well for most people.

14

> **NOTE**
>
> You can check to see whether PPP is installed on your system by running the pppd command as root from a command line with the --help argument, like this:
>
> ```
> # pppd --help
> ```
>
> That will list the current version number and describe a few available options if PPP is installed.
>
> If PPP isn't installed on your system, use the rpm command to install the PPP package from the Fedora DVD or use the Packages menu item from the System Settings menu. Chapter 34, "Advanced Software Management," covers the details of using rpm and the graphical package manager.

Configuring a Dialup Connection Manually

The first step in manually configuring PPP is to log in as root to copy and edit the necessary files. After you are logged in, you use the chat command, the pppd daemon, and several files to configure PPP:

- ▶ **/etc/ppp/ppp-on**—Used to start a PPP connection. This file contains the ISP's phone number, your username and password, as well as various options such as IP address options, the modem device, and its settings (such as baud rate) for the connection.

- ▶ **/etc/ppp/ppp-off**—Used to terminate a PPP connection.

- ▶ **/etc/ppp/ppp-on-dialer**—Used to perform dialing and connection with the chat command; this script contains error-handling and negotiation responses between the remote system and the chat command script.

CAUTION

Many software modems do not work with Linux because the manufacturers won't release programming information about them or provide Linux drivers. An external serial port modem or ISA bus modem almost always works; USB and PCI modems are still problematic. It is suggested that you do a thorough Google search, using your modem's name and model number, to see how others have solved problems with that particular modem. Links to software modem compatibility sites appear at the end of this chapter.

Begin by copying the scripts from the /usr/share/doc/ppp*/scripts directory to the /etc/ppp directory, like so:

```
# cp -ar /usr/share/doc/ppp*/scripts/ppp-o* /etc/ppp
```

Using your favorite text editor, edit the ppp-on file (making sure to disable the line wrapping function in your editor—that varies from editor to editor—and line-wrapping inserts carriage returns that cause these scripts to stop working) and change the first four entries to reflect your ISP's phone number and your username and password, as follows:

```
TELEPHONE=555-1212      # The telephone number for the connection
ACCOUNT=hudzilla          # The account name for logon
PASSWORD=spasm          # The password for this account
LOCAL_IP=0.0.0.0        # Local IP address if known. Dynamic = 0.0.0.0
```

Change the values for TELEPHONE, ACCOUNT, and PASSWORD, substituting your ISP's phone number and your username and password. Change the LOCAL_IP entry to an IP address only if your ISP provides one for use. (Dynamic IPs are typical of dialup accounts.) Otherwise, leave the entry blank. Next, scroll through the script until you find the dialing setup, which can look like this:

```
exec /usr/sbin/pppd debug lock modem crtscts /dev/ttyS0 38400 \
        asyncmap 20A0000 escape FF kdebug 0 $LOCAL_IP:$REMOTE_IP \
        noipdefault netmask $NETMASK defaultroute connect $DIALER_SCRIPT
```

These lines (actually a single script line) contain modem options for the chat script used in the ppp-on-dialer script and will start the pppd daemon on your computer after establishing a connection. Using a text editor, change the modem device (/dev/ttyS0 in this example) to /dev/modem.

CAUTION

You can use /dev/modem only if Fedora's kudzu utility has recognized and configured the computer's modem. (If /dev/modem does not exist, use the ln command to create the file as a symbolic link pointing to the correct serial port.) To create the symlink (from /dev/ttyS2, for example):

```
# ln -s /dev/ttyS2 /dev/modem
```

If your modem was not automatically detected and the /dev/modem link configured, it is possible that you have a software modem, also known as a *Winmodem* or *HSF* modem (refer to the earlier note).

Set the baud rate (38400 in the default case) to the desired connection speed—most likely 115200 or 57600. When finished, save the file.

Next, use the chmod command to make these scripts executable, like this:

```
# chmod +x /etc/ppp/ppp-o*
```

To debug or check the progress of your modem connection, dialing, and connection to your ISP, monitor the syslog messages by using the tail command with its -f "loop-forever" option, as follows:

```
# tail -f /var/log/messages
```

To connect to your ISP, run the ppp- script:

```
# /etc/ppp/ppp-on
```

Use the ppp-off script to stop the PPP connection, like so:

```
# /etc/ppp/ppp-off
```

You can also move the ppp-on and ppp-off scripts to a recognized $PATH, such as /usr/local/bin. Enabling use of these scripts by normal users will entail changing permissions of the serial port and other files (which can be a security problem because unauthorized users can access it).

TIP

If your modem is installed and working, you can access it with a terminal program such as minicom, which usually is not installed by default. After you install it using yum or from source code, start it the first time with the -s argument to configure it:

```
$ minicom -s
```

Set the serial port to that of your modem, and then save the configuration. You can then use minicom to communicate with your modem by using the AT command to set and see its responses.

If you do not want to go to that trouble, you can use the echo command to send commands to the modem, but the modem won't be capable of responding to you. For example, the AT&W command can be sent as follows:

```
# echo "AT&W" > /dev/modem
```

14

Using the Fedora Internet Configuration Wizard

The Fedora Modem Configuration Wizard can be used to set up the many kinds of network connection types that exist. Fedora provides wizards for the following connections:

- ▶ IPSec (VPN) connection (virtual private network using crypto IP encapsulation)
- ▶ Ethernet connection
- ▶ ISDN connection
- ▶ Modem connection
- ▶ Token Ring connection
- ▶ Wireless connection
- ▶ xDSL connection

The example provided here uses the wizard to configure a modem connection—the most commonly encountered home network connection. The other types are configured in essentially the same manner.

From the System menu, select the Administration submenu and click Network to open the Network Configuration tool. Enter the root password to gain access to the tool and click New in the toolbar to start the wizard. Select Modem Connection from the list of options, shown in Figure 14.4, and click Forward.

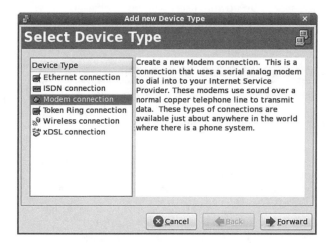

FIGURE 14.4   The Network Configuration tool can be used to quickly and easily configure many different kinds of Internet connections.

Select Modem Connection in the Device Type list, and then click the Forward button. You are then asked to select a provider, designate a name for the service, enter your ISP's phone number, and enter your username and password on the remote system, as shown in Figure 14.5. A dialing prefix (to disable call waiting, for example) can be added in the Prefix field. Additional special settings are also included for PPP users in various countries with different ISPs, as shown by the country flags on the left.

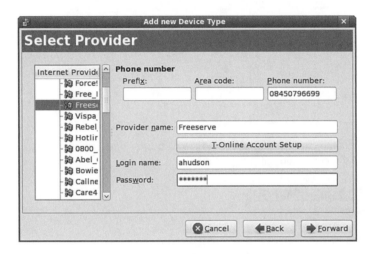

FIGURE 14.5   Enter a name for your ISP's service, along with the telephone number, username, and password for the service.

Enter the telephone number of your ISP's remote computer's modem. Enter a country code if needed, along with an area code and telephone number. Note that some areas require a 10-digit number for local telephone service. When finished, click the Forward button. You'll then be asked about IP address settings; unless you have specific instructions from your ISP, you should leave the automatic option enabled. Finally, you are able to confirm the settings. Click the Apply button to create the interface. When you have finished, you will see a new ppp0 entry in the Network Configuration window, as shown in Figure 14.6.

To edit the new connection identified as ppp0, select the interface and then click the Edit button. A configuration dialog appears, as shown in Figure 14.7. Each tab presents an easy-to-use interface for setting dialup options.

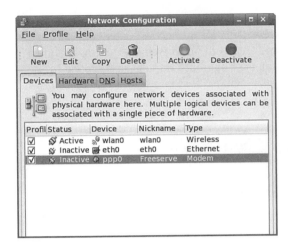

FIGURE 14.6   Your new PPP dialup connection appears in the Network Configuration dialog, which also shows the status of the connection.

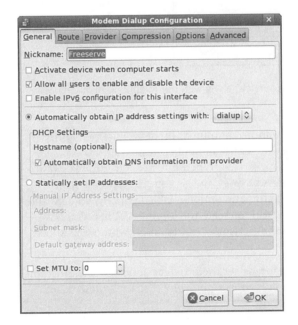

FIGURE 14.7   Here you can edit the dialup configuration, if necessary, to set IP addresses and other custom values; the defaults work for most people.

This window can be reached later from the System Settings menu as the Network menu item. Fedora also provides a simple control interface via the System, Administration menu as the Network Device Control menu item, as shown in Figure 14.8.

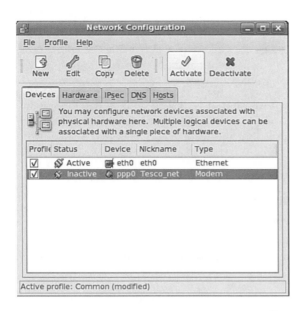

FIGURE 14.8   The Network Device Control enables you to start and stop a network interface.

Launch a PPP connection by selecting the ppp0 interface and then clicking the Activate button.

You can also use the ifup command manually (only as root) to bring up the connection like this:

```
# ifup ppp0
```

To close the connection manually, use ifdown:

```
# /sbin/ifdown ppp0
```

If you named the dialup connection something other than ppp0, use that name instead. Because this one is named Cavtel, it can be brought up manually with the following:

```
# ifup Cavtel
```

Troubleshooting Connection Problems

The Internet Configuration Wizard does not offer any Help dialogs, but the Linux Documentation Project at http://www.tldp.org/ offers many in-depth resources for configuring and troubleshooting these connections. The Internet search engine Google is also an invaluable tool for dealing with specific questions about these connections. For many other useful references, see the "Reference" section at the end of this chapter.

Here are a few troubleshooting tips culled from many years of experience:

▶ If your modem connects and then hangs up, you are probably using the wrong password or dialing the wrong number. If the password and phone number are correct, it is likely an authentication protocol problem.

▶ If you get connected but cannot reach websites, it is likely a domain name resolver problem, meaning that DNS is not working. If it worked yesterday and you haven't "adjusted" the associated files, it is probably a problem at the ISP's end. Call and ask.

▶ Always make certain that everything is plugged in. Check again—and again.

▶ If the modem works in Windows, but not in Linux no matter what you do, it is probably a software modem no matter what it said on the box.

▶ If everything just stops working (and you do not see smoke), it is probably a glitch at the ISP or the telephone company. Take a break and give them some time to fix it.

▶ Never configure a network connection when you have had too little sleep or too much caffeine; you will just have to redo it tomorrow.

Related Fedora and Linux Commands

You will use these commands when managing network connectivity in your Fedora system:

▶ **dhclient**—Automatically acquire, and then set IP info for a NIC

▶ **ethereal**—GNOME graphical network scanner

▶ **gnome-lokkit**—Fedora's basic graphical firewalling tool for X

▶ **ifconfig**—Displays and manages Linux networking devices

▶ **iwconfig**—Displays and sets wireless network device parameters

▶ **lokkit**—Fedora's basic graphical firewalling tool

▶ **netconfig**—Fedora's console-based graphical network interface configuration tool

▶ **route**—Displays and manages Linux kernel routing table

▶ **setup**—Fedora's console-based graphical management tool

▶ **ssh**—The OpenSSH remote-login client and preferred replacement for telnet

▶ **system-config-nfs**—Fedora's graphical Network File System configuration tool

▶ **system-config-network**—Fedora's graphical network and service management client for X

▶ **system-config-securitylevel**—Fedora's graphical firewall configuration utility

Reference

The following websites and books are great resources for more information on the topics covered in this chapter. Networking is complex. The more you take the time to learn, the easier setting up and maintaining your network will be.

General

▶ http://www.ietf.org/rfc.html—Go here to search for, or get a list of, *Request For Comments (RFC)*.

DHCP

▶ http://www.oth.net/dyndns.html—For a list of Dynamic DNS service providers, go to this site.

▶ http://www.isc.org/products/DHCP/dhcpv3-Read Me.html—The DHCP Read Me is available at this site.

Wireless

▶ http://www.ieee.org—The *Institute of Electrical and Electronics Engineers (IEEE)* website.

▶ http://www.mozillaquest.com/Network_02/Wireless_Network_Technology_ 03_Story-01.html—Wireless networking with Red Hat 7.2.

▶ https://agora.cs.uiuc.edu/display/tsg/Technology+Services+Group+Home— Wireless networking using Red Hat Linux at the *Computing Research Laboratory (CRL)*, the information technology support group for the Department of Computer Science at the University of Illinois at Urbana-Champaign.

▶ http://www.sorgonet.com/network/wirelessnoap/—Building a wireless network without using an access point, using Red Hat 8.0.

Books

▶ *Sams Teach Yourself TCP/IP Network Administration in 21 Days*, Sams Publishing, ISBN: 0-672-31250-6

▶ *TCP/IP Network Administration*, O'Reilly Publishing, ISBN: 1-56592-322-7

▶ *Practical Networking*, Que Publishing, ISBN: 0-7897-2252-6

▶ *The DHCP Handbook*, Sams Publishing, ISBN: 0-672-32327-3

# CHAPTER 15

Remote Access with SSH

The ability to control your system remotely is one of the high points of Fedora Core Linux—you can connect from any Linux box to another Linux box in a variety of ways. If you just want to check something quickly or if you have limited bandwidth, you have the option of using only the command line, but you can also connect directly to the X server and get full graphical control.

Understanding the selection of tools available is largely a history lesson. For example, Telnet was an earlier way of connecting to another computer through the command line, but it has since been superseded by SSH. That is not to say that you should ignore Telnet; you need to know how to use it so that you have it as a fallback. However, SSH is preferred because it is more secure. We cover both in this chapter.

Please keep in mind that although Telnet is worth keeping around as a fail-safe, last-resort option, SSH is superior in virtually every way. Telnet is fast but also insecure. It sends all your text, including your password, in plain text that can be read by anyone with the right tools. SSH, on the other hand, encrypts all your communication and so is more resource intensive but secure—even a government security agency sniffing your packets for some reason would still have a hard time cracking the encryption.

Andy Green, posting to the `fedora-list` mailing list, summed up the Telnet situation perfectly when he said, "As Telnet is universally acknowledged to encourage evil, the service telnetd is not enabled by default." It is worthwhile taking the hint: Use Telnet as a last resort only.

Setting Up a Telnet Server

Having been superseded by SSH, you will find the Telnet server installation packages under Legacy Network Server in the Add or Remove Packages dialog box. You need to select it from the Details selection because it is not one of the default selections for the package group. After it's installed, select System Settings, Server Settings, Services and enable Telnet for runlevel 5. Note your IP address while you are here (switch to root and run `ifconfig`).

With that done, you can now fire up your other Linux box and type **telnet** *<your IP>*. If you are unsure of your IP address, switch to root and use the `ifconfig` command. You are prompted to enter your username and password. The whole conversation should look like this:

```
[paul@susannah ~]$ telnet 10.0.0.1
Trying 10.0.0.1…
Connected to 10.0.0.1 (10.0.0.1)
Escape character is '^]'.

Welcome to Caitlin
Running Fedora

* All access is logged *

login: paul
Password:
Last login: Sat Jul 9 12:05:41 from 10.0.0.5
[paul@caitlin ~]$
```

TIP

Note that the server responds with `Welcome to Caitlin, running Fedora`, which is a customized message. Your machine will probably respond with `Fedora` and your kernel version. This is insecure: Giving away version numbers is never a smart move. In fact, even saying `Fedora` is questionable. Edit the `issue` and `issue.net` files in your `/etc` directory to change these messages.

Running the `w` command now shows you as connecting from the external IP address.

Setting Up an SSH Server

The OpenSSH server is set up to be automatically installed and run in Fedora, which means it should already be working on your system. However, if you have disabled it, you can re-enable it by selecting System Settings, Server Settings, Services and selecting the sshd box. As you might have gathered, `sshd` is the name for the SSH server daemon.

Two different versions of SSH exist, called SSH1 and SSH2. The latter is newer, is more secure, comes with more features, and is the default in Fedora Core Linux. However, support for SSH1 clients is also left enabled by default so that older clients can connect. Because it is less secure, you should disable SSH1 if you have no one who specifically relies on it.

To do this, edit the /etc/ssh/sshd_config file and look for this line:

```
#Protocol 2,1
```

Edit this line so that it becomes:

```
Protocol 2
```

This removes the comment sign (#) and tells sshd that you want it to only allow SSH2 connections. Save the file and exit your editor. The next step is to tell sshd to reread its configuration file, by executing this command:

```
kill -HUP `cat /var/run/sshd.pid`
```

If this returns cat: /var/run/sshd.pid: No such file or directory, it means you didn't have sshd running. Next time you start it, it reads the configuration file and uses SSH2 only.

You can test this change by trying to connect to your SSH server in SSH1 mode. From the same machine, type this:

ssh -1 localhost

The -1 switch forces SSH1 mode. If you successfully forced the SSH2 protocol, you should get the message Protocol major versions differ: 1 vs. 2.

The SSH Tools

To the surprise of many, OpenSSH actually comprises a suite of tools. You have already seen ssh, the secure shell command that connects to other machines, and sshd, the SSH server daemon that accepts incoming SSH connections. However, there is also sftp, a replacement for ftp, and scp, a replacement for rcp.

You should already be familiar with the ftp command because it is the lowest-common-denominator system for handling FTP file transfers. Like Telnet, though, ftp is insecure: It sends your data in plain text across the network and anyone can sniff your packets to pick out a username and password. The SSH replacement, sftp, puts FTP traffic over an SSH link, thus securing it.

The rcp command might be new to you, largely because it is not used much anymore. Back in its day, rcp was the primary way of copying a single file to another server. As with ftp, scp replaces rcp by simply channeling the data over a secure SSH connection. The difference between sftp and scp is that the former allows you to copy many files, whereas the latter sends just one.

Using scp to Copy Individual Files Between Machines

The most basic use of the scp command is to copy a file from your current machine to a remote machine. You can do that with the following command:

```
scp test.txt 10.0.0.1:
```

The first parameter is the name of the file you want to send, and the second is the server to which you want to send it. Note that there is a colon at the end of the IP address. This is where you can specify an exact location for the file to be copied. If you have nothing after the colon, as in the previous example, scp copies the file to your home directory. As with SSH, scp prompts you for your password before copying takes place.

You can rewrite the previous command so that you copy test.txt from the local machine and save it as newtest.txt on the server:

```
scp test.txt 10.0.0.1:newtest.txt
```

Alternatively, if there is a directory where you want the file to be saved, you can specify it like this:

```
scp test.txt 10.0.0.1:subdir/stuff/newtest.txt
```

The three commands so far have all assumed that your username on your local machine is the same as your username on the remote machine. If this is not the case, you need to specify your username before the remote address, like this:

```
scp test.txt japh@10.0.0.1:newtest.txt
```

You can use scp to copy remote files locally by simply specifying the remote file as the source and the current directory (.) as the destination:

```
scp 10.0.0.1:remote.txt .
```

The scp command is nominally also capable of copying files from one remote machine to another remote machine, but this functionality has yet to be properly implemented in Fedora Core Linux. If a patch is released—and we hope one is eventually—the correct command to use would be this:

```
scp 10.0.0.1:test.txt 10.0.0.2:remotetest.txt
```

That copies test.txt from 10.0.0.1 to remotetest.txt on 10.0.0.2. If this works, you are asked for passwords for both servers.

Using `sftp` to Copy Many Files Between Machines

`sftp` is a mix between `ftp` and `scp`. Connecting to the server uses the same syntax as `scp`—you can just specify an IP address to connect to using your current username, or you can specify a username using *username@ipaddress*. You can optionally add a colon and a directory, as with `scp`. After you are connected, the commands are the same as `ftp`: `cd`, `put`, `mput`, `get`, `quit`, and so on.

In one of the `scp` examples, we copied a remote file locally. You can do the same thing with `sftp` through the following conversation:

```
[paul@susannah ~]$ sftp 10.0.0.1
Connecting to 10.0.0.1...
paul@10.0.0.1's password:
sftp> get remote.txt
Fetching /home/paul/remote.txt to remote.txt
/home/paul/remote.txt        100%  23    0.0KB/s    00:00
sftp> quit
paul@susannah ~]$
```

Although FTP remains prominent because of the number of systems that do not have support for SSH (Windows, specifically), SFTP is gaining in popularity. Apart from the fact that it secures all communications between client and server, SFTP is popular because the initial connection between the client and server is made over port 22 through the `sshd` daemon. Someone using SFTP connects to the standard `sshd` daemon, verifies himself, and then is handed over to the SFTP server. The advantage to this is that it reduces the attack vectors because the SFTP server cannot be contacted directly and so cannot be attacked as long as the `sshd` daemon is secure.

Using `ssh-keygen` to Enable Key-Based Logins

There is a weak link in the SSH system, and, inevitably, it lies with users. No matter what lengths system administrators go to in training users to be careful with their passwords, Post-it notes with "pAssw0rd" written on them are attached to monitors around the world. Sure, it has a mix of letters and numbers, but it can be cracked in less than a second by any brute-force method. *Brute-forcing* is the method of trying every password possibility, starting with likely words (such as *password* and variants, or *god*) and then just trying random letters (for example, *a*, *aa*, *ab*, *ac*, and so on).

Even very strong passwords are no more than about 16 characters; such passwords take a long time to brute-force but can still be cracked. The solution is to use key-based logins, which generate a unique, 1024-bit private and public key pair for your machine. These keys take even the fastest computers a lifetime to crack, and you can back them up with a password to stop others from using them.

Creating an SSH key is done through the `ssh-keygen` command, like this:

```
ssh-keygen -t dsa
```

Press Enter when it prompts you where to save your key, and enter a passphrase when it asks you to. This passphrase is just a password used to protect the key—you can leave it blank if you want to, but doing so would allow other people to use your account to connect to remote machines if they manage to log in as you.

After the key is generated (it might take up to 30 seconds depending on the speed of your machine), change the directory to .ssh (cd ~/.ssh), which is a hidden directory where your key is stored and also where a list of safe SSH hosts is kept. There you will see the files id_dsa and id_dsa.pub. The first is your private key and should never be given out. The second is your public key, which is safe for distribution. You need to copy the public key to each server you want to connect to via key-based SSH.

Using scp, you can copy the public key over to your server, like this:

```
scp id_dsa.pub 10.0.0.1:
```

This places id_dsa.pub in your home directory on 10.0.0.1. The next step is to SSH into 10.0.0.1 normally and set up that key as an authorized key. So you can SSH in as yourself and then type the following:

```
touch .ssh/authorized_keys
cat id_dsa.pub >> .ssh/authorized_keys
chmod 400 .ssh/authorized_keys
```

The touch command creates the authorized_keys file (if it does not exist already); then you use cat to append the contents of id_dsa.pub to the list of already authorized keys. Finally, chmod is used to make authorized_keys read only.

With that done, you can type **exit** to disconnect from the remote machine and return to your local machine. Then you can try running ssh again. If you are prompted for your passphrase, you have successfully configured key-based authentication.

Now the current machine is secured, but what about every other machine? It is still possible to log in from another machine using only a password, which means your remote machine is still vulnerable.

The solution to this is to switch to root and edit the /etc/ssh/sshd_config file. Look for the PasswordAuthentication line and make sure it reads no (and that it is not commented out with a #). Save the file, and run kill -HUP `cat /var/run/sshd.pid` to have sshd reread its configuration files. With that done, sshd accepts connections only from clients with authorized keys, which stops crackers from brute-forcing their way in.

> **TIP**
>
> For extra security, consider setting `PermitRootLogin` to `no` in `/etc/ssh/sshd_config`. When this is set, it becomes impossible to SSH into your machine using the root account—you must connect with a normal user account and then use `su` or `sudo` to switch to root. This is advantageous because most brute-force attempts take place on the root account because it is the only account that is guaranteed to exist on a server.
>
> Also, even if a cracker knows your user account, she has to guess both your user password and your root password to take control of your system.

Remote X

Everything we have looked at so far has been about command-line remoting, with no mention of how to bring up a graphical user interface. There are two ways of doing this in Linux: the X Display Manager Control Protocol (XDMCP) and Virtual Network Computing (VNC). The former is specific to the X Window System and is very tightly integrated with the rest of the graphical system but is also very insecure. VNC is more modern and very widespread but insecure in some implementations. Both are being used with Fedora, so we cover both here.

XDMCP

Unless you have Fedora configured to log in a specific user automatically, you will be familiar with the user login screen that appears at bootup. What you are seeing is the GNOME Display Manager (GDM), which runs your X sessions, checks passwords, and so forth. What you are doing is logging in to the local machine because that is the default configuration.

However, GDM is also equipped to allow other network users to connect to your machine through the XDMCP protocol. There are various reasons for using XDMCP; the most popular is that many modern machines are large and noisy. They have big hard drives, CPUs with huge fans, powerful graphics cards, and so do not fit into a peaceful living room. On the flip side, a thin client (a machine with very little CPU power and no hard disk of its own) is silent but not powerful enough to run GNOME or OpenOffice.org.

The solution is to have your powerful machine locked away in a cupboard somewhere with a Wi-Fi connection attached and your quiet thin client sitting in the lounge also on the Wi-Fi link. The thin client connects to the powerful machine and runs all its programs from there, with all the graphics being relayed over the network.

With Fedora, this is easy to do. On the server side (the powerful machine), you need to check one box, and on the client side (the less-powerful machine), you need to check another box. We will start with the server side. Select System Settings, Login Screen; then select the XDMCP tab and click Enable XDMCP. On the client side, select System Settings, Login Screen; then select the Security tab and click the Allow Running XDMCP Chooser from the Login Screen. You should also make sure the Show Actions Menu box is checked.

Now, from the client side, log out from your desktop so that you return to the Fedora login screen. When it prompts you for your username, press F10. A menu appears with an option labeled XDMCP Chooser. Select that and a new dialog box appears with a list of local XDMCP servers that are willing to accept your connection—you should see your server in there. Select it and click Connect; you will see a login screen from that server, inviting you to log in. You need, of course, a valid account on the server to be able to log in; however, that is the only thing you need.

As you can see, because XDMCP is so core to the X Window System, it is easy to set up. However, as you will find as you use it, XDMCP is very slow—even on a Gigabit Ethernet network, it chews up a substantial percentage of bandwidth. It is also insecure. Anyone can monitor what you are doing with very little work. Because of these two flaws, XDMCP should never be used outside a trusted network.

VNC

The next step up from XDMCP is VNC, which was developed at AT&T's Cambridge Research Laboratory in England. VNC is widespread in the Linux world and, to a lesser extent, in the Windows world. Its main advantage is its widespread nature: Nearly all Linux distributions bundle VNC, and clients are available for a wide selection of platforms.

By default, Fedora installs the VNC server component but not the client component. Go to the Add or Remove Packages dialog box and select System Tools. Then select vnc to install the client, go to Network Servers, and select vnc-server to install the server.

With that done, all that remains is to tell Fedora who should be allowed to connect to your session. This is done from the Remote Desktop option on the Preferences menu. By default, your desktop is not shared, so check Allow Other Users to View Your Desktop to share it. You should also check Allow Other Users to Control Your Desktop; otherwise, people can see what you are doing but not interact with the desktop—which is not very helpful.

The second set of options on that screen is important. If you are using this as a remote way to connect to your own desktop, deselect Ask You for Confirmation. If this is not done, when you try to connect from your remote location, Fedora pops a message box up on the local machine asking Should this person be allowed to connect?. Because you are not there to click Yes, the connection fails. If you want to let someone else remotely connect to your system, keep this box enabled so that you know when people are connecting. You should always enter a password, no matter who might connect. VNC, like XDMCP, should not be considered secure over the Internet, or even on untrusted networks.

Reference

- ▶ http://www.openssh.com/—The home page of the OpenSSH implementation of SSH that Fedora Core Linux uses. It is run by the same team as OpenBSD, a secure BSD-based operating system.

- ▶ http://www.realvnc.com/—The home page of the team that made VNC at AT&T's Cambridge Research Laboratory. It has since started RealVNC Ltd., a company dedicated to developing and supporting VNC.

- ▶ http://www.tightvnc.com/—Here you can find an alternative to VNC called TightVNC that has several key advances over the stock VNC release. The most important feature is that TightVNC can use SSH for encryption, guaranteeing security.

- ▶ http://www.nomachine.com/—Another alternative to VNC is in the pipeline, called NX. The free implementation, FreeNX, is under heavy development at the time of writing but promises to work much faster than VNC.

One book on SSH that stands out from the crowd is known as "The Snail Book" because of the picture on the cover. It covers the entire SSH suite and is called *SSH: The Secure Shell* (O'Reilly), ISBN: 0-596-00011-1.

CHAPTER 16

Xen

Xen is a powerful new virtualization system that enables you to run multiple operating systems on one computer. If you have ever used virtualization software such as VMware or Virtual PC, you have an idea how Xen works, except that it is faster, more powerful, and, of course, completely free.

This chapter contains an introduction to the world of Xen: how it differs from normal virtualization solutions, how you can install it on your Fedora machine, and how to get it configured to best suit your environment.

Why Virtualization Is a Smart Idea

The last few years have seen an incredible growth in the market for *blade* servers—high-performance, low-cost, space-saving servers that can be hooked together to form massive computing networks. These server farms provide a terrific amount of power for a relatively small budget, but the main problem with them is that distributing workload makes idle servers much more likely. For example, server A is a monolithic server: It has four CPUs, 4GB RAM, and so on, and runs both your database and web servers. If your database server is quiet but your web server is overrun with requests, it simply gives more resources to the web server. The downside here is that running multiple servers on one computer is insecure—a hole in your web server (hardly an uncommon thing) would also expose your database server. Now imagine that situation in which there are two servers: one running a database and the other running the web server. In this scenario, the database blade server would stand idle while the web server is swamped with requests.

If you think this problem is quite rare, you ought to know that experts estimate that current server farm utilization is as low as 15%, which means that 85% of your computers are likely to be sitting around waiting for something to do. Virtualization allows you to create multiple independent virtual machine (*VM*) operating systems that run on a single server. If one VM needs more processing power, the server simply allocates it more resources. More importantly, because the VMs are completely isolated from each other—they are literally treated as independent hardware—a security hole in one server cannot affect the others.

Moving your server farm from 15% to 80% or higher utilization either means your users get a much faster and more reliable service, or you suddenly have a huge amount of hardware that you can sell or keep offline until needed. Either way, it is a huge cost savings, which makes virtualization the easiest way to cut your IT budget.

Virtualization Versus Paravirtualization

The method in which operating systems are kept isolated is quite simple: They really do each get a virtual machine. When you create a new VM, it is allocated a chunk of RAM all to itself, and lives completely self-contained from the outside world. VMware even has a virtual BIOS to complete the illusion. If your VM wants to communicate to other VMs on the same computer, it has to do so over a TCP/IP network connection, just like any other machine. In fact, when you install an operating system on a virtual machine, it cannot even tell that it *is* a virtual machine because it looks identical to raw hardware.

The problem with this type of virtualization is that it is very slow. For example, the VM has to access hardware frequently (to save files, show a display, and so on), but of course it cannot access the hardware directly because doing so would interfere with other VMs. Instead, its requests have to be translated and rerouted to the host operating system (*OS*), where they are handled. Similarly, if the VM tries to execute any special CPU instructions that would reveal that the VM is actually a virtual machine, the host OS has to stop those instructions and fake the answer so that the VM is not any wiser (a technique known as *binary patching*).

The solution is to move from virtualization to paravirtualization—the technique that Xen uses. Linux is open source, so the Xen developers modified the Linux source code so that Linux becomes aware of its existence as a virtual machine. When the virtual Linux needs access to the hardware, it just asks Xen for permission. The difference is huge: You can expect a normal VM to run at about 50% of the speed of a native machine, whereas a Xen virtual machine can run up to about 95%, simply by removing the need for binary patching and other virtual hacks.

The downside to Xen is that the source code has to be patched, which rules out closed-source operating systems. VMware runs Windows XP on Linux out of the box, but Xen cannot. That said, the new chips from Intel and AMD include virtualization on hardware, which enables Xen to run unmodified Windows at full speed on top of Linux. Without this technology, Xen can use only a modified, open source distribution, such as Linux, NetBSD, or FreeBSD.

How Xen Works

Xen is actually a very small operating system that has the sole goal of managing the resources of virtual machines. On top of the Xen OS runs what would previously have been called the *host* OS—the main operating system for the machine. Unlike VMware, the host OS (known as *domain 0* or just *dom0* in Xen terminology) is a virtual machine, but has special privileges assigned to it so that it is more responsive.

The domain 0 VM is where you control Xen, and where you start other guest VMs—known as *unprivileged domains* or *domU*. You can start as many as you want, with the only real limit being the amount of RAM in your machine. Because the domU OS is fully aware of its status as a Xen virtual machine, Xen lets you change the amount of RAM in a VM while it's running, with the exception that you can't go above the initial allocation of RAM.

Fedora Linux specifies a minimum system requirement of 256MB RAM, which means that if you are to run Fedora on top of Fedora, you need at least 512MB RAM. Keeping in mind that Xen uses a very small amount of RAM for itself, you should ideally have at least 768MB of RAM to be able to run two operating systems side by side at full speed.

Note that if you have tried Xen on old versions of Fedora, you no longer need to disable SELinux to get Xen to work.

Installing Xen

The first step is to convert your current OS to a virtualized guest OS. This is actually a very easy thing to do because, as discussed, domain 0 has special privileges—such as the capability to access hardware directly. As a result, you do not have to reformat your machine: dom0 reads straight from the disk, uses the graphics card, uses the sound card, and so on.

To get started, go to Applications, Add/Remove Software. From the window that appears, choose List view, and then select the following packages: `kernel-xen`, `vnc`, and `xen`. The `kernel-xen` package provides a Linux kernel that is configured to run on top of Xen without any special privileges, as well as a Linux kernel designed to be used as dom0 so it can access hardware directly. The `vnc` package is there to make VM management much easier. Finally, the `xen` package gives you all the tools you need to create and manage virtual machines. Along with these packages, there are several other dependencies that Fedora will automatically resolve for you, so just go ahead and install all the packages.

Because you have installed two new kernels, Fedora updates your Grub boot configuration to make them bootable, but leaves your original, non-Xen kernel as the default. Switch to root and bring up `/boot/grub/grub.conf` in your favorite text editor. Look for the line `"default=2"` and change it to read `"default=0"`. This might vary on your machine—set it to the position of the Xen hypervisor kernel in the `grub.conf` file, remembering that Grub counts from 0 rather than 1. That is, the first OS in the list is considered to be number 0. Note that you should not set the guest kernel as the default because it will *not* boot—it is designed only to be created on top of the hypervisor (dom0).

Save your changes and reboot, making sure that your new hypervisor kernel is the one that boots. Your system should restart as normal, and you will probably not notice anything different beyond a smattering of "XEN" at the very beginning of the boot phase. But when you are back in control, open a terminal and run **uname -r**—it should tell you that you are running the Xen hypervisor kernel.

At this point, you are already running as a virtual machine on top of the Xen kernel, but there is no way for you to communicate with the Xen kernel and thus manipulate the virtual machines on the system. To do that, you need to start the Xen daemon, which provides the link between dom0 (where you are working) and the Xen kernel underneath.

Run **ps aux | grep xend**—if you do not see xend in there, you need to start it yourself by switching to root with su - and then running **service xend start**. Now run the command **xm list**, which prints out a list of all the virtual machines that are running and how much RAM they have allocated—you should see Domain-0, which is your current system, in the list.

Setting Up Guest Operating Systems

The output from xm list probably shows that domain 0 is taking up all the RAM on your system, which means there is no room to create a new guest OS. Fortunately, you can resize that memory usage downward to make space: Run the command **xm mem-set Domain-0 256** to have domain 0 use 256MB RAM. This is the bare minimum for a Fedora install, so expect some slowdown—if you have more than 512MB RAM, we recommend you allocate more to each VM.

Creating a domU VM on Fedora is handled with the xenguest-install.py script, which you should run as root. You are asked to do the following things:

1. Give your virtual machine a friendly name (for example, FCUnleashed) so that you can differentiate between it and other virtual machines.

2. Allocate it some RAM, with the minimum being 256MB; more is better.

3. Choose where it should save its files. Xen uses a loopback filesystem so that all of a VM's files are stored in just one file on domain 0. Enter something like **/home/paul/ vms/fcu.img**.

4. Select how big the virtual disk should be. For a basic install, around 4.0GB should be enough.

5. Set the install location (the place from which Fedora should install). This needs to be an online resource, so choose a server from http://mirrors.fedoraproject.org/ publicist/Fedora/8.

Now sit back and wait. Downloading the necessary files can take quite a while, depending on your connection speed.

Once your files have been downloaded, the normal Fedora installer (Anaconda) will start, and will ask whether you want to install using text mode or VNC—choose Start VNC so that you have a graphical install. Xen's guests do not have direct access to the hardware, which means they have nowhere to display graphics. VNC lets you have your Xen VM render its graphics to your dom0 display inside a window, which means you can work with multiple VMs simultaneously. When you select Start VNC, you are prompted to enter a password. Click OK and you see the VNC address to which you need to connect. This address should look something like 10.0.0.1:1, where the :1 is the number of the VNC display.

Back on dom0, you should have installed VNC Viewer at the start of this chapter, so go to Applications, Accessories, VNC Viewer. Now enter that address (including the :1 or whatever it is for you) and click Connect. Enter your password when prompted. VNC starts and you see the Fedora installer. Depending on the resolution of your screen, the Fedora installer might not fit entirely on the screen; in that case, you have to use the scrollbars to get around.

The installer is as normal from here on in, except of course that it is using the virtual disk you created earlier so you have only a small amount of space. It might refer to your hard disk as something like /dev/xvda—do not worry about that.

Runtime Configuration

Now that your guest OS is up and running, you can start trying out more of the features of the xm command on dom0. You have already seen xm mem-set, which alters the amount of memory allocated to a machine. This works because the domU VM is aware of its virtualized state and can therefore handle having memory taken away. This extends further: You can use xm shutdown yourvm to have Xen politely request the VM to shutdown. On Linux, this goes through the whole shutdown sequence properly, ensuring that the machine is cleanly terminated. If you want an immediate shutdown, use xm destroy yourvm, but make sure the virtual machine is in a safe state first—if you have a text file open and unsaved, for example, it will be lost.

The xm command can also be used to save snapshots of a virtual machine, rather than just switching them off. To do this, use xm save yourvm yourvm.state. That command essentially saves the RAM of the *yourvm* VM (change *yourvm* to whatever you called your virtual machine) to a file and then turns off the VM. To restore a saved state, just use xm restore yourvm.state. If you want to create a virtual machine from a configuration file, use xm create -c yourconfig. Note that Xen searches the directory /etc/xen for configuration files, and that each VM must have a unique name assigned to it and set in the configuration file.

You can connect to the console of any virtual machine by running xm console yourvm. To exit from a console, press Ctrl+] (Control + right bracket). This does not shut down the VM; the VM continues to run, but you are no longer connected to it and have to use xm connect to reconnect.

> **TIP**
>
> The configuration files in /etc/xen are in text format and so are easily edited. For example, if you want to change the number of CPUs a VM sees, look for the vcpus setting. Note that these are *virtual* CPUs rather than real ones—you can set this to 8 and have your guest see eight CPUs, even if your actual machine has just one. This is a great way to test a cluster without going beyond your desktop!

> **Related Fedora and Xen Commands**
>
> The following commands are useful for working with Xen on Fedora:
>
> ▶ virt-manager—Red Hat's new graphical Xen management system
>
> ▶ vncviewer—Lets you connect to the graphical output of a Xen VM
>
> ▶ xend—Starts and stops the Xen daemon without using the service command
>
> ▶ xenguest-install.py—A helpful script that generates configuration files for you
>
> ▶ xm—Lets you manipulate the state of virtual machines while they are running

Reference

▶ **http://www.xensource.com**—A company (run by some of the Xen engineers) that offers help and support for Xen, as well as produces XenOptimizer to ease enterprise deployment.

▶ **http://www.cl.cam.ac.uk/Research/SRG/netos/xen**—The Xen home page at the Cambridge computer laboratory.

PART IV

Fedora As a Server

Apache Web Server Management

This chapter covers the configuration and management of the Apache web server. The chapter includes an overview of some of the major components of the server and discussions of text-based and graphical server configuration. You will see how to start, stop, and restart Apache, using the command line and the Red Hat utilities included with Fedora. The chapter begins with some introductory information about this popular server and then shows you how to install, configure, and start using Apache.

About the Apache Web Server

Apache is the most widely used web server on the Internet today, according to a Netcraft survey of active websites in October 2007, which is shown in Table 17.1.

TABLE 17.1   Netcraft Survey Results (October 2007)

Web Server	Number	Percentage
Apache	68,155,320	47.73%
Microsoft*	53,017,735	37.13%
Google	7,763,516	5.44%
SunONE	2,262,019	1.58%
lighttpd	1,515,963	1.08%

*All web server products

Note that these statistics do not reflect Apache's use on internal networks, known as *intranets*.

The name *Apache* appeared during the early development of the software because it was "a patchy" server, made up of patches for the freely available source code of the NCSA

HTTPd web server. For a while after the NCSA HTTPd project was discontinued, a number of people wrote a variety of patches for the code, to either fix bugs or add features they wanted. A lot of this code was floating around and people were freely sharing it, but it was completely unmanaged.

After a while, Brian Behlendorf and Cliff Skolnick set up a centralized repository of these patches, and the Apache project was born. The project is still composed of a small core group of programmers, but anyone is welcome to submit patches to the group for possible inclusion in the code.

There's been a surge of interest in the Apache project over the past several years, partially buoyed by a new interest in open source on the part of enterprise-level information services. It's also due in part to crippling security flaws found in Microsoft's Internet Information Services (IIS); the existence of malicious web task exploits; and operating system and networking vulnerabilities to the now-infamous Code Red, Blaster, and Nimda worms. IBM made an early commitment to support and use Apache as the basis for its web offerings and has dedicated substantial resources to the project because it makes more sense to use an established, proven web server.

In mid-1999, The Apache Software Foundation was incorporated as a nonprofit company. A board of directors, elected on an annual basis by the ASF members, oversees the company. This company provides a foundation for several open-source software development projects, including the Apache Web Server project.

The best places to find out about Apache are the Apache Software Foundation's website, http://www.apache.org/, and the Apache Week website, http://www.apacheweek.com/, where you can subscribe to receive Apache Week by email to keep up on the latest developments in the project, keep abreast of security advisories, and research bug fixes.

> **TIP**
>
> You'll find an overview of Apache in the Apache Software Foundation's frequently asked questions (FAQs) at http://httpd.apache.org/docs-2.2/faq/. In addition to extensive online documentation, you can also find the complete documentation for Apache in the HTML directory of your Apache server. You can access this documentation by looking at http://localhost/manual/index.html on your new Fedora system with one of the web browsers included on your system. You'll need to have Apache running on your system!

Fedora ships with Apache 2.2, and the server (named httpd) is included on this book's CD-ROMs and DVD. You can obtain the latest version of Apache as an RPM installation file from a Fedora FTP server; upgrade using up2date, yum, or apt-get; or get the source code from the Apache website and, in true Linux tradition, build it for yourself.

To determine the version of Apache included with your system, use the web server's -V command-line option like this:

```
$ /usr/sbin/httpd -V
Server version: Apache/2.2.4 (Unix)
Server built:   April 10 2007 12:47:09
```

```
Server's Module Magic Number: 20051115:4
Architecture:    32-bit
Server MPM: Prefork
  threaded: no
    forked: yes (variable process count)
Server compiled with....
```

The output displays the version number, build date and time, platform, and various options used during the build. You can use the -v option to see terser version information.

Installing the Apache Server

You can install Apache through Pirut, from your own RPMs, or build it yourself from source code. The Apache source builds on just about any Unix-like operating system and on Win32. If you elect to install the Web Server group of files when first installing Fedora, Apache and related software and documentation in 17 packages are installed automatically.

If you're about to install a new version of Apache, you should shut down the old server. Even if it's unlikely that the old server will interfere with the installation procedure, shutting it down ensures that there will be no problems. If you don't know how to stop Apache, see the "Starting and Stopping Apache" section later in this chapter.

Installing Through Pirut

Although the "Web Server" category was available during install, it's often best to install Fedora clean of any services so that you minimize your attack vectors out of the box. As soon as Fedora is installed, you can use Pirut to add Apache by choosing Web Server from the Servers category.

However, you might find it useful to use the List tab rather than the Browse tab, because all the Apache modules start with "mod" to help you find them easily. Fedora ships with many Apache modules, some of which are discussed in the following sections. However, only a handful are enabled by default—you need to use Pirut to install and activate them.

Installing from the RPM

You can find the Apache RPM on the Fedora installation media, on the Fedora FTP server, or at one of its many mirror sites. Check the Fedora site as often as possible to download updates as they become available. Updated RPM files usually contain important bug and security fixes. When an updated version is released, install it as quickly as possible to keep your system secure.

> **NOTE**
>
> Check the Apache site for security reports. Browse to http://httpd.apache.org/security_report.html for links to security vulnerabilities for Apache 1.3, 2.0, and 2.2. Subscribe to a support list or browse through up-to-date archives of all Apache mailing lists at http://httpd.apache.org/mail/ (for various articles) or http://httpd.apache.org/lists.html (for comprehensive and organized archives).

If you want the most recent, experimental version of Apache for testing, check Red Hat's Rawhide distribution, which is also available on the Fedora FTP server (http://download.fedora.redhat.com/pub/fedora/linux/core/development/). This distribution is experimental and always contains the latest versions of all RPMs. However, note that the Apache package might depend on new functionality available in other RPMs. Therefore, you might need to install many new RPMs to be able to use packages from Rawhide. If you still want to use an Apache version from the Rawhide distribution for testing, a better option might be to download the source code RPM (SRPM) and compile it yourself. That way, you avoid dependencies on other new packages.

CAUTION

You should be wary of installing experimental packages, and never install them on production servers (that is, servers used in "real life"). Very carefully test the packages beforehand on a host that isn't connected to a network!

After you have obtained an Apache RPM, you can install it with the command-line rpm tool by typing the following:

```
rpm -Uvh latest_apache.rpm
```

where `latest_apache.rpm` is the name of the latest Apache RPM.

The Apache RPM installs files in the following directories:

▶ /etc/httpd/conf—This directory contains the Apache configuration file, httpd.conf. See the section "Configuring Apache for Peak Performance" later in this chapter for more information.

▶ /etc/rc.d/—The tree under this directory contains the system startup scripts. The Apache RPM installs a startup script named httpd for the web server under the /etc/rc.d/init.d directory. This script, which you can use to start and stop the server from the command line, also automatically starts and stops the server when the computer is halted, started, or rebooted.

▶ /var/www—The RPM installs the default server icons, Common Gateway Interface (CGI) programs, and HTML files in this location. If you want to keep web content elsewhere, you can do so by making the appropriate changes in the server configuration files.

▶ /var/www/manual/—If you've installed the apache-manual RPM, you'll find a copy of the Apache documentation in HTML format here. You can access it with a web browser by going to http://localhost/manual/.

▶ /usr/share/man—Fedora's Apache RPM also contains man pages, which are placed underneath this directory. For example, the httpd man page is in section 8 of the man directory.

▶ /usr/bin—Some of the utilities from the Apache package are placed here—for example, the htpasswd program, which is used for generating authentication password files.

▶ /var/log/httpd—The server log files are placed in this directory. By default, there are two important log files (among several others): access_log and error_log. However, you can define any number of custom logs containing a variety of information. See the "Logging" section, later in this chapter, for more detail.

▶ /usr/src/redhat/SOURCES/—This directory might contain a tar archive containing the source code for Apache and, in some cases, patches for the source. You must have installed the Apache SRPM for these files to be created.

When Apache is running, it also creates the file httpd.pid, containing the process ID of Apache's parent process in the /var/run/ directory.

> **NOTE**
>
> If you are upgrading to a newer version of Apache, RPM doesn't write over your current configuration files. RPM moves your current files and appends the extension .rpmnew to them. For example, srm.conf becomes srm.conf.rpmnew.

Building the Source Yourself

There are several ways to obtain the source code for Apache. Fedora provides SRPMs containing the source of Apache, which include patches to make it work better with the Fedora distribution. The most up-to-date, stable binary version for Fedora can be installed through Pirut, or by installing a source RPM from Fedora's source repository. When you install one of these SRPMs, a tar archive containing the Apache source is created in /usr/src/redhat/SOURCES/.

After you have the tar file, you must unroll it in a temporary directory, such as /tmp. Unrolling this tar file creates a directory called apache_*version_number*, where *version_number* is the version you've downloaded (for example, apache_1.3.21).

You can also download the source directly from http://www.apache.org/. The latest version at the time of this writing, 2.2.6, is a 6MB compressed tape archive, and the latest pre-2.0 version of Apache is 1.3.31. Although many sites continue to use the older version (for script and other compatibility reasons), many new sites are migrating to or starting out with the latest stable version.

> **TIP**
>
> As with many software packages distributed in source code form for Linux and other Unix-like operating systems, extracting the source code results in a directory that contains a README and an INSTALL file. Be sure to peruse the INSTALL file before attempting to build and install the software.

Using `./configure` to Build Apache

To build Apache the easy way, run the `./configure` script in the directory just created. You can provide it with a `--prefix` argument to install it in a directory other than the default, which is `/usr/local/apache/`. Use this command:

```
# ./configure --prefix=/preferred/directory/
```

This generates the makefile that's used to compile the server code.

Next, type **make** to compile the server code. After the compilation is complete, type **make install** as root to install the server. You can now configure the server via the configuration files. See the "Runtime Server Configuration Settings" section, later in this chapter, for more information.

TIP

A safer way to install a new version of Apache from source is to use the `ln` command to create symbolic links of the existing file locations (listed in the "Installing from the RPM" section earlier in this chapter) to the new locations of the files. This method is safer because the default install locations are different from those used when the RPM installs the files. Failure to use this installation method could result in your web server process not being started automatically at system startup.

Another safe way to install a new version of Apache is to first back up any important configuration directories and files (such as `/etc/httpd`) and then use the `rpm` command to remove the server. You can then install and test your new version and, if needed, easily restore your original server and settings.

It is strongly recommended that you use Fedora's RPM version of Apache until you really know what happens at system startup. No "uninstall" option is available when installing Apache from source!

Apache File Locations After a Build and Install

Files are placed in various subdirectories of `/usr/local/apache` (or whatever directory you specified with the `--prefix` parameter) if you build the server from source.

The following is a list of the directories used by Apache, as well as brief comments on their usage:

- ▶ `/usr/local/apache/conf`—This contains several subdirectories and the Apache configuration file, `httpd.conf`. See the "Editing `httpd.conf`" section, later in this chapter, to learn more about configuration files.

- ▶ `/usr/local/apache`—The `cgi-bin`, `icons`, and `htdocs` subdirectories contain the CGI programs, standard icons, and default HTML documents, respectively.

- ▶ `/usr/local/apache/bin`—The executable programs are placed in this directory.

- ▶ `/usr/local/apache/logs`—The server log files are placed in this directory. By default, there are two log files—`access_log` and `error_log`—but you can define any number of custom logs containing a variety of information (see the "Logging" section later in this chapter). The default location for Apache's logs as installed by Fedora is /var/log/httpd.

A Quick Guide to Getting Started with Apache

Setting up, testing a web page, and starting Apache with Fedora can be accomplished in just a few steps. First, make sure that Apache is installed on your system. Either select it during installation or install the server and related RPM files.

Next, set up a home page for your system by editing (as root) the file named index.html under the /var/http/www/html directory on your system. Make a backup copy of the original page or www directory before you begin so that you can restore your web server to its default state if necessary.

Start Apache (again, as root) by using the service command with the keywords httpd and start, like this:

```
# service httpd start
```

You can also use the httpd script under the /etc/rc.d/init.d/ directory, like this:

```
# /etc/rc.d/init.d/httpd start
```

You can then check your home page by running a favorite browser and using localhost, your system's hostname, or its Internet Protocol (IP) address in the URL. For example, with the links text browser, use a command line like this:

```
# links http://localhost/
```

For security reasons, you shouldn't start and run Apache as root if your host is connected to the Internet or a company intranet. Fortunately, Apache is set to run as the user and group apache no matter how it's started (by the User and Group settings in /etc/httpd/httpd.conf). Despite this safe default, Apache should be started and managed by the user named apache, defined in /etc/passwd as:

```
apache:x:48:48:Apache:/var/www:/sbin/nologin
```

After you are satisfied with your website, use the setup (select Services) or ntsysv (select httpd) command to ensure that Apache is started properly.

Starting and Stopping Apache

At this point, you have installed your Apache server with its default configuration. Fedora provides a default home page named index.html as a test under the /var/www/html/usage directory. The proper way to run Apache is to set system initialization to have the server run after booting, network configuration, and any firewall configuration. See Chapter 11, "Automating Tasks," for more information about how Fedora boots.

It is time to start Apache up for the first time. The following sections show how to start and stop Apache, or configure Fedora to start or not start Apache when booting.

Starting the Apache Server Manually

You can start Apache from the command line of a text-based console or X terminal window, and you must have root permission to do so. The server daemon, httpd, recognizes several command-line options you can use to set some defaults, such as specifying where httpd reads its configuration directives. The Apache httpd executable also understands other options that enable you to selectively use parts of its configuration file, specify a different location of the actual server and supporting files, use a different configuration file (perhaps for testing), and save startup errors to a specific log. The -v option causes Apache to print its development version and quit. The -V option shows all the settings that were in effect when the server was compiled.

The -h option prints the following usage information for the server (assuming that you're running the command as root):

```
# httpd -h
Usage: httpd [-D name] [-d directory] [-f file]
             [-C "directive"] [-c "directive"]
             [-k start¦restart¦graceful¦stop]
             [-v] [-V] [-h] [-l] [-L] [-t]
Options:
  -D name            : define a name for use in <IfDefine name> directives
  -d directory       : specify an alternate initial ServerRoot
  -f file            : specify an alternate ServerConfigFile
  -C "directive"     : process directive before reading config files
  -c "directive"     : process directive after reading config files
  -e level           : show startup errors of level (see LogLevel)
  -E file            : log startup errors to file
  -v                 : show version number
  -V                 : show compile settings
  -h                 : list available command-line options (this page)
  -l                 : list compiled in modules
  -L                 : list available configuration directives
  -t -D DUMP_VHOSTS  : show parsed settings (currently only vhost settings)
  -t                 : run syntax check for config files
```

Other options include listing Apache's *static modules*, or special, built-in independent parts of the server, along with options that can be used with the modules. These options are called *configuration directives* and are commands that control how a static module works. Note that Apache also includes nearly 50 *dynamic modules*, or software portions of the server that can be optionally loaded and used while the server is running.

The -t option is used to check your configuration files. It's a good idea to run this check before restarting your server, especially if you've made changes to your configuration files.

Such tests are important because a configuration file error can result in your server shutting down when you try to restart it.

> **NOTE**
>
> When you build and install Apache from source and don't use Fedora's Apache RPM files, start the server manually from the command line as root (such as when testing). You do this for two reasons:
>
> ▶ The standalone server uses the default HTTP port (port 80), and only the superuser can bind to Internet ports that are lower than 1024.
>
> ▶ Only processes owned by root can change their UID and GID as specified by Apache's User and Group directives. If you start the server under another UID, it runs with the permissions of the user starting the process.
>
> Note that although some of the following examples show how to start the server as root, you should do so only for testing after building and installing Apache. Fedora is set up to run web services as the apache user if you use Fedora RPM files to install Apache.

Using /etc/rc.d/init.d/httpd

Fedora uses the scripts in the /etc/rc.d/init.d directory to control the startup and shutdown of various services, including the Apache web server. The main script installed for the Apache web server is /etc/rc.d/init.d/httpd, although the actual work is done by the apachectl shell script included with Apache.

> **NOTE**
>
> /etc/rc.d/init.d/httpd is a shell script and isn't the same as the Apache server located in /usr/sbin. That is, /usr/sbin/httpd is the program executable file (the server); /etc/rc.d/init.d/httpd is a shell script that uses another shell script, apachectl, to control the server. See Chapter 11 for a description of some service scripts under /etc/rc.d/init.d and how the scripts are used to manage services such as httpd.

You can use the /etc/rc.d/init.d/httpd script and the following options to control the web server:

▶ start—The system uses this option to start the web server during bootup. You, as root, can also use this script to start the server.

▶ stop—The system uses this option to stop the server gracefully. You should use this script, rather than the kill command, to stop the server.

▶ reload—You can use this option to send the HUP signal to the httpd server to have it reread the configuration files after modification.

▶ restart—This option is a convenient way to stop and then immediately start the web server. If the httpd server isn't running, it is started.

▶ condrestart—The same as the restart parameter, except that it restarts the httpd server only if it's actually running.

▶ status—This option indicates whether the server is running; if it is, it provides the various PIDs for each instance of the server.

For example, to check on the status of your server, use the command

```
# /etc/rc.d/init.d/httpd status
```

This prints the following for me:

```
httpd (pid 15997 1791 1790 1789 1788 1787 1786 1785 1784 1781) is running...
```

This indicates that the web server is running; in fact, 10 instances of the server are currently running in this configuration.

In addition to the previous options, the httpd script also offers these features:

▶ help—Prints a list of valid options to the httpd script (which are passed onto the server as if called from the command line).

▶ configtest—A simple test of the server's configuration, which reports Status OK if the setup is correct. You can also use httpd's -t option to perform the same test, like this:

```
# httpd -t
```

▶ fullstatus—Displays a verbose status report.

▶ graceful—The same as the restart parameter, except that the configtest option is used first and open connections are not aborted.

TIP

Use the reload option if you're making many changes to the various server configuration files. This saves time when you're stopping and starting the server by having the system simply reread the configuration files.

Controlling Apache with Fedora's service Command

Instead of directly calling the /etc/rc.d/init.d/httpd script, you can use Red Hat's service command to start, stop, and restart Apache. The service command is used with the name of a service (listed under /etc/rc.d/init.d) and an optional keyword:

```
# service <name_of_script> <option>
```

For example, you can use `service` with `httpd` and any option discussed in the previous section, like so:

```
# service httpd restart
```

This restarts Apache if it's running or starts the server if it isn't running.

Controlling Apache with Fedora's `chkconfig` Command

The `chkconfig` command provides a command-line–based interface to Fedora's service scripts. The command can be used to list and control which software services are started, restarted, and stopped for a specific system state (such as when booting up, restarting, or shutting down) and runlevel (such as single-user mode, networking with multitasking, or graphical login with X).

For example, to view your system's current settings, take a look at Fedora's default runlevel as defined in the system initialization table `/etc/inittab` using the `grep` command:

```
# grep id: /etc/inittab
id:3:initdefault:
```

This example shows that this Fedora system boots to a text-based login without running X11. You can then use the `chkconfig` command to look at the behavior of Apache for that runlevel:

```
# chkconfig --list ¦ grep httpd
httpd           0:off   1:off   2:off   3:off   4:off   5:off   6:off
```

Here you can see that Apache is turned off for runlevels 3 and 5 (the only two practical runlevels in a default Fedora system, although you could create a custom runlevel 4 for Apache). Use `--level`, `httpd`, and the control keyword `on` to set Apache to automatically start when booting to runlevel 3:

```
# chkconfig --level 3 httpd on
```

You can then again use `chkconfig` to verify this setting:

```
# chkconfig --list ¦ grep httpd
httpd           0:off   1:off   2:off   3:on    4:off   5:off   6:off
```

To have Apache also start when your system is booted to a graphical login, again use `level`, `httpd`, and the control keyword `on`, but this time, specify runlevel 5 like so:

```
# chkconfig --level 5 httpd on
```

17

Again, to verify your system settings, use the following:

```
# chkconfig --list | grep httpd
httpd              0:off    1:off    2:off    3:on     4:off    5:on     6:off
```

Use the `off` keyword to stop Apache from starting at a particular runlevel.

Graphic Interface Configuration of Apache

Some of Apache's basic behavior can be configured with Red Hat's `system-config-httpd`, a GUI tool for the X Window System. This is an easy way to configure settings, such as Apache's user and group name, the location of PID and process lock files, or performance settings (such as the maximum number of connections), without manually editing configuration files.

CAUTION

If you use `system-config-httpd`, you shouldn't try to manually edit the `httpd.conf` file. Manual changes are overwritten by the GUI client if you again use `system-config-httpd`!

Launch this client by using your X desktop panel's Server Settings' HTTP Server menu item or from the command line of an X terminal window, like this:

```
$ system-config-httpd &
```

After you press Enter, you're asked to type the `root` password. You then see the main client window shown in Figure 17.1.

FIGURE 17.1   The `system-config-httpd` main dialog box provides access to basic configuration of the Apache web server.

In the Main tab, you can set the server name, indicate where to send email addressed to the webmaster, and set the port that Apache uses. If you want, you can also configure specific virtual hosts to listen on different ports.

Configuring Virtual Host Properties

In the Virtual Hosts tab, you can configure the properties of each virtual host. The Name list box contains a list of all virtual hosts operating in Apache. Edit a virtual host by opening the Virtual Hosts Properties dialog box, shown in Figure 17.2. You do this by highlighting the name of a virtual host in the Name list box of the Virtual Hosts tab and clicking the Edit button at the right of the tab. Use the General Options item in the Virtual Hosts Properties dialog box to configure basic virtual host settings.

FIGURE 17.2   `system-config-httpd`'s Virtual Host Properties dialog box gives you access to numerous options for configuring the properties of an Apache virtual host.

Click the Site Configuration listing in the General Options list of this dialog box to set defaults, such as which files are loaded by default when no files are specified (the default is `index.*`) in the URL.

The SSL listing in the General Options pane gives you access to settings used to enable or disable SSL, specify certificate settings, and define the SSL log filename and location. Select the Logging listing to access options for configuring where the error messages are logged, as well as where the transfer log file is kept and how much information is put in it.

Use the Environment Variables options to configure settings for the env_mod module, used to pass environment directives to CGI programs. The Directories section configures the directory options (such as whether CGI programs are allowed to run) as well as the order entries mentioned in the httpd.conf section.

Configuring the Server

The Server tab, shown in Figure 17.3, enables you to configure things such as where the lock file and the PID file are kept. In both cases, you should use the defaults. You can also configure the directory where any potential core dumps will be placed.

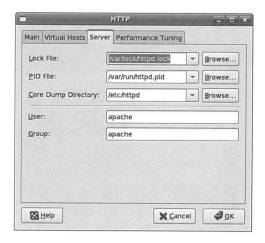

FIGURE 17.3   system-config-httpd's Server configuration tab.

Finally, you can set which user and group Apache is to run as. As mentioned in a previous note, for security reasons, you should run Apache as the user named apache and as a member of the group apache.

Configuring Apache for Peak Performance

Use the options in the Performance Tuning tab to configure Apache to provide peak performance in your system. Options in this tab set the maximum number of connections, connection timeouts, and number of requests per connection. When setting this number, keep in mind that for each connection to your server, another instance of the httpd program might be run, depending on how Apache is built. Each instance takes resources such as CPU time and memory. You can also configure details about each connection such as how long, in seconds, before a connection times out and how many requests each connection can make to the server. More tips on tuning Apache can be found in Chapter 31, "Performance Tuning."

Runtime Server Configuration Settings

At this point, the Apache server runs, but perhaps you want to change a behavior, such as the default location of your website's files. This section talks about the basics of configuring the server to work the way you want it to work.

Runtime configurations are stored in just one file—httpd.conf, which is found under the /etc/httpd/conf directory. This configuration file can be used to control the default behavior of Apache, such as the web server's base configuration directory (/etc/httpd), the name of the server's process identification (PID) file (/etc/httpd/run/httpd.pid), or its response timeout (300 seconds). Apache reads the data from the configuration file when started (or restarted). You can also cause Apache to reload configuration information with the command /etc/rc.d/init.d/httpd reload, which is necessary after making changes to its configuration file. (You learned how to accomplish this in the earlier section, "Starting and Stopping Apache.")

Runtime Configuration Directives

You perform runtime configuration of your server with configuration directives, which are commands that set options for the httpd daemon. The directives are used to tell the server about various options you want to enable, such as the location of files important to the server configuration and operation. Apache supports nearly 300 configuration directives with the following syntax:

```
directive option option...
```

Each directive is specified on a single line. See the following sections for some sample directives and how to use them. Some directives set only a value such as a filename, whereas others enable you to specify various options. Some special directives, called *sections*, look like HTML tags. Section directives are surrounded by angle brackets, such as <directive>. Sections usually enclose a group of directives that apply only to the directory specified in the section:

```
<Directory somedir/in/your/tree>
  directive option option
  directive option option
</Directory>
```

All sections are closed with a matching section tag that looks like this: </directive>. Note that section tags, like any other directives, are specified one per line.

TIP

After installing and starting Apache, you'll find an index of directives at http://localhost/manual/mod/directives.html.

17

Editing `httpd.conf`

Most of the default settings in the config file are okay to keep, particularly if you've installed the server in a default location and aren't doing anything unusual on your server. In general, if you don't understand what a particular directive is for, you should leave it set to the default value.

The following sections describe some of the configuration file settings you *might* want to change concerning operation of your server.

ServerRoot

The `ServerRoot` directive sets the absolute path to your server directory. This directive tells the server where to find all the resources and configuration files. Many of these resources are specified in the configuration files relative to the `ServerRoot` directory.

Your `ServerRoot` directive should be set to `/etc/httpd` if you installed the RPM or `/usr/local/apache` (or whatever directory you chose when you compiled Apache) if you installed from the source.

Listen

The `Listen` directive indicates on which port you want your server to run. By default, this is set to 80, which is the standard HTTP port number. You might want to run your server on another port—for example, when running a test server that you don't want people to find by accident. Don't confuse this with real security! See the "File System Authentication and Access Control" section for more information about how to secure parts of your web server.

User and Group

The `User` and `Group` directives should be set to the UID and group ID (*GID*) the server uses to process requests. In Fedora, set these configurations to a user with few or no privileges. In this case, they're set to user apache and group apache—a user defined specifically to run Apache. If you want to use a different UID or GID, be aware that the server runs with the permissions of the user and group set here. That means in the event of a security breach, whether on the server or (more likely) in your own CGI programs, those programs run with the assigned UID. If the server runs as root or some other privileged user, someone can exploit the security holes and do nasty things to your site. Always think in terms of the specified user running a command such as `rm -rf /` because that would wipe all files from your system. That should convince you that leaving apache as a user with no privileges is probably a good thing.

Instead of using names to specify the `User` and `Group` directives, you can specify them with the UID and GID numbers. If you use numbers, be sure that the numbers you specify correspond to the user and group you want and that they're preceded by the pound (#) symbol.

Here's how these directives look if specified by name:

```
User apache
Group apache
```

Here's the same specification by UID and GID:

```
User #48
Group #48
```

ServerAdmin

The ServerAdmin directive should be set to the address of the webmaster managing the
server. This address should be a valid email address or alias, such as
webmaster@gnulix.org, because this address is returned to a visitor when a problem
occurs on the server.

ServerName

The ServerName directive sets the hostname that the server returns. Set it to a fully qualified domain name (FQDN). For example, set it to www.your.domain rather than simply
www. This is particularly important if this machine will be accessible from the Internet
rather than just on your local network.

You don't need to set this unless you want a name other than the machine's canonical
name returned. If this value isn't set, the server will figure out the name by itself and set
it to its canonical name. However, you might want the server to return a friendlier
address, such as www.your.domain. Whatever you do, ServerName should be a real domain
name service (DNS) name for your network. If you're administering your own DNS,
remember to add an alias for your host. If someone else manages the DNS for you, ask
that person to set this name for you.

DocumentRoot

Set this directive to the absolute path of your document tree, which is the top directory
from which Apache serves files. By default, it's set to /var/www/html/usage. If you built
the source code yourself, DocumentRoot is set to /usr/local/apache/htdocs (if you didn't
choose another directory when you compiled Apache). Prior to version 1.3.4, this directive appears in srm.conf.

UserDir

The UserDir directive disables or enables and defines the directory (relative to a local
user's home directory) where that user can put public HTML documents. It's relative
because each user has her own HTML directory. This setting is disabled by default but can
be enabled to store user web content under any directory.

The default setting for this directive, if enabled, is public_html. Each user can create a
directory called public_html under her home directory, and HTML documents placed in

17

that directory are available as http://servername/~username, where *username* is the user-name of the particular user. Prior to version Apache version 1.3.4, this directive appears in srm.conf.

DirectoryIndex
The DirectoryIndex directive indicates which file should be served as the index for a directory, such as which file should be served if the URL http://servername/_ *SomeDirectory*/ is requested.

It's often useful to put a list of files here so that if index.html (the default value) isn't found, another file can be served instead. The most useful application of this is to have a CGI program run as the default action in a directory. If you have users who make their web pages on Windows, you might want to add index.htm as well. In that case, the directive would look like DirectoryIndex index.html index.cgi index.htm. Prior to version 1.3.4, this directive appears in srm.conf.

Apache Multiprocessing Modules

Apache version 2.0 and greater now uses a new internal architecture supporting multiprocessing modules (MPMs). These modules are used by the server for a variety of tasks, such as network and process management, and are compiled into Apache. MPMs enable Apache to work much better on a wider variety of computer platforms, and they can help improve server stability, compatibility, and scalability.

Apache can use only one MPM at any time. These modules are different from the base set included with Apache (see the "Apache Modules" section later in this chapter), but are used to implement settings, limits, or other server actions. Each module in turn supports numerous additional settings, called *directives*, which further refine server operation.

The internal MPM modules relevant for Linux include the following:

▶ mpm_common—A set of 20 directives common to all MPM modules

▶ prefork—A nonthreaded, preforking web server that works similar to earlier (1.3) versions of Apache

▶ worker—Provides a hybrid multiprocess multithreaded server

MPM enables Apache to be used on equipment with fewer resources, yet still handle massive numbers of hits and provide stable service. The worker module provides directives to control how many simultaneous connections your server can handle.

NOTE
Other MPMs are available for Apache related to other platforms, such as mpm_netware for NetWare hosts and mpm_winnt for Windows NT platforms. An MPM named perchild, which provides user ID assignment to selected daemon processes, is under development. For more information, browse to the Apache Software Foundation's home page at http://www.apache.org/.

Using `.htaccess` Configuration Files

Apache also supports special configuration files, known as `.htaccess` files. Almost any directive that appears in `httpd.conf` can appear in an `.htaccess` file. This file, specified in the `AccessFileName` directive in `httpd.conf` (or `srm.conf` prior to version 1.3.4) sets configurations on a per-directory (usually in a user directory) basis. As the system administrator, you can specify both the name of this file and which of the server configurations can be overridden by the contents of this file. This is especially useful for sites in which there are multiple content providers and you want to control what these people can do with their spaces.

To limit which server configurations the `.htaccess` files can override, use the `AllowOverride` directive. `AllowOverride` can be set globally or per directory. For example, in your `httpd.conf` file, you could use the following:

```
# Each directory to which Apache has access can be configured with respect
# to which services and features are allowed and/or disabled in that
# directory (and its subdirectories).
#
# First, it's best to configure the "default" to be a very restrictive set of
# permissions.
#
<Directory />
    Options FollowSymLinks
    AllowOverride None
</Directory>
```

Options Directives

To configure which configuration options are available to Apache by default, you must use the `Options` directive. `Options` can be None; All; or any combination of Indexes, Includes, FollowSymLinks, ExecCGI, and MultiViews. MultiViews isn't included in All and must be specified explicitly. These options are explained in Table 17.2.

TABLE 17.2   Switches Used by the `Options` Directive

Switch	Description
None	None of the available options are enabled for this directory.
All	All the available options, except for MultiViews, are enabled for this directory.
Indexes	In the absence of an `index.html` file or another `DirectoryIndex` file, a listing of the files in the directory is generated as an HTML page for display to the user.
Includes	Server-side includes (SSIs) are permitted in this directory. This can also be written as `IncludesNoExec` if you want to allow includes but don't want to allow the `exec` option in them. For security reasons, this is usually a good idea in directories over which you don't have complete control, such as `UserDir` directories.

TABLE 17.2   Continued

Switch	Description
FollowSymLinks	Allows access to directories that are symbolically linked to a document directory. You should never set this globally for the whole server and only rarely for individual directories. This option is a potential security risk because it allows web users to escape from the document directory and could potentially allow them access to portions of your file system where you really don't want people poking around.
ExecCGI	CGI programs are permitted in this directory, even if it isn't a directory defined in the ScriptAlias directive.
MultiViews	This is part of the mod_negotiation module. When a client requests a document that can't be found, the server tries to figure out which document best suits the client's requirements. See http://localhost/manuals/mod/_mod_negotiation.html for your local copy of the Apache documentation.

NOTE

These directives also affect all subdirectories of the specified directory.

AllowOverrides Directives

The AllowOverrides directives specify which configuration options .htaccess files can override. You can set this directive individually for each directory. For example, you can have different standards about what can be overridden in the main document root and in UserDir directories. This capability is particularly useful for user directories, where the user doesn't have access to the main server configuration files.

AllowOverrides can be set to All or any combination of Options, FileInfo, AuthConfig, and Limit. These options are explained in Table 17.3.

TABLE 17.3   Switches Used by the AllowOverrides Directive

Switch	Description
Options	The .htaccess file can add options not listed in the Options directive for this directory.
FileInfo	The .htaccess file can include directives for modifying document type information.
AuthConfig	The .htaccess file might contain authorization directives.
Limit	The .htaccess file might contain allow, deny, and order directives.

File System Authentication and Access Control

You're likely to include material on your website that isn't supposed to be available to the public. You must be able to lock out this material from public access and provide designated users with the means to unlock the material. Apache provides two methods for accomplishing this type of access: authentication and authorization. You can use different criteria to control access to sections of your website, including checking the client's IP address or hostname, or requiring a username and password. This section briefly covers some of these methods.

CAUTION

Allowing individual users to put web content on your server poses several important security risks. If you're operating a web server on the Internet rather than on a private network, you should read the WWW Security FAQ at http://www.w3.org/Security/Faq/www-security-faq.html.

Restricting Access with `allow` and `deny`

One of the simplest ways to limit access to website material is to restrict access to a specific group of users, based on IP addresses or hostnames. Apache uses the `allow` and `deny` directives to accomplish this.

Both directives take an address expression as a parameter. The following list provides the possible values and use of the address expression:

▶ `all` can be used to affect all hosts.

▶ A hostname or domain name, which can either be a partially or a fully qualified domain name; for example, `test.gnulix.org` or `gnulix.org`.

▶ An IP address, which can be either full or partial; for example, `212.85.67` or `212.85.67.66`.

▶ A network/netmask pair, such as `212.85.67.0/255.255.255.0`.

▶ A network address specified in classless inter-domain routing (CIDR) format; for example, `212.85.67.0/24`. This is the CIDR notation for the same network and netmask that were used in the previous example.

If you have the choice, it's preferable to base your access control on IP addresses rather than hostnames. Doing so results in faster performance because no name lookup is necessary—the IP address of the client is included with each request.

You also can use `allow` and `deny` to provide or deny access to website material based on the presence or absence of a specific environment variable. For example, the following statement denies access to a request with a context that contains an environment variable named NOACCESS:

```
deny from env=NOACCESS
```

The default behavior of Apache is to apply all the deny directives first and then check the allow directives. If you want to change this order, you can use the order statement. Apache might interpret the preceding statement in three different ways:

- ▶ Order deny,allow—The deny directives are evaluated before the allow directives. If a host isn't specifically denied access, it is allowed to access the resource. This is the default ordering if nothing else is specified.

- ▶ Order allow,deny—All allow directives are evaluated before deny directives. If a host isn't specifically allowed access, it is denied access to the resource.

- ▶ Order mutual-failure—Only hosts that are specified in an allow directive and at the same time do not appear in a deny directive are allowed access. If a host doesn't appear in either directive, it is not granted access.

Consider this example. Suppose that you want to allow only persons from within your own domain to access the server-status resource on your web. If your domain were named gnulix.org, you could add these lines to your configuration file:

```
<Location /server-status>
    SetHandler server-status
    Order deny,allow
    Deny from all
    Allow from gnulix.org
</Location>
```

Authentication

Authentication is the process of ensuring that visitors really are who they claim to be. You can configure Apache to allow access to specific areas of web content only to clients who can authenticate their identities. There are several methods of authentication in Apache; Basic Authentication is the most common (and the method discussed in this chapter).

Under Basic Authentication, Apache requires a user to supply a username and a password to access the protected resources. Apache then verifies that the user is allowed to access the resource in question. If the username is acceptable, Apache verifies the password. If the password also checks out, the user is authorized and Apache serves the request.

HTTP is a stateless protocol; each request sent to the server and each response is handled individually, and not in an intelligent fashion. Therefore, the authentication information must be included with each request. That means each request to a password-protected area is larger and therefore somewhat slower. To avoid unnecessary system use and delays, protect only those areas of your website that absolutely need protection.

To use Basic Authentication, you need a file that lists which users are allowed to access the resources. This file is composed of a plain text list containing name and password pairs. It looks very much like the /etc/passwd user file of your Linux system.

> **CAUTION**
>
> Don't use /etc/passwd as a user list for authentication. When you're using Basic Authentication, passwords and usernames are sent as base 64-encoded text from the client to the server—which is just as readable as plain text. The username and password are included in each request that is sent to the server. So anyone who might be snooping on Net traffic would be able to get this information!

To create a user file for Apache, use the htpasswd command. This is included with the Apache package. If you installed with the RPMs, it is in /usr/bin. Running htpasswd without any options produces the following output:

```
Usage:
        htpasswd [-cmdps] passwordfile username
        htpasswd -b[cmdps] passwordfile username password

        htpasswd -n[mdps] username
        htpasswd -nb[mdps] username password
 -c  Create a new file.
 -n  Don't update file; display results on stdout.
 -m  Force MD5 encryption of the password.
 -d  Force CRYPT encryption of the password (default).
 -p  Do not encrypt the password (plaintext).
 -s  Force SHA encryption of the password.
 -b  Use the password from the command line rather than prompting for it.
 -D  Delete the specified user.
On Windows, TPF, and NetWare systems, the '-m' flag is used by default.
On all other systems, the '-p' flag will probably not work.
```

As you can see, it isn't a very difficult command to use. For example, to create a new user file named gnulixusers with a user named wsb, you need to do something like this:

```
# htpasswd -c gnulixusers wsb
```

You would then be prompted for a password for the user. To add more users, you would repeat the same procedure, only omitting the -c flag.

You can also create user group files. The format of these files is similar to that of /etc/groups. On each line, enter the group name, followed by a colon, and then list all users, with each user separated by spaces. For example, an entry in a user group file might look like this:

```
gnulixusers: wsb pgj jp ajje nadia rkr hak
```

Now that you know how to create a user file, it's time to look at how Apache might use this to protect web resources.

To point Apache to the user file, use the `AuthUserFile` directive. `AuthUserFile` takes the file path to the user file as its parameter. If the file path isn't absolute—that is, beginning with a /—it's assumed that the path is relative to the `ServerRoot`. Using the `AuthGroupFile` directive, you can specify a group file in the same manner.

Next, use the `AuthType` directive to set the type of authentication to be used for this resource. Here, the type is set to `Basic`.

Now you need to decide to which realm the resource belongs. Realms are used to group different resources that share the same users for authorization. A realm can consist of just about any string. The realm is shown in the Authentication dialog box on the user's web browser. Therefore, you should set the realm string to something informative. The realm is defined with the `AuthName` directive.

Finally, state which type of user is authorized to use the resource. You do this with the `require` directive. The three ways to use this directive are as follows:

- If you specify `valid-user` as an option, any user in the user file is allowed to access the resource (that is, provided she also enters the correct password).

- You can specify a list of users who are allowed access with the `users` option.

- You can specify a list of groups with the `group` option. Entries in the group list, as well as the user list, are separated by a space.

Returning to the `server-status` example you saw earlier, instead of letting users access the `server-status` resource based on hostname, you can require the users to be authenticated to access the resource. You can do so with the following entry in the configuration file:

```
<Location /server-status>
    SetHandler server-status
    AuthType Basic
    AuthName "Server status"
    AuthUserFile "gnulixusers"
    Require valid-user
</Location>
```

Final Words on Access Control

If you have host-based as well as user-based access protection on a resource, the default behavior of Apache is to require the requester to satisfy both controls. But assume that you want to mix host-based and user-based protection and allow access to a resource if either method succeeds. You can do so by using the `satisfy` directive. You can set the `satisfy` directive to `All` (this is the default) or `Any`. When set to `All`, all access control methods must be satisfied before the resource is served. If `satisfy` is set to `Any`, the resource is served if any access condition is met.

Here's another access control example, again using the previous `server-status` example. This time, you combine access methods so that all users from the `Gnulix` domain are allowed access and those from outside the domain must identify themselves before gaining access. You can do so with the following:

```
<Location /server-status>
    SetHandler server-status
    Order deny,allow
    Deny from all
    Allow from gnulix.org
    AuthType Basic
    AuthName "Server status"
    AuthUserFile "gnulixusers"
    Require valid-user
    Satisfy Any
</Location>
```

There are more ways to protect material on your web server, but the methods discussed here should get you started and are probably more than adequate for most circumstances. Look to Apache's online documentation for more examples of how to secure areas of your site.

Apache Modules

The Apache core does relatively little; Apache gains its functionality from modules. Each module solves a well-defined problem by adding necessary features. By adding or removing modules to supply the functionality you want Apache to have, you can tailor the Apache server to suit your exact needs.

Nearly 50 core modules are included with the basic Apache server. Many more are available from other developers. The Apache Module Registry is a repository for add-on modules for Apache, and it can be found at http://modules.apache.org/. The modules are listed in the `modules` directory under `/etc/httpd/`, but the following directory is a link to the `/usr/lib/httpd/modules` directory where the modules reside (your list might look different):

mod_access.so	mod_cern_meta.so	mod_log_config.so	mod_setenvif.so
mod_actions.so	mod_cgi.so	mod_mime_magic.so	mod_speling.so
mod_alias.so	mod_dav_fs.so	mod_mime.so	mod_ssl.so
mod_asis.so	mod_dav.so	mod_negotiation.so	mod_status.so
mod_auth_anon.so	mod_dir.so	mod_perl.so	mod_suexec.so
mod_auth_dbm.so	mod_env.so	mod_proxy_connect.so	mod_unique_id.so
mod_auth_digest.so	mod_expires.so	mod_proxy_ftp.so	mod_userdir.so
mod_auth_mysql.so	mod_headers.so	mod_proxy_http.so	mod_usertrack.so
mod_auth_pgsql.so	mod_imap.so	mod_proxy.so	mod_vhost_alias.so
mod_auth.so	mod_include.so	mod_python.so	mod_autoindex.so
mod_info.so	mod_rewrite.so		

Each module adds new directives that can be used in your configuration files. As you might guess, there are far too many extra commands, switches, and options to describe them all in this chapter. The following sections briefly describe a subset of those modules available with Fedora's Apache installation.

mod_access

mod_access controls access to areas on your web server based on IP addresses, hostnames, or environment variables. For example, you might want to allow anyone from within your own domain to access certain areas of your web. Refer to the "File System Authentication and Access Control" section earlier in this chapter for more information.

mod_alias

mod_alias manipulates the URLs of incoming HTTP requests, such as when redirecting a client request to another URL. It also can map a part of the file system into your web hierarchy. For example,

```
Alias /images/ /home/wsb/graphics/
```

fetches contents from the /home/wsb/graphics directory for any URL that starts with /images/. This is done without the client knowing anything about it. If you use a redirection, the client is instructed to go to another URL to find the requested content. More advanced URL manipulation can be accomplished with mod_rewrite.

mod_asis

mod_asis is used to specify, in fine detail, all the information to be included in a response. This completely bypasses any headers Apache might have otherwise added to the response. All files with an .asis extension are sent straight to the client without any changes.

As a short example of the use of mod_asis, assume that you've moved content from one location to another on your site. Now you must inform people who try to access this resource that it has moved, as well as automatically redirect them to the new location. To provide this information and redirection, you can add the following code to a file with an .asis extension:

```
Status: 301 No more old stuff!
Location: http://gnulix.org/newstuff/
Content-type: text/html

<HTML>
 <HEAD>
  <TITLE>We've moved...</TITLE>
 </HEAD>
 <BODY>
   <P>We've moved the old stuff and now you'll find it at:</P>
```

```
  <A HREF="http://gnulix.org/newstuff/">New stuff</A>!.
 </BODY>
</HTML>
```

mod_auth

mod_auth uses a simple user authentication scheme, referred to as Basic Authentication, which is based on storing usernames and encrypted passwords in a text file. This file looks very much like Unix's /etc/passwd file and is created with the htpasswd command. Refer to the "File System Authentication and Access Control" section earlier in this chapter for more information about this subject.

mod_auth_anon

The mod_auth_anon module provides anonymous authentication similar to that of anonymous FTP. The module enables you to define user IDs of those who are to be handled as guest users. When such a user tries to log on, he is prompted to enter his email address as his password. You can have Apache check the password to ensure that it's a (more or less) proper email address. Basically, it ensures that the password contains an @ character and at least one . character.

mod_auth_dbm

mod_auth_dbm uses Berkeley DB files instead of text for user authentication files.

mod_auth_digest

mod_auth_digest builds upon the mod_auth module, and sends authentication data via the MD5 Digest Authentication process as defined in RFC 2617. Compared to using Basic Authentication, this is a much more secure way of sending user data over the Internet. Unfortunately, not all web browsers support this authentication scheme.

To create password files for use with mod_auth_dbm, you must use the htdigest utility. It has more or less the same functionality as the htpasswd utility. See the man page of htdigest for further information.

mod_autoindex

The mod_autoindex module dynamically creates a file list for directory indexing. The list is rendered in a user-friendly manner similar to those lists provided by FTP's built-in ls command.

mod_cgi

mod_cgi allows execution of CGI programs on your server. CGI programs are executable files residing in the /var/www/cgi-bin directory and are used to dynamically generate data (usually HTML) for the remote browser when requested.

mod_dir and mod_env

The mod_dir module is used to determine which files are returned automatically when a user tries to access a directory. The default is index.html. If you have users who create web pages on Windows systems, you should also include index.htm, like this:

```
DirectoryIndex index.html index.htm
```

mod_env controls how environment variables are passed to CGI and SSI scripts.

mod_expires

mod_expires is used to add an expiration date to content on your site by adding an Expires header to the HTTP response. Web browsers or cache servers don't cache expired content.

mod_headers

mod_headers is used to manipulate the HTTP headers of your server's responses. You can replace, add, merge, or delete headers as you see fit. The module supplies a Header directive for this. Ordering of the Header directive is important. A set followed by an unset for the same HTTP header removes the header altogether. You can place Header directives almost anywhere within your configuration files. These directives are processed in the following order:

1. Core server

2. Virtual host

3. <Directory> and .htaccess files

4. <Location>

5. <Files>

mod_info and mod_log_config

mod_info provides comprehensive information about your server's configuration. For example, it displays all the installed modules, as well as all the directives used in its configuration files.

mod_log_config defines how your log files should look. See the "Logging" section for further information about this subject.

mod_mime and mod_mime_magic

The mod_mime module tries to determine the MIME type of files from their extensions.

The mod_mime_magic module tries to determine the MIME type of files by examining portions of their content.

mod_negotiation

Using the mod_negotiation module, you can select one of several document versions that best suits the client's capabilities. You can select from among several options for which criteria to use in the negotiation process. You can, for example, choose among different languages, graphics file formats, and compression methods.

mod_proxy

mod_proxy implements proxy and caching capabilities for an Apache server. It can proxy and cache FTP, CONNECT, HTTP/0.9, and HTTP/1.0 requests. This isn't an ideal solution for sites that have a large number of users and therefore have high proxy and cache requirements. However, it's more than adequate for a small number of users.

mod_rewrite

mod_rewrite is the Swiss army knife of URL manipulation. It enables you to use powerful regular expressions to perform any imaginable manipulation of URLs. It provides rewrites, redirection, proxying, and so on. There's very little that you can't accomplish with this module.

> **TIP**
>
> See http://localhost/manual/misc/rewriteguide.html for a cookbook that gives you an in-depth explanation of what the mod_rewrite module is capable of.

17

mod_setenvif

mod_setenvif allows manipulation of environment variables. Using small snippets of text-matching code known as *regular expressions*, you can conditionally change the content of environment variables. The order in which SetEnvIf directives appear in the configuration files is important. Each SetEnvIf directive can reset an earlier SetEnvIf directive when used on the same environment variable. Be sure to keep that in mind when using the directives from this module.

mod_speling

mod_speling is used to enable correction of minor typos in URLs. If no file matches the requested URL, this module builds a list of the files in the requested directory and extracts those files that are the closest matches. It tries to correct only one spelling mistake.

mod_status

You can use mod_status to create a web page containing a plethora of information about a running Apache server. The page contains information about the internal status as well as statistics about the running Apache processes. This can be a great aid when you're trying to configure your server for maximum performance. It's also a good place to see whether something's amiss with your Apache server.

mod_ssl

mod_ssl provides Secure Sockets Layer (version 2 and 3) and transport layer security (version 1) support for Apache. At least 30 directives exist that deal with options for encryption and client authorization and that can be used with this module.

mod_unique_id

mod_unique_id generates a unique request identifier for every incoming request. This ID is put into the UNIQUE_ID environment variable.

mod_userdir

The mod_userdir module enables mapping of a subdirectory in each user's home directory into your web tree. The module provides several ways to accomplish this.

mod_vhost_alias

mod_vhost_alias supports dynamically configured mass virtual hosting, which is useful for Internet service providers (ISPs) with many virtual hosts. However, for the average user, Apache's ordinary virtual hosting support should be more than sufficient.

There are two ways to serve virtual hosts on an Apache server. You can have one IP address with multiple CNAMEs, or you can have multiple IP addresses with one name per address. Apache has different sets of directives to handle each of these options. (You learn more about virtual hosting in Apache in the next section of this chapter.)

Again, the available options and features for Apache modules are too numerous to describe completely in this chapter. You can find complete information about the Apache modules in the online documentation for the server included with Fedora or at the Apache Software Foundation's website.

Virtual Hosting

One of the more popular services to provide with a web server is to host a virtual domain. Also known as a *virtual host*, a virtual domain is a complete website with its own domain name, as if it were a standalone machine, but it's hosted on the same machine as other websites. Apache implements this capability in a simple way with directives in the httpd.conf configuration file.

Apache now can dynamically host virtual servers by using the mod_vhost_alias module you read about in the preceding section of the chapter. The module is primarily intended for ISPs and similar large sites that host a large number of virtual sites. This module is for more advanced users and, as such, it is outside the scope of this introductory chapter. Instead, this section concentrates on the traditional ways of hosting virtual servers.

Address-Based Virtual Hosts

After you've configured your Linux machine with multiple IP addresses, setting up Apache to serve them as different websites is simple. You need only put a VirtualHost directive in your httpd.conf file for each of the addresses you want to make an independent website:

```
<VirtualHost 212.85.67.67>
ServerName gnulix.org
DocumentRoot /home/virtual/gnulix/public_html
TransferLog /home/virtual/gnulix/logs/access_log
ErrorLog /home/virtual/gnulix/logs/error_log
</VirtualHost>
```

Use the IP address, rather than the hostname, in the VirtualHost tag.

You can specify any configuration directives within the <VirtualHost> tags. For example, you might want to set AllowOverrides directives differently for virtual hosts than you do for your main server. Any directives that aren't specified default to the settings for the main server.

Name-Based Virtual Hosts

Name-based virtual hosts enable you to run more than one host on the same IP address. You must add the names to your DNS as CNAMEs of the machine in question. When an HTTP client (web browser) requests a document from your server, it sends with the request a variable indicating the server name from which it's requesting the document. Based on this variable, the server determines from which of the virtual hosts it should serve content.

> **NOTE**
>
> Some older browsers are unable to see name-based virtual hosts because this is a feature of HTTP 1.1 and the older browsers are strictly HTTP 1.0–compliant. However, many other older browsers are partially HTTP 1.1–compliant, and this is one of the parts of HTTP 1.1 that most browsers have supported for a while.

Name-based virtual hosts require just one step more than IP address-based virtual hosts. You must first indicate which IP address has the multiple DNS names on it. This is done with the NameVirtualHost directive:

```
NameVirtualHost 212.85.67.67
```

You must then have a section for each name on that address, setting the configuration for that name. As with IP-based virtual hosts, you need to set only those configurations that must be different for the host. You must set the `ServerName` directive because it's the only thing that distinguishes one host from another:

```
<VirtualHost 212.85.67.67>
ServerName bugserver.gnulix.org
ServerAlias bugserver
DocumentRoot /home/bugserver/htdocs
ScriptAlias /home/bugserver/cgi-bin
TransferLog /home/bugserver/logs/access_log
</VirtualHost>

<VirtualHost 212.85.67.67>
ServerName pts.gnulix.org
ServerAlias pts
DocumentRoot /home/pts/htdocs
ScriptAlias /home/pts/cgi-bin
TransferLog /home/pts/logs/access_log
ErrorLog /home/pts/logs/error_log
</VirtualHost>
```

TIP

If you're hosting websites on an intranet or internal network, users are likely to use the shortened name of the machine rather than the FQDN. For example, users might type **http://bugserver/index.html** in their browser location fields rather than **http://bugserver.gnulix.org/index.html**. In that case, Apache would not recognize that those two addresses should go to the same virtual host. You could get around this by setting up `VirtualHost` directives for both `bugserver` and `bugserver.gnulix.org`, but the easy way around it is to use the `ServerAlias` directive, which lists all valid aliases for the machine:

```
ServerAlias bugserver
```

For more information about `VirtualHost`, refer to the help system on http://localhost/_manual.

Logging

Apache provides for logging just about any web access information in which you might be interested. Logging can help with the following:

▶ System resource management, by tracking usage

▶ Intrusion detection, by documenting bad HTTP requests

▶ Diagnostics, by recording errors in processing requests

Two standard log files are generated when you run your Apache server: `access_log` and `error_log`. They are found under the `/var/log/httpd` directory. (Others include the SSL logs `ssl_access_log`, `ssl_error_log`, and `ssl_request_log`.) All logs except for the `error_log` (by default, this is just the `access_log`) are generated in a format specified by the `CustomLog` and `LogFormat` directives. These directives appear in your `httpd.conf` file.

A new log format can be defined with the `LogFormat` directive:

```
LogFormat "%h %l %u %t \"%r\" %>s %b" common
```

The `common` log format is a good starting place for creating your own custom log formats. Note that most of the available log analysis tools assume that you are using the `common` log format or the `combined` log format—both of which are defined in the default configuration files.

The following variables are available for `LogFormat` statements:

%a	Remote IP address.
%A	Local IP address.
%b	Bytes sent, excluding HTTP headers. This is shown in Apache's Combined Log Format (CLF). For a request without any data content, a - is shown instead of 0.
%B	Bytes sent, excluding HTTP headers.
%{VARIABLE}e	The contents of the environment variable VARIABLE.
%f	The filename of the output log.
%h	Remote host.
%H	Request protocol.
%{HEADER}i	The contents of HEADER; header line(s) in the request sent to the server.
%l	Remote log name (from identd, if supplied).
%m	Request method.
%{NOTE}n	The contents of note NOTE from another module.
%{HEADER}o	The contents of HEADER; header line(s) in the reply.
%p	The canonical port of the server serving the request.
%P	The process ID of the child that serviced the request.
%q	The contents of the query string, prepended with a ? character. If there's no query string, this evaluates to an empty string.
%r	The first line of request.
%s	Status. For requests that were internally redirected, this is the status of the original request—%>s for the last.

17

%t	The time, in common log time format.
%{format}t	The time, in the form given by format, which should be in strftime(3) format.
%T	The seconds taken to serve the request.
%u	Remote user from auth; this might be bogus if the return status (%s) is 401.
%U	The URL path requested.
%V	The server name according to the UseCanonicalName directive.
%v	The canonical ServerName of the server serving the request.

You can put a conditional in front of each variable to determine whether the variable is displayed. If the variable isn't displayed, - is displayed instead. These conditionals are in the form of a list of numerical return values. For example, %!401u displays the value of REMOTE_USER unless the return code is 401.

You can then specify the location and format of a log file by using the CustomLog directive:

```
CustomLog logs/access_log common
```

If it isn't specified as an absolute path, the location of the log file is assumed to be relative to the ServerRoot.

Related Fedora and Linux Commands

You will use these commands when managing your Apache web server in Fedora:

- ▶ **apachectl**—Server control shell script included with Apache
- ▶ **system-config-httpd**—Red Hat's graphical web server configuration tool
- ▶ **httpd**—The Apache web server
- ▶ **konqueror**—KDE's graphical web browser
- ▶ **elinks**—A text-based, graphical menu web browser
- ▶ **firefox**—The premier open source web browser

Reference

- ▶ **http://news.netcraft.com/archives/web_server_survey.html**—A statistical graph of web server usage points out that Apache is, by far, the most widely used server for Internet sites.

- ▶ **http://www.apache.org/**—Extensive documentation and information about Apache are available at The Apache Project website.

▶ **http://apachetoday.com/**—Another good Apache site. Original content as well as links to Apache-related stories on other sites can be found at Apache Today's site.

▶ **http://modules.apache.org/**—Available add-on modules for Apache can be found at The Apache Module Registry website.

There are several good books about Apache. For example, see *Apache Server Unleashed* (Sams Publishing), ISBN 0-672-31808-3.

17

Administering Database Services

This chapter is an introduction to MySQL and PostgreSQL, two database systems that are included with Fedora. You'll learn what these systems do, how the two programs compare, and how to consider their advantages and disadvantages. This information can help you choose and deploy which one to use for your organization's database needs.

The database administrator (DBA) for an organization has several responsibilities, which vary according to the size and operations of the organization, supporting staff, and so on. Depending on the particular organization's structure, if you are the organization's DBA, your responsibilities might include the following:

▶ **Installing and maintaining database servers**—You might install and maintain the database software. Maintenance can involve installing patches as well as upgrading the software at the appropriate times. As DBA, you might need to have root access to your system and know how to manage software (refer to Chapter 2, "Fedora Quick Start"). You also need to be aware of kernel, file system, and other security issues.

▶ **Installing and maintaining database clients**—The database client is the program used to access the database (you'll learn more about that later in this chapter, in the section "Database Clients"), either locally or remotely over a network. Your responsibilities might include installing and maintaining these client programs on users' systems. This chapter discusses how to install and work with the clients from both the Linux command line and through its graphical interface database tools.

▶ **Managing accounts and users**—Account and user management includes adding and deleting users from the database, assigning and administering passwords, and so on. In this chapter, you will learn how to grant and revoke user privileges and passwords for MySQL and PostgreSQL while using Fedora.

▶ **Ensuring database security**—To ensure database security, you need to be concerned with things such as access control, which ensures that only authorized people can access the database, and permissions, which ensure that people who can access the database cannot do things they should not do. In this chapter, you will learn how to manage Secure Shell (SSH), web, and local GUI client access to the database. Planning and overseeing the regular backup of an organization's database and restoring data from those backups are other critical components of securing the database.

▶ **Ensuring data integrity**—Of all the information stored on a server's hard disk storage, chances are the information in the database is the most critical. Ensuring data integrity involves planning for multiple-user access and ensuring that changes are not lost or duplicated when more than one user is making changes to the database at the same time.

A Brief Review of Database Basics

Database services under Linux that use the software discussed in this chapter are based on a *client/server* model. Database clients are often used to input data and to query or display query results from the server. You can use the command line or a graphical client to access a running server. Databases generally come in two forms: flat file and relational. A *flat file* database can be as simple as a text file with a space, tab, or some other character delimiting different parts of the information. One example of a simple flat file database is the Fedora /etc/passwd file. Another example could be a simple address book that might look something like this:

```
Doe~John~505 Some Street~Anytown~NY~12345~555-555-1212
```

You can use standard Unix tools such as grep, awk, and perl to search for and extract information from this primitive database. Although this might work well for a small database such as an address book that only one person uses, flat file databases of this type have several limitations:

▶ **They do not scale well**—You do not have random access to data in flat file databases. You have only sequential access. This means that any search function has to scan each line in the file, one by one, to look for specific information. As the size of the database grows, access times increase and performance decreases.

▶ **Flat file databases are unsuitable for multi-user environments**—Depending on how the database is set up, it either enables only one user to access it at a time or allows two users to make changes simultaneously, making changes that could end up overwriting each other and causing data loss.

These limitations obviously make the flat file database unsuitable for any kind of serious work in even a small business—much less in an enterprise environment. Relational databases, or relational database management systems (RDBMSs), to give them their full name, are good at finding the relationships between individual pieces of data. An RDBMS stores data in tables with fields much like those in spreadsheets, making the data searchable and sortable. RDBMSs are the focus of this chapter.

Oracle, DB2, Microsoft SQL Server, and the freely available PostgreSQL and MySQL are all examples of RDBMSs. The following sections discuss how relational databases work and provide a closer look at some of the basic processes involved in administering and using databases. You will also learn about SQL, the standard language used to store, retrieve, and manipulate database data.

How Relational Databases Work

An RDBMS stores data in tables, which you can visualize as spreadsheets. Each column in the table is a field; for example, a column might contain a name or an address. Each row in the table is an individual record. The table itself has a name you use to refer to that table when you want to get data out of it or put data into it. Figure 18.1 shows an example of a simple relational database that stores name and address information.

last_name	first_name	address	city	state	zip	phone
Doe	John	501 Somestreet	Anytown	NY	55011	555-555-1212
Doe	Jane	501 Somestreet	Anytown	NY	55011	555-555-1212
Palmer	John	205 Anystreet	Sometown	NY	55055	123-456-7890
Johnson	Robert	100 Easystreet	Easytown	CT	12345	111-222-3333

FIGURE 18.1   In this visualization of how an RDBMS stores data, the database stores four records (rows) that include name and address information, divided into seven fields (columns) of data.

In the example shown in Figure 18.1, the database contains only a single table. Most RDBMS setups are much more complex than this, with a single database containing multiple tables. Figure 18.2 shows an example of a database named sample_database that contains two tables.

In the sample_database example, the phonebook table contains four records (rows) and each record hold three fields (columns) of data. The cd_collection table holds eight records, divided into five fields of data.

If you are thinking that there is no logical relationship between the phonebook table and the cd_collection table in the sample_database example, you are correct. In a relational database, users can store multiple tables of data in a single database—even if the data in one table is unrelated to the data in others.

For example, suppose that you run a small company that sells widgets and you have a computerized database of customers. In addition to storing each customer's name, address, and phone number, you want to be able to look up outstanding order and invoice information for any of your customers. You could use three related tables in an RDBMS to store and organize customer data for just those purposes. Figure 18.3 shows an example of such a database.

phonebook

last_name	first_name	phone
Doe	John	555-555-1212
Doe	Jane	555-555-1212
Palmer	John	555-123-4567
Johnson	Richard	555-111-4321

cd_collection

id	title	artist	year	rating
1	Mindbomb	The The	1989	4
2	For All You've Done	Hillsong	2004	
3	Trouser Jazz	Mr Scruff	2002	5
4	Natural Elements	Acoustic Alchemy	1988	3
5	Combat Rock	The Clash	1982	4
6	Life for Rent	Dido	2003	5
7	Adiemus 4	Karl Jenkins	2000	4
8	The Two Towers	Howard Shore	2002	5

FIGURE 18.2   A single database can contain two tables—in this case, phonebook and cd_collection.

In the example in Figure 18.3, we have added a Customer ID field to each customer record. This field holds a customer ID number that is the unique piece of information that can be used to link all other information for each customer to track orders and invoices. Each customer is given an ID unique to him; two customers might have the same data in their name fields, but their ID field values will never be the same. The Customer ID field data in the Orders and Overdue tables replaces the Last Name, First Name, and Shipping Address field information from the Customers table. Now, when you want to run a search for any customer's order and invoice data, you can search based on one key rather than multiple keys. You get more accurate results in faster, easier-to-conduct data searches.

Now that you have an idea of how data is stored in an RDBMS and how the RDBMS structure enables you to work with that data, you are ready to learn how to input and output data from the database. This is where SQL comes in.

customers

cid	last_name	first_name	shipping_address
1	Doe	John	505 Somestreet
2	Doe	Jane	505 Somestreet
3	Palmer	John	200 Anystreet
4	Johnson	Richard	1000 Another Street

orders

cid	order_num	stock_num	priority	shipped	date
1	1002	100,252,342	3	Y	8/31/01
1	1221	200,352	1	N	10/2/01
3	1223	200,121	2	Y	10/2/01
2	1225	221,152	1	N	10/3/01

overdue

cid	order_num	days_overdue	action
1	1002	32	sent letter

FIGURE 18.3   You can use three related tables to track customers, orders, and outstanding invoices.

Understanding SQL Basics

SQL (pronounced "S-Q-L") is a database query language understood by virtually all RDBMSs available today. You use SQL statements to get data into and retrieve data from a database. As with statements in any language, SQL statements have a defined structure that determines their meanings and functions.

As a DBA, you should understand the basics of SQL, even if you will not be doing any of the actual programming yourself. Fortunately, SQL is similar to standard English, so learning the basics is simple.

Creating Tables

As mentioned previously, an RDBMS stores data in tables that look similar to spreadsheets. Of course, before you can store any data in a database, you need to create the necessary tables and columns to store the data. You do this by using the CREATE statement. For example, the cd_collection table from Figure 18.2 has five columns, or fields: id, title, artist, year, and rating.

SQL provides several column types for data that define what kind of data will be stored in the column. Some of the available types are INT, FLOAT, CHAR, and VARCHAR. Both CHAR and VARCHAR hold text strings, with the difference being that CHAR holds a fixed-length string, whereas VARCHAR holds a variable-length string.

There are also special column types, such as DATE, which takes data in only a date format, and ENUMs (enumerations), which can be used to specify that only certain values are allowed. If, for example, you wanted to record the genres of your CDs, you could use an ENUM column that accepts only the values POP, ROCK, EASY_LISTENING, and so on. You will learn more about ENUM later in this chapter.

Looking at the cd_collection table, you can see that three of the columns hold numerical data and the other two hold string data. In addition, the character strings are of variable length. Based on this information, you can discern that the best type to use for the text columns is type VARCHAR, and the best type to use for the others is INT. You should notice something else about the cd_collection table: One of the CDs is missing a rating, perhaps because we have not listened to it yet. This value, therefore, is optional; it starts empty and can be filled in later.

You are now ready to create a table. As mentioned before, you do this by using the CREATE statement, which uses the following syntax:

```
CREATE TABLE table_name (column_name column_type(parameters) options, ...);
```

You should know the following about the CREATE statement:

- ▶ **SQL commands are not case sensitive**—For example, CREATE TABLE, create table, and Create Table are all valid.

- ▶ **Whitespace is generally ignored**—This means you should use it to make your SQL commands clearer.

The following example shows how to create the table for the cd_collection database:

```
CREATE TABLE cd_collection
(
id INT NOT NULL,
title VARCHAR(50) NOT NULL,
artist VARCHAR(50) NOT NULL,
year VARCHAR(50) NOT NULL,
rating VARCHAR(50) NULL
);
```

Notice that the statement terminates with a semicolon. This is how SQL knows you are finished with all the entries in the statement. In some cases, the semicolon can be omitted, and we will point out these cases when they arise.

TIP

SQL has a number of reserved keywords that cannot be used in table names or field names. For example, if you keep track of CDs you want to take with you on vacation, you would not be able to use the field name select because that is a reserved keyword. Instead, you should either choose a different name (selected?) or just prefix the field name with an f, such as fselect.

Inserting Data into Tables

After you create the tables, you can put data into them. You can insert data manually with the INSERT statement, which uses the following syntax:

```
INSERT INTO table_name VALUES('value1', 'value2', 'value3', ...);
```

This statement inserts *value1*, *value2*, and so on into the table *table_name*. The values that are inserted constitute one row, or *record*, in the database. Unless specified otherwise, values are inserted in the order in which the columns are listed in the database table. If, for some reason, you want to insert values in a different order (or if you want to insert only a few values and they are not in sequential order), you can specify in which columns you want the data to go by using the following syntax:

```
INSERT INTO table_name (column1,column4) VALUES('value1', 'value2');
```

You can also fill multiple rows with a single INSERT statement, using syntax such as the following:

```
INSERT INTO table_name VALUES('value1', 'value2'),('value3', 'value4');
```

In this statement, *value1* and *value2* are inserted into the first row and *value3* and *value4* are inserted into the second row.

The following example shows how you would insert the Nevermind entry into the cd_collection table:

```
INSERT INTO cd_collection VALUES(9, 'Nevermind', ''Nirvana', '1991,
''NULL);
```

MySQL requires the NULL value for the last column (rating) if you do not want to include a rating. PostgreSQL, on the other hand, lets you get away with just omitting the last column. Of course, if you had columns in the middle that were null, you would need to explicitly state NULL in the INSERT statement.

Normally, INSERT statements are coded into a front-end program so that users adding data to the database do not have to worry about the SQL statements involved.

Retrieving Data from a Database

Of course, the main reason for storing data in a database is so that you can later look up, sort, and generate reports on that data. Basic data retrieval is done with the SELECT statement, which has the following syntax:

```
SELECT column1, column2, column3 FROM table_name WHERE search_criteria;
```

The first two parts of the statement—the SELECT and FROM parts—are required. The WHERE portion of the statement is optional. If it is omitted, all rows in the table *table_name* are returned.

The *column1, column2, column3* indicates the name of the columns you want to see. If you want to see all columns, you can also use the wildcard * to show all the columns that match the search criteria. For example, the following statement displays all columns from the cd_collection table:

```
SELECT * FROM cd_collection;
```

If you wanted to see only the titles of all the CDs in the table, you would use a statement such as the following:

```
SELECT title FROM cd_collection;
```

To select the title and year of a CD, you would use the following:

```
SELECT title, year FROM cd_collection;
```

If you want something a little fancier, you can use SQL to print the CD title followed by the year in parentheses, as is the convention. Both MySQL and PostgreSQL provide string concatenation functions to handle problems such as this. However, the syntax is different in the two systems.

In MySQL, you can use the CONCAT() function to combine the title and year columns into one output column, along with parentheses. The following statement is an example:

```
SELECT CONCAT(title," (",year, ")") AS TitleYear FROM cd_collection;
```

That statement lists both the title and year under one column that has the label TitleYear. Note that there are two strings in the CONCAT() function along with the fields—these add whitespace and the parentheses.

In PostgreSQL, the string concatenation function is simply a double pipe (¦¦). The following command is the PostgreSQL equivalent of the preceding MySQL command:

```
SELECT (genus¦¦' ('¦¦species¦¦')') AS TitleYear FROM cd_collection;
```

Note that the parentheses are optional, but they make the statement easier to read. Once again, the strings in the middle and at the end (note the space between the quotes) are used to insert spacing and parentheses between the title and year.

Of course, more often than not, you do not want a list of every single row in the database. Rather, you want to find only rows that match certain characteristics. For this, you add the WHERE statement to the SELECT statement. For example, suppose that you want to find all the CDs in the cd_collection table that have a rating of 5. You would use a statement like the following:

```
SELECT * FROM cd_collection WHERE rating = 5;
```

Using the table from Figure 18.2, you can see that this query would return the rows for *Trouser Jazz*, *Life for Rent*, and *The Two Towers*. This is a simple query, and SQL is capable of handling queries much more complex than this. Complex queries can be written using logical AND and logical OR statements. For example, suppose that you want to refine the query so that it lists only those CDs that were not released in 2003. You would use a query like the following:

```
SELECT * FROM cd_collection WHERE rating = 5 AND year != 2003;
```

In SQL, != means "is not equal to." Once again looking at the table from Figure 18.2, you can see that this query returns the rows for *Trouser Jazz* and *The Two Towers* but doesn't return the row for *Life for Rent* because it was released in 2003.

So, what if you want to list all the CDs that have a rating of 3 or 4 except those released in the year 2000? This time, you combine logical AND and logical OR statements:

```
SELECT * FROM cd_collection WHERE rating = 3 OR rating = 4 AND year != 2000;
```

This query would return entries for *Mind Bomb, Natural Elements,* and *Combat Rock.* However, it wouldn't return entries for *Adiemus 4* because it was released in 2000.

TIP

One of the most common errors among new database programmers is confusing logical AND and logical OR. For example, in everyday speech, you might say "Find me all CDs released in 2003 and 2004." At first glance, you might think that if you fed this statement to the database in SQL format, it would return the rows for *For All You've Done* and *Life for Rent*. In fact, it would return no rows at all. This is because the database interprets the statement as "Find all rows in which the CD was released in 2003 and was released in 2004." It is, of course, impossible for the same CD to be released twice, so this statement would never return any rows, no matter how many CDs were stored in the table. The correct way to form this statement is with an OR statement instead of an AND statement.

SQL is capable of far more than is demonstrated here. But as mentioned before, this section is not intended to teach you all there is to know about SQL programming; rather, it teaches you the basics so that you can be a more effective DBA.

18

Choosing a Database: MySQL Versus PostgreSQL

If you are just starting out and learning about using a database with Linux, the first logical step is to research which database will best serve your needs. Many database software packages are available for Linux; some are free, and others cost hundreds of thousands of dollars. Expensive commercial databases, such as Oracle, are beyond the scope of this book. Instead, this chapter focuses on two freely available databases: MySQL and PostgreSQL.

Both of these databases are quite capable, and either one could probably serve your needs. However, each database has a unique set of features and capabilities that might serve your needs better or make developing database applications easier for you.

Speed

Until recently, the speed choice was simple: If the speed of performing queries was paramount to your application, you used MySQL. MySQL has a reputation for being an extremely fast database. Until recently, PostgreSQL was quite slow by comparison.

Newer versions of PostgreSQL have improved in terms of speed (when it comes to disk access, sorting, and so on). In certain situations, such as periods of heavy simultaneous access, PostgreSQL can be significantly faster than MySQL, as you will see in the next section. However, MySQL is still extremely fast when compared to many other databases.

Data Locking

To prevent data corruption, a database needs to put a lock on data while it is being accessed. As long as the lock is on, no other process can access the data until the first process has released the lock. This means that any other processes trying to access the data have to wait until the current process completes. The next process in line then locks the data until it is finished, and the remaining processes have to wait their turn, and so on.

Of course, operations on a database generally complete quickly, so in environments with a small number of users simultaneously accessing the database, the locks are usually of such short duration that they do not cause any significant delays. However, in environments in which many people are accessing the database simultaneously, locking can create performance problems as people wait their turns to access the database.

Older versions of MySQL lock data at the table level, which can be considered a bottleneck for updates during periods of heavy access. This means that when someone writes a row of data in the table, the entire table is locked so that no one else can enter data. If your table has 500,000 rows (or records) in it, all 500,000 rows are locked any time 1 row is accessed. Once again, in environments with a relatively small number of simultaneous users, this doesn't cause serious performance problems because most operations complete so quickly that the lock time is extremely short. However, in environments in which many people are accessing the data simultaneously, MySQL's table-level locking can be a significant performance bottleneck.

PostgreSQL, on the other hand, locks data at the row level. In PostgreSQL, only the row currently being accessed is locked. The rest of the table can be accessed by other users. This row-level locking significantly reduces the performance impact of locking in environments that have a large number of simultaneous users. Therefore, as a general rule, PostgreSQL is better suited for high-load environments than MySQL.

The MySQL release bundled with Fedora gives you the choice of using tables with table-level or row-level locking. In MySQL terminology, MyISAM tables use table-level locking and InnoDB tables use row-level locking.

> **NOTE**
>
> MySQL's data locking methods are discussed in more depth at http://www.mysql.com/doc/en/Internal_locking.html.
>
> You can find more information on PostgreSQL's locking at http://www.postgresql.org/docs/7.4/interactive/sql-lock.html.

ACID Compliance in Transaction Processing to Protect Data Integrity

Another way MySQL and PostgreSQL differ is in the amount of protection they provide for keeping data from becoming corrupted. The acronym ACID is commonly used to describe several aspects of data protection:

▶ **Atomicity**—This means that several database operations are treated as an indivisible (atomic) unit, often called a *transaction*. In a transaction, either all unit operations are carried out or none of them are. In other words, if any operation in the atomic unit fails, the entire atomic unit is canceled.

▶ **Consistency**—Ensures that no transaction can cause the database to be left in an inconsistent state. Inconsistent states can be caused by database client crashes, network failures, and similar situations. Consistency ensures that, in such a situation, any transaction or partially completed transaction that would cause the database to be left in an inconsistent state is *rolled back*, or undone.

▶ **Isolation**—Ensures that multiple transactions operating on the same data are completely isolated from each other. This prevents data corruption if two users try to write to the same record at the same time. The way isolation is handled can generally be configured by the database programmer. One way that isolation can be handled is through locking, as discussed previously.

▶ **Durability**—Ensures that, after a transaction has been committed to the database, it cannot be lost in the event of a system crash, network failure, or other problem. This is usually accomplished through transaction logs. Durability means, for example, that if the server crashes, the database can examine the logs when it comes back up and it can commit any transactions that were not yet complete into the database.

PostgreSQL is ACID-compliant, but again MySQL gives you the choice of using ACID-compliant tables or not. MyISAM tables are not ACID-compliant, whereas InnoDB tables are. Note that ACID compliancy is no easy task: All the extra precautions incur a performance overhead.

SQL Subqueries

Subqueries enable you to combine several operations into one atomic unit, and they enable those operations to access each other's data. By using SQL subqueries, you can perform some extremely complex operations on a database. In addition, using SQL subqueries eliminates the potential problem of data changing between two operations as a result of another user performing some operation on the same set of data. Both PostgreSQL and MySQL have support for subqueries in this release of Fedora.

Procedural Languages and Triggers

A *procedural language* is an external programming language that can be used to write functions and procedures. This enables you to do things that aren't supported by simple SQL. A *trigger* allows you to define an event that will invoke the external function or procedure you have written. For example, a trigger can be used to cause an exception if an INSERT statement containing an unexpected or out-of-range value for a column is given.

For example, in the CD tracking database, you could use a trigger to cause an exception if a user entered data that did not make sense. PostgreSQL has a procedural language called PL/pgSQL. Although MySQL has support for a limited number of built-in procedures and triggers, it does not have any procedural language. This means you cannot create custom procedures or triggers in MySQL, although the same effects can often be achieved through creative client-side programming.

Configuring MySQL

A free and stable version of MySQL is included with Fedora. MySQL is also available from the website http://www.mysql.com/. The software is available in source code, binary, and RPM format for Linux. You can elect to have MySQL installed when you install Fedora or later use the redhat-config-packages client to add the software to your system. See Chapter 2 for the details on adding (or removing) software.

After you install MySQL, you need to initialize the *grant tables*, or permissions to access any or all databases and tables and column data within a database. You can do this by issuing mysql_install_db as root. This command initializes the grant tables and creates a MySQL root user.

CAUTION

The MySQL data directory needs to be owned by the user as which MySQL will run (use the chown command to change ownership). In addition, only this user should have any permissions on this directory. (In other words, use chmod to set the permissions to 700.) Setting up the data directory any other way creates a security hole.

Running mysql_install_db should generate output similar to the following:

```
# mysql_install_db
Preparing db table
Preparing host table
Preparing user table
Preparing func table
```

```
Preparing tables_priv table
Preparing columns_priv table
Installing all prepared tables
020916 17:39:05 /usr/libexec/mysqld: Shutdown Complete
...
```

The command prepares MySQL for use on the system and reports helpful information. The next step is to set the password for the MySQL root user, which is discussed in the following section.

> **CAUTION**
>
> By default, the MySQL root user is created with no password. This is one of the first things you must change because the MySQL root user has access to all aspects of the database. The following section explains how to change the password of the user.

Setting a Password for the MySQL Root User

To set a password for the root MySQL user, you need to connect to the MySQL server as the root MySQL user; you can use the command `mysql -u root` to do so. This command connects you to the server with the MySQL client. When you have the MySQL command prompt, issue a command like the following to set a password for the root user:

```
mysql> SET PASSWORD FOR root = PASSWORD("secretword");
```

secretword should be replaced by whatever you want to be the password for the root user. You can use this same command with other usernames to set or change passwords for other database users.

After you enter a password, you can exit the MySQL client by typing **exit** at the command prompt.

Creating a Database in MySQL

In MySQL, you create a database by using the CREATE DATABASE statement. To create a database, you connect to the server by typing **mysql -u root -p** and pressing Enter. After you do so, you are connected to the database as the MySQL root user and prompted for a password. After you enter the password, you are placed at the MySQL command prompt. Then you use the CREATE DATABASE command. For example, the following commands create a database called animals:

```
# mysql -u root -p
Enter password:
Welcome to the MySQL monitor. Commands end with ; or \g.
Your MySQL connection id is 1 to server version: 3.23.58
```

```
Type 'help;' or '\h' for help. Type '\c' to clear the buffer.
```

```
mysql> CREATE DATABASE animals;
Query OK, 1 row affected (0.00 sec)
mysql>
```

Another way to create a database is to use the `mysqladmin` command, as the root user, with the `create` keyword and the name of a new database. For example, to create a new database named `reptiles`, you use a command line like this:

```
# mysqladmin -u root -p create reptiles
```

Granting and Revoking Privileges in MySQL

You probably want to grant yourself some privileges, and eventually you will probably want to grant privileges to other users. Privileges, also known as *rights*, are granted and revoked on four levels:

- ▶ **Global level**—These rights allow access to any database on a server.

- ▶ **Database level**—These rights allow access to all tables in a database.

- ▶ **Table level**—These rights allow access to all columns within a table in a database.

- ▶ **Column level**—These rights allow access to a single column within a database's table.

> **NOTE**
>
> Listing all the available privileges is beyond the scope of this chapter. See the MySQL documentation for more information.

To add a user account, you connect to the database by typing **mysql -u root -p** and pressing Enter. You are then connected as the root user and prompted for a password. (You did set a password for the root user as instructed in the last section, right?) After you enter the root password, you are placed at the MySQL command prompt.

To grant privileges to a user, you use the GRANT statement, which has the following syntax:

```
grant what_to_grant ON where_to_grant TO user_name IDENTIFIED BY 'password';
```

The first option, *what_to_grant*, is the privileges you are granting to the user. These privileges are specified with keywords. For example, the ALL keyword is used to grant global-, database-, table-, and column-level rights for a specified user.

The second option, *where_to_grant*, specifies the resources on which the privileges should be granted. The third option, *user_name*, is the username to which you want to grant the privileges. Finally, the fourth option, *password*, is a password that should be assigned to this user. If this is an existing user who already has a password and you are modifying permissions, you can omit the IDENTIFIED BY portion of the statement.

For example, to grant all privileges on a database named sampledata to a user named foobar, you could use the following command:

```
GRANT ALL ON animals.* TO foobar IDENTIFIED BY 'secretword';
```

The user foobar can now connect to the database sampledata by using the password secretword, and foobar has all privileges on the database, including the ability to create and destroy tables. For example, the user foobar can now log in to the server (by using the current hostname—shuttle2, in this example), and access the database like so:

```
$ mysql -h shuttle2 -u foobar -p animals
Enter password:
Welcome to the MySQL monitor. Commands end with ; or \g.
Your MySQL connection id is 43 to server version: 3.23.58

Type 'help;' or '\h' for help. Type '\c' to clear the buffer.

mysql>
```

> **NOTE**
>
> See the section "The MySQL Command-Line Client" later in this chapter for additional command-line options.

Later, if you need to revoke privileges from foobar, you can use the REVOKE statement. For example, the following statement revokes all privileges from the user foobar:

```
REVOKE ALL ON animals FROM foobar;
```

Advanced database administration, privileges, and security are very complex topics that are beyond the scope of this book. See the "Reference" section at the end of this chapter for links to online documentation. You can also check out Luke Welling's and Laura Thompson's book *PHP and MySQL Development* from Sams Publishing.

Configuring PostgreSQL

If you do not want to use the version of PostgreSQL bundled with Fedora, the latest PostgreSQL binary files and source are available at http://www.postgresql.org/. The PostgreSQL RPMs are distributed as several files. At a minimum, you probably want the postgresql, postgresql-server, and postgresql-libs RPMs. You should see the README.rpm-dist file in the FTP directory ftp://ftp.postgresql.org/pub/ to determine whether you need any other packages.

18

If you are installing from the Fedora RPM files, a necessary `postgres` user account (that is, an account with the name of the user running the server on your system) is created for you automatically:

```
$ fgrep postgres /etc/passwd
postgres:x:26:26:PostgreSQL Server:/var/lib/pgsql:/bin/bash
```

Otherwise, you need to create a user called `postgres` during the installation. This user shouldn't have login privileges because only root should be able to use su to become this user and no one will ever log in directly as the user. (Refer to Chapter 10, "Managing Users," for more information on how to add users to a Fedora system.) After you have added the user, you can install each of the PostgreSQL RPMs you downloaded using the standard `rpm -i` command for a default installation.

Initializing the Data Directory in PostgreSQL

After the RPMs are installed, you need to initialize the data directory. To do so, you must first create the data directory and you must be the root user. The following example assumes that the data directory is `/usr/local/pgsql/data`.

Create the `/usr/local/pgsql/data` directory (using `mkdir`) and change the ownerships of the directory (using `chown` and `chgrp`) so it is owned by the user `postgres`. Then use su and, as the user `postgres`, issue the following commands:

```
# mkdir /usr/local/pgsql
# chown postgres /usr/local/pgsql
# chgrp postgres /usr/local/pgsql
# su - postgres
-bash-2.05b$ initdb -D /usr/local/pgsql/data
The files belonging to this database system will be owned by user "postgres".
This user must also own the server process.

The database cluster will be initialized with locale en_US.UTF-8.
This locale setting will prevent the use of indexes for pattern matching
operations.  If that is a concern, rerun initdb with the collation order
set to "C".  For more information see the Administrator's Guide.

creating directory /usr/local/pgsql/data... ok
creating directory /usr/local/pgsql/data/base... ok
creating directory /usr/local/pgsql/data/global... ok
creating directory /usr/local/pgsql/data/pg_xlog... ok
creating directory /usr/local/pgsql/data/pg_clog... ok
creating template1 database in /usr/local/pgsql/data/base/1... ok
creating configuration files... ok
initializing pg_shadow... ok
enabling unlimited row size for system tables... ok
```

```
initializing pg_depend... ok
creating system views... ok
loading pg_description... ok
creating conversions... ok
setting privileges on built-in objects... ok
vacuuming database template1... ok
copying template1 to template0... ok

Success. You can now start the database server using:

 /usr/bin/postmaster -D /usr/local/pgsql/data
or
 /usr/bin/pg_ctl -D /usr/local/pgsql/data -l logfile start
```

This initializes the database and sets the permissions on the data directory to their correct values.

> **CAUTION**
>
> The `initdb` program sets the permissions on the data directory to `700`. You should not change these permissions to anything else to avoid creating a security hole.

You can start the `postmaster` program with the following command (make sure that you are still the user postgres):

$ postmaster -D /usr/local/pgsql/data &

If you have decided to use a directory other than /usr/local/pgsql/data as the data directory, you should replace the directory in the `postmaster` command line with whatever directory you are using.

> **TIP**
>
> By default, Fedora makes the PostgreSQL data directory /var/lib/pgsql/data. This isn't a very good place to store the data, however, because most people do not have the necessary space in the /var partition for any kind of serious data storage. Note that if you do change the data directory to something else (such as /usr/local/pgsql/data, as in the examples in this section), you need to edit the PostgreSQL startup file (named postgres) located in /etc/rc.d/init.d to reflect the change.

Creating a Database in PostgreSQL

Creating a database in PostgreSQL is straightforward, but it must be performed by a user who has permissions to create databases in PostgreSQL—for example, initially the user named postgres. You can then simply issue the following command from the shell prompt (not the PSQL client prompt, but a normal shell prompt):

```
# su - postgres
-bash-2.05b$ createdb database
```

where *database* is the name of the database you want to create.

The createdb program is actually a wrapper that makes it easier to create databases without having to log in and use psql. However, you can also create databases from within psql with the CREATE DATABASE statement. Here's an example:

```
CREATE DATABASE database;
```

You need to create at least one database before you can start the pgsql client program. You should create this database while you're logged in as the user postgres. To log in as this user, you need to use su to become root and then use su to become the user postgres. To connect to the new database, you start the psql client program with the name of the new database as a command-line argument, like so:

```
$ psql sampledata
```

If you don't specify the name of a database when you invoke psql, the command attempts to connect to a database that has the same name as the user as which you invoke psql (that is, the default database).

Creating Database Users in PostgreSQL

To create a database user, you use su to become the user postgres from the Linux root account. You can then use the PostgreSQL createuser command to quickly create a user who is allowed to access databases or create new database users, like this:

```
$ createuser phudson
Shall the new user be allowed to create databases? (y/n) y
Shall the new user be allowed to create more new users? (y/n) y
CREATE USER
```

In this example, the new user named phudson is created and allowed to create new databases and database users (you should carefully consider who is allowed to create new databases or additional users).

You can also use the PostgreSQL command-line client to create a new user by typing psql along with name of the database and then use the CREATE USER command to create a new user. Here is an example:

```
CREATE USER foobar ;
```

CAUTION

PostgreSQL allows you to omit the WITH PASSWORD portion of the statement. However, doing so causes the user to be created with no password. This is a security hole, so you should always use the WITH PASSWORD option when creating users.

NOTE

When you are finished working in the psql command-line client, you can type \q to get out of it and return to the shell prompt.

Deleting Database Users in PostgreSQL

To delete a database user, you use the dropuser command, along with the user's name, and the user's access is removed from the default database, like this:

```
$ dropuser msmith
DROP USER
```

You can also log in to your database by using psql and then use the DROP USER commands. Here's an example:

```
$ psql demodb
Welcome to psql, the PostgreSQL interactive terminal.

Type: \copyright for distribution terms
 \h for help with SQL commands
 \? for help on internal slash commands
 \g or terminate with semicolon to execute query
 \q to quit

demodb=# DROP USER msmith ;
DROP USER
demodb=# \q
$
```

Granting and Revoking Privileges in PostgreSQL

As in MySQL, granting and revoking privileges in PostgreSQL is done with the GRANT and REVOKE statements. The syntax is the same as in MySQL except that PostgreSQL doesn't use the IDENTIFIED BY portion of the statement because with PostgreSQL, passwords are assigned when you create the user with the CREATE USER statement, as discussed previously. Here is the syntax of the GRANT statement:

```
GRANT what_to_grant ON where_to_grant TO user_name;
```

The following command, for example, grants all privileges to the user `foobar` on the database `sampledata`:

```
GRANT ALL ON sampledata TO foobar;
```

To revoke privileges, you use the `REVOKE` statement. Here is an example:

```
REVOKE ALL ON sampledata FROM foobar;
```

This command removes all privileges from the user `foobar` on the database `sampledata`.

Advanced administration and user configuration are complex topics. This section cannot begin to cover all the aspects of PostgreSQL administration or of privileges and users. For more information on administering PostgreSQL, see the PostgreSQL documentation or consult a book on PostgreSQL, such as Korry Douglas's *PostgreSQL* (Sams Publishing).

Database Clients

Both MySQL and PostgreSQL use a client/server system for accessing databases. In the simplest terms, the database server handles the requests that come into the database and the database client handles getting the requests to the server as well as getting the output from the server to the user.

Users never interact directly with the database server even if it happens to be located on the same machine they are using. All requests to the database server are handled by a database client, which might or might not be running on the same machine as the database server.

Both MySQL and PostgreSQL have command-line clients. A command-line client is a very primitive way of interfacing with a database and generally isn't used by end users. As a DBA, however, you use the command-line client to test new queries interactively without having to write front-end programs for that purpose. In later sections of this chapter, you will learn a bit about the MySQL graphical client and the web-based database administration interfaces available for both MySQL and PostgreSQL.

The following sections examine two common methods of accessing a remote database, a method of local access to a database server, and the concept of web access to a database.

> **NOTE**
>
> You should consider access and permission issues when setting up a database. Should users be able to create and destroy databases? Or should they only be able to use existing databases? Will users be able to add records to the database and modify existing records? Or should users be limited to read-only access to the database? And what about the rest of the world? Will the general public need to have any kind of access to your database through the Internet? As DBA, you must determine the answers to these questions.

SSH Access to a Database

Two types of remote database access scenarios are briefly discussed in this section. In the first scenario, the user directly logs in to the database server through SSH (to take advantage of the security benefits of encrypted sessions) and then starts a program on the server to access the database. In this case, shown in Figure 18.4, the database client is running on the database server itself.

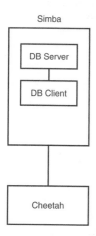

FIGURE 18.4   The user logs in to the database server located on host `simba` from the workstation (host `cheetah`). The database client is running on `simba`.

In the other scenario, shown in Figure 18.5, the user logs in to a remote host through SSH and starts a program on it to access the database, but the database is actually running on a different system. Three systems are now involved: the user's workstation, the remote host running the database client, and the remote host running the database server.

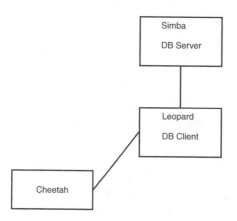

FIGURE 18.5   The user logs in to the remote host `leopard` from the workstation (host `cheetah`) and starts a database client on `leopard`. The client on `leopard` then connects to the database server running on host `simba`. The database client is running on `leopard`.

The important thing to note in Figure 18.5 is the middleman system leopard. Although the client is no longer running on the database server itself, it isn't running on the user's local workstation, either.

Local GUI Client Access to a Database

A user can log in to the database server by using a graphical client (which could be running on Windows, Macintosh OS, or a Unix workstation). The graphical client then connects to the database server. In this case, the client is running on the user's workstation. Figure 18.6 shows an example.

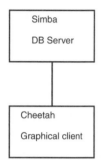

FIGURE 18.6   The user starts a GUI database program on his workstation (hostname cheetah). This program, which is the database client, then connects to the database server running on the host lion.

Web Access to a Database

In this section, we look at two basic examples of web access to the database server. In the first example, a user accesses the database through a form located on the World Wide Web. At first glance, it might appear that the client is running on the user's workstation. Of course, in reality it is not; the client is actually running on the web server. The web browser on the user's workstation simply provides a way for the user to enter the data that he wants to send to the database and a way for the results sent from the database to be displayed to the user. The software that actually handles sending the request to the database is running on the web server in the form of a CGI script; a Java servlet; or embedded scripting such as the PHP or Sun Microsystems, Inc.'s JavaServer Pages (JSP).

Often, the terms *client* and *front end* are used interchangeably when speaking of database structures. However, Figure 18.7 shows an example of a form of access in which the client and the front end aren't the same thing at all. In this example, the front end is the form displayed in the user's web browser. In such cases, the client is referred to as *middleware*.

In another possible web access scenario, it could be said that the client is a two-piece application in which part of it is running on the user's workstation and the other part is running on the web server. For example, the database programmer can use JavaScript in the web form to ensure that the user has entered a valid query. In this case, the user's query is partially processed on her own workstation and partially on the web server. Error checking is done on the user's own workstation, which helps reduce the load on the server and also helps reduce network traffic because the query is checked for errors before being sent across the network to the server.

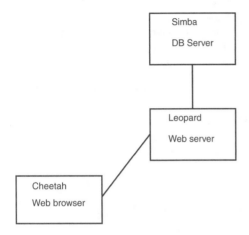

FIGURE 18.7   The user accesses the database through the World Wide Web. The front end is the user's web browser, the client is running on `leopard`, and the server is running on `simba`.

The MySQL Command-Line Client

The MySQL command-line client is `mysql`, and it has the following syntax:

```
mysql [options] [database]
```

Some of the available options for `mysql` are discussed in Table 18.1. *database* is optional, and if given, it should be the name of the database to which you want to connect.

TABLE 18.1   Command-Line Options to Use When Invoking `mysql`

Option	Action
-h *hostname*	Connects to the remote host *hostname* (if the database server isn't located on the local system).
-u *username*	Connects to the database as the user *username*.
-p	Prompts for a password. This option is required if the user as whom you are connecting needs a password to access the database. Note that this is a lowercase p.
-P *n*	Specifies *n* as the number of the port to which the client should connect. Note that this is an uppercase P.
-?	Displays a help message.

18

More options are available than are listed in Table 18.1, but these are the most common options. See the man page for `mysql` for more information on the available options.

CAUTION

Although `mysql` enables you to specify the password on the command line after the `-p` option, and thus enables you to avoid having to type the password at the prompt, you should never invoke the client this way. Doing so causes your password to display in the process list, and the process list can be accessed by any user on the system. This is a major security hole, so you should never give your password on the `mysql` command line.

You can access the MySQL server without specifying a database to use. After you log in, you use the `help` command to get a list of available commands, like this:

```
mysql> help
```

```
MySQL commands:
Note that all text commands must be first on line and end with ';'
help (\h) Display this help.
? (\?) Synonym for `help'.
clear (\c) Clear command.
connect (\r) Reconnect to the server. Optional arguments are db and host.
edit (\e) Edit command with $EDITOR.
ego (\G) Send command to mysql server, display result vertically.
exit (\q) Exit mysql. Same as quit.
go (\g) Send command to mysql server.
nopager (\n) Disable pager, print to stdout.
notee (\t) Don't write into outfile.
pager (\P) Set PAGER [to_pager]. Print the query results via PAGER.
print (\p) Print current command.
quit (\q) Quit mysql.
rehash (\#) Rebuild completion hash.
source (\.) Execute a SQL script file. Takes a file name as an argument.
status (\s) Get status information from the server.
tee (\T) Set outfile [to_outfile]. Append everything into given outfile.
use (\u) Use another database. Takes database name as argument.
```

You can then access a database by using the use command and the name of a database that has been created (such as `animals`) and to which you are authorized to connect, like this:

```
mysql> use animals
Database changed
mysql>
```

The PostgreSQL Command-Line Client

You invoke the PostgreSQL command-line client with the command psql. Like mysql, psql can be invoked with the name of the database to which you would like to connect. Also like mysql, psql can take several options. These options are listed in Table 18.2.

TABLE 18.2   Command-Line Options to Use When Invoking psql

Option	Action
-h *hostname*	Connects to the remote host *hostname* (if the database server isn't located on the local system).
-p *n*	Specifies *n* as the number of the port to which the client should connect. Note that this is a lowercase p.
-U *username*	Connects to the database as the user *username*.
-W	Prompts for a password after connecting to the database. In PostgreSQL 7 and later, password prompting is automatic if the server requests a password after a connection has been established.
-?	Displays a help message.

Several more options are available in addition to those listed in Table 18.2. See the psql's man page for details on all the available options.

Graphical Clients

If you'd rather interact with a database by using a graphical database client than with the command-line clients discussed in the previous section, you're in luck: A few options are available.

MySQL has an official graphical client, called MySQLGUI. MySQLGUI is available in both source and binary formats from the MySQL website at http://www.mysql.com/.

Web-based administration interfaces are also available for MySQL and PostgreSQL. phpMyAdmin and phpPgAdmin are two such products. Both of these products are based on the PHP-embedded scripting language and therefore require you to have PHP installed. Of course, you also need to have a web server installed.

18

Related Fedora and Database Commands

The following commands are useful for creating and manipulating databases in Fedora:

▶ **createdb**—Creates a new PostgreSQL database

▶ **createuser**—Creates a new PostgreSQL user account

▶ **dropdb**—Deletes a PostgreSQL database

▶ **dropuser**—Deletes a PostgreSQL user account

▶ **mysql**—Interactively queries the mysqld server

▶ **mysqladmin**—Administers the mysqld server

▶ **mysqldump**—Dumps or backs up MySQL data or tables

▶ **pgaccess**—Accesses a PostgreSQL database server

▶ **pg_ctl**—Controls a PostgreSQL server or queries its status

▶ **psql**—Accesses PostgreSQL via an interactive terminal

Reference

▶ **http://www.mysql.com/**—This is the official website of the MySQL database server. Here you can find the latest versions as well as up-to-date information and online documentation for MySQL. You can also purchase support contracts here. You might want to look into this if you will be using MySQL in a corporate setting. (Many corporations balk at the idea of using software for which the company has no support contract in place.)

▶ **http://www.postgresql.org/**—This is the official website of the PostgreSQL database server. You are asked to select a mirror when you arrive at this site. After you select a mirror, you are taken to the main site. From there, you can find information on the latest versions of PostgreSQL and read the online documentation.

▶ **http://www.postgresql.org/docs/8.1/interactive/tutorial-start.html**—This interactive HTML documentation tree is a great place to get started with learning how to use PostgreSQL.

▶ **http://www.pgsql.com/**—This is a commercial company that provides fee-based support contracts for the PostgreSQL database.

CHAPTER 19

File and Print

In the early days of computing, file and printer sharing was pretty much impossible because of the lack of good networking standards and interoperability. If you wanted to use a printer connected to another computer, you had to save the file to a floppy disk and walk over.

Nowadays, both file and printer sharing have become second nature in a world where it is not unusual for someone to own more than one computer. Whether it be for sharing photographs among various computers, or having a central repository available for collaboration, file sharing is an important part of our information age. Alongside this is the need to be able to share printers; after all, no one wants to have to plug and unplug a computer to a printer just to print out a quick letter.

Whatever your reasons for needing to share files and printers across a network, you will find out how to do both in this chapter. It looks at how you can share files using the popular UNIX *Network File System (NFS)* protocol, as well as the more Windows-friendly Samba system. You will also find out how to configure network attached printers with interfaces such as JetDirect. The chapter covers both graphical and command-line tools, so you should find something to suit the way you work.

Using the Network File System

NFS is the protocol developed by Sun Microsystems that allows computers to use a remote file system as if it were a real part of the local machine. A common use of NFS is to allow users' home directories to appear on every local machine they use, thus eliminating the need to have physical home directories. This opens up hot-desking and other flexible working arrangements, especially because no matter where the user is, his home directory follows him around.

Another popular use for NFS is to share binary files between similar computers. If you have a new version of a package that you want all machines to have, you have to do the upgrade only on the NFS server, and all hosts running the same version of Fedora will have the same upgraded package.

NFS Server Configuration

You configure the NFS server by editing the /etc/exports file. This file is similar to the /etc/fstab file in that it is used to set the permissions for the file systems being exported. The entries look like this:

```
/file/system yourhost(options) *.yourdomain.com(options) 192.168.2.0/24(options)
```

This shows three common clients to which to share /file/system. The first, yourhost, shares /file/system to just one host. The second, .yourdomain.com, uses the asterisk (*) as a wildcard to enable all hosts in yourdomain.com to access /file/system. The third share enables all hosts of the Class C network, 192.168.0.0, to access /file/share. For security, it is best not to use shares like the last two across the Internet because all data will be readable by any network the data passes by. Some common options are shown in Table 19.1.

TABLE 19.1   /etc/fstab Options

Option	Purpose
rw	Gives read and write access
ro	Gives read-only access
async	Writes data when the server, not the client, feels the need
sync	Writes data as it is received

The following is an example of an /etc/exports file:

```
# /etc/exports file for myhost.mydomain.com
/usr/local        yourhost(ro,show)
/home/ahudson      *.yourdomain.com(rw,hide,sync)
```

This file *exports* (makes available) /usr/local to yourhost. The mount is read-only (which is good for a directory of binary files that don't get written to). It also allows users on yourhost to see the contents of file systems that might be mounted on /usr/local. The second export mounts /home/ahudson to any host in yourdomain.com. It doesn't allow subsidiary file systems to be viewed, but you can read and write to the file system.

After you have finished with the /etc/exports file, you will check to see whether the NFS service is started by using the command:

```
# service nfs status
```

If you see a message saying that services are stopped, issue the following command:

```
# service nfs start
```

and watch as the related NFS services are started. When the services are started, you can enter the command

```
# /usr/sbin/exportfs -r
```

to export all the file systems in the /etc/exports file to a list named xtab under the /var/lib/nfs directory, which is used as a guide for mounting when a remote computer asks for a directory to be exported. The -r option to the command reads the entire /etc/exports file and mounts all the entries. The exportfs command can also be used to export specific files temporarily. Here's an example of using exportfs to export a file system:

```
# /usr/sbin/exportfs -o async yourhost:/usr/tmp
```

This command exports /usr/tmp to yourhost with the async option.

Be sure to restart the NFS server after making any changes to /etc/exports. If you prefer, you can use Fedora's system-config-nfs graphical client to set up NFS while using X. Start the client by going to System, Administration, Server Settings, NFS.

After you press Enter, you are prompted for the root password. Type in the password and click OK, and you see the main window. Click the Add button, and you see the Add NFS Share dialog box, as shown in Figure 19.1.

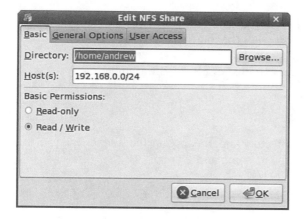

FIGURE 19.1   Fedora's *system-config-nfs* client can be used to quickly set up local directories for export via NFS.

In the Directory text box, type a name of a directory to be exported; in the Host(s) text box, type a hostname or the IP address of a remote host that is to be allowed access to the directory. By default, a directory is exported as read-only, but you can choose read and write access by clicking either option in the Basic Permissions area of the dialog box. When finished, click the OK button, click the Apply button, and then use the File menu to quit.

NOTE

As part of your configuration for using NFS, you might need to enable the port on your firewall. Go to System, Administration, Firewall to open the Firewall configuration utility. Check the box next to NFS4 and click Apply to apply the new firewall policy.

NFS Client Configuration

To configure your host as an NFS client (to acquire remote files or directories), edit the /etc/fstab file as you would to mount any local file system. However, rather than use a device name to be mounted (such as /dev/sda1), enter the remote hostname and the desired file system to be imported. For example, one entry might look like this:

```
# Device               Mount Point  Type  Options        Freq Pass
yourhost:/usr/local    /usr/local   nfs   nfsvers=4,ro   0    0
```

NOTE

If you use autofs on your system, you need to use proper autofs entries for your remote NFS mounts. See the section 5 man page for autofs.

The options column uses the same options as standard fstab file entries with some additional entries, such as nfsvers=4, which specifies the fourth version of NFS. You can also use the mount command, as root, to quickly attach a remote directory to a local file system by using a remote host's name and exported directory. For example:

```
# mount -t nfs 192.168.0.11:/home/andrew \
/home/andrew/test/foo
```

After you press Enter, the entire remote directory appears on your file system. You can verify the imported file system by using the df command, like so:

```
# df
Filesystem               1K-blocks        Used Available Use% Mounted on
/dev/mapper/VolGroup00-LogVol00
                         73575592    58627032  11150752  85% /
/dev/sda1                  101086       18697     77170  20% /boot
tmpfs                      512724           0    512724   0% /dev/shm
192.168.0.11:/home/andrew
                         35740416     5554304  28341248  17% /home/andrew/test/foo
```

Make sure that the desired mount point exists before using the mount command. When you finish using the directory (perhaps for copying backups), you can use the umount command to remove the remote file system. Note that if you specify the root directory (/) as a mount point, you cannot unmount the NFS directory until you reboot (because Linux complains that the file system is in use).

Putting Samba to Work

Samba uses the *Session Message Block* (*SMB*) protocol to enable the Windows operating system (or any operating system) to access Linux files. Using Samba, you can make your Fedora machine look just like a Windows computer to other Windows computers on your network. You do not need to install Windows on your PC.

Samba is a very complex program—so much so that the book *Samba Unleashed* (Sams Publishing, 2000, ISBN 0-672-31862-8) is more than 1,200 pages long. The Samba man page (when converted to text) for just the configuration file is 330KB and 7,013 lines long. Although Samba is complex, setting it up and using it does not have to be difficult. There are many options, which account for some of Samba's complexity. Depending on what you want, Samba's use can be as easy or as difficult as you would like it to be.

Fortunately, Fedora includes two tools: a simplified Samba management tool called system-config-samba, and a much more advanced tool known as *SWAT (Samba Web Administration Tool)*, which can be used to configure Samba with a web browser. SWAT provides an easy way to start and stop the Samba server; set up printing services; define remote access permissions; and create Samba usernames, passwords, and shared directories. This section delves into the basics of configuring Samba, and you should first read how to manually configure Samba to get an understanding of how the software works. At the end of this section, you will see how to enable, start, and use SWAT to set up simple file sharing.

Like most of the software that comes with Fedora, Samba is licensed under the GPL and is free. It comes as both an RPM and as source code. In both cases, installation is straightforward and the software can be installed when you install Fedora or use RPM software packages. The Samba RPMs should be on one of your Fedora install disks, or the latest version can be downloaded from the Internet, preferably from the Fedora Project (at http://fedoraproject.org/) or an authorized mirror site.

Installing from source code can be more time-consuming. If you do not want to install from Fedora's default locations, however, installing from the source code is a more configurable method. Just download the source from http://www.samba.org/ and unpack the files. Change into the source directory and, as root, run the command ./configure along with any changes from the defaults. Then run make, make test (if you want), followed by make install to install Samba in the specified locations.

If you install Samba from your Fedora DVD, you can find a large amount of documentation in the directory tree, starting at /usr/share/doc/samba*/doc/ in several formats, including PDF, HTML, and text, among others. Altogether, almost 3MB of documentation is included with the source code.

19

After Samba is installed, you can either create the file /etc/smb.conf or use the smb.conf file supplied with Samba, which is located by default under the /etc/samba directory with Fedora. Nearly a dozen sample configuration files can be found under the /usr/share/doc/samba*/examples directory.

> **NOTE**
>
> Depending on your needs, smb.conf can be a simple file of fewer than 20 lines or a huge file spanning many pages of text. If your needs are complex, I suggest picking up a copy of *Using Samba, 3rd Edition* by Carter, Ts, and Eckstein (O'Reilly, 2007).

Configuring Samba with system-config-samba

Fedora benefits from a slew of utilities that were developed as part of the original Red Hat Linux. Fortunately, work has carried on after Red Hat Linux was discontinued and the Samba configuration tool has lived on. And although it hasn't undergone major enhancements since Fedora Core 1, it is still a very useful tool to have to hand when configuring basic Samba services.

You can access it under System, Administration, Samba, and the opening screen is shown in Figure 19.2.

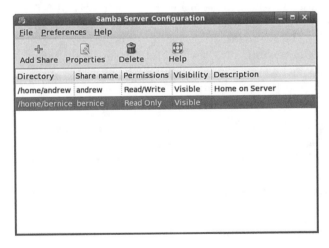

FIGURE 19.2   *System-config-samba*, a great way to get up and running quickly with Samba.

To get started, just click the Add Share icon in the toolbar, or select Add Share from the File menu. Either way takes you to the basic settings screen shown in Figure 19.3.

In the basic settings, you need to provide the path to the folder that you want to share via Samba. You also need to give it a share name, and an optional description. If you plan on setting up a number of shares, you might want to consider filling out the description to help you distinguish between them all.

FIGURE 19.3   Click the Browse button to locate the folder you want to share.

Next up you need to select one or both of the check boxes to allow users to view (visible) and or write (writable) to the folder. Subdirectories underneath the specified directory inherit the permissions stated here.

Configuring Samba with SWAT

The Samba team went all out to provide a handy GUI tool to administer almost every aspect of Samba, called SWAT. This section provides a simple example of how to use SWAT to set up SMB access to a user's home directory and how to share a directory.

You need to perform a few steps before you can start using SWAT. First, make sure you have the Samba and the samba-swat RPM packages installed. To then enable SWAT access to your system, edit the /etc/xinetd.d/swat file by changing the following line:

```
disable = yes
```

Change the word yes to the word no, like so:

```
disable = no
```

Note that you must do this as root, as regular users cannot change this file. Save the file, and then restart the xinetd daemon, using either the system-config-services client or the xinetd shell script under /etc/rc.d/init.d, as follows:

```
# service xinetd restart
```

Next, start an X session, launch any web browser, and browse to the http://localhost:901 *uniform resource locator (URL)*. You are presented a login prompt. Enter the root username and password, and then click the OK button. The screen clears, and you see the main SWAT page, as shown in Figure 19.4.

TIP

You can also configure Samba with Fedora's `system-config-samba` client. Launch the client from the command line of an X terminal window or select the System, Administration, Samba menu item (as shown later in Figure 19.10).

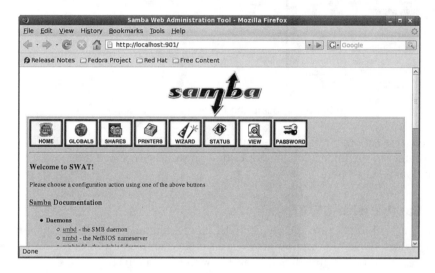

FIGURE 19.4   SWAT can be used to easily configure and administer Samba on your system.

First, click the GLOBALS icon in SWAT's main page. You see a page similar to the one shown in Figure 19.5. Many options are in the window, but you can quickly set up access for hosts from your LAN by simply entering one or more IP addresses or a subnet address (such as 192.168.0.—note the trailing period, which allows access for all hosts; in this example, on the 192.168.0 subnet) in the Hosts Allow field under the Security Options section. If you need help on how to format the entry, click the Help link to the left of the field. A new web page appears with the pertinent information.

When finished, click the Commit Changes button to save the global access settings. The next step is to create a Samba user and set the user's password. Click the PASSWORD icon on the main SWAT page (refer to Figure 19.4). The Server Password Management page opens, as shown in Figure 19.6. Type a new username in the User Name field; then type a password in the New Password and Re-type New Password fields.

NOTE

You must supply a username of an existing system user, but the password used for Samba access does not have to match the existing user's password.

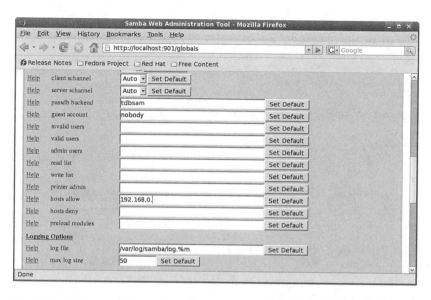

FIGURE 19.5   Configure Samba to allow access from specific hosts or subnets on your LAN.

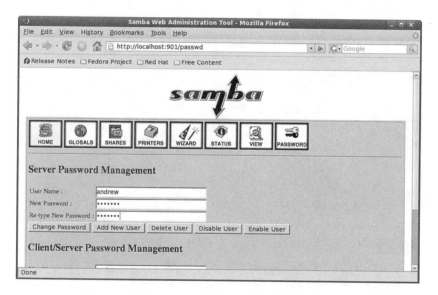

FIGURE 19.6   Enter a Samba username and password in the SWAT Password page.

When finished, click the Add New User button. SWAT then creates the username and password and displays Added user *username* (where *username* is the name you entered). The new Samba user should now be able to gain access to the home directory from any allowed host if the Samba (smb) server is running.

For example, if you have set up Samba on a host named rawhide that has a user named andrew, the user can access the home directory on rawhide from any remote host (if allowed by the GLOBALS settings), perhaps by using the smbclient command like so:

```
$ smbclient //rawhide/andrew -U andrew
Password:
Domain=[RAWHIDE] OS=[Unix] Server=[Samba 3.0.26a-6.fc8]
smb: \> pwd
Current directory is \\rawhide\andrew\
smb: \> quit
```

Click the Status icon in the toolbar at the top of the SWAT screen to view Samba's status or to start, stop, or restart the server. You can use various buttons on the resulting web page to control the server and view periodic or continuous status updates.

You can also use SWAT to share a Linux directory. First, click the Shares icon in the toolbar at the top of the main Samba page (refer to Figure 19.4). Type a share name in the Create Shares field, and then click the Create Shares button. The SWAT Shares page displays the detailed configuration information in a dialog box as shown in Figure 19.7, providing access to detailed configuration for the new Samba share.

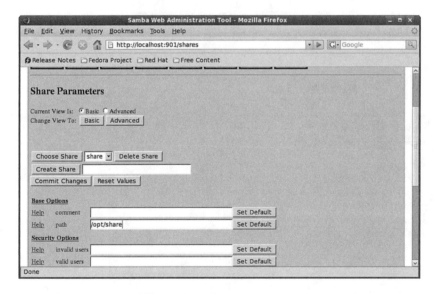

FIGURE 19.7   Use the SWAT Shares page to set up sharing of a portion of your Linux file system.

Type the directory name (such as /opt/share) you want to share in the Path field under the Base options. Select No or Yes in the Read Only field under Security options to allow or deny read and write access. Select Yes in the Guest OK option to allow access from other users and specify a hostname, IP address, or subnet in the Hosts Allow field to allow access. Click the Commit Changes button when finished. Remote users can then access the shared volume. This is how a Linux server running Samba can easily mimic shared volumes in a mixed computing environment!

Alternatively, use the system-config-samba client (from the command line or the Server Settings Samba Server menu item on the System Settings menu). Figure 19.8 shows the properties of a shared directory named /opt/share. Use the Add button to create new shares and the Properties button (both located on the main screen) to edit the share's access options. Use the Preferences menu to edit your Samba server's general settings or to create and manage Samba users.

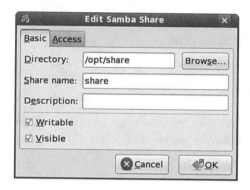

FIGURE 19.8   Configure a Samba share by editing the share defaults.

Manually Configuring Samba with /etc/samba/smb.conf

The /etc/samba/smb.conf file is broken into sections. Each section is a description of the resource shared (share) and should be titled appropriately. The three special sections are as follows:

▶ **[global]**—Establishes the global configuration settings (defined in detail in the smb.conf man page and Samba documentation, found under the /usr/share/doc/samba/docs directory)

▶ **[homes]**—Shares users' home directories and specifies directory paths and permissions

▶ **[printers]**—Handles printing by defining shared printers and printer access

Each section in your /etc/samba/smb.conf configuration file should be named for the resource being shared. For example, if the resource /usr/local/programs is being shared, you could call the section [programs]. When Windows sees the share, it is called by whatever you name the section (programs in this example). The easiest and fastest way to set up this share is with the following example from smb.conf:

```
[programs]
path = /usr/local/programs
writeable = true
```

This bit shares the /usr/local/programs directory with any valid user who asks for it and makes that directory writable. It is the most basic share because it sets no limits on the directory.

Here are some parameters you can set in the sections:

▶ Requiring a user to enter a password before accessing a shared directory

▶ Limiting the hosts allowed to access the shared directory

▶ Altering permissions users are allowed to have on the directory

▶ Limiting the time of day during which the directory is accessible

The possibilities are almost endless. Any parameters set in the individual sections override the parameters set in the [global] section. The following section adds a few restrictions to the [programs] section:

```
[programs]
path = /usr/local/programs
writeable = true
valid users = ahudsonahudson
browseable = yes
create mode = 0700
```

The valid users entry limits userid to just ahudson. All other users can browse the directory because of the browseable = yes entry, but only ahudson can write to the directory. Any files created by ahudson in the directory give ahudson full permissions, but no one else will have access to the files. This is exactly the same as setting permissions with the chmod command. Again, there are numerous options, so you can be as creative as you want to when developing sections.

Setting Global Samba Behavior with the [global] Section

The [global] section establishes configuration settings for all of Samba. If a given parameter is not specifically set in another section, Samba uses the default setting in the [global] section. The [global] section also sets the general security configuration for Samba. The [global] section is the only section that does not require the name in brackets.

Samba assumes that anything before the first bracketed section not labeled [global] is part of the global configuration. (Using bracketed headings in /etc/samba/smb.conf makes your configuration file more readable.) The following sections discuss common

Samba settings to share directories and printers. You will then see how to test your Samba configuration.

Sharing Home Directories Using the [homes] Section

The [homes] section shares out Fedora home directories for the users. The home directory is shared automatically when a user's Windows computer connects to the Linux server holding the home directory. The one problem with using the default configuration is that the user sees all the configuration files (such as .profile and others with a leading period in the filename) that he normally wouldn't see when logging on through Linux. One quick way to avoid this is to include a path option in the [homes] section. To use this solution, each user who requires a Samba share of his home directory needs a separate "home directory" to act as his Windows home directory.

For example, this pseudo home directory could be a directory named share in each user's home directory on your Fedora system. You can specify the path option when using SWAT by using the %u option when specifying a path for the default homes shares. The complete path setting would be as follows:

```
/home/%u/share
```

This setting specifies that the directory named share under each user's directory is the shared Samba directory. The corresponding manual smb.conf setting to provide a separate "home directory" looks like this:

```
[homes]
        comment = Home Directories
        path = /home/%u/share
        valid users = %S
        read only = No
        create mask = 0664
        directory mask = 0775
        browseable = No
```

If you have a default [homes] section, the share shows up in the user's Network Neighborhood as the user's name. When the user connects, Samba scans the existing sections in smb.conf for a specific instance of the user's home directory. If there is not one, Samba looks up the username in /etc/passwd. If the correct username and password have been given, the home directory listed in /etc/passwd is shared out at the user's home directory. Typically the [homes] section looks like this (the browseable = no entry prevents other users from being able to browse your home directory and using it is a good security practice):

```
[homes]
browseable = no
writable = yes
```

19

This example shares out the home directory and makes it writable to the user. Here's how you specify a separate Windows home directory for each user:

```
[homes]
browseable = no
writable = yes
path = /path/to/windows/directories
```

Sharing Printers by Editing the [printers] Section

The [printers] section works much like the [homes] section, but defines shared printers for use on your network. If the section exists, users have access to any printer listed in your Fedora /etc/printcap file.

Like the [homes] section, when a print request is received, all the sections are scanned for the printer. If no share is found (and with careful naming, there should not be unless you create a section for a specific printer), the /etc/printcap file is scanned for the printer name that is then used to send the print request.

For printing to work properly, printing services must be set up correctly on your Fedora computer. A typical [printers] section looks like the following:

```
[printers]
comment = Fedora Printers
browseable = no
printable = yes
path = /var/spool/samba
```

The /var/spool/samba is a spool path set just for Samba printing.

Testing Samba with the testparm Command

After you have created your /etc/smb.conf file, you can check it for correctness. Do so with the testparm command. This command parses through your /etc/smb.conf file and checks for any syntax errors. If none are found, your configuration file will probably work correctly. It does not, however, guarantee that the services specified in the file will work. It is merely making sure that the file is correctly written.

As with all configuration files, if you are modifying an existing, working file, it is always prudent to copy the working file to a different location and modify that file. Then you can check the file with the testparm utility. The command syntax is as follows:

```
# testparm /path/to/smb.conf.back-up
Load smb config files from smb.conf.back-up
Processing section "[homes]"
Processing section "[printers]"
Loaded services file OK.
```

This output shows that the Samba configuration file is correct, and, as long as all the services are running correctly on your Fedora machine, Samba should be working correctly. Now copy your old `smb.conf` file to a new location, put the new one in its place, and restart Samba with the command `/etc/init.d/smb restart`. Your new or modified Samba configuration should now be in place.

Starting the `smbd` Daemon

Now that your `smb.conf` file is correctly configured, you can start your Samba server daemon. You can do so with the `/usr/sbin/smbd` command, which (with no options) starts the Samba server with all the defaults. The most common option you will change in this command is the location of the `smb.conf` file; you change this option if you don't want to use the default location `/etc/smb/smb.conf`. The `-s` option allows you to change the `smb.conf` file Samba uses; this option is also useful for testing whether a new `smb.conf` file actually works. Another useful option is the `-l` option, which specifies the log file Samba uses to store information.

To start, stop, or restart Samba from the command line, use the `service` command, the `system-config-services` client, or the `/etc/rc.d/init.d/smb` script with a proper keyword, such as `start`, like so:

```
# /etc/rc.d/init.d/smb start
```

Using the `smbstatus` Command

The smbstatus command reports on the current status of your Samba connections. The syntax is as follows:

```
/usr/bin/smbstatus [options]
```

Table 19.2 shows some of the available options.

TABLE 19.2   `smbstatus` Options

Option	Result
-b	Brief output.
-d	Verbose output.
-s /path/to/config	Used if the configuration file used at startup is not the standard one.
-u username	Shows the status of a specific user's connection.
-p	Lists current smb processes. This can be useful in scripts.

Connecting with the `smbclient` Command

The smbclient command allows users on other Linux hosts to access your smb shares. You cannot mount the share on your host, but you can use it in a way that is similar to that you'd use with an FTP client. Several options can be used with the smbclient command.

19

The most frequently used is -I, followed by the IP address of the computer to which you are connecting. The smbclient command does not require root access to run:

```
smbclient -I 10.10.10.20 -U username%password
```

This gives you the following prompt:

```
smb: <current directory on share>
```

From here, the commands are almost identical to the standard UNIX/Linux FTP commands. Note that you can omit a password on the smbclient command line. You are then prompted to enter the Samba share password.

Mounting Samba Shares

There are two ways to mount Samba shares to your Linux host. Mounting a share is the same as mounting an available media partition or remote NFS directory, except that you use SMB to access the Samba share. (See Chapter 35, "Managing the File System," to see how to mount partitions.) The first method uses the standard Linux mount command:

```
mount -t smbfs //10.10.10.20/homes /mount/point -o username=ahudson,dmask=777,\
  fmask=777
```

> **NOTE**
>
> You can substitute a hostname for an IP address if your name service is running or the host is in your /etc/hosts file.

This command mounts ahudson's home directory on your host and gives all users full permissions to the mount. The permissions are equal to the permissions on the chmod command.

The second method produces the same results, using the smbmount command as follows:

```
# smbmount //10.10.10.20/homes /mount/point -o username=ahudson,dmask-777,\
  fmask=777
```

To unmount the share, use the standard:

```
# umount /mount/point
```

These mount commands can also be used to mount true Windows client shares to your Fedora host. Using Samba, you can configure your server to provide any service Windows can serve, and no one but you will ever know.

Network and Remote Printing with Fedora

Chapter 8, "Printing with Fedora," discussed how to set up and configure local printers and the associated print services. This section covers configuring printers for sharing and access across a network.

Offices all over the world benefit from using print servers and shared printers. In my office, I have two printers connected to the network via a Mac mini with Fedora PPC so that my wife can print from downstairs through her a wireless link, and I can print from my three computers in my office. It is a simple thing to do and can bring real productivity benefits, even in small settings.

Setting up remote printing service involves configuring a print server and then creating a remote printer entry on one or more computers on your network. This section introduces a quick method of enabling printing from one Linux workstation to another Linux computer on a LAN. You also learn about SMB printing using Samba and its utilities. Finally, this section discusses how to configure network-attached printers and use them to print single or multiple documents.

Enabling Network Printing on a LAN

To set up printing from one Linux workstation to another across a LAN, you need root permission and access to both computers, but the process is simple and easy to perform.

First, log in or ssh to the computer to which the printer is attached. This computer is the printer server. Use the hostname or ifconfig commands to obtain the hostname or IP address and write down or note the name of the printer queue. If the system uses LPRng rather than *CUPS (Common UNIX Printing System)*, you need to edit the file named /etc/lpd.perms. Scroll to the end of the file and look for the remote permission entry:

```
# allow local job submissions only
REJECT SERVICE=X NOT SERVER
```

Remote printing is not enabled by default, so you must comment out the service reject line with a pound sign (#):

```
# allow local job submissions only
#REJECT SERVICE=X NOT SERVER
```

Save the file, and then restart the lpd daemon.

This enables incoming print requests with the proper queue name (name of the local printer) from any remote host to be routed to the printer. After you finish, log out and go to a remote computer on your LAN without an attached printer.

19

> **TIP**
>
> LPRng, like CUPS, can be configured to restrict print services to single hosts, one or more specific local or remote users, all or part of a domain, or a LAN segment (if you specify an IP address range). An entry in /etc/lpd.perms, for example, to allow print requests only from hosts on 192.168.2.0, would look like this:
>
> ```
> ACCEPT SERVICE=X REMOTEIP=192.168.2.0/255.255.255.0
> ```
>
> The lpd.perms man page (included as part of the LPRng documentation) contains an index of keywords you can use to craft custom permissions. Don't forget to restart the lpd daemon after making any changes to /etc/lpd.perms (or /etc/lpd.conf).

If the computer with an attached printer is using Fedora and you want to set up the system for print serving, again use the system-config-printer client. You can create a new printer, but the easiest approach is to publish details of your printer across the network.

To enable sharing, start system-config-printer, and then select the Server Settings option in the left pane. All you need to do is select Share Published Printers Connected to This System to automatically allow access to all your printers, as shown in Figure 19.9.

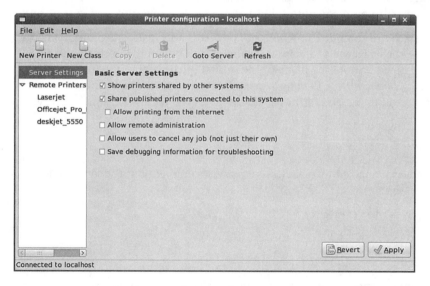

FIGURE 19.9   Sharing enables you to offer a locally attached printer as a remote printer on your network.

By default, all users are allowed access to the printer. You can change this setting by selecting the Access Control tab and adding users into the list.

Finally, you need to allow Fedora to publish your selected shared printers across the network. Click the Server Settings and make sure the Share Published Printers Connected to This System option is checked.

TIP

If you will share your CUPS-managed printer with other Linux hosts on a LAN using the Berkeley-type print spooling daemon, `lpd`, check the Enable LPD Protocol item under the Sharing dialog box's General tab. Next, check that the file `cups-lpd` under the `/etc/xinetd.d` directory contains the setting `disable = no` and then restart `xinetd`. This enables CUPS to run the `cups-lpd` server and accept remote print jobs sent by `lpd` from remote hosts. Do not forget to save your changes and restart CUPS!

When finished, click the Apply button and then select Quit from the Action menu to exit.

To create a printer queue to access a remote UNIX print server, use `system-config-printer` to create a printer but select the *Internet Printing Protocol (IPP)* type. Click Forward and enter a printer name and description; you are then asked to enter the hostname (or IP address) of the remote computer with a printer, along with the printer name, as shown in Figure 19.10.

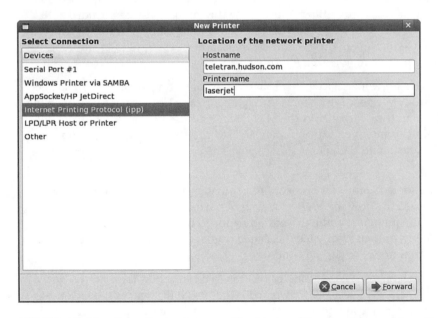

FIGURE 19.10   Enter the hostname or IP address of the remote computer with a printer, along with the remote printer's queue name.

> **NOTE**
>
> Browse to http://www.faqs.org/rfcs/rfc1179.html to read more about using the Strict RFC 1179 Compliance option when configuring Fedora to be able to print to a remote UNIX printer. This 13-year-old *Request For Comments (RFC)* document describes printing protocols for the BSD line-printer spooling system. The option is used to allow your documents to print to remote servers using the older print system or software conforming to the standard.

Click the Forward button after entering this information; then continue to configure the new entry as if the remote printer were attached locally (use the same print driver setting as the remote printer). When finished, do not forget to save the changes!

You can also test the new remote printer by clicking the Tests menu item and using one of the test page items, such as the ASCII or PostScript test pages. The ASCII test page prints a short amount of text to test the spacing and page width; the PostScript test page prints a page of text with some information about your printer, a set of radial lines one degree apart, and a color wheel (if you use a color printer).

Session Message Block Printing

Printing to an SMB printer requires Samba, along with its utilities such as the `smbclient` and associated `smbprint` printing filter. You can use the Samba software included with Fedora to print to a shared printer on a Windows network or set up a printer attached to your system as an SMB printer. This section describes how to use SMB to create a local printer entry to print to a remote shared printer.

The Control Panel's Network device is the usual means for setting up an SMB or shared printer under Windows operating systems through configuration settings. After enabling print sharing, reboot the computer. In the My Computer, Printers folder, right-click the name or icon of the printer you want to share and select Sharing from the pop-up menu. Set the Shared As item, and then enter a descriptive shared name, such as **HP2100**, and a password.

You must enter a shared name and password to configure the printer when running Linux. You also need to know the printer's workgroup name, IP address, and printer name, and have the username and password on hand. To find this information, select Start, Settings, Printers; then right-click the shared printer's listing in the Printers window and select Properties from the pop-up window.

On your Fedora system, use `system-config-printer` to create a new local printer queue and assign it a name; then select the Networked Windows (SMB) type in the list on the right side. Enter the connection details in the field at the top (preceded by `smb://`) and type your authentication details at the bottom (`mini` in the example shown in Figure 19.11). SMB printers offered by the server appear in the list and can be selected for use.

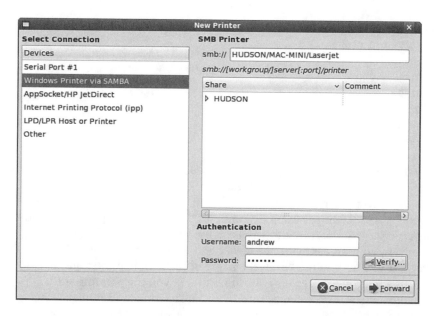

FIGURE 19.11   Create a shared remote printer, using required information for Windows.

Click Forward, and then create a printer with characteristics that match the remote printer. (For example, if the remote printer is an HP 2100 LaserJet, select the driver listed for that device in your configuration.)

Network-Attached Printer Configuration and Printing

Fedora supports other methods of remote printing, such as using a Novell Netware–based print queue or using a printer attached directly to your network with an HP JetDirect adapter. Some manufacturers even offer Linux-specific drivers and help. For example, HP provides graphical printer configuration tools and software drivers for other Linux distributions at http://h20000.www2.hp.com/bizsupport/TechSupport/Home.jsp.

You can set up network-attached printing quickly and easily, using a variety of devices. For example, NETGEAR's PS101 print server adapter works well with Linux. This tiny device (a self-hosted print server) is an adapter that directly attaches to a printer's Centronics port, eliminates the use of a parallel-port cable, and enables the use of the printer over a network. The PS101 offers a single 10Mbps ethernet jack and, after initial configuration and assignment of a static IP address, can be used to print to any attached printer supported by Fedora.

A JetDirect- or UNIX-based configuration using `system-config-printer` can be used to allow you to print to the device from Fedora or other remote Linux hosts. To see any open ports or services on the device, use the `nmap` command with the print server adapter's IP address like this:

```
$ nmap 192.168.0.9

Starting Nmap 4.20 ( http://insecure.org ) at 2007-10-23 21:11 BST
```

19

```
Interesting ports on 192.168.0.9:
Not shown: 1691 closed ports
PORT     STATE SERVICE
80/tcp   open  http
443/tcp  open  https
515/tcp  open  printer
9100/tcp open  jetdirect
9101/tcp open  jetdirect
9102/tcp open  jetdirect
Nmap finished: 1 IP address (1 host up) scanned in 1.532 seconds
```

To configure printing, select system-config-printer's JetDirect option; then specify the device's IP address (192.168.0.9 in the example) and port 9100 (as shown previously—you are clued that this is the correct port by the Service entry, which states jetdirect in the example). Alternatively, you can configure the device and attached printer as a UNIX-based print server, but you need to use PS1 as the name of the remote printer queue. Note that the device hosts a built-in web server (HTTP on port 80); you can administer the device by browsing to its IP address (such as http://192.168.2.52 in the example). Other services, such as FTP and Telnet, are supported but undocumented:

```
$ telnet 192.168.2.52
Trying 192.168.2.52...
Connected to 192.168.2.52 (192.168.2.52).
Escape character is '^]'.

Welcome to Print Server

PS>monitor
(P1)STATE: Idle
TYPE: Parallel
PRINTER STATUS: On-Line

PS>exit
Connection closed by foreign host.
```

TIP

Curiously, NETGEAR does not promote the PS101 as Linux-supported hardware even though it works. Other types of network-attached print devices include Bluetooth-enabled printers and 802.11b wireless ethernet print servers such as TRENDnet's TEW-PS3, HP/Compaq's parallel-port-based WP 110, and the JetDirect 380x with USB. As always, research how well a product, such as a printer or print server, works with Linux before purchasing!

Using the Common UNIX Printing System GUI

You can use CUPS to create printer queues, get print server information, and manage queues by launching a browser (such as Firefox) and browsing to http://localhost:631. CUPS provides a web-based administration interface, as shown in Figure 19.12.

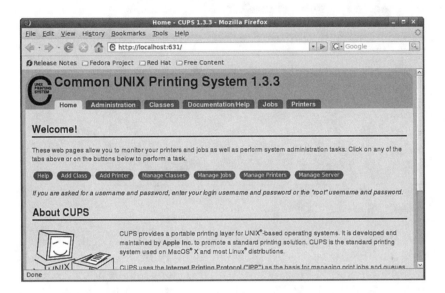

FIGURE 19.12   Use the web-based CUPS administrative interface to configure and manage printing.

This section provides a short example of creating a Linux printer entry, using CUPS's web-based interface. Use the CUPS interface to create a printer and device queue type (such as local, remote, serial port, or Internet); then you enter a device *uniform resource identifier (URI)*, such as lpd://192.168.2.35/lp, which represents the IP address of a remote UNIX print server, and the name of the remote print queue on the server. You also need to specify the model or make of printer and its driver. A Printers page link allows you to print a test page, stop the printing service, manage the local print queue, modify the printer entry, or add another printer.

In the Administration page, click the Add Printer button and then enter a printer name in the Name field (such as lp), a physical location of the printer in the Location field, and a short note about the printer (such as its type) in the Description field. Figure 19.13 shows a sample entry for a Brother Multi Function Printer.

19

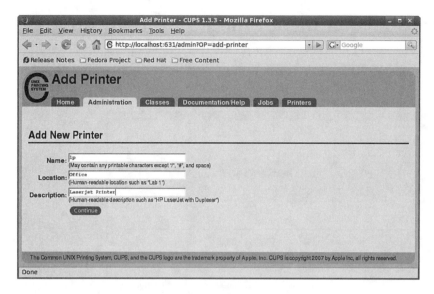

FIGURE 19.13   Use CUPS to create a new printer queue.

Click the Continue button. You can then select the type of printer access (local, remote, serial port, or Internet) in the Device page, as shown in Figure 19.14. For example, to configure printing to a local printer, select Parallel Port #1 or, for a remote printer, select the LPD/LPR Host or Printer entry. When you've made your selection, click Continue to proceed to the connection options screen, as shown in Figure 19.15.

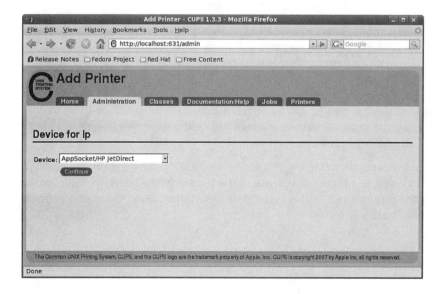

FIGURE 19.14   Select how the printer is connected.

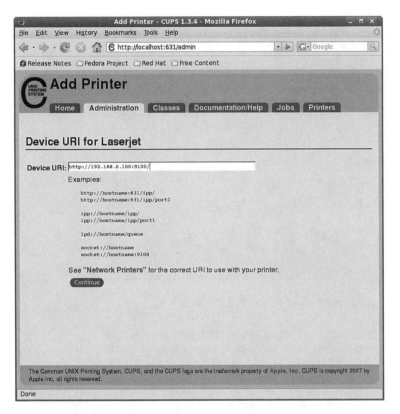

FIGURE 19.15   Enter the connection details as appropriate for your printer connection and as shown in the examples.

Again click Continue and select a printer make, as requested in the dialog box shown in Figure 19.16.

After you click Continue, you then select the driver. After creating the printer, you can then use the Printer page, as shown in Figure 19.17, to print a test page, stop printing service, manage the local print queue, modify the printer entry, or add another printer.

CUPS offers many additional features and after it is installed, configured, and running, and provides transparent traditional UNIX printing support for Fedora.

NOTE

To learn more about CUPS and to get a basic overview of the system, browse to http://www.cups.org/.

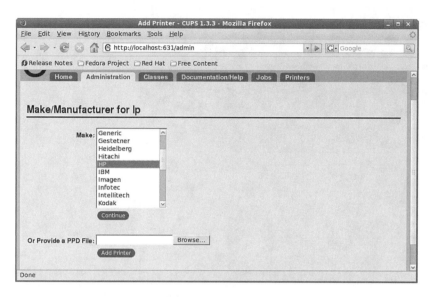

FIGURE 19.16   Select a printer make when creating a new queue.

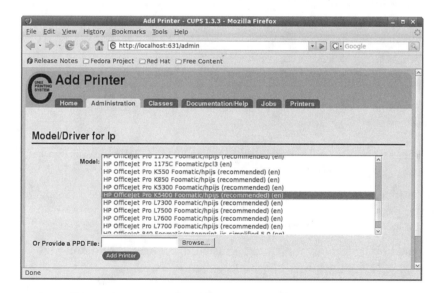

FIGURE 19.17   Manage printers easily, using the CUPS Printer page.

Console Print Control

Older versions of Red Hat Linux used the 4.3BSD line-printer spooling system and its suite of text-based printing utilities. Newer versions of these utilities, with the same names, are included with your Fedora DVD, but are part of the CUPS package. The commands support the launching of print jobs in the background (as a background process), the printing of multiple documents, the capability to specify local and networked printers, control of the printers, and management of the queued documents waiting in the printer's spool queue.

Using Basic Print Commands

After configuring your printer, you can print from the desktop, using any printer-capable graphical clients. If you do not use the desktop but prefer to use or access your Fedora system via a text-based interface, you can enter a number of print commands from the command line, too. The main CUPS commands used to print and control printing from the command line are as follows:

- ▶ `lp`—The line-printer spooling command; used to print documents that use a specific printer

- ▶ `lpq`—The line-printer queue display command; used to view the existing list of documents waiting to be printed

- ▶ `lpstat`—Displays server and printer status information

- ▶ `lprm`—The line-printer queue management command; used to remove print jobs from a printer's queue

- ▶ `lpc`—The line-printer control program; used by the root operator to manage print spooling, the `lpd` daemon, and printer activity

These commands offer a subset of the features provided by CUPS, but can be used to start and control printers and print queues from the command line.

You print files (documents or images) by using the `lp` command, along with a designated printer and filename. For example, to print the file `mydoc.txt` with the printer named lp, use the `lp` command, its `-d` command-line option, and the printer's name, like this:

```
# lp -dlp mydoc.txt
```

Managing Print Jobs

You can also print multiple documents from the command line. For example, to simultaneously print a number of files to the lp printer, use `lpr` like so:

```
# lp -dlp *.txt
```

This approach uses the wildcard capabilities of the shell to feed the `lpr` command all files in the current directory with a name ending in `.txt` for printing. Use the `lpq` command to view the printer's queue, as follows:

```
# lpq
lp is ready and printing
Rank    Owner    Job    File(s)                    Total Size
active  root     7      classes.conf               3072 bytes
```

The lpq command reports on the job, owner, job number, file being printed, and size of job. The job number (7 in this example) is used by CUPS to keep track of documents printing or waiting to be printed. Each job has a unique job number. To stop the print job in this example, use the lprm command, followed by the job number, like this:

```
# lprm 7
```

The lprm command removes the spooled files from the printer's queue and kills the job. Print job owners, such as regular users, can remove only spooled jobs that they own. As the root operator, you can kill any job.

Only the root operator can use the lpc command to administer printers and queues because the command is primarily used for printer and queue control. You, as a regular user, cannot use it to rearrange the order of your print jobs, but you can get a display of the status of any system printer. Start lpc on the command line like this:

```
# /usr/sbin/lpc
```

The lpc command has built-in help, but it consists of only five commands: exit, help, quit, status, and ?. The status command shows the status of a specified printer or all printers:

```
# lpc
lpc> ?
Commands may be abbreviated.   Commands are:

exit    help    quit    status   ?
lpc> status
lp:
        printer is on device 'parallel' speed -1
        queuing is enabled
        printing is enabled
        no entries
        daemon present
netlp:
        printer is on device 'parallel' speed -1
        queuing is enabled
        printing is enabled
        no entries
        daemon present
lpc> quit
```

The preceding sample session shows a status report for two printers: lp and netlp. Another helpful command is lpstat, which you use like this with its -t option:

```
# lpstat -t
scheduler is running
system default destination: lp
```

```
device for lp: parallel:/dev/lp0
device for netlp: parallel:/dev/lp0
lp accepting requests since Jan 01 00:00
netlp accepting requests since Jan 01 00:00
printer lp is idle.  enabled since Jan 01 00:00
printer netlp is idle.  enabled since Jan 01 00:00!)
```

This command lists all status information about printer queues on the local system.

Avoiding Printer Support Problems

Troubleshooting printer problems can be frustrating, especially if you find that your new printer is not working properly with Linux. First, keep in mind that nearly all printers on the market today work with Linux. However, some vendors have higher batting averages in the game of supporting Linux. If you care to see a scorecard, browse to http://www.linuxprinting.org/vendors.html.

All-in-One (Print/Fax/Scan) Devices

Problematic printers, or printing devices that might or might not work with Fedora, include multifunction (or *all-in-one*) printers that combine scanning, faxing, and printing services. You should research any planned purchase, and avoid any vendor unwilling to support Linux with drivers or development information.

One shining star in the field of Linux support for multifunction printers is the HP support of the HP OfficeJet Linux driver project at http://hpoj.sourceforge.net/. Printing and scanning are supported on many models, with fax support in development.

Using USB and Legacy Printers

Other problems can arise from the lack of a printer's USB vendor and device ID information—a problem shared by some USB scanners under Linux. For information regarding USB printer support, you can check with the Linux printing folks (http://www.linuxprinting.org/vendors.html) or with the Linux USB project at http://www.linux-usb.org/.

Although many newer printers require a *universal serial bus (USB)* port, excellent support still exists for legacy parallel-port (IEEE-1284) printers with Linux, enabling sites to continue to use older hardware. You can take advantage of Linux workarounds to set up printing even if the host computer does not have a traditional parallel printer port or if you want to use a newer USB printer on an older computer.

For example, to host a parallel port–based printer on a USB-only computer, attach the printer to the computer using an inexpensive USB-to-parallel converter. USB-to-parallel converters typically provide a Centronics connector; one end of that connector is plugged in to the older printer, whereas the other end is plugged in to a USB connector. The USB connector is then plugged in to your hub, desktop, or notebook USB port. On the other

19

hand, you can use an add-on PCI card to add USB support for printing (and other devices) if the legacy computer does not have a built-in USB port. Most PCI USB interface cards add at least two ports, and devices can be chained via a hub.

Related Fedora and Linux Commands

The following commands help you manage printing services:

- ▶ **accept**—Controls print job access to the CUPS server via the command line
- ▶ **cancel**—Cancels a print job from the command line
- ▶ **disable**—Controls printing from the command line
- ▶ **enable**—Controls CUPS printers
- ▶ **lp**—Sends a specified file to the printer and allows control of the print service
- ▶ **lpc**—Displays the status of printers and print service at the console
- ▶ **lpq**—Views print queues (pending print jobs) at the console
- ▶ **lprm**—Removes print jobs from the print queue via the command line
- ▶ **lpstat**—Displays printer and server status
- ▶ **system-config-printer**—Displays Fedora's graphical printer configuration tool
- ▶ **system-config-printer-tui**—Displays Fedora's text-dialog printer configuration tool

---

Reference

- ▶ **http://www.linuxprinting.org/**—Browse here for specific drivers and information about USB and other types of printers.

- ▶ **http://www.hp.com/wwsolutions/linux/products/printing_imaging/index.html**—Short but definitive information from HP regarding printing product support under Linux.

- ▶ **http://www.cups.org/**—A comprehensive repository of CUPS software, including versions for Red Hat Linux.

- ▶ **http://www.pwg.org/ipp/**—Home page for the Internet Printing Protocol standards.

- ▶ **http://www.linuxprinting.org/cups-doc.html**—Information about CUPS.

- ▶ **http://www.cs.wisc.edu/~ghost/**—Home page for the Ghostscript interpreter.

- ▶ **http://www.samba.org/**—Base entry point for getting more information about Samba and using the SMB protocol with Linux, UNIX, Mac OS, and other operating systems.

- ▶ In addition, an excellent book on Samba to help you learn more is *Using Samba, 3rd Edition* (O'Reilly & Associates, ISBN: 0-596-00769-8).

# CHAPTER 20

Remote File Serving with FTP

F*ile Transfer Protocol (FTP)* was once considered the primary method used to transfer files over a network from computer to computer. FTP is still heavily used today, although many graphical FTP clients now supplement the original text-based interface command. As computers have evolved, so has FTP, and Fedora includes many ways with which to use a graphical interface to transfer files over FTP.

This chapter contains an overview of the available FTP software included with Fedora, along with some details concerning initial setup, configuration, and use of FTP-specific clients. Fedora also includes an FTP server software package named vsftpd, the Very Secure FTP Daemon, and a number of associated programs you can use to serve and transfer files with the FTP protocol.

Choosing an FTP Server

FTP uses a client/server model. As a client, FTP accesses a server, and as a server, FTP provides access to files or storage. Just about every computer platform available has software written to enable a computer to act as an FTP server, but Fedora enables the average user to do this without paying hefty licensing fees and without regard for client usage limitations.

There are two types of FTP servers and access: standard and anonymous. A *standard* FTP server requires an account name and password from anyone trying to access the server. An *anonymous* server allows anyone to connect to the server to retrieve files. Anonymous servers provide the most flexibility, but they can also present a security risk. Fortunately, as you will read in this chapter, Fedora is set up to use proper file and directory permissions and common-sense default configurations, such as disallowing root from performing an FTP login.

> **NOTE**
>
> Many Linux users now use OpenSSH and its suite of clients, such as the sftp command, for a more secure solution when transferring files. The OpenSSH suite provides the sshd daemon and enables encrypted remote logins (see Chapter 15 for more information).

Choosing an Authenticated or Anonymous Server

When you are preparing to set up your FTP server, you must first make the decision to install either the authenticated or anonymous service. *Authenticated* service requires the entry of a valid username and password for access. As previously mentioned, *anonymous* service allows the use of the username anonymous and an email address as a password for access.

Authenticated FTP servers provide some measure of secure data transfer for remote users, but require maintenance of user accounts as usernames and passwords are used. Anonymous FTP servers are used when user authentication is not needed or necessary, and can be helpful in providing an easily accessible platform for customer support or public distribution of documents, software, or other data.

If you use an anonymous FTP server in your home or business Linux system, it is vital that you properly install and configure it to retain a relatively secure environment. Sites that host anonymous FTP servers generally place them outside the firewall on a dedicated machine. The dedicated machine contains only the FTP server and should not contain data that cannot be restored quickly. This dedicated-machine setup prevents malicious users who compromise the server from obtaining critical or sensitive data. For an additional, but by no means more secure setup, the FTP portion of the file system can be mounted read-only from a separate hard drive partition or volume, or mounted from read-only media, such as CD-ROM, DVD, or other optical storage.

Fedora FTP Server Packages

The Very Secure vsftpd server, like wu-ftpd (also discussed in this chapter), is licensed under the GNU GPL. The server can be used for personal or business purposes. Other FTP servers are available for Fedora, but only vsftpd comes bundled with this book's DVD. The wu-ftpd and vsftpd servers are covered in the remainder of this chapter.

Other FTP Servers

One alternative server is NcFTPd, available from http://www.ncftp.com. This server operates independently of xinetd (typically used to enable and start the wu-ftp server) and provides its own optimized daemon. Additionally, NcFTPd has the capability to cache directory listings of the FTP server in memory, thereby increasing the speed at which users can obtain a list of available files and directories. Although NcFTPd has many advantages over wu-ftpd, NcFTPd is not GPL-licensed software, and its licensing fees vary according to the maximum number of simultaneous server connections ($199 for 51 or more concurrent users and $129 for up to 50 concurrent users, but free to education institutions with a compliant domain name). Because of this licensing, NcFTPd is not packaged with Fedora, and you will not find it on this book's DVD.

> **NOTE**
>
> Do not confuse the ncftp client with ncftpd. The ncftp-3.1.7-4 package included with Fedora is the client software, a replacement for ftp-0.17-22, and includes the ncftpget and ncftpput commands for transferring files via the command line or with a remote file uniform resource locator address. ncftpd is the FTP server, which can be downloaded from www.ncftpd.com.

Another FTP server package for Linux is ProFTPD, licensed under the GNU GPL. This server works well with most Linux distributions and has been used by a number of Linux sites, including ftp.kernel.org and ftp.sourceforge.net. ProFTPD is actively maintained and updated for bug fixes and security enhancements. Its developers recommend that you use the latest release (1.2.10 at the time of this writing) to avoid exposure to exploits and vulnerabilities. Browse to http://www.proftpd.org to download a copy.

Yet another FTP server package is Bsdftpd-ssl, which is based on the BSD ftpd (and distributed under the BSD license). Bsdftpd-ssl offers simultaneous standard and secure access through security extensions; secure access requires a special client. For more details, browse to http://bsdftpd-ssl.sc.ru/.

Finally, another alternative is to use Apache and the HTTP protocol for serving files. Using a web server to provide data downloads can reduce the need to monitor and maintain a separate software service (or directories) on your server. This approach to serving files also reduces system resource requirements and gives remote users a bit more flexibility when downloading (such as enabling them to download multiple files at once). See Chapter 17, "Apache Web Server Management," for more information about using Apache.

Installing FTP Software

As part of the Workstation installation, the client software for FTP is already installed. You can verify that FTP-related software is installed on your system by using the RPM (Red Hat Package Manager), grep, and sort commands in this query:

```
$ rpm -qa ¦ grep ftp ¦ sort
```

The sample results might differ, depending on what software packages are installed. In your Fedora file system, the /usr/bin/pftp file is symbolically linked to /usr/bin/ftp as well as the vsftpd server under the /usr/sbin directory. The base anonymous FTP directory structure is located under the /var/ftp directory. Other installed packages include additional text-based and graphical FTP clients.

If vsftpd is not installed, you can find it under FTP Server in the Add/Remove Applications dialog.

> **NOTE**
>
> If you host an FTP server connected to the Internet, make it a habit to always check the Fedora site, http://fedora.redhat.com, for up-to-date system errata and security and bug fixes for your server software.

Because the anonftp and wu-ftpd RPM packages are not included with Fedora, you must download and install them if you want to use the wu-ftpd server. Retrieve the most recent packages for Linux from http://www.wu-ftpd.org/ to build from the latest source code or obtain RPM packages from a reputable mirror.

The FTP User

After Fedora is installed, an FTP user is created. This user is not a normal user per se, but a name for anonymous FTP users. The FTP user entry in /etc/passwd looks like this:

```
ftp:x:14:50:FTP User:/var/ftp:/sbin/nologin
```

> **NOTE**
>
> The FTP user, as discussed here, applies to anonymous FTP configurations and server setup.
>
> Also, note that other Linux distributions might use a different default directory, such as /usr/local/ftp, for FTP files and anonymous users.

This entry follows the standard /etc/passwd entry: username, password, user ID, group ID, comment field, home directory, and shell. To learn more about /etc/password, see the section "The Password File" in Chapter 10, "Managing Users."

Items in this entry are separated by colons. In the preceding example, you can see that the Fedora system hosting the server uses shadowed password because an x is present in the traditional password field. The shadow password system is important because it provides Fedora an additional level of security; the shadow password system is normally installed during the Fedora installation.

The FTP server software uses this user account to assign permissions to users connecting to the server. By using a default shell of /sbin/nologin (as opposed to /bin/bash or some other standard interactive shell) for anonymous FTP users, the software renders those users unable to log in as regular users. /sbin/nologin is not a shell, but a program usually assigned to an account that has been locked. As root inspection of the /etc/shadow file shows (see Listing 20.1), it is not possible to log in to this account, denoted by the use of * as the password.

LISTING 20.1   Shadow Password File `ftp` User Entry

```
# cat /etc/shadow
bin:*:11899:0:99999:7:::
daemon:*:11899:0:99999:7:::
adm:*:11899:0:99999:7:::
lp:*:11899:0:99999:7:::
...
ftp:*:12276:0:99999:7:::
...
```

The shadow file (only a portion of which is shown in Listing 20.1) contains additional information not found in the standard /etc/passwd file, such as account expiration, password expiration, whether the account is locked, and the encrypted password. The * in the password field indicates that the account is not a standard login account; thus, it does not have a password.

Although shadow passwords are in use on the system, passwords are not transmitted in a secure manner when using FTP. Because FTP was written before the necessity of encryption and security, it does not provide the mechanics necessary to send encrypted passwords. Account information is sent in plain text on FTP servers; anyone with enough technical knowledge and a network sniffer can find the password for the account to which you connect on the server. Many sites use an anonymous-only FTP server specifically to prevent normal account passwords from being transmitted over the Internet.

Figure 20.1 shows a portion of an `ethereal` capture of an FTP session where you can see it has caught a user's password being sent in clear text. The `ethereal` client is a graphical browser used to display network traffic in real time, and it can be used to watch packet data, such as an FTP login on a LAN.

Quick and Dirty FTP Service

Conscientious Linux administrators take the time to carefully install, set up, and configure a production FTP server before offering public service or opening up for business on the Internet. However, you can set up a server very quickly on a secure LAN by following a few simple steps:

1. Ensure that the FTP server RPM package is installed, networking is enabled, and firewall rules on the server allow FTP access. See Chapter 14, "Networking," to see how to use Red Hat's `system-config-securitylevel` client for firewalling.

2. If anonymous access to server files is desired, populate the /var/ftp/pub directory. Do this by mounting or copying your content, such as directories and files, under this directory.

3. Edit and then save the appropriate configuration file (such as `vsftpd.conf` for vsftpd) to enable access.

4. If you are using `wu-ftpd`, you must start or restart `xinetd` like so: `/etc/rc.d/init.d/xinetd restart`. If you are using `vsftpd`, you must start or restart the server like so: `service vsftpd start`.

20

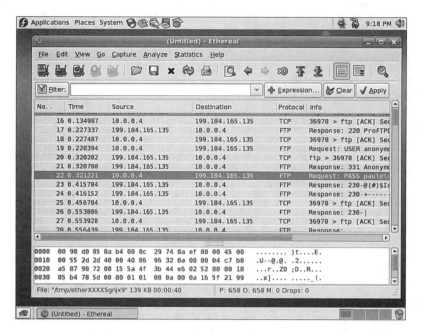

FIGURE 20.1   The `ethereal` client can filter and sniff FTP sessions to capture usernames and passwords.

`xinetd` Configuration for `wu-ftpd`

`xinetd` (pronounced "zy-net-d") is the extended Internet services daemon, and handles incoming connections for network services. `xinetd` is the preferred replacement for a similar tool (used with other Linux distributions and older Red Hat releases) called `inetd`. However, in addition to several other improvements over `inetd`, `xinetd` enables you to apply individual access policies to different network connection requests, such as FTP.

This daemon controls a number of services on your system, according to settings in configuration files under the `/etc/xinetd.d` directory. This section shows you how to edit the appropriate files to enable the use of the `wu-ftpd` FTP server.

Configuring `xinetd` for the `wu-ftp` Server

When you use RPM to install `wu-ftp`, the RPM package might contain a `xinetd` configuration file, `/etc/xinetd.d/wu-ftpd`, as shown in Listing 20.2. You need to edit the file because its default settings disable incoming FTP requests.

NOTE

Do not be confused by the first line of the `wu-ftpd` file's text. Even though the line reads `default: on`, FTP service is off unless you specifically configure its use. The line is a comment because it begins with a pound sign (#) and is ignored by `xinetd`. Whether FTP service is on is determined by the text line `disable = yes`.

LISTING 20.2   xinetd Configuration File for wu-ftpd

```
# default: on
# description: The wu-ftpd FTP server serves FTP connections. It uses \
#       normal, unencrypted usernames and passwords for authentication.
service ftp
{
disable = yes
        socket_type             = stream
        wait                    = no
        user                    = root
        server                  = /usr/sbin/in.ftpd
        server_args             = -l -a
        log_on_success          += DURATION
        nice                    = 10


}
```

Using an editor, change the disable = yes line to disable = no. Save the file and exit
the editor. You then must restart xinetd because configuration files are parsed only at
startup. To restart xinetd as root, issue the command **/etc/rc.d/init.d/xinetd restart**.
This makes a call to the same shell script that is called at any runlevel to start or stop the
xinetd daemon (and thus start up or shut down the system). xinetd should report its
status as:

```
# /etc/rc.d/init.d/xinetd restart
Stopping xinetd:                                    [  OK  ]
Starting xinetd:                                    [  OK  ]
```

After it is restarted, the FTP server is accessible to all incoming requests.

Starting the Very Secure FTP Server (vsftpd) Package

Previous versions of Red Hat's Linux distributions required you to edit a file named vsftp
under the /etc/xinetd.d directory to enable and start the Very Secure FTP server, vsftpd.
With Fedora, you can now simply use the system-config-services client or service
command to start vsftpd. For example, start the server using the service command
like this:

```
# service vsftpd start
Starting vsftpd for vsftpd:                         [  OK  ]
```

Use the system-config-services client or service command to start, stop, or restart the
vsftpd server. Do not run two FTP servers on your system at the same time!

20

> **TIP**
>
> You can also use the shell script named `vsftpd` under the `/etc/rc.d/init.d` directory to start, stop, restart, and query the `vsftpd` server. You must have root permission to use the `vsftpd` script to control the server, but any user can query the server (to see whether it is running and to see its process ID number) using the `status` keyword like this:
>
> $ /etc/rc.d/init.d/vsftpd status

Configuring the Very Secure FTP Server

The `vsftpd` server, although not as popular as `wu-ftpd`, is used by Red Hat, Inc. for its FTP server operations. (The `vsftpd` server home page is located at http://vsftpd.beasts.org/.) The server offers features such as simplicity, security, and speed. It has been used by a number of sites, such as ftp.debian.org, ftp.gnu.org, rpmfind.net, and ftp.gimp.org. Note that despite its name, the Very Secure FTP server does *not* enable use of encrypted usernames or passwords.

Its main configuration file is `vsftpd.conf`, which resides under the `/etc/vsftpd` directory. The server has a number of features and default policies, but you can override them by changing the installed configuration file.

By default, anonymous logins are enabled, but users are not allowed to upload files, create new directories, or delete or rename files. The configuration file installed by Fedora allows local users (that is, users with a login and shell account) to log in and access their home directories. This configuration presents potential security risks because usernames and passwords are passed without encryption over a network. The best policy is to deny your users access to the server from their user accounts. The standard `vsftpd` configuration disables this feature.

Controlling Anonymous Access

You an toggle anonymous access features for your FTP server by editing the `vsftpd.conf` file and changing related entries to YES or NO in the file. Settings to control how the server works for anonymous logins include:

▶ `anonymous_enable`—Enabled by default. Use a setting of NO, and then restart the server to turn off anonymous access.

▶ `anon_mkdir_write_enable`—Allows or disallows creating of new directories.

▶ `anon_other_write_enable`—Allows or disallows deleting or renaming of files and directories.

▶ `anon_upload_enable`—Controls whether anonymous users can upload files (also depends on the global `write_enable` setting). This is a potential security and liability hazard and should rarely be used; if enabled, consistently monitor any designated upload directory.

▶ `anon_world_readable_only`—Allows anonymous users to download only files with world-readable (444) permission.

After making any changes to your server configuration file, make sure to restart the server; doing so forces `vsftpd` to reread its settings.

Other `vsftpd` Server Configuration Files

You can edit `vsftpd.conf` to enable, disable, and configure many features and settings of the `vsftpd` server, such as user access, filtering of bogus passwords, and access logging. Some features might require the creation and configuration of other files, such as:

▶ `/etc/vsftpd.user_list`—Used by the `userlist_enable` and/or the `userlist_deny` options; the file contains a list of usernames to be denied access to the server.

▶ `/etc/vsftpd.chroot_list`—Used by the `chroot_list_enable` and/or `chroot_local_user` options, this file contains a list of users who are either allowed or denied access to a home directory. You can specify an alternative file by using the `chroot_list_file` option.

▶ `/etc/vsftpd.banned_emails`—A list of anonymous password entries used to deny access if the `deny_email_enable` setting is enabled. You can specify an alternative file by using the `banned_email` option.

▶ `/var/log/vsftpd.log`—Data transfer information is captured to this file if you enable logging by using the `xferlog_enable` setting.

TIP

Before editing the FTP server files, make a backup file first. Also, it is always a good idea to comment out (using a pound sign at the beginning of a line) what is changed instead of deleting or overwriting entries. Follow these comments with a brief description explaining why the change was made. This leaves a nice audit trail of what was done, by whom, when, and why. If you have any problems with the configuration, these comments and details can help you troubleshoot and return to valid entries if necessary. You can use the `rpm` command or other Linux tools (such as `mc`) to extract a fresh copy of a configuration file from the software's RPM archive. Be aware, however, that the extracted version replaces the current version and overwrites your configuration changes.

20

Default `vsftpd` Behaviors

The contents of a file named `.message` (if it exists in the current directory) are displayed when a user enters the directory. This feature is enabled in the installed configuration file, but disabled by the daemon. FTP users are also not allowed to perform recursive directory listings, which can help reduce bandwidth use.

The PASV data connection method is enabled to let external users know the IP address of the FTP server. This is a common problem when using FTP from behind a firewall/gateway that uses IP masquerading or when incoming data connections are disabled. For example, here is a connection to an FTP server (running ProFTPD), an attempt to view a directory listing, and the resulting need to use ftp's internal passive command:

```
$ ftp ftp.tux.org
Connected to gwyn.tux.org.
220 ProFTPD 1.2.5rc1 Server (ProFTPD on ftp.tux.org) [gwyn.tux.org]
500 AUTH not understood.
KERBEROS_V4 rejected as an authentication type
Name (ftp.tux.org:gbush): gbush
331 Password required for gbush.
Password:
230 User gbush logged in.
Remote system type is UNIX.
Using binary mode to transfer files.
ftp> cd public_html
250 CWD command successful.
ftp> ls
500 Illegal PORT command.
ftp: bind: Address already in use
ftp>
ftp> pass
Passive mode on.
ftp> ls
227 Entering Passive Mode (204,86,112,12,187,89).
150 Opening ASCII mode data connection for file list
-rw-r--r--   1 gbush     gbush         8470 Jan 10  2000 LinuxUnleashed.gif
-rw-r--r--   1 gbush     gbush         4407 Oct  4  2001 RHU72ed.gif
-rw-r--r--   1 gbush     gbush         6732 May 18  2000 SuSEUnleashed.jpg
-rw-r--r--   1 gbush     gbush         6175 Jan 10  2000 TYSUSE.gif
-rw-r--r--   1 gbush     gbush         3135 Jan 10  2000 TZones.gif
...
```

> **NOTE**
>
> Browse to http://slacksite.com/other/ftp.html for a detailed discussion regarding active and passive FTP modes and the effect of firewall blocking of service ports on FTP server and client connections.

Another default setting is that specific user login controls are not set, but you can configure the controls to deny access to one or more users.

The data transfer rate for anonymous client access is unlimited, but you can set a maximum rate (in bytes per second) by using the anon_max_rate setting in vsftpd.conf. This can be useful for throttling bandwidth use during periods of heavy access. Another default is that remote clients are logged out after five minutes of idle activity or a stalled data transfer. You can set idle and transfer timeouts (stalled connections) separately.

Other settings that might be important for managing your system's resources (networking bandwidth or memory) when offering FTP access include the following:

▶ dirlist_enable—Toggles directory listings on or off.

▶ dirmessage_enable—Toggles display of a message when the user enters a directory. A related setting is ls_recurse_enable, which can be used to disallow recursive directory listings.

▶ download_enable—Toggles downloading on or off.

▶ max_clients—Sets a limit on the maximum number of connections.

▶ max_per_ip—Sets a limit on the number of connections from the same IP address.

Configuring the wu-ftpd Server

wu-ftp uses a number of configuration files to control how it operates, including the following:

▶ ftpaccess—Contains the majority of server configuration settings

▶ ftpconversions—Contains definitions of file conversions during transfers

▶ ftphosts—Holds settings to control user access from specific hosts

These files may be created in the /etc directory during RPM installation, or may be created by a system administrator. The following sections describe each of these files and how to use the commands they contain to configure the wu-ftp server so that it is accessible to all incoming requests.

CAUTION

When configuring an anonymous FTP server, it is extremely important to ensure that all security precautions are taken to prevent malicious users from gaining privileged-level access to the server. Although this chapter shows you how to configure your FTP server for secure use, all machines connected to the Internet are potential targets for malicious attacks. Vulnerable systems can be a source of potential liability, especially if anyone accesses and uses them to store illegal copies of proprietary software— even temporarily. There is little value in configuring a secure FTP server if the rest of the system is still vulnerable to attack. Use Red Hat's lokkit or system-config-securitylevel client to implement a firewall on your system.

20

Using Commands in the `ftpaccess` File to Configure `wu-ftpd`

The `ftpaccess` file contains most of the server configuration details. Each line contains a definition or parameter that is passed to the server to specify how the server is to operate. The directives can be broken down into the following categories, including:

▶ **Access Control**—Settings that determine who can access the FTP server and how it is accessed

▶ **Information**—Settings that determine what information is provided by the server or displayed to a user

▶ **Logging**—Settings that determine whether logging is enabled and what information is logged

▶ **Permission Control**—Settings that control the behavior of users when accessing the server; in other words, what actions users are allowed to perform, such as create a directory, upload a file, delete a file or directory, and so on

---

TIP

Many more options can be specified for the `wu-ftpd` FTP server in its `ftpaccess` file. The most common commands have been covered here. A full list of configuration options can be found in the `ftpaccess` man page after you install the server.

You can edit the `ftpaccess` file at the command line to make configuration changes in any of these categories. The following sections describe some configuration changes and how to edit these files to accomplish them.

Configure Access Control

Controlling which users can access the FTP server and how they can do so are critical parts of system security. Use the following entries in the `ftpaccess` file to specify to which group the user accessing the server is assigned.

Limit Access for Anonymous Users

This command imposes increased security on the anonymous user:

```
autogroup <groupname> <class> [<class>]
```

If the anonymous user is a member of a group, he is allowed access to only files and directories owned by him or his group. The group must be a valid group from `/etc/groups` or `/var/ftp/etc/groups`.

Define User Classes

This command defines a class of users by the address to which the user is connected:

```
class <class> <typelist> <addrglob> [<addrglob>]
```

There might be multiple members for a class of users, and multiple classes might apply to individual members. When multiple classes apply to one user, the first class that applies is used.

The `typelist` field is a comma-separated list of the keywords anonymous, guest, and real. anonymous applies to the anonymous user, and guest applies to the guest access account, as specified in the guestgroup directive. real defines those users who have a valid entry in the /etc/passwd file.

The `addrglob` field is a regular expression that specifies addresses to which the class is to be applied. The (*) entry specifies all hosts.

Block a Host's Access to the Server

Sometimes it is necessary to block entire hosts from accessing the server. This can be useful to protect the system from individual hosts or entire blocks of IP addresses, or to force the use of other servers. Use this command to do so:

```
deny <addrglob> <message_file>
```

deny always denies access to hosts that match a given address.

addrglob is a regular expression field that contains a list of addresses, either numeric or DNS names. This field can also be a file reference that contains a listing of addresses. If an address is a file reference, it must be an absolute file reference; that is, starting with a /. To ensure that IP addresses can be mapped to a valid domain name, use the !nameserver parameter.

A sample deny line resembles the following:

```
deny *.exodous.net /home/ftp/.message_exodous_deny
```

This entry denies access to the FTP server from all users who are coming from the exodous.net domain, and displays the message contained in the .message_exoduous_deny file in the /home/ftp directory.

---

ftpusers File Purpose Now Implemented in ftpaccess

Certain accounts for the system to segment and separate tasks with specific permissions are created during Linux installation. The `ftpusers` file (located in /etc/ftpusers) is where accounts for system purposes are listed. It is possible that the version of wu-ftp you use with Fedora deprecates the use of this file, and instead implements the specific functionality of this file in the ftpaccess file with the commands of deny-uid/deny-gid.

20

Restrict Permissions Based on Group IDs

The guestgroup line assigns a given group name or group names to behave exactly like the anonymous user. Here is the command:

```
guestgroup <groupname> [<groupname>]
```

This command confines the users to a specific directory structure in the same way anonymous users are confined to /var/ftp. This command also limits these users to access files for which their assigned group has permissions.

The groupname parameter can be the name of a group or that group's corresponding group ID (*GID*). If you use a GID as the groupname parameter, put a percentage symbol (%) in front of it. You can use this command to assign permissions to a range of group IDs, as in this example:

```
guestgroup %500-550
```

This entry restricts all users with the group IDs 500–550 to being treated as a guest group, rather than individual users. For guestgroup to work, you must set up the users' home directories with the correct permissions, exactly like the anonymous FTP user.

Limit Permissions Based on Individual ID

The guestuser line works exactly like the guestgroup command you just read about, except it specifies a user ID (*UID*) instead of a group ID. Here's the command:

```
guestuser <username> [<username>]
```

This command limits the guest user to files for which the user has privileges. Generally, a user has more privileges than a group, so this type of assignment can be less restrictive than the guestgroup line.

Restrict the Number of Users in a Class

The limit command restricts the number of users in a class during given times. Here is the command, which contains fields for specifying a class, a number of users, a time range, and the name of a text file that contains an appropriate message:

```
limit <class> <n> <times> <message_file>
```

If the specified number of users from the listed class is exceeded during the given time period, the user sees the contents of the file given in the message_file parameter.

The times parameter is somewhat terse. Its format is a comma-delimited string in the form of days, hours. Valid day strings are Su, Mo, Tu, We, Th, Fr, Sa, and Any. The hours string is formatted in a 24-hour format. An example is as follows:

```
limit anonymous 10 MoTuWeThFr,Sa0000-2300 /home/ftp/.message_limit_anon_class
```

This line limits the anonymous class to 10 concurrent connections on Monday through Friday, and on Saturday from midnight to 11:00 p.m. For example, if the number of concurrent connections is exceeded at 11:00 p.m. on Saturday, the users will see the contents of the file `/home/ftp/.message_limit_anon_class`.

Syntax for finer control over limiting user connections can be found in the `ftpaccess` man page.

Limit the Number of Invalid Password Entries

This line allows control over how many times a user can enter an invalid password before the FTP server terminates the session:

```
loginfails <number>
```

The default for `loginfails` is set to 5. This command prevents users without valid passwords from experimenting until they get it right.

Configure User Information

Providing users with information about the server and its use is a good practice for any administrator of a public FTP server. Adequate user information can help prevent user problems and eliminate tech support calls. You also can use this information to inform users of restrictions governing the use of your FTP server. User information gives you an excellent way to document how your FTP server should be used.

You can use the commands detailed in the following sections to display messages to users as they log in to the server and as they perform specific actions. The following commands enable messages to be displayed to users when logging in to the server and when an action is performed.

Display a Prelogin Banner

This command is a reference to a file that is displayed before the user receives a login prompt from the FTP server:

```
banner <path>
```

This file generally contains information to identify the server. The path is an absolute pathname relative to the system root (/), not the base of the anonymous FTP user's home. The entry might look like this:

```
banner /etc/rh8ftp.banner
```

This example uses the file named `rh8ftp.banner` under the `/etc` directory. The file can contain one or more lines of text, such as:

```
Welcome to Widget, Inc.'s Red Hat Linux FTP server.
This server is only for use of authorized users.
Third-party developers should use a mirror site.
```

20

When an FTP user attempts to log in, the banner is displayed like so:

```
$ ftp shuttle2
Connected to shuttle2.home.org.
220-Welcome to Widget, Inc.'s Red Hat Linux FTP server.
220-This server is only for use of authorized users.
220-Third-party developers should use a mirror site.
220-
220-
220 shuttle2 FTP server (Version wu-2.6.2-8) ready.
504 AUTH GSSAPI not supported.
504 AUTH KERBEROS_V4 not supported.
KERBEROS_V4 rejected as an authentication type
Name (shuttle2:phudson):
```

> **NOTE**
>
> Note that the banner does not replace the greeting text that, by default, displays the hostname and server information, such as:
>
> ```
> 220 shuttle2 FTP server (Version wu-2.6.2-8) ready.
> ```
>
> To hide version information, use the `greeting` command in `ftpaccess` with a keyword, such as `terse`, like so:
>
> ```
> greeting terse
> ```
>
> FTP users then see a short message like this as part of the login text:
>
> ```
> 220 FTP server ready.
> ```
>
> Also, not all FTP clients can handle multiline responses from the FTP server. The banner <path> command is what the banner line uses to pass the file contents to the client. If clients cannot interrupt multiline responses, the FTP server is useless to them. You should also edit the default banner to remove identity and version information.

Display a File

This line specifies a text file to be displayed to the user during login and when the user issues the `cd` command:

```
message <path> {<when> {<class> ...}}
```

The optional `when` clause can be `LOGIN` or `CWD=(dir)`, where `dir` is the name of a directory that is current. The optional `class` parameter enables messages to be shown to only a given class or classes of users.

Using messages is a good way to give information about where things are on your site as well as information that is system dependent, such as alternative sites, general policies regarding available data, server availability times, and so on.

You can use magic cookies to breathe life into your displayed messages. *Magic cookies* are symbolic constants that are replaced by system information. Table 20.1 lists the `message` command's valid magic cookies and their representations.

TABLE 20.1   Magic Cookies and Their Descriptions

Cookie	Description
%T	Local time (form Thu Nov 15 17:12:42 1990)
%F	Free space in partition of CWD (kilobytes)
	[Not supported on all systems]
%C	Current working directory
%E	Maintainer's email address as defined in `ftpaccess`
%R	Remote hostname
%L	Local hostname
%u	Username as determined via RFC931 authentication
%U	Username given at login time
%M	Maximum allowed number of users in this class
%N	Current number of users in this class
%B	Absolute limit on disk blocks allocated
%b	Preferred limit on disk blocks
%Q	Current block count
%I	Maximum number of allocated inodes (+1)
%i	Preferred inode limit
%q	Current number of allocated inodes
%H	Time limit for excessive disk use
%h	Time limit for excessive files
Ratios	
%xu	Uploaded bytes
%xd	Downloaded bytes
%xR	Upload/download ratio (1:n)
%xc	Credit bytes
%xT	Time limit (minutes)
%xE	Elapsed time since login (minutes)
%xL	Time left
%xU	Upload limit
%xD	Download limit

To understand how this command works, imagine that you want to display a welcome message to everyone who logs in to the FTP server. An entry of:

```
message /home/ftp/welcome.msg   login
message /welcome.msg            login
```

shows the contents of the `welcome.msg` file to all authenticated users who log in to the server. The second entry shows the same message to the anonymous user.

The `welcome.msg` file is not created with the installation of the RPM, but you can create it using a text editor. Type the following:

```
Welcome to the anonymous ftp service on %L!

There are %N out of %M users logged in.

Current system time is %T

Please send email to %E if there are
any problems with this service.

Your current working directory is %C
```

Save this file as `/var/ftp/welcome.msg`. Verify that it works by connecting to the FTP server:

```
220 FTP server ready.
504 AUTH GSSAPI not supported.
504 AUTH KERBEROS_V4 not supported.
KERBEROS_V4 rejected as an authentication type
Name (shuttle:phudson): anonymous
331 Guest login ok, send your complete e-mail address as password.
Password:
230-Welcome to the anonymous ftp service on shuttle.home.org!
230-
230-There are 1 out of unlimited users logged in.
230-
230-Current system time is Mon Nov  3 10:57:06 2003
230-
230-Please send email to root@localhost if there are
230-any problems with this service.
230-Your current working directory is /
```

Display Administrator's Email Address

This line sets the email address for the FTP administrator:

```
email <name>
```

This string is printed whenever the %E magic cookie is specified. This magic cookie is used in the message line or in the shutdown file. You should display this string to users in the login banner message so that they know how to contact you (the administrator) in case of problems with the FTP server.

CAUTION

Do not use your live email address in the display banner; you want others to be able to access user emails as necessary. Instead, use an alias address that routes the messages to the appropriate IT department or other address.

Notify User of Last Modification Date

The `readme` line tells the server whether a notification should be displayed to the user when a specific file was last modified. Here's the command:

```
readme <path> {<when {<class>}}
```

The `path` parameter is any valid path for the user. The optional `when` parameter is exactly as seen in the message line. `class` can be one or more classes as defined in the class file. The `path` is absolute for real users. For the anonymous user, the `path` is relative to the anonymous home directory, which is `/var/ftp` by default.

Configure System Logging

Part of system administration involves reviewing log files for what the server is doing, who accessed it, what files were transferred, and other pieces of important information. You can use a number of commands within `/etc/ftpacess` to control your FTP server's logging actions.

Redirect Logging Records

This line allows the administrator to redirect where logging information from the FTP server is recorded:

```
log <syslog>{+<xferlog>}
```

By default, the information for commands is stored in `/var/log/messages`, although the man pages packaged in some RPMs state that this information is written to `/var/log/xferlog`. Check your server's settings for information regarding the location of your file transfer logs.

Log All User-Issued Commands

This line enables logging for all commands issued by the user:

```
log commands [<typelist>]
```

`typelist` is a comma-separated list of anonymous, guest, and real. If no `typelist` is given, commands are logged for all users. Some `wu-ftpd` RPMs set the logging of all file transfers to `/var/log/xferlog` (see the next section). However, you can add the `log` command to ftpaccess with the `commands` keyword to capture user actions. Logging is

20

then turned on and user actions are captured in /var/log/messages. Here is a sample log file:

```
Oct  6 12:21:42 shuttle2 ftpd[5229]: USER anonymous
Oct  6 12:21:51 shuttle2 ftpd[5229]: PASS phudson@widget.com
Oct  6 12:21:51 shuttle2 ftpd[5229]: ANONYMOUS FTP LOGIN FROM 192.168.2.31
➥[192.168.2.31], phudson@widget.com
Oct  6 12:21:51 shuttle2 ftpd[5229]: SYST
Oct  6 12:21:54 shuttle2 ftpd[5229]: CWD pub
Oct  6 12:21:57 shuttle2 ftpd[5229]: PASV
Oct  6 12:21:57 shuttle2 ftpd[5229]: LIST
Oct  6 12:21:59 shuttle2 ftpd[5229]: QUIT
Oct  6 12:21:59 shuttle2 ftpd[5229]: FTP session closed
```

The sample log shows the username and password entries for an anonymous login. The CWD entry shows that a cd command is used to navigate to the pub directory. Note that the commands shown do not necessarily reflect the syntax the user typed, but instead list corresponding system calls the FTP server received. For example, the LIST entry is actually the ls command.

Log Security Violations and File Transfers

Two other logging commands are useful in the /etc/ftpaccess configuration file. This line enables the logging of security violations:

```
log security [<typelist>]
```

Violations are logged for anonymous, guest, and real users, as specified in the typelist— the same as other log commands. If you do not specify a typelist, security violations for all users are logged.

This line writes a log of all files transferred to and from the server:

```
log transfers [<typelist> [<directions>]]
```

typelist is the same as in log commands and log security lines. directions is a comma-separated list of the keywords inbound for uploaded files and outbound for downloaded files. If no directions list is given, both uploaded and downloaded files are logged. Inbound and outbound logging is turned on by default.

Configure Permission Control

Controlling user activity is an important component of securing your system's server. The ftpaccess file includes a number of commands that enable you to determine what users can and cannot execute during an FTP session. You can use these permission controls to allow users to change file permissions, delete and overwrite files, rename files, and create new files with default permissions. You learn how to use all these ftpaccess file command lines in the following sections.

> **NOTE**
>
> By default, all the `ftpaccess` file command lines prohibit anonymous users from executing actions and enable authorized users to do so.

Allow Users to Change File Permissions

The `chmod` line determines whether a user can change a file's permissions. Here is the command line:

```
chmod <yes¦no> <typelist>
```

This command acts the same as the standard `chmod` command.

The `yes¦no` parameter designates whether the command can be executed. `typelist` is a comma-delimited string of the keywords anonymous, guest, and real. If you do not specify a `typelist` string, the command is applied to all users. An exhaustive description of its purpose and parameters can be found in the man page.

Assign Users File-Delete Permission

The `delete` line determines whether the user can delete files with the `rm` command. Here's the command line:

```
delete<yes¦no> <typelist>
```

The `yes¦no` parameter is used to turn this permission on or off, and `typelist` is the same as the `chmod` command.

Assign Users File-Overwrite Permission

This command line of the `ftpaccess` file allows or denies users the ability to overwrite an existing file. Here's the command line:

```
overwrite <yes¦no> <typelist>
```

The FTP client determines whether users can overwrite files on their own local machines; this line specifically controls overwrite permissions for uploads to the server. The yes|no parameter toggles the permission on or off, and `typelist` is the same as in the `chmod` line.

Allow Users to Rename Files

You can enable or prevent a user from renaming files by using this command line:

```
rename <yes¦no> <typelist>
```

The `yes¦no` parameter toggles the permission on or off, and `typelist` is the same comma-delimited string as in `chmod`.

Allow Users to Compress Files

This line determines whether the user is able to use the compress command on files:

```
compress <yes¦no> [<classglob>]
```

The yes|no parameter toggles the permission on or off, and classglob is a regular expression string that specifies one or more defined classes of users. The conversions that result from the use of this command are specified in the ftpconversions file, which contains directions on what compression or extraction command is to be used on a file with a specific extension, such as .Z for the compress command, .gz for the gunzip command, and so on. See the section "Configuring FTP Server File-Conversion Actions" later in this chapter.

Assign or Deny Permission to Use tar

This line determines whether the user is able to use the tar (tape archive) command on files:

```
tar <yes¦no> [<classglob> ...]
```

The yes¦no parameter toggles the permission on or off, and classglob is a regular expression string that specifies one or more defined classes of users. Again, the conversions that result from the use of this command are specified in the ftpconversions file.

Determine What Permissions Can Apply to User-Created Upload Files

This line is a bit different from the other commands in the permission control section. The umask command determines with what permissions a user can create new files; here it is.

```
umask <yes¦no> <typelist>
```

The yes¦no parameter toggles based on whether a user is allowed to create a file with his default permissions when uploading a file. Like the overwrite command you read about earlier in this section, this command line is specific to uploaded files because the client machine determines how new files are created from a download.

Configure Commands Directed Toward the cdpath

This alias command allows the administrator to provide another name for a directory other than its standard name:

```
alias <string> <dir>
```

The alias line applies to only the cd command. This line is particularly useful if a popular directory is buried deep within the anonymous FTP user's directory tree. The following is a sample entry:

```
alias linux-386 /pub/redhat/7.3/en/i386/
```

This line would allow the user to type `cd linux-386` and be automatically taken to the `/pub/redhat/7.3/en/i386` directory.

The `cdpath <dir>` line specifies the order in which the `cd` command looks for a given user-entered string. The search is performed in the order in which the `cdpath` lines are entered in the `ftpacess` file.

For example, if the following `cdpath` entries are in the `ftpaccess` file,

```
cdpath /pub/redhat/
cdpath /pub/linux/
```

and the user types `cd i386`, the server searches for an entry in any defined aliases, first in the `/pub/redhat` directory and then in the `/pub/linux` directory. If a large number of aliases are defined, it is recommended that symbolic links to the directories be created instead of aliases. Doing so reduces the amount of work on the FTP server and decreases the wait time for the user.

Structure of the `shutdown` File

The `shutdown` command tells the server where to look for the `shutdown` message generated by the `ftpshut` command or by the user. The `shutdown` command is used with a pathname to a shutdown file, such as:

```
shutdown /etc/rh8ftpshutdown
```

If this file exists, the server checks the file to see when the server should shut down. The syntax of this file is as follows:

```
<year> <month> <day> <hour> <minute> <deny_offset> <disc_offset> <text>
```

year can be any year after 1970 (called the *epoch*), month is from 0–11, hour is 0–23, and minute is 0–59. deny_offset is the number of minutes before shutdown in which the server disallows new connections. disc_offset is the number of minutes before connected users are disconnected, and text is the message displayed to the users at login. In addition to the valid magic cookies defined in the messages section, those listed in Table 20.2 are also available.

TABLE 20.2   Magic Cookies for the `shutdown` File

Cookie	Description
%s	The time the system will be shut down
%r	The time new connections will be denied
%d	The time current connections will be dropped

20

Configuring FTP Server File-Conversion Actions

The FTP server can convert files during transfer to compress and uncompress files automatically. Suppose that the user is transferring a file to his Microsoft Windows machine that was TARed and GZIPed on a Linux machine. If the user does not have an archive utility installed to uncompress these files, he cannot access or use the files.

As the FTP server administrator, you can configure the FTP server to automatically unarchive these files before download if the site supports users who do not have unarchive capabilities. Additionally, you can configure an upload area for the users, and then configure the FTP server to automatically compress any files transferred to the server.

The structure of the format of the `ftpconversions` file is:

```
1:2:3:4:5:6:7:8
```

where 1 is the strip prefix, 2 is the strip postfix, 3 is the add-on prefix, 4 is the add-on postfix, 5 is the external command, 6 is the types, 7 is the options, and 8 is the description.

Strip Prefix

The *strip prefix* is one or more characters at the beginning of a filename that should be automatically removed by the server when the file is requested. By specifying a given prefix to strip in a conversions rule, such as devel, the user can request the file `devel_procman.tar.gz` by the command `get procman.tar.gz`, and the FTP server performs any other rules that apply to that file and retrieve it from the server. Although this feature is documented, as of version 2.6.2, it has yet to be implemented.

Strip Postfix

The *strip postfix* works much the same as the strip prefix, except that one or more characters are taken from the end of the filename. This feature is typically used to strip the `.gz` extension from a file that was TARed and GZIPed when the server performed automatic decompression before sending the file to the client.

Add-On Prefix

The *add-on prefix* conversion instructs the server to insert one or more characters to a filename before it is transferred to the server or client. For example, assume that a user requests the file `procman.tar.gz`. The server has a conversion rule to add a prefix of gnome to all `.tar.gz` files; therefore the server would append this string to the file before sending it to the client. The user would receive a file called `gnome_procman.tar.gz`. Keywords such as uppercase and lowercase can be used in this function to change the case of the filename for those operating systems in which case makes a difference. As with the strip prefix conversion, this feature is not yet implemented in version 2.6.2.

Add-On Postfix

An *add-on postfix* instructs the server to append one or more characters to the end of a filename during the transfer or reception of a file. A server can contain TARed packages of applications that are uncompressed. If an add-on postfix conversion is configured on the server, the server could compress the file, append a .gz extension after the file was compressed, and then send that file to the client. The server could also perform the same action for uncompressed files sent to the server. This would have the effect of conserving disk space on the server.

External Command

The *external command* entries in the ftpconversions file contain the bulk of the FTP server conversion rules. The external command entry tells the server what should be done with a file after it is transferred to the server. The specified conversion utility can be any command on the server, although generally it is a compression utility. As the file is sent, the server passes the file through the external command. If the file is being uploaded to the server, the command needs to send the result to standard in, whereas a download sends the result to standard out. For example, here is an entry specifying the tar command:

```
:   : :.tar:/bin/tar -c -f - %s:T_REG|T_DIR:O_TAR:TAR
```

The following sections describe the fields in a conversion entry.

Types

You must use the types field of the ftpconversions file to tell the server to what types of files the conversion rules apply. Separate the file type entries with the (|) character, and give each type a value of T_REG, T_ASCII, and T_DIR.

T_REG signifies a regular file, T_ASCII an ASCII file, and T_DIR a directory. A typical entry is T_REG | T_ASCII, which signifies a regular ASCII file.

Options

The options field informs the server what action is being done to the file. Similar to the types field, options are separated by the (|) character. Here are the valid ranges you can assign to items in the options field:

▶ O_COMPRESS to compress the file

▶ O_UNCOMPRESS to uncompress the file

▶ O_TAR to tar the file

An example of this field is O_COMPRESS | O_TAR, where files are both compressed and TARed.

Description

The description field allows an administrator to quickly understand what the rule is doing. This field does not have any syntax restriction, although it is usually a one-word entry—such as TAR, TAR+COMPRESS, or UNCOMPRESS—which is enough to get the concept across.

An Example of Conversions in Action

Crafting complex conversion entries is a task perhaps best left to the Linux/Unix expert, but the sample ftpconversions file included with wu-ftpd provides more than enough examples for the average Red Hat administrator. Building your own simple conversion entry is not really too difficult, so let's examine and decode an example:

```
:.Z:   :   :/bin/compress -d -c %s:T_REG¦T_ASCII:O_UNCOMPRESS:UNCOMPRESS
```

In this example, the strip prefix (field 1) is null because it is not yet implemented, so this rule does not apply to prefixes. The second field of this rule contains the .Z postfix; therefore it deals with files that have been compressed with the compress utility. The rule does not address the add-on prefix or postfix, so fields 3 and 4 are null. Field 5, the external command field, tells the server to run the compress utility to decompress all files that have the .Z extension, as the -d parameter signifies. The -c options tells compress to write its output to standard out, which is the server in this case. The %s is the name of the file against which the rule was applied. Field 6 specifies that this file is a regular file in ASCII format. Field 7, the options field, tells the server that this command uncompresses the file. Finally, the last field is a comment that gives the administrator a quick decode of what the conversion rule is doing—that is, uncompressing the file.

Examples

Several conversion rules may be specified in wu-ftpd's default ftpconversions file. Additional examples of conversion rules, such as for Sun's Solaris operating system, might be available in the wu-ftpd documentation.

Using ftphosts to Allow or Deny FTP Server Connection

The purpose of the ftphosts file is to allow or deny specific users or addresses from connecting to the FTP server. The format of the file is the word allow or deny, optionally followed by a username, followed by an IP or a DNS address.

```
allow username address
deny username address
```

Listing 20.3 shows a sample configuration of this file.

LISTING 20.3   ftphosts Configuration File for Allowing or Denying Users

```
# Example host access file
#
# Everything after a '#' is treated as comment,
# empty lines are ignored
allow tdc 128.0.0.1
allow tdc 192.168.101.*
allow tdc insanepenguin.net
allow tdc *.exodous.net
deny anonymous 201.*
deny anonymous *.pilot.net
```

The * is a wildcard that matches any combination of that address. For example, `allow tdc *.exodous.net` allows the user `tdc` to log in to the FTP server from any address that contains the domain name exodous.net. Similarly, the anonymous user is not allowed to access the FTP if he is coming from a 201 public class C IP address.

Changes made to your system's FTP server configuration files become active only after you restart `xinetd` because configuration files are parsed only at startup. To restart `xinetd` as root, issue the command **/etc/rc.d/init.d/xinetd restart**. This makes a call to the same shell script that is called at system startup and shutdown for any runlevel to start or stop the `xinet` daemon. `xinetd` should report its status as:

```
# /etc/rc.d/init.d/xinetd restart
Stopping xinetd:                                    [  OK  ]
Starting xinetd:                                    [  OK  ]
```

When the FTP server restarts, it is accessible to all incoming requests.

Using Commands for Server Administration

`wu-ftp` provides a few commands to aid in server administration. Those commands are:

▶ **ftpwho**—Displays information about current FTP server users

▶ **ftpcount**—Displays information about current server users by class

▶ **ftpshut**—Provides automated server shutdown and user notification

▶ **ftprestart**—Provides automated server restart and shutdown message removal

Each of these commands must be executed with superuser privileges because they reference the `ftpaccess` configuration file to obtain information about the FTP server.

Display Information About Connected Users

The ftpwho command provides information about the users currently connected to the FTP server. Here's the command line:

```
/usr/bin/ftpwho
```

Table 20.3 shows the format of the output ftpwho displays.

TABLE 20.3   ftpwho Fields

Name	Description
Process ID	The process ID of the FTP server process.
TTY	The terminal ID of the process. This is always a question mark (?) because the FTP daemon is not an interactive login.
Status	The status of the FTP process. The values are:
	S: Sleeping
	Z: Zombie, indicating a crash
	R: Running
	N: Normal process
Time	The elapsed processor time the process has used in minutes and seconds.
Details	Tells from what host the process is connecting, the user who connected, and the currently executing command.

Listing 20.4 shows typical output from this command. It lists the process ID for the ftp daemon handling requests, the class to which the particular user belongs, the total time connected, the connected username, and the status of the session.

In addition to the information given about each connected user, ftpwho also displays the total number of users connected out of any maximum that has been set in the ftpaccess file. This information can be used to monitor the use of your FTP server.

You can pass one parameter to ftpwho. (You can find the parameter by using the ftpwho--help command.) The single parameter you can pass to ftpwho is -v. This parameter prints out version and licensing information for wu-ftp, as shown here:

```
# ftpwho
Service class all:
10447 ?        SN     0:00 ftpd: localhost: anonymous/winky@disney.com: IDLE
1 users (no maximum)
```

The output of ftpwho, using the -V option, which shows version information, is shown in Listing 20.4.

LISTING 20.4   ftpwho -V Command Output

Copyright © 1999,2000,2001 WU-FTPD Development Group.
All rights reserved.

Portions Copyright © 1980, 1985, 1988, 1989, 1990, 1991, 1993, 1994
  The Regents of the University of California.
Portions Copyright © 1993, 1994 Washington University in Saint Louis.
Portions Copyright © 1996, 1998 Berkeley Software Design, Inc.
Portions Copyright © 1989 Massachusetts Institute of Technology.
Portions Copyright © 1998 Sendmail, Inc.
Portions Copyright © 1983, 1995, 1996, 1997 Eric P. Allman.
Portions Copyright © 1997 by Stan Barber.
Portions Copyright © 1997 by Kent Landfield.
Portions Copyright © 1991, 1992, 1993, 1994, 1995, 1996, 1997
Free Software Foundation, Inc.

Use and distribution of this software and its source code are governed
by the terms and conditions of the WU-FTPD Software License ("LICENSE").

If you did not receive a copy of the license, it may be obtained online
at http://www.wu-ftpd.org/license.html.
Version wu-2.6.2-8

Count the Number of Connections

/usr/bin/ftpcount counts the number of connected users to the FTP server and the maximum number of users allowed. This same information is found at the end of the output for the ftpwho command. This command takes only one parameter, -V, which displays the same output as the previous ftpwho example.

```
# ftpcount
Service class all                 -   4 users (no maximum)
```

Use /usr/sbin/ftpshut to Schedule FTP Server Downtime

As with any public server administration, it is always good practice to let users of the FTP server know about upcoming outages, when the server will be updated, and other relevant site information. The ftpshut command allows the administrator to let the FTP server do much of this automatically.

20

The `ftpshut` command enables the administrator to take down the FTP server at a specific time, based on some parameters passed to it. The format of the command is as follows and is documented in the `ftpshut` man page:

```
ftpshut [ -V ] [ -l min] [ -d min] time [ warning-message ... ]
```

The `-V` parameter displays the command's version information. The `time` parameter is the time when the `ftpshut` command will stop the FTP servers. This parameter takes either a + number for the number of minutes from the current time, or a specific hour and minute in 24-hour clock format with the syntax of *HH:MM*.

The `-l` parameter enables the FTP server administrator to specify how long, in minutes, before shutdown the server disallows new connections. The default is 10 minutes. If the time given to shut down the servers is less than 10 minutes, new connections are disallowed immediately.

The `-d` parameter is similar to the `-l` parameter, but controls when the FTP server terminates the current connections. By default, this occurs five minutes before the server shuts down. If the shutdown time is less than five minutes, the server terminates the current connections immediately.

When you execute this command, the FTP server creates a file containing the shutdown information in the location specified under the shutdown section in the `ftpaccess` file. The default configuration for this file is `/etc/shutmsg`. If you execute the `ftpshut` command with warning messages, the messages are displayed when the user logs in to the server.

```
Name (pheniox:tdc): anonymous
331 Guest login ok, send your complete e-mail address as password.
Password:
230-system doing down at Mon Sep  3 06:23:00 2001
230-0 users of unlimited on pheniox.
230 Guest login ok, access restrictions apply.
Remote system type is UNIX.
Using binary mode to transfer files.
```

Here is a sample `ftpshut` command:

```
ftpshut -l 5 -d 5 +10 "system going down at %s %N users of %M on %R"
```

This command tells the FTP server to disconnect new connections in 5 minutes, drop all current connections in 5 minutes, shut down the server in 10 minutes, and display a warning message to the users at login. The message can be a mixture of text and the magic cookies defined in Table 20.4. It is important to keep in mind that the message can be a maximum of 75 characters in length. Additionally, it is not important to know how many characters the magic cookies take because the system knows this information and truncates the message at 75 characters.

TABLE 20.4   Magic Cookies for the `ftpshut` Command

Cookie	Description
%s	Time the system will be shut down
%r	Time new connections will be denied
%d	Time current connections will be dropped
%C	Current working directory
%E	Server administrator's email address as specified in the `ftpaccess` file
%F	Available free space in the current working directories partition, in kilobytes
%L	Local host time
%M	Maximum number of allowed connections in this user class
%N	Current number of connections for this user class
%R	Remote hostname
%T	Local time, in the form of `Fri Aug 31 21:04:00 2001`
%U	Username given at login

When `ftpshut` is issued to the system, it creates a file that stores the necessary information. The `ftprestart` command removes this file for all servers, either canceling the impending shutdown or removing the shutdown file and restarting the FTP server. The `ftprestart` has only one optional argument, `-V`, to show version information.

Use `/var/log/xferlog` to View a Log of Server Transactions

The `xferlog` file gives a log of what transactions have occurred with the FTP server. Depending on the settings in the `/etc/ftpaccess` file, the contents of this file can contain the files sent or received, by whom, with a date stamp. Table 20.5 lists the fields of this file. The same information can also be found in the corresponding man page included in the `wu-ftp` RPM.

TABLE 20.5   `/var/log/xferlog` Fields

Field	Description
current-time	Current local time in the form of *DDD MMM dd hh:mm:ss YYYY*, where *DDD* is the day of the week, *MMM* is the month, *dd* is the day of the month, *hh* is the hour, *mm* is the minutes, *ss* is the seconds, and *YYYY* is the year.
transfer-time	Total time in seconds for the transfer.
remote-host	Remote hostname.
file-size	Size of the transferred file in bytes.
filename	Name of the file.
transfer-type	A single character indicating the transfer type. The types are: a for ASCII transfers b for binary transfers

20

TABLE 20.5   Continued

Field	Description
special-action-flag	One or more character flags indicating any special action taken by the server. The values are: C for compressed files U for uncompressed files T for TARed files - for no special action taken
direction	Indicates whether the file was sent from or received by the server.
access-mode	The way in which the user logged in to the server. The values are: a for an anonymous guest user g for a guest user, corresponding to the `guestgroup` command in the `/etc/ftpaccess` file r for a real user on the local machine
username	If logged in as a real user, the username. If the access mode was `guest`, the password is given.
service-name	The name of the service used, usually FTP.
authentication-method	Type of authentication used. The values are: 0 for none 1 for RFC931 authentication (a properly formed email address)
authenticated-user-id	This is the user ID returned to the server based on the authentication method used to access the server. An * is used when an authenticated user ID cannot be found.
completion-status	A single-character field indicating the status of the transfer. The values are: c for a completed transfer i for an incomplete transfer

An example of this file is seen in Listing 20.5.

LISTING 20.5   Sample `/var/log/xferlog` File with Inbound and Outbound Logging

```
Mon Sep  3 07:13:05 2001 1 localhost.localdomain 100
 /var/ftp/pub/README b  o a testing@test.com ftp 0 * c
Mon Sep  3 02:35:35 2001 1 helios 8 /var/ftp/pub/configuration a
_ o a testing@test.com ftp 0 * c
Mon Sep  3 02:35:35 2001 1 helios 8 /var/ftp/pub/temp.txt a  o a
testing@test.com ftp 0 * c
Mon Sep  3 02:35:35 2001 1 helios 8 /var/ftp/pub/tftp-server-
0.17-14.i386.rpm a  o a testing@test.com ftp 0 * c
Mon Sep  3 02:35:35 2001 1 helios 8 /var/ftp/pub/wu-ftpd-2.6.1-
22.i386.rpm a  o a testing@test.com ftp 0 * c
```

You use these commands to install, configure, and manage FTP services in Fedora:

- ▶ **epiphany**—A graphical GNOME browser supporting FTP
- ▶ **ftp**—A text-based interactive FTP command
- ▶ **ftpcopy**—Copy directories and files from an FTP server
- ▶ **ftpcp**—Retrieve data from a remote FTP server, but do not overwrite existing local files
- ▶ **gftp**—A graphical FTP client for GNOME
- ▶ **konqueror**—KDE's graphical web browser
- ▶ **lftp**—An advanced text-based FTP program
- ▶ **nautilus**—Red Hat's graphical file explorer and browser
- ▶ **ncftp**—A sophisticated, text-based FTP program
- ▶ **sftp**—Secure file transfer program
- ▶ **smbclient**—Samba FTP client to access SMB/CIFS resources on servers
- ▶ **system-config-services**—Red Hat's system service GUI admin utility
- ▶ **vsftpd**—The Very Secure FTP daemon
- ▶ **webcam**—A webcam-oriented FTP client included with xawtv

Reference

- ▶ http://www.wu-ftpd.org/—wu-ftp official website.

- ▶ http://www.cert.org/—Computer emergency response team.

- ▶ http://www.openssh.com/—OpenSSH home page and source for the latest version of OpenSSH and its component clients, such as sftp.

- ▶ http://www.cert.org/tech_tips/anonymous_ftp_config.html—CERT anonymous FTP configuration guidelines.

- ▶ http://vsftpd.beasts.org/—Home page for the vsftd FTP server.

- ▶ ftp://vsftpd.beasts.org/users/cevans/—Download site for the latest releases of the vsftpd server.

20

Handling Electronic Mail

Email is still the dominant form of communication over the Internet. It is fast, free, and very easy to use. However, much of what goes on behind the scenes is extremely complicated and would appear scary to anyone who does not know much about how email is handled. Fedora comes equipped with a number of powerful applications to help you build anything from a small email server right through to large servers handling thousands of messages.

This chapter shows you how to configure Fedora to act as an email server. We look at the options available in Fedora, as well as the pros and cons of each one. You will also learn how mail is handled in Linux, and to a lesser extent, UNIX.

How Email Is Sent and Received

Email is transmitted as plain text across networks around the world using *SMTP* (*Simple Mail Transfer Protocol*). As the name implies, the protocol itself is fairly basic, and it has been extended to add further authentication and error reporting/messaging to satisfy the growing demands of modern email. *Mail transfer agents*, or *MTAs*, work in the background, transferring email from server to server, allowing emails to be sent all over the world. You might have come across such MTA software such as Sendmail, Postfix, Fetchmail, Exim, or Qmail.

SMTP enables each computer through which the email passes to forward it in the right direction to the final destination. When you consider that there are millions of email servers across the world, you have to marvel at how simple it all seems.

Here is a simplified example of how email is successfully processed and sent to its destination:

1. andrew@hudson.org composes and sends an email message to paul@hudzilla.org.

2. The MTA at hudson.org receives andrew's email message and queues it for delivery behind any other messages that are also waiting to go out.

3. The MTA at hudson.org contacts the MTA at hudzilla.org on port 25. After hudzilla.org acknowledges the connection, the MTA at hudson.org sends the mail message. After hudzilla.org accepts and acknowledges receipt of the message, the connection is closed.

4. The MTA at hudzilla.org places the mail message into paul's incoming mailbox; paul is notified that he has new mail the next time he logs on.

Of course, several things can go wrong during this process. Consider these examples:

▶ What if paul does not exist at hudzilla.org? In this case, the MTA at hudzilla.org rejects the email and notifies the MTA at hudson.org of what the problem is. The MTA at hudson.org then generates an email message and sends it to andrew@hudson.org, informing him that no paul exists at hudzilla.org (or perhaps just silently discards the message and gives the sender no indication of the problem, depending on how the email server is configured).

▶ What happens if hudzilla.org doesn't respond to hudson.org's connection attempts? (Perhaps the server is down for maintenance.) The MTA at hudson.org notifies the sender that the initial delivery attempt has failed. Further attempts will be made at intervals decided by the server administrator until the deadline is reached, and the sender then is notified that the mail is undeliverable.

The Mail Transport Agent

Several MTAs are available for Fedora, each with pros and cons to being used. Normally they are hidden under the skin of Fedora, silently moving mail between servers all over the world with need for little or no maintenance. Some MTAs are extremely powerful, and are able to cope with hundreds of thousands of messages each day, whereas others are geared toward smaller installations. Other MTAs are perhaps not as powerful, but are packed full with features. The next section takes a look at some of the more popular MTAs available for Fedora.

Sendmail

The overwhelming majority of emails transmitted over the Internet today are handled by Sendmail, which just so happens to be the default MTA supplied with Fedora. It is extremely popular across the Linux/UNIX/BSD world and is well supported. There is a commercial version available, which has a GUI interface for ease of configuration.

As well as being popular, Sendmail is particularly powerful compared to some of the other MTAs. However, it is not without its downsides, and other MTAs can handle more email per second in a larger environment. The other issue with Sendmail is that it can be extremely complicated to set it up exactly as you want it. In fact, the level of complexity associated with Sendmail often leads to system administrators replacing it with one of the other alternatives that is easier to configure. There are a few books available specifically for Sendmail, but the most popular one has more than a thousand pages, reflecting the complex nature of Sendmail configuration.

The good news, however, is that the default configuration for Sendmail works fine for most basic installations out of the box, making further configurations unnecessary. Even if you want to use it as a basic email server, you have to do only some minor tweaks. We take a look at some basic Sendmail configuration later in this chapter in the section titled "Basic Sendmail Configuration and Operation."

Postfix

Postfix has its origins as the IBM Secure Mailer, but was released to the developer community by IBM. Compared to Sendmail, it is much easier to administer and has a number of speed advantages. Postfix offers a pain-free replacement for Sendmail, and you are able to replace Sendmail with Postfix without the system breaking a sweat. In fact, when you install Postfix in place of Sendmail, applications that relied on Sendmail automatically use Postfix instead and carry on working correctly. Postfix uses a Sendmail *wrapper*, which deceives other programs into thinking that Postfix is Sendmail. This wrapper, or more correctly, interface, makes switching to Postfix extremely easy.

> **CAUTION**
>
> Fedora provides Postfix version 2.4, which uses a slightly different configuration than the earlier version. If you are upgrading Postfix from an earlier Fedora or Red Hat version, check your configuration files.
>
> Fedora also now compiles Postfix and Sendmail against version 2.1 of the Cyrus SASL library (an authentication library). The Release Notes contain detailed information on file location and option changes that affect you if you use these libraries.

For enhanced security, many Postfix processes used to use the `chroot` facility (which restricts access to only specific parts of the file system) for improved security, and there are no `setuid` components in Postfix. With the current release of Fedora, a `chroot` configuration *is no longer used* and is, in fact, discouraged by the Postfix author. You can manually reconfigure Postfix to a `chroot` configuration, but that is no longer supported by Fedora.

If you are starting from scratch, Postfix is considered a better choice than Sendmail.

Qmail and Exim

Qmail is a direct competitor to Postfix but is not provided with Fedora. Postfix is designed to be easier to use than Sendmail, as well as faster and more secure. However, Qmail isn't a drop-in replacement for Sendmail, so migrating an existing Sendmail installation to Qmail is not quite as simple as migrating from Sendmail to Postfix. Qmail is relatively easy to administer, and it integrates with a number of software add-ons, including web mail systems and POP3 servers. Qmail is available from http://www.qmail.org/.

Exim is yet another MTA, and it is available using yum. Exim is considered faster and more secure than Sendmail or Postfix, but is much different to configure than either of those. Exim and Qmail use the maildir format rather than mbox, so both are considered "NFS safe" (see the following sidebar).

MDIR Versus Mailbox

Qmail also introduced maildir, which is an alternative to the standard UNIX method of storing incoming mail. maildir is a more versatile system of handling incoming email, but it requires your email clients to be reconfigured, and it is not compatible with the traditional UNIX way of storing incoming mail. You have to use mail programs that recognize the maildir format. (Modern programs do.)

The traditional mbox format keeps all mail assigned to a folder concatenated as a single file and maintains an index of individual emails. With maildir, each mail folder has three subfolders: /cur, /new, and /tmp. Each email is kept in a separate, unique file. If you are running a mail server for a large number of people, you should select a file system that can efficiently handle a large number of small files.

mbox does have one major disadvantage. While you are accessing the monolithic mbox file that contains all your email, suppose that some type of corruption occurs, either to the file itself or to the index. Recovery from this problem can be difficult. The mbox files are especially prone to problems if the files are being accessed over a network and can result in file corruption; you should avoid accessing mbox mail mounted over NFS, the network file system, because sudden connection loss can seriously corrupt your mbox file.

Depending on how you access your mail, maildir does permit the simultaneous access of maildir files by multiple applications; mbox does not.

The choice of a mail user agent, or email client, also affects your choice of mail directory format. For example, the pine program does not cache any directory information and must reread the mail directory any time it accesses it. If you are using pine, maildir would be a poor choice. More advanced email clients perform caching, so maildir might be a good choice, although the email client cache can get out of synchronization. It seems that there is no perfect choice.

Fedora provides you with mail alternatives that have both strong and weak points. Be aware of the differences among the alternatives and frequently reevaluate your selection to make certain that it is the best one for your circumstances.

Choosing an MTA

Other MTAs are available for use with Fedora, but those discussed in the preceding sections are the most popular. Which one should you choose? That depends on what you need to do. Sendmail's main strengths are that it is considered the standard and it can do things that many other MTAs cannot. However, if ease of use or speed is a concern to you, you might want to consider replacing Sendmail with Postfix, Exim, or Qmail. Because Sendmail is the default MTA included with Fedora, it is covered in more detail over the following sections.

The Mail Delivery Agent

SMTP is a server-to-server protocol that was designed to deliver mail to systems that are always connected to the Internet. Dialup systems connect only at the user's command; they connect for specific operations, and are frequently disconnected. To accommodate this difference, many mail systems also include a *mail delivery agent*, or *MDA*. The MDA transfers mail to systems without permanent Internet connections. An MDA is similar to an MTA (see the following note), but does not handle deliveries between systems and does not provide an interface to the user.

> **NOTE**
>
> Procmail and Spamassassin are examples of MTAs; both provide filtering services to the MTA while they store messages locally and then make them available to the MUA or email client for reading by the user.

The MDA uses the POP3 or IMAP protocols for this process. In a manner similar to a post office box at the post office, POP3 and IMAP implement a "store and forward" process that alleviates the need to maintain a local mail server if all you want to do is read your mail. For example, dialup Internet users can intermittently connect to their ISPs' mail servers to retrieve mail by using Fetchmail—the MDA provided by Fedora (see the section "Using Fetchmail to Retrieve Mail," later in this chapter).

The Mail User Agent

The *mail user agent*, or *MUA*, is another necessary part of the email system. The MUA is a mail client, or mail reader, that enables the user to read and compose email and provides the user interface. (It is the email application itself that most users are familiar with as "email.") Some popular UNIX command-line MUAs are elm, pine, and mutt. Fedora also provides modern GUI MUAs: Evolution, Thunderbird, Mozilla Mail, Balsa, Sylpheed, and KMail. For comparison, common non-UNIX MUAs are Microsoft Outlook, Outlook Express, Pegasus, and Eudora.

The Microsoft Windows and Macintosh MUAs often include some MTA functionality; UNIX does not. For example, Microsoft Outlook can connect to your Internet provider's mail server to send messages. On the other hand, UNIX MUAs generally rely on an external MTA such as Sendmail. This might seem like a needlessly complicated way to do things, and it is if used to connect a single user to her ISP. For any other situation, however, using an external MTA provides you much greater flexibility because you can use any number of external programs to handle and process your email functions and customize the service. Having the process handled by different applications gives you great control over how you provide email service to users on your network, as well as to individual and *SOHO (small office/home office)* users.

For example, you could

- ▶ Use Evolution to read and compose mail.

- ▶ Use Sendmail to send your mail.

- ▶ Use xbiff to notify you when you have new mail.

- ▶ Use Fetchmail to retrieve your mail from a remote mail server.

- ▶ Use Procmail to automatically sort your incoming mail based on sender, subject, or many other variables.

- ▶ Use Spamassassin to eliminate the unwanted messages before you read them.

Basic Sendmail Configuration and Operation

Because Sendmail is the Fedora default client (and the mostly widely used client), the following sections provide a brief explanation and examples for configuring and operating your email system. As mentioned earlier, however, Sendmail is an extremely complex program with a very convoluted configuration. As such, this chapter covers only some of the basics. For more information on Sendmail, as well as other MTAs, see the "Reference" section at the end of this chapter.

Sendmail configuration is handled by files in the /etc/mail directory, with much of the configuration being handled by the file sendmail.cf. The actual syntax of the configuration file, sendmail.cf, is cryptic (see the following example). In an attempt to make it easier to configure Sendmail, the sendmail.mc file was created. The following example belies that goal, however. The sendmail.mc file must be processed with the m4 macro processor to create the sendmail.cf file; the needs of that processor account for the unusual syntax of the file. You will learn how to use it later, and we see a Perl script that automates and simplifies the entire process. First, let's examine some basic configuration you might want to do with Sendmail.

> **NOTE**
>
> sendmail.cf has some strange syntax because of the requirements of the m4 macro processor. You do not need to understand the details of m4 here, but note the quoting system. The starting quote is a backtick (`` ` ``), and the ending quote is simply a single quote ('). Also, the dnl sequence means to "delete to new line" and causes anything from the sequence up to and including the newline character to be deleted in the output.
>
> Here's a look at an excerpt from the sendmail.cf file:
>
> ```
> CP.
> # "Smart" relay host (may be null)
> DS
> ```

```
# operators that cannot be in local usernames (i.e., network indicators)
CO @ % !
# a class with just dot (for identifying canonical names)
C..
# a class with just a left bracket (for identifying domain literals)
C[[
# access_db acceptance class
C{Accept}OK RELAY
C{ResOk}OKR
# Hosts for which relaying is permitted ($=R)
FR-o /etc/mail/relay-domains
```

And here's a quote from the sendmail.mc file for comparison:

```
dnl define(`SMART_HOST',`smtp.your.provider')
define(`confDEF_USER_ID',``8:12'')dnl
undefine(`UUCP_RELAY')dnl
undefine(`BITNET_RELAY')dnl
dnl define(`confAUTO_REBUILD')dnl
define(`confTO_CONNECT', `1m')dnl
define(`confTRY_NULL_MX_LIST',true)dnl
```

You can see why the file is described as cryptic.

Complicated email server setup is beyond the scope of this book; for more information on this topic, we suggest *Sendmail, 3rd Edition* by Costales and Allman, a 1,200-page comprehensive tome on Sendmail configuration. However, the following five sections address some commonly used advanced options.

Configuring Masquerading

Sometimes you might want to have Sendmail masquerade as a host other than the actual hostname of your system. Such a situation could occur if you have a dialup connection to the Internet and your ISP handles all your mail for you. In this case, you want Sendmail to masquerade as the domain name of your ISP. For example:

```
MASQUERADE_AS(`samplenet.org')dnl
```

Using Smart Hosts

If you do not have a full-time connection to the Internet, you probably want to have Sendmail send your messages to your ISP's mail server and let it handle delivery for you. Without a full-time Internet connection, you could find it difficult to deliver messages to some locations (such as some underdeveloped areas of the world where email services are unreliable and sporadic). In those situations, you can configure Sendmail to function as a smart host by passing email on to another sender rather than attempting to deliver the email directly. You can use a line such as the following in the `sendmail.mc` file to enable a smart host:

```
define(`SMART_HOST', `smtp.samplenet.org')
```

This line causes Sendmail to pass any mail it receives to the server `smtp.samplenet.org` rather than attempt to deliver it directly. Smart hosting will not work for you if your ISP, like many others, blocks any mail relaying. Some ISPs block relaying because it is frequently used to disseminate spam.

Setting Message Delivery Intervals

As mentioned earlier, Sendmail typically attempts to deliver messages as soon as it receives them, and again at regular intervals after that. If you have only periodic connections to the Internet, as with a dialup connection, you likely would prefer that Sendmail hold all messages in the queue and attempt to deliver them at specific time intervals or at your prompt. You can configure Sendmail to do so by adding the following line to `sendmail.mc`:

```
define(`confDELIVERY_MODE', `d')dnl
```

This line causes Sendmail to attempt mail delivery only at regularly scheduled queue processing intervals (by default, somewhere between 20 and 30 minutes).

However, this delay time might not be sufficient if you are offline for longer periods of time. In those situations, you can invoke Sendmail with no queue processing time. For example, by default, Sendmail might start with the following command:

```
# sendmail -bd -q30m
```

This tells Sendmail that it should process the mail queue (and attempt message delivery) every 30 minutes. You can change 30 to any other number to change the delivery interval. If you want Sendmail to wait for a specific prompt before processing the queue, you can invoke Sendmail with no queue time, like this:

```
# sendmail -bd -q
```

This command tells Sendmail to process the queue once when it is started, and again only when you manually direct it to do so. To manually tell Sendmail to process the queue, you can use a command like the following:

```
# sendmail -q
```

> **TIP**
>
> If you use networking over a modem, there is a configuration file for pppd called `ppp.linkup`, which is located in `/etc/ppp`. Any commands in this file are automatically run each time the PPP daemon is started. You can add the line `sendmail -q` to this file to have your mail queue automatically processed each time you dial up your Internet connection.

Building the `sendmail.cf` File

Books are available to explore the depths of Sendmail configuration, but the *Sendmail Installation and Operation Guide* (check on Google for this) is the canonical reference. Configuration guidance can also be found through a Google search; many people use Sendmail in many different configurations. Fortunately, Fedora has provided a default Sendmail configuration that works out of the box for a home user as long as your networking is correctly configured and you do not require an ISP-like Sendmail configuration.

After you have made all your changes to `sendmail.mc`, you have to rebuild the `sendmail.cf` file. First, back up your old file:

```
# cp /etc/mail/sendmail.cf /etc/mail/sendmail.cf.old
```

You must run `sendmail.mc` through the `m4` macro processor to generate a useable configuration file. A command, such as the following, is used to do this:

```
# m4 /etc/mail/sendmail.mc > /etc/mail/sendmail.cf
```

This command loads the `cf.m4` macro file from `/usr/share/sendmail-cf/m4/cf.m4` and then uses it to process the `sendmail.mc` file. The output, normally sent to STDOUT, is then redirected to the file `sendmail.cf`, and your new configuration file is ready. You have to restart Sendmail before the changes take effect.

> **TIP**
>
> Fedora also provides an alternative to using awk to rebuild the Sendmail configuration. As root, execute the following:
>
> ```
> # make -C /etc/mail
> ```

Mail Relaying

By default, Sendmail does not relay mail that did not originate from the local domain. This means that if a Sendmail installation running at hudson.org receives mail intended for hudzilla.com, and that mail did not originate from hudson.org, the mail is rejected and not relayed. If you want to allow selected domains to relay through you, add an entry for the domain to the file `/etc/mail/relay-domains`. If the file does not exist, create it in your favorite text editor and add a line containing the name of the domain that you want to allow to relay through you. Sendmail has to be restarted for this change to take effect.

> **CAUTION**
>
> You need a very good reason to relay mail; otherwise, do not do it. Allowing all domains to relay through you makes you a magnet for spammers who want to use your mail server to send spam. This could lead to your site being blacklisted by many other sites, which then will not accept any mail from you or your site's users—even if the mail is legitimate!

Forwarding Email with Aliases

Aliases enable you to have an infinite number of valid recipient addresses on your system, without having to worry about creating accounts or other support files for each address. For example, most systems have postmaster defined as a valid recipient, yet do not have an actual login account named postmaster. Aliases are configured in the file /etc/aliases. Here is an example of an alias entry:

```
postmaster: root
```

This entry forwards any mail received for postmaster to the root user. By default, almost all the aliases listed in the /etc/aliases file forward to root.

CAUTION

Reading email as root is a security hazard; a malicious email message can exploit an email client and cause it to execute arbitrary code as the user running the client. To avoid this danger, you can forward all of root's mail to another account and read it from there. You can choose one of two ways for doing this.

You can add an entry to the /etc/mail/aliases file that sends root's mail to a different account. For example, root: foobar would forward all mail intended for root to the account foobar.

The other way is to create a file named .forward in root's home directory that contains the address to which the mail should forward.

Any time you make a change to the /etc/mail/aliases file, you have to rebuild the aliases database before that change takes effect. This is done with the following:

```
# newaliases
```

Rejecting Email from Specified Sites

You read earlier in this chapter that you must be careful with mail relaying to avoid becoming a spam magnet. But what do you do if you are having problems with a certain site sending you spam? You can use the /etc/mail/access file to automatically reject mail from certain sites.

You can use several rules in the access file. Table 21.1 lists these rules.

TABLE 21.1   The Various Possible Options for Access Rules

Option	Action
OK	Accepts mail from this site, overriding any rules that would reject mail from this site.
RELAY	Allows this domain to relay through the server.
REJECT	Rejects mail from this site and sends a canned error message.
DISCARD	Simply discards any message received from the site.

TABLE 21.1   Continued

Option	Action
ERROR: "*n* message"	Sends an error message back to the originating server, where *n* is an RFC 821-compliant error code number. The message itself can be anything you want.

The following is an example of three rules used to control access to a Sendmail account. The first rejects messages from spam.com. The second rejects messages from lamer.com and displays an error message to that site. The third allows mail from the specific host user5.lamer.com, even though there is a rule that rejects mail from the site lamer.com.

> **NOTE**
>
> For a more personal example of why you would bother to do this, I find that I get a lot of spam from the Hotmail domain, so I would just as soon reject it all. However, my wife uses a Hotmail account for her mail. If I did not allow her mail through, that would be a problem for me.

```
spam.com          REJECT
lamer.com         ERROR:"550 Mail from spammers is not accepted at this site."
user5.lamer.com   OK
```

Open the /etc/access file, enter the rules of your choice, and then restart Sendmail so that your changes to the access file take effect. That can be done with

```
# service sendmail restart
```

or any of the other ways discussed in Chapter 11, "Automating Tasks."

Introducing Postfix

Sendmail has been the de facto MTA of choice for the Internet for a long time. At one point, it was the power behind 90% of the email traffic across the world, although it has now become largely superseded by worthier programs.

One of the more popular programs that have become available is Postfix, which was developed and is exclusively maintained by Wietse Venema. Designed to be a drop-in replacement for Sendmail, Postfix allows the system administrator to replace Sendmail without any detriment to the system.

Postfix was designed from the ground up to retain compatibility with Sendmail but to work in a more efficient fashion. Sendmail is notoriously system intensive when handling either large volumes of mail or large numbers of clients. One command pretty much handles everything, making Sendmail something of a monolith. On the other hand, Postfix works with several individual modules all working together, using modules only when needed.

Making the Switch

Postfix is easy to install and configure. The first thing to do is to make a backup of all your Sendmail information that you want to keep, just in case. After you have done this, you need to use yum to remove Sendmail and install Postfix.

After Postfix has been successfully installed, you can begin configuring it. The scripts for Postfix are all located in /etc/postfix and include

- ▶ **install.cf**—The script generated when Postfix is installed. This file lists the locations Postfix uses and can be a big help when working with the main.cf file.

- ▶ **main.cf**—The principal configuration script for Postfix. Within the remarks at the start of the script, you are advised to change only a couple of options at any time. This is sage advice, given that there are more than 300 possibilities!

- ▶ **master.cf**—The throttle control for Postfix. This script enables you to change settings for Postfix that directly affect the speed at which it works. Unless you have a reason to tinker with this file, leave it alone. Trust me: You will know when you need to make changes.

- ▶ **postfix-script**—The script used by Postfix as a wrapper. You cannot execute it directly; instead it is called by Postfix itself.

You can keep your original Sendmail aliases file for use with Postfix because it will not make much difference to it.

You will also require the services of system-switch-mail, which can also be installed by using yum.

After system-switch-mail has been successfully installed, switch to a root terminal and type the following:

```
# system-switch-mail
```

You are then greeted with a simple text screen, asking which MTA you want to use. Select Postfix and simply press Enter. After a few seconds, a new window appears, informing you that your MTA has been successfully switched. All you then need to do is ensure that Postfix is enabled in runlevel 5 by checking the service (system-config-services).

Further configuration of Postfix focuses on the main.cf file, which is extensively documented throughout the file using comments.

The beauty of Postfix is that it can be used in any situation from a single home user to a large corporation that has thousands of clients, even up to the ISP level. It can even be linked to MySQL for authentication purposes and virtual hosting.

Using Fetchmail to Retrieve Mail

SMTP is designed to work with systems that have a full-time connection to the Internet. What if you are on a dialup account? What if you have another system store your email for you and then you log in to pick it up once in a while? (Most users who are not setting up servers are in this situation.) In this case, you cannot easily receive email with SMTP, and you need to use a protocol, such as POP3 or IMAP, instead.

> **NOTE**
>
> Remember when we said that some mail clients can include some MTA functionality? Microsoft Outlook and Outlook Express can be configured to use SMTP and, if you use a dialup connection, offer to start the connection and then use SMTP to send your mail. Therefore, a type of MTA functionality is included in those mail clients.

Unfortunately, many MUAs do not know anything about POP3 or IMAP. To eliminate that problem, you can use a program called Fetchmail to contact mail servers using POP3 or IMAP, download mail off the servers, and then inject those messages into the local MTA just as if they had come from a standard SMTP server. The following sections explain how to install, configure, and use the Fetchmail program.

Installing Fetchmail

Similar to other packages, Fetchmail can be installed with the `yum install` command. This command installs all files to their default locations. If, for whatever reason, you need to perform a custom installation, see Chapter 34, "Advanced Software Management," for more information on changing the default options for `rpm`.

You can get the latest version of Fetchmail at http://fetchmail.berlios.org. It is available in both source and RPM binary formats. The version of Fedora on the DVD accompanying this book provides a reasonably current version of Fetchmail and installs useful Fetchmail documentation in the `/usr/share/doc/fetchmail` directory. That directory includes an `FAQ`, `features` list, and `Install` documentation.

Configuring Fetchmail

After you have installed Fetchmail, you must create the file `.fetchmailrc` in your home directory, which provides the configuration for the Fetchmail program.

You can create and subsequently edit the `.fetchmailrc` file by using any text editor. The configuration file is straightforward and quite easy to create; the following sections explain the manual method for creating and editing the file. The information presented in the following sections does not discuss all the options available in the `.fetchmailrc` file, but covers the most common ones needed to get a basic Fetchmail installation up and running. You have to use a text editor to create the file to include entries like the ones shown as examples—modified for your personal information, of course. For advanced configuration, see the man page for Fetchmail. The man page is well written and documents all the configuration options in detail.

> **CAUTION**
>
> The .fetchmailrc file is divided into three different sections: global options, mail server options, and user options. It is important that these sections appear in the order listed. Do not add options to the wrong section. Putting options in the wrong place is one of the most common problems that new users make with Fetchmail configuration files.

Configuring Global Options

The first section of .fetchmailrc contains the global options. These options affect all the mail servers and user accounts that you list later in the configuration file. Some of these global options can be overridden with local configuration options, as you learn later in this section. Here is an example of the options that might appear in the global section of the .fetchmailrc file:

```
set daemon 600
set postmaster foobar
set logfile ./.fetchmail.log
```

The first line in this example tells Fetchmail that it should start in daemon mode and check the mail servers for new mail every 600 seconds, or 10 minutes. Daemon mode means that after Fetchmail starts, it moves itself into the background and continues running. Without this line, Fetchmail would check for mail once when it started and would then terminate and never check again.

The second option tells Fetchmail to use the local account foobar as a last resort address. In other words, any email that it receives and cannot deliver to a specified account should be sent to foobar.

The third line tells Fetchmail to log its activity to the file ./.fetchmail.log. Alternatively, you can use the line set syslog—in which case, Fetchmail logs through the syslog facility.

Configuring Mail Server Options

The second section of the .fetchmailrc file contains information on each of the mail servers that should be checked for new mail. Here is an example of what the mail section might look like:

```
poll mail.samplenet.org
proto pop3
no dns
```

The first line tells Fetchmail that it should check the mail server mail.samplenet.org at each poll interval that was set in the global options section (which was 600 seconds in our example). Alternatively, the first line can begin with skip. If a mail server line begins with skip, it is not polled as the poll interval, but is polled only when it is specifically specified on the Fetchmail command line.

The second line specifies the protocol that should be used when contacting the mail server. In this case, we are using the POP3 protocol. Other legal options are IMAP, APOP, and KPOP. You can also use AUTO here—in which case, Fetchmail attempts to automatically determine the correct protocol to use with the mail server.

The third line tells Fetchmail that it should not attempt to do a DNS lookup. You probably want to include this option if you are running over a dialup connection.

Configuring User Accounts

The third and final section of .fetchmailrc contains information about the user account on the server specified in the previous section. Here is an example:

```
user foobar
pass secretword
fetchall
flush
```

The first line, of course, is simply just the username that is used to log in to the email server, and the second line specifies the password for that user. Many security-conscious people cringe at the thought of putting clear-text passwords in a configuration file, and they should if it is group or world-readable. The only protection for this information is to make certain that the file is readable only by the owner; that is, with file permissions of 600.

The third line tells Fetchmail that it should fetch all messages from the server, even if they have already been read.

The fourth line tells Fetchmail that it should delete the messages from the mail server after it has completed downloading them. This is the default, so you do not really have to specify this option. If you want to leave the messages on the server after downloading them, use the option no flush.

The configuration options you just inserted configured the entire .fetchmailrc file to look like this:

```
set daemon 600
set postmaster foobar
set logfile ./.fetchmail.log

poll mail.samplenet.org
proto pop3
no dns

user foobar
pass secretword
fetchall
flush
```

What this file tells Fetchmail to do is

- ▸ Check the POP3 server `mail.samplenet.org` for new mail every 600 seconds.

- ▸ Log in using the username `foobar` and the password `secretword`.

- ▸ Download all messages off the server.

- ▸ Delete the messages from the server after Fetchmail has finished downloading them.

- ▸ Send any mail Fetchmail receives that cannot be delivered to a local user to the account `foobar`.

As mentioned earlier, many more options can be included in the `.fetchmailrc` file than are listed here. However, these options get you up and running with a basic configuration.

For additional flexibility, you can define multiple `.fetchmailrc` files to retrieve mail from different remote mail servers while using the same Linux user account. For example, you can define settings for your most often-used account and save them in the default `.fetchmailrc` file. Mail can then quickly be retrieved like so:

```
$ fetchmail -a
1 message for ahudson at mail.myserver.com (1108 octets).
reading message 1 of 1 (1108 octets) . flushed
```

By using Fetchmail's `-f` option, you can specify an alternative resource file and then easily retrieve mail from another server, as follows:

```
$ fetchmail -f .myothermailrc
2 messages for bball at othermail.otherserver.org (5407 octets).
reading message 1 of 2 (3440 octets) ... flushed
reading message 2 of 2 (1967 octets) . flushed
You have new mail in /var/spool/mail/bball
```

By using the `-d` option, along with a time interval (in seconds), you can use Fetchmail in its daemon—or background—mode. The command launches as a background process and retrieves mail from a designated remote server at a specified interval. For more advanced options, see the Fetchmail man page, which is well written and documents all options in detail.

CAUTION

Because the `.fetchmailrc` file contains your mail server password, it should be readable only by you. This means that it should be owned by you and should have permissions no greater than `600`. Fetchmail complains and refuses to start if the `.fetchmailrc` file has permissions greater than this.

Choosing a Mail Delivery Agent

Because of the modular nature of mail handling, it is possible to use multiple applications to process mail and accomplish more than simply delivering it. Getting mail from the storage area and displaying it to the user is the purpose of the *mail delivery agent (MDA)*. MDA functionality can be found in some of the mail clients (*MUAs*), which can cause some confusion to those still unfamiliar with the concept of UNIX mail. As an example, the Procmail MDA provides filtering based on rulesets; KMail and Evolution, both MUAs, provide filtering, but the MUAs pine, mutt, and Balsa do not. Some MDAs perform simple sorting, and other MDAs are designed to eliminate unwanted emails, such as spam and viruses.

You would choose an MDA based on what you want to do with your mail. The following sections look at five MDAs that offer functions you might find useful in your particular situation. If you have simple needs (just organizing mail by rules), one of the MUAs that offers filtering might be better for your needs. Fedora provides the Evolution MUA as the default selection (and it contains some MDA functionality as previously noted), so try that first and see whether it meets your needs. If not, investigate one of the following MDAs provided by Fedora.

Unless otherwise noted, all the MDA software is provided with the Fedora discs. Chapter 34 details the general installation of any software.

Procmail

As a tool for advanced users, the Procmail application acts as a filter for email as it is retrieved from a mail server. It uses rulesets (known as *recipes*) as it reads each email message. No default configuration is provided; you must manually create a ~/.procmail file for each user, or each user can create her own.

There is no systemwide default configuration file. The creation of the rulesets is not trivial and requires an understanding of the use of regular expressions that is beyond the scope of this chapter. Fedora does provide three examples of the files in /usr/share/doc/procmail/examples, as well as a fully commented example in the /usr/share/doc/procmail directory, which also contains a Read Me and FAQ. Details for the rulesets can be found in the man page for Procmail, as well as the man pages for procmailrc, procmailsc, and procmailex, which contain examples of Procmail recipes.

Spamassassin

If you have used email for any length of time, you have likely been subjected to *spam*— unwanted email that is sent to thousands of people at the same time. Fedora provides an MDA named Spamassassin to assist you in reducing and eliminating unwanted emails. Easily integrated with Procmail and Sendmail, it can be configured for both systemwide and individual use. It employs a combination of rulesets and *blacklists* (Internet domains known to mail spam).

Enabling Spamassassin is simple. You must first have installed and configured Procmail. The Read Me file found in /usr/share/doc/spamassasin provides details on configuring the .procmail file to process mail through Spamassassin. It tags probable spam with a unique header; you can then have Procmail filter the mail in any manner you choose. One interesting use of Spamassassin is to use it to tag email received at special email accounts established solely for the purpose of attracting spam. This information is then shared with the Spamassassin site, where these "spam trap"–generated hits help the authors fine-tune the rulesets.

Squirrelmail

Perhaps you do not want to read your mail in an MUA. If you use your web browser often, it might make sense to read and send your mail via a web interface, such as the one used by Hotmail or Yahoo! Mail. Fedora provides Squirrelmail for just that purpose. Squirrelmail is written in the PHP 4 language and supports IMAP and SMTP, with all pages rendering in HTML 4.0 without using Java. It supports MIME attachments, as well as an address book and folders for segregating email.

You must configure your web server to work with PHP 4. Detailed installation instructions can be found in /usr/share/doc/squirrelmail/INSTALL. After it is configured, point your web browser to http://www.yourdomain.com/squirellmail/ to read and send email.

Virus Scanners

Although the currently held belief is that Linux is immune to email viruses targeted at Microsoft Outlook users, it certainly makes no sense for UNIX mail servers to permit infected email to be sent through them. Although Fedora does not provide a virus scanner, one of the more popular of many such scanners is MailScanner, available from http://www.sng.ecs.soton.ac.uk/mailscanner/; a Fedora RPM package is available as well as the source code. It supports Sendmail and Exim, but not Postfix or Qmail. Searching on the terms "virus" and "email" at Freshmeat.net will turn up a surprising list of GPLed virus scanners that might serve your needs.

Special Mail Delivery Agents

If you already use Hotmail or another web-based email account, the currently available MUAs are not useful to you: Formal POP3 access to a Hotmail account is not available free of charge. However, Microsoft Outlook Express can access Hotmail at no charge, using a special protocol called *HTTPMail*. How that is done is covered in RFC 2518 as "WebDAV extensions to HTTP/1.1." No specific solution is provided by Fedora, but the basic tools it provides are adequate when supplemented by some clever Perl programming.

Hotwayd is available from http://sourceforge.net/projects/hotwayd/ and implements this functionality, allowing you to use your favorite mail client to read mail from Hotmail.

A newer Hotmail access tool is Gotmail from http://sourceforge.net/projects/gotmail. It is a Perl script that is easy to configure. There are brief tutorials on configuring it for use with KMail and Evolution at http://www.madpenguin.org/cms/?m=show&id=437.

## 21

A similar tool exists for Yahoo! Mail. FetchYahoo is available from http://fetchyahoo. twizzler.org/.

After it is implemented, you can use a regular MUA, or mail client, to access your web-based mail. None of them, however, enable you to send mail through Hotmail or Yahoo! Mail.

Mail Daemons

Fedora provides an `imap` package that installs IMAP and POP daemons (servers) for your system. These servers facilitate receiving mail from a remote site. After it is installed, the documentation is found in `/usr/share/doc/imap` and the Read Me is brief; Fedora has already done the configuration for you; you need only start the services (see Chapter 15, "Remote Access with SSH").

Biff and its KDE cousin KOrn are small daemons that monitor your mail folder and notify you when a message has been placed there. It is common to include `biff  y` in the `.login` or `.profile` files to automatically start it upon user login if you want to use Biff. You can start KOrn by adding the applet to the KDE taskbar.

> **NOTE**
>
> Autoresponders automatically generate replies to received messages; they are commonly used to notify others that the recipient is out of the office. Mercifully, Fedora does not include one, but you can find and install an autoresponder at `Freshmeat.net`. If you subscribe to a mailing list, be aware that automatic responses from your account can be very annoying to others on the list. Please unsubscribe from mail lists before you leave the office with your autoresponder activated.

Alternatives to Microsoft Exchange Server

One of the last areas in which a Microsoft product has yet to be usurped by open source software is a replacement for MS Exchange Server. Many businesses use MS Outlook and MS Exchange Server to access email and to provide calendaring, notes, file sharing, and other collaborative functions. General industry complaints about Exchange Server center around scalability, administration (backup and restore in particular), and licensing fees.

A drop-in alternative needs to have compatibility with MS Outlook because it's intended to replace Exchange Server in an environment in which there are Microsoft desktops in existence using Outlook. A work-alike alternative provides similar features to Exchange Server, but does not offer compatibility with the MS Outlook client itself; this incompatibility with Outlook is typical of many of the open source alternatives.

Several drop-in alternatives exist, none of which is fully open source because some type of proprietary connector is needed to provide the services to MS Outlook clients (or provide Exchange services to the Linux Evolution client). For Outlook compatibility, the key seems to be the realization of a full, open implementation of *MAPI*, Microsoft's *Messaging*

Application Program Interface. That goal is going to be difficult to achieve because MAPI is a poorly documented Microsoft protocol. For Linux-only solutions, the missing ingredient for many alternatives is a useable group calendaring/scheduling system similar in function to that provided by Exchange Server/Outlook.

Of course, independent applications for these functions abound in the open source world, but one characteristic of groupware is its central administration; another is that all components can share information.

The following sections examine several of the available servers, beginning with MS Exchange Server itself and moving toward those applications that have increasing incompatibility with it. None of these servers are provided with Fedora.

Microsoft Exchange Server/Outlook Client

Exchange Server and Outlook seem to be the industry benchmark because of their widespread deployment. They offer a proprietary server providing email, contacts, scheduling, public folders, task lists, journaling, and notes using MS Outlook as the client and MAPI as the API. If you consider what MS Exchange offers as the full set of features, no other replacement offers 100% of the features exactly as provided by MS Exchange Server—even those considered drop-in replacements. The home page for the Microsoft Exchange Server is http://www.microsoft.com/exchange/.

CommuniGate Pro

CommuniGate Pro is a proprietary, drop-in alternative to MS Exchange Server, providing, email, webmail, LDAP directories, a web server, file server, contacts, calendaring (third-party), and a list server. The CommuniGate Pro MAPI Connector provides access to the server from MS Outlook and other MAPI-enabled clients. The home page for this server is http://www.stalker.com/.

Oracle Collaboration Suite

Oracle Collaboration Suite, or *OCS* as it is known, is a proprietary application that supports deployment on Linux. It provides a number of services, including email (both POP and IMAP based), file sharing, calendaring, and instant messaging to name but a few. You can find it at http://www.oracle.com/collabsuite/.

Open Xchange

The Open Xchange message server is based on Cyrus-imap and Postfix. Most of the server's groupware features are provided by a proprietary web-based groupware server (ComFire). Open Xchange also uses Apache, OpenLDAP, and Samba to provide public directories, notes, webmail, scheduler, tasks, project management, document management, forums, and bookmarks. Some compatibility with MS Outlook is provided. The home page is http://www.open-xchange.org/.

Relevant Fedora and Linux Commands

You will use the following commands to manage electronic mail in Fedora:

- ▶ **balsa**—A GNOME mail user agent for X
- ▶ **biff**—A console-based mail notification utility
- ▶ **evolution**—A comprehensive and capable Ximian GNOME mail PIM for X
- ▶ **fetchmail**—A console-based and daemon-mode mail retrieval command for Linux
- ▶ **fetchmailconf**—A graphical Fetchmail configuration client for X
- ▶ **kmail**—A graphical mail user client for KDE and X
- ▶ **korn**—A biff applet for KDE and X
- ▶ **mail**—A console-based mail user agent
- ▶ **mutt**—A console-based mail user agent
- ▶ **sendmail**—A comprehensive mail transport agent for UNIX and Linux
- ▶ **xbiff**—A mail notification X client

Reference

The following references are recommended reading for email configuration. Of course, not all references apply to you. Select the ones that apply to the email server that you are using.

Web Resources

- ▶ **http://www.sendmail.org/**—This is the Sendmail home page. Here you can find configuration information and FAQs regarding the Sendmail MTA.

- ▶ **http://www.postfix.org/**—This is the Postfix home page. If you are using the Postfix MTA, documentation and sample configurations can be found at this site.

- ▶ **http://www.qmail.org/**—This is the home page for the Qmail MTA. It contains documentation and links to other resources on Qmail.

- ▶ **http://www.linuxgazette.com/issue35/jao.html**—IMAP on Linux: A Practical Guide. The Internet Mail Access Protocol allows a user to access his email stored on a remote server rather than a local disk.

- ▶ **http://www.imap.org/about/whatisIMAP.html**—A page describing what IMAP is.

- ▶ **http://www.rfc-editor.org/**—A repository of RFCs that define the technical "rules" of modern computer usage.

- ▶ **http://www.procmail.org/**—The Procmail home page.

- ▶ **http://www.ibiblio.org/pub/Linux/docs/HOWTO/other-formats/html_single/Qmail-VMailMgr-Courier-imap-HOWTO.html**—If you want some help configuring a mail system based on the lesser-used applications, this HOWTO can help.

Books

▶ *Sendmail*, from O'Reilly Publishing. This is the de facto standard guide for everything Sendmail. It is loaded with more than 1,000 pages, which gives you an idea of how complicated Sendmail really is.

▶ *Postfix*, from Sams Publishing. An excellent book that covers the Postfix MTA.

▶ *Running Qmail*, from Sams Publishing. This is similar to the Postfix book from Sams Publishing except that it covers the Qmail MTA.

# CHAPTER 22

Setting Up a Proxy Server

There are two things in this world that you can never have enough of: time and bandwidth. Fedora comes with a proxy server—Squid—that enables you to cache web traffic on your server so that websites load faster and users consume less bandwidth.

What Is a Proxy Server?

A *proxy server* lies between client machines—the desktops in your company—and the Internet. As clients request websites, they do not connect directly to the web and send the HTTP request. Instead, they connect to the local proxy server. The proxy then forwards their requests on to the web, retrieves the result, and hands it back to the client. At its simplest, a proxy server really is just an extra layer between client and server, so why bother?

The three main reasons for deploying a proxy server are

▶ **Content control**—You want to stop people whiling away their work hours reading the news or downloading MP3s.

▶ **Speed**—You want to cache common sites to make the most of your bandwidth.

▶ **Security**—You want to monitor what people are doing.

Squid is capable of achieving all of these goals and more.

Installing Squid

Squid installation is handled through the Add/Remove Applications dialog under the System Settings menu. The Squid package is confusingly located under the Web Server group; this has the downside of installing Apache alongside Squid whether you like it or not. That said, you can (and should) deselect other autoinstall packages that you do not need from the Web Server category.

After Squid is installed, switch to the console and use su to get to the root account. You should run the command chkconfig --level 345 squid on to run Squid at runlevels 3, 4, and 5, like this:

```
[root@susannah ~]# chkconfig --list squid
squid    0:off 1:off 2:off 3:off 4:off 5:off 6:off
[root@susannah ~]# chkconfig --level 345 squid on
[root@susannah ~]# chkconfig --list squid
squid    0:off 1:off 2:off 3:on 4:on 5:on 6:off
```

That runs Squid the next time the system switches to runlevel 3, 4, or 5, but it will not run it just yet.

Configuring Clients

Before you configure your new Squid server, you should set up the local web browser to use Squid for its web access. This allows you to test your rules as you are working with the configuration file.

To configure Firefox, select Preferences from the Edit menu. From the dialog that appears, click the Connection Settings button (near the bottom on the General tab) and select the option Manual Proxy Configuration. Check the box beneath it, Use the Same Proxy for All Protocols; then enter **127.0.0.1** as the IP address and **3128** as the port number. See Figure 22.1 for how this should look. If you are configuring a remote client, specify the IP address of the Squid server instead of 127.0.0.1.

For Konqueror, go to the Settings menu and select Configure Konqueror. From the left tab, scroll down to Proxy, select Manually Specify the Proxy Settings, and then click Setup. Enter **127.0.0.1** as the proxy IP address and **3128** as the port. As with Firefox, if you are configuring a remote client, specify the IP address of the Squid server instead of 127.0.0.1.

Internet Explorer's proxy settings are in Tools/Internet Options. From the Connections tab, click the LAN Settings button and enable the Use a Proxy Server for Your LAN option. Enter the address as the IP of your Squid machine, and then specify **3128** as the port.

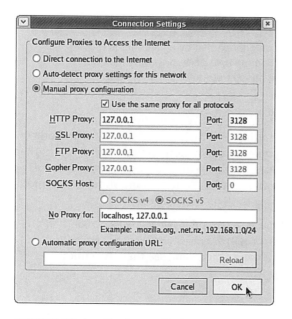

FIGURE 22.1   Setting up Firefox to use 127.0.0.1 routes all its web requests through Squid.

Access Control Lists

The main Squid configuration file is /etc/squid/squid.conf, and the default Fedora configuration file is full of comments to help guide you. The default configuration file allows full access to the local machine but denies the rest of your network. This is a secure place to start; we recommend you try all the rules on yourself (localhost) before rolling them out to other machines.

Before you start, open two terminal windows as root. In the first, change to the directory /var/log/squid and run this command:

```
tail -f access.log cache.log
```

That command reads the last few lines from both files and (thanks to the -f flag) follows them so that any changes appear in there. This allows you to watch what Squid is doing as people access it. We will refer to this window as the *log window*, so keep it open. In the other window (as root, remember), bring up the file /etc/squid/squid.conf in your favorite editor. This window will be referred to as the *config editor*, and you should keep it open also.

To get started, search for the string acl all—this brings you to the access control section, which is where most of the work needs to be done. There is a lot you can configure elsewhere, but unless you have unusual requirements, you can leave the defaults in place.

> **NOTE**
>
> The default port for Squid is 3128, but you can change that by editing the http_port line. Alternatively, you can have Squid listen on multiple ports by having multiple http_port lines: 80, 8000, and 8080 are all popular ports for proxy servers.

The acl lines make up your access control lists. The first 16 or so lines define the minimum recommended configuration for setting up which ports to listen to, and other fairly standard configuration settings that you can safely ignore. If you scroll down farther (past another short block of comments), you come to the http_access lines, which are combined with the acl lines to dictate who can do what. You can (and should) mix and match acl and http_access lines to keep your configuration file easy to read.

Just below the first block of http_access lines is a comment like # INSERT YOUR OWN RULE(S) HERE TO ALLOW ACCESS FROM YOUR CLIENTS. This is just what we are going to do. First, though, scroll just a few lines farther and you should see these two lines:

```
http_access allow localhost
http_access deny all
```

The first says, "allow HTTP access to the local computer, but deny everyone else." This is the default rule, as mentioned earlier. Leave that in place for now, and run service squid start to start the server with the default settings. If you have not yet configured the local web browser to use your Squid server, do so now so you can test the default rules.

In your web browser (Firefox is assumed from here on, but it makes little difference), go to the URL http://fedora.redhat.com. You should see it appear as normal in the browser, but in the log window you should see a lot of messages scroll by as Squid downloads the site for you and stores it in its cache. This is all allowed because the default configuration allows access to the localhost.

Go back to the config editor window and add the following before the last two http_access lines:

```
http_access deny localhost
```

So the last three lines should look like this:

```
http_access deny localhost
http_access allow localhost
http_access deny all
```

Save the file and quit your editor. Then run this command:

```
kill -SIGHUP `cat /var/run/squid.pid`
```

That command looks for the PID of the Squid daemon and then sends the SIGHUP signal to it, which forces it to reread its configuration file while running. You should see a string of messages in the log window as Squid rereads its configuration files. If you now go back to Firefox and enter a new URL, you should see the Squid error page informing you that you do not have access to the requested site.

The reason you are now blocked from the proxy is because Squid reads its ACL lines in sequence, from top to bottom. If it finds a line that conclusively allows or denies a request, it stops reading and takes the appropriate action. So, in the previous lines, localhost is being denied in the first line and allowed in the second. When Squid sees localhost asking for a site, it reads the deny line first and immediately sends the error page—it does not even get to the allow line. Having a deny all line at the bottom is highly recommended so that only those you explicitly allow are able to use the proxy.

Go back to editing the configuration file and remove the deny localhost and allow localhost lines. This leaves only deny all, which blocks everyone (including the localhost) from accessing the proxy. Now we are going to add some conditional allow statements: We want to allow localhost only if it fits certain criteria.

Defining access criteria is done with the acl lines, so above the deny all line, add this:

```
acl newssites dstdomain news.bbc.co.uk slashdot.org
http_access allow newssites
```

The first line defines an access category called newssites, which contains a list of domains (dstdomain). The domains are news.bbc.co.uk and slashdot.org, so the full line reads, "create a new access category called newssites, which should filter on domain, and contain the two domains listed." It does *not* say whether access should be granted or denied to that category; that comes in the next line. The line http_access allow newssites means, "allow access to the category newssites with no further restrictions." It is not limited to localhost, which means this applies to every computer connecting to the proxy server.

Save the configuration file and rerun the kill -SIGHUP line from before to restart Squid; then go back to Firefox and try loading http://fedora.redhat.com. You should see the same error as before because that was not in the newssites category. Now try http://news. bbc.co.uk, and it should work. However, if you try http://www.slashdot.org, it will *not* work, and you might also have noticed that the images did not appear on the BBC News website either. The problem here is that specifying slashdot.org as the website is very specific: It means that http://slashdot.org will work, whereas http://www.slashdot.org will not. The BBC News site stores its images on the site http://newsimg.bbc.co.uk, which is why they do not appear.

Go back to the configuration file, and edit the newssites ACL to this:

```
acl newssites dstdomain .bbc.co.uk .slashdot.org
```

Putting the period in front of the domains (and in the BBC's case, taking the news off also) means that Squid allows any subdomain of the site to work, which is usually what you will want. If you want even more vagueness, you can just specify .com to match *.com addresses.

Moving on, you can also use time conditions for sites. For example, if you want to allow access to the news sites in the evenings, you can set up a time category using this line:

```
acl freetime time MTWHFAS 18:00-23:59
```

This time, the category is called `freetime` and the condition is `time`, which means we need to specify what time the category should contain. The seven characters following that are the days of the week: Monday, Tuesday, Wednesday, tHursday, Friday, sAturday, and sUnday. Thursday and Saturday use capital *H* and *A* so that they do not clash with Tuesday and Sunday.

With the `freetime` category defined, you can change the `http_access` line to include it, like this:

```
http_access allow newssites freetime
```

For Squid to allow access now, it must match both conditions—the request must be for either `*.bbc.co.uk` or `slashdot.org`, and during the time specified. If either condition does not match, the line is not matched and Squid continues looking for other matching rules beneath it. The times you specify here are inclusive on both sides, which means users in the `freetime` category can surf from 18:00:00 until 23:59:59.

You can add as many rules as you like, although you should be careful to try to order them so that they make sense. Keep in mind that all conditions in a line must be matched for the line to be matched. Here is a more complex example:

▶ You want a category `newssites` that contains serious websites people need for their work.

▶ You want a category `playsites` that contains websites people do not need for their work.

▶ You want a category `worktime` that stretches from 09:00 to 18:00.

▶ You want a category `freetime` that stretches from 18:00 to 20:00, when the office closes.

▶ You want people to be able to access the news sites, but not the play sites, during working hours.

▶ You want people to be able to access both the news sites and the play sites during the free time hours.

To do that, you need the following rules:

```
acl newssites dstdomain .bbc.co.uk .slashdot.org
acl playsites dstdomain .tomshardware.com fedora.redhat.com
acl worktime time MTWHF 9:00-18:00
acl freetime time MTWHF 18:00-20:00
http_access allow newssites worktime
http_access allow newssites freetime
http_access allow playsites freetime
```

NOTE

The letter D is equivalent to MTWHF in meaning "all the days of the working week."

Notice that there are two http_access lines for the newssites category: one for worktime and one for freetime. All the conditions must be matched for a line to be matched. The alternative would be to write this:

```
http_access allow newssites worktime freetime
```

However, if you do that and someone visits news.bbc.co.uk at 2:30 p.m. (14:30) on a Tuesday, Squid works like this:

▶ Is the site in the newssites category? Yes, continue.

▶ Is the time within the worktime category? Yes, continue.

▶ Is the time within the freetime category? No; do not match rule, and continue searching for rules.

Two lines therefore are needed for the worktime category.

One particularly powerful way to filter requests is with the url_regex ACL line. This enables you to specify a regular expression that is checked against each request: If the expression matches the request, the condition matches.

For example, if you want to stop people downloading Windows executable files, you would use this line:

```
acl noexes url_regex -i exe$
```

The dollar sign means "end of URL," which means it would match http://www.somesite.com/virus.exe but not http://www.executable.com/innocent.html. The -i part means "case-insensitive," so the rule matches .exe, .Exe, .EXE, and so on. You can use the caret sign (^) for "start of URL."

For example, you could stop some pornography sites by using this ACL:

```
acl noporn url_regex -i sex
```

Do not forget to run the kill -SIGHUP command each time you make changes to Squid; otherwise, it does not reread your changes. You can have Squid check your configuration files for errors by running squid -k parse as root. If you see no errors, it means your configuration is fine.

NOTE

It is critical that you run the command kill -SIGHUP and provide it the process ID of your Squid daemon each time you change the configuration; without this, Squid does not reread its configuration files.

Specifying Client IP Addresses

The configuration options so far have been basic, and there are many more you can use to enhance the proxying system you want.

After you are past deciding which rules work for you locally, it is time to spread them out to other machines. This is done by specifying IP ranges that should be allowed or disallowed access, and you enter these into Squid by using more ACL lines.

If you want to, you can specify all the IP addresses on your network, one per line. However, for networks of more than about 20 people or that use DHCP, that is more work than necessary. A better solution is to use classless interdomain routing (CIDR) notation, which enables you to specify addresses like this:

```
192.0.0.0/8
192.168.0.0/16
192.168.0.0/24
```

Each line has an IP address, followed by a slash and then a number. That last number defines the range of addresses you want covered and refers to the number of bits in an IP address. An IP address is a 32-bit number, but we are used to seeing it in dotted-quad notation: A.B.C.D. Each of those quads can be between 0 and 255 (although in practice some of these are reserved for special purposes), and each is stored as an 8-bit number.

The first line in the previous code covers IP addresses starting from 192.0.0.0; the /8 part means that the first 8 bits (the first quad, 192) is fixed and the rest is flexible. So Squid treats that as addresses 192.0.0.0, 192.0.0.1, through to 192.0.0.255, and then 192.0.1.0, 192.0.1.1, all the way through to 192.255.255.255.

The second line uses /16, which means Squid allows IP addresses from 192.168.0.0 to 192.168.255.255. The last line has /24, which allows addresses from 192.168.0.0 to 192.168.0.255.

You can place these addresses into Squid by using the src ACL line, like this:

```
acl internal_network src 10.0.0.0/24
```

That line creates a category of addresses from 10.0.0.0 to 10.0.0.255. You can combine multiple address groups together, like this:

```
acl internal_network src 10.0.0.0/24 10.0.3.0/24 10.0.5.0/24 192.168.0.1
```

That example allows 10.0.0.0–10.0.0.255, and then 10.0.3.0–10.0.3.255, and finally the single address 192.168.0.1.

Keep in mind that if you are using the local machine and you have the web browser configured to use the proxy at 127.0.0.1, the client IP address will be 127.0.0.1, too. So, make sure that you have rules in place for localhost.

As with other ACL lines, you need to enable them with appropriate http_access allow and http_access deny lines.

Sample Configurations

To help you fully understand how Squid access control works, and also to help give you a head start developing your own rules, the following are some ACL lines you can try. Each line is preceded with one or more comment lines (starting with a #) explaining what it does:

```
# include the domains news.bbc.co.uk and slashdot.org
# and not newsimg.bbc.co.uk or www.slashdot.org.
acl newssites dstdomain news.bbc.co.uk slashdot.org


# include any subdomains or bbc.co.uk or slashdot.org
acl newssites dstdomain .bbc.co.uk .slashdot.org


# include only sites located in Canada
acl canadasites dstdomain .ca

# include only working hours
acl workhours time MTWHF 9:00-18:00


# include only lunchtimes
acl lunchtimes time MTWHF 13:00-14:00


# include only weekends
acl weekends time AS 00:00-23:59


# include URLs ending in ".zip". Note: the \ is important,
# because "." has a special meaning otherwise
acl zipfiles url_regex -i \.zip$


# include URLs starting with https
acl httpsurls url_regex -i ^https


# include all URLs that match "hotmail"
url_regex hotmail url_regex -i hotmail


# include three specific IP addresses
acl directors src 10.0.0.14 10.0.0.28 10.0.0.31


# include all IPs from 192.168.0.0 to 192.168.0.255
acl internal src 192.168.0.0/24


# include all IPs from 192.168.0.0 to 192.168.0.255
# and all IPs from 10.0.0.0 to 10.255.255.255
acl internal src 192.168.0.0/24 10.0.0.0/8
```

22

When you have your ACL lines in place, you can put together appropriate `http_access` lines. For example, you might want to use a multilayered access system so that certain users (for example, company directors) have full access, whereas others are filtered. For example:

```
http_access allow directors
http_access deny hotmail
http_access deny zipfiles
http_access allow internal lunchtimes
http_access deny all
```

Because Squid matches those lines in order, directors will have full, unfiltered access to the web. If the client IP address is not in the `directors` list, the two deny lines are processed so that the user cannot download `.zip` files or read online mail at Hotmail. After blocking those two types of requests, the `allow` on the fourth line allows internal users to access the web, as long as they do so only at lunch time. The last line (which is highly recommended) blocks all other users from the proxy.

Reference

▶ **http://www.squid-cache.org/**—The home page of the Squid Web Proxy Cache.

▶ **http://www.deckle.co.za/squid-users-guide/Main_Page**—The home page of *Squid: A User's Guide*, a free online book about Squid.

▶ **http://www.faqs.org/docs/securing/netproxy-squid.html**—A brief online guide to configuring a local Squid server.

▶ **http://squid.visolve.com/squid/index.htm/**—The home page of a company that can provide commercial support and deployment of Squid.

▶ **http://squid.visolve.com/squid/reverseproxy.htm**—ViSolve's guide to setting up Squid to reverse proxy to cache a local web server for external visitors.

As well as these URLs, there are two excellent books on the topic of web caching. The first is *Squid: The Definitive Guide* (O'Reilly) by Duane Wessels, ISBN: 0-596-00162-2. The second is *Web Caching* (O'Reilly) also by Duane Wessels, ISBN: 1-56592-536-X.

Of the two, the former is more practical and covers the Squid server in depth. The latter is more theoretical, discussing how caching is implemented. Wessels is one of the leading developers on Squid, so both books are of impeccable technical accuracy.

CHAPTER 23

Managing DNS

Computers on a network need to be useful, which means you need to be able to identify each computer so that you can connect to and communicate with it. Most of today's networks use the *Internet Protocol (IP)*, so each computer on this network has a unique IP address to identify it.

An IP address is a very large 32-bit number, but there is a shortcut method of displaying that number called the *dotted-quad address*. The dotted-quad form of the address is made of four 8-bit numbers separated by dots. For example, a computer with the address 3232250992 has the dotted-quad form 192.168.60.112. It's easier to use and remember the dotted-quad form of an IP address, but even then remembering a lot of numbers becomes quite difficult. The *domain name system (DNS)* enables you to allocate host-names that are much easier to remember to these IP addresses. These names, such as fedoraproject.org, are translated by DNS into the dotted-quad IP address, saving time—and memory!

This translation process is called *name resolution* and is performed by software known as a *resolver*. For the average user, local configuration involves the DNS client, which queries a remote DNS server to exchange information. The DNS servers are typically maintained by *Internet service providers (ISPs)* and large corporate networks, although anyone can configure and run his own DNS server. All computers on networks need to have a properly configured DNS client.

This chapter introduces DNS concepts and practice using *Berkeley Internet Name Domain (BIND)*, the de facto standard DNS software for UNIX. In this chapter, you learn some of the concepts that are basic to DNS and its functions, including how DNS structure information is stored, how DNS serves name information to users, and how name resolution actually works. You learn how to use BIND to configure nameservers and how to provide DNS for a domain. This chapter also teaches you some important techniques for keeping DNS functions secure, as well as some of the most important troubleshooting techniques for tracking down potential problems related to your DNS functions.

If you are not going to be a DNS administrator, much of the information in this chapter will be of no practical use to you. That said, the knowledge of DNS that you can gain in this chapter might help you understand DNS problems that occur—so you will realize that it is not your computer that is broken! You will also see how, after you register a domain name, you can obtain third-party DNS service so that you do not have to maintain a DNS server. Also, the commonly used DNS-related tools are explained with a focus on how they can be used to troubleshoot domain name resolution problems that you're likely to encounter.

DNS is essential for many types of network operations, and especially so when your network provides connectivity to the outside world via the Internet. DNS was designed to make the assignment and translation of hostnames fast and reliable and to provide a consistent, portable namespace for network resources. Its database is maintained in a distributed fashion to accommodate its size and the need for frequent updates. Performance and bandwidth utilization are improved by the extensive use of local caches. Authority over portions of the database is delegated to people who are able and willing to maintain the database in a timely manner, so updates are no longer constrained by the schedules of a central authority.

DNS is a simple—but easily misconfigured—system. Hostname resolution errors might manifest themselves in ways that are far from obvious, long after the changes that caused the errors were made. Such naming errors can lead to unacceptable and embarrassing service disruptions.

An understanding of the concepts and processes involved in working with BIND will help to make sure that your experiences as a DNS manager are pleasant ones.

Configuring DNS for Clients

Later in the chapter, we focus on setup and configuration to provide DNS. This section briefly examines the setup and configuration required for a computer to use DNS services. The important user setup and configuration processes for DNS are likely to have been accomplished during the initial installation of Fedora. After the initial installation, further DNS configuration can be accomplished by one or more of these methods:

- Using *Dynamic Host Control Protocol (DHCP)*, in which case some system settings are updated by the dhclient command without intervention by a local or remote administrator or user

- Using the system-config-network GUI configuration tool

- Manually editing the system's /etc/host.conf configuration file to specify the methods and order of name resolution

▶ Manually editing the system's `/etc/nsswitch.conf` configuration file to specify the methods and order of name resolution

▶ Manually editing the system's `/etc/hosts` file, which lists specific hostnames and IP addresses

▶ Manually editing the system's `/etc/resolv.conf` configuration file to add name-server, domain, or search definition entries

Successful DNS lookups depend on the system's networking being enabled and correctly configured. You can learn more about how to accomplish that in Chapter 14, "Networking."

When an application needs to resolve a hostname, it calls system library functions to do the name resolution. If the GNU C library installed is version 2 or later, the `/etc/nsswitch.conf` configuration file is used. Older versions of the library use `/etc/host.conf`. Fedora uses the newer GNU C library, but `/etc/host.conf` is still provided for applications that have been statically linked with other libraries. The two files should be kept in sync.

The `/etc/host.conf` File

The `/etc/host.conf` file, known as the *resolver configuration file*, specifies which services to use for name resolution and the order in which they are to be used. This file has been superseded by `/etc/nsswitch.conf`, but is still provided for applications that use other libraries.

By default with Fedora, this file contains the following:

```
order hosts,bind
```

The order shown here is to first consult `/etc/hosts` for a hostname. If the hostname is found in `/etc/hosts`, use the IP address specified there. If the hostname is not found in `/etc/hosts`, try to resolve the name with DNS (BIND).

One other option is available, although it is not set by default. This is *NIS*, which is Sun's *Network Information Service*.

The `/etc/nsswitch.conf` File

The file `/etc/nsswitch.conf` is the system databases and name service switch configuration file. It contains methods for many types of lookups, but here we are concerned with DNS resolution, so the line we are interested in is the `hosts` line. This line defines the methods to be used for resolving hostnames and the order in which to apply them. The methods used are the following:

▶ **db**—Local database files (`*.db`)

▶ **files**—Use the local file `/etc/hosts`

▶ **dns**—Use BIND

▶ **nis**—Use Sun's NIS

▶ **nisplus**—Use Sun's NIS+

The default line with Fedora is this:

```
hosts: files dns
```

With this default, the same methods and order are specified as in the default `/etc/host.conf`. First `/etc/hosts` is searched, and then DNS is used.

Another example is as follows:

```
hosts: files dns nisplus nis
```

In this example, name searches that fail in `/etc/hosts` and with DNS continue to the NIS services (`nisplus` and `nis`). NIS included with Fedora is the `ypserv` daemon.

When you are testing your configuration, you might want to halt name searching at a specific point. You can use the entry `[NOTFOUND=return]`. For example, to stop searching after looking in `/etc/hosts`, you would use the following line:

```
hosts: files [NOTFOUND=return] dns nisplus nis
```

The `/etc/hosts` File

The file `/etc/hosts` contains a table of local hosts (hostnames and IP addresses) used for local DNS-type lookups. The file is used if the keyword `hosts` is included in the order line of `/etc/host.conf`.

Using `/etc/hosts` to provide hostnames and hostname aliases can be effective when used on small networks. For example, a short `/etc/hosts` might look like this:

```
...
192.168.0.3    teletran.hudson.com      teletran webserver #always breaks
192.168.0.4    optimus.hudson.com     optimus mailserver
192.168.0.5    prowl.hudson.com     prowl music repository
192.168.0.6    megatron.hudson.com     fileserver
...
```

This example shows a short list of hosts. The format of the file is an IP address, a `hostname/domain` name, and aliases (such as teletran and optimus). Using this approach, a system administrator would maintain and update a master hosts list, and then replicate the complete `/etc/hosts` file to every computer on the LAN. Users are then able to access other systems by simply using the hostname alias (such as `teletran`). The format of `/etc/hosts` is easy to understand and easy to maintain, and can be used in conjunction with DNS, and in conjunction with a *Dynamic Host Configuration Protocol (DHCP)* server on the same network.

Two disadvantages of using /etc/hosts become readily apparent on a large network: maintenance and replication. Maintaining huge lists of IP addresses, hostnames, and aliases—along with ensuring that changes are regularly updated to every host on the network—can be a challenge.

The /etc/hosts file can be edited with a text editor or with the system-config-network GUI configuration tool, which can be launched by going to System, Administration and choosing Network. Choose the Hosts tab to edit the file.

The /etc/resolv.conf File

The file /etc/resolv.conf specifies how DNS searches are made. The file contains a list of nameservers (DNS servers to connect to) and some options. For example, a simple but usable /etc/resolv.conf generally contains at least two nameserver entries, specifying a primary and secondary nameserver. This example uses fictitious internal IP addresses:

```
nameserver 192.168.0.1
nameserver 192.168.0.2
search mydomain.com
```

The IP addresses listed in the /etc/resolv.conf file are usually assigned by an ISP and represent the remote nameservers. Other optional keywords, such as domain and search, are used to specify a local domain and search list for queries; the two terms are mutually exclusive, however (and these terms are explained shortly). If you have both, the last term listed is used.

You can configure the information in /etc/resolv.conf from the system-config-network tool by launching the tool from the Network menu item in the System Settings menu. The DNS tab enables you to enter or edit the DNS information, as shown in Figure 23.1.

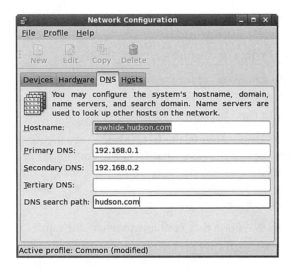

FIGURE 23.1   The GUI Network Configuration tool is one of Fedora's best-designed GUI tools, permitting extensive network configuration.

Understanding the Changes Made by DHCP

If your system is set to use DHCP, any existing `/etc/resolv.conf` is saved as `resolv.conf.predhclient` and a new `/etc/resolv.conf` is created with the DNS information supplied by DHCP when the DHCP connection is made. When DHCP is released, the saved file is moved back as `/etc/resolv.conf`.

Essential DNS Concepts

We begin with a look at the ideas behind DNS prior to discussing the details of the software used to implement it. An understanding at this level is invaluable in avoiding the majority of problems that administrators commonly experience with DNS, as well as in diagnosing and quickly solving the ones that do occur. The following overview omits several small details in the protocol because they are not relevant to the everyday tasks of a DNS administrator. If you need more information about DNS, consult the DNS standards, especially RFC 1034. The RFCs related to DNS are distributed with BIND. Fedora installs them in `/usr/share/doc/bind-*/rfc/`.

The domain namespace is structured as a tree. Each domain is a node in the tree and has a name. For every node, there are *resource records (RRs)*—each of which stores a single fact about the domain. (Who owns it? What is its IP address?) Domains can have any number of children, or subdomains. The root of the tree is a domain named . (similar to the / root directory in a file system).

Each of the resource records belonging to a domain stores a different type of information. For example:

- ▶ **A (Address)** records store the IP address associated with a name.

- ▶ **NS (Nameserver)** records name an authoritative nameserver for a domain.

- ▶ **SOA (Start of Authority)** records contain basic properties of the domain and the domain's zone.

- ▶ **PTR (Pointer)** records contain the real name of the host to which the IP belongs.

- ▶ **MX (Mail Exchanger)** records specify a mail server for the zone.

Each record type is discussed in detail later in this chapter.

Every node has a unique name that specifies its position in the tree, just as every file has a unique path that leads from the root directory to that file. That is, in the domain name, one starts with the root domain (.) and prepends to it each name in the path, using a dot to separate the names. The root domain has children named com., org., net., de., and so on. They, in turn, have children named ibm.com., wiw.org., and gmx.de..

In general, a *fully qualified domain name (FQDN)* is one that contains the machine name and the domain name, such as the following:

```
foo.example.com.
```

This is similar to the following path:

```
/com/example/foo
```

Contrary to the example, the trailing dot in an FQDN is often omitted. This reverse order is the source of confusion to many people who first examine DNS.

How Nameservers Store DNS Structure Information

Information about the structure of the tree and its associated resource records is stored by programs called *nameservers*. Every domain has an authoritative nameserver that holds a complete local copy of the data for the domain; the domain's administrators are responsible for maintaining the data. A nameserver can also cache information about parts of the tree for which the server has no authority. For administrative convenience, nameservers can delegate authority over certain subdomains to other, independently maintained, nameservers.

The authoritative nameserver for a zone knows about the nameservers to which authority over subdomains has been delegated. The authoritative nameserver might refer queries about the delegated zones to those nameservers. So you can always find authoritative data for a domain by following the chain of delegations of authority from . (the root domain) until you reach an authoritative nameserver for the domain. This is what gives DNS its distributed tree structure.

How DNS Provides Name Service Information to Users

Users of DNS need not be aware of these details. To them, the namespace is just a single tree—any part of which they can request information about. The task of finding the requested RRs from the resource set for a domain is left to programs called *resolvers*. Resolvers are aware of the distributed structure of the database. They know how to contact the root nameservers (which are authoritative for the root domain) and how to follow the chain of delegations until they find an authoritative nameserver that can give them the information for which they are looking.

As an analogy, you can think of domains as directories in a file system and RRs as files in these directories. The delegation of authority over subdomains is similar to having an NFS file system mounted under a subdirectory: Requests for files under that directory would go to the NFS server, rather than this file system. The resolver's job is to start from the root directory and walk down the directory tree (following mount points) until it reaches the directory that contains the files in which the user is interested. For efficiency, the nameservers can then cache the information they find for some time. This is why things appear to be listed in reverse order. This process is examined in detail next.

In practice, there are several authoritative nameservers for a domain. One of them is the *master* (or *primary*) nameserver, where the domain's data is held. The others are known as *slave* (or *secondary*) nameservers, and they hold automatically updated copies of the master data. Both the master and the slaves serve the same information, so it doesn't matter which one a resolver asks. The distinction between master and slave is made purely for reasons of reliability—to ensure that the failure of a single nameserver does not result in the loss of authoritative data for the domain. As a bonus, this redundancy also distributes the network load between several hosts so that no one nameserver is overwhelmed with requests for authoritative information.

> **NOTE**
>
> As a DNS administrator, it is your responsibility to ensure that your nameservers provide sufficient redundancy for your zones. Your slaves should be far away from the master so that power failures, network outages, and other catastrophes do not affect your name service.

Despite these precautions, the load on DNS servers would be crushing without the extensive use of local caches. As mentioned before, nameservers are allowed to cache the results of queries and intermediate referrals for some time so that they can serve repeated requests for data without referring to the source each time. If they did not do this, root nameservers (and the nameservers for other popular zones) would be contacted by clients all over the world for every name lookup, wasting enormous resources.

Name Resolution in Practice

When a web browser issues a request for an IP address, the request is sent to a local nameserver, which resolves the name, stores the result in its cache, and returns the IP address. DNS can be a fascinating and extremely in-depth subject—see the "Reference" section at the end of this chapter for further reading.

Using DNS Tools

Fedora includes a number of standard tools that enable you to work with DNS. These tools, found in the `bind-utils` and `whois` packages, have everyday uses that do not require DNS administrator skills. If you want to know what domain name belongs to an IP address, or vice versa, these are the tools to use to track down that information. *Forward lookups* are where you map a name to an IP address; *reverse lookups* are where you map an address to a name.

Here are tools you can use:

- `dig` *(Domain Information Groper)*
- `host`
- `nslookup`
- `whois`

The following sections briefly describe these tools and provide examples of their use.

dig

The Domain Information Groper is a command-line utility that queries DNS nameservers. By default, dig uses the nameservers listed in `/etc/resolv.conf` and performs an NS *(nameserver)* query. Reverse lookups are accomplished with the `-x` argument with a default A *(Address)* query.

Here is an example of a forward lookup with dig:

```
$ dig www.pearson.com
; <<>> DiG 9.5.0a6 <<>> www.pearson.com
;; global options:  printcmd
;; Got answer:
;; ->>HEADER<<- opcode: QUERY, status: NOERROR, id: 5889
;; flags: qr rd ra; QUERY: 1, ANSWER: 1, AUTHORITY: 3, ADDITIONAL: 3

;; QUESTION SECTION:
;www.pearson.com.                IN      A

;; ANSWER SECTION:
www.pearson.com.        86400   IN      A       195.69.212.200

;; AUTHORITY SECTION:
pearson.com.            46430   IN      NS      ns2.pearson.com.
pearson.com.            46430   IN      NS      oldtxdns2.pearsontc.com.
pearson.com.            46430   IN      NS      ns.pearson.com.

;; ADDITIONAL SECTION:
ns.pearson.com.         162044  IN      A       195.69.213.15
ns2.pearson.com.        78028   IN      A       195.69.215.15
oldtxdns2.pearsontc.com. 139762 IN      A       192.251.135.15

;; Query time: 50 msec
;; SERVER: 192.168.0.1#53(192.168.0.1)
;; WHEN: Sun Oct 28 20:02:53 2007
;; MSG SIZE  rcvd: 166
```

And here is a reverse lookup with dig:

```
$ dig 195.69.212.200

; <<>> DiG 9.5.0a6 <<>> 195.69.212.200
;; global options:  printcmd
;; Got answer:
;; ->>HEADER<<- opcode: QUERY, status: NXDOMAIN, id: 53249
;; flags: qr rd ra; QUERY: 1, ANSWER: 0, AUTHORITY: 1, ADDITIONAL: 0

;; QUESTION SECTION:
```

23

```
;195.69.212.200.                          IN      A

;; AUTHORITY SECTION:
.                       10800   IN      SOA     A.ROOT-SERVERS.NET. NSTLD.VERISIGN-
GRS.COM. 2007102800 1800 900 604800 86400

;; Query time: 47 msec
;; SERVER: 192.168.0.1#53(192.168.0.1)
;; WHEN: Sun Oct 28 20:03:49 2007
;; MSG SIZE  rcvd: 107
```

host

A command-line utility, `host` performs forward and reverse lookups by querying DNS nameservers, similar to `dig`.

Here's an example of a forward lookup with `host`:

```
$ host www.pearson.com
www.pearson.com has address 195.69.212.200
```

Here's a reverse lookup with `host`:

```
$ host 195.69.212.200
200.212.69.195.in-addr.arpa domain name\
pointer www.environment.pearson.com.
200.212.69.195.in-addr.arpa domain name\
pointer booktime.pearson.com.
200.212.69.195.in-addr.arpa domain name\
pointer environment.pearson.com.
```

nslookup

A command-line utility, `nslookup` can be used in an interactive or noninteractive manner to query DNS nameservers. Note that `nslookup` is outdated; try using `dig` instead.

Here's an example of a forward lookup using `nslookup`:

```
$ nslookup www.pearson.com
Server:         192.168.0.1
Address:        192.168.0.1#53

Non-authoritative answer:
Name:   www.pearson.com
Address: 195.69.212.200
```

Here's a reverse lookup using `nslookup`:

```
nslookup 195.69.212.200
Server:         192.168.2.1
Address:        192.168.2.1#53

Non-authoritative answer:
200.212.69.195.in-addr.arpa    name = environment.pearson.com.
200.212.69.195.in-addr.arpa    name = www.environment.pearson.com.
200.212.69.195.in-addr.arpa    name = booktime.pearson.com.

Authoritative answers can be found from:
212.69.195.in-addr.arpa nameserver = ns2.pearson.com.
212.69.195.in-addr.arpa nameserver = ns.pearson.com.
ns2.pearson.com internet address = 195.69.215.15
```

Note that using a reverse lookup does not tell you the FQDN of the server using that IP address. To determine that, you have to use the `whois` client.

whois

A command-line utility from the `whois` package, `whois` queries various `whois` servers across the Internet.

For an IP lookup:

```
$ whois 165.193.130.83

[Querying whois.arin.net]
[whois.arin.net]

OrgName:    Savvis
OrgID:      SAVVI-3
Address:    3300 Regency Parkway
City:       Cary
StateProv:  NC
PostalCode: 27511
Country:    US

NetRange:   165.193.0.0 - 165.193.255.255
CIDR:       165.193.0.0/16
NetName:    SAVVIS
NetHandle:  NET-165-193-0-0-1
Parent:     NET-165-0-0-0-0
NetType:    Direct Allocation
NameServer: NS01.SAVVIS.NET
NameServer: NS02.SAVVIS.NET
```

```
NameServer: NS03.SAVVIS.NET
NameServer: NS04.SAVVIS.NET
NameServer: NS05.SAVVIS.NET
Comment:
RegDate:
Updated:    2007-09-18


OrgAbuseHandle: ABUSE11-ARIN
OrgAbuseName:   Abuse
OrgAbusePhone:  +1-877-393-7878
OrgAbuseEmail:  abuse@savvis.net


OrgNOCHandle: NOC99-ARIN
OrgNOCName:   SAVVIS Support Center
OrgNOCPhone:  + 1-888-638-6771
OrgNOCEmail:  ipnoc@savvis.net


OrgTechHandle: UIAA-ARIN
OrgTechName:   US IP Address Administration
OrgTechPhone:  + 1-888-638-6771
OrgTechEmail:  ipadmin@savvis.net


# ARIN WHOIS database, last updated 2007-10-27 19:10
# Enter ? for additional hints on searching ARIN's WHOIS database.
```

And for a domain name lookup (which is not what whois is used for):

```
$ whois www.pearson.com

Whois Server Version 2.0

Domain names in the .com and .net domains can now be registered
with many different competing registrars. Go to http://www.internic.net
for detailed information.

No match for "WWW.PEARSON.COM".
```

Configuring a Local Caching Nameserver

A caching nameserver builds a local cache of resolved domain names and provides them to other hosts on your LAN. This speeds up DNS searches and saves bandwidth by reusing lookups for frequently accessed domains and is especially useful on a slow dialup connection or when your ISP's own nameservers malfunction.

If you have BIND and BIND-utils installed on your computer, you can configure a caching nameserver by installing the `caching-nameserver` package. This sets up the `/etc/named.conf` configuration file, the `/var/named` directory, and the configuration files in `/var/named` (`localhost.zone`, `named.ca`, and `named.local`).

To start the caching nameserver, you can start the named service manually (see Chapter 11, "Automating Tasks") or use the system-config-services GUI configuration tool. Choose the Services menu option in the Server Settings menu, which is in the System Settings menu, and then select named and click the Start button.

To get your local computer to use the caching nameserver, reconfigure the `/etc/resolv.conf` file to comment out any references to your ISP's nameservers, and set the only nameserver to be the localhost (`127.0.0.1`). The `/etc/resolv.conf` for the caching nameserver host is as follows:

```
#/etc/resolv.conf
#nameserver 83.64.1.10
#nameserver 83.64.0.10
nameserver 127.0.0.1
```

Other machines on your network should have the IP of the local caching nameserver in their `/etc/resolv.conf` files. Assuming that the IP address for the computer running the caching nameserver is 192.168.1.5, the `/etc/resolv.conf` files on the other machines on your network should be the following:

```
#/etc/resolv.conf
#nameserver 83.64.1.10
#nameserver 83.64.0.10
nameserver 192.168.1.5
```

Ad Blocking with a Caching Nameserver

Another advantage of setting up a caching nameserver is that you can use it to block ads and objectionable sites by using bogus DNS zones to block specific domains. You do this by overriding the DNS lookup of the sites you want to block. Configuration is simple. First, determine the sites that you want to block. For example, you might want to block all access to doubleclick.net. Create an entry in `/etc/named.conf` like this:

```
zone "doublelick.net" { type master; file "fakes"; };
```

Then create a new `/var/named/fakes` file. This should contain

```
$TTL 1D
@       IN      SOA     dns.companyname.com. hostmaster.companyname.com. (
                        2004081701 8H 2H 4W 1D)

@       IN      NS      dns.companyname.example.com.
@       IN      A       127.0.0.1
*       IN      A       127.0.0.1
```

where *dns.companyname.com* should be replaced by the hostname of the caching nameserver. This points all DNS lookups of doubleclick.net to `127.0.0.1`, where they will not be found. To make the change effective, you have to restart named so that the new configuration information is read. Chapter 11 describes several different ways of restarting the named service; here is one of them:

```
# kill -HUP 'pidof named'
```

When named is restarted, attempts to resolve all doubleclick.net addresses fail, the ads are neither loaded nor displayed, and your browsing experience is faster.

Your Own Domain Name and Third-Party DNS

It is possible to have your own domain name and provide third-party DNS service for it, meaning that you do not have to configure and administer a DNS nameserver for yourself. You can even have a mail address for your domain without having a mail server.

Here is a summary of the major tasks involved in providing a third-party DNS service to your own domain name:

▶ **Register and pay for a unique domain name**—Several companies now offer to register these names, so shop around for the most reasonable price and perform some Google background checks on the company before using it.

▶ **Use a third-party DNS provider to provide DNS services**—One popular provider is ZoneEdit, which provides detailed steps to use the service. ZoneEdit also provides mail-forwarding services, so mail addressed to you@your.own.domain is forwarded to your regular ISP mail account. ZoneEdit also allows you to use Dynamic DNS, which enables you to run a server on a dynamically assigned IP (from a cable or dialup provider), yet still have DNS servers locate you. ZoneEdit can also provide a startup web page space for you or forward requests to an already established page with a long, complicated address.

▶ **Return to your domain name registrar and tell it what nameservers are authoritative for your domain**.

After you have completed the preceding tasks, it takes about three days for the information to propagate around the Internet.

Providing DNS for a Real Domain with BIND

BIND is the de facto standard DNS software suite for UNIX. It contains a nameserver daemon (named) that answers DNS queries, a resolver library that enables programs to make such queries, and some utility programs. BIND is maintained by the *ISC (Internet Software Consortium)* at the website http://www.isc.org/bind/.

Three major versions of BIND are in common use today: 4, 8, and 9. The use of BIND 4 is now *strongly* discouraged because of numerous security vulnerabilities and other bugs, and is not discussed here. BIND 8, with many new features and bug fixes, is now quite widely deployed. It is actively maintained, but still vulnerable to a variety of attacks; its use is *strongly* discouraged, too. Fedora now provides BIND 9.

> **NOTE**
>
> If you are upgrading from BIND 8 to BIND 9, make sure to read the file /usr/share/ doc/bind-9.5.0/misc/migration for any issues regarding configuration files (which will cause BIND not to run) and use of existing shell scripts. An HTML version of the BIND 9 manual is the Bv9ARM.html file under the /usr/share/doc/bind-9.5.0/arm directory.

In this chapter, we discuss the use of BIND 9, which ships with Fedora. BIND 9 was rewritten from scratch in an attempt to make the code more robust and leave behind the problems inherent in the old code. It is compliant with new DNS standards and represents a substantial improvement in features, performance, and security.

The bind RPM package contains the named daemon and a wealth of BIND documentation. The bind-utils RPM package contains, among other things, the invaluable dig(1) utility. If you choose to compile BIND yourself, you can download the source distribution from the ISC's website and follow the build instructions therein.

> **NOTE**
>
> You can find build instructions in the Read Me file under the /usr/share/doc/bind- 9.5.0 directory, too.

After you install the RPMs, the following directories are of special interest because they contain the file used by BIND and contain the information shown in the listing:

```
- - - - - - - - - -

/etc/                          The rndc.conf, named.conf configuration files.
/usr/bin/                      dig, host, nslookup, nsupdate.
/usr/sbin/                     named, rndc, and various support programs.
/usr/share/doc/bind-9.5.0/     BIND documentation.
/usr/share/man/                Manual pages.
/var/named/*                   Zone files.
- - - - - - - - - -
```

If you install from source, the files will be in the locations you specified at configure time, with the default directories under /usr/local/.

The following example uses BIND to configure a nameserver and then expand it as necessary to provide useful DNS service. To accomplish this, you must configure named (the nameserver daemon) and rndc components (a control utility that permits various interactions with a running instance of named). You also might need to configure the resolver software, as discussed later. Three configuration files are used:

- ▶ rndc.key to specify the key used to authenticate between rndc and named

- ▶ rndc.conf to configure rndc

- ▶ named.conf to configure named

When rndc communicates with named, it uses cryptographic keys to digitally sign commands before sending them over the network to named. The configuration file, /etc/rndc.key, specifies the key used for the authentication.

The only authentication mechanism currently supported by named is the use of a secret key, encrypted with the HMAC-MD5 algorithm and shared between rndc and named. The easiest way to generate a key is to use the dnssec-keygen utility. In the following example, the utility is asked to generate a 128-bit HMAC-MD5 user key named rndc:

```
$ dnssec-keygen -a hmac-md5 -b 128 -n user rndc
Krndc.+157+14529
$ cat Krndc.+157+14529.private
Private-key-format: v1.2
Algorithm: 157 (HMAC_MD5)
Key: mKKd2FiHMFe1JqXl/z4cfw==
```

The utility creates two files with .key and .private extensions, respectively. The Key: line in the .private file reveals the secret that rndc and named need to share (mKKd2FiHMFe1JqXl/z4cfw==). When you have this, you can set up the rndc.key configuration file, which is shared by both rndc.conf and named.conf:

```
key "rndc" {  algorithm    hmac-md5;  secret    "mKKd2FiHMFe1JqXl/z4cfw=="; };
----------
```

rndc.conf

rndc uses a TCP connection (on port 953) to communicate with named. The configuration file, /etc/rndc.conf by default, must specify a server to talk to as well as include the corresponding key (which must be recognized by named) to use while talking to it:

```
----------
# Use the key named "rndc" when talking to the nameserver "localhost."
server localhost {
    key               "rndc";
};

# Defaults.
options {
    default-server    localhost;
```

```
    default-key          "rndc";
};


# Include the key to use
include "/etc/rndc.key;
----------
```

The file needs to have three sections:

- **Server section**—Defines a nameserver (localhost) and specifies a key (rndc) to be used while communicating with it

- **Options section**—Sets up reasonable defaults because the file might list multiple servers and keys

- **Key section**—Includes the file already created, /etc/rndc.key

Should you need it, the rndc(8) and rndc.conf(5) manual pages contain more information.

named.conf

You next must configure named itself. Its single configuration file (/etc/named.conf) has syntax very similar to rndc.conf; this section describes only a small subset of the configuration directives essential to the configuration of a functional nameserver. For a more exhaustive reference, consult the BIND 9 *ARM (Administrator Reference Manual)*; it is distributed with BIND, and Fedora installs it under /usr/share/doc/bind-*/arm/).

Only the options and named sections in the named.conf file are absolutely necessary. The options section must tell named where the zone files are kept, and named must know where to find the root zone (.). We also set up a controls section to enable suitably authenticated commands from rndc to be accepted. Because clients (notably nslookup) often depend on resolving the nameserver's IP, we set up the 0.0.127.in-addr.arpa reverse zone, too.

We start with a configuration file similar to this:

```
----------options {     # This is where zone files are kept.     directory
         "/var/named"; };


# Allow rndc running on localhost to send us commands. controls {     inet
 127.0.0.1          allow { localhost; }          keys { rndc; }; };""include
 "/etc/rndc.key";


# Information about the root zone. zone "." {     type             hint;
file              "root.hints"; }; # Lots of software depends on being
able to resolve 127.0.0.1 zone "0.0.127.in-addr.arpa" {     type
master;     file             "rev/127.0.0"; };
----------
```

The options section is where to specify the directory in which named should look for zone files (as named in other sections of the file). You learn about using other options in later examples in this chapter.

Next, we instruct named to accept commands from an authenticated rndc. We include the key file, /etc/rndc.key, and the controls section saying that rndc connects from localhost and uses the specified key. (You can specify more than one IP address in the allow list or use an access control list as described in the "Managing DNS Security" section, later in this chapter.)

The . zone tells named about the root nameservers with names and addresses in the root.hints file. This information determines which root nameserver is initially consulted, although this decision is frequently revised based on the server's response time. Although the hints file can be obtained via FTP, the recommended, network-friendly way to keep it synchronized is to use dig. We ask a root nameserver (it doesn't matter which one) for the NS records of . and use the dig output directly:

```
# dig @j.root-servers.net. ns > /var/named/root.hints
# cat /var/named/root.hints
; <<>> DiG 8.2 <<>> @j.root-servers.net . ns
; (1 server found)
;; res options: init recurs defnam dnsrch
;; got answer:
;; ->>HEADER<<- opcode: QUERY, status: NOERROR, id: 6
;; flags: qr aa rd; QUERY: 1, ANSWER: 13, AUTHORITY: 0, ADDITIONAL: 13
;; QUERY SECTION:       ;; ., type = NS, class = IN


;; ANSWER SECTION:
.                       6D IN NS        H.ROOT-SERVERS.NET.
.                       6D IN NS        C.ROOT-SERVERS.NET.
.                       6D IN NS        G.ROOT-SERVERS.NET.
.                       6D IN NS        F.ROOT-SERVERS.NET.
.                       6D IN NS        B.ROOT-SERVERS.NET.
.                       6D IN NS        J.ROOT-SERVERS.NET.
.                       6D IN NS        K.ROOT-SERVERS.NET.
.                       6D IN NS        L.ROOT-SERVERS.NET.
.                       6D IN NS        M.ROOT-SERVERS.NET.
.                       6D IN NS        I.ROOT-SERVERS.NET.
.                       6D IN NS        E.ROOT-SERVERS.NET.
.                       6D IN NS        D.ROOT-SERVERS.NET.
.                       6D IN NS        A.ROOT-SERVERS.NET.


;; ADDITIONAL SECTION:
H.ROOT-SERVERS.NET.     5w6d16h IN A    128.63.2.53
C.ROOT-SERVERS.NET.     5w6d16h IN A    192.33.4.12
G.ROOT-SERVERS.NET.     5w6d16h IN A    192.112.36.4
```

```
     F.ROOT-SERVERS.NET.          5w6d16h IN A    192.5.5.241
     B.ROOT-SERVERS.NET.          5w6d16h IN A    128.9.0.107
     J.ROOT-SERVERS.NET.          5w6d16h IN A    198.41.0.10
     K.ROOT-SERVERS.NET.          5w6d16h IN A    193.0.14.129
     L.ROOT-SERVERS.NET.          5w6d16h IN A    198.32.64.12
     M.ROOT-SERVERS.NET.          5w6d16h IN A    202.12.27.33
     I.ROOT-SERVERS.NET.          5w6d16h IN A    192.36.148.17
     E.ROOT-SERVERS.NET.          5w6d16h IN A    192.203.230.10
     D.ROOT-SERVERS.NET.          5w6d16h IN A    128.8.10.90
     A.ROOT-SERVERS.NET.          5w6d16h IN A    198.41.0.4

     ;; Total query time: 4489 msec
     ;; FROM: lustre to SERVER: j.root-servers.net  198.41.0.10
     ;; WHEN: Mon Sep 10 04:18:26 2001
     ;; MSG SIZE  sent: 17  rcvd: 436
```

23

The Zone File

The zone `0.0.127.in-addr.arpa` section in `named.conf` says that we are a master name-server for that zone and that the zone data is in the file `127.0.0`. Before examining the first real zone file in detail, look at the general format of a RR specification:

```
name    TTL    class    type    data
```

Here, `name` is the DNS name with which this record is associated. In a zone file, names ending with a `.` are fully qualified, whereas others are relative to the name of the zone. In the zone `example.com`, `foo` refers to the fully qualified name `foo.example.com`. The special name `@` is a short form for the name of the zone itself. If the name is omitted, the last specified name is used again.

The `TTL` *(Time To Live)* field is a number that specifies the time for which the record can be cached. This is explained in greater detail in the discussion of the `SOA` record in the next section. If this field is omitted, the default `TTL` for the zone is assumed. `TTL` values are usually in seconds, but you can append an `m` for minutes, `h` for hours, or `d` for days.

BIND supports different record classes, but for all practical purposes, the only important class is `IN`, for Internet. If no class is explicitly specified, a default value of `IN` is assumed; to save a little typing, we do not mention the class in any of the zone files we write here.

The `type` field is mandatory and names the RR in use, such as `A`, `NS`, `MX`, or `SOA`. (We use only a few of the existing RRs here. Consult the DNS standards for a complete list.)

The `data` field (or fields) contains data specific to this type of record. The appropriate syntax will be introduced as we examine the use of each RR in turn.

Here is the zone file for the `0.0.127.in-addr.arpa` zone:

```
          $TTL 2D
          @        SOA      localhost. hostmaster.example.com. (
                                 2001090101   ; Serial
                                 24h          ; Refresh
                                 2h           ; Retry
                                 3600000      ; Expire (1000h)
                                 1h)          ; Minimum TTL
                   NS       localhost.

1         PTR      localhost.
```

The `$TTL` directive that should begin every zone file sets the default minimum time to live for the zone to two days. This is discussed further in the next section.

The Zone File's SOA Record

The second line in the zone file uses the special @ name that you saw earlier. Here, it stands for `0.0.127.in-addr.arpa`, to which the SOA *(Start of Authority)* record belongs. The rest of the fields (continued until the closing parenthesis) contain SOA-specific data.

The first data field in the SOA record is the fully qualified name of the master nameserver for the domain. The second field is the email address of the contact person for the zone. Replacing the @ sign with a . writes it as a DNS name; foo@example.com would be written as `foo.example.com` (note the trailing .).

Do not use an address such as a.b@example.com because it is written as `a.b.example.com` and will later be misinterpreted as a@b.example.com.

TIP

It is important to ensure that mail to the contact email address specified in the SOA field is frequently read because it is used to report DNS setup problems and other potentially useful information.

The next several numeric fields specify various characteristics of this zone. These values must be correctly configured, and to do so, you must understand each field. As shown in the comments (note that zone file comments are not the in the same syntax as `named.conf` comments), the fields are serial number, refresh interval, retry time, expire period, and minimum TTL.

Serial numbers are 32-bit quantities that can hold values between 0 and 4,294,967,295 ($2^{32} - 1$). Every time the zone data is changed, the serial number must be incremented. This change serves as a signal to slaves that they need to transfer the contents of the zone again. It is conventional to assign serial numbers in the format YYYYMMDDnn; that is, the date of the change and a two-digit revision number (for example, 2007060101). For changes made on the same day, you increment only the revision. This reasonably assumes that you make no more than 99 changes to a zone in one day. For changes on the next day, the date is changed and the revision number starts from 01 again.

The refresh interval specifies how often a slave server should check whether the master data has been updated. It has been set to 24 hours here, but if the zone changes often, the value should be lower. Slaves can reload the zone much sooner if both they and the master support the DNS NOTIFY mechanism, and most DNS software does.

The retry time is relevant only when a slave fails to contact the master after the refresh time has elapsed. It specifies how long it should wait before trying again. (It is set to two hours here.) If the slave is consistently unable to contact the master for the length of the expire period (usually because of some catastrophic failure), it discards the zone data it already has and stops answering queries for the zone. Thus, the expire period should be long enough to allow for the recovery of the master nameserver. It has been repeatedly shown that a value of one or two weeks is too short. One thousand hours (about six weeks) is accepted as a good default.

As you read earlier, every RR has a TTL field that specifies how long it can be cached before the origin of the data must be consulted again. If the RR definition does not explicitly specify a TTL value, the default TTL (set by the $TTL directive) is used instead. This enables individual RRs to override the default TTL value as required.

The SOA TTL, the last numeric field in the SOA record, is used to determine how long negative responses (NXDOMAIN) should be cached. (That is, if a query results in an NXDOMAIN response, that fact is cached for as long as indicated by the SOA TTL.) Older versions of BIND used the SOA minimum TTL to set the default TTL, but BIND 9 no longer does so. The default TTL of 2 (two days) and SOA TTL of 1 (one hour) are recommended for cache friendliness.

The values used previously are good defaults for zones that do not change often. You might have to adjust them a bit for zones with different requirements. In that case, the website at http://www.ripe.net/docs/ripe-203.html is recommended reading.

The Zone File's Other Records
The next two lines in the zone file create NS and PTR records. The NS record has no explicit name specified, so it uses the last one, which is the @ of the SOA record. Thus, the nameserver for 0.0.127.in-addr.arpa is defined to be localhost.

The PTR record has the name 1, which becomes 1.0.0.127.in-addr.arpa (which is how you write the address 127.0.0.1 as a DNS name). When qualified, the PTR record name 1 becomes localhost. (You will see some of the numerous other RR types later when we configure our nameserver to be authoritative for a real domain.)

TXT Records and SPF

One record not already mentioned is the TXT record. This record is usually used for documentation purposes in DNS, but a recent proposal uses the TXT record to help in the fight against email address forgery, spam, and phishing attacks.

One problem with email and SMTP is that when email is being delivered, the sender can claim that the email is coming from trusted.bank.com, when really it is coming from smalltime.crook.com. When the recipient of the email gets the email, it looks like valid instructions from trusted.bank.com; but if the receiver trusts the email and follows its instructions, his bank accounts can become vulnerable. These situations can be controlled by using *SPF (Sender Policy Framework)*.

Domains can publish the valid IP address of their email servers in specially formatted TXT records. A TXT record could look like this:

```
trusted.bank.com. IN TXT "v=spf1 ip4:37.21.50.80 -all"
```

This record specifies that only one IP address is allowed to send mail for trusted.bank.com.

Receiving email servers can then do one extra check with incoming email. When an email arrives, they know the IP address that the email is coming from. They also know that the sender claims to be coming from trusted.bank.com, for example. The receiving email server can look up the DNS TXT record for trusted.bank.com, extract the allowed IP addresses, and compare them to the IP address that the email really is coming from. If they match, it is an extremely good indication that the email really is coming from trusted.bank.com. If they do not match, it is a very good indication that the email is bogus and should be deleted or investigated further.

The SPF system does rely on cooperation between senders and receivers. Senders must publish their TXT records in DNS, and receivers must check the records with incoming email. If you want more details on SPF, visit the home page at http://spf.pobox.com/.

Logging

The example now has all the elements of a minimal functioning DNS server, but before experimenting further, some extra logging will allow you to see exactly what named is doing. Log options are configured in a logging section in named.conf, and the various options are described in detail in the BIND 9 ARM.

All log messages go to one or more channels—each of which can write messages to the syslog, to an ordinary file, stderr, or null. (Log messages written to null are discarded.) Categories of messages exist, such as those generated while parsing configuration files, those caused by OS errors, and so on. Your logging statement must define some channels and associate them with the categories of messages that you want to see.

BIND logging is very flexible, but complicated, so we examine only a simple log configuration here. The following addition to `named.conf` sets up a channel called `custom`, which writes time-stamped messages to a file and sends messages in the listed categories to it:

```
logging {
    channel custom {
        file "/tmp/named.log";   # Where to send messages.
        print-time yes;          # Print timestamps?
        print-category yes;      # Print message category?
    };

    category config      { custom; };   # Configuration files
    category notify      { custom; };   # NOTIFY messages
    category dnssec      { custom; };   # TSIG messages
    category general     { custom; };   # Miscellaneous
    category security    { custom; };   # Security messages
    category xfer-out    { custom; };   # Zone transfers
    category lame-servers { custom; };
};
```

NOTE

Retaining and frequently examining your logs is especially important because syntax errors often cause BIND to reject a zone and not answer queries for it, causing your server to become *lame* (meaning that it is not authoritative for the zone for which it is supposed to be).

Resolver Configuration

The last step before running BIND is to set up the local resolver software. This involves configuring the `/etc/hosts`, `/etc/resolv.conf`, and `/etc/nsswitch.conf` files.

To avoid gratuitous network traffic, most UNIX resolvers still use a `hosts`-like text file named `/etc/hosts` to store the names and addresses of commonly used hosts. Each line in this file contains an IP address and a list of names for the host. Add entries to this file for any hosts you want to be able to resolve independently from DNS. If the entry is found in `/etc/hosts`, the resolver does not have to contact a DNS server to resolve the name, which reduces network traffic.

/etc/resolv.conf specifies the addresses of preferred nameservers and a list of domains relative to which unqualified names are resolved. You specify a nameserver with a line of the form nameserver 1.2.3.4 (where 1.2.3.4 is the address of the nameserver). You can use multiple nameserver lines (usually up to three). You can use a search line to specify a list of domains to search for unqualified names.

A search line such as search example.com example.net causes the resolver to attempt to resolve the unqualified name xyz, first as xyz.example.com, and then, if that fails, as xyz.example.net. Do not use too many domains in the search list because it slows down resolution.

A hosts: files dns line in /etc/nsswitch.conf causes the resolver to consult /etc/hosts before using the DNS during the course of a name lookup. This allows you to override the DNS by making temporary changes to /etc/hosts, which is especially useful during network testing. (Older resolvers might require an order hosts, bind line in the /etc/host.conf file instead.)

Running the named Nameserver Daemon

Finally! You can now start named with /etc/rc.d/init.d/named start. You should see messages similar to the ones that follow in the syslog (or another location, according to the logging configuration you have set up). One way to do this is to monitor the log file with the tail command; that scrolls the changes in the file down the screen:

```
# tail -f /var/log/messages
- - - - - - - - - -
July 9 23:48:33 titan named[2605]: starting BIND 9.2.3 -u named
July 9 23:48:33 titan named[2605]: using 1 CPU
July 9 23:48:33 titan named[2608]: loading configuration from '/etc/named.conf'
July 9 23:48:33 titan named[2608]: no IPv6 interfaces found
July 9 23:48:33 titan named[2608]: listening on IPv4 interface lo, 127.0.0.1#53
July 9 23:48:33 titan named: named startup succeeded
July 9 23:48:33 titan named[2608]: listening on IPv4 interface\
  eth0, 192.168.2.68#53
July 9 23:48:33 titan named[2608]: command channel listening on 127.0.0.1#953
October 9 23:48:33 titan named[2608]: zone 0.0.127.in-addr.arpa/IN: \
loaded serial 1997022700
October 9 23:48:33 titan named[2608]: zone localhost/IN: loaded serial 42
October 9 23:48:33 titan named[2608]: running
- - - - - - - - - -
```

You can use rndc to interact with this instance of named. Running rndc without arguments displays a list of available commands, including ones to reload or refresh zones, dump statistics and the database to disk, toggle query logging, and stop the server. Unfortunately, rndc does not yet implement all the commands that were supported by ndc—the control program shipped with earlier versions of BIND.

You should now be able to resolve `1.0.0.127.in-addr.arpa` locally (try `dig @localhost 1.0.0.127.in-addr.arpa PTR +norec`) and other names via recursive resolution. If you cannot accomplish this resolution, something is wrong, and you should read the "Troubleshooting DNS" section later in this chapter to diagnose and correct your problem before proceeding further. Remember to read the logs!

Providing DNS for a Real Domain

You can expand the minimal nameserver configuration you just created into one that performs useful name service for a real domain. Suppose that your ISP has assigned to you the IP addresses in the 192.0.2.0/29 range (which has six usable addresses: 192.0.2.1–6) and that you want to serve authoritative data for the domain example.com. A friend has agreed to configure her nameserver (192.0.2.96) to be a slave for the domain, as well as a backup mail server. In return, she wants the foo.example.com subdomain delegated to her own nameservers.

Forward Zone

First, you must introduce the zone to `named.conf`:

```
zone "example.com" {
    type master;
    file "example.com";
};
```

and create the zone file:

```
$TTL 2D
@       SOA     ns1.example.com. hostmaster.example.com. (
                        2001090101  ; Serial
                        24h         ; Refresh
                        2h          ; Retry
                        3600000     ; Expire (1000h)
                        1h)         ; Minimum TTL
        NS      ns1.example.com.
        NS      ns2.example.com.
        MX 5    mx1.example.com.
        MX 10   mx2.example.com.
        A       192.0.2.1

; Addresses
ns1     A       192.0.2.1               ; Nameservers
```

```
    ns2      A       192.0.2.96
    mx1      A       192.0.2.2          ; Mail servers
    mx2      A       192.0.2.96
    www      A       192.0.2.3          ; Web servers
    dev      A       192.0.2.4
    work     A       192.0.2.5          ; Workstations
    play     A       192.0.2.6


    ; Delegations
    foo      NS      dns1.foo.example.com.
    foo      NS      dns2.foo.example.com.
    dns1.foo A       192.0.2.96
    dns2.foo A       192.0.2.1
- - - - - - - - - -
```

The SOA record is similar to the one you saw before. Note that the next five records use the implicit name @, which is short for example.com.

The two NS records define ns1.example.com (your own server, 192.0.2.1) and ns2.example.com (your friend's server, 192.0.2.96) as authoritative nameservers for example.com.

The MX *(Mail Exchanger)* records specify a mail server for the zone. An MX RR takes two arguments: a priority number and the name of a host. In delivering mail addressed to example.com, the listed MXes are tried in increasing order of priority. In this case, mx1.example.com (your own machine, 192.0.2.2) has the lowest priority and is always tried first. If the attempt to deliver mail to mx1 fails for some reason, the next listed MX, mx2.example.com (your friend's server), is tried.

The A record says that the address of example.com is 192.0.2.1, and the next few lines specify addresses for other hosts in the zone: your nameservers ns1 and ns2, mail servers mx1 and mx2, two web servers, and two workstations.

Next you add NS records to delegate authority over the foo.example.com domain to dns1 and dns2.foo.example.com. The A records for dns1 and dns2 are known as *glue* records, and they enable resolvers to find the address of the authoritative nameserver so that they can continue the query. (If you were using dig, the NS records for dns1 and dns2 would be listed in the AUTHORITY section of the response, whereas the ADDITIONAL section would contain their addresses.)

Notice that dns2.foo.example.com is 192.0.2.1, your own nameserver. You are acting as a slave for the foo.example.com zone and must configure named accordingly. You introduce the zone as a slave in named.conf and specify the address of the master nameserver:

```
- - - - - - - - - -

    zone "foo.example.com" {
        type slave;
```

```
           file "foo.example.com";
           masters {
               192.0.2.96;
           };
       };
----------
```

Similarly, your friend must configure 192.0.2.96, which is a master for foo.example.com and a slave for example.com. She must also configure her server to accept mail addressed to example.com. Usually, mx2 would just queue the mail until it could be delivered to mx1.

Reverse Zone

Take a moment to pretend that we live in a perfect world: Your highly competent ISP has successfully delegated authority of your reverse zone to you, and you must set up named to handle reverse resolution, too. This process is very similar to what you used to set up the reverse zone for 0.0.127.in-addr.arpa. Now, however, you must determine your zone's name.

DNS can delegate authority only at the . in domain names; as a result, you can set up reverse zones for the whole of a class A, B, or C network because they are divided at octet boundaries in the IP address. This approach is clearly unsuitable for classless subnets such as yours because the divisions are not at octet boundaries, but in the middle of an octet. In other words, your network cannot be described as x.* (Class A), x.y.* (Class B), or x.y.z.* (Class C). The latter comes closest, but includes several addresses (such as 192.0.2.22) that do not belong to the tiny 192.0.2.0/29 network. To set up a reverse zone for your network, you must resort to the use of classless delegation (described in RFC 2317).

The ISP, which is authoritative for the 2.0.192.in-addr.arpa zone, must either maintain your reverse zone for you or add the following records into its zone file:

```
----------

   1            CNAME   1.1-6
   2            CNAME   2.1-6
   3            CNAME   3.1-6
   4            CNAME   4.1-6
   5            CNAME   5.1-6
   6            CNAME   6.1-6

   1-6          NS      192.0.2.1
   1-6          NS      192.0.2.96
----------
```

The first CNAME record says that 1.2.0.192.in-addr.arpa is an alias for 1.1-6.2.0.192._in-addr.arpa. (The others are similar. There are no CNAME records for network and broadcast addresses 0 and 7 because they do not need to resolve.) Resolvers already know how to follow CNAME aliases while resolving names. When they ask about the 1-6 domains, they find the NS records defined previously and continue with their query by asking the nameserver about 1.1-6.2.0.192.in-addr.arpa.

So you must set up a zone file for 1-6.2.0.192.in-addr.arpa. Apart from the peculiar name, this zone file is similar in every respect to the reverse zone set up earlier, and should contain six PTR records (apart from the SOA and NS records). Note that you make 192.0.2.96 (ns2) a slave for the reverse zone, too, so the administrator must add a suitable zone statement to named.conf for it.

> **CAUTION**
>
> Be aware that in the real world you might have to wait for months for your ISP to get the reverse delegation right, and your reverse zone remains broken until then.

Registering the Domain

You now have a working DNS setup, but external resolvers cannot see it because there is no chain of delegations from the root nameservers to yours. You need to create this chain by registering the domain; that is, by paying the appropriate registration fees to an authority known as a *registrar*, which then delegates authority over the chosen zone to your nameservers.

Nothing is magical about what a registrar does. It has authority over a certain portion of the DNS database (say, the com. *top-level domain [TLD]*), and, for a fee, it delegates authority over a subdomain (example.com) to you. This delegation is accomplished by the same mechanisms that were explained earlier in the delegation of foo.example.com.

The site http://www.iana.org/domain-names.htm contains a list of all the TLDs and the corresponding registrars (of which there are now several). The procedure and fees for registering a domain vary wildly between them. Visit the website of the registrar in question and follow the procedures outlined there. After wading through the required amounts of red tape, your domain should be visible to the rest of the world.

Congratulations! Your job as a DNS administrator has just begun.

Troubleshooting DNS

Several sources offer good information about finding and fixing DNS errors. The DNSRD Tricks and Tips page at http://www.dns.net/dnsrd/trick.html and the comp.protocols.tcp-ip.domains FAQ (an HTML version is located at http://www.intac.com/~cdp/cptd-faq/) are good places to start. This section discusses some of the more common errors and their cures.

> **NOTE**
>
> RFC 1912, "Common DNS Operational and Configuration Errors," discusses several of the most common DNS problems at length. It is available at http://www.intac.com/~cdp/cptd-faq/.

Delegation Problems

Your zone must be delegated to the nameservers authoritative for them, either by the root nameservers or the parents of the zone in question. Improper delegation can cause the name service for your domain to become dysfunctional, prevent some networks from using the name service, and numerous other problems. These problems typically occur only in the initial stages of setting up a domain when the delegations have not propagated widely yet.

If you experience such problems, you can use dig to follow delegation chains and find the point at which problems occur. A tool such as dnswalk might also be useful (see "Tools for Troubleshooting" later in this chapter).

Lame delegation is another common DNS delegation problem. *Lame delegation* occurs when a nameserver is listed as being authoritative for a zone, but in fact is not authoritative (it has not been configured to be a master for the zone); the nameserver in a lame delegation is called a *lame server*. Unfortunately, lame delegations are very common on the Internet. They can be the temporary result of domains being moved or (especially in the case of reverse zones) more permanent configuration errors that are never detected because of a lack of attention to detail.

If your registrar's bills for your domain are not promptly paid, the registrar might discontinue the delegation of authority for your zone. If this happens (and the whois record for your domain usually mentions this), the best thing to do is quickly pay the registrar and ask for a renewal of the delegation. It is better not to let it happen, however, because such changes can take a relatively long time to make and propagate.

Reverse Lookup Problems

Reverse lookup problems are often hard to diagnose because they manifest themselves as failures in systems other than DNS. Many security-sensitive services perform reverse lookups on the originating host for all incoming connections and deny the connection if the query fails.

Even if reverse resolution succeeds, many servers might reject connections from your host if your A and PTR records do not match. That is, the PTR record for a particular IP address refers to a name and the A record for that name refers to a different IP address. They perform a double lookup to verify that the PTR and A records match to eliminate spoofing attacks. Carefully maintain your reverse zones at all times.

Delegation problems are a frequent source of woe. Unfortunately, many ISPs appear unable to understand, configure, or delegate reverse zones. In such cases, you often have little choice but to try and tell your ISP what to do to fix the problem. If the ISP staff refuses to listen, find a new ISP (or live with broken DNS).

Another typical symptom of failing reverse lookups is an abnormally long delay on connection attempts. This happens when the server's query for a PTR record is not answered and times out (often because of network problems or the nameserver being down). This can be baffling to diagnose, but you should suspect DNS problems whenever you hear questions such as "Hey! Why is my web browser taking so long to connect?"

Maintaining Accurate Serial Numbers

Accurate serial numbers are very important to the correct operation of slave servers. An increase in the serial number of a zone causes slaves to reload the zone and update their local caches.

A common mistake that system administrators make is forgetting to increment the serial number after a change to the zone data. If you make this mistake, secondary nameservers don't reload the zone, and continue to serve old data. If you suspect that the data on the master and slave servers is out of sync, you can use dig to view the SOA record for the zone on each server (dig @master domain SOA and dig @slave domain SOA) and compare the serial numbers in the responses.

Another common problem is setting the serial number to an incorrect value—either too small or too large. A too-small serial number causes slaves to think that they possess a more up-to-date copy of the zone data, but this is easily corrected by increasing the serial number as necessary. A too-large serial number is more problematic and requires more elaborate measures to repair.

Serial number comparisons are defined in such a way that if a serial number—when subtracted from another with no overflow correction—results in a positive number, the second number is newer than the first, and a zone transfer is required. (See RFC 1982, "Serial Number Arithmetic," for details.) You can exploit this property by temporarily setting the serial number to 2^{32} (4,294,967,296), waiting for all the slaves to reload the zone, and then setting it to the correct number.

Troubleshooting Problems in Zone Files

The most common error in zone data is forgetting that names in a zone file are relative to the origin of the zone, not to the root. Writing www.example.com in the zone file for example.com and expecting it to be fully qualified causes names such as www.example.com.example.com to show up in the DNS. You should either write www, which is qualified to the correct www.example.com, or write www.example.com. (with the trailing period) to indicate that the name is fully qualified.

The SOA record should contain (as the first field) the domain name of the master server (not a CNAME) and a contact address (with the @ replaced by a .) to report problems to.

Mail sent to this address should be read frequently. The other fields should contain sensible values for your zone, and the serial number should be correctly incremented after each change.

As discussed earlier, A and PTR records should always match; that is, the A record pointed to by a PTR record should point back to the address of the PTR record. Remember to quote the two arguments of HINFO records if they contain any whitespace. Avoid the use of CNAME records for MX, NS, and SOA records.

In general, after making changes to zone data, it is a good idea to reload named and examine the logs for any errors that cause named to complain or reject the zone. Even better, you could use one of the verification tools, such as dnswalk, discussed briefly next.

Tools for Troubleshooting

BIND includes the always useful dig program, as well as named-checkconf (to check /etc/named.conf for syntax errors) and named-checkzone (to do the same for zone files). We also especially recommend dnswalk and nslint. dnswalk is a Perl script that scans the DNS setup of a given domain for problems. It should be used in conjunction with RFC 1912, which explains most of the problems it detects. nslint, like the analogous lint utility for C programs, searches for common BIND and zone file configuration errors.

By occasionally using these programs to troubleshoot DNS problems (especially after nontrivial zone changes), you go far toward keeping your DNS configuration healthy and trouble free.

Using Fedora's BIND Configuration Tool

Fedora provides a dozen or more different graphical configuration tools system administrators can use to configure network (and system) services. One of these tools is system-config-bind, a deceptively simple BIND configuration tool that requires an active X session and must be run with root privileges.

You can launch this client by using the command system-config-bind from a terminal window or by selecting the Domain Name Service menu item from the Server Settings menu. system-config-bind is automatically installed if you select the Fedora configuration tools.

> **NOTE**
>
> Using system-config-bind and then saving any changes overwrites existing settings! If you prefer to manually edit your named configuration files, do not use system-config-bind. Always make a backup of the configuration files in any event—you'll be glad you did.

After you type the root password and press the Enter key, the client launches. You then see its main window, as shown in Figure 23.2.

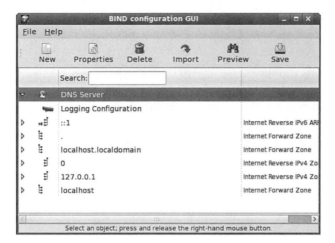

FIGURE 23.2   Fedora's `system-config-bind` utility can be used to create, modify, and save basic domain nameserver settings.

`system-config-bind` can be used to add a forward master zone, reverse master zone, MX records, or slave zone. Click the New button to select an entry for configuration, as shown in Figure 23.3.

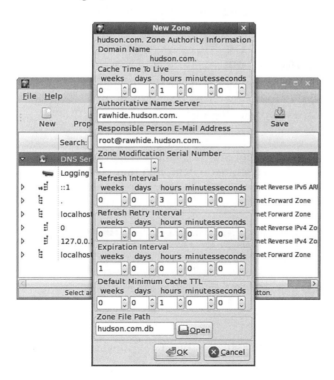

FIGURE 23.3   Use `system-config-bind` to add a new DNS record to your server or edit the existing settings.

You can edit or delete existing settings by first selecting and then clicking the Properties or Delete button in the `system-config-bind` dialog. When you finish entering or editing your custom settings, select the Save menu item from the File menu. Configuration files are saved in `/etc/named.conf` and under the `/var/named` directory.

Managing DNS Security

Security considerations are of vital importance to DNS administrators because DNS was not originally designed to be a secure protocol and a number of successful attacks against BIND have been found over the years. The most important defense is to keep abreast of developments in security circles and act on them promptly.

DNS is especially vulnerable to attacks known as poisoning and spoofing. *Poisoning* refers to placing incorrect data into the DNS database, which then spreads to clients and caches across the world, potentially causing hundreds of thousands of people to unwittingly use the bad data. Although DNS poisoning can occur because of carelessness, it has serious implications when performed deliberately. What if someone set up a clone of a common website, redirected users to it by DNS poisoning, and then asked them for their credit card numbers? *Spoofing*, the practice of forging network packets and making nameservers believe that they are receiving a valid answer to a query, is one of the ways malicious poisoning can be performed.

BIND has often been criticized as being very insecure, and although recent versions are greatly improved in this regard, DNS administrators today must take several precautions to ensure that its use is adequately protected from attacks. Of course, it is important to always run the latest recommended version of BIND.

> **TIP**
>
> One of your strongest defenses against DNS security risks is to keep abreast of developments in security circles and act on them promptly. The BugTraq mailing list, hosted at http://www.securityfocus.com/, and the SANS Institute, at http://www.sans.org/, are good places to start.

UNIX Security Considerations

The most important step in securing any UNIX system is to configure the environment BIND in which runs to use all the security mechanisms available to it through the operating system to its advantage. In short, this means that you should apply general security measures to your computer.

Run `named` with as few privileges as it needs to function. Do not run `named` as `root`. Even if an attacker manages to exploit a security hole in BIND, the effects of the break-in can be minimized if `named` is running as user `nobody` rather than as `root`. Of course, `named` has to be started as `root` because it needs to bind to port 53, but it can be instructed to switch to a given user and group with the `-u` and `-g` command-line options.

Starting named with a command such as named -u nobody -g nogroup is highly recommended. Remember, however, that if you run multiple services as nobody, you increase the risks of a compromise. In such a situation, it is best to create separate accounts for each service and use them for nothing else. Fedora runs named as the user named.

You can also use the chroot feature of UNIX to isolate named into its own part of the file system. If correctly configured, such a file system "jail" restricts attackers—if they manage to break in—to a part of the file system that contains little of value. It is important to remember that a *chroot jail* is not a panacea, and it does not eliminate the need for other defensive measures.

CAUTION

Programs that use chroot but do not take any other precautions have been shown to be unsecure. BIND does take such additional precautions. See the chroot-BIND HOWTO at http://www.ibiblio.org/pub/Linux/docs/HOWTO/other-formats/ html_single/Chroot-BIND-HOWTO.html.

For a chroot environment to work properly, you have to set up a directory that contains everything BIND needs to run. It is recommended that you start with a working configuration of BIND, create a directory—say /usr/local/bind—and copy over the files it needs into subdirectories under that one. For instance, you have to copy the binaries, some system libraries, the configuration files, and so on. Consult the BIND documentation for details about exactly which files you need.

When your chroot environment is set up, you can start named with the -t /usr/local/ bind option (combined with the -u and -g options) to instruct it to chroot to the directory you have set up.

You might also want to check your logs and keep track of resource usage. named manages a cache of DNS data that can potentially grow very large; it happily hogs CPU and bandwidth also, making your server unusable. This is something that can be exploited by clever attackers, but you can configure BIND to set resource limits. Several such options in the named.conf file are available, including datasize, which limits the maximum size of the data segment and, therefore, the cache. One downside of this approach is that named might be killed by the kernel if it exceeds these limits, meaning that you have to run it in a loop that restarts it if it dies or run it from /etc/inittab.

DNS Security Considerations

Several configuration options exist for named that can make it more resistant to various potential attacks. The most common ones are briefly described next. For more detailed discussions of the syntax and use of these options, refer to the BIND 9 documentation.

> **TIP**
>
> The Security Level Configuration Tool (`system-config-securitylevel`) has been updated to make implementation of the firewall simpler. The new on/off choice (rather than levels as used before) allows you to employ a firewall without requiring any special configuration for your DNS server.

Defining Access Control Lists

Specifying network and IP addresses multiple times in a configuration file is tedious and error prone. BIND allows you to define *access control lists (ACLs)*, which are named collections of network and IP addresses. You use these collections to ease the task of assigning permissions. Four predefined ACLs exist:

- ▶ **any**—Matches anything

- ▶ **none**—Matches nothing

- ▶ **localhost**—Matches all the network interfaces local to your nameserver

- ▶ **localnets**—Matches any network directly attached to a local interface

In addition, you can define your own lists in named.conf, containing as many network and IP addresses as you prefer, using the acl command as shown:

```
- - - - - - - - - -

acl trusted {
    192.0.2.0/29;         // Our own network is OK.
    localhost;            // And so is localhost.
    !192.0.2.33/29;       // But not this range.
};
- - - - - - - - - -
```

Here you see that you can use an exclamation point (!) to negate members in an ACL. After they are defined, you can use these ACLs in allow-query, allow-transfer, allow-recursion, and similar options, as discussed next.

Controlling Queries

As mentioned before, most nameservers perform recursive resolution for any queries they receive unless specifically configured not to do so. (We suppressed this behavior by using dig +norec.) By repeatedly fetching data from a number of unknown and untrusted nameservers, recursion makes your installation vulnerable to DNS poisoning. (In other words, you get deliberately or inadvertently incorrect lists.) You can avoid this problem by explicitly denying recursion.

You can disable recursive queries by adding a `recursion no` statement to the options section of `named.conf`. It might still be desirable to allow recursive queries from some trusted hosts, however, and this can be accomplished by the use of an `allow-recursion` statement. This excerpt would configure `named` to disallow recursion for all but the listed hosts:

```
- - - - - - - - - -

options {
    ...

    recursion no;
    allow-recursion {
        192.0.2.0/29;
        localnets;         // Trust our local networks.
        localhost;         // And ourselves.
    };
};
- - - - - - - - - -
```

You can choose to be still more restrictive and allow only selected hosts to query your nameserver by using the `allow-query` statement (with syntax similar to `allow-recursion`, as described previously). Of course, this solution does not work if your server is authoritative for a zone. In that case, you have to explicitly `allow-query { all; }` in the configuration section of each zone for which you want to serve authoritative data.

Controlling Zone Transfers

You also can use queries to enable only known slave servers to perform zone transfers from your server. Not only do zone transfers consume a lot of resources (they require a `named-xfer` process to be forked each time) and provide an avenue for denial-of-service attacks, but also there have been remote exploits via buffer overflows in `named-xfer` that allow attackers to gain root privileges on the compromised system. To prevent this, add a section such as the following to all your zone definitions:

```
- - - - - - - - - -

zone "example.com" {
    ...
    allow-transfer {
        192.0.2.96;        // Known slave.
        localhost;         // Often required for testing.
    };
};
- - - - - - - - - -
```

Alert named to Potential Problem Hosts

Despite all this, it might be necessary to single out a few troublesome hosts for special treatment. The `server` and `blackhole` statements in `named.conf` can be used to tell `named` about known sources of poisoned information or attack attempts. For instance, if the host `203.122.154.1` is repeatedly trying to attack the server, the following addition to the options section of `named.conf` causes the server to ignore traffic from that address. Of course, you can specify multiple addresses and networks in the black-hole list:

```
. . . . . . . . . .

options {    ...
blackhole {       203.122.154.1;    };};
. . . . . . . . . .
```

For a known source of bad data, you can do something such as the following to cause your nameserver to stop asking the listed server any questions. This is different from adding a host to the black-hole list. A server marked as bogus is never sent queries, but it can still ask questions. A black-holed host is simply ignored altogether:

```
. . . . . . . . . .

server bogus.info.example.com {    bogus yes;};
. . . . . . . . . .
```

The AUS-CERT advisory AL-1999.004, which discusses denial-of-service attacks against DNS servers, also discusses various ways of restricting access to nameservers and is a highly recommended read. A copy is located at ftp://ftp.auscert.org.au/pub/auscert/_advisory/AL-1999.004.dns_dos. Among other things, it recommends the most restrictive configuration possible and the permanent black-holing of some addresses known to be popular sources of spoofed requests and answers. It is a good idea to add the following ACL to the black-hole list of all your servers:

```
. . . . . . . . . .

/* These are known fake source addresses. */acl "bogon" {
    0.0.0.0/8;     # Null address
    1.0.0.0/8;     # IANA reserved, popular fakes
    2.0.0.0/8;     192.0.2.0/24;  # Test address
    224.0.0.0/3;   # Multicast addresses

    /* RFC 1918 addresses may be fake too. Don't list these if you
       use them internally. */
       10.0.0.0/8;
       172.16.0.0/12;
       192.168.0.0/16;
};
. . . . . . . . . .
```

Using DNS Security Extensions

DNS Security Extensions (DNSSEC), a set of security extensions to the DNS protocol, provides data integrity and authentication by using cryptographic digital signatures. It provides for the storage of public keys in the DNS and their use for verifying transactions. DNSSEC still isn't widely deployed, but BIND 9 does support it for interserver transactions (zone transfers, NOTIFY, recursive queries, dynamic updates). It is worth configuring the *transaction signature (TSIG)* if your slaves also run BIND 9. We briefly discuss using TSIG for authenticated zone transfers here.

To begin, we use `dnssec-keygen`, as we did with `rndc`, to generate a shared secret key. This key is stored on both the master and slave servers. As before, we extract the `Key:` data from the `.private` file. The following command creates a 512-bit host key named `transfer`:

```
$ dnssec-keygen -a hmac-md5 -b 512 -n host transfer
```

Next we set up matching `key` statements in `named.conf` for both the master and slave servers (similar to the contents of the `/etc/rndc.key` file created earlier). Remember not to transfer the secret key from one machine to the other over an unsecure channel. Use `ssh`, `sftp` (secure FTP), or something similar. Remember also that the shared secrets shouldn't be stored in world-readable files. The statements, identical on both machines, would look something similar to this:

```
key transfer {
    algorithm "hmac-md5";
    secret "...";          # Key from .private file
};
```

Finally, we set up a `server` statement on the master to instruct it to use the key we just created when communicating with the slave, and to enable authenticated zone transfers with the appropriate `allow-transfer` directives:

```
server 192.0.2.96 {
    key { transfer; };
};
```

The BIND 9 ARM contains more information on TSIG configuration and DNSSEC support in BIND.

Using Split DNS

BIND is often run on firewalls—both to act as a proxy for resolvers inside the network and to serve authoritative data for some zones. In such situations, many people prefer to avoid exposing more details of their private network configuration via DNS than is unavoidable (although there is some debate about whether this is actually useful). Those accessing your system from outside the firewall should see only information they are explicitly allowed access to, whereas internal hosts are allowed access to other data. This kind of setup is called *split DNS*.

Suppose that you have a set of zones you want to expose to the outside world and another set you want to allow hosts on your network to see. You can accomplish that with a configuration such as the following:

```
----------
acl private {    localhost;    192.168.0.0/24;
    # Define your internal network suitably.
};
view private_zones {    match { private; };    recursion yes;
      # Recursive resolution for internal hosts.
zone internal.zone {        # Zone statements;    };
  # More internal zones.
};
view public_zones {    match { any; }    recursion no;
      zone external.zone {        # Zone statements;    };
      # More external zones.
};
----------
```

Further, you might want to configure internal hosts running named to forward all queries to the firewall and never try to resolve queries themselves. The forward only and forwarders options in named.conf do this. (forwarders specifies a list of IP addresses of the nameservers to forward queries to.)

The BIND 9 ARM discusses several details of running BIND in a secure split-DNS configuration.

Related Fedora and Linux Commands

You can use the following commands to manage DNS in Fedora:

▶ **dig**—The domain information groper command, used to query remote DNS servers

▶ **host**—A domain nameserver query utility

▶ **named**—A domain nameserver included with Fedora

▶ **system-config-bind**—A GUI tool to configure DNS information

▶ **nsupdate**—A Dynamic DNS update utility

▶ **rndc**—The nameserver control utility included with BIND

Reference

▶ **http://www.dns.net/dnsrd/**—The DNS resources database.

▶ **http://www.isc.org/products/BIND/**—The ISC's BIND web page.

▶ **http://www.bind9.net/manuals**—The BIND 9 Administrator Reference Manual.

▶ **http://www.ibiblio.org/pub/Linux/docs/HOWTO/other-formats/html_single/ Chroot-BIND-HOWTO.html**—A guide to how `chroot` works with BIND 9.

▶ **http://langfeldt.net/DNS-HOWTO/**—The home page of the DNS HOWTO for BIND versions 4, 8, and 9.

▶ **http://www.ibiblio.org/pub/Linux/docs/HOWTO/other-formats/html_single/ DNS-HOWTO.html#s3**—Setting up a resolving, caching nameserver. Note that the file referenced as `/var/named/root.hints` is called `/var/named/named.ca` in Fedora.

▶ **http://spf.pobox.com/**—The home page of Sender Policy Framework, a method of preventing email address forgery.

▶ *The Concise Guide to DNS and BIND*, **by Nicolai Langfeldt (Que Publishing, 2000)**—An in-depth discussion of both theoretical and operational aspects of DNS administration.

CHAPTER 24

LDAP

The Lightweight Directory Access Protocol (LDAP, pronounced *ell-dap*) is one of those technologies that, although hidden, forms part of the core infrastructure in enterprise computing. Its job is simple: It stores information about users. However, its power comes from the fact that it can be linked into dozens of other services. LDAP can power login authentication, public key distribution, email routing, and address verification and, more recently, has formed the core of the push toward single sign-on technology.

> **TIP**
>
> Most people find the concept of LDAP easier to grasp when they think of it as a highly specialized form of database server. Behind the scenes, Fedora uses a database for storing all its LDAP information; however, LDAP does not offer anything as straightforward as SQL for data manipulation!
>
> OpenLDAP uses Sleepycat Software's Berkeley DB (BDB), and sticking with that default is highly recommended. That said, there are alternatives if you have specific needs.

This chapter looks at a relatively basic installation of an LDAP server, including how to host a companywide directory service that contains the names and email addresses of employees. LDAP is a client/server system, meaning that an LDAP server hosts the data and an LDAP client queries it. Fedora comes with OpenLDAP as its LDAP server, along with several LDAP-enabled email clients, including Evolution and Mozilla Thunderbird. This chapter covers all three of these applications.

Because LDAP data is usually available over the Internet—or at least your local network—it is imperative that you make every effort to secure your server. This chapter gives specific instruction on password configuration for OpenLDAP, and we recommend you follow our instructions closely.

Configuring the Server

If you have been using LDAP for years, you are aware of its immense power and flexibility. On the other hand, if you are just trying LDAP for the first time, it will seem like the most broken component you could imagine. LDAP has very specific configuration requirements, is vastly lacking in graphical tools, and has a large number of acronyms to remember. On the bright side, all the hard work you put in will be worth it because, when it works, LDAP will hugely improve your networking experience.

The first step in configuring your LDAP server is to install the client and server applications. Select Add/Remove Applications, click the Details button next to Network Servers, and check openldap-servers. Then click the Details button next to System Tools and select openldap-clients. After you have installed them, close the dialog box and bring up a terminal.

Now switch to the root user and edit /etc/openldap/slapd.conf in the text editor of your choice. This is the primary configuration file for slapd, the OpenLDAP server daemon. Scroll down until you see the lines database, suffix, and rootdn.

This is the most basic configuration for your LDAP system. What is the name of your server? The dc stands for *domain component*, which is the name of your domain as stored in DNS—for example, example.com. For our examples, we used hudzilla.org. LDAP considers each part of a domain name (separated by a period) to be a domain component, so the domain hudzilla.org is made up of a domain component hudzilla and a domain component org.

Change the suffix line to match your domain components, separated by commas. For example:

```
suffix    "dc=hudzilla,dc=org"
```

The next line defines the root DN, which is another LDAP acronym meaning *distinguished name*. A DN is a complete descriptor of a person in your directory: her name and the domain in which she resides. For example:

```
rootdn    "cn=root,dc=hudzilla,dc=org"
```

CN is yet another LDAP acronym, this time meaning *common name*. A common name is just that—the name a person is usually called. Some people have several common names. Andrew Hudson is a common name, but that same user might also have the common name Andy Hudson. In our rootdn line, we define a complete user: common name root at domain hudzilla.org. These lines are essentially read backward. LDAP goes to org first, searches org for hudzilla, and then searches hudzilla for root.

The `rootdn` is important because it is more than just another person in your directory. The root LDAP user is like the root user in Linux. It is the person who has complete control over the system and can make whatever changes he wants to.

Now comes a slightly more complex part: The LDAP root user needs to be given a password. The easiest way to do this is to open a new terminal window alongside your existing one. Switch to root in the new terminal also, and type **slappasswd**. This tool generates password hashes for OpenLDAP, using the SHA1 hash algorithm. Enter a password when it prompts you. When you have entered and confirmed your password, you should see output like this:

{SSHA}qMVxFT2K1UUmrA89Gd7z6EK3gRLDIo2W

That is the password hash generated from your password. Yours will be different from the one shown here, but what is important is that it has {SSHA} at the beginning to denote it uses SHA1. You now need to switch back to the other terminal (the one editing `slapd.conf`) and add this line below the `rootdn` line:

`rootpw <your password hash>`

You should replace *<your password hash>* with the full output from `slappasswd`, like this:

`rootpw {SSHA}qMVxFT2K1UUmrA89Gd7z6EK3gRLDIo2W`

That sets the LDAP root password to the one you just generated with `slappasswd`. That is the last change you need to make in the `slapd.conf` file, so save your changes and close your editor.

Back in the terminal, run the `slaptest` command. This checks your `slapd.conf` file for errors and ensures you edited it correctly. Presuming there are no errors, run these two commands:

```
chkconfig ldap on
service ldap start
```

These tell Fedora to start OpenLDAP each time you boot up, and to start it right now.

The final configuration step is to tell Fedora which DN it should use if none is specified. You do so by going to System Settings and selecting Authentication. In the dialog box that appears, check Enable LDAP Support in both the User Information tab and Authentication tab. Next, click the Configure LDAP button, enter your DCs (for example, **dc=hudzilla,dc=org**) for the LDAP Search Base DN, and enter **127.0.0.1** for the LDAP Server. Click OK and then click OK again.

TIP

Checking Enable LDAP Support does not actually change the way in which your users log in. Behind the scenes, this forces Fedora to set up the `ldap.conf` file in `/etc/openldap` so that LDAP searches that do not specify a base search start point are directed to your DC.

Populating Your Directory

With LDAP installed, configured, and running, you can now fill the directory with people. This involves yet more LDAP acronyms and is by no means an easy task, so do not worry if you have to reread this several times before it sinks in.

First, create the file `base.ldif`. You use this file to define the base components of your system: the domain and the address book. LDIF is an acronym standing for LDAP Data Interchange Format, and it is the standard way of recording user data for insertion into an LDAP directory. Here are the contents we used for our example:

```
dn: dc=hudzilla,dc=org
objectClass: top
objectClass: dcObject
objectClass: organization
dc: hudzilla
o: Hudzilla Dot Org

dn: ou=People,dc=hudzilla,dc=org
ou: People
objectClass: top
objectClass: organizationalUnit
```

This file contains two individual entities, separated by an empty line. The first is the organization, `hudzilla.org`. The dn lines you know already; they define each object uniquely in the scope of the directory. The `objectClass` directive specifies which attributes should be allowed for this entity and which attributes should be required. In this case, we use it to set the DC to hudzilla and to set o (the name of the organization) to Hudzilla Dot Org.

The next entity defines the address book, `People`, in which all our people will be stored. It is defined as an organizational unit, which is what the ou stands for. An *organizational unit* really is just an arbitrary partition of your company. You might have OUs for marketing, accounting, and management, for example.

You need to customize the file to your own requirements. Specifically, change the DCs to those you specified in your `slapd.conf`.

Next, create and edit a new file called `people.ldif`. This is where you will define entries for your address book, also using LDIF. Here are the people we used in our example:

```
dn: cn=Paul Hudson,ou=People,dc=hudzilla,dc=org
objectClass: inetOrgPerson
cn: Paul Hudson
cn: Hudzilla
mail: paul@hudzilla.org
jpegPhoto:< file:///home/paul/paulhudson.jpg
sn: Hudson

dn: cn=Andrew Hudson,ou=People,dc=hudzilla,dc=org
objectClass: inetOrgPerson
cn: Andrew Hudson
cn: IzAndy
mail: andrew@hudzilla.org
sn: Hudson

dn: cn=Nick Veitch,ou=People,dc=hudzilla,dc=org
objectClass: inetOrgPerson
cn: Nick Veitch
cn: CrackAttackKing
mail: nick@hudzilla.org
sn: Veitch
```

There are three entries there, again separated by empty lines. Each person has a DN that is made up of his common name (CN), organizational unit (OU), and domain components (DCs). He also has an `objectClass` definition, `inetOrgPerson`, which gives him standard attributes such as an email address, a photograph, and a telephone number. Entities of type `inetOrgPerson` must have a CN and an SN (surname), so you will see them in this code.

Note also that each person has two common names: his actual name and a nickname. Not all LDAP clients support more than one CN, but there is no harm in having several as long as the main one comes first and is listed in the DN.

> **TIP**
>
> Having multiple key/value pairs, like multiple CNs, is one of the defining features of LDAP. In today's interconnected world, few people can be defined in a single set of attributes because they have home phone numbers, work phone numbers, cell phone numbers, plus several email addresses, and potentially even a selection of offices where they hot desk. Using multiple CNs and other attributes allows you to properly record these complex scenarios.

The `jpegPhoto` attribute for the first entity has very particular syntax. Immediately after the colon you use an opening angle bracket (<), followed by a space and then the location of the person's picture. Because the picture is local, it is prefixed with `file://`. It is in `/home/paul/paulhudson.jpg`, so the whole URL is `file:///home/paul/paulhudson.jpg`.

After you have edited the file to include the people in your organization, save it and close the editor. As root, issue these two commands:

```
ldapadd -x -W -D "cn=root,dc=hudzilla,dc=org" -f base.ldif
ldapadd -x -W -D "cn=root,dc=hudzilla,dc=org" -f people.ldif
```

The ldapadd command is used to convert LDIF into live directory content and, most importantly, can be executed while your LDAP server is running. The -x parameter means to use only basic authentication, which means you need to supply the root username and password. -W means to prompt you for the password. -D lets you specify a DN for your username, and immediately after the -D, we specify the root DN as set earlier in slapd.conf. Finally, -f means to use the LDIF from the following file.

When you run them, you are prompted for the root password you set earlier. On entering it, you should see confirmation messages as your entries are added, like this:

```
adding new entry "cn=Paul Hudson,ou=People,dc=hudzilla,dc=org"
```

If you see an error such as ldap_bind: Can't contact LDAP server (-1), you need to start the LDAP server by typing **service ldap start**. The most likely sources of other errors are typing errors. LDIF is a precise format, even down to its use of whitespace.

To test that the directory has been populated and that your configuration settings are correct, run this command:

ldapsearch -x 'objectclass=*'

The ldapsearch command does what you might expect: It queries the LDAP directory from the command line. Again, -x means to use simple authentication, although in this situation you do not need to provide any credentials because you are only reading from the directory. The objectclass=* search specifies that you're searching for any entry of any objectclass, so the search will return all the entries in your directory.

You can amend the search to be more specific, for example:

```
ldapsearch -x 'cn=Ni*'
```

This returns all people with a common name that begins with *Ni*. If you get results for your searches, you are ready to configure your clients.

TIP

OpenLDAP needs specific permissions for its files. The /var/lib/ldap directory should be owned by user ldap and group ldap, with permissions 600. If you experience problems, try running chmod 600 /var/lib/ldap.

Configuring Clients

Although Fedora comes with a selection of email clients, there is not enough room here to cover them all. So we will discuss the two most frequently used clients: Evolution, the default, and Thunderbird. Both are powerful messaging solutions and so both work well with LDAP. Of the two, Thunderbird seems to be the easier to configure. We have had various problems with Evolution in situations where Thunderbird has worked the first time.

Evolution

To configure Evolution for LDAP, click the arrow next to the New button and select Address Book. A new screen appears, the first option of which prompts you for the type of address book to create. Select On LDAP Servers.

For Name, just enter **Address book**, and for Server, enter the IP address of your LDAP server (or **127.0.0.1** if you are working on the server), as shown in Figure 24.1. Leave the port as 389, which is the default for slapd. Switch to the Details tab, and set Search Base to be the DN for your address book—for example, ou=People,dc=hudzilla,dc=org. Set Search Scope to be Sub so that Evolution will perform a comprehensive search. To finish, click Add Address Book.

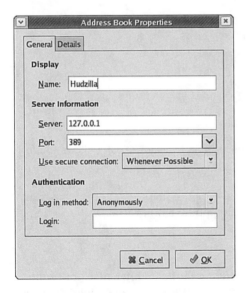

FIGURE 24.1   Configuring Evolution to use LDAP for addresses is easy for anonymous connections.

Although Evolution is now configured to use your directory, it will not use it for email address autocompletion just yet. To enable that, go to the Tools menu and click Settings. From the options that appear on the left, click Autocompletion and select your LDAP server from the list. Click Close and then create a new email message. If everything has worked, typing part of someone's name should pop up a box with LDAP matches.

Thunderbird

Thunderbird is a little easier to configure than Evolution and tends to work better, particularly with entries that have multiple CNs. To enable autocompletion, go to the Tools menu, click Options, and then select Composition from the tab on the left.

Check the Directory Server box and click the Edit Directories button to its right. From the dialog box that appears, click Add to add a new directory. You can give it any name you want because this is merely for display purposes. As shown in Figure 24.2, set the Hostname field to be the IP address of your LDAP server (or **127.0.0.1** if you are working on the server). Set the Base DN to be the DN for your address book (for instance, **ou=People,dc=hudzilla,dc=org**), and leave the port number as 389. Click OK three times to get back to the main interface.

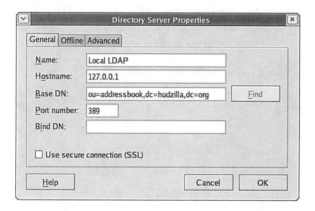

FIGURE 24.2   Thunderbird's options are buried deeper than Evolution's, but it allows you to download the LDAP directory for offline use.

Now, click Write to create a new email message, and type the first few letters of a user in the To box. If everything works, Thunderbird should pop up a box with LDAP matches.

Administration

After your LDAP server and clients are set up, they require little maintenance until something changes externally. Specifically, if someone in your directory changes jobs, changes her phone number, gets married (changing her surname), quits, or so forth, you need to be able to update your directory to reflect the change.

OpenLDAP comes with a selection of tools for manipulating directories, of which you have already met ldapadd. To add to that, you can use ldapdelete for deleting entries in your directory and ldapmodify for modifying entries. Both are hard to use but come with moderate amounts of documentation in their man pages.

A much smarter option is to use `phpLDAPadmin`, which is a GPL LDAP administration tool that allows you to add and modify entries entirely through your web browser. You can learn more and download the product to try at http://www.phpldapadmin.com/.

Reference

▶ **http://www.openldap.org/**—The home page of the OpenLDAP project, where you can download the latest version of the software and meet other users.

▶ **http://www.kingsmountain.com/ldapRoadmap.shtml**—A great set of links and resources across the Internet that explain various aspects of LDAP and its parent protocol, X500.

▶ **http://ldap.perl.org/**—The home of the Perl library for interacting with LDAP provides comprehensive documentation to get you started.

▶ **http://www.ldapguru.com/**—A gigantic portal for LDAP administrators around the world. From forums dedicated to LDAP to jobs specifically for LDAP admins, this site could very well be all you need.

▶ The definitive book on LDAP is *LDAP System Administration* (O'Reilly), ISBN: 1-56592-491-6. It is an absolute must for the bookshelf of any Linux LDAP administrator.

▶ For more general reading, try *LDAP Directories Explained* (Addison-Wesley), ISBN: 0-201-78792-X. It has a much stronger focus on Microsoft's Active Directory LDAP implementation, though.

24

PART V

Programming Linux

Using Perl

Perl (Practical Extraction and Report Language or Pathologically Eclectic Rubbish Lister, depending on who you speak to!) is a powerful scripting tool you can use to manage files, create reports, edit text, and perform many other tasks when using Linux. Perl is included with Fedora and could be considered an integral part of the distribution because Fedora depends on Perl for many types of software services, logging activities, and software tools. If you do a full install from this book's DVD, you will find nearly 150 software tools written in Perl installed under the /usr/bin and /usr/sbin directories.

Perl is not the easiest of programming languages to learn because it is designed for flexibility. This chapter shows how to create and use Perl scripts on your system. You will see what a Perl program looks like, how the language is structured, as well as where you can find modules of prewritten code to help you write your own Perl scripts.

Using Perl with Linux

Although originally designed as a data extraction and report generation language, Perl appeals to many Linux system administrators because it can be used to create utilities that fill a gap between the capabilities of shell scripts and compiled C programs. Another advantage of Perl over other Unix tools is that it can process and extract data from binary files, whereas sed and awk cannot.

> **NOTE**
>
> In Perl, "there is more than one way to do it." This is the unofficial motto of Perl, and it comes up so often that it is usually abbreviated as TIMTOWTDI.

You can use Perl at your shell's command line to execute one-line Perl programs, but most often the programs (usually ending in .pl) are run as commands. These programs generally work on any computer platform because Perl has been ported to just about every operating system. Perl is available by default when you install Fedora, and you will find its RPM files on the DVD included with this book.

Perl programs are used to support a number of Fedora services, such as system logging. For example, the logwatch.pl program is run every morning at 4:20 a.m. by the crond (scheduling) daemon on your system. Other Fedora services supported by Perl include:

- ▶ Amanda for local and network backups

- ▶ Fax spooling with the faxrunqd program

- ▶ Printing supported by Perl document filtering programs

- ▶ Hardware sensor monitoring setup that uses the sensors-detect Perl program

Perl Versions

As of this writing, the current production version of Perl is 5.8.8 (which is Perl version 5 point 8, patch level 8). You can download the code from http://www.perl.com/ and build it yourself from source. You will occasionally find updated versions in RPM format for Fedora, which you can install by updating your system.

You can determine what version of Perl you installed by typing **perl -v** at a shell prompt. If you are installing the latest Fedora distribution, you should have the latest version of Perl.

A Simple Perl Program

This section introduces a very simple sample Perl program to get you started using Perl. Although trivial for experienced Perl hackers, a short example is necessary for new users who want to learn more about Perl.

To introduce you to the absolute basics of Perl programming, Listing 25.1 illustrates a simple Perl program that prints a short message.

LISTING 25.1   A Simple Perl Program

```
#!/usr/bin/perl
print "Look at all the camels!\n";
```

Type that in and save it to a file called trivial.pl. Then make the file executable using the chmod command (see the following sidebar) and run it at the command prompt.

Command-Line Error

If you get the message bash: `trivial.pl`: `command not found` or bash: `./trivial.pl`: `Permission denied`, it means that you either typed the command line incorrectly or forgot to make `trivial.pl` executable (with the `chmod` command):

```
$ chmod +x trivial.pl
```

You can force the command to execute in the current directory as follows:

```
$ ./trivial.pl
```

Or you can use Perl to run the program like this:

```
$ perl trivial.pl
```

The sample program in the listing is a two-line Perl program. Typing in the program and running it (using Perl or making the program executable) shows how to create your first Perl program, a process duplicated by Linux users around the world every day!

NOTE

`#!` is often pronounced *she-bang*, which is short for *sharp* (the musicians name for the # character), and *bang*, which is another name for the exclamation point. This notation is also used in shell scripts. Refer to Chapter 33, "Writing and Executing a Shell Script," for more information about writing shell scripts.

The `#!` line is technically not part of the Perl code at all. The # character indicates that the rest of the screen line is a comment. The comment is a message to the shell, telling it where it should go to find the executable to run this program. The interpreter ignores the comment line.

Exceptions to this practice include when the # character is in a quoted string and when it is being used as the delimiter in a regular expression. Comments are useful to document your scripts, like this:

```
#!/usr/bin/perl
# a simple example to print a greeting
print "hello there\n";
```

A block of code, such as what might appear inside a loop or a branch of a conditional statement, is indicated with curly braces ({}). For example, here is an infinite loop:

```
#!/usr/bin/perl
# a block of code to print a greeting forever
while (1) {
        print "hello there\n";
};
```

25

Perl statements are terminated with a semicolon. A Perl statement can extend over several actual screen lines because Perl is not concerned about whitespace.

The second line of the simple program prints the text enclosed in quotation marks. \n is the escape sequence for a newline character.

TIP

Using the `perldoc` and `man` commands is an easy way to get more information about the version of Perl installed on your system. To learn how to use the `perldoc` command, enter the following:

```
$ perldoc perldoc
```

To get introductory information on Perl, you can use either of these commands:

```
$ perldoc perl
$ man perl
```

For an overview or table of contents of Perl's documentation, use the `perldoc` command like this:

```
$ perldoc perltoc
```

The documentation is extensive and well organized. Perl includes a number of standard Linux manual pages as brief guides to its capabilities, but perhaps the best way to learn more about Perl is to read its *perlfunc* document, which lists all the available Perl functions and their usage. You can view this document by using the `perldoc` script and typing **perldoc perlfunc** at the command line. You can also find this document online at http://www.cpan.org/doc/manual/html/pod/perlfunc.html.

Perl Variables and Data Structures

Perl is a *weakly typed* language, meaning that it does not require that you declare a data type, such as a type of value (data) to be stored in a particular variable. C, for example, makes you declare that a particular variable is an integer, a character, a structure, or whatever the case may be. Perl variables are whatever type they need to be, and can change type when you need them to.

Perl Variable Types

There are three variable types in Perl: *scalars*, *arrays*, and *hashes*. A different character is used to signify each variable type.

Scalar variables are indicated with the $ character, as in $penguin. Scalars can be numbers or strings, and they can change type from one to the other as needed. If you treat a number like a string, it becomes a string. If you treat a string like a number, it is translated into a number if it makes sense to do so; otherwise, it usually evaluates to 0. For example, the string "76trombones" evaluates as the number 76 if used in a numerical calculation, but the string "polar bear" will evaluate to 0.

Perl arrays are indicated with the @ character, as in @fish. An *array* is a list of values that are referenced by index number, starting with the first element numbered 0, just as in C and awk. Each element in the array is a scalar value. Because scalar values are indicated with the $ character, a single element in an array is also indicated with a $ character.

For example, $fish[2] refers to the third element in the @fish array. This tends to throw some people off, but is similar to arrays in C in which the first array element is 0.

Hashes are indicated with the % character, as in %employee. A *hash* is a list of name and value pairs. Individual elements in the hash are referenced by name rather than by index (unlike an array). Again, because the values are scalars, the $ character is used for individual elements.

For example, $employee{name} gives you one value from the hash. Two rather useful functions for dealing with hashes are *keys* and *values*. The keys function returns an array containing all the keys of the hash, and values returns an array of the values of the hash. Using this approach, the Perl program in Listing 25.2 displays all the values in your environment, much like typing the bash shell's env command.

LISTING 25.2   Displaying the Contents of the env Hash

```
#!/usr/bin/perl
foreach $key (keys %ENV)  {
  print "$key = $ENV{$key}\n";
}
```

Special Variables

Perl has a wide variety of special variables, which usually look like punctuation— $_, $!, and $]—and are all extremely useful for shorthand code. $_ is the default variable, $! is the error message returned by the operating system, and $] is the Perl version number.

$_ is perhaps the most useful of these, and you will see that variable used often in this chapter. $_ is the Perl default variable, which is used when no argument is specified. For example, the following two statements are equivalent:

```
chomp;
chomp($_);
```

The following loops are equivalent:

```
for $cow (@cattle) {
        print "$cow says moo.\n";
}
for (@cattle)        {
        print "$_ says moo.\n";
}
```

For a complete listing of the special variables, you should see the `perlvar` document that comes with your Perl distribution (such as in the `perlvar` manual page), or you can go online to http://theoryx5.uwinnipeg.ca/CPAN/perl/pod/perlvar.html.

Operators

Perl supports a number of operators to perform various operations. There are *comparison* operators (used to compare values, as the name implies), *compound* operators (used to combine operations or multiple comparisons), *arithmetic* operators (to perform math), and special string constants.

Comparison Operators

The comparison operators used by Perl are similar to those used by C, awk, and the csh shells, and are used to specify and compare values (including strings). Most frequently, a comparison operator is used within an `if` statement or loop. Perl has comparison operators for numbers and strings. Table 25.1 shows the numeric comparison operators and their behavior.

TABLE 25.1   Numeric Comparison Operators in Perl

Operator	Meaning
==	Is equal to
<	Less than
>	Greater than
<=	Less than or equal to
>=	Greater than or equal to
!=	Not equal to
..	Range of >= first operand to <= second operand
<=>	Returns -1 if less than, 0 if equal, and 1 if greater than

Table 25.2 shows the string comparison operators and their behaviors.

TABLE 25.2   String Comparison Operators in Perl

Operator	Meaning
eq	Is equal to
lt	Less than
gt	Greater than
le	Less than or equal to
ge	Greater than or equal to
ne	Not equal to
cmp	Returns -1 if less than, 0 if equal, and 1 if greater than
=~	Matched by regular expression
!~	Not matched by regular expression

Compound Operators

Perl uses compound operators, similar to those used by C or awk, which can be used to combine other operations (such as comparisons or arithmetic) into more complex forms of logic. Table 25.3 shows the compound pattern operators and their behavior.

TABLE 25.3   Compound Pattern Operators in Perl

Operator	Meaning
&&	Logical AND
¦¦	Logical OR
!	Logical NOT
()	Parentheses; used to group compound statements

Arithmetic Operators

Perl supports a wide variety of math operations. Table 25.4 summarizes these operators.

TABLE 25.4   Perl Arithmetic Operators

Operator	Purpose
x**y	Raises x to the y power (same as x^y)
x%y	Calculates the remainder of x/y
x+y	Adds x to y
x-y	Subtracts y from x
x*y	Multiplies x times y
x/y	Divides x by y
-y	Negates y (switches the sign of y); also known as the *unary minus*
++y	Increments y by 1 and uses value (prefix increment)
y++	Uses value of y and then increments by 1 (postfix increment)
--y	Decrements y by 1 and uses value (prefix decrement)
y--	Uses value of y and then decrements by 1 (postfix decrement)
x=y	Assigns value of y to x. Perl also supports operator-assignment operators (+=, -=, *=, /=, %=, **=, and others)

You can also use comparison operators (such as == or <) and compound pattern operators (&&, ¦¦, and !) in arithmetic statements. They evaluate to the value 0 for false and 1 for true.

Other Operators

Perl supports a number of operators that don't fit any of the prior categories. Table 25.5 summarizes these operators.

25

TABLE 25.5   Other Perl Operators

Operator	Purpose
~x	Bitwise not (changes 0 bits to 1 and 1 bits to 0)
x & y	Bitwise and
x ¦ y	Bitwise or
x ^ y	Bitwise exclusive or (XOR)
x << y	Bitwise shift left (shifts x by y bits)
x >> y	Bitwise shift right (shifts x by y bits)
x . y	Concatenate y onto x
a x b	Repeats string a for b number of times
x , y	Comma operator—evaluates x and then y
x ? y : z	Conditional expression—if x is true, y is evaluated; otherwise, z is evaluated.

Except for the comma operator and conditional expression, these operators can also be used with the assignment operator, similar to the way addition (+) can be combined with assignment (=), giving +=.

Special String Constants

Perl supports string constants that have special meaning or cannot be entered from the keyboard. Table 25.6 shows most of the constants supported by Perl.

TABLE 25.6   Perl Special String Constants

Expression	Meaning
\\	The means of including a backslash
\a	The alert or bell character
\b	Backspace
\c	Control character (like holding the Ctrl key down and pressing the C character)
\e	Escape
\f	Formfeed
\n	Newline
\r	Carriage return
\t	Tab
\xNN	Indicates that NN is a hexadecimal number
\0NNN	Indicates that NNN is an octal (base 8) number

Conditional Statements

Perl offers two conditional statements, if and unless, which function opposite one another. if enables you to execute a block of code only if certain conditions are met so that you can control the flow of logic through your program. Conversely, unless performs the statements when certain conditions are not met. The following sections explain and demonstrate how to use these conditional statements when writing scripts for Linux.

if/else

The syntax of the Perl if/else structure is as follows:

```
if (condition) {
  statement or block of code
} elsif (condition) {
  statement or block of code
} else {
  statement or block of code
}
```

condition can be a statement that returns a true or false value.

Truth is defined in Perl in a way that might be unfamiliar to you, so be careful. Everything in Perl is true except 0 (the digit zero), "0" (the string containing the number 0), "" (the empty string), and an undefined value. Note that even the string "00" is a true value because it is not one of the four false cases.

The statement or block of code is executed if the test condition returns a true value. For example, Listing 25.3 uses the if/else structure and shows conditional statements using the eq string comparison operator.

LISTING 25.3   if/elsif/else

```
if  ($favorite eq "chocolate") {
    print "I like chocolate too.\n";
} elsif ($favorite eq "spinach") {
    print "Oh, I don't like spinach.\n";
} else {
    print "Your favorite food is $favorite.\n";
}
```

unless

unless works just like if, only backward. unless performs a statement or block if a condition is false:

```
unless ($name eq "Rich")        {
  print "Go away, you're not allowed in here!\n";
}
```

> **NOTE**
>
> You can restate the preceding example in more natural language like this:
>
> ```
> print "Go away!\n" unless $name eq "Rich";
> ```

Looping

A *loop* is a way to repeat a program action multiple times. A very simple example is a countdown timer that performs a task (waiting for one second) 300 times before telling you that your egg is done boiling.

Looping constructs (also known as *control structures*) can be used to iterate a block of code as long as certain conditions apply, or while the code steps through (evaluates) a list of values, perhaps using that list as arguments. Perl has four looping constructs: for, foreach, while, and until.

for

The for construct performs a *statement* (block of code) for a set of conditions defined as follows:

```
for (start condition; end condition; increment function) {
  statement(s)
}
```

The start condition is set at the beginning of the loop. Each time the loop is executed, the increment function is performed until the end condition is achieved. This looks much like the traditional for/next loop. The following code is an example of a for loop:

```
for ($i=1; $i<=10; $i++) {
      print "$i\n"
}
```

foreach

The foreach construct performs a statement block for each element in a list or array:

```
@names = ("alpha","bravo","charlie");
foreach $name (@names) {
  print "$name sounding off!\n";
}
```

The loop variable ($name in the example) is not merely set to the value of the array elements; it is aliased to that element. That means if you modify the loop variable, you're actually modifying the array. If no loop array is specified, the Perl default variable $_ may be used:

```
@names = ("alpha","bravo","charlie");
foreach (@names) {
  print "$_ sounding off!\n";
}
```

This syntax can be very convenient, but it can also lead to unreadable code. Give a thought to the poor person who'll be maintaining your code. (It will probably be you.)

> **NOTE**
>
> foreach is frequently abbreviated as for.

while

while performs a block of statements as long as a particular condition is true:

```
while ($x<10) {
    print "$x\n";
    $x++;
}
```

Remember that the condition can be anything that returns a true or false value. For example, it could be a function call:

```
while ( InvalidPassword($user, $password) )           {
        print "You've entered an invalid password. Please try again.\n";
        $password = GetPassword;
}
```

until

until is the exact opposite of the while statement. It performs a block of statements as long as a particular condition is false—or, rather, until it becomes true:

```
until (ValidPassword($user, $password))  {
  print "You've entered an invalid password. Please try again.\n";
  $password = GetPassword;
}
```

last and next

You can force Perl to end a loop early by using a last statement. last is similar to the C break command—the loop is exited. If you decide you need to skip the remaining contents of a loop without ending the loop itself, you can use next, which is similar to the C continue command. Unfortunately, these statements don't work with do ... while.

On the other hand, you can use redo to jump to a loop (marked by a label) or inside the loop where called:

```perl
$a = 100;
while (1) {
  print "start\n";
  TEST: {
    if (($a = $a / 2) > 2) {
      print "$a\n";
      if (--$a < 2) {
        exit;
      }
      redo TEST;
    }
  }
}
```

In this simple example, the variable $a is repeatedly manipulated and tested in an endless loop. The word "start" is printed only once.

do ... while and do ... until

The while and until loops evaluate the conditional first. You change the behavior by applying a do block before the conditional. With the do block, the condition is evaluated last, which results in the contents of the block always executing at least once (even if the condition is false). This is similar to the C language do ... while (*conditional*) statement.

Regular Expressions

Perl's greatest strength is in text and file manipulation, which it accomplishes by using the regular expression (*regex*) library. Regexes, which are quite different from the wildcard handling and filename expansion capabilities of the shell, allow complicated pattern matching and replacement to be done efficiently and easily. For example, the following line of code replaces every occurrence of the string bob or the string mary with fred in a line of text:

```perl
$string =~ s/bob|mary/fred/gi;
```

Without going into too many of the details, Table 25.7 explains what the preceding line says.

TABLE 25.7   Explanation of `$string =~ s/bob¦mary/fred/gi;`

Element	Explanation
`$string =~`	Performs this pattern match on the text found in the variable called `$string`.
`s`	Substitutes one text string for another.
`/`	Begins the text to be matched.
`bob¦mary`	Matches the text bob or `mary`. You should remember that it is looking for the text `mary`, not the word `mary`; that is, it will also match the text `mary` in the word `maryland`.
`/`	Ends text to be matched; begins text to replace it.
`fred`	Replaces anything that was matched with the text `fred`.
`/`	Ends replace text.
`g`	Does this substitution globally; that is, replaces the match text wherever in the string you match it (and any number of times).
`i`	Make the search text case insensitive. It matches bob, Bob, or bOB.
`;`	Indicates the end of the line of code.

If you are interested in the details, you can get more information from the regex (7) section of the manual.

Although replacing one string with another might seem a rather trivial task, the code required to do the same thing in another language (for example, C) is rather daunting unless supported by additional subroutines from external libraries.

Access to the Shell

Perl can perform any process you might ordinarily perform if you type commands to the shell through the `` ` `` syntax. For example, the code in Listing 25.4 prints a directory listing.

LISTING 25.4   Using Backticks to Access the Shell

```
$curr_dir = `pwd`;
@listing = `ls -al`;
print "Listing for $curr_dir\n";
foreach $file (@listing) {
    print "$file";
}
```

> **NOTE**
>
> The `` ` `` notation uses the backtick found above the Tab key (on most keyboards), not the single quotation mark.

You can also use the Shell module to access the shell. Shell is one of the standard modules that comes with Perl; it allows creation and use of a shell-like command line. Look at the following code for an example:

```
use Shell qw(cp);
cp ("/home/httpd/logs/access.log", "/tmp/httpd.log");
```

This code almost looks as if it is importing the command-line functions directly into Perl. Although that is not really happening, you can pretend that the code is similar to a command line and use this approach in your Perl programs.

A third method of accessing the shell is via the system function call:

```
$rc = 0xffff & system('cp /home/httpd/logs/access.log /tmp/httpd.log');
if ($rc == 0) {
  print "system cp succeeded \n";
} else {
  print "system cp failed $rc\n";
}
```

The call can also be used with the or die clause:

```
system('cp /home/httpd/logs/access.log /tmp/httpd.log') == 0
  or die "system cp failed: $?"
```

However, you can't capture the output of a command executed through the system function.

Modules and CPAN

A great strength of the Perl community (and the Linux community) is that it is an open source community. This community support is expressed for Perl via CPAN, which is a network of mirrors of a repository of Perl code.

Most of CPAN is made up of *modules*, which are reuseable chunks of code that do useful things, similar to software libraries containing functions for C programmers. These modules help speed development when building Perl programs and free Perl hackers from repeatedly reinventing the wheel when building a bicycle.

Perl comes with a set of standard modules installed. Those modules should contain much of the functionality that you will initially need with Perl. If you need to use a module not installed with Fedora, use the CPAN module (which is one of the standard modules) to download and install other modules onto your system. At http://www.perl.com/CPAN, you will find the CPAN Multiplex Dispatcher, which attempts to direct you to the CPAN site closest to you.

Typing the following command puts you into an interactive shell that gives you access to CPAN. You can type **help** at the prompt to get more information on how to use the CPAN program.

```
$ perl -MCPAN -e shell
```

After you have installed a module from CPAN (or written one of your own), you can load that module into memory, where you can use it with the use function:

```
use Time::CTime;
```

use looks in the directories listed in the variable @INC for the module. In this example, use looks for a directory called Time, which contains a file called CTime.pm, which in turn is assumed to contain a package called Time::CTime. The distribution of each module should contain documentation on using that module.

For a list of all the standard Perl modules (those that come with Perl when you install it), see perlmodlib in the Perl documentation. You can read this document by typing **perldoc perlmodlib** at the command prompt.

Related Fedora and Linux Commands

You will use these commands and tools when using Perl with Linux:

- ▶ **a2p**—A filter used to translate awk scripts into Perl
- ▶ **find2perl**—A utility used to create Perl code from command lines, using the find command
- ▶ **pcregrep**—A utility used to search data, using Perl-compatible regular expressions
- ▶ **perlcc**—A compiler for Perl programs
- ▶ **perldoc**—A Perl utility used to read Perl documentation
- ▶ **s2p**—A filter used to translate sed scripts into Perl
- ▶ **vi**—The vi (actually vim) text editor

Reference

- ▶ http://www.perl.com/—Tom Christiansen maintains the Perl language home page. This is the place to find all sorts of information about Perl, from its history and culture to helpful tips. This is also the place to download the Perl interpreter for your system.

- ▶ http://www.perl.com/CPAN—This is part of the site just mentioned, but it merits its own mention. CPAN (Comprehensive Perl Archive Network) is the place for you to find modules and programs in Perl. If you write something in Perl that you think is particularly useful, you can make it available to the Perl community here.

- **http://www.perl.com/pub/q/FAQs**—Frequently Asked Questions index of common Perl queries; this site offers a handy way to quickly search for answers about Perl.

- **http://learn.perl.org/**—One of the best places to start learning Perl online. If you master Perl, go to http://jobs.perl.org.

- **http://www.pm.org/**—The Perl Mongers are local Perl users groups. There might be one in your area. The Perl advocacy site is http://www.perl.org/.

- **http://www.tpj.com/**—*The Perl Journal* is "a reader-supported monthly e-zine" devoted to the Perl programming language. *TPJ* is always full of excellent, amusing, and informative articles, and is an invaluable resource to both new and experienced Perl programmers.

- **http://www-106.ibm.com/developerworks/linux/library/l-p101**—A short tutorial about one-line Perl scripts and code.

Books

- *Advanced Perl Programming*, by Sriram Srinivasan, O'Reilly & Associates.

- *Sams Teach Yourself Perl in 21 Days*, *Second Edition*, by Laura Lemay, Sams Publishing.

- *Learning Perl*, *Third Edition*, by Randal L. Schwartz, Tom Phoenix, O'Reilly & Associates.

- *Programming Perl*, *Third Edition*, by Larry Wall, Tom Christiansen, and Jon Orwant, O'Reilly & Associates.

CHAPTER 26

Working with Python

As PHP has come to dominate the world of web scripting, Python is increasingly dominating the domain of command-line scripting. Python's precise and clean syntax makes it one of the easiest languages to learn, and it enables programmers to code more quickly and spend less time maintaining their code. Although PHP is fundamentally similar to Java and Perl, Python is closer to C and Modula-3, and so it might look unfamiliar at first.

Most other languages have a group of developers at their cores, but Python has Guido van Rossum—creator, father, and Benevolent Dictator For Life (BDFL). Although Guido spends less time working on Python now, he still essentially has the right to veto changes to the language, which has enabled it to remain consistent over the many years of its development. The end result is that, in Guido's own words, "Even if you are in fact clueless about language design, you can tell that Python is a very simple language."

The following pages constitute a "quick start" tutorial to Python, designed to give you all the information you need to put together basic scripts and to point you toward resources that can take you further.

Python on Linux

Fedora comes with Python installed by default, as do many other versions of Linux and Unix—even Mac OS X comes with Python preinstalled. This is partly for the sake of convenience: Because Python is such a popular scripting language, preinstalling it saves having to install it later if the user wants to run a script. However, in Fedora's case, part of the reason for preinstallation is that several of the core system programs are written in Python, including yum itself.

The Python binary is installed into /usr/bin/python; if you run that, you enter the Python interactive interpreter, where you can type commands and have them executed immediately. Although PHP also has an interactive mode (use php -a to activate it), it is neither as powerful nor as flexible as Python's.

As with Perl, PHP, and other scripting languages, you can also execute Python scripts by adding a shebang line to the start of your scripts that points to /usr/bin/python and then setting the file to be executable. If you haven't seen one of these before, they look something like this: #!/usr/bin/python.

The third and final way to run Python scripts is through mod_python, which is installed by default when you select the Web Server application group from the Add/Remove Packages dialog.

For the purposes of this introduction, we will be using the interactive Python interpreter because it provides immediate feedback on commands as you type them.

Getting Interactive

We will be using the interactive interpreter for this chapter, so it is essential that you are comfortable using it. To get started, open a terminal and run the command python. You should see this:

```
[paul@caitlin ~]$ python
Python 2.3.4 (#1, Oct 26 2004, 16:42:40)
[GCC 3.4.2 20041017 (Red Hat 3.4.2-6.fc3)] on linux2
Type "help", "copyright", "credits" or "license" for more information.
>>>
```

The >>> is where you type your input, and you can set and get a variable like this:

```
>>> python = 'great'
>>> python
'great'
>>>
```

On line 1, the variable python is set to the text great, and on line 2 that value is read back from the variable when you type the name of the variable you want to read. Line 3 shows Python printing the variable; on line 4, you are back at the prompt to type more commands. Python remembers all the variables you use while in the interactive interpreter, which means you can set a variable to be the value of another variable.

When you are finished, press Ctrl+D to exit. At this point, all your variables and commands are forgotten by the interpreter, which is why complex Python programs are always saved in scripts!

The Basics of Python

Python is a language wholly unlike most others, and yet it is so logical that most people can pick it up very quickly. You have already seen how easily you can assign strings, but in Python nearly everything is that easy—as long as you remember the syntax!

Numbers

The way Python handles numbers is more precise than some other languages. It has all the normal operators—such as + for addition, - for subtraction, / for division, and * for multiplication—but it adds % for modulus (division remainder), ** for raise to the power, and // for floor division. It is also very specific about which type of number is being used, as this example shows:

```
>>> a = 5
>>> b = 10
>>> a * b
50
>>> a / b
0
>>> b = 10.0
>>> a / b
0.5
>>> a // b
0.0
```

The first division returns 0 because both a and b are integers (whole numbers), so Python calculates the division as an integer, giving 0. Because b is converted to 10.0, Python considers it to be a floating-point number and so the division is now calculated as a floating-point value, giving 0.5. Even with b being floating-point, using //—floor division—rounds it down.

Using **, you can easily see how Python works with integers:

```
>>> 2 ** 30
1073741824
>>> 2 ** 31
2147483648L
```

The first statement raises 2 to the power of 30 (that is, $2 \times 2 \times 2 \times 2 \times 2 \times ...$), and the second raises 2 to the power of 31. Notice how the second number has a capital L on the end of it—this is Python telling you that it is a long integer. The difference between long integers and normal integers is slight but important: Normal integers can be calculated with simple instructions on the CPU, whereas long integers—because they can be as big as you need them to be—need to be calculated in software and therefore are slower.

When specifying big numbers, you need not put the *L* at the end—Python figures it out for you. Furthermore, if a number starts off as a normal number and then exceeds its boundaries, Python automatically converts it to a long integer. The same is not true the other way around: If you have a long integer and then divide it by another number so that it could be stored as a normal integer, it remains a long integer:

```
>>> num = 99999999999999999999999999999999999L
>>> num = num / 100000000000000000000000000000000
>>> num
999L
```

You can convert between number types by using typecasting, like this:

```
>>> num = 10
>>> int(num)
10
>>> float(num)
10.0
>>> long(num)
10L
>>> floatnum = 10.0
>>> int(floatnum)
10
>>> float(floatnum)
10.0
>>> long(floatnum)
10L
```

You need not worry whether you are using integers or long integers; Python handles it all for you, so you can concentrate on getting the code right.

More on Strings

Python stores a string as an immutable sequence of characters—a jargon-filled way of saying "it is a collection of characters that, after they are set, cannot be changed without creating a new string." Sequences are important in Python. There are three primary types, of which strings are one, and they share some properties. Mutability makes much more sense when you learn about lists in the next section.

As you saw in the previous example, you can assign a value to strings in Python with just an equal sign, like this:

```
>>> mystring = 'hello';
>>> myotherstring = "goodbye";
>>> mystring
'hello'
>>> myotherstring;
```

```
'goodbye'
>>> test = "Are you really Bill O'Reilly?"
>>> test
"Are you really Bill O'Reilly?"
```

The first example encapsulates the string in single quotation marks and the second and third in double quotation marks. However, printing the first and second strings shows them both in single quotation marks because Python does not distinguish between the two. The third example is the exception—it uses double quotation marks because the string itself contains a single quotation mark. Here, Python prints the string with double quotation marks because it knows the string contains the single quotation mark.

Because the characters in a string are stored in sequence, you can index into them by specifying the character in which you are interested. Like most other languages, these indexes are zero-based, which means you need to ask for character 0 to get the first letter in a string. For example:

```
>>> string = "This is a test string"
>>> string
'This is a test string'
>>> string[0]
'T'
>>> string [0], string[3], string [20]
('T', 's', 'g')
```

The last line shows how, with commas, you can ask for several indexes at the same time. You could print the entire first word by using this:

```
>>> string[0], string[1], string[2], string[3]
('T', 'h', 'i', 's')
```

However, for that purpose you can use a different concept: slicing. A *slice* of a sequence draws a selection of indexes. For example, you can pull out the first word like this:

```
>>> string[0:4]
'This'
```

The syntax there means "take everything from position 0 (including 0) and end at position 4 (excluding it)." So [0:4] copies the items at indexes 0, 1, 2, and 3. You can omit either side of the indexes, and it copies either from the start or to the end:

```
>>> string [:4]
'This'
>>> string [5:]
'is a test string'
>>> string [11:]
'est string'
```

You can also omit both numbers, and it gives you the entire sequence:

```
>>> string [:]
'This is a test string'
```

Later you will learn precisely why you would want to do that, but for now there are a number of other string intrinsics that will make your life easier. For example, you can use the + and * operators to concatenate (join) and repeat strings, like this:

```
>>> mystring = "Python"
>>> mystring * 4
'PythonPythonPythonPython'
>>> mystring = mystring + " rocks! "
>>> mystring * 2
'Python rocks! Python rocks! '
```

In addition to working with operators, Python strings come with a selection of built-in methods. You can change the case of the letters with capitalize() (uppercases the first letter and lowercases the rest), lower() (lowercases them all), title() (uppercases the first letter in each word), and upper() (uppercases them all). You can also check whether strings match certain cases with islower(), istitle(), and isupper(); that also extends to isalnum() (returns true if the string is letters and numbers only) and isdigit() (returns true if the string is all numbers).

This example demonstrates some of these in action:

```
>>> string
'This is a test string'
>>> string.upper()
'THIS IS A TEST STRING'
>>> string.lower()
'this is a test string'
>>> string.isalnum()
False
>>> string = string.title()
>>> string
'This Is A Test String'
```

Why did isalnum() return false—the string contains only alphanumeric characters, doesn't it? Well, no. There are spaces in there, which is what is causing the problem. More importantly, the calls were to upper() and lower(), and those methods did not change the contents of the string—they just returned the new value. So, to change the string from This is a test string to This Is A Test String, you actually have to assign it back to the string variable.

Lists

Python's built-in list data type is a sequence, like strings. However, Python's lists are mutable, which means they can be changed. Lists are like arrays in that they hold a selection of elements in a given order. You can cycle through them, index into them, and slice them:

```
>>> mylist = ["python", "perl", "php"]
>>> mylist
['python', 'perl', 'php']
>>> mylist + ["java"]
['python', 'perl', 'php', 'java']
>>> mylist * 2
['python', 'perl', 'php', 'python', 'perl', 'php']
>>> mylist[1]
'perl'
>>> mylist[1] = "c++"
>>> mylist[1]
'c++'
>>> mylist[1:3]
['c++', 'php']
```

The brackets notation is important: You cannot use parentheses ((and)) or braces ({ and }) for lists. Using + for lists is different from using + for numbers. Python detects you are working with a list and appends one list to another. This is known as *operator overloading*, and it is one of the reasons Python is so flexible.

Lists can be *nested*, which means you can put a list inside a list. However, this is where mutability starts to matter, and so this might sound complicated! If you recall, the definition of an immutable string sequence is a collection of characters that, after they are set, cannot be changed without creating a new string. Lists are mutable, as opposed to immutable, which means you can change your list without creating a new list.

This becomes important because Python, by default, copies only a reference to a variable rather than the full variable. For example:

```
>>> list1 = [1, 2, 3]
>>> list2 = [4, list1, 6]
>>> list1
[1, 2, 3]
>>> list2
[4, [1, 2, 3], 6]
```

Here you can see a nested list. list2 contains 4, and then list1, and then 6. When you print the value of list2, you can see it also contains list1. Now, proceeding on from that:

26

```
>>> list1[1] = "Flake"
>>> list2
[4, [1, 'Flake', 3], 6]
```

Line one sets the second element in list1 (remember, sequences are zero-based!) to be Flake rather than 2; then the contents of list2 are printed. As you can see, when list1 changed, list2 was updated also. The reason for this is that list2 stores a reference to list1 as opposed to a copy of list1; they share the same value.

You can show that this works both ways by indexing twice into list2, like this:

```
>>> list2[1][1] = "Caramello"
>>> list1
[1, 'Caramello', 3]
```

The first line says, "get the second element in list2 (list1) and the second element of that list, and set it to be 'Caramello'." Then list1's value is printed, and you can see it has changed. This is the essence of mutability: We are changing our list without creating a new list. On the other hand, editing a string creates a new string, leaving the old one unaltered. For example:

```
>>> mystring = "hello"
>>> list3 = [1, mystring, 3]
>>> list3
[1, 'hello', 3]
>>> mystring = "world"
>>> list3
[1, 'hello', 3]
```

Of course, this raises the question of how you copy without references when references are the default. The answer, for lists, is that you use the [:] slice, which you saw earlier. This slices from the first element to the last, inclusive, essentially copying it without references. Here is how that looks:

```
>>> list4 = ["a", "b", "c"]
>>> list5 = list4[:]
>>> list4 = list4 + ["d"]
>>> list5
['a', 'b', 'c']
>>> list4
['a', 'b', 'c', 'd']
```

Lists have their own collections of built-in methods, such as sort(), append(), and pop(). The latter two add and remove single elements from the end of the list, with pop() also returning the removed element. For example:

```
>>> list5 = ["nick", "paul", "julian", "graham"]
>>> list5.sort()
>>> list5
['graham', 'julian', 'nick', 'paul']
>>> list5.pop()
'paul'
>>> list5
['graham', 'julian', 'nick']
>>> list5.append("Rebecca")
```

In addition, one interesting method of strings returns a list: split(). This takes a character by which to split and then gives you a list in which each element is a chunk from the string. For example:

```
>>> string = "This is a test string";
>>> string.split(" ")
['This', 'is', 'a', 'test', 'string']
```

Lists are used extensively in Python, although this is slowly changing as the language matures.

Dictionaries

Unlike lists, *dictionaries* are collections with no fixed order. Instead, they have a *key* (the name of the element) and a *value* (the content of the element), and Python places them wherever it needs to for maximum performance. When defining dictionaries, you need to use braces ({ }) and colons (:). You start with an opening brace and then give each element a key and a value, separated by a colon, like this:

```
>>> mydict = { "perl" : "a language", "php" : "another language" }
>>> mydict
{'php': 'another language', 'perl': 'a language'}
```

This example has two elements, with keys perl and php. However, when the dictionary is printed, we find that php comes before perl—Python hasn't respected the order in which they were entered. You can index into a dictionary using the normal code:

```
>>> mydict["perl"]
'a language'
```

However, because a dictionary has no fixed sequence, you cannot take a slice, or index by position.

Like lists, dictionaries are mutable and can also be nested; however, unlike lists, you cannot merge two dictionaries by using +. A key is used to locate dictionary elements, so having two elements with the same key would cause a clash. Instead, you should use the update() method, which merges two arrays by overwriting clashing keys.

You can also use the keys() method to return a list of all the keys in a dictionary.

26

Conditionals and Looping

So far, we have been looking at just data types, which should show you how powerful Python's data types are. However, you simply cannot write complex programs without conditional statements and loops.

Python has most of the standard conditional checks, such as > (greater than), <= (less than or equal to), and == (equal), but it also adds some new ones, such as in. For example, you can use in to check whether a string or a list contains a given character/element:

```
>>> mystring = "J Random Hacker"
>>> "r" in mystring
True
>>> "Hacker" in mystring
True
>>> "hacker" in mystring
False
```

The last example demonstrates how in is case sensitive. You can use the operator for lists, too:

```
>>> mylist = ["soldier", "sailor", "tinker", "spy"]
>>> "tailor" in mylist
False
```

Other comparisons on these complex data types are done item by item:

```
>>> list1 = ["alpha", "beta", "gamma"]
>>> list2 = ["alpha", "beta", "delta"]
>>> list1 > list2
True
```

list1's first element (alpha) is compared against list2's first element (alpha) and, because they are equal, the next element is checked. That is equal also, so the third element is checked, which is different. The g in gamma comes after the d in delta in the alphabet, so gamma is considered greater than delta and list1 is considered greater than list2.

Loops come in two types, and both are equally flexible. For example, the for loop can iterate through letters in a string or elements in a list:

```
>>> string = "Hello, Python!"
>>> for s in string: print s,
...
H e l l o ,   P y t h o n !
```

The for loop takes each letter in string and assigns it to s. The letter is then printed to the screen when you use the print command, but note the comma at the end: this tells

Python not to insert a line break after each letter. The "..." is there because Python allows you to enter more code in the loop; you need to press Enter again here to have the loop execute.

The same construct can be used for lists:

```
>>> mylist = ["andi", "rasmus", "zeev"]
>>> for p in mylist: print p
...
andi
rasmus
zeev
```

Without the comma after the print statement, each item is printed on its own line.

The other loop type is the while loop, and it looks similar:

```
>> while 1: print "This will loop forever!"
...
This will loop forever!
This will loop forever!
This will loop forever!
This will loop forever!
This will loop forever!
(etc)
Traceback (most recent call last):
  File "<stdin>", line 1, in ?
KeyboardInterrupt
>>>
```

That is an infinite loop (it will carry on printing that text forever), so you have to press Ctrl+C to interrupt it and regain control.

If you want to use multiline loops, you need to get ready to use your Tab key: Python handles loop blocks by recording the level of indent used. Some people find this odious; others admire it for forcing clean coding on users. Most of us, though, just get on with programming!

For example:

```
>>> i = 0
>>> while i < 3:
...     j = 0
...     while j < 3:
...             print "Pos: " + str(i) + "," + str(j) + ")"
...             j += 1
...     i += 1
...
```

26

```
Pos: (0,0)
Pos: (0,1)
Pos: (0,2)
Pos: (1,0)
Pos: (1,1)
Pos: (1,2)
Pos: (2,0)
Pos: (2,1)
Pos: (2,2)
```

You can control loops by using the break and continue keywords. break exits the loop and continues processing immediately afterward, and continue jumps to the next loop iteration.

Functions

Other languages—such as PHP—read and process an entire file before executing it, which means you can call a function before it is defined because the compiler reads the definition of the function before it tries to call it. Python is different: If the function definition has not been reached by the time you try to call it, you get an error. The reason behind this behavior is that Python actually creates an object for your function, and that in turns means two things. First, you can define the same function several times in a script and have the script pick the correct one at runtime. Second, you can assign the function to another name just by using =.

A function definition starts with def, followed by the function name, parentheses and a list of parameters, and then a colon. The contents of a function need to be indented at least one level beyond the definition. So, using function assignment and dynamic declaration, you can write a script that prints the correct greeting in a roundabout manner:

```
>>> def hello_english(Name):
...       print "Hello, " + Name + "!"
...
>>> def hello_hungarian(Name):
...       print "Szia, " + Name + "!"
...
>>> hello = hello_hungarian
>>> hello("Paul")
Szia, Paul!
>>> hello = hello_english
>>> hello("Paul")
```

Notice that function definitions include no type information. Functions are typeless, as we said. The upside of this is that you can write one function to do several things:

```
>>> def concat(First, Second):
...       return First + Second
```

```
...
>>> concat(["python"], ["perl"])
['python', 'perl']
>>> concat("Hello, ", "world!")
'Hello, world!'
```

That demonstrates how the `return` statement sends a value back to the caller, but also how a function can do one thing with lists and another thing with strings. The magic here is being accomplished by the objects. You can write a function that tells two objects to add themselves together, and the objects intrinsically know how to do that. If they don't—if, perhaps, the user passes in a string and an integer—Python catches the error for you. However, it is this hands-off, "let the objects sort themselves out" attitude that makes functions so flexible. The `concat()` function could conceivably concatenate strings, lists, or *zonks*—a data type someone created herself that allows addition. The point is that you do not limit what your function can do—cliché as it might sound, the only limit is your imagination!

Object Orientation

After having read this far, you should not be surprised to hear that Python's object orientation is flexible and likely to surprise you if you have been using C-like languages for several years.

The best way to learn Python OOP is to just do it. So, here is a basic script that defines a class, creates an object of that class, and calls a function:

```
class dog(object):
    def bark(self):
        print "Woof!"


fluffy = dog()
fluffy.bark()
```

Defining a class starts, predictably, with the `class` keyword, followed by the name of the class you are defining and a colon. The contents of that class need to be indented one level so that Python knows where each class stops. Note that the `object` inside parentheses is there for object inheritance, which is discussed later. For now, the least you need to know is that if your new class is not based on an existing class, you should put `object` inside parentheses as shown in the previous code.

Functions inside classes work in much the same way as normal functions do (although they are usually called *methods*), with the main difference being that they should all take at least one parameter, usually called `self`. This parameter is filled with the name of the object on which the function was called, and you need to use it explicitly.

Creating an instance of a class is done by assignment. You do not need any new keyword, as in some other languages—you just provide empty parentheses. You call a function of that object by using a period and the name of the class to call, with any parameters passed inside parentheses.

Class and Object Variables

Each object has its own set of functions and variables, and you can manipulate those variables independent of objects of the same type. Additionally, some class variables are set to a default value for all classes and can also be manipulated globally.

This script demonstrates two objects of the dog class being created, each with its own name:

```
class dog(object):
    name = "Lassie"
    def bark(self):
        print self.name + " says 'Woof!'"
    def setName(self, name):
        self.name = name
fluffy = dog()
fluffy.bark()
poppy = dog()
poppy.setName("Poppy")
poppy.bark()
```

That outputs the following:

```
Lassie says 'Woof!'
Poppy says 'Woof!'
```

Each dog starts with the name Lassie, but it gets customized. Keep in mind that Python assigns by reference by default, meaning each object has a reference to the class's name variable, and as you assign that with the setName() method, that reference is lost. What this means is that any references you do not change can be manipulated globally. Thus, if you change a class's variable, it also changes in all instances of that class that have not set their own value for that variable. For example:

```
class dog(object):
    name = "Lassie"
    color = "brown"
fluffy = dog()
poppy = dog()
print fluffy.color
dog.color = "black"
print poppy.color
poppy.color = "yellow"
print fluffy.color
print poppy.color
```

So, the default color of dogs is brown—both the `fluffy` and `poppy` dog objects start off as brown. Then, with `dog.color`, the default color is set to black, and because neither of the two objects has set its own color value, they are updated to be black. The third to last line uses `poppy.color` to set a custom color value for the `poppy` object—`poppy` becomes yellow, but `fluffy` and the `dog` class in general remain black.

Constructors and Destructors

To help you automate the creation and deletion of objects, you can easily override two default methods: __init__ and __del__. These are the methods called by Python when a class is being instantiated and freed, known as the *constructor* and *destructor*, respectively.

Having a custom constructor is great when you need to accept a set of parameters for each object being created. For example, you might want each dog to have its own name on creation, and you could implement that with this code:

```python
class dog(object):
    def __init__(self, name):
        self.name = name
fluffy = dog("Fluffy")
print fluffy.name
```

If you do not provide a `name` parameter when creating the dog object, Python reports an error and stops. You can, of course, ask for as many constructor parameters as you want, although it is usually better to ask for only the ones you need and have other functions fill in the rest.

On the other side of things is the destructor method, which allows you to have more control over what happens when an object is destroyed. Using the two, you can show the life cycle of an object by printing messages when it is created and deleted:

```python
class dog(object):
    def __init__(self, name):
        self.name = name
        print self.name + " is alive!"
    def __del__(self):
        print self.name + " is no more!"
fluffy = dog("Fluffy")
```

The destructor is there to give you the chance to free up resources allocated to the object or perhaps log something to a file.

Class Inheritance

Python allows you to reuse your code by inheriting one class from one or more others. For example, cars, trucks, and motorbikes are all vehicles, and so share a number of similar properties. In that scenario, you would not want to have to copy and paste functions between them; it would be smarter (and easier!) to have a vehicle class that defines all the shared functionality and then inherit each vehicle from that.

Consider the following code:

```
class car(object):
    color = "black"
    speed = 0
    def accelerateTo(self, speed):
        self.speed = speed
    def setColor(self, color):
        self.color = color
mycar = car()
print mycar.color
```

This creates a car class with a default color and also provides a setColor() function so that people can change their own colors. Now, what do you drive to work? Is it a car? Sure it is, but chances are it is a Ford, or a Dodge, or a Jeep, or some other make—you don't get cars without a make. On the other hand, you do not want to have to define a class Ford, give it the methods accelerateTo(), setColor(), and however many other methods a basic car has and then do exactly the same thing for Ferrari, Nissan, and so on.

The solution is to use inheritance: Define a car class that contains all the shared functions and variables of all the makes and then inherit from that. In Python, you do this by putting the name of the class from which to inherit inside parentheses in the class declaration, like this:

```
class car(object):
    color = "black"
    speed = 0
    def accelerateTo(self, speed):
        self.speed = speed
    def setColor(self, color):
        self.color = color

class ford(car): pass
class nissan(car): pass
mycar = ford()
print mycar.color
```

The pass directive is an empty statement—it means the class contains nothing new. However, because the ford and nissan classes inherit from the car class, they get color, speed, accelerateTo(), and setColor() provided by their parent class. Note that you do not need object after the classnames for ford and nissan because they are inherited from an existing class: car.

By default, Python gives you all the methods the parent class has, but you can override that by providing new implementations for the classes that need them. For example:

```
class modelt(car):
    def setColor(self, color):
        print "Sorry, Model Ts come only in black!"


myford = ford()
ford.setColor("green")
mycar = modelt()
mycar.setColor("green")
```

The first car is created as a Ford, so setColor() works fine because it uses the method from the car class. However, the second car is created as a Model T, which has its own setColor() method, so the call will fail.

This provides an interesting scenario: What do you do if you have overridden a method and yet want to call the parent's method also? If, for example, changing the color of a Model T was allowed but just cost extra, you would want to print a message saying, "You owe $50 more," but then change the color. To do this, you need to use the class object from which the current class is inherited—car, in this example. Here's an example:

```
class modelt(car):
    def setColor(self, color):
        print "You owe $50 more"
        car.setColor(self, color)


mycar = modelt()
mycar.setColor("green")
print mycar.color
```

That prints the message and then changes the color of the car.

Multiple Inheritance

You can inherit as many classes as you need, building up functionality as you go. For example, you could have a class animalia, a subclass chordata, a sub-subclass mammalia, and a sub-sub-subclass homosapiens. Each one is more specific than its parent. However, an interesting addition in Python is the capability to have multiple inheritance—to take functionality from two classes simultaneously.

Again, this is best shown in code:

```
class car(object):
    def drive(self):
        print "We're driving..."
```

```
class timemachine(object):
    def timeTravel(self):
        print "Traveling through time..."

class delorian(car,timemachine): pass
mydelorian = delorian()
mydelorian.drive()
mydelorian.timeTravel()
```

In that example, you can see a class car and a class timemachine. Both work by themselves, so you can have a car and drive around in it or a time machine and travel through time with it. However, there is also a delorian class that inherits from car and timemachine. As you can see, it is able to call both drive() (inherited from car) and timeTravel() (inherited from timemachine).

This introduces another interesting problem: What happens if both car and timemachine have a refuel() function? The answer is that Python picks the correct function to use based on the order in which you listed the parent classes. The previous code used class delorian(car,timemachine), which means "inherit from car and then from timemachine." As a result, if both classes had a refuel() function, Python would pick car.refuel().

This situation becomes more complex when further inheritance is involved. That is, if car inherits its refuel() method from vehicle, Python still chooses it. What happens behind the scenes is that Python picks the first class from which you inherited and searches it and all its parent classes for a matching method call. If it finds none, it goes to the next class and checks it and its parents. This process repeats until it finds a class that has the required method.

The Standard Library and the Vaults of Parnassus

A default Python install includes many modules (blocks of code) that enable you to interact with the operating system, open and manipulate files, parse command-line options, perform data hashing and encryption, and much more. This is one of the reasons most commonly cited when people are asked why they like Python so much—it comes stocked to the gills with functionality you can take advantage of immediately. In fact, the number of modules included in the Standard Library is so high that entire books have been written about them—try *Python Standard Library* (O'Reilly, ISBN: 0-596-00096-0) for a comprehensive, if slightly dated, list of them.

For unofficial scripts and add-ons for Python, the recommended starting place is called the Vaults of Parnassus: http://py.vaults.ca/. There you can find about 20,000 public scripts and code examples for everything from mathematics to games.

Reference

▶ **http://www.python.org/**—The Python website is packed with information and updated regularly. This should be your first stop, if only to read the latest Python news.

▶ **http://www.zope.org/**—The home page of the Zope Content Management System (CMS), it's one of the most popular CMSes around and, more importantly, written entirely in Python.

▶ **http://www.jython.org/**—Python also has an excellent Java-based interpreter to allow it to run on other platforms. If you prefer Microsoft's .NET, try http://www.codeplex.com/Wiki/View.aspx?ProjectName=IronPython.

▶ **http://www.pythonline.com/**—Guido van Rossum borrowed the name for his language from Monty Python's Flying Circus, and as a result, many Python code examples use oblique Monty Python references. A visit to the official Monty Python site to hone your Python knowledge is highly recommended!

▶ **http://www.python.org/moin/PythonBooks**—There are few truly great books about Python; however, you can find a list of what's on offer at this site. If you are desperate to pick up a book immediately, you could do much worse than to choose *Learning Python* (O'Reilly, ISBN: 0-596-00281-5).

26

Writing PHP Scripts

This chapter introduces you to the world of PHP programming, from the point of view of using it as a web scripting language and as a command-line tool. PHP originally stood for *personal home page* because it was a collection of Perl scripts designed to ease the creation of guest books, message boards, and other interactive scripts commonly found on home pages. However, since those early days, it has received two major updates (PHP 3 and PHP 4), plus a substantial revision in PHP 5, which is the version bundled with Fedora.

Part of the success of PHP has been its powerful integration with databases—its earliest uses nearly always took advantage of a database back end. In PHP 5, however, two big new data storage mechanisms were introduced: SQLite, which is a powerful and local database system, and SimpleXML, which is an API designed to make XML parsing and querying easy. As you will see over time, the PHP developers did a great job because both SQLite and SimpleXML are easy to learn and use.

> **NOTE**
>
> PHP's installation packages are under the Web Server category in Add/Remove Applications. The basic package is just called php, but you might also want to add extensions such as php_ldap, php_mysql, or php_pgsql. Choose only the extensions you plan to use; otherwise, you will waste system resources.

Introduction to PHP

In terms of the way it looks, PHP is a cross between Java and Perl, having taken the best aspects of both and merged them successfully into one language. The Java parts include a powerful object-orientation system, the capability to throw program exceptions, and the general style of writing that both languages borrowed from C. Borrowed from Perl is the "it should just work" mentality where ease of use is favored over strictness. As a result, you will find a lot of "there is more than one way to do it" in PHP.

Entering and Exiting PHP Mode

Unlike PHP's predecessors, you embed your PHP code inside your HTML as opposed to the other way around. Before PHP, many websites had standard HTML pages for most of their content, linking to Perl CGI pages to do back-end processing when needed. With PHP, all your pages are capable of processing and containing HTML.

Each .php file is processed by PHP that looks for code to execute. PHP considers all the text it finds to be HTML until it finds one of four things:

- ▶ `<?php`

- ▶ `<?`

- ▶ `<%`

- ▶ `<script language="php">`

The first option is the preferred method of entering PHP mode because it is guaranteed to work.

After you are in PHP mode, you can exit it by using `?>` (for `<?php` and `<?`); `%>` for `<%`) or `</script>` (for `<script language="php">`). This code example demonstrates entering and exiting PHP mode:

```
In HTML mode
<?php
  echo "In PHP mode";
?>
In HTML mode
In <?php echo "PHP"; ?> mode
```

Variables

All variables in PHP start with a dollar sign ($). Unlike many other languages, PHP does not have different types of variable for integers, floating-point numbers, arrays, or Booleans. They all start with a $, and all are interchangeable. As a result, PHP is a weakly typed language, which means you do not declare a variable as containing a specific type of data; you just use it however you want to.

Save the code in Listing 27.1 into the script fedora1.php.

LISTING 27.1   Testing Types in PHP

```php
<?php
  $i = 10;
  $j = "10";
  $k = "Hello, world";
  echo $i + $j;
  echo $i + $k;
?>
```

To run that script, bring up a console and browse to where you saved it. Then type this command:

```
$ php fedora1.php
```

If PHP is installed correctly, you should see the output 2010, which is really two things. The 20 is the result of 10 + 10 ($i plus $j), and the 10 is the result of adding 10 to the text string Hello, world. Neither of those operations is really straightforward. Whereas $i is set to the number 10, $j is actually set to be the text value "10", which is not the same thing. Adding 10 to 10 gives 20, as you would imagine, but adding 10 to "10" (the string) forces PHP to convert $j to an integer on the fly before adding it.

Running $i + $k adds another string to a number, but this time the string is Hello, world and not just a number inside a string. PHP still tries to convert it, though, and converting any nonnumeric string into a number converts it to 0. So, the second echo statement ends up saying $i + 0.

As you should have guessed by now, calling echo outputs values to the screen. Right now, that prints directly to your console, but internally PHP has a complex output mechanism that enables you to print to a console, send text through Apache to a web browser, send data over a network, and more.

Now that you have seen how PHP handles variables of different types, it is important that you understand the selection of types available to you—see Table 27.1.

TABLE 27.1   Data Types in PHP

Type	Stores
integer	Whole numbers; for example, 1, 9, or 324809873
float	Fractional numbers; for example, 1.1, 9.09, or 3.141592654
string	Characters; for example, "a", "sfdgh", or "Fedora Unleashed"
boolean	True or false
array	Several variables of any type
object	An instance of a class
resource	Any external data

The first four can be thought of as simple variables, and the last three as complex variables. Arrays are simply collections of variables. You might have an array of numbers (the ages of all the children in a class); an array of strings (the names of all Wimbledon tennis champions); or even an array of arrays, known as a *multidimensional array*. Arrays are covered in more depth in the next section because they are unique in the way in which they are defined.

Objects are used to define and manipulate a set of variables that belong to a unique entity. Each object has its own personal set of variables, as well as functions that operate on those variables. Objects are commonly used to model real-world things. You might define an object that represents a TV, with variables such as $CurrentChannel (probably an integer), $SupportsHiDef (a Boolean), and so on.

Of all the complex variables, the easiest to grasp are resources. PHP has many extensions available to it that allow you to connect to databases, manipulate graphics, or even make calls to Java programs. Because they are all external systems, they need to have types of data unique to them that PHP cannot represent by using any of the six other data types. So, PHP stores their custom data types in resources—data types that are meaningless to PHP but can be used by the external libraries that created them.

Arrays

Arrays are one of our favorite parts of PHP because the syntax is smart and easy to read and yet manages to be as powerful as you could want. You need to know four pieces of jargon to understand arrays:

▶ An array is made up of many *elements*.

▶ Each element has a *key* that defines its place in the array. An array can have only one element with a given key.

▶ Each element also has a *value*, which is the data associated with the key.

▶ Each array has a *cursor*, which points to the current key.

The first three are used regularly; the last one less so. The array cursor is covered later in this chapter in the "Basic Functions" section, but we look at the other three now. With PHP, your keys can be virtually anything: integers, strings, objects, or other arrays. You can even mix and match the keys so that one key is an array, another is a string, and so on. The one exception to all this is floating-point numbers: You cannot use floating-point numbers as keys in your arrays.

There are two ways of adding values to an array: with the [] operator, which is unique to arrays, and with the array() pseudo-function. You should use [] when you want to add items to an existing array and use array() to create a new array.

To sum all this up in code, Listing 27.2 shows a script that creates an array without specifying keys, adds various items to it both without keys and with keys of varying types, does a bit of printing, and then clears the array.

LISTING 27.2   Manipulating Arrays

```php
<?php
  $myarr = array(1, 2, 3, 4);

  $myarr[4] = "Hello";
  $myarr[] = "World!";
  $myarr["elephant"] = "Wombat";
  $myarr["foo"] = array(5, 6, 7, 8);

  echo $myarr[2];
  echo $myarr["elephant"];
  echo $myarr["foo"][1];

  $myarr = array();
?>
```

The initial array is created with four elements, assigned the values 1, 2, 3, and 4. Because no keys are specified, PHP automatically assigns keys for us starting at 0 and counting upward—giving keys 0, 1, 2, and 3. Then we add a new element with the [] operator, specifying 4 as the key and "Hello" as the value. Next, [] is used again to add an element with the value "World!" and no key, and then again to add an element with the key "elephant" and the value "wombat". The line after that demonstrates using a string key with an array value—an array inside an array (a multidimensional array).

The next three lines demonstrate reading back from an array, first using a numeric key, then using a string key, and then using a string key and a numeric key. Remember, the "foo" element is an array in itself, so that third reading line retrieves the array and then prints the second element (arrays start at 0, remember). The last line blanks the array by simply using array() with no parameters, which creates an array with elements and assigns it to $myarr.

The following is an alternative way of using array() that enables you to specify keys along with their values:

```php
$myarr = array("key1" => "value1", "key2" => "value2",
7 => "foo", 15 => "bar");
```

Which method you choose really depends on whether you want specific keys or want PHP to pick them for you.

Constants

Constants are frequently used in functions that require specific values to be passed in. For example, a popular function is extract(), which takes all the values in an array and places them into variables in their own right. You can choose to change the name of the variables as they are extracted by using the second parameter—send it 0 and it overwrites

27

variables with the same names as those being extracted, send it 1 and it skips variables with the same names, send it 5 and it prefixes variables only if they exist already, and so on. Of course, no one wants to have to remember a lot of numbers for each function, so you can instead use EXTR_OVERWRITE for 0, EXTR_SKIP for 1, EXTR_PREFIX_IF_EXISTS for 5, and so on, which is much easier.

You can create constants of your own by using the define() function. Unlike variables, constants do not start with a dollar sign, which makes the code to define a constant look like this:

```php
<?php
  define("NUM_SQUIRRELS", 10);
  define("PLAYER_NAME", "Jim");
  define("NUM_SQUIRRELS_2", NUM_SQUIRRELS);
  echo NUM_SQUIRRELS_2;
?>
```

That script demonstrates how you can set constants to numbers, strings, or even the value of other constants, although that doesn't really get used much!

Comments

Adding short comments to your code is recommended and usually a requirement in larger software houses. In PHP you have three options for commenting style: //, /* */, and #. The first option (two slashes) instructs PHP to ignore everything until the end of the line. The second (a slash and an asterisk) instructs PHP to ignore everything until it reaches */. The last (a hash symbol) works like // and is included because it is common among shell scripting languages.

This code example demonstrates the difference between // and /* */:

```php
<?php
  echo "This is printed!";
  // echo "This is not printed";
  echo "This is printed!";
  /* echo "This is not printed";
  echo "This is not printed either"; */
?>
```

It is generally preferred to use // because it is a known quantity. On the other hand, it is easy to introduce coding errors with /* */ by losing track of where a comment starts and ends.

NOTE

Contrary to popular belief, having comments in your PHP script has almost no effect on the speed at which the script executes. What little speed difference exists is wholly removed if you use a code cache.

Escape Sequences

Some characters cannot be typed, and yet you will almost certainly want to use some of them from time to time. For example, you might want to use an ASCII character for newline, but you can't type it. Instead, you need to use an escape sequence: \n. Similarly, you can print a carriage return character with \r. It's important to know both of these because on the Windows platform, you need to use \r\n to get a new line. If you do not plan to run your scripts anywhere else, you need not worry about this!

Going back to the first script we wrote, you will recall it printed 2010 because we added 10 + 10 and then 10 + 0. We can rewrite that using escape sequences, like this:

```php
<?php
  $i = 10;
  $j = "10";
  $k = "Hello, world";
  echo $i + $j;
  echo "\n";
  echo $i + $k;
  echo "\n";
?>
```

This time PHP prints a new line after each of the numbers, making it obvious that the output is 20 and 10 rather than 2010. Note that the escape sequences must be used in double quotation marks because they do not work in single quotation marks.

Three common escape sequences are \\, which means "ignore the backslash"; \", which means "ignore the double quote"; and \', which means "ignore the single quote." This is important when strings include quotation marks inside them. If you had a string such as "Are you really Bill O'Reilly?", which has a single quotation mark in, this code would not work:

```php
<?php
  echo 'Are you really Bill O'Reilly?';
?>
```

PHP would see the opening quotation mark, read all the way up to the *O* in O'Reilly, and then see the quotation mark following the *O* as being the end of the string. The Reilly? part would appear to be a fragment of text and would cause an error. You have two options here: You can either surround the string in double quotation marks or escape the single quotation mark with \'.

If you choose the escaping route, it will look like this:

```php
echo 'Are you really Bill O\'Reilly?';
```

Although they are a clean solution for small text strings, you should be careful with overusing escape sequences. HTML is particularly full of quotation marks, and escaping them can get messy:

```
$mystring = "<img src=\"foo.png\" alt=\"My picture\"
width=\"100\" height=\"200\" />";
```

In that situation, you are better off using single quotation marks to surround the text simply because it is a great deal easier on the eye!

Variable Substitution

PHP allows you to use two methods to define strings: single quotation marks, double quotation marks, or heredoc notation, but the latter isn't often used. Single quotation marks and double quotation marks work identically, with one minor exception: variable substitution.

Consider the following code:

```
<?php
  $age = 25
  echo "You are ";
  echo $age;
?>
```

That is a particularly clumsy way to print a variable as part of a string. Fortunately, if you put a variable inside a string, PHP performs *variable substitution*, replacing the variable with its value. That means you can rewrite the code like so:

```
<?php
  $age = 25
  echo "You are $age";
?>
```

The output is the same. The difference between single quotation marks and double quotation marks is that single-quoted strings do not have their variables substituted. Here's an example:

```
<?php
  $age = 25
  echo "You are $age";
  echo 'You are $age';
?>
```

The first echo prints "You are 25", but the second one prints "You are $age".

Operators

Now that we have data values to work with, we need some operators to use, too. We have already used + to add variables together, but many others in PHP handle arithmetic, comparison, assignment, and other operators. *Operator* is just a fancy word for something that performs an operation, like addition or subtraction. However, *operand* might be new to you. Consider this operation:

```
$a = $b + c;
```

In this operation, = and + are operators and $a, $b, and $c are operands. Along with +, you also already know - (subtract), * (multiply), and / (divide), but Table 27.2 shows more.

TABLE 27.2   Operators in PHP

Operator	What It Does
=	Assigns the right operand to the left operand.
==	Returns true if the left operand is equal to the right operand.
!=	Returns true if the left operand is not equal to the right operand.
===	Returns true if the left operand is identical to the right operand. This is not the same as ==.
!==	Returns true if the left operand is not identical to the right operand. This is not the same as !=.
<	Returns true if the left operand is smaller than the right operand.
>	Returns true if the left operand is greater than the right operand.
<=	Returns true if the left operand is equal to or smaller than the right operand.
&&	Returns true if both the left operand and the right operand are true.
||	Returns true if either the left operand or the right operand is true.
++	Increments the operand by one.
- -	Decrements the operand by one.
+=	Increments the left operand by the right operand.
-=	Decrements the left operand by the right operand.
.	Concatenates the left operand and the right operand (joins them).
%	Divides the left operand by the right operand and returns the remainder.
|	Performs a bitwise OR operation. It returns a number with bits that are set in either the left operand or the right operand.
&	Performs a bitwise AND operation. It returns a number with bits that are set both in the left operand and the right operand.

There are at least 10 other operators not listed, but to be fair, you're unlikely to use them. Even some of the ones in this list are used infrequently—bitwise AND, for example. Having said that, the bitwise OR operator is used regularly because it allows you to combine values.

27

Here is a code example demonstrating some of the operators:

```php
<?php
  $i = 100;
  $i++; // $i is now 101
  $i--; // $i is now 100 again
  $i += 10; // $i is 110
  $i = $i / 2; // $i is 55
  $j = $i; // both $j and $i are 55
  $i = $j % 11; // $i is 0
?>
```

The last line uses modulus, which for some people takes a little bit of effort to understand. The result of $i % 11 is 0 because $i is set to 55 and modulus works by dividing the left operand (55) by the right operand (11) and returning the remainder. 55 divides by 11 exactly five times, and so has the remainder 0.

The concatenation operator, a period, sounds scarier than it is: It just joins strings together. For example:

```php
<?php
  echo "Hello, " . "world!";
  echo "Hello, world!" . "\n";
?>
```

Two "special" operators in PHP are not covered here and yet are used frequently. Before you look at them, though, it's important that you see how the comparison operators (such as <, <=, and !=) are used inside conditional statements.

Conditional Statements

In a *conditional statement*, you instruct PHP to take different actions, depending on the outcome of a test. For example, you might want PHP to check whether a variable is greater than 10 and, if so, print a message. This is all done with the if statement, which looks like this:

```php
if (your condition) {
  // action to take if condition is true
} else {
  // optional action to take otherwise
}
```

The your condition part can be filled with any number of conditions you want PHP to evaluate, and this is where the comparison operators come into their own. For example:

```php
if ($i > 10) {
  echo "11 or higher";
} else {
  echo "10 or lower";
}
```

PHP looks at the condition and compares $i to 10. If it is greater than 10, it replaces the whole operation with 1; otherwise, it replaces it with 0. So, if $i is 20, the result looks like this:

```
if (1) {
  echo "11 or higher";
} else {
  echo "10 or lower";
}
```

In conditional statements, any number other than 0 is considered to be equivalent to the Boolean value true, so if (1) always evaluates to true. There is a similar case for strings: If your string has any characters in it, then it evaluates to true, with empty strings evaluating to false. This is important because you can then use that 1 in another condition through && or ¦¦ operators. For example, if you want to check whether $i is greater than 10 but less than 40, you could write this:

```
if ($i > 10 && $i < 40) {
  echo "11 or higher";
} else {
  echo "10 or lower";
}
```

If we presume that $i is set to 50, the first condition ($i > 10) is replaced with 1 and the second condition ($i < 40) is replaced with 0. Those two numbers are then used by the && operator, which requires both the left and right operands to be true. While 1 is equivalent to true, 0 is not, so the && operand is replaced with 0 and the condition fails.

=, ==, ===, and similar operators are easily confused and often the source of programming errors. The first, a single equal sign, assigns the value of the right operand to the left operand. However, all too often you see code like this:

```
if ($i = 10) {
  echo "The variable is equal to 10!";
} else {
  echo "The variable is not equal to 10";
}
```

That is incorrect. Rather than checking whether $i is equal to 10, it assigns 10 to $i and returns true. What is needed is ==, which compares two values for equality. In PHP, this is extended so that there is also === (three equal signs), which checks whether two values are identical—more than just equal.

The difference is slight but important: If you have a variable with the string value "10" and compare it against the number value of 10, they are equal. Thus, PHP converts the type and checks the numbers. However, they are not identical. To be considered identical, the two variables must be equal (that is, have the same value) and be of the same data type (that is, both are strings, both are integers, and so on).

NOTE

It is common practice to put function calls in conditional statements rather than direct comparisons. For example:

```
if (do_something()) {
```

If the do_something() function returns true (or something equivalent to true, such as a nonzero number), the conditional statement evaluates to true.

Special Operators

The ternary operator and the execution operator work differently from those you have seen so far. The ternary operator is rarely used in PHP, thankfully, because it is really just a condensed conditional statement. Presumably it arose through someone needing to make his code occupy as little space as possible because it certainly does not make PHP code any easier to read!

The ternary operator works like this:

```
$age_description = ($age < 18) ? "child" : "adult";
```

Without explanation, that code is essentially meaningless; however, it expands into the following five lines of code:

```
if ($age < 18) {
  $age_description = "child";
} else {
  $age_description = "adult";
}
```

The ternary operator is so named because it has three operands: a condition to check ($age < 18 in the previous code), a result if the condition is true ("child"), and a result if the condition is false ("adult"). Although we hope you never have to use the ternary operator, it is at least important to know how it works in case you stumble across it.

The other special operator is the execution operator, which is the backtick symbol, `. The position of the backtick key varies depending on your keyboard, but it is likely to be just to the left of the 1 key (above Tab). The execution operator executes the program inside the backticks, returning any text the program outputs. For example:

```
<?php
  $i = `ls -l`;
  echo $i;
?>
```

That executes the ls program, passing in -l (a lowercase *L*) to get the long format, and stores all its output in $i. You can make the command as long or as complex as you like, including piping to other programs. You can also use PHP variables inside the command.

Switching

Having multiple if statements in one place is ugly, slow, and prone to errors. Consider the code in Listing 27.3.

LISTING 27.3   How Multiple Conditional Statements Lead to Ugly Code

```php
<?php
  $cat_age = 3;

  if ($cat_age == 1) {
    echo "Cat age is 1";
  } else {
    if ($cat_age == 2) {
      echo "Cat age is 2";
    } else {
      if ($cat_age == 3) {
        echo "Cat age is 3";
      } else {
        if ($cat_age == 4) {
          echo "Cat age is 4";
        } else {
          echo "Cat age is unknown";
        }
      }
    }
  }
?>
```

Even though it certainly works, it is a poor solution to the problem. Much better is a switch/case block, which transforms the previous code into what's shown in Listing 27.4.

LISTING 27.4   Using a switch/case Block

```php
<?php
  $cat_age = 3;

  switch ($cat_age) {
    case 1:
      echo "Cat age is 1";
      break;
    case 2:
      echo "Cat age is 2";
      break;
    case 3:
      echo "Cat age is 3";
      break;
```

27

LISTING 27.4   Continued

```
    case 4:
      echo "Cat age is 4";
      break;
    default:
      echo "Cat age is unknown";
  }
?>
```

Although it is only slightly shorter, it is a great deal more readable and much easier to maintain. A switch/case group is made up of a switch() statement in which you provide the variable you want to check, followed by numerous case statements. Notice the break statement at the end of each case. Without that, PHP would execute each case statement beneath the one it matches. Calling break causes PHP to exit the switch/case. Notice also that there is a default case at the end that catches everything that has no matching case.

It is important that you do not use case default: but merely default:. Also, it is the last case label, so it has no need for a break statement because PHP exits the switch/case block there anyway.

Loops

PHP has four ways you can execute a block of code multiple times: while, for, foreach, and do...while. Of the four, only do...while sees little use; the others are popular and you will certainly encounter them in other people's scripts.

The most basic loop is the while loop, which executes a block of code for as long as a given condition is true. So you can write an infinite loop—a block of code that continues forever—with this PHP:

```
<?php
  $i = 10;
  while ($i >= 10) {
    $i += 1;
    echo $i;
  }
?>
```

The loop block checks whether $i is greater or equal to 10 and, if that condition is true, adds 1 to $i and prints it. Then it goes back to the loop condition again. Because $i starts at 10 and only numbers are added to it, that loop continues forever. With two small changes, you can make the loop count down from 10 to 0:

```
<?php
  $i = 10;
  while ($i >= 0) {
```

```
    $i -= 1;
    echo $i;
  }
?>
```

So, this time you check whether $i is greater than or equal to 0 and subtract 1 from it with each loop iteration. while loops are typically used when you are unsure of how many times the code needs to loop because while keeps looping until an external factor stops it.

With a for loop, you specify precise limits on its operation by giving it a declaration, a condition, and an action. That is, you specify one or more variables that should be set when the loop first runs (the *declaration*), you set the circumstances that will cause the loop to terminate (the *condition*), and you tell PHP what it should change with each loop iteration (the *action*). That last part is what really sets a for loop apart from a while loop: You usually tell PHP to change the condition variable with each iteration.

You can rewrite the script that counts down from 10 to 0 using a for loop:

```
<?php
  for($i = 10; $i >= 0; $i -= 1) {
    echo $i;
  }
?>
```

This time you do not need to specify the initial value for $i outside the loop, and neither do you need to change $i inside the loop—it is all part of the for statement. The actual amount of code is really the same, but for this purpose the for loop is arguably tidier and therefore easier to read. With the while loop, the $i variable was declared outside the loop and so was not explicitly attached to the loop.

The third loop type is foreach, which is specifically for arrays and objects, although it is rarely used for anything other than arrays. A foreach loop iterates through each element in an array (or each variable in an object), optionally providing both the key name and the value.

In its simplest form, a foreach loop looks like this:

```
<?php
  foreach($myarr as $value) {
    echo $value;
  }
?>
```

This loops through the $myarr array created earlier, placing each value in the $value variable. You can modify that to get the keys as well as the values from the array, like this:

27

```php
<?php
  foreach($myarr as $key => $value) {
    echo "$key is set to $value\n";
  }
?>
```

As you can guess, this time the array keys go in $key and the array values go in $value. One important characteristic of the foreach loop is that it goes from the start of the array to the end and then stops—and by *start* we mean the first item to be added rather than the lowest index number. This script shows this behavior:

```php
<?php
  $array = array(6 => "Hello", 4 => "World",
                 2 => "Wom", 0 => "Bat");
  foreach($array as $key => $value) {
    echo "$key is set to $value\n";
  }
?>
```

If you try this script, you will see that foreach prints the array in the original order of 6, 4, 2, 0 rather than the numerical order of 0, 2, 4, 6.

If you ever want to exit a loop before it has finished, you can use the same break statement you saw earlier to exit a switch/case block. This becomes more interesting if you find yourself with *nested* loops—loops inside of loops. This is a common situation to be in. For example, you might want to loop through all the rows in a table and, for each row in that table, loop through each column. Calling break exits only one loop or switch/case, but you can use break 2 to exit two loops or switch/cases, or break 3 to exit three, and so on.

Including Other Files

Unless you are restricting yourself to the simplest programming ventures, you will want to share code among your scripts at some point. The most basic need for this is to have a standard header and footer for your website, with only the body content changing. However, you might also find yourself with a small set of custom functions you use frequently, and it would be an incredibly bad move to simply copy and paste the functions into each of the scripts that use them.

The most common way to include other files is with the include keyword. Save this script as include1.php:

```php
<?php
  for($i = 10; $i >= 0; $i -= 1) {
    include "echo_i.php";
  }
?>
```

Then save this script as `echo_i.php`:

```php
<?php
  echo $i;
?>
```

If you run `include1.php`, PHP loops from 10 to 0 and includes `echo_i.php` each time. For its part, `echo_i.php` just prints the value of `$i`, which is a crazy way of performing an otherwise simple operation, but it does demonstrate how included files share data. Note that the `include` keyword in `include1.php` is inside a PHP block, but PHP is reopened inside `echo_i.php`. This is important because PHP exits PHP mode for each new file, so you always have a consistent entry point.

Basic Functions

PHP has a vast number of built-in functions that enable you to manipulate strings, connect to databases, and more. There is not room here to cover even 10% of the functions; for more detailed coverage of functions, check the "Reference" section at the end of this chapter.

Strings

Several important functions are used for working with strings, and there are many less frequently used ones for which there is not enough space here. We look at the most important here, ordered by difficulty—easiest first!

The easiest function is `strlen()`, which takes a string as its parameter and returns the number of characters in there, like this:

```php
<?php
  $ourstring = "  The Quick Brown Box Jumped Over The Lazy Dog  ";
  echo strlen($ourstring);
?>
```

27

We will use that same string in subsequent examples to save space. If you execute that script, it outputs 48 because 48 characters are in the string. Note the two spaces on either side of the text, which pad the 44-character phrase up to 48 characters.

We can fix that padding with the `trim()` function, which takes a string to trim and returns it with all the whitespace removed from either side. This is a commonly used function because all too often you encounter strings that have an extra new line at the end or a space at the beginning. This cleans it up perfectly.

Using `trim()`, we can turn the 48-character string into a 44-character string (the same thing, without the extra spaces), like this:

```php
echo trim($ourstring);
```

Keep in mind that trim() returns the trimmed string, so that it outputs "The Quick Brown Box Jumped Over The Lazy Dog". We can modify it so that trim() passes its return value to strlen() so that the code trims it and then outputs its trimmed length:

```
echo strlen(trim($ourstring));
```

PHP always executes the innermost functions first, so the previous code takes $ourstring, passes it through trim(), uses the return value of trim() as the parameter for strlen(), and prints it.

Of course, everyone knows that boxes do not jump over dogs—the usual phrase is "the quick brown fox." Fortunately, there is a function to fix that problem: str_replace(). Note that it has an underscore in it; PHP is inconsistent on this matter, so you really need to memorize the function name.

The str_replace() function takes three parameters: the text to search for, the text to replace it with, and the string you want to work with. When working with search functions, people often talk about *needles* and *haystacks*—in this situation, the first parameter is the needle (the thing to find), and the third parameter is the haystack (what you are searching through).

So, we can fix our error and correct *box* to *fox* with this code:

```
echo str_replace("Box", "Fox", $ourstring);
```

There are two little addendums to make here. First, note that we have specified "Box" as opposed to "box" because that is how it appears in the text. The str_replace() function is a *case-sensitive* function, which means it does not consider "Box" to be the same as "box". If you want to do a search and replace that is not case sensitive, you can use the stri_replace() function, which works in the same way.

The second addendum is that because we are actually changing only one character (*B* to *F*), we need not use a function at all. PHP enables you to read (and change) individual characters of a string by specifying the character position inside braces ({ and }). As with arrays, strings are zero-based, which means in the $ourstring variable $ourstring{0} is *T*, $ourstring{1} is *h*, $ourstring{2} is *e*, and so on. We could use this instead of str_replace(), like this:

```
<?php
    $ourstring = "  The Quick Brown Box Jumped Over The Lazy Dog  ";
    $ourstring{18} = "F";
    echo $ourstring;
?>
```

You can extract part of a string by using the substr() function, which takes a string as its first parameter, a start position as its second parameter, and an optional length as its third parameter. Optional parameters are common in PHP. If you do not provide them, PHP assumes a default value. In this case, if you specify only the first two parameters, PHP copies from the start position to the end of the string. If you specify the third parameter, PHP copies that many characters from the start.

We can write a simple script to print `"Lazy Dog   "` by setting the start position to 38, which, remembering that PHP starts counting string positions from 0, copies from the 39th character to the end of the string:

```
echo substr($ourstring, 38);
```

If we just want to print the word `"Lazy"`, we need to use the optional third parameter to specify the length as 4, like this:

```
echo substr($ourstring, 38, 4);
```

The `substr()` function can also be used with negative second and third parameters. If you specify just parameter one and two and provide a negative number for parameter two, `substr()` counts backward from the end of the string. Rather than specifying 38 for the second parameter, we can use –10 so that it takes the last 10 characters from the string. Using a negative second parameter and positive third parameter counts backward from the end string and then uses a forward length. We can print `"Lazy"` by counting 10 characters back from the end and then taking the next four characters forward:

```
echo substr($ourstring, -10, 4);
```

Finally, we can use a negative third parameter, too, which also counts back from the end of the string. For example, using `"-4"` as the third parameter means to take everything except the last four characters. Confused yet? This code example should make it clear:

```
echo substr($ourstring, -19, -11);
```

That counts 19 characters backward from the end of the string (which places it at the *O* in Over) and then copies everything from there until 11 characters before the end of the string. That prints `"Over The"`. The same thing could be written using –19 and 8, or even 29 and 8—there is more than one way to do it!

Moving on, the `strpos()` function returns the position of a particular substring inside a string; however, it is most commonly used to answer the question, "Does this string contain a specific substring?" You need to pass it two parameters: a haystack and a needle (yes, that's a different order from `str_replace()`!).

In its most basic use, `strpos()` can find the first instance of `"Box"` in our phrase, like this:

```
echo strpos($ourstring, "Box");
```

This outputs 18 because that is where the *B* in Box starts. If `strpos()` cannot find the substring in the parent string, it returns `false` rather than the position. Much more helpful, though, is the ability to check whether a string contains a substring; a first attempt to check whether our string contains the word *The* might look like this:

```php
<?php
  $ourstring = "The Quick Brown Box Jumped Over The Lazy Dog";
  if (strpos($ourstring, "The")) {
    echo "Found 'The'!\n";
  } else {
    echo "'The' not found!\n";
  }
?>
```

Note that we have temporarily taken out the leading and trailing whitespace from $ourstring and we are using the return value of strpos() for the conditional statement. This reads, "If the string is found, print a message; if not, print another message." Or does it?

Run the script, and you will see it print the "not found" message. The reason for this is that strpos() returns false if the substring is not found and otherwise returns the position where it starts. If you recall, any nonzero number equates to true in PHP, which means that 0 equates to false. With that in mind, what is the string index of the first *The* in the phrase? Because PHP's strings are zero-based and we no longer have the spaces on either side of the string, the *The* is at position 0, which the conditional statement evaluates to false—hence, the problem.

The solution here is to check for identicality. You know that 0 and false are equal, but they are not identical because 0 is an integer, whereas false is a Boolean. So, we need to rewrite the conditional statement to see whether the return value from strpos() is identical to false. If it is, the substring is not found:

```php
<?php
  $ourstring = "The Quick Brown Box Jumped Over The Lazy Dog";
  if (strpos($ourstring, "The") !== false) {
    echo "Found 'The'!\n";
  } else {
    echo "'The' not found!\n";
  }
?>
```

Arrays

Working with arrays is no easy task, but PHP makes it easier by providing a selection of functions that can sort, shuffle, intersect, and filter them. As with other functions, there is only space here to choose a selection; this is by no means a definitive reference to PHP's array functions.

The easiest function to use is array_unique(), which takes an array as its only parameter and returns the same array with all duplicate values removed. Also in the realm of "so easy you do not need a code example" is the `shuffle()` function, which takes an array as its parameter and randomizes the order of its elements. Note that `shuffle()` does not return the randomized array; it uses the actual parameter you pass and scrambles it directly. The last too-easy-to-demonstrate function is `in_array()`, which takes a value as its first parameter and an array as its second and returns `true` if the value is in the array.

With those out of the way, we can focus on the more interesting functions, two of which are `array_keys()` and `array_values()`. They both take an array as their only parameter and return a new array made up of the keys in the array or the values of the array, respectively. The `array_values()` function is an easy way to create a new array of the same data, just without the keys. This is often used if you have numbered your array keys, deleted several elements, and want to reorder it.

The `array_keys()` function creates a new array where the values are the keys from the old array, like this:

```php
<?php
  $myarr = array("foo" => "red", "bar" => "blue", "baz" => "green");
  $mykeys = array_keys($myarr);
  foreach($mykeys as $key => $value) {
    echo "$key = $value\n";
  }
?>
```

That prints "`0 = foo`", "`1 = bar`", and "`2 = baz`".

Several functions are used specifically for array sorting, but only two get much use: `asort()` and `ksort()`, the first of which sorts the array by its values and the second of which sorts the array by its keys. Given the array $myarr from the previous example, sorting by the values would produce an array with elements in the order bar/blue, baz/green, and foo/red. Sorting by key would give the elements in the order bar/blue, baz/green, and foo/red. As with the `shuffle()` function, both `asort()` and `ksort()` do their work *in place*, meaning they return no value, directly altering the parameter you pass in. For interest's sake, you can also use `arsort()` and `krsort()` for reverse value sorting and reverse key sorting, respectively.

This code example reverse sorts the array by value and then prints it as before:

```php
<?php
  $myarr = array("foo" => "red", "bar" => "blue", "baz" => "green");
  arsort($myarr);
  foreach($myarr as $key => $value) {
    echo "$key = $value\n";
  }
?>
```

Previously when discussing constants, we mentioned the `extract()` function that converts an array into individual variables; now it is time to start using it for real. You

27

need to provide three variables: the array you want to extract, how you want the variables prefixed, and the prefix you want used. Technically, the last two parameters are optional, but practically you should always use them to properly namespace your variables and keep them organized.

The second parameter must be one of the following:

▶ EXTR_OVERWRITE—If the variable exists already, overwrites it.

▶ EXTR_SKIP—If the variable exists already, skips it and moves onto the next variable.

▶ EXTR_PREFIX_SAME—If the variable exists already, uses the prefix specified in the third parameter.

▶ EXTR_PREFIX_ALL—Prefixes all variables with the prefix in the third parameter, regardless of whether it exists already.

▶ EXTR_PREFIX_INVALID—Uses a prefix only if the variable name would be invalid (for example, starting with a number).

▶ EXTR_IF_EXISTS—Extracts only variables that already exist. We have never seen this used.

This next script uses extract() to convert $myarr into individual variables, $arr_foo, $arr_bar, and $arr_baz:

```php
<?php
  $myarr = array("foo" => "red", "bar" => "blue", "baz" => "green");
  extract($myarr, EXTR_PREFIX_ALL, 'arr');
?>
```

Note that the array keys are "foo", "bar", and "baz" and that the prefix is "arr", but that the final variables will be $arr_foo, $arr_bar, and $arr_baz. PHP inserts an underscore between the prefix and array key.

Files

As you will have learned from elsewhere in the book, the Unix philosophy is that everything is a file. In PHP, this is also the case: A selection of basic file functions is suitable for opening and manipulating files, but those same functions can also be used for opening and manipulating network sockets. We cover both here.

Two basic read and write functions for files make performing these basic operations easy. They are file_get_contents(), which takes a filename as its only parameter and returns the file's contents as a string, and file_put_contents(), which takes a filename as its first parameter and the data to write as its second parameter.

Using these two, we can write a script that reads all the text from one file, filea.txt, and writes it to another, fileb.txt:

```php
<?php
  $text = file_get_contents("filea.txt");
  file_put_contents("fileb.txt", $text);
?>
```

Because PHP enables us to treat network sockets like files, we can also use `file_get_contents()` to read text from a website, like this:

```php
<?php
  $text = file_get_contents("http://www.slashdot.org");
  file_put_contents("fileb.txt", $text);
?>
```

The problem with using `file_get_contents()` is that it loads the whole file into memory at once; that's not practical if you have large files or even smaller files being accessed by many users. An alternative is to load the file piece by piece, which can be accomplished through the following five functions: `fopen()`, `fclose()`, `fread()`, `fwrite()`, and `feof()`. The *f* in those function names stands for *file*, so they open, close, read from, and write to files and sockets. The last function, `feof()`, returns `true` if the end of the file has been reached.

The `fopen()` function takes a bit of learning to use properly, but on the surface it looks straightforward. Its first parameter is the filename you want to open, which is easy enough. However, the second parameter is where you specify how you want to work with the file, and you should specify one of the following:

- ▶ r—Read only; it overwrites the file
- ▶ r+—Reading and writing; it overwrites the file
- ▶ w—Write only; it erases the existing contents and overwrites the file
- ▶ w+—Reading and writing; it erases the existing content and overwrites the file
- ▶ a—Write only; it appends to the file
- ▶ a+—Reading and writing; it appends to the file
- ▶ x—Write only, but only if the file does not exist
- ▶ a+—Reading and writing, but only if the file does not exist

Optionally, you can also add b (for example, a+b or rb) to switch to binary mode. This is recommended if you want your scripts and the files they write to work smoothly on other platforms.

When you call `fopen()`, you should store the return value. It is a resource known as a *file handle*, which the other file functions all need to do their jobs. The `fread()` function, for example, takes the file handle as its first parameter and the number of bytes to read as its second, returning the content in its return value. The `fclose()` function takes the file handle as its only parameter and frees up the file.

27

So, we can write a simple loop to open a file, read it piece by piece, print the pieces, and then close the handle:

```php
<?php
  $file = fopen("filea.txt", "rb");
  while (!feof($file)) {
    $content = fread($file, 1024);
    echo $content;
  }
  fclose($file);
?>
```

That leaves only the fwrite() function, which takes the file handle as its first parameter and the string to write as its second. You can also provide an integer as the third parameter, specifying the number of bytes you want to write of the string, but if you exclude this, fwrite() writes the entire string.

If you recall, you can use a as the second parameter to fopen() to append data to a file. So we can combine that with fwrite() to have a script that adds a line of text to a file each time it is executed:

```php
<?php
  $file = fopen("filea.txt", "ab");
  fwrite($file, "Testing\n");
  fclose($file);
?>
```

To make that script a little more exciting, we can stir in a new function, filesize(), that takes a filename (not a file handle, but an actual filename string) as its only parameter and returns the file's size in bytes. Using that new function brings the script to this:

```php
<?php
  $file = fopen("filea.txt", "ab");
  fwrite($file, "The filesize was" . filesize("filea.txt") . "\n");
  fclose($file);
?>
```

Although PHP automatically cleans up file handles for you, it is still best to use fclose() yourself so that you are always in control.

Miscellaneous

Several functions do not fall under the other categories and so are covered here. The first one is isset(), which takes one or more variables as its parameters and returns true if they have been set. It is important to note that a variable with a value set to something that would be evaluated to false—such as 0 or an empty string—still returns true from isset() because it does not check the value of the variable. It merely checks that it is set; hence, the name.

The unset() function also takes one or more variables as its parameters, simply deleting the variable and freeing up the memory. With these two, we can write a script that checks for the existence of a variable and, if it exists, deletes it (see Listing 27.5).

LISTING 27.5   Setting and Unsetting Variables

```php
<?php
  $name = "Ildiko";
  if (isset($name)) {
    echo "Name was set to $name\n";
    unset($name);
  } else {
    echo "Name was not set";
  }

  if (isset($name)) {
    echo "Name was set to $name\n";
    unset($name);
  } else {
    echo "Name was not set";
  }
?>
```

That script runs the same isset() check twice, but it unset()s the variable after the first check. As such, it prints "Name was set to Ildiko" and then "Name was not set".

Perhaps the most frequently used function in PHP is exit, although purists will tell you that it is in fact a language construct rather than a function. exit terminates the processing of the script as soon as it is executed, meaning subsequent lines of code are not executed. That is really all there is to it; it barely deserves an example, but here is one just to make sure you understand it:

```php
<?php
  exit;
  echo "Exit is a language construct!\n";
?>
```

That script prints nothing because the exit comes before the echo.

One function we can guarantee you will use often is var_dump(), which dumps out information about a variable, including its value, to the screen. This is invaluable for arrays because it prints every value and, if one or more of the elements is an array, it prints all the elements from those, and so on. To use this function, just pass it a variable as its only parameter:

```php
<?php
  $drones = array("Graham", "Julian", "Nick", "Paul");
  var_dump($drones);
?>
```

The output from that script looks like this:

```
array(4) {
  [0]=>
  string(6) "Graham"
  [1]=>
  string(6) "Julian"
  [2]=>
  string(4) "Nick"
  [3]=>
  string(4) "Paul"
}
```

The var_dump() function sees a lot of use as a basic debugging technique because it is the easiest way to print variable data to the screen to verify it.

Finally, we briefly discuss regular expressions, with the emphasis on *briefly* because regular expression syntax is covered elsewhere in this book and the only unique thing relevant to PHP are the functions you will use to run the expressions. You have the choice of either Perl-Compatible Regular Expressions (PCRE) or POSIX Extended regular expressions, but there really is little to differentiate between them in terms of functionality offered. For this chapter, we use the PCRE expressions because, to the best of our knowledge, they see more use by other PHP programmers.

The main PCRE functions are preg_match(), preg_match_all(), preg_replace(), and preg_split(). We start with preg_match() because it provides the most basic functionality by returning true if one string matches a regular expression. The first parameter to preg_match() is the regular expression you want to search for, and the second is the string to match. So, if we wanted to check whether a string had the word *Best, Test, rest, zest,* or any other word containing *est* preceded by any letter of either case, we could use this PHP code:

```php
$result = preg_match("/[A-Za-z]est/", "This is a test");
```

Because the test string matches the expression, $result is set to 1 (true). If you change the string to a nonmatching result, you get 0 as the return value.

The next function is preg_match_all(), which gives you an array of all the matches it found. However, to be most useful, it takes the array to fill with matches as a by-reference parameter and saves its return value for the number of matches that were found.

We suggest you use preg_match_all() and var_dump() to get a feel for how the function works. This example is a good place to start:

```php
<?php
  $string = "This is the best test in the West";
  $result = preg_match_all("/[A-Za-z]est/", $string, $matches);
  var_dump($matches);
?>
```

That outputs the following:

```
array(1) {
  [0]=>
  array(3) {
    [0]=>
    string(4) "best"
    [1]=>
    string(4) "test"
    [2]=>
    string(4) "West"
  }
}
```

If you notice, the $matches array is actually multidimensional in that it contains one element, which itself is an array containing all the matches to our regular expression. The reason is that our expression has no *subexpressions*, meaning no independent matches using parentheses. If we had subexpressions, each would have its own element in the $matches array containing its own array of matches.

Moving on, preg_replace() is used to change all substrings that match a regular expression into something else. The basic manner of using this is quite easy: You search for something with a regular expression and provide a replacement for it. However, a more useful variant is *backreferencing*; that is, using the match as part of the replacement. For this example, imagine you have written a tutorial on PHP but want to process the text so that each reference to a function is followed by a link to the PHP manual.

PHP manual page URLs take the form http://www.php.net/*<somefunc>*—for example, http://www.php.net/preg_replace. The string to match is a function name, which is a string of alphabetic characters, potentially also mixed with numbers and underscores and terminated with two parentheses, (). As a replacement, we will use the match we found, surrounded in HTML emphasis tags (<em></em>), and then with a link to the relevant PHP manual page. Here is how that looks in code:

```php
<?php
  $regex = "/([A-Za-z0-9_]*)\(\)/";
  $replace = "<em>$1</em> (<a href=\"http://www.php.net/$1\">manual</A>)";
  $haystack = "File_get_contents()is easier than using fopen().";
```

```
  $result = preg_replace($regex, $replace, $haystack);
  echo $result;
?>
```

The $1 is our backreference; it will be substituted with the results from the first subexpression. The way we have written the regular expression is very exact. The [A-Za-z0-9_]* part, which matches the function name, is marked as a subexpression. After that is \(\), which means the exact symbols (and), not the regular expression meanings of them, which means that $1 in the replacement will contain fopen rather than fopen(), which is how it should be. Of course, anything that is not backreferenced in the replacement is removed, so we have to put the () after the first $1 (not in the hyperlink) to repair the function name.

After all that work, the output is perfect:

```
<em>File_get_contents()</em> (<a href="http://www.php.net/
file_get_contents">manual</A>) is easier than using <em>fopen()
</em> (<a href="http://www.php.net/fopen">manual</A>).
```

Handling HTML Forms

Given that PHP's primary role is handling web pages, you might wonder why this section has been left so late in the chapter. It is because handling HTML forms is so central to PHP that it is essentially automatic.

Consider this form:

```
<form method="POST" action="thispage.php">
User ID: <input type="text" name="UserID" /><br />
Password: <input type="password" name="Password" /><br />
<input type="submit" />
</form>
```

When a visitor clicks the Submit button, thispage.php is called again and this time PHP has the variables available to it inside the $_REQUEST array. Given that script, if the user enters 12345 and frosties as her user ID and password, PHP provides you with $_REQUEST['UserID'] set to 12345 and $_REQUEST['Password'] set to frosties. Note that it is important that you use HTTP POST unless you specifically want GET. POST enables you to send a great deal more data and stops people from tampering with your URL to try to find holes in your script.

Is that it? Well, almost. That tells you how to retrieve user data, but be sure to sanitize it so that users do not try to sneak HTML or JavaScript into your database as something you think is innocuous. PHP gives you the strip_tags() function for this purpose. It takes a string and returns the same string with all HTML tags removed.

Reference

Being as popular as it is, PHP gets a lot of coverage on the Internet. The best place to look for information, though, is the PHP online manual, at http://www.php.net/. It is comprehensive, well-written, and updated regularly:

▶ **http://www.phpbuilder.net/**—A large PHP scripts and tutorials site where you can learn new techniques and also chat with other PHP developers.

▶ **http://www.zend.com/**—The home page of a company founded by two of the key developers of PHP. Zend develops and sells proprietary software, including a powerful IDE and a code cache, to aid PHP developers.

▶ **http://pear.php.net/**—The home of the PEAR project contains a large collection of software you can download and try, and the site has thorough documentation for it all.

▶ **http://www.phparch.com/**—There are quite a few good PHP magazines around, but *PHP Architect* probably leads the way. It posts some of its articles online for free, and its forums are good, too.

Quality books on PHP abound, and you are certainly spoiled for choice. For beginning developers, the best available is *PHP and MySQL Web Development* (Sams Publishing), ISBN 0-672-32672-8. For a concise, to-the-point book covering all aspects of PHP, check out *PHP in a Nutshell* (O'Reilly). Finally, for advanced developers, you can consult *Advanced PHP Programming* (Sams Publishing), ISBN 0-672-32561-6.

27

CHAPTER 28

C/C++ Programming Tools for Fedora

If you're looking to learn C or C++ programming, this part of the book isn't the right place to start—unlike Perl, Python, PHP, or even C#, it takes more than a little dabbling to produce something productive with C, so this chapter is primarily focused on the tools Fedora offers you as a C or C++ programmer.

Whether you're looking to compile your own code or someone else's, the GNU Compiler Collection (gcc) is there to help—it understands C, C++, Fortran, Pascal, and dozens of other popular languages, which means you can try your hand at whatever interests you. Fedora also ships with hundreds of libraries you can link to, from the GUI toolkits behind GNOME and KDE to XML parsing and game coding. Some use C, others C++, and still others offer support for both, meaning you can choose what you're most comfortable with.

Programming in C/C++ with Linux

C is the programming language most frequently associated with Unix-like operating systems such as Linux or BSD. Since the 1970s, the bulk of the Unix operating system and its applications have been written in C. Because the C language doesn't directly rely on any specific hardware architecture, Unix was one of the first portable operating systems. In other words, the majority of the code that makes up Unix doesn't know and doesn't care on which computer it is actually running. Machine-specific features are isolated in a few modules within the Unix kernel, which makes it easy for you to modify them when you are porting to different hardware architectures.

C is a *compiled* language, which means that your C source code is first analyzed by the *preprocessor*. It is then translated into assembly language and then into machine instructions that are appropriate to the target CPU. An assembler then creates a binary, or *object*, file from the machine instructions. Finally, the object file is linked to any required external software support by the *linker*. A C program is stored in a text file that ends with a .c extension and always contains at least one routine, or function, such as main(), unless the file is an *include* file (with an .h extension—also known as a *header* file) containing shared variable definitions or other data or declarations. *Functions* are the commands that perform each step of the task that the C program was written to accomplish.

> **NOTE**
>
> The Linux kernel is mostly written in C, which is why Linux works with so many different CPUs. To learn more about building the Linux kernel from source, see Chapter 36, "Kernel and Module Management."

C++ is an object-oriented extension to C. Because C++ is a superset of C, C++ compilers compile C programs correctly, and it is possible to write non–object-oriented code in C++. The reverse is not true: C compilers cannot compile C++ code.

C++ extends the capabilities of C by providing the necessary features for object-oriented design and code. C++ also provides some features, such as the capability to associate functions with data structures, that do not require the use of class-based object-oriented techniques. For these reasons, the C++ language enables existing Unix programs to migrate toward the adoption of object orientation over time.

Support for C++ programming using Fedora is provided by gcc, which you run with the name g++ when you are compiling C++ code.

Using the C Programming Project Management Tools Provided with Fedora Linux

Fedora is replete with tools that make your life as a C/C++ programmer easier. There are tools to create programs (editors), compile programs (gcc), create libraries (ar), control the source (Subversion), automate builds (make), debug programs (gdb and ddd), and determine where inefficiencies lie (gprof).

The following sections introduce some of the programming and project management tools included with Fedora. The DVD included with this book contains many of these tools, which you can use to help automate software development projects. If you have some previous Unix experience, you will be familiar with most of these programs because they are traditional complements to a programmer's suite of software.

Building Programs with make

You use the make command to automatically build and install a C program, and for that use it is an easy tool. If you want to create your own automated builds, however, you need to learn the special syntax that make uses; the following sections walk you through a basic make setup.

Using Makefiles

The make command automatically builds and updates applications by using a makefile. A *makefile* is a text file that contains instructions about which options to pass on to the compiler preprocessor, the compiler, the assembler, and the linker. The makefile also specifies, among other things, which source code files have to be compiled (and the compiler command line) for a particular code module and which code modules are required to build the program—a mechanism called *dependency checking*.

The beauty of the make command is its flexibility. You can use make with a simple makefile, or you can write complex makefiles that contain numerous macros, rules, or commands that work in a single directory or traverse your file system recursively to build programs, update your system, and even function as document management systems. The make command works with nearly any program, including text processing systems such as TeX.

You could use make to compile, build, and install a software package, using a simple command like this:

```
# make install
```

You can use the default makefile (usually called Makefile, with a capital *M*), or you can use make's -f option to specify any makefile, such as MyMakeFile, like this:

```
# make -f MyMakeFile
```

Other options might be available, depending on the contents of your makefile.

Using Macros and Makefile Targets

Using make with macros can make a program portable. Macros enable users of other operating systems to easily configure a program build by specifying local values, such as the names and locations, or *pathnames*, of any required software tools. In the following example, macros define the name of the compiler (CC), the installer program (INS), where the program should be installed (INSDIR), where the linker should look for required libraries (LIBDIR), the names of required libraries (LIBS), a source code file (SRC), the intermediate object code file (OBS), and the name of the final program (PROG):

```
# a sample makefile for a skeleton program
CC= gcc
INS= install
INSDIR= /usr/local/bin
LIBDIR= -L/usr/X11R6/lib
LIBS= -lXm -lSM -lICE -lXt -lX11
SRC= skel.c
OBJS= skel.o
PROG= skel
```

28

```
skel:   ${OBJS}
        ${CC} -o ${PROG} ${SRC} ${LIBDIR} ${LIBS}

install: ${PROG}
        ${INS} -g root -o root ${PROG} ${INSDIR}
```

NOTE

The indented lines in the previous example are indented with tabs, not spaces. This is very important to remember! It is difficult for a person to see the difference, but make can tell. If make reports confusing errors when you first start building programs under Linux, you should check your project's makefile for the use of tabs and other proper formatting.

Using the makefile from the preceding example, you can build a program like this:

```
# make
```

To build a specified component of a makefile, you can use a target definition on the command line. To build just the program, you use make with the skel target, like this:

```
# make skel
```

If you make any changes to any element of a target object, such as a source code file, make rebuilds the target automatically. This feature is part of the convenience of using make to manage a development project. To build and install a program in one step, you can specify the target of install like this:

```
# make install
```

Larger software projects might have a number of traditional targets in the makefile, such as the following:

▶ test—To run specific tests on the final software

▶ man—To process an include or a troff document with the man macros

▶ clean—To delete any remaining object files

▶ archive—To clean up, archive, and compress the entire source code tree

▶ bugreport—To automatically collect and then mail a copy of the build or error logs

Large applications can require hundreds of source code files. Compiling and linking these applications can be a complex and error-prone task. The make utility helps you organize the process of building the executable form of a complex application from many source files.

Using the `autoconf` Utility to Configure Code

The `make` command is only one of several programming automation utilities included with Fedora. There are others, such as `pmake` (which causes a parallel make), `imake` (which is a dependency-driven makefile generator that is used for building X11 clients), `automake`, and one of the newer tools, `autoconf`, which builds shell scripts that can be used to configure program source code packages.

Building many software packages for Linux that are distributed in source form requires the use of GNU's `autoconf` utility. This program builds an executable shell script named `configure` that, when executed, automatically examines and tailors a client's build from source according to software resources, or *dependencies* (such as programming tools, libraries, and associated utilities) that are installed on the target host (your Linux system).

Many Linux commands and graphical clients for X downloaded in source code form include `configure` scripts. To configure the source package, build the software, and then install the new program, the `root` user might use the script like this (after uncompressing the source and navigating into the resulting build directory):

```
# ./configure ; make ; make install
```

The `autoconf` program uses a file named `configure.in` that contains a basic *ruleset*, or set of macros. The `configure.in` file is created with the `autoscan` command. Building a properly executing `configure` script also requires a template for the makefile, named `Makefile.in`. Although creating the dependency-checking `configure` script can be done manually, you can easily overcome any complex dependencies by using a graphical project development tool such as KDE's KDevelop or GNOME's Glade. (See the "Graphical Development Tools" section, later in this chapter, for more information.)

Managing Software Projects with Subversion

Although `make` can be used to manage a software project, larger software projects require document management, source code controls, security, and revision tracking as the source code goes through a series of changes during its development. Subversion provides source code version control utilities for this kind of large software project management.

The Subversion system is used to track changes to multiple versions of files, and it can be used to backtrack or branch off versions of documents inside the scope of a project. It can also be used to prevent or resolve conflicting entries or changes made to source code files by multiple developers. Source code control with Subversion requires the use of at least the following five command options on the `svn` command line:

- **checkout**—Checks out revisions
- **update**—Updates your sources with changes made by other developers
- **add**—Adds new files to the repository
- **delete**—Eliminates files from the repository
- **commit**—Publishes changes to other repository developers

28

Note that some of these commands require you to use additional fields, such as the names of files. With the commit command, you should always try to pass the -m parameter (lets you provide a message describing the change) followed by some information about your changes. For example:

```
svn commit -m "This fixes bug 204982."
```

One of the most impressive features of Subversion is its ability to work offline—any local Subversion checkout automatically has a .svn directory hidden in there, which contains copies of all checked out files. Thanks to this, you can check your current files against the ones you checked out without having to contact the server—it all runs locally.

Debugging Tools

Debugging is both a science and an art. Sometimes, the simplest tool—the code listing—is the best debugging tool. At other times, however, you need to use other debugging tools. Three of these tools are splint, gprof, and gdb.

Using splint to Check Source Code

The splint command is similar to the traditional Unix lint command: It statically examines source code for possible problems, and it also has many additional features. Even if your C code meets the standards for C and compiles cleanly, it might still contain errors. splint performs many types of checks and can provide extensive error information. For example, this simple program might compile cleanly and even run:

```
$ gcc -o tux tux.c
$ ./tux
```

But the splint command might point out some serious problems with the source:

```
$ splint tux.c
Splint 3.1.1 --- 17 Feb 2004

tux.c: (in function main)
tux.c:2:19: Return value (type int) ignored: putchar(t[++j] -...
  Result returned by function call is not used. If this is intended, can cast
  result to (void) to eliminate message. (Use -retvalint to inhibit warning)
Finished checking --- 1 code warning
```

You can use the splint command's -strict option, like this, to get a more verbose report:

```
$ splint -strict tux.c
```

GCC also supports diagnostics through the use of extensive warnings (through the -Wall and -pedantic options):

```
$ gcc -Wall tux.c
tux.c:1: warning: return type defaults to `int'
tux.c: In function `main':
tux.c:2: warning: implicit declaration of function `putchar'
```

Using gprof to Track Function Time

You use the gprof (profile) command to study how a program is spending its time. If a program is compiled and linked with -p as a flag, a mon.out file is created when it executes, with data on how often each function is called and how much time is spent in each function. gprof parses and displays this data. An analysis of the output generated by gprof helps you determine where performance bottlenecks occur. Using an optimizing compiler can speed up a program, but taking the time to use gprof's analysis and revising bottleneck functions significantly improves program performance.

Doing Symbolic Debugging with gdb

The gdb tool is a symbolic debugger. When a program is compiled with the -g flag, the symbol tables are retained and a symbolic debugger can be used to track program bugs. The basic technique is to invoke gdb after a *core dump* (a file containing a snapshot of the memory used by a program that has crashed) and get a stack trace. The stack trace indicates the source line where the core dump occurred and the functions that were called to reach that line. Often, this is enough to identify a problem. It isn't the limit of gdb, though.

gdb also provides an environment for debugging programs interactively. Invoking gdb with a program enables you to set breakpoints, examine the values of variables, and monitor variables. If you suspect a problem near a line of code, you can set a breakpoint at that line and run gdb. When the line is reached, execution is interrupted. You can check variable values, examine the stack trace, and observe the program's environment. You can single-step through the program to check values. You can resume execution at any point. By using breakpoints, you can discover many bugs in code.

A graphical X Window System interface to gdb is called the Data Display Debugger, or ddd.

28

Using the GNU C Compiler

If you elected to install the development tools package when you installed Fedora 7 (or perhaps later on, using RPM or other package tools), you should have the GNU C compiler (gcc). Many different options are available for the GNU C compiler, and many of them are similar to those of the C and C++ compilers that are available on other Unix systems. Look at the man page or information file for gcc for a full list of options and descriptions.

When you use gcc to build a C program, the compilation process takes place in several steps:

1. First, the C preprocessor parses the file. To do so, it sequentially reads the lines, includes header files, and performs macro replacement.

2. The compiler parses the modified code to determine whether the correct syntax is used. In the process, it builds a symbol table and creates an intermediate object format. Most symbols have specific memory addresses assigned, although symbols defined in other modules, such as external variables, do not.

3. The last compilation stage, linking, ties together different files and libraries and then links the files by resolving the symbols that had not previously been resolved.

> **NOTE**
>
> Most C programs compile with a C++ compiler if you follow strict ANSI rules. For example, you can compile the standard hello.c program (everyone's first program) with the GNU C++ compiler. Typically, you name the file something like hello.cc, hello.C, hello.c++, or hello.cxx. The GNU C++ compiler accepts any of these names.

Graphical Development Tools

Fedora includes a number of graphical prototyping and development environments for use during X sessions. If you want to build client software for KDE or GNOME, you might find the KDevelop and Glade programs extremely helpful. You can use each of these programs to build graphical frameworks for interactive windowing clients, and you can use each of them to automatically generate the necessary skeleton of code needed to support a custom interface for your program.

Using the KDevelop Client

You can launch the KDevelop client (shown in Figure 28.1) from the desktop panel's start menu's Extras, Programming menu item or from the command line of a terminal window, like this:

```
$ kdevelop &
```

After you press Enter, the KDevelop Setup Wizard runs, and you are taken through several short wizard dialogs that set up and ensure a stable build environment. You must then run kdevelop again (either from the command line or by clicking its menu item under the desktop panel's Programming menu). You will then see the main KDevelop window and can start your project by selecting KDevelop's Project menu and clicking the New menu item.

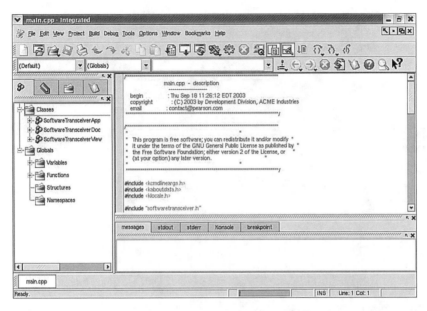

FIGURE 28.1   KDE's KDevelop is a rapid prototyping and client-building tool for use with Linux.

You can begin building your project by stepping through the wizard dialogs. When you click the Create button, KDevelop automatically generates all the files that are normally found in a KDE client source directory (including the `configure` script, which checks dependencies and builds the client's makefile). To test your client, you can either first click the Build menu's Make menu item (or press F8) or just click the Execute menu item (or press F9), and the client is built automatically. You can use KDevelop to create KDE clients, plug-ins for the `konqueror` browser, KDE `kicker` panel applets, KDE desktop themes, Qt library–based clients, and even programs for GNOME.

The Glade Client for Developing in GNOME

If you prefer to use GNOME and its development tools, the Glade GTK+ GUI builder can save you time and effort when building a basic skeleton for a program. You launch Glade from the desktop panel's Programming menu.

When you launch Glade, a directory named `Projects` is created in your home directory, and you see a main window, along with two floating palette and properties windows (see Figure 28.2, which shows a basic GNOME client with a calendar widget added to its main window). You can use Glade's File menu to save the blank project and then start building your client by clicking and adding user interface elements from the Palette window. For example, you can first click the Palette window's Gnome button and then click to create your new client's main window. A window with a menu and a toolbar appears—the basic framework for a new GNOME client!

28

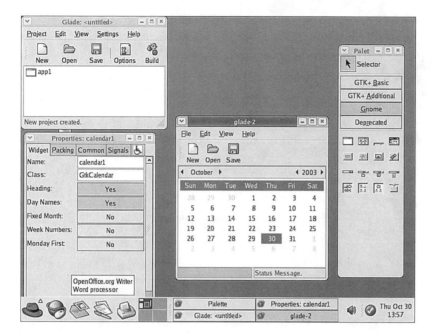

FIGURE 28.2   Glade is 100% backward compatible, which means Glade 2 can read Glade 3 interfaces, and vice versa.

Related Fedora and Linux Commands

You will use many of these commands when programming in C and C++ for Linux:

- **ar**—The GNU archive development tool
- **as**—The GNU assembler
- **autoconf**—The GNU configuration script generator
- **cervisia**—A KDE client that provides a graphical interface to a CVS project
- **cvs**—An older project revision control system, now replaced by Subversion
- **designer**—Trolltech's graphical prototyping tool for use with Qt libraries and X
- **gcc**—The GNU C/C++ compiler system
- **gdb**—The GNU interactive debugger
- **glade-3**—The GNOME graphical development environment for building GTK+ clients
- **gprof**—The GNU program profiler
- **kdevelop**—The KDE C/C++ graphical development environment for building KDE, GNOME, or terminal clients
- **make**—A GNU project management command
- **patch**—Larry Wall's source patching utility
- **pmake**—A BSD project management command
- **splint**—The C source file checker
- **svn**—The Subversion version control system

Reference

▶ **http://www.trolltech.com/products/qt/tools.html**—Trolltech's page for Qt Designer and a number of programming automation tools (including translators) that you can use with Fedora.

▶ **http://glade.gnome.org**—Home page for the Glade GNOME developer's tool.

▶ **http://www.kdevelop.org**—Site that hosts the KDevelop Project's latest versions of the KDE graphical development environment, KDevelop.

▶ *Sams Teach Yourself C++ for Linux in 21 Days*, by Jesse Liberty and David B. Horvath, Sams Publishing.

▶ *C How to Program* and *C++ How to Program*, both by Harvey M. Deitel and Paul J. Deitel, Deitel Associates.

▶ *The Annotated C++ Reference Manual*, by Margaret A. Ellis and Bjarne Stroustrup, ANSI Base Document.

▶ *Programming in ANSI C*, by Stephen G. Kochan, Sams Publishing.

Although Microsoft intended it for Windows, Microsoft's .NET platform has grown to encompass many other operating systems. No, this isn't a rare sign of Microsoft letting customers choose which OS is best for them—instead, the spread of .NET is because of the Mono project, which is a free re-implementation of .NET available under the GPL license.

Because of the potential for patent complications, it took Red Hat a long time to incorporate Mono into Fedora, but it's here now and works just fine. What's more, Mono supports both C# and Visual Basic .NET, as well as the complete .NET 1.0 and 1.1 frameworks (and much of the 2.0 framework too), making it quick to learn and productive to use.

Why Use Mono?

Linux already has numerous programming languages available to it, so why bother with Mono and .NET? Here are my top five reasons:

▶ .NET is "compile once, run anywhere"; that means you can compile your code on Linux and run it on Windows, or the reverse.

▶ Mono supports C#, which is a C-like language with many improvements to help make it object-oriented and easier to use.

▶ .NET includes automatic garbage collection to remove the possibility of memory leaks.

▶ .NET uses comes with built-in security checks to ensure that buffer overflows and many types of exploits are a thing of the past.

▶ Mono uses a high-performance just-in-time compiler to optimize your code for the platform on which it's running. This lets you compile it on a 32-bit machine, then run it on a 64-bit machine and have the code dynamically re-compiled for maximum 64-bit performance.

At this point, Mono is probably starting to sound like Java, and indeed it shares several properties with it. However, Mono has the following improvements:

▶ The C# language corrects many of the irritations in Java, while keeping its garbage collection.

▶ .NET is designed to let you compile multiple languages down to the same bytecode, including C#, Visual Basic .NET, and many others. The Java VM is primarily restricted to the Java language.

▶ Mono even has a special project (known as "IKVM") that compiles Java source code down to .NET code that can be run on Mono.

▶ Mono is completely open source!

Whether you're looking to create command-line programs, graphical user interface apps, or even web pages, Mono has all the power and functionality you need.

Mono on the Command Line

Mono should already be installed on your system; however, it is installed only for end users rather than for developers—you need to install a few more packages to make it usable for programming. Start up Add/Remove Software, and, from the List view, make sure the following packages are selected:

▶ mono-core

▶ mono-data

▶ mono-data-sqlite

▶ mono-debugger

▶ mono-devel

▶ monodevelop

▶ monodoc

▶ mono-extras

▶ mono-jscript

▶ mono-locale-extras

▶ mono-nunit

▶ mono-web

▶ mono-winforms

That gives you the basics to do Mono development, plus a few extra bits and pieces if you want to branch out a bit.

If you want to do some exciting things with Mono, lots of Mono-enabled libraries are available. Try going to the Search view and search for "sharp" to bring up the list of .NET-enabled libraries that you can use with Mono—the suffix is used because C# is the most popular .NET language. In this list, you'll see things such as avahi-sharp, dbus-sharp, evolution-sharp, gecko-sharp2, gmime-sharp, gnome-sharp, gtk-sharp2, gtksourceview-sharp, and ipod-sharp—we recommend you at least install the gtk-sharp2 libraries (including the development package) as these are used to create graphical user interfaces for Mono.

But for now, let's get you up and running with Mono on the command line. Mono is split into two distinct parts: the compiler and the interpreter. The compiler turns your source code into an executable, and is called gmcs. The interpreter actually runs your code as a working program, and is just called Mono. You should by now have installed MonoDevelop, so go the Applications menu, choose Programming, then MonoDevelop to start it up.

TIP

You don't have to use MonoDevelop to write your code, but it helps—syntax highlighting, code completion, and drag-and-drop GUI designers are just a few of its features.

When MonoDevelop has loaded, go to the File menu and choose New Project. From the left of the window that appears, choose C#, then Console Project. Give it a name and choose a location to save it—all being well, you should see something similar to Figure 29.1. When you're ready, click New to have MonoDevelop generate your project for you.

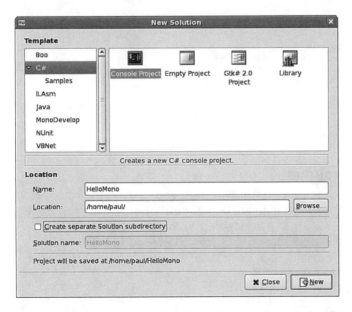

FIGURE 29.1   MonoDevelop ships with a number of templates to get you started, including one for a quick Console Project.

The default Console Project template creates a program that prints a simple message to the command line: the oh-so-traditional "Hello World!" Change it to something more insightful if you want, then press F5 to build and run the project. Just following the code view is a set of tabs where debug output is printed. One of those tabs, Application Output, becomes selected when the program runs, and you'll see "Hello World!" (or the message you chose) printed there—not bad given that you haven't written any code yet! You can see how this should look in Figure 29.2.

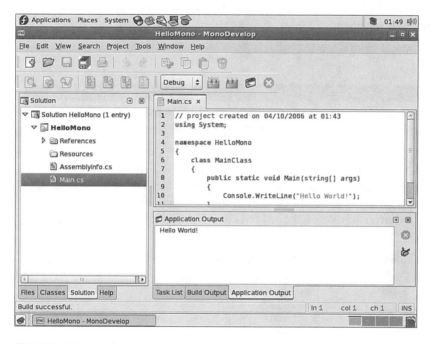

FIGURE 29.2   Your console template prints a message to the Application Output window in the bottom part of the window.

The Structure of a C# Program

As you can guess from its name, C# draws very heavily on C and C++ for its syntax, but it borrows several ideas from Java too. C# is object-oriented, which means your program is defined as a class, which is then instantiated through the Main() method call. To be able to draw on some of the .NET framework's many libraries, you need to add using statements at the top of your files—by default there's just using System; that enables you to get access to the console to write your message.

If you've come from C or C++, you'll notice that there are no header files in C#: your class definition and its implementation are all in the same file. You might also have noticed that the Main() method accepts the parameter "string[] args", which is C#-speak for "an array of strings." C never had a native "string" data type, whereas C++ acquired it rather late in the game, and so both languages tend to use the antiquated char* data type to point to a string of characters. In C#, "string" is a data type all its own, and comes with built-in functionality such as the capability to replace substrings, the capability to trim off whitespace, and the capability to convert itself to upper- or lowercase if you want it to. Strings are also Unicode friendly out of the box in .NET, so that's one fewer thing for you to worry about.

The final thing you might have noticed—at least, if you had looked in the directory where MonoDevelop placed your compiled program (usually /path/to/your/project/bin/Debug)—is that Mono uses the Windows-like .exe file extension for its programs. because Mono aims to be 100% compatible with Microsoft .NET, which means you can take your Hello World program and run it unmodified on a Windows machine and have the same message printed out.

Printing Out the Parameters

We're going to expand your little program by having it print out all the parameters passed to it, one per line. In C#, this is—rather sickeningly—just one line of code. Add this just after the existing Console.WriteLine() line in your program:

```
foreach (string arg in args) Console.WriteLine(arg);
```

The foreach keyword is a special kind of loop designed to iterate over an array of finite size. The for array exists in C#, and lets you loop a certain number of times; the while array exists too, and lets you loop continuously until you tell it to break. But the foreach loop is designed to loop over arrays that have a specific number of values, but you don't know how many values that will be. You get each value as a variable of any type you want—the preceding code says string arg in args, which means "for each array element in args, give it to me as the variable arg of type string. Of course, args is already an array of strings, so no datatype conversion will actually take place here—but it could if you wanted to convert classes or do anything of the like.

After you have each individual argument, call WriteLine() to print it out. This works whether there's one argument or one hundred arguments—or even if there are no arguments at all (in which case the loop doesn't execute at all).

Creating Your Own Variables

As you saw in the parameter list for Main() and the arg variable in your foreach loop, C# insists that each variable has a distinct data type. You can choose from quite a variety: Boolean for true/false values; string for text; int for numbers, float for floating-point numbers; and so on. If you want to be very specific, you can use int32 for a 32-bit integer (covering from –2147483648 to 2147483648) or int64 for a 64-bit integer (covering even larger numbers). But on the whole you can just use int and leave C# to work it out itself.

So now you can modify your program to accept two parameters, add them together as numbers, then print the result. This gives you a chance to see variable definitions, conversion, and mathematics, all in one. Edit the Main() method to look like this:

```
public static void Main (string[] args)
{
    int num1 = Convert.ToInt32(args[0]);
    int num2 = Convert.ToInt32(args[1]);
    Console.WriteLine("Sum of two parameters is: " + (num1 + num2)");
}
```

As you can see, each variable needs to be declared with a type (int) and a name (num1 and num2), so that C# knows how to handle them. Your args array contains strings, so you need to explicitly convert the strings to integers with the Convert.ToInt32() method. Finally, the actual addition of the two strings is done at the end of the method, while they are being printed out. Note how C# is clever enough to have integer + integer be added together (in the case of num + num2), whereas string + integer attaches the integer to the end of the string (in the case of "Sum of two parameters is:" + the result of num1 + num2). This isn't by accident: C# tries to convert data types cleverly, and warns you only if it can't convert a data type without losing some data. For example, if you try to treat a 64-bit integer as a 32-bit integer, it warns you because you might be throwing a lot of data away.

Adding Some Error Checking

Right now your program crashes in a nasty way if users don't provide at least two parameters. The reason for this is that we use arg[0] and arg[1] (the first and second parameters passed to your program) without even checking whether *any* parameters were passed in. This is easily solved: args is an array, and arrays can reveal their size. If the size doesn't match what you expect, you can bail out.

Add this code at the start of the Main() method:

```
if (args.Length != 2) {
    Console.WriteLine("You must provide exactly two parameters!");
    return;
}
```

The new piece of code in there is return, which is a C# keyword that forces it to exit the current method. As Main() is the only method being called, this has the effect of terminating the program because the user didn't supply two parameters.

Using the Length property of args, it is now possible for you to write your own Main() method that does different things, depending on how many parameters are provided. To do this properly, you need to use the else statement and nest multiple if statements like this:

```
if (args.Length == 2) {
    /// whatever…
} else if (args.Length == 3) {
    /// something else
} else if (args.Length == 4) {
```

```
   /// even more
} else {
   /// only executed if none of the others are
}
```

Building on Mono's Libraries

Fedora ships with several Mono-built programs, including Tomboy and Beagle. It also comes with a fair collection of .NET-enabled libraries, some of which you probably already installed earlier. The nice thing about Mono is that it lets you build on these libraries really easily: You just import them with a `using` statement, then get started.

To demonstrate how easy it is to build more complicated Mono applications, we're going to produce two: one using Beagle, the super-fast file indexer, and one using Gtk#, the GUI toolkit that's fast becoming the standard for Gnome development. Each has its own API that takes some time to master fully, but you can get started with them in minutes.

Searching with Beagle

Beagle is the de facto Linux search tool for Gnome, and is also used by several KDE-based programs. It works by scanning your computer in the background, then monitoring for file system changes so that its data always stays up to date. However, the magic is that it indexes data cleverly—if you tag your images, it reads those tags. If you have album and artist data in your MP3s, it reads that data too. It also reads your emails, your instant messenger conversations, your web browser history, and much more—and provides all this data in one place, so if you search for "firefox" you'll find the application itself, all the times you've mentioned Firefox in your emails, and so on.

In MonoDevelop, go to File, New Project, select C#, then choose Console Project. Give it the name BeagleTest, and tell MonoDevelop not to create a separate directory for the solution. You'll be back at the default Hello World program, but you're going to change that. First, you need to tell Mono that you want to use Beagle and Gtk#. No, you're not going to create a GUI for your search, but you do want to take advantage of Gtk#'s idle loop system—we'll explain why soon.

To add references to these two libraries, right-click on the word References in the left pane (just above Resources) and select Edit References. A new window appears (shown in Figure 29.3), and from that you should make sure Beagle and gtk-sharp are selected. Now click OK, and the References group on the left should expand so that you can see you have Beagle, gtk-sharp, and System (the last one is the default reference for .NET programs).

Now it's time to write the code. At the top of the `Main.cs` file (your main code file), you need to edit the `"using"` statements to look like this:

```
using System;
using System.Collections;
using Beagle;
using Gtk;
```

FIGURE 29.3   You need to tell Mono exactly which resource libraries you want to import for your program.

The `BeagleTest` namespace and `MainClass` class aren't changing, but you do need to edit the `Main()` method so that you can run your Beagle query. Here's how it should look, with C# comments (//, as in C++) sprinkled throughout to help you understand what's going on:

```
public static void Main(string[] args)
{
    Application.Init();

    // "Query" is the main Beagle search type.
    //It does lots of magic for you - you just need to provide it with a search
➡term and tell it where to search
    Query q = new Query();

    // these two are callback functions.
    // What you're saying is, when a hit is returned
    // (that is, when Beagle finds something, it should
    // run your OnHitsAdded() method. That code isn't written
    // yet, but you'll get there soon.
    q.HitsAddedEvent += OnHitsAdded;
    q.FinishedEvent += OnFinished;

    // these two tell Beagle where to search
    q.AddDomain(QueryDomain.Neighborhood);
    q.AddDomain(QueryDomain.Global);
```

```
// finally, you tell Beagle to search for the first word
// provided to your command (args[0]), then ask it
// to asynchronously run its search. That is, it runs
// in the background and lets your program continue running
q.AddText(args[0]);
q.SendAsync();

// tell Gtk# to run
Application.Run();
}
```

The only thing I haven't explained in there is the Gtk# stuff, but you might already have guessed why it's needed. The problem is this: Beagle runs its search asynchronously, which means that it returns control to your program straight away. Without the `Application.Run()` call, the `SendAsync()` method is the last thing your program does, which meant that it terminates itself before Beagle actually has chance to return any data. So, Gtk# serves as an idle loop: when you call `Run()`, Gtk# makes sure your program carries on running until you tell it to quit, giving Beagle enough time to return its results.

Now, let's take a look at the `OnHitsAdded` and `OnFinished` methods, called whenever Beagle finds something to return and when it's finished searching, respectively:

```
static void OnHitsAdded (HitsAddedResponse response)
{
    // sometimes Beagle can return multiple hits (files)
    // in each response, so you need to go through each
    // one and print it out line by line
    foreach(Hit hit in response.Hits)
    {
        // the Uri of hits is its location, which might
        // be on the web, on your filesystem, or somewhere else
        Console.WriteLine("Hit: " + hit.Uri);
    }
}

static void OnFinished(FinishedResponse response)
{
    // the application is done, we can tell Gtk# to quit now
    Application.Quit();
}
```

When you're done, press F8 to compile your program. If you encounter any errors, you have typed something incorrectly, so check carefully against the preceding text. Now open a terminal, change to the directory where you created your project, then look inside

29

there for the bin/Debug subdirectory. All being well, you should find the `BeagleTest.exe` file in there, which you can run like this:

```
mono BeagleTest.exe hello
```

If you get a long string of errors when you run your program, try running this command first: `export MONO_PATH=/usr/lib/beagle`. That tells Mono where to look for the Beagle library, which is probably your problem.

Creating a GUI with Gtk#

Gtk# was included with Gnome by default for the first time in Gnome 2.16, but it had been used for a couple of years prior to that and so was already mature. MonoDevelop comes with its own GUI designer called Stetic, which lets you drag and drop GUI elements onto your windows to design them.

To get started, go to File, New Project in MonoDevelop, choose C#, then Gtk# 2.0 project. Call it GtkTest, and deselect the box asking MonoDevelop to make a separate directory for the solution. You'll find that Main.cs contains a little more code this time because it needs to create and run the Gtk# application. However, the actual code to create your GUI lives in User Interface in the left pane. If you open that group, you'll see MainWindow, which, when double-clicked, brings up MonoDevelop's GUI designer.

There isn't space for me to devote much time to GUI creation, but it's very easy for you to drag and drop the different window widgets onto your form to see what properties they have. The widgets are all listed on the top right of the GUI designer, with widget properties on the bottom-right.

For now, drag a button widget onto your form. It automatically takes up all the space on your window. If you don't want this to happen, try placing one of the containers down first, then putting your button in there. For example, if you want a menu bar at the top, then a calendar, then a status bar, you ought to drop the VBox pane onto the window first, then drop each of those widgets into the separate parts of the VPane, as shown in Figure 29.4.

Your button will have the text "button1" by default, so click on it to select it, then look in the properties pane for Label. It might be hidden away in the Button Properties group, so you'll need to make sure that's open. Change the label to "Hello." Just at the top of the properties pane is a tab saying Properties (where you are right now), and another saying Signals. Signals are the events that happen to your widgets, such as the mouse moving over them, someone typing, or, of interest to us, when your button has been clicked. Look inside the Button Signals group for Clicked and double-click on it. MonoDevelop automatically switches you to the code view, with a pre-created method to handle button clicks.

Type this code into the method:

```
button1.Label = "World!";
```

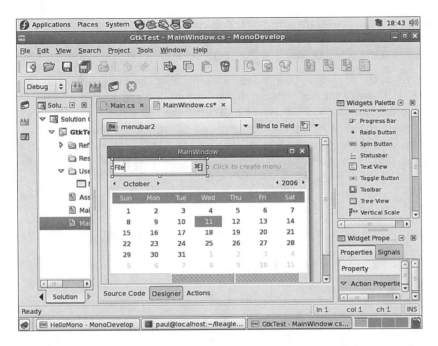

FIGURE 29.4   Using a VPane lets you space your widgets neatly on your form. Gtk# automatically handles window and widget resizing for you.

You need to make one last change before you try compiling. MonoDevelop doesn't automatically give you variables to work with each item in your window—you need to ask for them explicitly. Beneath the code window you will see a button saying Designer—click that to get back to your GUI designer window. Now click the button you created, then click the button marked Bind to Field. This edits your code to create the `button1` variable (if you click Source Code, you see the variable near the top). Now press F5 to compile and run, and try clicking the button!

Reference

- ▶ **http://www.mono-project.com/**—The homepage of the Mono project is packed with information to help you get started. You can also download new Mono versions from here, if there's something you desperately need.

- ▶ **http://www.monodevelop.com/**—The MonoDevelop project has its own site, which is the best place to look for updates.

- ▶ **http://www.icsharpcode.net/OpenSource/SD/**—MonoDevelop started life as a port of SharpDevelop. If you happen to dual-boot on Windows, this might prove very useful to you.

▶ **http://msdn.microsoft.com/vcsharp/**—We don't print many Microsoft URLs in this book, but this one is important: It's the homepage of their C# project, which can be considered the spiritual home of C# itself.

The #1 book we refer to for C# information is Jesse Liberty's *Programming C#* (O'Reilly, ISBN 0-596-00699-3). It's compact, it's comprehensive, and it's competitively priced. If you're very short on time and want the maximum detail (admittedly, with rather limited readability), you should try *The C# Programming Language*, which was co-authored by the creator of C#, Anders Hejlsberg (Addison-Wesley, ISBN: 0-321-33443-4). For a more general book on the .NET framework and all the features it provides, you might find *.NET Framework Essentials* (O'Reilly, ISBN: 0-596-00505-9) useful.

PART VI

Fedora Housekeeping

Securing Your Machines

No home computer with a connection to the Internet is 100% safe. If this information does not concern you, it should! Although there is no way to stop a serious cracker who is intent on getting into your computer or network, there are ways to make it harder for him and to warn you when he does.

In this chapter, we discuss all aspects of securing your Linux machines. You might have wondered why we did not spread this information around the book wherever it was appropriate, but the reason is simple: If you ever have a security problem with Linux, you know you can turn to this page and start reading without having to search or try to remember where you saw a tip. Everything you need is here in this one chapter, and we strongly advise you read it from start to finish.

Understanding Computer Attacks

There are many ways in which computer attacks can be divided, but perhaps the easiest is *internal*, which are computer attacks done by someone with access to a computer on the local network, and *external*, which are attacks by someone with access to a computer through the Internet. This might sound like a trivial separation to make, but it is actually important: Unless you routinely hire talented computer hackers or allow visitors to plug computers into your network, the worst internal attack you are likely to encounter is from a disgruntled employee.

Hacker Versus Cracker

In earlier days, there was a distinction made between the words *hacker* and *cracker*. A hacker was someone who used technology to innovate in new or unusual ways, whereas a cracker was someone who used technology to attack another's computers and cause harm.

This distinction was lost on the general public, so the term *hacker* has now come to mean the same as *cracker* when talking about security.

Although you should never ignore the internal threat, you should arguably be more concerned with the outside world. The big bad Internet is a security vortex. Machines connected directly to the outside world can be attacked by people across the world, and invariably are, even only a few minutes after having been connected.

This situation is not a result of malicious users lying in wait for your IP address to do something interesting. Instead, canny virus writers have created worms that exploit a vulnerability, take control of a machine, and then spread themselves to other machines around them. As a result, most attacks today are the result of these autohacking tools; there are only a handful of true hackers around, and, to be frank, if one of these ever actually targets you seriously, it will take a mammoth effort to repel him regardless of which operating system you run.

Autohacking scripts also come in another flavor: prewritten code that exploits a vulnerability and gives its users special privileges on the hacked machine. These scripts are rarely used by their creators; instead, they are posted online and downloaded by wannabe hackers, who then use them to attack vulnerable machines.

So, the external category is itself made up of worms, serious day job hackers, and wannabe hackers (usually called *script kiddies*). Combined, they will assault your Internet-facing servers, and it is your job to make sure that your boxes stay up, happily ignoring the firefight around them.

On the internal front, things are somewhat more difficult. Users who sit inside your firewall are already past your primary source of defense and, worse, they might even have physical access to your machines.

Regardless of the source of the attack, there is a five-step checklist you can follow to secure your Fedora box:

1. Assess your vulnerability. Decide which machines can be attacked, which services they are running, and who has access to them.

2. Configure the server for maximum security. Only install what you need, only run what you must, and configure a local firewall.

3. Secure physical access to the server.

4. Create worst-case-scenario policies.

5. Keep up to date with security news.

These topics are covered in the following sections, and each is as important as the others.

Assessing Your Vulnerability

It is a common mistake for people to assume that switching on a firewall makes them safe. This is not the case and, in fact, has never been the case. Each system has distinct security needs, and taking the time to customize its security layout gives you maximum security and the best performance.

The following list summarizes the most common mistakes:

▶ **Installing every package**—Do you plan to use the machine as a DNS server? If not, why have BIND installed? Go through the Add/Remove Applications dialog and ensure that you have only the software you need.

▶ **Enabling unused services**—Do you want to administer the machine remotely? Do you want people to upload files? If not, turn off SSH and FTP because they just add needless attack vectors. This goes for many other services.

▶ **Disabling the local firewall on the grounds that you already have a firewall at the perimeter**—In security, depth is crucial: The more layers someone has to hack through, the higher the likelihood she will give up or get caught.

▶ **Letting your machine give out more information than it needs to**—Many machines are configured to give out software names and version numbers by default, which is just giving hackers a helping hand.

▶ **Placing your server in an unlocked room**—If so, you might as well just hand your data over to your friendly local hackers and save the bother. The exception to this is if all the employees at your company are happy and trustworthy. But why take the risk?

▶ **Plugging your machine into a wireless network**—Unless you need wireless, avoid it, particularly if your machine is a server. Never plug a server into a wireless network because it is just too fraught with security problems.

After you have ruled out these mistakes, you are onto the real problem: Which attack vectors are open on your server? In Internet terms, this comes down to which services are Internet-facing and on which ports they are running.

Two tools are often used to determine your vulnerabilities: Nmap and Nessus. Nessus scans your machine, queries the services running, checks their version numbers against its list of vulnerabilities, and reports problems.

30

Although Nessus sounds clever, it does not work well in many modern distributions (Fedora included) because of the way patches are made available to software. For example, if you're running Apache 2.0.52 and a bug is found that's fixed in 2.0.53, Fedora backports that patch to 2.0.52. This is done because the new release probably also includes new features that might break your code, so the Red Hat team takes only what is necessary and copies it into your version. If Nessus has not been updated to take this information into account, it reports a false positive—it claims you're vulnerable to a problem against which you're patched.

The better solution is to use Nmap, which scans your machine and reports on any open TCP/IP ports it finds. Any service you have installed that responds to Nmap's query is pointed out, which enables you to ensure that you have locked everything down as much as possible.

To install Nmap, select System Settings, Add/Remove Applications. Near the bottom of the list of applications is System Tools, where you can select Nmap-frontend and Nmap. Although you can use Nmap from a command line, it is easier to use with the front end— at least until you become proficient. To run the front end, select Actions, Run Application and run `nmapfe`. If you want to enable all Nmap's options, you need to switch to root and run `nmapfe` from the console.

The best way to run Nmap is to use the SYN Stealth scan, with OS Detection and Version Probe turned on. You need to be root to enable the first two options (they are on by default when you are root), but it is well worth it. When you run Nmap (click the Scan button), it tests every port on your machine and checks whether it responds. If it does respond, Nmap queries it for version information and then prints its results onscreen.

The output lists the port numbers, service name (what usually occupies that port), and version number for every open port on your system. The information Nmap shows you should not be a surprise. If there is something open that you do not recognize, a hacker might have placed a backdoor on your system to allow easy access.

You should use the output from Nmap to help you find and eliminate unwanted services. The fewer services that are open to the outside world, the more secure you are.

Protecting Your Machine

After you have disabled all the unneeded services on your system, what remains is a core set of connections and programs that you want to keep. However, you are not finished yet: You need to clamp down your wireless network, lock your server physically, and put scanning procedures in place (such as Tripwire and promiscuous mode network monitors).

Securing a Wireless Network

Wireless networking, although convenient, can be very insecure by its very nature because transmitted data (even encrypted data) can be received by remote devices. Those devices could be in the same room; in the house, apartment, or building next door; or even several blocks away. Extra care must be used to protect the actual frequency used by your network. Great progress has been made in the past couple of years, but the possibility of a security breech is increased when the attacker is in the area and knows the frequency on which to listen. It should also be noted that the encryption method used by more wireless NICs is weaker than other forms of encryption (such as SSH) and should not be considered as part of your security plan.

TIP

Always use OpenSSH-related tools, such as `ssh` or `sftp`, to conduct business on your wireless LAN. Passwords are not transmitted as plain text, and your sessions are encrypted. Refer to Chapter 15, "Remote Access with SSH," to see how to connect to remote systems with `ssh`.

The better the physical security is around your network, the more secure it will be (this applies to wired networks as well). Keep wireless transmitters (routers, switches, and so on) as close to the center of your building as possible. Note or monitor the range of transmitted signals to determine whether your network is open to mobile network sniffing—now a geek sport known as *war driving*. (Linux software is available at http://sourceforge.net/project/showfiles.php?group_id=57253.) An occasional walk around your building not only gives you a break from work, but can also give you a chance to notice any people or equipment that should not be in the area.

Keep in mind that it takes only a single rogue wireless access point hooked up to a legitimate network hub to open access to your entire system. These access points can be smaller than a pack of cigarettes, so the only way to spot them is to scan for them with another wireless device.

Passwords and Physical Security

The next step toward better security is to use secure passwords on your network and ensure that users use them as well, especially the root password. If the root password on just one machine is cracked, the whole network is in trouble. For somewhat more physical security, you can force the use of a password with the LILO or GRUB bootloaders, remove bootable devices such as floppy and CD-ROM drives, or configure a network-booting server for Fedora. This approach is not well supported or documented at the time of this writing, but you can read about one way to do this in Brieuc Jeunhomme's Network Boot and Exotic Root HOWTO, available at http://www.tldp.org/HOWTO/Network-boot-HOWTO/. You can also read more about GRUB and LILO in Chapter 36, "Kernel and Module Management."

Also, keep in mind that some studies show that as many as 90% of network break-ins are by current or former employees. If a person no longer requires access to your network, lock out access or, even better, remove the account immediately. A good security policy also dictates that any data associated with the account first be backed up and retained for a set period of time to ensure against loss of important data. If you are able, remove the terminated employee from the system before he leaves the building.

30

Finally, be aware of physical security. If a potential attacker can get physical access to your system, getting full access becomes trivial. Keep all servers in a locked room, and ensure that only authorized personnel are given access to clients.

Configuring and Using Tripwire

Tripwire is a security tool that checks the integrity of normal system binaries and reports any changes to syslog or by email. Tripwire is a good tool for ensuring that your binaries have not been replaced by Trojan horse programs. *Trojan horses* are malicious programs inadvertently installed because of identical filenames to distributed (expected) programs, and they can wreak havoc on a breached system.

Fedora does not include the free version of Tripwire, but it can be used to monitor your system. To set up Tripwire for the first time, go to http://www.tripwire.org/, and then download and install an open-source version of the software. After installation, run the twinstall.sh script (found under /etc/tripwire) as root like so:

```
# /etc/tripwire/twinstall.sh
----------------------------------------------
The Tripwire site and local passphrases are used to
sign a variety of files, such as the configuration,
policy, and database files.

Passphrases should be at least 8 characters in length
and contain both letters and numbers.

See the Tripwire manual for more information.

----------------------------------------------
Creating key files...

(When selecting a passphrase, keep in mind that good passphrases typically
have upper- and lowercase letters, digits, and punctuation marks, and are
at least 8 characters in length.)

Enter the site keyfile passphrase:
```

You then need to enter a password of at least eight characters (perhaps best is a string of random madness, such as 5fwkc4ln) at least twice. The script generates keys for your site (host) and then asks you to enter a password (twice) for local use. You are then asked to enter the new site password. After following the prompts, the (rather extensive) default configuration and policy files (tw.cfg and tw.pol) are encrypted. You should then back up and delete the original plain-text files installed by Fedora's RPM package.

To then initialize Tripwire, use its `--init` option like so:

```
# tripwire --init
Please enter your local passphrase:
Parsing policy file: /etc/tripwire/tw.pol
Generating the database...
*** Processing Unix File System ***

....
Wrote database file: /var/lib/tripwire/shuttle2.twd
The database was successfully generated.
```

Note that not all the output is shown here. After Tripwire creates its database (which is a snapshot of your file system), it uses this baseline along with the encrypted configuration and policy settings under the /etc/tripwire directory to monitor the status of your system. You should then start Tripwire in its integrity-checking mode, using a desired option. (See the tripwire manual page for details.) For example, you can have Tripwire check your system and then generate a report at the command line, like so:

```
# tripwire -m c
```

No output is shown here, but a report is displayed in this example. The output could be redirected to a file, but a report is saved as /var/lib/tripwire/report/hostname-YYYYM-MDD-HHMMSS.twr (in other words, using your host's name, the year, the month, the day, the hour, the minute, and the seconds). Use the twprint utility to read this report, like so:

```
# twprint --print-report -r \
/var/lib/tripwire/report/shuttle2-20020919-181049.twr ¦ less
```

Other options, such as emailing the report, are supported by Tripwire, which your system's scheduling table, /etc/crontab, should run as a scheduled task on off-hours. (It can be resource intensive on less powerful computers.) The Tripwire software package also includes a twadmin utility you can use to fine-tune or change settings or policies or to perform other administrative duties.

Devices

Do not ever advertise that you have set a NIC to promiscuous mode. Promiscuous mode (which can be set on an interface by using ifconfig's promisc option) is good for monitoring traffic across the network and can often allow you to monitor the actions of someone who might have broken into your network. The tcpdump command also sets a designated interface to promiscuous mode while the program runs; unfortunately, the ifconfig command does not report this fact while tcpdump is running! Keep in mind that this is one way a cracker will monitor your network to gain the ever-so-important root password.

30

NOTE

Browse to http://www.redhat.com/docs/manuals/ to read about how to detect unauthorized network intrusions or packet browsing (known as network *sniffing*). You can use the information to help protect your system. Scroll down the page and click the Security Guide link.

Do not forget to use the right tool for the right job. Although a network bridge can be used to connect your network to the Internet, doing so would not be a good option. Bridges have almost become obsolete because they forward any packet that comes their way, which is not good when a bridge is connected to the Internet. A router enables you to filter which packets are relayed.

Viruses

Even in the right hands, Linux is every bit as vulnerable to viruses as Windows is. That might come as a surprise to you, particularly if you made the switch to Linux on the basis of its security record. However, the difference between Windows and Linux is that it is much easier to secure against viruses on Linux. Indeed, as long as you are smart, you need never worry about them. Here is why:

▶ Linux never puts the current directory in your executable path, so typing **ls** runs /bin/ls rather than any ls in the current directory.

▶ A non-root user is able to infect only files he has write access to, which is usually only the files in his home directory. This is one of the most important reasons for never using the root account longer than you need to!

▶ Linux forces you to mark files as executable, so you can't accidentally run a file called myfile.txt.exe, thinking it was just a text file.

▶ By having more than one common web browser and email client, Linux has strength through diversity: Virus writers cannot target one platform and hit 90% of the users.

Despite saying all that, Linux is susceptible to being a carrier for viruses. If you run a mail server, your Linux box can send virus-infected mails on to Windows boxes. The Linux-based server would be fine, but the Windows client would be taken down by the virus.

In this situation, you should consider a virus scanner for your machine. You have several to choose from, both free and commercial. The most popular free suite is Clam AV (http://www.clamav.net/), but Central Command, BitDefender, F-Secure, Kaspersky, McAfee, and others all compete to provide commercial solutions—look around for the best deal before you commit.

Configuring Your Firewall

Always use a hardware-based or software-based firewall on computers connected to the Internet. Fedora includes a graphical firewall configuration client named system-config-securitylevel, along with a console-based firewall client named lokkit. Use these tools to implement selective or restrictive policies regarding access to your computer or LAN.

Start the lokkit command from a console or terminal window. You must run this command as root; otherwise, you will see an error message like this:

```
$ /usr/sbin/lokkit
ERROR - You must be root to run lokkit.
```

Use the su command to run lokkit like this:

```
$ su -c "/usr/sbin/lokkit"
```

After you press Enter, you see a dialog as shown in Figure 30.1. Press the Tab key to navigate to enable or disable firewalling. You can also customize your firewall settings to allow specific protocols access through a port and to designate an ethernet interface for firewalling if multiple NICs are installed. Note that you can also use a graphical interface version of lokkit by running the gnome-lokkit client during an X session.

FIGURE 30.1   Fedora's lokkit command quickly generates firewall rules in memory for Linux.

Using system-config-securitylevel is a fast and easy way to implement a simple packet-filtering ruleset with filtering rules used to accept or reject TCP and UDP packets flowing through your host's ethernet or designated device, such as eth0 or ppp0. The rules are created on the fly and implemented immediately in memory with iptables.

Start system-config-securitylevel from the Administration menu's Firewall menu item. You are prompted for the root password and the client's window then appears. Figure 30.2 shows firewalling enabled for the eth0 ethernet device, allowing incoming secure shell and HTTP requests.

30

FIGURE 30.2   Fedora's `system-config-securitylevel` client can also be used to quickly generate and implement standard or simple custom firewall rules for Linux.

You can use Fedora to create a custom firewall, perhaps supporting IP masquerading (also known as *NAT*) by using either `ipchains` or `iptables`. You'll find two sample scripts under the `/usr/share/doc/rp-pppoe/configs` directory; these are used when a digital subscriber line (DSL) is used for Internet connection.

Forming a Disaster Recovery Plan

No one likes planning for the worst, which is why two-thirds of the population do not have a will. It is a scary thing to have your systems hacked: One or more criminals have broken through your carefully laid blocks and caused untold damage to the machine. Your boss, if you have one, will want a full report of what happened and why, and your users will want their email when they sit down at their desks in the morning. What to do?

If you ever do get hacked, nothing will take the stress away entirely. However, if you take the time to prepare a proper response in advance, you should at least avoid premature aging. Here are some tips to get you started:

▶ **Do not just pull the network cable out**—This alerts the hacker that he has been detected, which rules out any opportunities for security experts to monitor for that hacker returning and actually catch him.

▶ **Inform only the people that need to know**—Your boss and other IT people are at the top of the list; other employees are not. Keep in mind that it could be one of the employees behind the attack, and this tips them off.

▶ **If the machine is not required and you do not want to trace the attack, you can safely remove it from the network**—However, do not switch it off because some backdoors are enabled only when the system is rebooted.

▶ **Make a copy of all the log files on the system and store them somewhere else—** These might have been tampered with, but they might contain nuggets of information.

▶ **Check the `/etc/passwd` file and look for users you do not recognize**—Change all the passwords on the system, and remove bad users.

▶ **Check the output of `ps aux` for unusual programs running**—Also check to see whether any `cron` jobs are set to run.

▶ **Look in `/var/www` and see whether any web pages are there that should not be.** If you see any you don't recognize, check them closely and move them into a quarantined area if need be.

▶ **Check the contents of the `.bash_history` files in the home directories of your users**—Are there any recent commands for the root user?

▶ **If you have worked with external security companies previously, call them in for a fresh audit**—Hand over all the logs you have, and explain the situation. They will be able to extract all the information from the logs that is possible.

▶ **Start collating backup tapes from previous weeks and months**—Your system might have been hacked long before you noticed, so you might need to roll back the system more than once to find out when the attack actually succeeded.

▶ **Download and install Rootkit Hunter from http://www.rootkit.nl/projects/ rootkit_hunter.html**—This searches for (and removes) the types of files that bad guys leave behind for their return.

Keep your disaster recovery plan somewhere safe; saving it as a file on the machine in question is a very bad move!

Keeping Up-to-Date on Linux Security Issues

A multitude of websites relate to security. One in particular hosts an excellent mailing list. The site is called Security Focus, and the mailing list is called BugTraq. BugTraq is well-known for its unbiased discussion of security flaws. Be warned: It receives a relatively large amount of traffic (20–100+ messages daily). The archive is online at http://www.securityfocus.com/archive/1.

Security holes are often discussed on BugTraq before the software makers have even released the fix. The Security Focus site has other mailing lists and sections dedicated to Linux in general and is an excellent resource.

Understanding SELinux

Users moving from Windows to Linux often make the mistake of wanting to maximize the security of their system by changing the default Linux settings "to what they ought to be." If that's you, stop right there: Fedora is designed to be secure out of the box, which means you need to change nothing to be secure.

One of the most commonly misunderstood components of the Fedora security ecosystem is SELinux, which was designed by the US government's National Security Agency to ensure that Linux meets its high requirements for technology security. What people misunderstand about SELinux is that it works automatically, out of the box, whether you understand it or not; you don't need to enable it, tweak it, or even know how it works for it to help keep your system secure. SELinux is designed to complement, rather than replace, the existing Linux security permissions system, which means that anything allowed by SELinux but disallowed by your filesystem permissions is denied.

SELinux works by monitoring every system request of every program. For example, each time Apache wants to serve a web page, it has to ask SELinux whether it can read the requested file. Don't worry, the speed hit is minimal; but in terms of security, it means that even if Apache is compromised, it still can't be used to read sensitive files because SELinux stops it.

The only time you are likely to run into SELinux is when a program tries to do something it shouldn't. This *might* mean you have a security problem, but might also mean your system is trying to do something that the Fedora developers hadn't anticipated. Either way, you'll see a small bubble appear in the top-right corner of your screen, saying AVC denial, click icon to view. When you click the icon, the SELinux troubleshooter app appears, explaining what happened and why it was blocked. The troubleshooter also tells you what to do if the request was legitimate and you want to allow it in the future.

One last word of advice: even if SELinux does get in your way now and then, don't disable it. Several previous Linux security vulnerabilities have been exploited on other distros, but stopped on Fedora thanks to SELinux, which proves it works. Having your filesystem permissions set correctly, keeping SELinux enabled, and using the built-in firewall all helps to keep your system secure—make the most of it!

Related Fedora and Linux Commands

These commands are used to manage security in your Fedora system:

- ▶ **Ethereal**—GNOME graphical network scanner
- ▶ **gnome-lokkit**—Fedora's basic graphical firewalling tool for X
- ▶ **lokkit**—Fedora's basic graphical firewalling tool
- ▶ **ssh**—The OpenSSH remote login client and preferred replacement for telnet
- ▶ **system-config-securitylevel**—Fedora's graphical firewall configuration utility

Reference

▶ http://www.redhat.com/docs/manuals/linux/RHL-9-Manual/custom-guide/
s1-basic-firewall-gnomelokkit.html—Red Hat's guide to basic firewall configuration. Newer documentation will appear at http://fedora.redhat.com/.

▶ http://www.insecure.org/nmap/—This site contains information on Nmap.

▶ http://www.securityfocus.com/—The Security Focus website.

▶ http://www.tripwire.org/—Information and download links for the open-source version of Tripwire.

# CHAPTER 31

Performance Tuning

Squeezing extra performance out of your hardware might sound like a pointless task given how cheap commodity upgrades are today. To a certain degree that is true—for most of us, it is cheaper to buy a new computer than to spend hours fighting to get a 5% speed boost. But what if the speed boost were 20%? How about if it were 50%?

The benefit you can get by optimizing your system varies depending on what kinds of tasks you are running, but there is something for everyone. Over the next few pages, we look at quick ways to optimize the Apache web server, both the GNOME and KDE desktop systems, both MySQL and PostgreSQL database servers, and more.

Before you start, you need to understand that *optimization* is not an absolute term: If you optimize a system, you improve its performance, but it is still possible it could further be increased. Getting 99.999% performance out of a system is not the objective because optimization suffers from the law of diminishing returns—the basic changes make the biggest differences, but after that it takes increasing amounts of work to obtain decreasing speed improvements.

Hard Disk

Many Linux users love to tinker under the hood to increase the performance of their computers, and Linux gives you some great tools to do just that. Whereas mothers tell us, "Don't fix what's not broken," fathers often say, "Fix it until it breaks." In this section, you learn about many of the commands used to tune, or "tweak," your file system.

Before you undertake any "under the hood" work with Linux, however, keep a few points in mind. First, perform a benchmark on your system before you begin. Linux does not offer a well-developed benchmarking application, but availability changes rapidly. You can search online for the most up-to-date information for benchmarking applications for Linux. If you are a system administrator, you might choose to create your own benchmarking tests. Second, tweak only one thing at a time so that you can tell what works, what does not work, and what breaks. Some of these tweaks might not work or might lock up your machine.

Always have a working boot disk handy and remember that you are personally assuming all risks for attempting any of these tweaks.

Using the BIOS and Kernel to Tune the Disk Drives

One method of tuning involves adjusting the settings in your BIOS. Because the BIOS is not Linux and every BIOS seems different, always read your motherboard manual for better possible settings and make certain that all the drives are detected correctly by the BIOS. Change only one setting at a time.

Linux does provide a limited means to interact with BIOS settings during the boot process (mostly overriding them). In this section, you will learn about those commands.

Other options are in the following list, and are more fully outlined in the BOOTPROMPT HOWTO and the kernel documentation. These commands can be used to force the IDE controllers and drives to be optimally configured. Of course, YMMV (your mileage may vary) because these do not work for everyone:

- ▶ **idex=dma**—This forces DMA support to be turned on for the primary IDE bus, where $x = 0$, or the secondary bus, where $x = 1$.

- ▶ **idex=autotune**—This command attempts to tune the interface for optimal performance.

- ▶ **idex=ata66**—If you have ATA66 drives and controllers, this command enables support for it.

- ▶ **hdx=ide-scsi**—This command enables SCSI emulation of an IDE drive. This is required for some CD-RW drives to work properly in write mode and it might provide some performance improvements for regular CD-R drives, too.

- ▶ **idebus=xx**—This can be any number from 20 to 66; autodetection is attempted, but this can set it manually if dmesg says that it isn't autodetected correctly or if you have it set in the BIOS to a different value (overclocked). Most PCI controllers are happy with 33.

- ▶ **pci=biosirq**—Some motherboards might cause Linux to generate an error message saying that you should use this. Look in dmesg for it; if you do not see it, you don't need to use it.

These options can be entered into /boot/grub/grub.conf in the same way as other options are appended.

The `hdparm` Command

The `hdparm` utility can be used by root to set and tune the settings for IDE hard drives. You would do this to tune the drives for optimal performance.

Once a kernel patch and an associated support program, the `hdparm` program is now included with Fedora. You should experiment only with the drives mounted read-only because some settings can damage some file systems when used improperly. The `hdparm` command also works with CD-ROM drives and some SCSI drives.

The general format of the command is this:

```
# hdparm command device
```

This command runs a hard disk test:

```
# hdparm -tT /dev/sda
```

You need to replace `/dev/sda` with the location of your hard disk. `hdparm` then runs two tests: cached reads and buffered disk reads. A good IDE hard disk should be getting 400–500MB/sec for the first test, and 20–30MB/sec for the second. Note your scores, and then try this command:

```
# hdparm -m16 -d1 -u1 -c1 /dev/sda
```

That enables various performance-enhancing settings. Now try executing the original command again—if you see an increase, you should run this command:

```
$ hdparm -m16 -d1 -u1 -c1 -k1 /dev/sda
```

The extra parameter tells `hdparm` to write the settings to disk so that they will be used each time you boot up—ensuring optimal disk performance in the future.

The man entry for `hdparm` is extensive and contains useful detailed information, but because the kernel configuration selected by Fedora already attempts to optimize the drives, it might be that little can be gained through tweaking. Because not all hardware combinations can be anticipated by Fedora or by Linux and performance gains are always useful, you're encouraged to try.

TIP

You can use the `hdparm` command to produce a disk transfer speed result with the following:

```
# hdparm -tT device
```

Be aware, however, that although the resulting numbers appear quantitative, they are subject to several technical qualifications beyond the scope of what is discussed and explained in this chapter. Simply put, do not accept values generated by `hdparm` as absolute numbers, but as only a relative measure of performance.

Systemwide tweaks to `hdparm` are formally handled through the `/etc/sysconfig/harddisks` files, but this file's use is poorly documented and, therefore, of little use.

File System Tuning

Never content to leave things alone, Linux provides several tools to adjust and customize the file system settings. The belief is that hardware manufacturers and distribution creators tend to select conservative settings that will work well all the time, leaving some of the potential of your system leashed—that's why you have chosen *Fedora Unleashed, 2008 Edition* to help you.

The Linux file system designers have done an excellent job of selecting default values used for file system creation and the 2.6 version of the Linux kernel now contains new code for the IDE subsystem that significantly improves *I/O (input/output)* transfer speeds over older versions, obviating much of the need for special tweaking of the file system and drive parameters if you use IDE disks. Although these values work well for most users, some server applications of Linux benefit from file system tuning. As always, observe and benchmark your changes.

Synchronizing the File System with `sync`

Because Linux uses buffers when writing to devices, the write does not occur until the buffer is full, until the kernel tells it to, or if you tell it to by using the `sync` command. Traditionally, the command is given twice, as in the following:

```
# sync ; sync
```

It is really overkill to do it twice. Still, it can be helpful prior to the unmounting of certain types of media with slow write speeds (such as some USB hard drives or PCMCIA storage media), but only because it delays the user from attempting to remove the media too soon, not because two syncs are better than one.

The `tune2fs` Command

With `tune2fs`, you can adjust the tunable file system parameters on an ext2 or ext3 file system. A few performance-related items of note are as follows:

▶ To disable file system checking, the `-c 0` option sets the maximum mount count to zero.

▶ The interval between forced checks can be adjusted with the `-I` option.

▶ The -m option sets the reserved blocks percentage with a lower value, freeing more space at the expense of fsck having less space to write any recovered files.

▶ Decrease the number of superblocks to save space with the -O sparse_super option. (Modern file systems use this by default.) Always run e2fsck after you change this value.

▶ More space can be freed with the -r option, which sets the number of reserved (for root) blocks.

Note that most of these uses of tune2fs free up space on the drive at the expense of the capability of fsck to recover data. Unless you really need the space and can deal with the consequences, just accept the defaults; large drives are now relatively inexpensive.

The e2fsck Command

This utility checks an ext2/ext3 file system. Some useful arguments taken from man e2fsck are as follows:

▶ -c—Checks for bad blocks and then marks them as bad

▶ -f—Forces checking on a clean file system

▶ -v—Verbose mode

The badblocks Command

Although not a performance-tuning program per se, the badblocks utility checks an (preferably) unmounted partition for bad blocks. It is not recommended that you run this command by itself, but rather allow it to be called by fsck. It should be used directly only if you specify the block size accurately—don't guess or assume anything.

The options available for badblocks are detailed in the man page. They allow for very low-level manipulation of the file system, which is useful for data recovery by file system experts or for file system hacking, but is beyond the scope of this chapter and the average user.

Disabling File Access Time

Whenever Linux reads a file, it changes the last access time—known as the *atime*. This is also true for your web server: If you are getting hit by 50 requests a second, your hard disk updates the atime 50 times a second. Do you really need to know the last time a file was accessed? If not, you can disable the atime setting for a directory by typing this:

```
$ chattr -R +A /path/to/directory
```

The chattr command changes file system attributes, of which "don't update atime" is one. To set that attribute, use +A and specify -R so that it is recursively set. /path/to/directory gets changed, and so do all the files and subdirectories it contains.

If you want to change a whole drive so that it never updates the atime, edit the file /etc/fstab as root and look for the part that says defaults for the drive you want to change. It might say defaults or something more complex like defaults,errors= remount-ro; you need to change that to add noatime, as in defaults,noatime. Make sure you don't put any extra spaces in there!

Kernel

As the Linux kernel developed over time, developers sought a way to fine-tune some of the kernel parameters. Before sysctl, those parameters had to be changed in the kernel configuration and then the kernel had to be recompiled.

The sysctl command can change some parameters of a running kernel. It does this through the /proc file system, which is a "virtual window" into the running kernel. Although it might appear that a group of directories and files exist under /proc, that is only a representation of parts of the kernel. You can read values from and write values to those "files," referred to as *variables*. You can display a list of the variables as shown in the following. (An annotated list is presented because roughly 250 items—or more—exist in the full list.)

```
# sysctl -A
net.ipv4.tcp_max_syn_backlog = 1024
net.ipv4.tcp_rfc1337 = 0
net.ipv4.tcp_stdurg = 0
net.ipv4.tcp_abort_on_overflow = 0
net.ipv4.tcp_tw_recycle = 0
net.ipv4.tcp_syncookies = 0
net.ipv4.tcp_fin_timeout = 60
net.ipv4.tcp_retries2 = 15
net.ipv4.tcp_retries1 = 3
net.ipv4.tcp_keepalive_intvl = 75
net.ipv4.tcp_keepalive_probes = 9
net.ipv4.tcp_keepalive_time = 7200
net.ipv4.ipfrag_time = 30
```

The items shown are networking parameters, and actually tweaking these values is beyond the scope of this book. If you want to change a value, however, the -w command is used:

```
# sysctl -w net.ipv4.tcp_retries 2=20
```

This increases the value of that particular kernel parameter.

31

> **NOTE**
>
> Fedora provides a graphical interface to the `sysctl` command in `system-config-proc`. It's still a beta-quality application, and it must be launched from the command line. The interface itself is unremarkable, and it does not provide a means to manipulate all the possible values, but it does offer useful help for the kernel variables it addresses.

If you find that a particular setting is useful, you can enter it into the `/etc/sysctl.conf` file. The format is as follows, using the earlier example:

```
net.ipv4.tcp_retries 2=20
```

Of more interest to kernel hackers than regular users, `sysctl` is a potentially powerful tool that continues to be developed and documented.

> **TIP**
>
> The kernel does a good job of balancing performance for graphical systems, so there's not a great deal you can do to tweak your desktop to run faster.
>
> Both GNOME and KDE are "heavyweight" desktop systems: They are all-inclusive, all-singing, and all-dancing environments that do far more than browse your file system. The drawback to this is that their size makes them run slowly on older systems. On the flip side, Fedora also comes with the Xfce desktop, which is a great deal slimmer and faster than the other two. If you find GNOME and KDE are struggling just to open a file browser, Xfce is for you.
>
> Alternatively, if you simply cannot live without GNOME or KDE, take a look in the `/usr/share/autostart` directory, where you will see a list of files that are started when your graphical system boots. If you do not need any of them, just move them out of there and into somewhere safe in case you ever need them again.

Apache

Despite being the most popular web server on the Internet, Apache is by no means the fastest. Part of the problem is that Apache has been written to follow every applicable standard to the letter, so much of its development work has been geared toward standards-compliancy rather than just serving web pages quickly. That said, with a little tweaking you can convert a $1,000 Dell server into something capable of surviving the Slashdot Effect.

> **NOTE**
>
> Slashdot.org is a popular geek news website that spawned the *Slashdot Effect*—the result of thousands of geeks descending on an unsuspecting website simultaneously. Our $1,000 Dell server had dual 2.8GHz Xeons with 1GB of RAM and SCSI hard disks—if you have more RAM, faster chips, and a high-end network card, you can kick sand in Slashdot's face.

The first target of your tuning should be the `httpd.conf` file in `/etc/httpd/conf`, as well as the other files in `/etc/httpd/conf.d`. The more modules you have loaded, the more load Apache is placing on your server—take a look through the LoadModule list and comment out (start the line with a #) the ones you do not want. Some of these modules can be uninstalled entirely through the Add or Remove Packages dialog.

As a rough guide, you are almost certain to need `mod_mime` and `mod_dir`, and probably also `mod_log_config`. The default Apache configuration in Fedora is quite generic, so unless you are willing to sacrifice some functionality you might also need `mod_negotiation` (a speed killer if there ever was one), and `mod_access` (a notorious problem). It's possible to configure both of those last two modules so that they work with little or no performance decrease, but all too often they get abused and just slow things down.

Whatever you do, when you are disabling modules ensure you leave either `mod_deflate` or `mod_gzip` enabled, depending on your Apache version. Your bottleneck is almost certainly going to be your bandwidth rather than your processing power, and having one of these two compressing your content will usually turn 10Kb of HTML into 3Kb for supported browsers (most of them).

Next, ensure keepalives are turned off. Yes, you read that right: Turn keepalives off. This adds some latency to people viewing your site because they cannot download multiple files through the same connection. However, it in turn reduces the number of simultaneous open connections and so allows more people to connect.

If you are serving content that does not change, you can take the extreme step of enabling MMAP support. This allows Apache to serve pages directly from RAM without bothering to check whether they have changed, which works wonders for your performance. However, the downside is that when you do change your pages you need to restart Apache. Look for the `EnableMMAP` directive—it is probably commented out and set to off, so you need to remove the comment and set it to On.

Finally, you should do all you can to ensure that your content is static: Avoid PHP if you can, avoid databases if you can, and so on. If you know you are going to get hit by a rush of visitors, use plain HTML so the speed with which Apache can serve pages is limited only by your bandwidth.

TIP

Some people, when questioned about optimizing Apache, recommend you tweak the `HARD_SERVER_LIMIT` in the Apache source code and recompile. Although we agree that compiling your own Apache source code is a great way to get a measurable speed boost if you know what you are doing, you should need to change this directive only if you are hosting a huge site.

The default value, 256, is enough to handle the Slashdot Effect—and if you can handle that, you can handle most things.

MySQL

Tuning your MySQL server for increased performance is exceptionally easy to do, largely because you can see huge speed increases simply by getting your queries right. That said, there are various things you can tune in the server itself to help it cope with higher loads as long as your system has enough RAM.

The key is understanding its buffers—there are buffers and caches for all sorts of things, and finding out how full they are is crucial to maximizing performance. MySQL performs best when it makes full use of its buffers, which in turn places a heavy demand on system RAM. Unless you have 4GB of RAM or more in your machine, you do not have enough capacity to set very high values for all your buffers—you need to pick and choose.

Measuring Key Buffer Usage

When you add indexes to your data, it enables MySQL to find data faster. However, ideally you want to have these indexes stored in RAM for maximum speed, and the variable `key_buffer_size` defines how much RAM MySQL can allocate for index key caching. If MySQL cannot store its indexes in RAM, you experience serious performance problems. Fortunately, most databases have relatively small key buffer requirements, but you should measure your usage to see what work needs to be done.

To do this, log in to MySQL and type **SHOW STATUS LIKE '%key_read%';**. That returns all the status fields that describe the hit rate of your key buffer—you should get two rows back: `Key_reads` and `Key_read_requests`, which are the number of keys being read from disk and the number of keys being read from the key buffer. From these two numbers you can calculate the percentage of requests being filled from RAM and from disk, using this simple equation:

    100 – ((Key_reads / Key_read_requests) × 100)

That is, you divide `Key_reads` by `Key_read_requests`, multiply the result by 100, and then subtract the result from 100. For example, if you have `Key_reads` of 1000 and `Key_read_requests` of 100000, you divide 1000 by 100000 to get 0.01; then you multiply that by 100 to get 1.0, and subtract that from 100 to get 99. That number is the percentage of key reads being served from RAM, which means 99% of your keys are served from RAM.

Most people should be looking to get more than 95% served from RAM, although the primary exception is if you update or delete rows very often—MySQL can't cache what keeps changing. If your site is largely read only, you should get around 98%. Lower figures mean you might need to bump up the size of your key buffer.

If you are seeing problems, the next step is to check how much of your current key buffer is being used. Use the SHOW VARIABLES command and look up the value of the `key_buffer_size` variable. It is probably something like 8388600, which is eight million bytes, or 8MB. Now, use the SHOW STATUS command and look up the value of `Key_blocks_used`.

You can now determine how much of your key buffer is being used by multiplying Key_blocks_used by 1024, dividing by key_buffer_size, and multiplying by 100. For example, if Key_blocks_used is 8000, you multiply that by 1024 to get 8192000; then you divide that by your key_buffer_size (8388600) to get 0.97656, and finally multiply that by 100 to get 97.656. Thus, almost 98% of your key buffer is being used.

Now, on to the important part: You have ascertained that you are reading lots of keys from disk, and you also now know that the reason for reading from disk is almost certainly because you do not have enough RAM allocated to the key buffer. A general rule of thumb is to allocate as much RAM to the key buffer as you can, up to a maximum of 25% of system RAM—128MB on a 512MB system is about the ideal for systems that read heavily from keys. Beyond that, you will actually see drastic performance decreases because the system has to use virtual memory for the key buffer.

Open /etc/my.cnf in your text editor and look for the line that contains key_buffer_size. If you do not have one, you need to create a new one—it should be under the line [mysqld]. When you set the new value, do not just pick some arbitrarily high number. Try doubling what is there right now (or try 16MB if there's no line already); then see how it goes. To set 16MB as the key buffer size, you need a line like this:

```
[mysqld]
set-variable = key_buffer_size=16M
datadir=/var/lib/mysql
```

Restart your MySQL server with service mysqld restart, and then go back into MySQL and run SHOW VARIABLES again to see the key_buffer_size. It should be 16773120 if you have set it to 16M. Now, because MySQL just got reset, all its values for key hits and the like will also have been reset. You need to let it run for a while so that you can assess how much has changed. If you have a test system you can run, this is the time to run it.

After your database has been accessed with normal usage for a short while (if you get frequent accesses, this might be only a few minutes), recalculate how much of the key buffer is being used. If you get another high score, double the size again, restart, and retest. You should keep repeating this until you see your key buffer usage is below 50% or you find you don't have enough RAM to increase the buffer further—remember that you should never allocate more than 25% of system RAM to the key buffer.

Using the Query Cache

Newer versions of MySQL enable you to cache the results of queries so that, if new queries come in that use exactly the same SQL, the result can be served from RAM. In some ways the query cache is quite intelligent: If part of the result changes because of another query, for example, the cached results are thrown away and recalculated next time. However, in other ways it isn't so smart. For example, it uses cached results only if the new query is exactly the same as a cached query, even down to the capitalization of the SQL.

The query cache works well in most scenarios. If your site has an equal mix of reading and writing, the query cache does its best but is not optimal. If your site is mostly reading with few writes, more queries are cached (and for longer), thus improving overall performance.

First, you need to find out whether you have the query cache enabled. To do this, use SHOW VARIABLES and look up the value of have_query_cache. All being well, you should get YES back, meaning that the query cache is enabled. Next, look for the value of query_cache_size and query_cache_limit—the first is how much RAM in bytes is allocated to the query cache, and the second is the maximum result size that should be cached. A good starting set of values for these two is 8388608 (8MB) and 1048576 (1MB).

Next, type **SHOW STATUS LIKE 'Qcache%';** to see all the status information about the query cache. You should get output like this:

```
mysql> SHOW STATUS LIKE 'qcache%';
+-------------------------+--------+
| Variable_name           | Value  |
+-------------------------+--------+
| Qcache_free_blocks      | 1      |
| Qcache_free_memory      | 169544 |
| Qcache_hits             | 698    |
| Qcache_inserts          | 38     |
| Qcache_lowmem_prunes    | 20     |
| Qcache_not_cached       | 0      |
| Qcache_queries_in_cache | 18     |
| Qcache_total_blocks     | 57     |
+-------------------------+--------+
8 rows in set (0.00 sec)
```

From that, you can see that only 18 queries are in the cache (Qcache_queries_in_cache), 169544 bytes of memory are free in the cache (Qcache_free_memory), 698 queries have been read from the cache (Qcache_hits), 38 queries have been inserted into the cache (Qcache_inserts), but 20 of them were removed for lack of memory (Qcache_lowmem_prunes), giving the 18 from before. Qcache_not_cached is 0, which means 0 queries were not cached—MySQL is caching them all.

From that, you can calculate how many total queries came in—it is the sum of Qcache_hits, Qcache_inserts, and Qcache_not_cached, which is 736. You can also calculate how well the query cache is being used by dividing Qcache_hits by that number and multiplying by 100. In this case, 94.84% of all queries are being served from the query cache, which is a great number.

In this example, you can see that many queries have been trimmed because there is not enough memory in the query cache. This can be changed by editing the /etc/my.cnf file and adding a line like this one, somewhere in the [mysqld] section:

```
set-variable = query_cache_size=32M
```

An 8MB query cache should be enough for most people, but larger sites might want 16MB or even 32MB if you are storing a particularly large amount of data. Very few sites have need to go beyond a 32MB query cache, but keep an eye on the `Qcache_lowmem_prunes` value to ensure that you have enough RAM allocated.

Using the query cache does not incur much of a performance hit. When MySQL calculates the result of a query normally, it simply throws the result away when the connection closes. With the query cache, it skips the throwing away, and so there is no extra work being done. If your site does have many updates and deletes, be sure to check whether you get any speed boost at all from the query cache.

Miscellaneous Tweaks

If you have tuned your key buffer and optimized your query cache and yet still find your site struggling, you can make a few additional small changes that will add some more speed.

When reading from tables, MySQL has to open the file that stores the table data. How many files it keeps open at a time is defined by the `table_cache` setting, which is set to 64 by default. You can increase this setting if you have more than 64 tables, but you should be aware that Fedora does impose limits on MySQL about how many files it can have open at a time. Going beyond 256 is not recommended unless you have a particularly database-heavy site and know exactly what you are doing.

The other thing you can tweak is the size of the read buffer, which is controlled by `read_buffer_size` and `read_buffer_rnd_size`. Both of these are allocated per connection, which means you should be very careful to have large numbers. Whatever you choose, `read_buffer_rnd_size` should be three to four times the size of `read_buffer_size`, so if `read_buffer_size` is 1MB (suitable for very large databases), `read_buffer_rnd_size` should be 4MB.

Query Optimization

The biggest speed-ups can be seen by reprogramming your SQL statements so they are more efficient. If you follow these tips, your server will thank you:

▶ Select as little data as possible. Rather than SELECT *, select only the fields you need.

▶ If you only need a few rows, use LIMIT to select the number you need.

▶ Declare fields as NOT NULL when creating tables to save space and increase speed.

▶ Provide default values for fields, and use them where you can.

▶ Be careful with table joins because they are the easiest way to write inefficient queries.

▶ If you must use joins, be sure you join on fields that are indexed. They should preferably be integer fields because these are faster than strings for comparisons.

▶ Find and fix slow queries. Add `log-long-format` and `log-slow-queries =
/var/log/slow-queries.log` to your `/etc/my.cnf` file, under `[mysqld]`, and MySQL
can tell you the queries that took a long time to complete.

▶ Use `OPTIMIZE TABLE` *tablename* to defragment tables and refresh the indexes.

Reference

▶ **http://www.coker.com.au/bonnie++/**—The home page of bonnie, a disk benchmarking tool. It also contains a link to RAID benchmarking utilities and Postal, a
benchmarking utility for SMTP servers.

▶ **http://httpd.apache.org/docs-2.0/misc/perf-tuning.html**—The official Apache
guide to tuning your web server.

▶ **http://dev.mysql.com/doc/refman/5.0/en/optimization.html**—Learn how to
optimize your MySQL server directly from the source, the MySQL manual.

One particular MySQL optimization book will really help you get more from your system
if you run a large site: *High Performance MySQL*, by Jeremy Zawodny and Derek Balling
(O'Reilly), ISBN: 0-596-00306-4.

CHAPTER 32

Command-Line Master Class

In the earlier years of Linux, people made a big fuss of the graphical environments that were available—they rushed to tell new users that you really did not need to keep going back to the command line to type things. Now that Linux is more mature, people accept that the command line is still a reality, and a welcome one. Although the GUI does make life easier for day-to-day tasks, your options are limited by what the developers want you to have—you cannot bring commands together in new ways, and neither can you use any of the GUI features if, for example, your GUI is broken. It does happen!

In his book *The Art of UNIX Programming,** Eric Raymond wrote a short story that perfectly illustrates the power of the command line versus the GUI. It's reprinted here with permission, for your reading pleasure:

> One evening, Master Foo and Nubi attended a gathering of programmers who had met to learn from each other. One of the programmers asked Nubi to what school he and his master belonged. Upon being told they were followers of the Great Way of UNIX, the programmer grew scornful.
>
> "The command-line tools of UNIX are crude and backward," he scoffed. "Modern, properly designed operating systems do everything through a graphical user interface."
>
> Master Foo said nothing, but pointed at the moon. A nearby dog began to bark at the master's hand.

Raymond, Eric. The Art of UNIX Programming. Addison-Wesley, 2004.

"I don't understand you!" said the programmer.

Master Foo remained silent, and pointed at an image of the Buddha. Then he pointed at a window.

"What are you trying to tell me?" asked the programmer.

Master Foo pointed at the programmer's head. Then he pointed at a rock.

"Why can't you make yourself clear?" demanded the programmer.

Master Foo frowned thoughtfully, tapped the programmer twice on the nose, and dropped him in a nearby trash can.

As the programmer was attempting to extricate himself from the garbage, the dog wandered over and piddled on him.

At that moment, the programmer achieved enlightenment.

Whimsical as the story is, it illustrates that there are some things that the GUI just does not do well. Enter the command line: It is a powerful and flexible operating environment on Linux, and—if you practice—can actually be quite fun, too!

In this chapter, you learn how to master the command line so that you are able to perform common tasks through it, and also link commands together to create new command groups. We also look at the two most popular Linux text editors: Vim and Emacs. The command line is also known as the shell, the console, the command prompt, and the *CLI (command-line interpreter)*. For the purposes of this chapter, these terms are interchangeable, although there are fine-grained differences among them!

Why Use the Shell?

Moving from the GUI to the command line is a conscious choice for most people, although it is increasingly rare that it is an either/or choice. While in X, you can press Ctrl+Alt+F1 at any time to switch to a terminal, but most people tend to run an X terminal application that enables them to have the point-and-click applications and the command-line applications side by side.

Reasons for running the shell include

▶ You want to chain two or more commands together.

▶ You want to use a command or parameter available only on the shell.

▶ You are working on a text-only system.

▶ You have used it for a long time and feel comfortable there.

Chaining two or more commands together is what gives the shell its real power. Hundreds of commands are available and, by combining them in different ways, you get hundreds of new commands. Some of the shell commands are available through the GUI, but these commands usually have only a small subset of their parameters available, which limits what you are able to do with them.

Working from a text-only system encapsulates both working locally with a broken GUI and also connecting to a remote, text-only system. If your Linux server is experiencing problems, the last thing you want to do is load it down with a GUI connection—working in text mode is faster and more efficient.

The last use is the most common: People use the shell just because it is familiar to them, with many people even using the shell to start GUI applications just because it saves them taking their hands off the keyboard for a moment! This is not a bad thing; it provides fluency and ease with the system and is a perfectly valid way of working.

Basic Commands

It is impossible to know how many commands the average shell citizen uses, but if we had to guess, we would place it at about 25:

- ▶ **cat**—Prints the contents of a file
- ▶ **cd**—Changes directories
- ▶ **chmod**—Changes file access permissions
- ▶ **cp**—Copies files
- ▶ **du**—Prints disk use
- ▶ **emacs**—Text editor
- ▶ **find**—Finds files by searching
- ▶ **gcc**—The C/C++/Fortran compiler
- ▶ **grep**—Searches for a string in input
- ▶ **less**—The filter for paging through output
- ▶ **ln**—Creates links between files
- ▶ **locate**—Finds files from an index
- ▶ **ls**—Lists files in the current directory
- ▶ **make**—Compiles and installs programs
- ▶ **man**—The manual page reader
- ▶ **mkdir**—Makes directories
- ▶ **mv**—Moves files
- ▶ **ps**—Lists processes
- ▶ **rm**—Deletes files and directories

32

▶ **ssh**—Connects to other machines

▶ **tail**—Prints the last lines of a file

▶ **top**—Prints resource use

▶ **vim**—A text editor

▶ **which**—Prints the location of a command

▶ **xargs**—Executes commands from its input

Of course, many other commands are available to you and are used fairly often—diff, nmap, ping, su, uptime, who, and so on—but if you are able to understand the 25 listed here, you will have sufficient skill to concoct your own command combinations.

Note that we say *understand* the commands—not *know all their possible parameters and uses*. This is because several of the commands, although commonly used, are used only by people with specific needs. gcc and make are good examples of this: Unless you plan to become a programmer, you need not worry about these beyond just typing make and make install now and then. If you want to learn more about these two commands, refer to Chapter 28, "C/C++ Programming Tools for Fedora."

Similarly, both Emacs and Vim are text editors that have a text-based interface all their own, and SSH has already been covered in detail in Chapter 15, "Remote Access with SSH."

What remains are 20 commands, each of which has many parameters to customize what it actually does. Again, you can eliminate many of these because many of the parameters are esoteric and rarely used, and, the few times in your Linux life that you need them, you can just read the manual page!

We go over these commands one by one, explaining the most common ways to use them. There is one exception to this: The xargs command requires you to understand how to join commands together, so it is bundled in the section "Combining Commands."

Most of these commands have been touched on elsewhere in the book, primarily in Chapter 4, "Command-Line Quick Start." The goal of that chapter was to give you "the least you need to know" to get by, whereas in this chapter each command is treated individually with an aim to giving you the confidence needed to be able to mix them together to create your own commands.

Printing the Contents of a File with cat

Many of Fedora's shell commands manipulate text strings, so if you want to be able to feed them the contents of files, you need to be able to output those files as text. Enter the cat command, which prints the contents of any files you pass to it. Its most basic use is like this:

```
$ cat myfile.txt
```

That prints the contents of `myfile.txt`. For this use, there are two extra parameters that are often used: `-n` numbers the lines in the output, and `-s` ("squeeze") prints a maximum of one blank line at a time. That is, if your file has 1 line of text, 10 blank lines, 1 line of text, 10 blank lines, and so on, `-s` shows the first line of text, a single blank line, the next line of text, a single blank line, and so forth. When you combine `-s` and `-n`, `cat` numbers only the lines that are printed—the 10 blank lines shown as one will count as 1 line for numbering.

This command prints information about your CPU, stripping out multiple blank lines and numbering the output:

```
$ cat -sn /proc/cpuinfo
```

You can also use `cat` to print the contents of several files at once, like this:

```
$ cat -s myfile.txt myotherfile.txt
```

In that command, `cat` merges `myfile.txt` and `myotherfile.txt` on the output, stripping out multiple blank lines. The important thing is that `cat` does not distinguish between the files in the output—no filenames are printed, and no extra breaks between the two files. This allows you to treat the two as one or, by adding more files to the command line, to treat 20 files as 1.

Changing Directories with cd

Changing directories is surely something that has no options, right? Not so. `cd` is actually more flexible than most people realize. Unlike most of the other commands here, `cd` is not a command in itself—it is built in to `bash` (or whichever shell interpreter you are using), but it is still used like a command.

The most basic use of `cd` is this:

```
$ cd somedir
```

That command looks in the current directory for the `somedir` subdirectory, and then moves you into it. You can also specify an exact location for a directory, like this:

```
$ cd /home/paul/stuff/somedir
```

The first part of `cd`'s magic lies in the characters (`-` and `~`, a dash and a tilde). The first means "switch to my previous directory," and the second means "switch to my home directory." This conversation with `cd` shows this in action:

```
[paul@caitlin ~]$ cd /usr/local
[paul@caitlin local]$ cd bin
[paul@caitlin bin]$ cd -
/usr/local
[paul@caitlin local]$ cd ~
[paul@caitlin ~]$
```

In the first line, we change to /usr/local and get no output from the command. In the second line, we change to bin, which is a subdirectory of /usr/local. Next, cd - is used to change back to the previous directory. This time, bash prints the name of the previous directory so we know where we are. Finally, cd ~ is used to change back to the home directory, although if you want to save an extra few keystrokes, just typing **cd** by itself is equivalent to cd ~.

The second part of cd's magic is its capability to look for directories in predefined locations. When you specify an absolute path to a directory (that is, one starting with a /), cd always switches to that exact location. However, if you specify a relative subdirectory—for example, cd subdir—you can tell cd to what location you would like that to be relative. This is accomplished with the CDPATH environment variable. If this variable is not set, cd always uses the current directory as the base; however, you can set it to any number of other directories.

The next example shows a test of this. It starts in /home/paul/empty, an empty directory, and the lines are numbered for later reference:

```
 1 [paul@caitlin empty]$ pwd
 2 /home/paul/empty
 3 [paul@caitlin empty]$ ls
 4 [paul@caitlin empty]$ mkdir local
 5 [paul@caitlin empty]$ ls
 6 local
 7 [paul@caitlin empty]$ cd local
 8 [paul@caitlin local]$ cd ..
 9 [paul@caitlin empty]$ export CDPATH=/usr
10 [paul@caitlin empty]$ cd local
11 /usr/local
12 [paul@caitlin empty]$ cd -
13 /home/paul/empty
14 [paul@caitlin empty]$ export CDPATH=.:/usr
15 [paul@caitlin empty]$ cd local
16 /home/paul/empty/local
17 [paul@caitlin local]$
```

Lines 1–3 show that you are in /home/paul/empty and that it is indeed empty—ls had no output. Lines 4–6 show the local subdirectory being made so that /home/paul/empty/local exists. Lines 7 and 8 show you can cd into /home/paul/empty/local and back out again.

In line 9, CDPATH is set to /usr. This was chosen because Fedora has the directory /usr/local, which means the current directory (/home/paul/empty) and the CDPATH directory (/usr) both have a local subdirectory. In line 10, while in the /home/paul/empty directory, cd local is used. This time, bash switches to /usr/local and even prints the new directory to ensure that you know what it has done.

Lines 12 and 13 move you back to the previous directory, /home/paul/empty. In line 14, CDPATH is set to be .:/usr. The : is the directory separator, so this means bash should look first in the current directory, ., and then in the /usr directory. In line 15, cd local is issued again, this time moving to /home/paul/empty/local. Note that bash has still printed the new directory—it does that whenever it looks up a directory in CDPATH.

Changing File Access Permissions with chmod

What you learned about chmod earlier can be greatly extended through one simple parameter: -c. This instructs chmod to print a list of all the changes it made as part of its operation, which means you can capture the output and use it for other purposes. For example:

```
[paul@caitlin tmp]$ chmod -c 600 *
mode of `1.txt' changed to 0600 (rw-------)
mode of `2.txt' changed to 0600 (rw-------)
mode of `3.txt' changed to 0600 (rw-------)
[paul@caitlin tmp]$ chmod -c 600 *
[paul@caitlin tmp]$
```

There the chmod command is issued with -c, and you can see it has output the result of the operation: Three files were changed to rw------- (read and write by user only). However, when the command is issued again, no output is returned. This is because -c prints only the changes that it made. Files that already match the permissions you are setting are left unchanged and therefore are not printed.

There are two other parameters of interest: --reference and -R. The first enables you to specify a file to use as a template for permissions rather than specifying permissions yourself. For example, if you want all files in the current directory to have the same permissions as the file /home/paul/myfile.txt, you would use this:

```
$ chmod --reference /home/paul/myfile.txt *
```

You can use -R to enable recursive operation, which means you can use it to chmod a directory and it changes the permissions of that directory and all files and subdirectories under that directory. You could use chmod -R 600 /home to change every file and directory under /home to become read/write to their owners.

Copying Files with cp

Like mv, which is covered later, cp is a command that is easily used and mastered. However, two marvelous parameters rarely see much use (which is a shame!) despite their power. These are --parents and -u, the first of which copies the full path of the file into the new directory. The second copies only if the source file is newer than the destination.

Using --parents requires a little explanation, so here is an example. You have a file, /home/paul/desktop/documents/work/notes.txt, and want to copy it to your /home/paul/backup folder. You could just do a normal cp, but that would give you

/home/paul/backup/notes.txt, so how would you know where that came from later? If you use --parents, the file is copied to /home/paul/backup/desktop/documents/work/notes.txt.

The -u parameter is perfect for synchronizing two directories because it enables you to run a command like cp -Ru myfiles myotherfiles and have cp recopy only files that have changed. The -R parameter means *recursive* and enables you to copy directory contents.

Printing Disk Use with du

The du command prints the size of each file and directory that is inside the current directory. Its most basic use is as easy as it gets:

```
$ du
```

That query outputs a long list of directories and how much space their files take up. You can modify that with the -a parameter, which instructs du to print the size of individual files and directories. Another useful parameter is -h, which makes du use human-readable sizes like 18M (18MB) rather than 17532 (the same number in bytes, unrounded). The final useful basic option is -c, which prints the total size of files.

So, using du, you can get a printout of the size of each file in your home directory, in human-readable format, and with a summary at the end, like this:

```
$ du -ahc /home/paul
```

Two advanced parameters deal with filenames you want excluded from your count. The first is --exclude, which enables you to specify a pattern that should be used to exclude files. This pattern is a standard shell file-matching pattern as opposed to a regular expression, which means you can use ? to match a single character or * to match 0 or many characters. You can specify multiple --exclude parameters to exclude several patterns. For example:

```
$ du --exclude="*.xml" --exclude="*.xsl"
```

Of course, typing numerous --exclude parameters repeatedly is a waste of time, so you can use -X to specify a file that has the list of patterns you want excluded. The file should look like this:

```
*.xml
*.xsl
```

That is, each pattern you want excluded should be on a line by itself. If that file were called xml_exclude.txt, you could use it in place of the previous example like this:

```
$ du -X xml_exclude.txt
```

You can make your exclusion file as long as you need, or you can just specify multiple -X parameters.

> **TIP**
>
> Running du in a directory where several files are hard-linked to the same inode counts the size of the file only once. If you want to count each hard link separately for some reason, use the -1 parameter (lowercase *L*) .

Finding Files by Searching with `find`

The `find` command is one of the darkest and least understood areas of Linux, but it is also one of the most powerful. Admittedly, the `find` command does not help itself by using X-style parameters. The UNIX standard is -c, -s, and so on, whereas the GNU standard is --dosomething, --mooby, and so forth. X-style parameters merge the two by having words preceded by only one dash.

However, the biggest problem with `find` is that it has more options than most people can remember—it truly is capable of doing most things you could want. The most basic use is this:

```
$ find -name "*.txt"
```

That query searches the current directory and all subdirectories for files that end in .txt. The previous search finds files ending in .txt but not .TXT, .Txt, or other case variations. To search without case sensitivity, use -iname instead of -name. You can optionally specify where the search should start before the -name parameter, as follows:

```
$ find /home -name "*.txt"
```

Another useful test is -size, which lets you specify how big the files should be to match. You can specify your size in kilobytes and optionally also use + or - to specify greater than or less than. For example:

```
$ find /home -name "*.txt" -size 100k
$ find /home -name "*.txt" -size +100k
$ find /home -name "*.txt" -size -100k
```

The first brings up files of exactly 100KB, the second only files greater than 100KB, and the last only files less than 100KB.

Moving on, the -user option enables you to specify the user that owns the files you are looking for. So, to search for all files in /home that end with .txt, are under 100KB, and are owned by user paul, you would use this:

```
$ find /home -name "*.txt" -size -100k -user paul
```

You can flip any of the conditions by specifying -not before them. For example, you can add a -not before -user paul to find matching files owned by everyone *but* paul:

```
$ find /home -name "*.txt" -size -100k -not -user paul
```

You can add as many -not parameters as you need, even using -not -not to cancel each other out! (Yes, that is pointless.) Keep in mind, though, that -not -size -100k is essentially equivalent to -size +100k, with the exception that the former will match files of exactly 100KB, whereas the latter will not.

You can use -perm to specify which permissions a file should have for it to be matched. This is tricky, so read carefully. The permissions are specified in the same way as with the chmod command: u for user, g for group, o for others, r for read, w for write, and x for execute. However, before you give the permissions, you need to specify a plus, a minus, or a blank space. If you specify neither a plus nor a minus, the files must exactly match the mode you give. If you specify -, the files must match all the modes you specify. If you specify +, the files must match any the modes you specify. Confused yet?

The confusion can be cleared up with some examples. This next command finds all files that have permission o=r (readable for other users). Notice that if you remove the -name parameter, it is equivalent to * because all filenames are matched:

```
$ find /home -perm -o=r
```

Any files that have o=r set are returned from that query. Those files also might have u=rw and other permissions, but as long as they have o=r, they will match. This next query matches all files that have o=rw set:

```
$ find /home -perm -o=rw
```

However, that query does not match files that are o=r or o=w. To be matched, a file must be readable *and* writable by other users. If you want to match readable *or* writable (or both), you need to use +, like this:

```
$ find /home -perm +o=rw
```

Similarly, this next query matches files that are only readable by user, group, and others:

```
$ find /home -perm -ugo=r
```

Whereas this query matches files as long as they are readable by the user, or by the group, or by others, or by any combination of the three:

```
$ find /home -perm +ugo=r
```

If you use neither + nor -, you are specifying the exact permissions to search for. For example, the next query searches for files that are readable by user, group, and others but not writable or executable by anyone:

```
$ find /home -perm ugo=r
```

You can be as specific as you need to be with the permissions. For example, this query finds all files that are readable for the user, group, and others and writable by the user:

```
$ find /home -perm ugo=r,u=w
```

To find files that are not readable by others, use the -not condition, like this:

```
$ find /home -not -perm +o=r
```

Now, on to the most advanced aspect of the find command: the -exec parameter. This enables you to execute an external program each time a match is made, passing in the name of the matched file wherever you want it. This has very specific syntax: Your command and its parameters should follow immediately after -exec, terminated by \;. You can insert the filename match at any point, using {} (an opening and a closing brace side by side).

So, you can match all text files on the entire system (that is, searching recursively from / rather than from /home as in the previous examples) over 10KB, owned by paul, that are not readable by other users, and then use chmod to enable reading, like this:

```
$ find / -name "*.txt" -size +10k -user paul -not -perm +o=r -exec chmod o+r {} \;
```

When you type your own -exec parameters, be sure to include a space before \;. Otherwise, you might see an error such as missing argument to `-exec'.

Do you see now why some people think the find command is scary? Many people learn just enough about find to be able to use it in a very basic way, but we hope you will see how much it can do if you give it a chance.

Searches for a String in Input with grep

The grep command, like find, is an incredibly powerful search tool in the right hands. Unlike find, though, grep processes any text, whether in files, or just in standard input.

The basic use of grep is this:

```
$ grep "some text" *
```

That query searches all files in the current directory (but not subdirectories) for the string some text and prints matching lines along with the name of the file. To enable recursive searching in subdirectories, use the -r parameter, like this:

```
$ grep -r "some text" *
```

Each time a string is matched within a file, the filename and the match are printed. If a file contains multiple matches, each of the matches is printed. You can alter this behavior with the -l parameter (lowercase *L*), which forces grep to print the name of each file that contains at least one match, without printing the matching text. If a file contains more than one match, it is still printed only once. Alternatively, the -c parameter prints each filename that was searched and includes the number of matches at the end, even if there were no matches.

You have a lot of control when specifying the pattern to search for. You can, as previously, specify a simple string like some text, or you can invert that search by specifying the -v parameter. For example, this returns all the lines of the file `myfile.txt` that do not contain the word `hello`:

```
$ grep -v "hello" myfile.txt
```

You can also use regular expressions for your search term. For example, you can search `myfile.txt` for all references to `cat`, `sat`, or `mat` with this command:

```
$ grep "[cms]at" myfile.txt
```

Adding the `-i` parameter to that removes case sensitivity, matching `Cat`, `CAT`, `MaT`, and so on:

```
$ grep -i [cms]at myfile.txt
```

The output can also be controlled to some extent with the `-n` and `--color` parameters. The first tells `grep` to print the line number for each match, which is where it appears in the source file. The `--color` parameter tells `grep` to color the search terms in the output, which helps them stand out when among all the other text on the line. You choose which color you want, using the GREP_COLOR environment variable: export GREP_COLOR=36 gives you cyan, and export GREP_COLOR=32 gives you lime green.

This next example uses these two parameters to number and color all matches to the previous command:

```
$ grep -in --color [cms]at myfile.txt
```

Later you will see how important `grep` is for piping with other commands.

Paging Through Output with `less`

The `less` command enables you to view large amounts of text in a more convenient way than the `cat` command. For example, your /etc/passwd file is probably more than a screen long, so if you run `cat /etc/passwd`, you are not able to see what the lines at the top were. Using `less /etc/passwd` enables you to use the cursor keys to scroll up and down the output freely. Type **q** to quit and return to the shell.

On the surface, `less` sounds like a very easy command; however, it has the infamy of being one of the few Linux commands that have a parameter for every letter of the alphabet. That is, `-a` does something, `-b` does something else, `-c`, `-d`, `-e` … `-x`, `-y`, `-z`—they all do things, with some letters even differentiating between upper- and lowercase. Furthermore, these are only the parameters used to invoke `less`. After you begin viewing your text, even more commands are available to you. Make no mistake—`less` is a complex beast to master.

Input to `less` can be divided into two categories: what you type before running `less` and what you type while running it. The former category is easy, so we start there.

We have already discussed how many parameters `less` is capable of taking, but they can be distilled down to three that are very useful: `-M`, `-N`, and `+`. Adding `-M` (this is different from `-m`!) enables verbose prompting in `less`. Instead of just printing a colon and a flashing cursor, `less` prints the filename, the line numbers being shown, the total number of lines, and the percentage of how far you are through the file. Adding `-N` (again, this is different from `-n`) enables line numbering.

The last option, `+`, enables you to pass a command to `less` for it to execute as it starts. To use this, you first need to know the commands available to you in `less`, which means we need to move onto the second category of `less` input: what you type while `less` is running.

The basic navigation keys are the up, down, left, and right cursors; Home and End (for navigating to the start and end of a file); and Page Up and Page Down. Beyond that, the most common command is `/`, which initiates a text search. You type what you want to search for and press Enter to have `less` find the first match and highlight all subsequent matches. Type `/` again and press Enter to have `less` jump to the next match. The inverse of that is `?`, which searches backward for text. Type `?`, enter a search string, and press Enter to go to the first previous match of that string, or just use `?` and press Enter to go to the next match preceding the current position. You can use `/` and `?` interchangeably by searching for something with `/` and then using `?` to go backward in the same search.

Searching with `/` and `?` is commonly done with the `+` command-line parameter from earlier, which passes `less` a command for execution after the file has loaded. For example, you can tell `less` to load a file and place the cursor at the first match for the search `hello`, like this:

```
$ less +/hello myfile.txt
```

Or, you can tell it to place the cursor at the last match for the search `hello`:

```
$ less +?hello myfile.txt
```

Beyond the cursor keys, the controls primarily involve typing a number and then pressing a key. For example, to go to line 50, type **50g**, or to go to the 75% point of the file, type **75p**. You can also place invisible mark points through the file by pressing `m` and then typing a single letter. Later, while in the same less session, you can press `'` (a single quote) and then type the letter, and you will move back to the same position. You can set up to 52 marks, named a–z and A–Z.

One clever feature of `less` is that you can, at any time, press `v` to have your file opened inside your text editor. This defaults to Vim, but you can change that by setting the `EDITOR` environment variable to something else.

If you have made it this far, you can already use `less` better than most users. You can, at this point, justifiably skip to the next section and consider yourself proficient with `less`. However, if you want to be a `less` guru, there are two more things to learn: how to view multiple files simultaneously and how to run shell commands.

Like most other file-based commands in Linux, less can take several files as its parameters. For example:

```
$ less -MN 1.txt 2.txt 3.txt
```

That command loads all three files into less, starting at 1.txt. When viewing several files, less usually tells you in which file you are, as well as numbering them: 1.txt (file 1 of 3) should be at the bottom of the screen. That said, certain things do make that go away, so you should use -M anyway.

You can navigate between files by typing a colon and then pressing n to go to the next file or p to go to the previous file; these are referred to from now on as :n and :p. You can open another file for viewing by typing :e and providing a filename. This can be any file you have permission to read, including files outside the local directory. Use the Tab key to complete filenames. Files you open in this way are inserted one place after your current position, so if you are viewing file 1 of 4 and open a new file, the new file is numbered 2 of 5 and is opened for viewing straightaway. To close a file and remove it from the list, use :d.

Viewing multiple files simultaneously has implications for searching. By default, less searches within only one file, but it is easy to search within all files. When you type / or ? to search, follow it with a *—you should see EOF-ignore followed by a search prompt. You can now type a search and it will search in the current file; if nothing is found, it looks in subsequent files until it finds a match. You can repeat searches by pressing the Esc key and then either n or N. The lowercase option repeats the search forward across files, and the uppercase repeats it backward.

The last thing you need to know is that you can get to a shell from the less and execute commands. The simplest way to do this is just to type ! and press Enter. This launches a shell and leaves you free to type all the commands you want, as per normal. Type **exit** to return to less. You can also type specific commands by entering them after the exclamation mark, using the special character % for the current filename. For example, du -h % prints the size of the current file. Finally, you can use !! to repeat the previous command.

Creating Links Between Files with ln

Linux enables you to create links between files that look and work like normal files for the most part. Moreover, it allows you to make two types of links, known as *hard* links and *symbolic* links (*symlinks*). The difference between the two is crucial, although it might not be obvious at first!

Each filename on your system points to what is known as an *inode*, which is the absolute location of a file. Linux allows you to point more than one filename to a given inode, and the result is a *hard link*—two filenames pointing to exactly the same file. Each of these files shares the same contents and attributes. So, if you edit one, the other changes because they are both the same file.

On the other hand, a *symlink*—sometimes called a *soft* link—is a redirect to the real file. When a program tries to read from a symlink, it automatically is redirected to what the symlink is pointing at. The fact that symlinks are really just dumb pointers has two advantages: You can link to something that does not exist (and create it later if you want), and you can link to directories.

Both types of links have their uses. Creating a hard link is a great way to back up a file on the same disk. For example, if you delete the file in one location, it still exists untouched in the other location. Symlinks are popular because they allow a file to appear to be in a different location; you could store your website in /var/www/live and an under-construction holding page in /var/www/construction. Then you could have Apache point to a symlink /var/www/html that is redirected to either the live or construction directory depending on what you need.

> **TIP**
>
> The shred command overwrites a file's contents with random data, allowing for safe deletion. Because this directly affects a file's contents, rather than just a filename, this means that all filenames hard linked to an inode are affected.

Both types of link are created with the ln command. By default, the ln command creates hard links, but you can create symlinks by passing it the -s parameter. The syntax is ln [-s] <something> <somewhere>, for example:

```
$ ln -s myfile.txt mylink
```

That command creates the symlink mylink that points to myfile.txt. Remove the -s to create a hard link. You can verify that your link has been created by running ls -l. Your symlink should look something like this:

```
lrwxrwxrwx  1 paul paul    5 2007-11-12 12:39 mylink -> myfile.txt
```

Note how the file properties start with l (lowercase *L*) for link and how ls -l also prints where the link is going. Symlinks are always very small in size; the previous link is 5 bytes in size. If you created a hard link, it should look like this:

```
-rw-rw-r  2 paul paul   341 2007-11-12 12:39 mylink
```

This time the file has normal attributes, but the second number is 2 rather than 1. That number is how many hard links point to this file, which is why it is 2 now. The file size is also the same as that of the previous filename because it *is* the file, as opposed to just being a pointer.

Symlinks are used extensively in Linux. Programs that have been superseded, such as sh, now point to their replacements (in this case, bash), and library versioning is accomplished through symlinks. For example, applications that link against zlib load /usr/lib/libz.so. Internally, however, that is just a symlink that points to the actual zlib library: /usr/lib/libz.so.1.2.1.2. This enables multiple versions of libraries to be installed without applications needing to worry about the version name.

Finding Files from an Index with `locate`

When you use the `find` command, it searches recursively through each directory each time you request a file. This is slow, as you can imagine. Fortunately, Fedora ships with a `cron` job that creates an index of all the files on your system every night. Searching this index is extremely fast, which means that, if the file you are looking for has been around since the last index, this is the preferable way of searching.

To look for a file in your index, use the command `locate` followed by the names of the files you want to find, like this:

```
$ locate myfile.txt
```

On a relatively modern computer (1.5GHz or higher), `locate` should be able to return all the matching files in less than a second. The trade-off for this speed is lack of flexibility. You can search for matching filenames, but, unlike with `find`, you cannot search for sizes, owners, access permissions, or other attributes. The one thing you can change is case sensitivity; use the `-i` parameter to do a search that is not case sensitive.

Although Fedora rebuilds the filename index nightly, you can force a rebuild whenever you want by running the command `updatedb` as root. This usually takes a few minutes, but when it's done the new database is immediately available.

Listing Files in the Current Directory with `ls`

The `ls` command, like `ln`, is one of those you expect to be very straightforward. It lists files, but how many options can it possibly have? In true Linux style, the answer is many, although again you need know only a few to wield great power!

The basic use is simply `ls`, which outputs the files and directories in the current location. You can filter that with normal wildcards, so all these are valid:

```
$ ls *
```

```
$ ls *.txt
```

```
$ ls my*ls *.txt *.xml
```

Any directories that match these filters are recursed into one level. That is, if you run `ls my*` and you have the files `myfile1.txt` and `myfile2.txt` and a directory `mystuff`, the matching files are printed first. Then `ls` prints the contents of the `mystuff` directory.

The most popular parameters for customizing the output of `ls` are the following:

> ▶ `-a`—Includes hidden files

> ▶ `-h`—Uses human-readable sizes

> ▶ `-l`—A lowercase *L*, it enables long listing

> ▶ `-r`—Reverses the order of results

▶ **-R**—Recursively lists directories

▶ **-s**—Shows sizes

▶ **--sort**—Sorts the listing

All files that start with a period are hidden in Linux, so that includes the .gnome directory in your home directory, as well as .bash_history and the . and .. implicit directories that signify the current directory and the parent. By default, ls does not show these files, but if you run ls -a, they are shown. You can also use ls -A to show all the hidden files except . and ...

The -h parameter has to be combined with the -s parameter, like this:

```
$ ls -sh *.txt
```

That query outputs the size of each matching file in a human-readable format, such as 108KB or 4.5MB.

Using the -1 parameter shows much more information about your files. Instead of just providing the names of the files, you get output like this:

```
drwxrwxr-x 24 paul paul  4096 2007-11-12 21:33 arch
-rw-r--r--  1 paul paul 18691 2007-11-12 21:34 COPYING
-rw-r--r--  1 paul paul 88167 2007-11-12 21:35 CREDITS
drwxrwxr-x  2 paul paul  4096 2007-11-12 21:35 crypto
```

That output shows four matches and prints a lot of information about each of them. The first row shows the arch directory; you can tell it is a directory because its file attributes start with a d. The rwxrwxr-x following that shows the access permissions, and this has special meaning because it is a directory. Read access for a directory allows users to see the directory contents, write access allows you to create files and subdirectories, and execute access allows you to cd into the directory. If a user has execute access but not read access, he can cd into the directory but not list files.

Moving on, the next number on the line is 24, which also has a special meaning for directories: It is the number of subdirectories, including . and ... After that is paul paul, which is the name of the user owner and the group owner for the directory. Next are the size and modification time, and finally the directory name itself.

The next line shows the file COPYING, and most of the numbers have the same meaning, with the exception of the 1 immediately after the access permissions. For directories, this is the number of subdirectories, but for files, this is the number of hard links to this file. A 1 in this column means this is the only filename pointing to this inode, so if you delete it, it is gone.

Fedora comes configured with a shortcut command for ls -1: 11.

The `--sort` parameter enables you to reorder the output from the default alphabetic sorting. You can sort by various things, although the most popular are extension (alphabetically), size (largest first), and time (newest first). To flip the sorting (making size sort by smallest first), use the `-r` parameter also. So, this command lists all `.ogg` files, sorted smallest to largest:

```
$ ls --sort size -r *.ogg
```

Finally, the `-R` parameter recurses through subdirectories. For example, `ls /etc` lists all the files and subdirectories in `/etc`, but `ls -R /etc` lists all the files and subdirectories in `/etc`, all the files and subdirectories in `/etc/acpi`, all the files and subdirectories in `/etc/acpi/actions`, and so on until every subdirectory has been listed.

Reading Manual Pages with `man`

Time for a much-needed mental break: The `man` command is easy to use. Most people use only the topic argument, like this: `man gcc`. However, two other commands that are very useful work closely with `man`—whatis and apropos.

The `whatis` command returns a one-line description of another command, which is the same text you get at the top of that command's man page. For example:

```
[paul@caitlin ~]$ whatis ls
ls      (1) - list directory contents
```

The output there explains what `ls` does but also provides the man page section number for the command so that you can query it further.

On the other hand, the `apropos` command takes a search string as its parameter and returns all man pages that match the search. For example, `apropos mixer` gives this list:

```
alsamixer (1) - soundcard mixer for ALSA soundcard driver
mixer (1) - command-line mixer for ALSA soundcard driver
aumix (1) - adjust audio mixer
```

So, use apropos to help you find commands and use `whatis` to tell you what a command does.

Making Directories with `mkdir`

Making directories is as easy as it sounds, although there is one parameter you should be aware of: `-p`. If you are in `/home/paul` and you want to create the directory `/home/paul/audio/sound`, you get an error like this:

```
mkdir: cannot create directory `audio/sound`: No such file or directory
```

At first glance, this seems wrong because `mkdir` cannot create the directory because it does not exist. What it actually means is that it cannot create the directory sound because the directory audio does not exist. This is where the `-p` parameter comes in: If you try to make a directory within another directory that does not exist, as in the previous example, -p creates the parent directories, too. So:

```
$ mkdir -p audio/sound
```

That first creates the audio directory and then creates the sound directory inside it.

Moving Files with mv

This command is one of the easiest around. There are two helpful parameters to mv: -f, which overwrites files without asking; and -u, which moves the source file only if it is newer than the destination file. That's it!

Listing Processes with ps

This is the third and last "command that should be simple, but isn't" that is discussed here. The ps command lists processes and gives you an extraordinary amount of control over its operation.

The first thing to know is that ps is typically used with what are known as *BSD-style parameters*. Back in the section "Finding Files by Searching with find," we discussed UNIX-style, GNU-style, and X-style parameters (-c, --dosomething, and -dosomething, respectively), but BSD-style parameters are different because they use single letters without a dash.

The default use of ps therefore lists all processes you are running that are attached to the terminal. However, you can ask it to list all your processes attached to any terminal (or indeed no terminal) by adding the x parameter: ps x. You can ask it to list all processes for all users with the a parameter or combine that with x to list all processes for all users, attached to a terminal or otherwise: ps ax.

However, both of these are timid compared with the almighty u option, which enables user-oriented output. In practice, that makes a huge difference because you get important fields such as the username of the owner, how much CPU time and RAM are being used, when the process was started, and more. This outputs a lot of information, so you might want to try adding the f parameter, which creates a process forest by using ASCII art to connect parent commands with their children. You can combine all the options so far with this command: ps faux (yes, with a little imagination, you spell words with the parameters!).

You can control the order in which the data is returned by using the --sort parameter. This takes either a + or a - (although the + is default) followed by the field by which you want to sort: command, %cpu, pid, and user are all popular options. If you use the minus sign, the results are reversed. This next command lists all processes, in descending order by CPU use:

```
$ ps aux --sort=-%cpu
```

There are many other parameters for ps, including a huge number of options for compatibility with other UNIXes. If you have the time to read the man page, you should give it a try!

Deleting Files and Directories with rm

The rm command has only one parameter of interest: --preserve-root. By now, you should know that issuing rm -rf / as root will destroy your Linux installation because -r means *recursive* and -f means *force* (do not prompt for confirmation before deleting). It is possible for a clumsy person to issue this command by accident—not by typing the command on purpose, but by putting a space in the wrong place. For example:

```
$ rm -rf /home/paul
```

That command deletes the home directory of the user paul. This is not an uncommon command; after you have removed a user and backed up her data, you will probably want to issue something similar. However, if you add an accidental space between the / and the h in home, you get this:

```
£ rm -rf / home/paul
```

This time the command means "delete everything recursively from / and then delete home/paul"—quite a different result! You can stop this from happening by using the --preserve-root parameter, which stops you from catastrophe with this message:

```
rm: it is dangerous to operate recursively on `/'
rm: use --no-preserve-root to override this failsafe.
```

Of course, no one wants to keep typing --preserve-root each time he runs rm, so you should add this line to the .bashrc file in your home directory:

```
alias rm='rm --preserve-root'
```

That alias automatically adds --preserve-root to all calls to rm in future bash sessions.

Printing the Last Lines of a File with tail

If you want to watch a log file as it is written to, or want to monitor a user's actions as they are occurring, you need to be able to track log files as they change. In these situations, you need the tail command, which prints the last few lines of a file and updates as new lines are added. This command tells tail to print the last few lines of /var/log/httpd/access_log, the Apache hit log:

```
$ tail /var/log/httpd/access_log
```

To get tail to remain running and update as the file changes, add the -f parameter (which means "follow"):

```
$ tail -f /var/log/httpd/access_log
```

You can tie the lifespan of a tail call to follow the existence of a process by specifying the --pid parameter. When you do this, tail continues to follow the file you asked for until it sees that the process (identified by PID) is no longer running, at which point tail stops tailing.

If you specify multiple files on the command line, `tail` follows both, printing file headers whenever the input source changes. Press Ctrl+C to terminate `tail` when in follow mode.

Printing Resource Usage with `top`

The `top` command is unusual in this list because the few parameters it takes are rarely, if ever, used. Instead, it has a number of commands you can use while it is running to customize the information it shows you. To get the most from these instructions, open two terminal windows. In the first, run the program `yes` and leave it running; in the second, switch to root, and run `top`.

The default sort order in `top` shows the most CPU-intensive tasks first. The first command there should be the `yes` process you just launched from the other terminal, but there should be many others, too. First, you want to filter out all the other users and focus on the user running yes. To do this, press **u** and enter the username you used when you ran yes. When you press Enter, `top` filters out processes not being run by that user.

The next step is to kill the process ID of the `yes` command, so you need to understand what each of the important fields means:

▸ **PID**—The process ID

▸ **User**—The owner of the process

▸ **PR**—Priority

▸ **NI**—Niceness

▸ **Virt**—Virtual image size in kilobytes

▸ **Res**—Resident size in kilobytes

▸ **Shr**—Shared memory size in kilobytes

▸ **S**—Status

▸ **%CPU**—CPU use

▸ **%Mem**—Memory use

▸ **Time+**—CPU time

▸ **Command**—The command being run

Several of these fields are unimportant unless you have a specific problem. The ones we are interested in are PID, User, Niceness, %CPU, %MEM, Time+, and Command. The Niceness of a process is how much time the CPU allocates to it compared to everything else on the system: 19 is the lowest, and –19 is the highest.

With the columns explained, you should be able to find the process ID of the errant yes command launched earlier; it is usually the first number below PID. Now type **k**, enter that process ID, and press Enter. You are prompted for a signal number (the manner in which you want the process killed), with 15 provided as the default. Signal 15 (also known as SIGTERM, for "terminate") is a polite way of asking a process to shut down, and all processes that are not wildly out of control should respond to it. Give top a few seconds to update itself, and the yes command should be gone. If not, you need to be more forceful: type **k** again, enter the PID, and press Enter. When prompted for a signal to send, enter **9** and press Enter to send SIGKILL, which means "terminate whether you like it or not."

You can choose the fields to display by pressing f. A new screen appears that lists all possible fields, along with the letter you need to press to toggle their visibility. Selected fields are marked with an asterisk and have their letter, for example:

```
* A: PID        = Process Id
```

If you press the a key, the screen changes to this:

```
a: PID          = Process Id
```

When you have made your selections, press Enter to return to the normal top view with your normal column selection.

You can also press F to select the field you want to use for sorting. This works in the same way as the field selection screen, except that you can select only one field at a time. Again, press Enter to get back to top after you have made your selection, and the output will be updated with the new sorting.

If you press B, text bolding is enabled. By default, this bolds some of the header bar and any programs that are currently running (as opposed to sleeping), but if you press x you can also enable bolding of the sorted column. You can use y to toggle bolding of running processes.

The last command to try is r, which enables you to *re-nice*—or adjust the nice value—of a process. You need to enter the PID of the process, press Enter, and enter a new nice value. Keep in mind that 19 is the lowest and –20 is the highest; anything less than 0 is considered "high" and should be used sparingly.

Printing the Location of a Command with which

The purpose of which is to tell you the exact command that would be executed if you typed it. For example, which mkdir returns /bin/mkdir, telling you that running the command mkdir runs /bin/mkdir.

Combining Commands

So far, we have been using commands only individually, and for the large part that is what you will be doing in practice. However, some of the real power of these commands lies in the capability to join them to get exactly what you want. There are some extra little commands we have not yet covered that are often used as glue because they do one simple thing that enables a more complex process to work.

All the commands we have examined have printed their information to the screen, but this is often flexible. There are two ways to control where output should go: piping and output redirection. A *pipe* is a connector between one command's output and another's input. Rather than send its output to your terminal, a command sends that output directly to another command for input. Output redirection works in a similar way to pipes but is usually used for files. We look at pipes first and then output redirection.

Two of the commands covered so far are ps and grep: the process lister and the string matcher. You can combine the two to find out which users are playing Nethack right now:

```
$ ps aux ¦ grep nethack
```

That creates a list of all the processes running right now and sends that list to the grep command, which filters out all lines that do not contain the word *nethack*. Fedora allows you to pipe as many commands as you can sanely string together. For example, you could add in the wc command, which counts the numbers of lines, words, and characters in its input, to count precisely how many times Nethack is being run:

```
$ ps aux ¦ grep nethack ¦ wc -l
```

The -l (lowercase *L*) parameter to wc prints only the line count.

Using pipes in this way is often preferable to using the -exec parameter to find, simply because many people consider find to be a black art and so anything that uses it less frequently is better! This is where the xargs command comes in: It converts output from one command into arguments for another.

For a good example, consider this mammoth find command from earlier:

```
$ find / -name "*.txt" -size +10k -user paul -not -perm +o=r -exec chmod o+r {} \;
```

That command searches every directory from / onward for files matching *.txt that are greater than 10KB, are owned by user paul, and do not have read permission for others. Then it executes chmod on each of the files. It is a complex command, and people who are not familiar with the workings of find might have problems understanding it. So, what we can do is break up the single command into two parts: a call to find and a call to xargs. The conversion would look like this:

```
$ find / -name "*.txt" -size +10k -user paul -not -perm +o=r ¦ xargs chmod o+r
```

That has eliminated the confusing {} \; from the end of the command, but it does the same thing, and faster, too. The speed difference between the two exists because using -exec with find causes it to execute chmod once for each file. However, chmod accepts many files at a time and, because the same parameter is used each time, you should take advantage of that. The second command, using xargs, is called once with all the output from find, and so saves many command calls. The xargs command automatically places the input at the end of the line, so the previous command might look something like this:

```
$ xargs chmod o+r file1.txt file2.txt file3.txt
```

Not every command accepts multiple files, however, and if you specify the -1 parameter, xargs executes its command once for each line in its input. If you want to check what it is doing, use the -p parameter to have xargs prompt you before executing each command.

For even more control, the -i parameter enables you to specify exactly where the matching lines should be placed in your command. This is important if you need the lines to appear before the end of the command or need them to appear more than once. Either way, using the -i parameter also enables the -1 parameter so that each line is sent to the command individually. This next command finds all files in /home/paul that are larger than 10,000KB in size (10MB) and copies them to /home/paul/archive:

```
$ find /home/paul -size +10000k ¦ xargs -i cp {} ./home/paul/archive
```

Using find with xargs is a unique case. All too often, people use pipes when parameters would do the job just as well. For example, these two commands are identical:

```
$ ps aux --sort=-%cpu ¦ grep -v `whoami`
```

```
$ ps -N ux --sort=-%cpu
```

The former prints all users and processes and then pipes that to grep, which in turn filters out all lines that contain the output from the program whoami (our username). So, line one prints all processes being run by other uses, sorted by CPU use. Line two does not specify the a parameter to ps, which makes it list only our parameters. It then uses the -N parameter to flip that, which means it lists everyone but us, without the need for grep.

The reason people use the former is often just simplicity: Many people know only a handful of parameters to each command, so they can string together two commands simply rather than write one command properly. Unless the command is to be run regularly, this is not a problem. Indeed, the first line would be better because it does not drive people to the manual to find out what ps -N does!

Multiple Terminals

It is both curious and sad that many Linux veterans have not heard of the screen command. Curious because they needlessly go to extra effort to replicate what screen takes in its stride and sad because they are missing a powerful tool that would benefit them greatly.

Picture this scene: You connect to a server via SSH and are working at the remote shell. You need to open another shell window so that you can have the two running side by side; perhaps you want the output from top in one window while typing in another.

What do you do? Most people would open another SSH connection, but doing so is both wasteful and unnecessary. screen is a *terminal multiplexer*, which is a fancy term for a program that lets you run multiple terminals inside one terminal.

The best way to learn screen is to try it yourself, so open a console, type **screen**, and then press Enter. Your display blanks momentarily and then is replaced with a console; it will look like nothing has changed. Now, let's do something with that terminal. Run top and leave it running for the time being. Hold down the Ctrl key and press a (referred to as Ctrl+a from now on); then let go of them both and press **c**. Your prompt clears again, leaving you able to type. Run the uptime command.

Pop quiz: What happened to the old terminal running top? It is still running, of course. You can press Ctrl+a and then press **0** (zero) to return to it. Press Ctrl+a and then press **1** to go back to your uptime terminal. While you are viewing other terminals, the commands in the other terminals carry on running as normal so that you can multitask.

Many of screen's commands are case sensitive, so the lettering used here is very specific: Ctrl+a means "press Ctrl and the *a* key," but Ctrl+A means press "Ctrl and Shift and the *a* key" so that you get a capital *A*. Ctrl+a+A means "press Ctrl and the *a* key, let them go, and then press Shift and the *a* key."

You have seen how to create new displays and how to switch between them by number. However, you can also bring up a window list and select windows using your cursor with Ctrl+a+" (that is, press Ctrl and a together, let go, and press the double quotes key [usually Shift and the single quote key]). You will find that the screens you create have the name bash by default, which is not very descriptive. Select a window and press Ctrl+a+A. You are prompted to enter a name for the current window, and your name is used in the window list.

When you get past window 9, it becomes impossible to switch to windows using Ctrl+a and 0–9; as soon as you type the 1 of 10, screen switches to display 1. The solution is to use either the window list or the quick-change option, in which you press Ctrl+a+' (single quote), enter either the screen number or the name you gave it, and then press Enter. You can also change back to the previous window by pressing Ctrl+a+Ctrl+a. If you work within only a small set of windows, you can use Ctrl+a+n and Ctrl+a+p to move to the next and previous windows, respectively. Of course, if you are changing to and from windows only to see whether something has changed, you are wasting time because screen can monitor windows for you and report if anything changes. To enable (or disable) monitoring for a window, use Ctrl+a+M; when something happens, screen flashes a message. If you miss it (the messages disappear when you type something), use Ctrl+a+m to bring up the last message.

Windows close when you kill the main program inside. Having pressed Ctrl+a+c, your window will be bash; type **exit** to quit. Alternatively, you can use Ctrl+a+K to kill a window. When all your windows are closed, screen terminates and prints a screen is terminating message so that you know you are out.

However, there are two alternatives to quitting: locking and disconnecting. The first, activated with Ctrl+a+x, locks access to your screen data until you enter your system password. The second is the most powerful feature of screen: You can exit it and do other things for a while and then reconnect later and screen will pick up where you left off. For example, you could be typing at your desk, disconnect from screen, and then go home, reconnect, and carry on as if nothing had changed. What's more, all the programs you ran from screen carry on running even while screen is disconnected. It even automatically disconnects for you if someone closes your terminal window while it is in a locked state (with Ctrl+a+x).

To disconnect from screen, press Ctrl+a+d. You are returned to the prompt from which you launched screen and can carry on working, close the terminal you had opened, or even log out completely. When you want to reconnect, run the command screen -r. You can, in the meantime, just run screen and start a new session without resuming the previous one, but that is not wise if you value your sanity! You can disconnect and reconnect the same screen session as many times you want, which potentially means you need never lose your session again.

Although this has been a mere taste of screen, we hope you can see how useful it can be.

Date and Time

The Fedora installer will query you during installation for default time zone settings, and whether your computer's hardware clock is set to *Greenwich mean time (GMT)*—more properly known as *UTC* or *coordinated universal time*.

Linux provides a system date and time; your computer hardware provides a hardware clock-based time. In many cases, it is possible for the two times to drift apart. Linux system time is based on the number of seconds elapsed since January 1, 1970. Your computer's hardware time depends on the type of clock chips installed on your PC's motherboard, and many motherboard chipsets are notoriously subject to drift.

Keeping accurate time is not only important on a single workstation, but also critically important in a network environment. Backups, scheduled downtimes, and other network-wide actions need to be accurately coordinated.

Fedora provides two date and time utilities you can use at the command line:

▶ **date**—Used to display, set, or adjust the system date and time from the command line

▶ **hwclock**—A root command to display, set, adjust, and synchronize hardware and system clocks

Using the date Command

Use the date command to display or set your Linux system time. This command requires you to use a specific sequence of numbers to represent the desired date and time. To see your Linux system's idea of the current date and time, use the date command like this:

```
# date
Wed Jan 10 14:17:01 EDT 2005
```

To adjust your system's time (say, to January 27, 2006 at 8 a.m.), use a command line with the month, day, hour, minute, and year, as follows:

```
# date 012606002003
Fri Jan 27 08:00:00 EDT 2003
```

Using the `hwclock` Command

Use the `hwclock` command to display or set your Linux system time, display or set your PC's hardware clock, or to synchronize the system and hardware times. To see your hardware date and time, use `hwclock` with its `--show` option like so:

```
# hwclock --show
Fri 27 Jan 2006 02:17:53 PM GMT  -0.193809 seconds
```

Use `hwclock` with its `--set` and `--date` options to manually set the hardware clock like so:

```
# hwclock --set --date "01/27/06 08:00:00"
# hwclock --show
Tue 27 Jan 2006 08:00:08 AM GMT -0.151718 seconds
```

In these examples, the hardware clock has been set with `hwclock`, which is then used again to verify the new hardware date and time. You can also `hwclock` to set the Linux system date and time date, using your hardware clock's values with the Linux system date and time.

For example, to set the system time from your PC's hardware clock, use the `--hctosys` option as follows:

```
# hwclock --hctosys
```

Capturing Screen Images

Although you're working at the command line rather than a swish GUI, you can still grab images from your graphical desktop through the `import` command, and that's exactly what we did to capture the images for this book.

First, we ran `xhost +` on the remote computer to allow another computer access to the X server on the remote machine; the command to take the screenshot is run on our local machine like this:

```
$ import -window root -display 192.168.2.4:0 12fig07.jpg
```

This utility made a difficult task easy because the publisher required the screenshots be done from an 800×600 screen (too small to comfortably work in) to accommodate its printing and production equipment.

We could also have used the classic UNIX tool xwd to take screenshots. The command would have looked similar to that of import:

```
$ xwd -root -display 192.168.2.4:0 -out 12fig07.jpg
```

Reference

▶ **http://www.gnu.org/**—The website of the GNU project, it contains manuals and downloads for lots of command-line software.

▶ **http://www.linuxdevcenter.com/linux/cmd/**—A wide selection of Linux commands and explanations of what they do.

▶ **http://www.tuxfiles.org/linuxhelp/cli.html**—Several short command-line tutorials, courtesy of tuXfiles.

▶ **http://www.linuxcommand.org/**—Describes itself as "your one-stop command line shop!" It contains a wealth of useful information about the console.

▶ **http://www.tripwire.org/**—Information and download links for the open source version of Tripwire.

Books

Understanding the way UNIX works at the nuts-and-bolts level can be both challenging and rewarding, and there are several good books that will help guide you on your way. Perhaps the best is *The Art of UNIX Programming*, by Eric Raymond (Addison-Wesley, ISBN: 0-13-142901-9), which focuses on the philosophy behind UNIX and manages to mix in much about the command line.

O'Reilly's *UNIX CD Bookshelf* (ISBN: 0-596-00392-7) contains seven highly respected books in one, although it retails for more than $120 as a result! That said, it is incomparable in its depth and breadth of coverage.

CHAPTER 33

Writing and Executing a Shell Script

W hy should you write and use shell scripts? Shell scripts can save you time and typing, especially if you routinely use the same command lines multiple times every day. Although you could also use the history function (press the Up or Down keys while using bash or use the history command), a shell script can add flexibility with command-line argument substitution and built-in help.

Although a shell script doesn't execute faster than a program written in a computer language such as C, a shell program can be smaller in size than a compiled program. The shell program does not require any additional library support other than the shell or, if used, existing commands installed on your system. The process of creating and testing shell scripts is also generally simpler and faster than the development process for equivalent C language commands.

NOTE

Hundreds of commands included with Fedora are actually shell scripts, and many other good shell script examples are available over the Internet—a quick search yields numerous links to online tutorials and scripting guides from fellow Linux users and developers. For example, the startx command, used to start an X Window session from the text console, is a shell script used every day by most users. To learn more about shell scripting with bash, see the Advanced Bash-Scripting Guide, listed in the "Reference" section at the end of this chapter. You will also find *Sams Teach Yourself Shell Programming in 24 Hours* a helpful guide to learning more about using the shell to build your own commands.

When you are learning to write and execute your first shell scripts, start with scripts for simple but useful tasks. Begin with short examples, and then expand the scripts as you build on your experience and knowledge. Make liberal use of comments (lines preceded with a pound # sign) to document each section of your script. Include an author statement and overview of the script as additional help, along with a creation date or version number. Use a text editor such as vi to write shell scripts because it does not automatically wrap lines of text. Line wrapping can break script syntax and cause problems. If you use the nano editor, include its -w flag to disable line wrap.

In this section, you learn how to write a simple shell script to set up a number of *aliases* (command synonyms) whenever you log on. Instead of typing all the aliases every time you log on, you can put them in a file by using a text editor, such as vi, and then execute the file. Normally these changes are saved in systemwide shell configuration files under the /etc directory to make the changes active for all users or in your .bashrc, .cshrc (if you use tcsh), or .bash_profile files in your home directory.

Here is what is contained in myenv, a sample shell script created for this purpose (for bash):

```
#!/bin/sh
alias ll='ls -l'
alias ldir='ls -aF'
alias copy='cp'
```

This simple script creates command *aliases*, or convenient shorthand forms of commands, for the ls and cp commands. The ll alias provides a long directory listing: The ldir alias is the ls command, but prints indicators (for directories or executable files) in listings. The copy alias is the same as the cp command. You can experiment and add your own options or create aliases of other commands with options you frequently use.

You can execute myenv in a variety of ways under Linux. As shown in this example, you can make myenv executable by using the chmod command and then execute it as you would any other native Linux command:

```
$ chmod +x myenv
```

This line turns on the executable permission of myenv, which can be checked with the ls command and its -l option like this:

```
$ ls -l myenv
-rwxrwxr-x   1 andrew    andrew    65   2007-11-12 17:38 myenv
```

Running a Shell Program

You can run your new shell program in several ways. Each method produces the same results, which is a testament to the flexibility of using the shell with Linux. One way to run your shell program is to execute the file `myenv` from the command line as if it were a Linux command:

```
$ ./myenv
```

A second way to execute `myenv` under a particular shell, such as zsh, is as follows:

```
$ zsh  myenv
```

This invokes a new `zsh` shell and passes the filename `myenv` as a parameter to execute the file. A third way requires you to create a directory named `bin` in your home directory, and to then copy the new shell program into this directory. You can then run the program without specifying a specific location or using a shell. You do this like so:

```
$ mkdir bin
$ mv myenv bin
$ myenv
```

This works because Fedora is set up by default to include the executable path `$HOME/bin` in your shell's environment. You can view this environment variable, named `PATH`, by piping the output of the `env` command through `fgrep`, like so:

```
$ env ¦ fgrep PATH
/usr/kerberos/bin:/usr/local/bin:/bin:/usr/bin: \
/usr/X11R6/bin:/sbin:/home/andrew/bin
```

As you can see, the user (andrew in this example) can use the new `bin` directory to hold executable files. Another way to bring up an environment variable is to use the `echo` command along with the variable name (in this case, `$PATH`):

```
$ echo $PATH
/usr/kerberos/bin:/usr/local/bin:/usr/bin:/bin:/usr/X11R6/bin:/home/andrew/bin
```

CAUTION

Never put `.` in your $PATH to execute files or a command in the current directory—this presents a serious security risk, especially for the root operator, and even more so if `.` is first in your $PATH search order. Trojan scripts placed by crackers in directories such as /tmp can be used for malicious purposes, and are executed immediately if the current working directory is part of your $PATH.

After you execute the command `myenv`, you should be able to use `ldir` from the command line to get a list of files under the current directory and `ll` to get a list of files with attributes displayed. However, the best way to use the new commands in `myenv` is to put them into your shell's login or profile file. For Fedora, and nearly all Linux users, the default shell is `bash`, so you can make these commands available for everyone on your system by putting them in the /etc/bashrc file. Systemwide aliases for tcsh are contained in files with the extension .csh under the /etc/profile.d directory. The shell can use these command aliases, too.

Interpreting Shell Scripts Through Specific Shells

The majority of shell scripts use a *shebang line* (#!) at the beginning to control the type of shell used to run the script; this bang line calls for an sh-incantation of bash:

```
#!/bin/sh
```

A shebang line (short for *sharp* and *bang*, two names for # and !) tells the Linux kernel that a specific command (a shell, or in the case of other scripts, perhaps awk or Perl) is to be used to interpret the contents of the file. Using a shebang line is common practice for all shell scripting. For example, if you write a shell script using bash, but want the script to execute as if run by the Bourne shell, sh, the first line of your script will contain #!/bin/sh, which is a link to the bash shell. Running bash as sh causes bash to act as a Bourne shell. This is the reason for the symbolic link sh, which points to bash.

The Shebang Line

The shebang line is a magic number, as defined in /usr/share/magic—a text database of magic numbers for the Linux file command. Magic numbers are used by many different Linux commands to quickly identify a type of file, and the database format is documented in the section five man page named magic (read by using man 5 magic). For example, magic numbers can be used by the Linux file command to display the identity of a script (no matter what filename is used) as a shell script if a specific shell or other interpreter is used, such as awk or Perl.

You might also find different or new environment variables available to your scripts by using different shells. For example, if you launch csh from the bash command line, you will find several new variables or variables with slightly different definitions, such as the following:

```
$ env
...
VENDOR=intel
MACHTYPE=i386
HOSTTYPE=i386-linux
HOST=werewolf.hudson.com
```

On the other hand, bash might provide these variables or variables of the same name with a slightly different definition, such as these:

```
$ env
...
```

```
HOSTTYPE=i386
HOSTNAME=werewolf.hudson.com
```

Although the behavior of a shebang line is not defined by POSIX, variations of its use can be helpful when you are writing shell scripts. For example, as described in the want man page, you can use a shell to help execute programs called within a shell script without needing to hard-code pathnames of programs. The want command is a windowing *Tool Control Language* (tcl) interpreter that can be used to write graphical clients. Avoiding the use of specific pathnames to programs increases shell script portability because not every UNIX or Linux system has programs in the same location.

For example, if you want to use the want command, your first inclination might be to write the following:

```
#!/usr/local/bin/wish
```

Although this works on many other operating systems, the script fails under Linux because want is located under the /usr/bin directory. However, if you write the command line this way

```
#!/bin/sh
exec wish "$@"
```

the script always finds the correct binary.

Using Variables in Shell Scripts

When writing shell scripts for Linux, you work with three types of variables:

- ▶ **Environment variables**—Part of the system environment, you can use them in your shell program. New variables can be defined, and some of them, such as PATH, can also be modified within a shell program.

- ▶ **Built-in variables**—These variables, such as options used on the command (interpreted by the shell as a *positional argument*), are provided by Linux. Unlike environment variables, you cannot modify them.

- ▶ **User variables**—Defined by you when you write a shell script. You can use and modify them at will within the shell program.

A major difference between shell programming and other programming languages is that in shell programming, variables are not *typed*—that is, you do not have to specify whether a variable is a number or a string, and so on.

Assigning a Value to a Variable

Assume that you want to use a variable called lcount to count the number of iterations in a loop within a shell program. You can declare and initialize this variable as follows:

Command	Environment
lcount=0	bash
set lcount=0	tcsh

> **NOTE**
>
> Under bash, you must ensure that the equal sign (=) does not have spaces before and after it.

To store a string in a variable, you can use the following:

Command	Environment
myname=Andrew	bash
set myname=Andrew	tcsh

Use the preceding variable form if the string doesn't have embedded spaces. If a string has embedded spaces, you can do the assignment as follows:

Command	Environment
myname="Andrew Hudson"	bash
set myname="Andrew Hudson"	tcsh

Accessing Variable Values

You can access the value of a variable by prefixing the variable name with a $ (dollar sign). That is, if the variable name is var, you can access the variable by using $var.

If you want to assign the value of var to the variable lcount, you can do so as follows:

Command	Environment
lcount=$var	bash
set lcount=$var	tcsh

Positional Parameters

It is possible to pass options from the command line or from another shell script to your shell program.

These options are supplied to the shell program by Linux as *positional parameters*, which have special names provided by the system. The first parameter is stored in a variable called 1 (number 1), and you can access it by using $1 within the program. The second parameter is stored in a variable called 2, and you can access it by using $2 within the program, and so on. One or more of the higher numbered positional parameters can be omitted while you're invoking a shell program.

Understanding how to use these positional parameters and how to access and use variables retrieved from the command line is necessary when developing more advanced shell programs.

A Simple Example of a Positional Parameter

For example, if a shell program mypgm expects two parameters—such as a first name and a last name—you can invoke the shell program with only one parameter, the first name. However, you cannot invoke it with only the second parameter, the last name.

Here is a shell program called mypgm1, which takes only one parameter (a name) and displays it on the screen:

```
#!/bin/sh
#Name display program
if [ $# -eq 0 ]
then
    echo "Name not provided"
else
    echo "Your name is "$1
fi
```

If you execute mypgm1, as follows

```
$ bash  mypgm1
```

you get the following output:

```
Name not provided
```

However, if you execute mypgm1, as follows

```
$ bash  mypgm1 Andrew
```

you get the following output:

```
Your name is Andrew
```

The shell program mypgm1 also illustrates another aspect of shell programming: the built-in variables provided to the shell by the Linux kernel. In mypgm1, the built-in variable $# provides the number of positional parameters passed to the shell program. You learn more about working with built-in variables in the next major section of this chapter.

33

Accessing and Retrieving Variables

Using positional parameters in scripts can be helpful if you need to use command lines with piped commands requiring complex arguments. Shell programs containing positional parameters can be even more convenient if the commands are infrequently used. For example, if you use your Fedora system with an attached voice modem as an answering machine, you can write a script to issue a command that retrieves and plays the voice messages. The following lines convert a saved sound file (in RMD or voice-phone format) and pipe the result to your system's audio device:

```
#!/bin/sh
# play voice message in /var/spool/voice/incoming
rmdtopvf /var/spool/voice/incoming/$1 ¦ pvfspeed -s 8000 ¦ \
pvftobasic >/dev/audio
```

A voice message can then easily be played back if you use this script (perhaps named pmm):

```
$ pmm name_of_message
```

Shell scripts that contain positional parameters are often used for automating routine and mundane jobs, such as system log report generation, file system checks, user resource accounting, printer use accounting, and other system, network, or security administration tasks.

Using a Simple Script to Automate Tasks

You could use a simple script to examine your system log for certain keywords. If the script is run via your system's scheduling table, /etc/crontab, it can help automate security monitoring. By combining the output capabilities of existing Linux commands with the language facilities of the shell, you can quickly build a useful script to perform a task normally requiring a number of command lines. For example, you can create a short script, named greplog, like this:

```
#!/bin/sh
#    name:  greplog
#     use:  mail grep of designated log using keyword
# version:  v.01 08aug02
#
#  author: bb
#
# usage: greplog [keyword] [logpathname]
#
#  bugs: does not check for correct number of arguments

# build report name using keyword search and date
log_report=/tmp/$1.logreport.`date '+%m%d%y'`

# build report header with system type, hostname, date and time
```

```
echo "=================================================================" \
     >$log_report
echo "              S Y S T E M   M O N I T O R   L O G" >>$log_report
echo uname -a >>$log_report
echo "Log report for" `hostname -f` "on" `date '+%c'`        >>$log_report
echo "=================================================================" \
     >>$log_report ; echo "" >>$log_report

# record log search start
echo "Search for->" $1 "starting" `date '+%r'` >>$log_report
echo "" >>$log_report

# get and save grep results of keyword ($1) from logfile ($2)
grep -i $1 $2 >>$log_report

# build report footer with time
echo "" >>$log_report
echo "End of" $log_report at `date '+%r'` >>$log_report

# mail report to root
mail -s "Log Analysis for $1" root <$log_report

# clean up and remove report
rm $log_report
exit 0
```

In this example, the script creates the variable $log_report, which will be the filename of the temporary report. The keyword ($1) and first argument on the command line is used as part of the filename, along with the current date (with perhaps a better approach in using $$ instead of the date, which appends the script's PID as a file extension). Next, the report header containing some formatted text, the output of the uname command, and the hostname and date is added to the report. The start of the search is then recorded, and any matches of the keyword in the log are added to the report. A footer containing the name of the report and the time is then added. The report is mailed to root with the search term as the subject of the message, and the temporary file is deleted.

NOTE

By default, Fedora uses the logwatch log monitoring command (actually a Perl script) in your system's /etc/cron.daily directory to generate various reports each day at 0402 (4:02 a.m.). Configure logwatch by editing the file /etc/log.d/logwatch. conf. Other system monitoring tools are included, such as tripwire. You can control system logging by editing /etc/syslog.conf.

33

You can test the script by running it manually and feeding it a keyword and a pathname to the system log, /var/log/messages, like this:

```
# greplog FAILED /var/log/messages
```

Note that your system should be running the syslogd daemon. If any login failures have occurred on your system, the root operator might get an email message that looks like this:

```
Date: Mon, 12 Nov 2007 16:23:24 -0000
From: root <root@werewolf.hudson.com>
To: root@werewolf.hudson.com
Subject: FAILED


=================================================================
              S Y S T E M   M O N I T O R   L O G
Linux werewolf 2.6.23-1.41 #1 Thu Nov 8 21:41:26 EST 2007 i686 i686 i386
+GNU/Linux
Log report for werewolf.hudson.com on Tue 12 Nov 2007 04:23:24 PM GMT
=================================================================


Search for-> FAILED starting 04:23:24 PM


12 16:23:04 werewolf login[1769]: FAILED LOGIN 3 FROM (null) FOR ahudson,
+Authentication failure


End of /tmp/FAILED.logreport.102303 at 04:23:24 PM
```

To further automate the process, you can include command lines using the script in another script to generate a series of searches and reports.

Built-In Variables

Built-in variables are special variables provided to the shell by Linux that can be used to make decisions within a shell program. You cannot modify the values of these variables within the shell program.

Some of these variables are the following:

- ▶ **$#**—Number of positional parameters passed to the shell program
- ▶ **$?**—Completion code of the last command or shell program executed within the shell program (returned value)
- ▶ **$0**—The name of the shell program
- ▶ **$***—A single string of all arguments passed at the time of invocation of the shell program

To show these built-in variables in use, here is a sample program called mypgm2:

```
#!/bin/sh
#my test program
echo "Number of parameters is $#"
echo "Program name is $0"
echo "Parameters as a single string is $*"
```

If you execute mypgm2 from the command line in bash as follows

```
$ bash mypgm2 Andrew Hudson
```

you get the following result:

```
Number of parameters is 2
Program name is mypgm2
Parameters as a single string is Sanjiv Guha
```

Special Characters

Some characters have special meaning to Linux shells; these characters represent commands, denote specific use for surrounding text, or provide search parameters. Special characters provide a sort of shorthand by incorporating these rather complex meanings into a simple character. Table 33.1 shows some special characters.

TABLE 33.1   Special Shell Characters

Character	Explanation
$	Indicates the beginning of a shell variable name
¦	Pipes standard output to next command
#	Starts a comment
&	Executes a process in the background
?	Matches one character
*	Matches one or more characters
>	Output redirection operator
<	Input redirection operator
`	Command substitution (the backquote or backtick—the key above the Tab key on most keyboards)
>>	Output redirection operator (to append to a file)
<<	Wait until following end-of-input string (HERE operator)
[ ]	Range of characters
[a-z]	All characters a through z
[a,z] or [az]	Characters a or z
Space	Delimiter between two words

Special characters are very useful to you when you are creating shell scripts, but if you inadvertently use a special character as part of variable names or strings, your program behaves incorrectly. As you learn in later parts of this section, you can use one of the special characters in a string if you precede it with an *escape character* (/, or backslash) to indicate that it isn't being used as a special character and shouldn't be treated as such by the program.

A few special characters deserve special note. They are the double quotes ("), the single quotes ('), the backslash (\), and the backtick (`)—all discussed in the following sections.

Using Double Quotes to Resolve Variables in Strings with Embedded Spaces

If a string contains embedded spaces, you can enclose the string in double quotes (") so that the shell interprets the whole string as one entity instead of more than one.

For example, if you assigned the value of abc def (abc followed by one space, followed by def) to a variable called x in a shell program as follows, you would get an error because the shell would try to execute def as a separate command:

Command	Environment
x=abc def	bash
set x=abc def	tcsh

The shell executes the string as a single command if you surround the string in double quotes, as follows:

Command	Environment
x="abc def"	bash
set x="abc def"	tcsh

The double quotes resolve all variables within the string. Here is an example for bash:

```
var="test string"
newvar="Value of var is $var"
echo $newvar
```

If you execute a shell program containing the preceding three lines, you get the following result:

```
Value of var is test string
```

Using Single Quotes to Maintain Unexpanded Variables

You can surround a string with single quotes (') to stop the shell from expanding variables and interpreting special characters. When used for the latter purpose, the single quote is an *escape character*, similar to the backslash, which you learn about in the next section. Here, you learn how to use the single quote to avoid expanding a variable in a shell script. An unexpanded variable maintains its original form in the output.

In the following examples, the double quotes in the preceding examples have been changed to single quotes:

```
var='test string'
newvar='Value of var is $var'
echo $newvar
```

If you execute a shell program containing these three lines, you get the following result:

```
Value of var is $var
```

As you can see, the variable var maintains its original format in the results, rather than having been expanded.

Using the Backslash As an Escape Character

As you learned earlier, the backslash (\) serves as an escape character that stops the shell from interpreting the succeeding character as a special character. Imagine that you want to assign a value of $test to a variable called var. If you use the following command, the shell reads the special character $ and interprets $test as the value of the variable test. No value has been assigned to test; a null value is stored in var as follows:

Command	Environment
var=$test	bash
set var=$test	tcsh

Unfortunately, this assignment might work for bash, but it returns an error of undefined variable if you use it with tcsh. Use the following commands to correctly store $test in var:

Command	Environment
var=\$test	bash
set var = \$test	tcsh

The backslash before the dollar sign (\$) signals the shell to interpret the $ as any other ordinary character and not to associate any special meaning to it. You could also use single quotes (') around the $test variable to get the same result.

Using the Backtick to Replace a String with Output

You can use the backtick (`) character to signal the shell to replace a string with its output when executed. This special character can be used in shell programs when you want the result of the execution of a command to be stored in a variable. For example, if you want to count the number of lines in a file called `test.txt` in the current directory and store the result in a variable called `var`, you can use the following command:

Command	Environment
var='wc -l test.txt'	bash
set var = 'wc -l test.txt'	tcsh

Comparison of Expressions in bash

Comparing values or evaluating the differences between similar bits of data—such as file information, character strings, or numbers—is a task known as *comparison of expressions*. Comparison of expressions is an integral part of using logic in shell programs to accomplish tasks. The way the logical comparison of two operators (numeric or string) is done varies slightly in different shells. In bash, a command called `test` can be used to achieve comparisons of expressions. In tcsh, you can write an expression to accomplish the same thing.

The bash shell syntax provides a command named `test` to compare strings, numbers, and files. The syntax of the `test` command is as follows:

`test expression`

or

`[ expression ]`

Both forms of the `test` commands are processed the same way by bash. The `test` commands support the following types of comparisons:

- ▶ String comparison
- ▶ Numeric comparison
- ▶ File operators
- ▶ Logical operators

String Comparison

The following operators can be used to compare two string expressions:

- ▶ **=**—To compare whether two strings are equal
- ▶ **!=**—To compare whether two strings are not equal
- ▶ **-n**—To evaluate whether the string length is greater than zero
- ▶ **-z**—To evaluate whether the string length is equal to zero

Next are some examples using these operators when comparing two strings, string1 and string2, in a shell program called compare1:

```
#!/bin/sh
string1="abc"
string2="abd"
if [ $string1 = $string2 ]; then
   echo "string1 equal to string2"
else
   echo "string1 not equal to string2"
fi

if [ $string2 != string1 ]; then
   echo "string2 not equal to string1"
else
   echo "string2 equal to string2"
fi

if [ $string1 ]; then
   echo "string1 is not empty"
else
   echo "string1 is empty"
fi

if [ -n $string2 ]; then
   echo "string2 has a length greater than zero"
else
   echo "string2 has length equal to zero"
fi

if [ -z $string1 ]; then
   echo "string1 has a length equal to zero"
else
  echo "string1 has a length greater than zero"
fi
```

If you execute compare1, you get the following result:

```
string1 not equal to string2
string2 not equal to string1
string1 is not empty
string2 has a length greater than zero
string1 has a length greater than zero
```

If two strings are not equal in size, the system pads out the shorter string with trailing spaces for comparison. That is, if the value of string1 is abc and that of string2 is ab, string2 will be padded with a trailing space for comparison purposes—it will have a value of ab.

Number Comparison

The following operators can be used to compare two numbers:

▶ **-eq**—To compare whether two numbers are equal

▶ **-ge**—To compare whether one number is greater than or equal to the other number

▶ **-le**—To compare whether one number is less than or equal to the other number

▶ **-ne**—To compare whether two numbers are not equal

▶ **-gt**—To compare whether one number is greater than the other number

▶ **-lt**—To compare whether one number is less than the other number

The following shell program compares three numbers, number1, number2, and number3:

```
#!/bin/sh
number1=5
number2=10
number3=5

if [ $number1 -eq $number3 ]; then
    echo "number1 is equal to number3"
else
    echo "number1 is not equal to number3"
fi

if [ $number1 -ne $number2 ]; then
    echo "number1 is not equal to number2"
else
    echo "number1 is equal to number2"
fi

if [ $number1 -gt $number2 ]; then
    echo "number1 is greater than number2"
else
    echo "number1 is not greater than number2"
fi

if [ $number1 -ge $number3 ]; then
    echo "number1 is greater than or equal to number3"
else
```

```
    echo "number1 is not greater than or equal to number3"
fi


if [ $number1 -lt $number2 ]; then
    echo "number1 is less than number2"
else
    echo "number1 is not less than number2"
fi


if [ $number1 -le $number3 ]; then
    echo "number1 is less than or equal to number3"
else
    echo "number1 is not less than or equal to number3"
fi
```

When you execute the shell program, you get the following results:

```
number1 is equal to number3
number1 is not equal to number2
number1 is not greater than number2
number1 is greater than or equal to number3
number1 is less than number2
number1 is less than or equal to number3
```

File Operators

The following operators can be used as file comparison operators:

▶ **-d**—To ascertain whether a file is a directory

▶ **-f**—To ascertain whether a file is a regular file

▶ **-r**—To ascertain whether read permission is set for a file

▶ **-s**—To ascertain whether a file exists and has a length greater than zero

▶ **-w**—To ascertain whether write permission is set for a file

▶ **-x**—To ascertain whether execute permission is set for a file

Assume that a shell program called compare3 is in a directory with a file called file1 and a subdirectory dir1 under the current directory. Assume that file1 has a permission of r-x (read and execute permission) and dir1 has a permission of rwx (read, write, and execute permission). The code for the shell program would look like this:

```
#!/bin/sh
if [ -d $dir1 ]; then
    echo "dir1 is a directory"
else
```

```
   echo "dir1 is not a directory"
fi


if [ -f $dir1 ]; then
   echo "dir1 is a regular file"
else
   echo "dir1 is not a regular file"
fi


if [ -r $file1 ]; then
   echo "file1 has read permission"
else
   echo "file1 does not have read permission"
fi


if [ -w $file1 ]; then
   echo "file1 has write permission"
else
   echo "file1 does not have write permission"
fi


if [ -x $dir1 ]; then
   echo "dir1 has execute permission"
else
   echo "dir1 does not have execute permission"
fi
```

If you execute the shell program, you get the following results:

```
dir1 is a directory
file1 is a regular file
file1 has read permission
file1 does not have write permission
dir1 has execute permission
```

Logical Operators

Logical operators are used to compare expressions using Boolean logic, which compares values by using characters representing NOT, AND, and OR.

- ▶ **!**—To negate a logical expression

- ▶ **-a**—To logically AND two logical expressions

- ▶ **-o**—To logically OR two logical expressions

This example named `logic` uses the file and directory mentioned in the previous compare3 example:

```
#!/bin/sh
if [ -x file1 -a -x dir1 ]; then
    echo file1 and dir1 are executable
else
    echo at least one of file1 or dir1 are not executable
fi

if [ -w file1 -o -w dir1 ]; then
    echo file1 or dir1 are writable
else
    echo neither file1 or dir1 are executable
fi

if [ ! -w file1 ]; then
    echo file1 is not writable
else
    echo file1 is writable
fi
```

If you execute `logic`, it yields the following result:

```
file1 and dir1 are executable
file1 or dir1 are writable
file1 is not writable
```

Special Statements: for, while, and Others

Bash comes with a variety of built-in statements to handle more complex condition checks such as loops and switch blocks. As with many things, bash shares the same syntax, so these next sections are applicable to both shells.

The for Statement

The for statement is used to execute a set of commands once each time a specified condition is true. The for statement has a number of formats. The first format used by bash is as follows:

```
for curvar in list
do
    statements
done
```

33

This form should be used if you want to execute *statements* once for each value in list. For each iteration, the current value of the list is assigned to vcurvar. list can be a variable containing a number of items or a list of values separated by spaces. The second format is as follows:

```
for curvar
do
    statements
done
```

In this form, the *statements* are executed once for each of the positional parameters passed to the shell program. For each iteration, the current value of the positional parameter is assigned to the variable curvar.

This form can also be written as follows:

```
for curvar in $@
do
    statements
done
```

Remember that $@ gives you a list of positional parameters passed to the shell program, quoted in a manner consistent with the way the user originally invoked the command.

Suppose that you want to create a backup version of each file in a directory to a subdirectory called backup. You can do the following in bash:

```
#!/bin/sh
for filename in *
do
    cp $filename backup/$filename
    if [ $? -ne 0 ]; then
        echo "copy for $filename failed"
    fi
done
```

In the preceding example, a backup copy of each file is created. If the copy fails, a message is generated.

The while Statement

The while statement can be used to execute a series of commands while a specified condition is true. The loop terminates as soon as the specified condition evaluates to False. It is possible that the loop will not execute at all if the specified condition initially evaluates to False. You should be careful with the while command because the loop will never terminate if the specified condition never evaluates to False.

Endless Loops Have Their Place in Shell Programs

Endless loops can sometimes be useful. For example, you can easily construct a simple command that constantly monitors the 802.11b link quality of a network interface by using a few lines of script:

```
#!/bin/sh
while :
 do
   /sbin/iwconfig eth0 ¦ grep Link ¦ tr '\n' '\r'
 done
```

The script outputs the search, and then the tr command formats the output. The result is a simple animation of a constantly updated single line of information:

```
Link Quality:92/92  Signal level:-11 dBm  Noise level:-102 dBm
```

This technique can also be used to create a graphical monitoring client for X that outputs traffic information and activity about a network interface:

```
#!/bin/sh
xterm -geometry 75x2 -e \
bash -c \
"while :; do \
    /sbin/ifconfig eth0 ¦ \
    grep 'TX bytes' ¦
    tr '\n' '\r' ; \
done"
```

The simple example uses a bash command-line script (enabled by -c) to execute a command line repeatedly. The command line pipes the output of the ifconfig command through grep, which searches ifconfig's output and then pipes a line containing the string "TX bytes" to the tr command. The tr command then removes the carriage return at the end of the line to display the information inside an /xterm X11 terminal window, automatically sized by the -geometry option:

```
RX bytes:4117594780 (3926.8 Mb)  TX bytes:452230967 (431.2 Mb)
```

Endless loops can be so useful that Linux includes a command that repeatedly executes a given command line. For example, you can get a quick report about a system's hardware health by using the sensors command. But rather than use a shell script to loop the output endlessly, you can use the watch command to repeat the information and provide simple animation:

```
$ watch "sensors -f ¦ cut -c 1-20"
```

In bash, the following format is used for the while flow-control construct:

```
while expression
do
    statements
done
```

If you want to add the first five even numbers, you can use the following shell program in bash:

```
#!/bin/bash
loopcount=0
result=0
while [ $loopcount -lt 5 ]
do
    loopcount=`expr $loopcount + 1`
    increment=`expr $loopcount \* 2`
    result=`expr $result + $increment`
done

echo "result is $result"
```

The until Statement

The until statement can be used to execute a series of commands until a specified condition is true. The loop terminates as soon as the specified condition evaluates to True.

In bash, the following format is used:

```
until expression
do
    statements
done
```

As you can see, the format of the until statement is similar to that of the while statement, but the logic differs: In a while loop, you execute until an expression iterates to False, but in an until loop, you loop until the expression iterates to True.

If you want to add the first five even numbers, you can use the following shell program in bash:

```
#!/bin/bash
loopcount=0
result=0
until [ $loopcount -ge 5 ]
do
    loopcount=`expr $loopcount + 1`
    increment=`expr $loopcount \* 2`
```

```
    result=`expr $result + $increment`
done

echo "result is $result"
```

The example here is identical to the example for the while statement, except that the condition being tested is just the opposite of the condition specified in the while statement.

The shift Statement

The shift statement is used to process the positional parameters, one at a time, from left to right. As you'll remember, the positional parameters are identified as $1, $2, $3, and so on. The effect of the shift command is that each positional parameter is moved one position to the left and the current $1 parameter is lost.

The shift statement is useful when you are writing shell programs in which a user can pass various options. Depending on the specified option, the parameters that follow can mean different things or might not be there at all.

The format of the shift command is as follows:

```
shift    number
```

The parameter *number* is the number of places to be shifted and is optional. If not specified, the default is 1; that is, the parameters are shifted one position to the left. If specified, the parameters are shifted number positions to the left.

The if Statement

The if statement evaluates a logical expression to make a decision. An if condition has the following format in bash:

```
if [ expression ]; then
    Statements
elif [ expression ]; then
    Statements
else
    Statements
fi
```

The if conditions can be nested. That is, an if condition can contain another if condition within it. It isn't necessary for an if condition to have an elif or else part. The else part is executed if none of the expressions that are specified in the if statement and are optional in subsequent elif statements are true. The word fi is used to indicate the end of an if statement, which is very useful if you have nested if conditions. In such a case, you should be able to match fi to if to ensure that all if statements are properly coded.

In the following example for bash, a variable var can have either of two values: Yes or No. Any other value is invalid. This can be coded as follows:

```
if [ $var = "Yes" ]; then
    echo "Value is Yes"
elif [ $var = "No" ]; then
    echo "Value is No"
else
    echo "Invalid value"
fi
```

The case Statement

The case statement is used to execute statements depending on a discrete value or a range of values matching the specified variable. In most cases, you can use a case statement instead of an if statement if you have a large number of conditions.

The format of a case statement for bash is as follows:

```
case str in
    str1 ¦ str2)
        Statements;;
    str3¦str4)
        Statements;;
    *)
        Statements;;
esac
```

You can specify a number of discrete values—such as str1, str2, and so on—for each condition, or you can specify a value with a wildcard. The last condition should be * (asterisk) and is executed if none of the other conditions is met. For each of the specified conditions, all the associated statements until the double semicolon (;;) are executed.

You can write a script that echoes the name of the month if you provide the month number as a parameter. If you provide a number that isn't between 1 and 12, you get an error message. The script is as follows:

```
#!/bin/sh

case $1 in
    01 ¦ 1) echo "Month is January";;
    02 ¦ 2) echo "Month is February";;
    03 ¦ 3) echo "Month is March";;
    04 ¦ 4) echo "Month is April";;
    05 ¦ 5) echo "Month is May";;
    06 ¦ 6) echo "Month is June";;
    07 ¦ 7) echo "Month is July";;
    08 ¦ 8) echo "Month is August";;
```

```
    09 ¦ 9) echo "Month is September";;
    10) echo "Month is October";;
    11) echo "Month is November";;
    12) echo "Month is December";;
    *) echo "Invalid parameter";;
esac
```

You need to end the statements under each condition with a double semicolon (;;). If you do not, the statements under the next condition will also be executed.

The last condition should be `default` and is executed if none of the other conditions is met. For each of the specified conditions, all the associated statements until `breaksw` are executed.

The break and exit Statements

You should be aware of two other statements: the `break` statement and the `exit` statement.

The `break` statement can be used to terminate an iteration loop, such as a `for`, `until`, or `repeat` command.

`exit` statements can be used to exit a shell program. You can optionally use a number after `exit`. If the current shell program has been called by another shell program, the calling program can check for the code (the `$?` or `$status` variable, depending on the shell) and make a decision accordingly.

Using Functions in Shell Scripts

As with other programming languages, shell programs also support functions. A *function* is a piece of a shell program that performs a particular process; you can reuse the same function multiple times within the shell program. Functions help eliminate the need for duplicating code as you write shell programs.

The following is the format of a function in `bash`:

```
func(){
    Statements
}
```

You can call a function as follows:

```
func param1 param2 param3
```

The parameters *param1*, *param2*, and so on are optional. You can also pass the parameters as a single string—for example, $@. A function can parse the parameters as if they were positional parameters passed to a shell program from the command line as command-line arguments, but instead use values passed inside the script. For example, the following script uses a function named `Displaymonth()` that displays the name of the month or an

error message if you pass a month number out of the range 1 to 12. This example works
with bash:

```
#!/bin/sh
Displaymonth() {
   case $1 in
      01 ¦ 1) echo "Month is January";;
      02 ¦ 2) echo "Month is February";;
      03 ¦ 3) echo "Month is March";;
      04 ¦ 4) echo "Month is April";;
      05 ¦ 5) echo "Month is May";;
      06 ¦ 6) echo "Month is June";;
      07 ¦ 7) echo "Month is July";;
      08 ¦ 8) echo "Month is August";;
      09 ¦ 9) echo "Month is September";;
      10) echo "Month is October";;
      11) echo "Month is November";;
      12) echo "Month is December";;
      *) echo "Invalid parameter";;
   esac
}
Displaymonth 8
```

The preceding program displays the following output:

```
Month is August
```

Reference

► **http://www.gnu.org/software/bash/bash.html**—The bash home page at the GNU
   Software Project.

► **http://www.tldp.org/LDP/abs/html/**—Mendel Cooper's "Advanced Bash-Scripting
   Guide."

► **http://www.linuxnewbie.org/nhf/intel/shells/basic.html**—Learn basic shell
   commands at this site.

► **http://www.cs.princeton.edu/~jlk/lj/**—"The New Korn Shell—ksh93," an article
   by David G. Korn, Charles J. Northrup, and Jeffery Korn regarding the korn shell.

► **http://lug.umbc.edu/~mabzug1/bash-httpd.html**—The Bash-httpd FAQ, with
   links to the latest version of the bash web server, bash-httpd-0.02.

► **http://www.tcsh.org/**—Find out more about tcsh here.

► **http://www.zsh.org/**—Examine zsh in more detail here.

CHAPTER **34**

Advanced Software Management

Fedora is provided with a large number of packages already supplied and ready to go. However, Fedora also comes with a great package management tool, called yum, which enables you to quickly and easily download and install more packages. The yum tool (Yellowdog Updater, Modified) has been included with Fedora since version 1 and has become the tool of choice for installing and updating applications. This chapter takes a look at how yum works, its basic usage, and more advanced package and repository management, including using some of the GUI tools available with Fedora. But before that, we take a look at RPM, which is the underlying technology that yum utilizes.

Using RPM for Software Management

The rpm command uses the RPM system to install, remove (erase), upgrade, verify, and build software archives known as *RPM files*. These archives, or packages, contain package identification (a signature), checksums (mathematically derived validation values), and an archive of the software, either in source or binary form. An RPM package also contains quite a bit of additional information, such as a name, version, and basic description, and can include pre- and post-installation scripts used for software installation, erasure, or upgrading.

What Is RPM?

RPM has a long history and is closely associated with Red Hat, the sponsors of Fedora. RPM itself can link itself back to early Linux package management software—named RPP, PMS, and PM—that were written in Perl. RPM came onto the scene in Red Hat Linux 2.0, released late 1995, and was then rewritten in C for the Red Hat Linux 3.0.3 (Picasso) release in 1996. Since then, the rpm command has been the prime feature of Red Hat's unique software management system, which is based on the concept of pristine sources, or the capability to use a single, initial archive of a program's source code to build packages for different systems and to track versions.

In addition to improving the package management of early software management scripts, RPM version 4.1 introduced software features designed to ease the task of building software for different platforms from a single set of source-code files. Changes can be tracked and kept outside a developer's initial source code, and multiple packages can be built from scratch and installed at the same time. Simultaneously, RPM also verifies installation dependencies. Additional features, such as a checksum and *GNU Privacy Guard (GPG)* signatures, enable binary software packages to be safely distributed without the fear of virus infection or the inclusion of Trojan code. Red Hat has committed to further active development of RPM.

The RPM database installed on your computer keeps track of which versions of which packages are installed. RPM uses your system's /var/lib/rpm directory to store files (actually databases) containing information about the software installed on your system. You can use the ls command to view these files. (You might see file sizes different from those shown here, depending on the amount of software you have installed.)

```
total 75476
-rw-r--r-- 1 root root 10432512 2007-10-29 21:36 Basenames
-rw-r--r-- 1 root root    12288 2007-10-29 21:17 Conflictname
-rw-r--r-- 1 root root        0 2007-10-29 21:17 __db.000
-rw-r--r-- 1 root root    24576 2007-10-29 21:15 __db.001
-rw-r--r-- 1 root root  1318912 2007-10-29 21:15 __db.002
-rw-r--r-- 1 root root   450560 2007-10-29 21:15 __db.003
-rw-r--r-- 1 root root  3145728 2007-10-29 21:36 Dirnames
-rw-r--r-- 1 root root 10584064 2007-10-29 21:36 Filemd5s
-rw-r--r-- 1 root root    32768 2007-10-29 21:36 Group
-rw-r--r-- 1 root root    20480 2007-10-29 21:36 Installtid
-rw-r--r-- 1 root root    86016 2007-10-29 21:36 Name
-rw-r--r-- 1 root root 54706176 2007-10-29 21:36 Packages
-rw-r--r-- 1 root root   344064 2007-10-29 21:36 Providename
-rw-r--r-- 1 root root   131072 2007-10-29 21:36 Provideversion
-rw-r--r-- 1 root root    12288 2007-10-29 21:17 Pubkeys
-rw-r--r-- 1 root root   479232 2007-10-29 21:36 Requirename
-rw-r--r-- 1 root root   278528 2007-10-29 21:36 Requireversion
-rw-r--r-- 1 root root   163840 2007-10-29 21:36 Sha1header
-rw-r--r-- 1 root root    81920 2007-10-29 21:36 Sigmd5
-rw-r--r-- 1 root root    12288 2007-10-29 21:36 Triggername
```

The primary database of installed software is contained in the file named `Packages`. As you can see from the preceding example, this database can grow to 50MB (and perhaps larger) if you perform a full installation of Fedora (more than 4GB of software). After you install Fedora, `rpm` and related commands use this directory during software management operations.

rpm at the Command Line

As a Fedora system administrator, you will use the `rpm` command or the Fedora graphical clients to perform one of five basic tasks. These operations, which must be conducted by the root operator, include the following:

▶ Installing new software

▶ Erasing or removing outdated or unneeded packages

▶ Upgrading an installed software package

▶ Querying to get information about a software package

▶ Verifying the installation or integrity of a package installation

The `rpm` command has more than 60 command-line options, but its administrative functions can be grouped according to the previous five types of action. Graphical RPM clients provide easy-to-use interfaces to these operations. As a system administrator, you have a choice between using a graphical interface and using `rpm`'s various command-line options.

The general format of an `rpm` command is as follows:

```
# rpm option packagename
```

The basic options look like this:

▶ `-i`—Installs the selected package or packages

▶ `-e`—Erases (removes) the selected package or packages

▶ `-U`—Removes the currently installed package, and then installs software with the contents of the selected package or packages, leaving the existing configuration files

▶ `-q`—Queries the system or selected package or packages

▶ `-V`—Verifies installed or selected package or packages

Two Handy Options

By appending v or h to any option, you get the following:

▶ `v`—Some status feedback

▶ `h`—Hash marks as the work proceeds

Many additional options can also be added to or used in conjunction with these options. Table 34.1 summarizes these.

TABLE 34.1 Handy Options to Use with rpm

Option	Used To
rpm-i	Install a package
	Useful options to -i:
	--excludedocs: Does not install documentation to save space
	--replacepkgs: Replaces the package with a new copy of itself
	--force: The "big hammer"—Ignores all warnings and installs anyway
	--noscripts: Does not execute any pre- or post-install scripts
	--nodeps: Ignores any dependencies
	--root *path*: Sets an alternative root to *path*
rpm -e	Erase (deletes) a package
	Useful option to -e:
	--nodeps: Ignores any dependencies
rpm -U	Upgrade a package, removing the older one but keeping modified files, such as configurations
	Useful options to -U:
	--oldpackage: Permits downgrading to an older version
	Other options are the same as with rpm -i
rpm -q	Query about package information
	Useful options to -q:
	-p *file*: Displays all information about the package *file*
	-f *file*: Asks what package owns the file *file*?
	--whatprovides *x*: Determines what packages provide *x*
	--whatrequires *x*: Determines what packages require *x*
	-i: Summarizes the package information
	-l: Lists the files in package
	--scripts: Displays the contents of any install, uninstall, or verifies scripts
	--provides: Displays the capabilities package provides
	--requires: Displays the capabilities package requires
rpm -V	Verify packages against the RPM database
	Useful options to -V:
	-a: Verifies all installed packages
rpm -K	Use GPG to verify a downloaded package
	Useful options to -K:
	--nosignature: If you lack public GPG encryption keys, do not have GPG installed, or are legally prohibited from using GPG, this still verifies the package using size and MD5 checksums.

RPM Is for Programmers, Too!

Remember that RPM was created not only to provide an easy-to-use administrative tool, but also as a developer's tool for use in multiplatform source-code package management. Programmers using rpm for development and distribution use its rpmbuild command, along with a myriad of additional command-line flags. RPM can be used to build binaries, execute programs, test installations, verify and sign packages, build source packages, track versions, and target builds for specific architectures. You can find details at the RPM home page (http://www.rpm.org).

Using rpm on the Command Line

Although several GUI clients make use of rpm, you can perform all five basic rpm operations by using the rpm command from the command line. This section gives you an introduction to performing those operations. It also provides examples of how to install, verify, query, remove, and upgrade a software package.

The most common rpm operation is software installation. Using rpm is an easy way to keep track of installed software, and it can be used to quickly remove undesired packages. Use the -i option, along with the full or partial name (using regular expressions) of a software package, to install software with rpm. For example, to install the RPM file for configuring the usage of the FreshRPMs repository, use the rpm command like this:

```
# rpm -ivh http://ftp.freshrpms.net/pub/freshrpms/fedora/linux/ \
8/freshrpms-release/freshrpms-release-1.1-1.fc.noarch.rpm
Retrieving http://ftp.freshrpms.net/pub/freshrpms/fedora/linux/ \
7/freshrpms-release/freshrpms-release-1.1-1.fc.noarch.rpm
warning: /var/tmp/rpm-xfer.48amVs: V3 DSA signature: NOKEY, key ID 8df56d05
Preparing...                  ######################################### [100%]
   1:freshrpms-release
######################################### [100%]
```

This example uses the v and h options, which provide a more verbose output and display of hash marks to show the progress of the installation. The example also demonstrates the capability of rpm to use HTTP or FTP servers to fetch files for installation. It also shows that rpm can use GPG keys to validate a file. (The key was not installed in the example.)

You can also use rpm to query its database after installing packages to verify an installation. Use the -V option, along with the name of a software package, to verify installation of your system. For example, to verify the freshrpms-release package, use the rpm command like this:

```
# rpm -V freshrpms-release
```

34

NOTE

If everything is correct with your software installation, your system displays no response to `rpm -V` after you run the command; only problems are displayed.

As you can see from the following program output, you can get additional information about a package by adding additional verification options (such as two more v's) to the `-V` option. To get more information about an installed package, use one or more forms of the `rpm` query options. For example, to display concise information about an installed package, use the `-q` option, along with the `i` option and the installed package name, like this. (Note that your version will differ from that shown here.)

```
# rpm -qi yum
```

```
Name        : yum                   Relocations: (not relocatable)
Version     : 3.2.7                       Vendor: Fedora Project
Release     : 1.fc8                   Build Date: Fri 12 Oct 2007 09:22:34 PM
BST
Install Date: Sun 21 Oct 2007 05:20:19 PM BST      Build Host:
➥ppc3.fedora.redhat.com
Group       : System Environment/Base   Source RPM: yum-3.2.7-1.fc8.src.rpm
Size        : 1712619                      License: GPLv2+
Signature   : (none)
Packager    : Fedora Project
URL         : http://linux.duke.edu/yum/
Summary     : RPM installer/updater
Description :
Yum is a utility that can check for and automatically download and
install updated RPM packages. Dependencies are obtained and downloaded
automatically prompting the user as necessary.
```

This form of the `rpm` query provides quite a bit of information about the software package. (You can also query packages before installation by providing a pathname for them.)

If this package is not up-to-date, you can easily and quickly upgrade the package by downloading a newer version and then using rpm's `-U` or upgrade option like this:

```
# rpm -Uvh yum-3.2.0-1.fc8.rpm
Preparing...                ########################################### [100%]
   1:yum                    ########################################### [100%]
```

Note that it was not necessary to remove the currently installed software package—the U option removes the old version of the software (saving the old configuration files), and then automatically installs the new software.

You can also upgrade your system software by using the rpm command's -F or "freshen" option, which fetches a designated package from a remote FTP or HTTP server. For example, to upgrade the fetchmail-conf package, use rpm like this:

```
# rpm -Fv ftp://ftp.tux.org/linux/redhat/updates/9/en/os/i386/\
initscripts-7.14-1.i386.rpm
Retrieving ftp://ftp.tux.org/linux/redhat/updates/9/en/os/i386/\
initscripts-7.14-1.i386.rpm
Preparing packages for installation...
initscripts-7.14-1
```

Use the -e option, along with the name of a software package, to remove or erase software from your system with rpm. For example, to remove the unace archiving package, use the rpm command like this:

```
# rpm -e unace
```

Note that if the operation succeeds, no messages are displayed on your system. You can quickly search for the names of installed packages by piping the output of rpm -qa through the grep and sort commands (see Chapter 4, "Command-Line Quick Start," for additional information on grep and sort); here's how to do that search:

```
# rpm -qa | grep mail | sort
fetchmail-6.3.8-3.fc8
mailcap-2.1.25-1.fc8
mailx-8.1.1-46.fc7
procmail-3.22-20.fc8
sendmail-8.14.1-4.2.fc8
```

This example returns a sorted list of all packages with names containing the word mail.

> **NOTE**
>
> Another essential feature of the rpm command is its --rebuilddb option. If your system's RPM database becomes corrupted, this is your first (and perhaps only) option for restoring software management services. We hope that you never have to use this option; help ensure that by always backing up your data!

Extracting a Single File from an RPM File

Occasionally, it is useful to extract a single file from an RPM package. You can do so using the command-line version of mc, the Midnight Commander. In Figure 34.1, the Midnight Commander displays the contents of the yum RPM file. The Midnight Commander is a UNIX clone of the famous DOS Norton Commander, a file management utility. Using mc, just highlight the RPM file and press Enter; the contents of the RPM file are displayed. In the listing, you can browse the file structure of the RPM file and use mc to copy files from it.

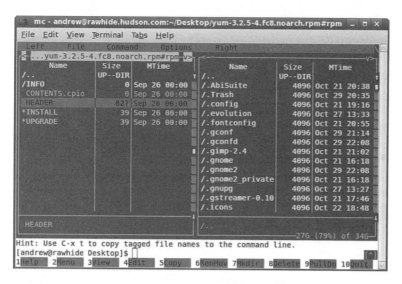

FIGURE 34.1   A classic two-panel directory view and drop-down menus betray Midnight Commander's DOS inspiration, but it's a full-featured Linux file manager.

You might want to know what an .rpm script will do before you install the application. You can use the F3 key in mc to view the script files. If you want to look at the scripts without using mc, use this command:

```
# rpm -q --scripts filename > scripts.txt
```

This command pipes the scripts into a file, where you can examine it with a text editor. You could also pipe it to the less pagination command to view the scripts on your display:

```
# rpm -q — scripts filename ¦ less
```

Getting Started with yum

As noted earlier, yum acts like a wrapper around rpm, allowing you to work easily with multiple files, both to install and include dependencies. This section introduces you to yum and makes sure you have the basics.

yum

yum is controlled entirely from the command line, so you have to memorize some useful switches to get the most from it. But before you go into yum itself, it is worthwhile understanding what goes on behind the scenes. How does yum actually work?

It is easiest to think of yum as a software layer that utilizes the rpm command. When you issue commands to yum, it automatically accesses various repositories and downloads the rpm headers that you requested and then queries them with the rpm command. The advantage to this is that all the processing takes place locally, without the need to download the entire RPM itself. Typically, the RPM header makes up a very small portion of the file, which makes it easy to handle and quick to download. yum builds and maintains a local cache of header files, attributed to the supplying repository, and queries this when you use yum. Each time yum is invoked, it checks the repositories for any updates. If any are found, it adds new headers to its cache, thereby making it as up-to-date as possible when you need to use it. Because yum uses rpm, there should be no dependency problems, making it a fast and easy way to install and update software.

yum is primarily controlled by its configuration file, yum.conf, and by the contents of the yum.repos.d directory, both of which can be found in /etc. By default, yum uses the Fedora repositories for updates, but you can easily add more of your own if you want to install other software that is not available from the default repositories.

yum is incredibly easy to use, requiring a single command with a switch to update all the software in Fedora.

To get going with yum, you will need to open a terminal. Check that yum is installed and working by simply typing the following:

```
$ yum
```

This brings up the usage options for yum and lets you know that you have it installed.

After you have verified that yum is available, you should switch to super user and enter the following command:

```
# yum check-update
```

This command initializes yum and asks it to scan the installed RPMs on your machine, scan the repositories for header files, and then start building a cache of header files. After several minutes of frantic activity, yum will have completed its local cache of header files and will be ready for you to start downloading and installing updates and new software.

To perform a quick and easy update of all the software on your system, enter the following command:

```
# yum update
```

This asks yum to download header information from the registered repositories, check that against your currently installed packages, and update any that are marked as having new versions. This can take some time, depending on how often you run the command and how many packages you have installed on your system.

When yum has finished downloading the headers and working out dependencies, you are prompted with a list of the packages to be updated or installed and asked to give the go-ahead. Enter **y** at the command prompt and yum commences downloading the RPM files.

After the download finishes, yum runs the installation and a test to ensure that everything completed correctly. When yum is satisfied that everything is present and correct, you are returned to the command prompt with a freshly updated system.

This is great when you want to update your entire system, but what if you want to update only certain packages? Again, yum can easily take care of this for you. You can identify the package you want and then use yum to check for its availability by using the command shown here:

```
# yum list <packagename>
```

This command asks yum to cross-reference the package name with packages registered at the repositories and let you know what is available. You can use wildcards as part of the command to find out which associated packages are available. For instance, the command

```
# yum list kde*
```

searches for any packages containing kde, which is useful if you want to selectively update packages. Use the command shown here to update a single package:

```
# yum update <packagename>
```

Or use this command to update more than one package at a time:

```
# yum update <packagename1> <packagename2>
```

Of course, when yum is processing the required packages, it also solves any dependency issues. You will get the opportunity to see not only the packages that will be updated, but also which packages were required to satisfy dependency issues.

About yum

yum is not developed solely by Red Hat. Instead, Duke University has the honor of being the creator and maintainer of yum and its related technology. In particular, Seth Vidal has spent a lot of time and effort ensuring that yum improves in both speed and functionality. Subscribe to the yum mailing list at https://lists.dulug.duke.edu/ mailman/listinfo/yum for the latest information and updates on yum. Seth has now moved across to Red Hat and spends most of his time working on yum!

Running yum Noninteractively

Running yum can involve dependency resolution and a number of updates, which can itself take a long time to download, especially if you are connected to the Internet via a slow connection. Even with a relatively good connection (8Mbps DSL), it can take a while to download a few hundred megabytes of packages. There is, however, an option within yum that you can use to make it run with minimal user intervention. The syntax looks like this:

```
# yum -y update
```

This tells yum that when a question is asked, it is to automatically assume the answer to be yes. This way you can go away and do other tasks rather than waiting for yum to finish downloading all the headers and ask you whether you want to go ahead and install the packages.

Using yum to Remove Packages

So far we have looked at using yum only for installing software, but that is only a small part of its capabilities. It can also be used to remove packages that are no longer required and to give detailed information on installed and available packages. The syntax is similar to the installation and update functions of yum.

As mentioned earlier, yum interfaces with the rpm command to use it for querying the local package database. If you need to remove a package, you can use yum remove <packagename>. yum then scans the local file system, finds the package named, and checks for potential dependency problems. This way, you will never remove a package that could crash your system. You are prompted to give confirmation that you want to remove the required package; then yum processes the package and its dependencies to remove them safely.

Maintaining yum

Over time yum can build up a large cache of RPM headers and other assorted information that can gradually build up to occupy a sizable amount of room on your hard drive. This cache is kept in /var/cache/yum, and you can manage it by using the yum command with your choice of options.

After yum finishes with the packages it downloads, it does not automatically delete them from the system, even though you might have no further use for them. After only one invocation of yum update, I found that my cache file had blossomed to just over 500MB in size. A few months down the line and this could grow exponentially as new updates, bug fixes, and security patches become available.

As with all things in Fedora, you get a choice as to what you want to remove: the packages themselves, the RPM header files, or both. To clean the system of just the packages, use the following command:

```
# yum clean packages
```

When I did this, yum removed all the downloaded packages on my system, saving me 450MB immediately.

If you also want to remove the header files, you can use the following command:

```
# yum clean headers
```

This saved an extra 10MB on top of the 450MB that removing the packages gave me.

> **NOTE**
>
> If you decide to remove the header files, yum has to re-download them the next time that you decide to update your system. This can take a little bit of time, but should not be a problem if you have a fast broadband connection.

Finally, if you want to remove both the packages and the headers in one quick step, you should use this command:

```
# yum clean all
```

This removes all packages and headers from the cache. We suggest using the command just to clean the packages, especially if you are on a slow Internet connection, because keeping the headers saves you time in future updating sessions.

Using yum to Manage Package Inventory

Another useful feature of yum is its capability to list several sets of packages. There are a few options that you can list, including packages that are currently installed, packages that are available to be installed, and packages that have updates available.

The command is as follows:

```
$ yum list <available> <updates> <installed> <extras>
```

- ▶ **available**—This lists the available packages in the configured repositories.

- ▶ **updates**—This lists the available updates for currently installed packages.

- ▶ **installed**—This lists the packages currently installed on the system.

- ▶ **extras**—This lists the installed packages that are not present in any of the configured repositories.

So if I want to find out which packages I have installed on my system, I use the command yum list installed to return a detailed summary of packages installed and their version numbers. You can take this one step further and query for individual packages. You might want to find out which version of OpenOffice.org you have installed and which version is available for installation. For this, you use yum list openoffice.org— the results of which would show you which version was installed and which version was available for updating.

yum can also search the headers and summaries for each RPM file so that you can find specific information about packages that would not usually be available in just the package name itself. For example, using yum search kdebindings would bring up entries matching kdebindings. The results of this command are shown here:

```
$ yum search kdebindings
Loading "refresh-updatesd" plugin
```

```
kdebindings-devel.i386 : Development files for kdebindings
kdebindings-dcopperl.i386 : DCOP Bindings for Perl
kdebindings-devel.i386 : Development files for kdebindings
kdebindings.i386 : KDE bindings to non-C++ languages
kdebindings-dcopperl.i386 : DCOP Bindings for Perl
kdebindings.i386 : KDE bindings to non-C++ languages
```

Configuring yum

As mentioned earlier, yum is primarily controlled by the contents of the yum.conf file and the /etc/yum.repos.d directory. Let's take a closer look at the contents of both of these so that you can get a better understanding of how best to configure yum.

When you initially install Fedora, a default yum.conf file provides several switches for the yum command. It basically saves you from having to type in a number of switches and keeps yum simple. By default, yum is configured to do the following:

▶ Keep a cache of headers in /var/cache/yum

▶ Give minimal onscreen information during processing

▶ Keep a log file in /var/log/yum.log

▶ Download only the most up-to-date packages

▶ Be tolerant of errors in the process

▶ Match packages to your processor architecture

▶ Have a maximum retry limit of 20 times

▶ Check for obsolete packages

▶ Use GPG keys to ensure the identities of packages

All these options are contained within the yum.conf file, letting you easily modify or even remove certain lines. For instance, you might need yum to try only a maximum of five times, or you might need yum to give you more visual information.

You can add repository information into the yum.conf file, but an easier way to handle repos is to use the /etc/yum.repos.d folder. This folder enables you to create individual configuration files for each repository. By default, Fedora comes with repositories for their base packages, updated packages, updated packages that are in testing, and the more unstable development packages. Only the base and updated packages are enabled by default.

> **CAUTION**
>
> Unless you really know what you are doing, avoid the more unstable repositories of `fedora-updates-testing` and `fedora-development`. These repositories contain bleeding-edge packages that can break your system. You have been warned!

Opening a repository file shows you some details about the repository itself, including the path to it (either via HTTP, FTP, or local access), any lists of mirrors for that repository, whether that repository is enabled, and whether GPG checking is enabled.

If you want to add a new repository, you need to find out a few things before you can successfully add it to either its own repository file under `/etc/yum.repos.d` or in the `yum.conf` file.

You can also configure yum to ignore or exclude updates to certain packages. So, for instance, if you have a graphics driver that works only with a specific kernel version and you do not want to have to fix it every time a new kernel is released, you can elect for yum to exclude any kernel updates. Within the `yum.conf` file, you need to add a line within the top section similar to this:

```
exclude=kernel
```

This tells yum to ignore any packages that start with `kernel`, and should limit the amount of repair work you have to do when a new kernel version is installed.

Using pirut for Software Management

Up to now we've focused solely on command-line utilities that you can use to manage your software. Fedora also offers a number of graphical tools for package management, including pirut, yumex (Yum Extender), and pup. Chapter 2, "Fedora Quick Start" covered pup, so the next two sections cover pirut and yumex. The default graphical package management tool in Fedora is an application named pirut, which cunningly has been renamed Add/Remove Software in the Applications menu. This application replaces kpackage, gnorpm, and xrpm—all of which are no longer provided. Add/Remove Software allows you to select packages arranged in categories and install or remove them.

Launch pirut by clicking the Applications menu on your desktop, and then choose Add/Remove Software. You are asked for the super-user password, and then the package management tool launches with the package-browsing screen, shown in Figure 34.2.

The packages listed in the screen are organized into broad categories, with subcategories listed on the right side. Tick the box next to each subcategory to select the default packages for it. The numbers to the bottom of the package group window indicate the number of packages installed on your system and the total number of packages available in the group. In Figure 34.3, you can see that 24 of 78 possible KDE packages have been installed.

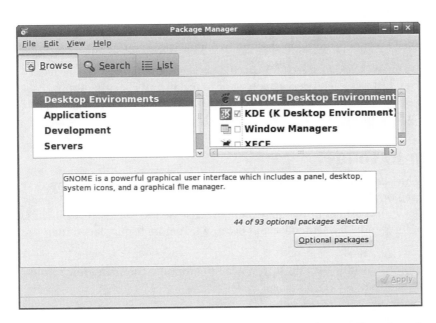

FIGURE 34.2   The initial screen of *pirut* allows you to browse through packages sorted by groups.

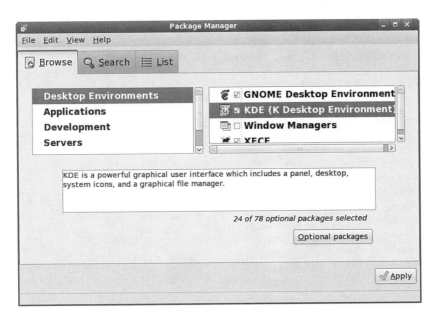

FIGURE 34.3   All three main window managers have been selected in this view.

You can see brief information about the subcategories in the box below the selection. Use the Optional Packages button to get access to all the optional packages related to that subcategory. Just check each box to select that package, and click Close to return to the main window. Clicking the Apply button starts the download and installation process, which can take some time, depending on the number of packages you specify.

The pirut tool also enables you to search for specific packages and to browse through a long list of packages. Just tick each package you want to install and click the Apply button. With the search function, pirut remembers each package that you check, so you can search again and again within one session to build up a list of required packages.

Using Yum Extender

Although pirut is the default package management tool for Fedora, development work has also been carried out by the community on a more powerful tool called *Yum Extender* (yumex). Yum Extender has gained in popularity since its release just over two years ago, mainly because of its friendly user interface and because it is more feature laden than pirut.

Yum Extender is not installed by default, so you need to drop to a command line to run the following command

```
# yum install yumex
```

to download and install the Yum Extender package. After yum has finished, you will find an entry under the Applications, System Tools menu. Figure 34.4 shows Yum Extender in action.

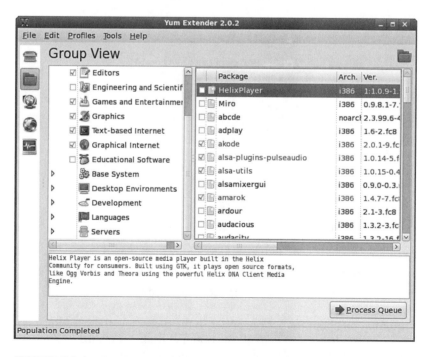

FIGURE 34.4   The Yum Extender, making *yum* even more useful!

Creating a Local yum Repository

When yum is active, it can download a lot of information in the form of RPM headers and files, which can easily eat up bandwidth. If you have three or more Fedora-based machines on a local network, creating a local yum repository can be a good way to conserve bandwidth and save time.

Before you start setting up the repository, you need to have the rsync and createrepo packages installed because you will need them both. Use the command yum install rsync createrepo to make sure that they are installed.

To begin, create a directory that will house your repository. In the example, we use /home/andrew/repo/ as the target directory. Next, find the site you want to mirror (a selection of sites for Fedora can be found at http://fedora.redhat.com/download/mirrors.html). This example uses the UK Mirror service in Canterbury, Kent.

```
# rsync -avz rsync://rsync.mirrorservice.org/sites/ \
download.fedora.redhat.com/pub/fedora/linux/updates/ \
7/i386/ /home/andrew/repo
```

rsync then starts to download the files it finds within that directory to /home/andrew/repo. This can take some time. (At the time of writing, about 5GB of updates are available at the previous address.) To ensure that rsync really is working, use Nautilus to navigate to /home/andrew/repo; here you should see a number of packages appearing one after the other.

After you have completed downloading the updates you want, you need to create your repository. This is where the createrepo command comes in.

createrepo is a program designed to quickly and efficiently draw the relevant information from a collection of RPM files to make the metadata yum requires to successfully install or update your currently installed package base.

The command is simply the following:

**createrepo /*yourtargetdirectoryhere*

So, if we were to use the example in the previous section, the syntax would look something like this:

$ createrepo /home/andrew/repo

This would give you the following output:

```
88/88 - alsa-lib-1.0.6-5.i386.rpm
Saving Primary metadata
Saving file lists metadata
Saving other metadata
```

This shows that 88 RPMs were cataloged and that the relevant metadata was saved. The program automatically uses the given directory, so you do not have to worry about making several copies of directories.

At this point, you need to move your newly created repository into a subdirectory of /var/www/html/ so that they are accessible via apache and the HTTP protocol. Use this command:

```
#mv /home/andrew/repo /var/lib/html/
```

After this is done, you are ready to include your new repository into the /etc/yum.conf file or into its own file under /etc/yum.repo.d. Let's take a look at a typical configuration file for use with yum:

```
$ cat /etc/yum.repos.d/local.repo
[local]
name=Fedora $releasever - $basearch - Updates
baseurl=http://192.168.0.5/repo
enabled=1
gpgcheck=0
```

This file is fairly easy to read. Line one is the name of the repository that is passed to yum. The name must be enclosed in square brackets for it to be picked up; in this case, it is simply local. Line two provides the display name for yum to show while it is busy working; for this repository, it uses Fedora $releasever - $basearch - Updates, which prints the release version (in this case 4) and the base architecture (i386). Next comes the base URL, or the primary download point. This is used for yum to scan and download the metadata it needs. The fourth line shows whether this repository is enabled: enabled=0 means it is disabled, and enabled=1 means it is enabled and able to be used. The final line determines whether the RPMs are checked with a GnuPG key. You are advised to obtain the relevant GnuPG key from the original repository to ensure that the packages you install have not been tampered with. Use the following command to import this into the RPM database:

```
# rpm --import thiskey.txt
```

After the key has been imported into the database, yum can use it to verify that the packages are intact and safe to use.

> **CAUTION**
>
> Notice that we say the use of GPG keys can make packages safer to use. This is certainly true, but be aware that sometimes packages can conflict with each other. Be careful about which repositories you use because some are incompatible with others. When selecting a repository, always read any FAQs for warnings of incompatibilities.

Reference

- ▶ **http://www.linux.duke.edu/projects/yum/**—The home page of the yum project, hosted at Linux@Duke (Duke University).

- ▶ **http://rpm.livna.org/**—The Livna yum repository.

- ▶ **http://freshrpms.net/**—The FreshMeat yum repository. It's part of the OSTG, which also includes Slashdot and linux.com.

- ▶ **http://dag.wieers.com**—The yum repository of Dag Wieers.

- ▶ **http://atrpms.net**—ATrpms yum repository. It includes some highly unstable packages, so use it at your own risk!

- ▶ **http://apt.sw.be/dries/**—Dries's yum/apt repository.

- ▶ **http://www.fedorafaq.org/**—A useful, but unofficial, source of information. It gives locations of GPG keys for all the previously mentioned repositories.

34

CHAPTER 35

Managing the File System

A Linux file system is more than just a format for your hard drive or floppy disk and more than just the disk itself or the formatting process. The file system is the structure and organization of data on a data storage device. In other words, it is how your data is organized and stored in files, disk drives, and removable media.

In this chapter, you learn about the structure of the disks themselves, the file systems that can be placed on them, and how to work with those file systems. You also learn some background and history about the file systems that Linux can use. This chapter provides some basic information about the file system's default settings, as well as how you can adapt those settings to better match your system and its needs. At the end of the chapter, you learn how to build a test file system and use the loopback file system so that you can safely explore all the file system commands without risking any damage to your system.

Also covered are the use of the file system table, fstab, and instructions for formatting ext3, reiserfs, and DOS drives. The "Reference" section is full of sources with extensive information on file system-related topics.

The Fedora File System Basics

The Fedora file system, like all Unix file systems, is used for storing not only data, but also metadata—information about the files, such as who the file owner is, what permissions are associated with the file, and other file attributes.

The Fedora file system is much more complex than most people care to know about. Its features are patterned after features found on commercial Unix systems, as well as those included in research or experimental file systems.

Fortunately, the native Linux file system is robust and works well with the default settings. Fedora has conveniently provided an easy-to-use setup tool for use during the installation, but here you also learn how to manage file system settings manually.

Providing a great deal of flexibility, the file system support enables Linux users to access files on file systems used by other operating systems, many of which are obscure. A sampling of the Fedora kernel modules for supported file systems is as follows:

- ▶ `cramfs`—Compressed ROM file system.

- ▶ `ext3`—Linux Extended File System 3 (adds journaling to ext2). Note: work is now underway to develop ext4, which will build upon ext3.

- ▶ `fat`—Microsoft File Allocation Table file system: FAT 12 and FAT 16.

- ▶ `hfs`—Macintosh: Hierarchical file system.

- ▶ `jfs`—IBM's journaled file system.

- ▶ `msdos`—Microsoft File Allocation Table -16.

- ▶ `nfs`—Network file system.

- ▶ `ntfs`—Windows NT, Windows 2000, Windows XP.

- ▶ `reiserfs`—Reiser file system.

- ▶ `smbfs`—File system based on the use of the Shared Message Block protocol used by Microsoft and Samba.

- ▶ `udf`—Universal Disk Format (DVD-ROM file system).

- ▶ `umsdos`—MS-DOS file system with Linux permissions.

- ▶ `vfat`—Microsoft File Allocation Table file system known as FAT32.

Support for `ext3`, `ext2`, `NFS`, and `iso9660` file systems is compiled into the Linux kernel; all others are available as modules.

There is not an exact correlation between the file system source code and the modules compiled for the default kernel. The kernel documentation for the file systems can be found at `/usr/src/linux-2.6/Documentation/file systems/`. The usage of some of these file system modules is mentioned in the `man` page for `mount`.

Physical Structure of the File System on the Disk

If you were to visualize the file system on the physical disk, it would resemble a series of boxes known as blocks. The first block on the disk is a special block that contains the boot sector; subsequent blocks contain the operating system, applications, and your data.

Each individual block is made up of smaller groups of data:

▶ A superblock (called by that name because it contains redundant information about the overall file system).

▶ Redundant file system descriptors—All the redundant information is useful for reliability and recovery from disasters and errors.

▶ A bitmap of the block.

▶ A bitmap of the inode table.

▶ Information from the inode table.

▶ The data blocks themselves.

Inodes and File Attributes

The information that constitutes a file in the ext2/ext3 file system begins with the inode. The inode contains the following description of the file: the file type, its access rights, its owners, several different time stamps, the file size, and pointers to data blocks that hold the file information. When you want to access a file, the kernel uses those pointers to calculate where the data resides physically on the disk.

File attributes are also stored in the inode. The chattr command enables the root operator to manipulate some special attributes of files on an ext2/3 file system. One of the most interesting uses of the chattr command is to make a file *immutable*, meaning that it cannot be deleted, renamed, written to, or modified by anyone, even root (at least until the immutable attribute is unset). To make a file immutable (the word means unalterable; not capable of change):

```
# chattr +i filename
```

and to change it back:

```
# chattr -i filename
```

Another interesting flag is the s flag, which tells the system to zero out all the blocks used for that file when the file is deleted.

To observe the existing attributes of a file, use:

```
# lsattr filename
```

The chattr utility is part of the e2fsprogs package.

A file's attributes include its access *permissions*. The traditional Unix system of permissions is controlled with chmod. Posix Access Control Lists extend this functionality.

ACL supports permissions for users and groups beyond the traditional owner/group/world scheme. They enable finer-grained control of permissions for files.

To learn more about Access Control Lists, visit the Posix ACLs for Linux website: http://acl.bestbits.at/.

35

How big are these blocks? The default size is 1,024 bytes, but the size can be made smaller or larger when the file system is first created. The optimum size is determined by the application of the particular machine. If you typically use very large files, a larger block size can speed up disk I/O operations at the expense of slower I/O for smaller files; the reverse is also true. For an individual system, block size might require monitoring over time and benchmarking before an optimal value is determined. For most users, the defaults have been found satisfactory.

File System Partitions

File system partitions are ways to organize blocks of data on the physical drive media and are parts of the overall file system on your computer. No single universal partition format exists. In addition to the commonly used DOS partition format (used by Linux as well), Fedora also provides support for the following partition types:

- ► Amiga

- ► Macintosh (compiled into the kernel)

- ► BSD (compiled into the kernel)

- ► SunOS/Solaris (compiled into the kernel)

- ► UnixWare slices (compiled into the kernel)

- ► SGI (compiled into the kernel)

- ► Windows Logical Disk Manager

NOTE

Other modules and support are likely available if you care to search the Internet for them; try searching on the keyword file systems on http://freshmeat.net/ and http://www.google.com/linux/. As is always the case with open-source operating systems, any skilled and enterprising soul can write his own file system modules.

Network and Disk File Systems

File systems can be separated into two broad categories: those that can be used over a network and local disk file systems. You are provided with all the applications necessary to work with both categories of file systems when using Fedora.

Network file systems are physically stored somewhere other than your local computer but appear as if they are mounted on your local computer.

NOTE

Mounting is the Unix method of attaching a file system (also referred to as a *volume*) to the file system tree at a mount point. Using the mount command is covered later in this chapter.

Some common network file system types are:

▶ NFS—The Network File System was developed by Sun and is in common use. It has no built-in security because it was originally designed to run over friendly networks. Although considered problematic by some, it is easy to implement. It is typically used between Unix peers. Fedora supports client and server installations of this file system.

▶ Coda—Similar to NFS, Coda offers support for disconnected operation and security caching (keeping a local copy of files in case the network connection is lost). Fedora provides only kernel compatibility with Coda; the actual client and server code is available from http://www.coda.cs.cmu.edu/.

▶ InterMezzo—Similar in features to Coda, InterMezzo is a GPL project. The server daemon can be obtained from http://www.inter-mezzo.org/.

▶ SMB—The network-focused Server Message Block protocol was developed by Microsoft. The Linux implementation is known as Samba and is one of the most advanced open-source projects available. It is typically used between Linux and Microsoft Windows peers. Netatalk is the Macintosh equivalent protocol.

Disk file systems are found on a physical device; they are the hard drive in your desktop or laptop computer. Some common disk file system types are:

▶ FAT is a disk-oriented, table-based (a linked list) file system used by Microsoft. It has been regularly extended to add functionality. Microsoft's Enterprise-level file system is known as NTFS. (You learn more about this system in "DOS File Systems," later in this chapter.)

▶ ext2, ext3, and reiserfs are inode-based. (You learn about reiserfs in "The Reiser File System (reiserfs)," later in this chapter.)

The JFS (Journaled File System from IBM) and XFS (from Silicon Graphics) file systems are available for use with Fedora, but primarily serve as migration aids for those migrating existing file systems to Linux.

A journaling file system adds a journal, or hidden file, to the data on the drive. Because of the way data is written to a disk, the kernel might be holding some of the data while it is deciding where to place it. If your computer were to suffer a failure, that cached data would be lost. A journaling file system keeps that data in a special place until the kernel decides to formally write it to the disk. If a system failure occurs, a special application (fsck) knows that the data was never formally written and makes certain that it is written in the correct place. This ensures that no data is lost. Journaling file systems are actually much more complex than this, but the mechanics of them are beyond the scope of this chapter. Journaling file systems such as ext3, reiserfs, JFS, and XFS are major improvements over older, nonjournaling file systems.

Viewing Your System's File Systems

Your installation of Fedora might have its own unique set of useable virtual file system modules. You can view the file systems that your system can access right now (and verify your kernel's support for these file systems) by using the following command:

```
# cat /proc/file systems
```

Your output will vary, depending on your system's hardware and kernel settings. The test system we used for this chapter presented this output:

```
nodev   rootfs
nodev   bdev
nodev   proc
nodev   sockfs
nodev   tmpfs
nodev   shm
nodev   pipefs
        ext2
nodev   ramfs
        iso9660
nodev   devpts
        ext3
nodev   usbdevfs
nodev   usbfs
        ReiserFS
        vfat
nodev   nfs
nodev   autofs
nodev   binfmt_misc
```

The entries not preceded by `nodev` are not of interest to us because they do not provide any information about the file system. On this machine, the `ext2`, `ext3`, `vfat`, `reiserfs`, and `iso9660` file systems are supported. Modules for other file systems could be loaded if needed.

Working with the `ext3` File System

Red Hat had invested heavily in the development of the `ext3` file system and provides support for the `ext3` file system as the journaling file system for its distribution. Red Hat (and now Fedora) does not provide that level of support for other file systems. Other distributions, such as SUSE and Mandriva, support the Reiser file system, which is covered later.

The `ext3` file system is an update to the `ext2` file system, which has been one of the most popular Linux file systems for some time. You can choose to use the `ext3` file system during a fresh install or automatically convert to an `ext3` file system when you upgrade your present system to the current version of Fedora. All the ext2 tools provided by Fedora have been upgraded to work with both ext2 and ext3. We mention the ext2 tools only because you will see the ext2 file system mentioned frequently; ext3, as supplied with Fedora, is completely compatible with ext2.

Understanding the ext3 File System Structure

Fedora's rationale for choosing ext3 might be compelling. Although it provides availability, data integrity, and speed similar to other file system choices, ext3 has one unique advantage: It is an easy transition from ext2 to ext3, and the transition is forgiving of mistakes made along the way. It is also potentially possible to recover a deleted file from an ext3 file system; such a recovery is not possible at all for a reiserfs file system.

> **NOTE**
>
> The downside to using ext3 seems to be performance related. A recent benchmarking evaluation (see http://fsbench.netnation.com/) of all Linux file systems placed ext3 at the bottom for general performance. What the study really demonstrates is that you must match the file system to the application for best all-around performance.

The ext3 file system can accommodate files as large as 2TB, directories as large as 2TB, and a maximum filename length of 255 characters. (With special kernel patches, this limit can be increased to 1,024 characters if the standard length is insufficient for your use.) The ext3 file system can allocate and use empty space in a very efficient manner.

The usage of space is so efficient that ext3 file systems typically do not need defragmenting (rearranging the files to make them contiguous). The dynamic allocation of resources is also the source of one Achilles heel for the file system. When a file is deleted, its inode is erased and the data blocks associated with it are freed; they might very well be reallocated immediately, and the old data lost forever.

> **NOTE**
>
> A defragmentation program for the ext2 file system does exist, but it is infrequently used, is not typically included with standard Linux distributions such as Fedora, and is not recommended for general use. The ext2/3 file system assigns blocks of space for files based on their parent directories; this spaces files out all over the physical disk, leaving room to keep files contiguous and reduce fragmentation. However, a file system full of files at 90% of its capacity can become badly fragmented.

Every file system varies in structure, depending on its efficiency, security, and even proprietary designs to limit cross-compatibility deliberately. The ext3 file systems were designed to follow Unix design concepts, particularly "everything is a file."

For example, a directory in the ext3 file system is simply a file; that file contains the names of the files to be found in that directory, and the locations of those files. The list of names is linked so that space is not wasted because of varying filename lengths.

Journaling Options in `ext3`

The `ext3` file system has several options that, depending on your needs, allow you to select how much information is journaled. Generally speaking, the typical journal requires a second or so to be read and recovered. The time needed to recover from an improper shutdown of a journaled file system is not dependent on the file system size, but the amount of data in the journal.

The default setting provided by Fedora is adequate for most needs. The optimal choice depends on so many factors (computer usage, hardware used, and testing and evaluation methods) that a meaningful discussion is beyond the scope of this chapter. You learn in this chapter what the choices are and how they differ, but whether a choice is right for you can only be determined on an individual basis.

Like all journaling file systems, the traditional file system check (`fsck`) is not necessary on an `ext3` file system. Although only mildly annoying on a 20GB drive on your machine at home, imagine the seemingly endless hours that an `fsck` would take to run on a terabyte of data. This feature is shared in common with the other journaling file systems.

When choosing journaling options, you can trade off data integrity (keeping your data current and valid) for data transfer speed in your file system's operation; you cannot have both because of the nature of the file system design. You can choose to expose some of your data to potential damage in the case of an improper shutdown in exchange for faster data handling, or you can sacrifice some speed to keep the state of the file system consistent with the state of the operating system.

Three modes available as options to `ext3` are as follows:

- `writeback`—Enables old data to stay in the file system, attaining the fastest speed possible. It does not schedule any data writes; it just enables the kernel's 30-second `writeback` code to flush the buffer.

- `ordered`—Keeps the data consistent, but with some sacrifice in speed (the default mode for Fedora).

- `journal`—Requires more disk space to journal more data. You might see slower performance because data is written twice, but there are some speed benefits if you are doing synchronous data writes, as in database operations.

For most of us, the default selection represents a good trade-off. Fedora supports booting from an `ext3` formatted root file system with the proper drivers loaded in the `initrd` image.

You select the mode by using the appropriate mount option in `/etc/fstab`. For example, to set the file system mode to the fastest of the three modes, use `data=writeback` as the option. For more details, enter **man mount**.

Verifying File Integrity in `ext3` File Systems with the `fsck` Utility

You assure file system integrity by using the `fsck`, or file system check, program—one of five commands in the library that are used to maintain and modify the `ext3` file system.

When fsck is run, it performs a sequential analysis of the file system information available in the file system if it detects a directory that cannot be traced back to the root or an undeleted file with a zero link count. It places these directories and files in the /lost+found directory that is created on each physical partition by the file system formatting process. Some blocks are reserved for this and other uses of the super-user. It is possible to reduce this allocation to free additional space for regular users by providing special arguments to the formatting program mke2fs.

To run the fsck command, use the name of the file system as the argument. You must ensure that the file system you want to check is unmounted by using the umount command. If you want to fsck the file system at /dev/hdc, for example, do this:

```
# fsck /dev/hdc
```

> **TIP**
>
> If you are logged on as a regular user and su to root using su, you do not inherit root's environment and path, meaning that the preceding command does not work unless you use the full path: /usr/sbin/fsck.
>
> Either type the full path each time, or become root with su -, which causes you to inherit root's environment and path; you have less to type.

35

The file system state is tracked in the ext3 file systems. A special field in the superblock tells the kernel that, after the file system is mounted read/write, it is marked as not clean; when it is properly unmounted, it is marked as clean. If a file system is not unmounted properly, it could contain corrupt data because all the file data might not have been written to it. (This is what the journaling file systems such as ext3 strive to eliminate.) When the system is booted, this flag is checked and if it is not clean, the program fsck is run. Internally, fsck is actually a wrapper program that runs the appropriate version of fsck for the file system in use: fsck.minix, fsck.ext2, fsck.ext3, fsck.reiserfs, fsck.msdos, or fsck.vfat. If the kernel detects an inconsistency in the superblock field, the file system is marked erroneous, and the file system check is forced even if other indicators suggest that fsck does not need to be run.

By default, the system runs fsck on a file system after a periodic number of reboots, regardless of the status of the clean flag. This behavior is triggered by a mount counter kept in the superblock or after a predetermined amount of time has elapsed since the last reboot (information also kept in the superblock). These parameters can be adjusted through the tune2fs command; this command can also be used to modify how the kernel handles the erroneous flag and, interestingly, the number of blocks reserved for the super-user, also known as *root*. This latter option is useful on very large or very small disks to make more disk space available to the user.

Other File Systems Available to Fedora

Although ext3 is certainly an acceptable root file system, there are other alternatives. No operating systems can support as many root file systems as Linux, but you should be aware that every file system has its strengths and weaknesses. Some are better with small files, some are better with large files; some are better at writing data, and some better at reading data. Unfortunately, there is no one perfect file system. The following sections discuss some of the other common file systems available for use with Fedora.

The Reiser File System (`reiserfs`)

The other popular journaling file system for Linux is the written-from-scratch Reiser file system, `reiserfs`. For a long time it was used by the SUSE distribution, but SUSE now uses ext3. `reiserfs` offers similar features to `ext3`, but there is no easy migration path from an already existing `ext2` partition. In the past, `reiserfs` didn't work well over NFS mounts, but recent versions of the `nfsd` daemon have fixed those problems. Fedora does offer `reiserfs`, but does not offer support for booting from it as the root partition file system, nor does it offer the choice to format non-root partitions as `reiserfs` during the installation process.

`reiserfs` is offered primarily for compatibility with existing `reiserfs` partitions you might want to access. Although the Reiser file system can be used as a root file system (meaning that Linux can be booted from a Reiser file system), Fedora has chosen not to support that option. The main problem is that `reiserfs` does not, at the time of writing, play nicely with SELinux and is therefore not recommended either by Red Hat or the NSA (SELinux's developers).

> **NOTE**
>
> Namesys, the company behind `reiserfs`, has struggled since its founder (Hans Reiser) was arrested as part of the police investigation into the murder of his wife. Few distros now recommend using `reiserfs`, so we would recommend avoiding it for the foreseeable future.

JFS and XFS File Systems

Two commercial Unix file systems have been ported (rewritten) to allow them to be used in Linux. IBM has provided its Journaled File System (JFS) that is used with its commercial Unix named AIX. Silicon Graphics, Inc. (SGI) has provided its XFS file system used by its commercial Unix named IRIX. Because these file systems are generally suited for enterprise systems rather than home or small office systems, it seems likely that they are offered in Fedora to ease the transition of IRIX and AIX users to Linux by eliminating the need for these users to reformat their very large file systems.

Beginning with kernel 2.6, XFS is fully supported in the kernel.

DOS File Systems

The extent of DOS file system support in Linux is often surprising to newcomers, but the DOS file system proved to be a viable option in the early years of Linux. Because

Microsoft has been the dominant operating system on Intel computers, Linux has always worked toward coexistence with DOS.

Microsoft DOS and the consumer-oriented Windows operating systems use a file system known as FAT (File Allocation Table). FAT32 is the typical system used today. The number following the FAT name indicates the size of the space for naming address pointers; the more space, the larger a section of contiguous space can be identified and accessed. FAT32 is the most recent version of FAT, and it is backward compatible with other versions of FAT. Older versions are not forward compatible.

The Fedora kernel can access all versions of FAT-formatted partitions (including floppy disks), using the vfat kernel module.

CD-ROM File Systems

If you use CD-ROM or DVD-ROM media, you need to understand a little bit about the file system and how it works with Linux. To the average user, the file system of a CD-ROM looks just like a native Linux file system. It is not the native file system, but the features of the Virtual File System make it possible for it to appear that way. The CD-ROM file system standards continue to evolve to accommodate new technology.

iso9660

The file system typically used on a CD-ROM is known as iso9660, the name of the standard that defines the format. Each operating system translates the iso9660 file system into the native file system of the operating system (with some restrictions). Several extensions have been created to address certain special needs. The Rock Ridge extension allows long filenames and Unix-like symbolic links. The Joliet extension allows Unicode characters and long filenames, useful when dealing with non-English languages. El Torito CDs contain a bootable image and, with a suitable BIOS, can boot an operating system from the CD.

Universal Disk Format

The Universal Disk Format (UDF) is the file system used on DVD discs. UDF has a number of built-in features such as allowing larger files, having improved file descriptors, and packet writing that the iso9660 file system cannot easily accommodate. The UDF format is the next step in compact disc technology.

Creating a File System

To create a file system on a disk that has never had a partition table on it or to change the partition table (called repartitioning the disk), you must first create the new partition table. In this section, you begin by learning about the basic structure and workings of the disk as a storage device. This information is fundamental to your understanding of the file system creation process. You then learn to create a partition table by using the fdisk and GNUparted commands. As with all similar Linux commands, each has its own strengths and weaknesses and none is a perfect choice for all situations. In the end, the partition table you create will be the same no matter which command you use. You then learn to create the file system, using commands appropriate for the type of file system you want to create.

> **NOTE**
>
> The Microsoft version of `fdisk` creates both a partition table and the bootloader. In Linux, `fdisk` creates only the partition table. The bootloader is created later by LILO, GRUB, or another bootloader; no bootloader is necessary to create a file system and store data on a disk, just a partition table.
>
> In fact, IDE disks physically installed as something other than `/dev/hda` (such as `/dev/hdc`, the secondary master drive) do not have a bootloader written to them; the space where the bootloader code normally resides is likely to be blank. For SCSI disks, the drive designated in the BIOS as the bootable drive has the bootloader written to it.

The Disk as a Storage Device

Because data storage devices are central to the file system, it is important to understand the workings of the most common data storage device: the hard disk drive. Although they work with a different medium, the basic storage functions of floppy disks and removable disk drives are similar to those of the hard disk.

Mechanically, the hard drive is a metal box that encloses disks, also known as platters, which have a magnetic coating on each side. Multiple disks are typically connected to the same spindle and rotated by a motor. The read and write heads for each side of the disk are moved by a second motor to position them over the area of the disk where the data you are looking for is stored. Each platter is organized into cylinders (the default size is 512 bytes) and sectors, and each platter has a head. Each drive has some electronics on a controller card that, along with the disk controller card on the motherboard of the computer, are capable of placing the heads at the correct space to retrieve the data.

The three components, cylinders, heads, and sectors (CHS), are referred to as the *drive geometry* and are used to identify specific locations on the drive. The CHS information for the drive is detected by the system BIOS and passed on to the operating system.

The first sector of the disk is called the MBR, or Master Boot Record. It is the most important sector on the disk because it contains the bootloader code and the partition table (the table containing pointers to beginning and end of the logical partitions on the disk). The BIOS gets the system's hardware ready, and then executes the bootloader code. The bootloader code and the bootloader program load the kernel and turn over control of the system to the kernel. Then, Linux is on its way to providing us with one of the best operating system experiences in the world.

The MBR sector is 512 bytes long; the first 446 bytes contain the bootloader code. The next 64 bytes contain the partition table, and the final 2 bytes contain a special code (the hexadecimal values of 55 and AA, respectively) that identifies that sector as the MBR. More details about the MBR can be found Chapter 13, "Backing Up."

Creating the Partition Table

Fedora provides several tools to create, examine, and modify the partition table. Because not all the tools we review are likely to be installed on your system (or other system you might be working on for now), this chapter describes making a partition table, using some command-line and graphical tools that Fedora provides.

The partition table has enough room for only four partitions. When the format was first created, it must have been assumed that four would be plenty. Complex, modern systems with very large hard drives make multiple partitions desirable for any number of unique reasons. To get around this problem, one of the four partitions—typically, partition number four—can be used as an *extended* partition. In other words, in the partition table, it looks like a big partition taking up the rest of the disk. Actually, it is a link to a table that contains the offsets to as many as 63 partitions for IDE disks and 15 for SCSI disks. One extended partition is chained to the next one in this manner.

The `fdisk` Command

The Linux `fdisk` command edits the partition table. You must be the super-user (root) before you can run `fdisk` (also said in Linux shorthand as "run `fdisk` as root"). Only hard drives (IDE and SCSI) can be accessed with `fdisk`, and you must use the device name as an argument. USB hard drives are accessed under SCSI emulation and are treated just as if they were SCSI devices. For example, to open `fdisk` and use it on the first IDE hard drive on the system, you would type this:

```
# fdisk /dev/hda
```

and you would see something like this:

```
# fdisk /dev/hda
The number of cylinders for this disk is set to 4982. There is nothing wrong
→with that, but this is larger than 1024, and in certain setups could
→cause problems with software that runs at boot time:
1) software that runs at boot time (e.g., old versions of LILO)
2) booting and partitioning software from other OSes (e.g., DOS FDISK or the
   →OS/2 FDISK)
```

Pressing the m key displays the help screen as follows:

```
Command (m for help): m
Command action
   a   toggle a bootable flag
   b   edit bsd disklabel
   c   toggle the dos compatibility flag
   d   delete a partition
   l   list known partition types
   m   print this menu
   n   add a new partition
   o   create a new empty DOS partition table
```

35

```
p  print the partition table
q  quit without saving changes
s  create a new empty Sun disklabel
t  change a partition's system id
u  change display/entry units
v  verify the partition table
w  write table to disk and exit
x  extra functionality (experts only)
```

Pressing the p key will display the volume's partition information as follows (note that your drive information will be different):

```
Command (m for help): p

Disk /dev/hda: 255 heads, 63 sectors, 4982 cylinders
Units = cylinders of 16065 * 512 bytes

   Device Boot   Start     End    Blocks  Id System
/dev/hda1   *        1     383   3076416   b Win95 FAT32
/dev/hda2          384     387     32130  83 Linux
/dev/hda3          388    1025   5124735  83 Linux
/dev/hda4         1026    4982 31784602+  5 Extended
/dev/hda5         1026    1042    136521  82 Linux swap
/dev/hda6         1043    1552  4096543+ 83 Linux
/dev/hda7         1553    4102 20482843+ 83 Linux
/dev/hda8         4103    4500  3196903+ 83 Linux
/dev/hda9         4501    4982  3871633+ 83 Linux
```

Older versions of fdisk would default to /dev/hda. The author of fdisk decided that wasn't a good thing, so now you must always type the device name.

TIP

The fdisk command is dangerous to explore only if you write the changes to the partition table. Because you are specifically asked whether you want to do this, poke around to satisfy your curiosity and avoid pressing the w key when you're done; just use q to quit. Armed with this knowledge, do not feel too shy if you're curious about the partition table. But if you really do not want to take a chance on breaking anything, play it safe and use the -l (that's the letter L, not the numeral 1) as in:

```
# fdisk -l /dev/had
```

fdisk happily prints the contents of the partition table to the screen (often referred to as stdout, or standard output) and exits without placing you in the edit mode.

It is always a good idea to keep a hard copy of your edited partition table. You can redirect the output of fdisk -l to a file:

```
# fdisk -l device > mypartitiontable.txt
```

or send it to the printer with:

```
# fdisk -l device ¦ kprinter
```

In the first example, a redirector symbol (>) is used to redirect the listing from stdout to a file. In the second example, we used a pipe (¦) to send the output directly to the printer (assuming that you have one connected).

Now that you are running fdisk as root, you can create a partition table. We will assume that you have installed a brand-new drive as /dev/hdb (the Primary Slave IDE device) and want to partition the entire drive as a single partition. Launch fdisk with:

```
# fdisk /dev/hdb
```

Use the n key to create a new partition, and fdisk prompts you for the beginning cylinder:

```
First Cylinder (1-9729, default 1) :
```

Press the Enter key to accept the default of 1. Now, fdisk prompts:

```
Using the default value of 1
Last Cylinder or +size or +sixeM or +sizeK (2-9729, default 9729) :
```

Here, you can give the size in cylinders, the size in kilobytes, the size in megabytes, or accept the default value (which is the last cylinder on the disk). Press the Enter key to accept the default.

```
Using default value of 9729
```

And we are back at the fdisk prompt:

```
Command (m for help) :
```

Enter the w command to write the new partition table to the disk, and fdisk exits, returning you to the command prompt.

The parted Command

In the past, Red Hat used a partition editor during its installation process named Disk Druid; the underlying code for Disk Druid has been replaced by GNUparted (also known simply as parted, the name of the command itself). GNUparted is the GNU partition editor and a very powerful utility. You use parted to create, delete, move, resize, and copy ext2, ext3, and FAT32 partitions. Although GNUparted displays a GUI interface during the installation process, it really is a console utility. GNUparted can be used from the command line.

35

Creating the File System on the Partitioned Disk

After you partition the disk for a specific file system, you can create the file system on it. In the DOS world, this two-part process is described by DOS as *low-level formatting* (creating the partitions and partition table) and *formatting* (creating the file system). In the Unix world, the latter is known as *creating a file system*. In this section, you learn how to create a file system in Linux.

An unformatted disk storage device (a floppy disk, hard disk drive, or removable media) typically arrives to you with a low-level format, which has been done with a tool such as `fdisk` or `superformat`. Although the disk might have a boot block and partition information, it typically lacks the file structure needed for a file system.

> **NOTE**
>
> If you are preparing to create a file system on any device other than a floppy disk, examine it with `fdisk` or another utility of your choice and modify the partition table accordingly (following the instructions you saw in the preceding sections of this chapter).

To create the file system structure, you need to do what is sometimes referred to as a high-level format. For FAT file systems, this is accomplished by the `format` command. In Linux, you use the `mke2fs -j` command to create an ext3 file system.

> **NOTE**
>
> If you are creating a Reiser file system, use the `mkreiserfs` command. To create a DOS file system, use the `mkdosfs` command. Other commands for other file systems include:
>
> ▶ **mkfs.ext2**—The ext2 file system
>
> ▶ **mkfs.msdos**—The MS-DOS file system
>
> ▶ **mkfs.vfat**—The FAT32 file system

Using `mke2fs` to Create the File System

The `mke2fs` command is used to create both the ext2 and the ext3 file systems. At its simplest, the command is used as:

```
# mke2fs partition
```

such as:

```
# mke2fs /dev/hdc4
```

Here are some of the most useful options for mke2fs:

▶ -c—This option checks for bad blocks during file system creation.

▶ -N—This option overrides the default number of inodes created. (The default number is usually a good choice, but you might need to use this option to allow additional useable disk space.)

▶ -m—This option frees up some space on the disk, but you do so at your peril. By default, the system allocates 5% of the blocks to the super-user—to be used in file recovery during fsck. You can lower that allocation, but you might not leave enough blocks for fsck to recover enough files.

▶ -L—This option gives the volume a label, which is useful if you need to be reminded what the file system is used for; it also provides some flexibility in identifying volumes in /etc/fstab.

▶ -S—This option is a last-ditch effort for recovering a broken file system; it writes only the superblock and descriptors, leaving the information in the inodes unchanged. Always run fsck after using this option.

As you can see, mke2fs offers a few options to make more space available for the regular users. But that extra space always comes from the super user's space for recovering damaged files. The default settings accommodate most users, so think carefully before using one of these options. Hard disks are getting less expensive all the time, so adding another might be a better solution.

Using mkfs.ext3

To make a new ext3 file system, you use the mke2fs command with the -j or -J option, or call the command as mkfs.ext3. Use the tune2fs command on an existing ext2 file system to add journaling. You learn how to convert an existing ext2 file system into an ext3 file system later in this chapter. Here, x represents a partition:

```
# tune2fs /dev/hdx -j
```

Some arguments you can use with this command include:

▶ -j—This option adds an ext3 journal to the new file system, using the default values. Note that you must be using a kernel that has ext3 support to actually make use of the journal.

▶ -J journal-options—This option overrides the default ext3 journal parameters so that you can choose the options you desire. The following journal options are comma separated and you can provide an argument by using the = sign.

▶ size=journal-size—This option creates a journal of journal-size megabytes. With a minimum size of 1,024 blocks, it cannot be more than 102,400 blocks. There must be enough free space in the file system to create a journal of that size.

▶ `device=external-journal`—This option associates the file system with a journal not contained within the file system (one that must have already been created with the command `mke2fs -O journal_device journal_name`); in other words, the journal and the data files do not have to be on the same device.

NOTE

The latter two options in the arguments list are mutually exclusive.

To select the `ext3` journaling mode, you must add the appropriate entry in `/etc/fstab`.

Because the `ext3` file system is a new version of the `ext2` file system with journaling added, it supports the same options as `ext2`, as well as the following additions:

▶ `noload`—This option disables the `ext3` file system's journal when mounting; it becomes an `ext2` file system.

▶ `data=journal` / `data=ordered` / `data=writeback`—This option specifies the journaling mode; `ordered` is the default. Metadata is always journaled.

▶ `journal`—The slowest, but most secure mode because all the data is written to the journal before it is written to the regular file system.

▶ `ordered`—This is the default mode in which all data is written to the main file system prior to its metadata being committed to the journal.

▶ `writeback`—With this option, data can be written into the main file system after its metadata has been committed to the journal. This option enables old data to appear in files after a crash and journal recovery, but it is the fastest option.

Using `mkreiserfs`

The Reiser file system journals file data and handles smaller files more efficiently than the `ext3` file system. Although it is suitable for use as the root file system, Fedora does not officially support its use in that way. You use the `mkreiserfs` command to create a Reiser file system. The default values for `mkreiserfs` work well. To create a Reiser file system, use:

```
# mkreiserfs device
```

Creating a DOS File System with `mkdosfs`

It is possible to create DOS file systems without owning any Microsoft software if you use the `mkdosfs` command. To create a DOS file system in an image file, use the `-C` option. The `-n` option enables you to specify a volume label. To create a 1.4MB DOS file system as an image file with the label `dosfloppy`, the sector size (`-S`) should be `512` and the block count should be `1440`. Use the `-v` option to provide verbose output so that you can observe what happens.

```
# mkdosfs -n dosfloppy -v -C floppy.img -S 512 1440
```

A complete review of all the argument options and syntax for creating a DOS file system can be found in the man page for mkdosfs. The new file system must be mounted (as described in the following section) and then formatted with the mformat command.

Mounting File Systems

File systems in Unix are very flexible in that they need not be physically present on your computer; you can have network access to other file systems on other machines. The Linux file system structure (the Virtual File System we spoke of at the beginning of the chapter) makes it appear as if all the file systems, regardless of type and location, are local and mounted somewhere on the root file system. As the system administrator, you decide what file systems are to be made available and where they will be attached, or mounted, to the root file system. The standard arrangement of the file system tree is that installed by default by Fedora. The source of that standard arrangement is found in the file system hierarchy standards. Although a detailed discussion of those standards is beyond the scope of this section, they can be examined at http://www.pathname.com/fhs/. In this section, you learn how to mount file systems to the root file system and add file systems to the system, and you learn the traditional mount points of commonly used file systems as well.

In Linux (and its Unix cousins), all file systems—whether local, remote, images on a disk, or in memory—are mounted on a single point known as root (which is not the same as the root operator, also known as the *super-user*). This mount point is written as a forward slash, /, which is read and pronounced "root." The resulting file directory hierarchy all starts from /. After they are mounted, the physical location of the files is unimportant because they all appear to be local.

Even if the file systems are different (FAT, ext2, HPFS, NTFS, and so on), the Linux kernel modules and the VFS make them all appear as part of the directory tree as native files. Listing the file systems as native files obviates the need for any applications to be aware of the physical location of the file or the true nature of the native file system. As a result, programming these applications is simplified because the applications have to work only with what they think are local, native files.

Any file system can be mounted anywhere, but some places are more traditional than others. Removable media devices are traditionally mounted under the /mnt directory (for example, CD-ROM drives on /mnt/cdrom). The /mnt directory is the traditional place to mount removable or remote file systems that are unrelated to the local system directories that branch from the root mount point.

The mount Command

File systems are mounted with the mount command and unmounted, curiously enough, with the umount command.

During the installation, you have the opportunity to decide where and how your partitions will be mounted. You indicate your choices, and Fedora automatically stores them in /etc/fstab, the file system table, for you. The mount command looks at /etc/fstab and mounts the file system according to those set preferences. You learn more about the file system table later in this section.

The syntax for `mount` is:

```
mount -t type file system_to_be mounted mount_point
```

Here are the components of the `mount` command, and a brief explanation of each:

- ▶ *type*—Always preceded by the -t argument and followed by a space, and then the type of file system you are mounting. Typical file system types are ext2, ext3, vfat, iso9660, hpfs, hfs, ntfs, and others. For many file systems, `mount` can detect what type they are automatically, and the -t argument is superfluous (and is replaced with auto).

- ▶ file system_to_be mounted (as represented by the partition on which it resides)— This is the device name of the file system you want to `mount`, typically in the form of /dev/hdx, /dev/scx, or /dev/fdx.

- ▶ mount_point—The place in the directory tree where you want to mount the file system. Curiously, you can mount a file system over part of an existing file system. For example, if you have an existing directory at /foo with a single file named bar, and you mount a file system at /foo that includes a file named snafu, a listing of the directory /foo does not show the file bar, but only the file snafu. To show both files is a feature called *transparency*, which unfortunately is not in the current Linux repertoire.

The only real restriction to "mount anything anywhere" is that the critical system files in /bin, /etc, /lib, /dev, /proc, and /tmp need to be accessed at bootup, which typically means that they need to be on the same physical disk. If they cannot be accessed at bootup, Linux does not load and run.

Here are a few examples of using the `mount` command:

Mounting a floppy:

```
# mount -t vfat /dev/fd0 /mnt/floppy
```

Mounting a CD-ROM:

```
# mount -t iso9660 /dev/scd0 /mnt/cdrom
```

Mounting a Network File System (NFS) volume:

```
# mount -t nfs remote_host:/dir [options] mount_point
```

Numerous mount options exist. These options are used primarily in the /etc/fstab file. You can invoke a `mount` option by preceding it (or a comma-delimited string of options) with the -o switch. The mount options are listed in the fstab section of this chapter.

The umount Command

To unmount a file system, use the umount command with the following syntax:

umount *mount_point*

You can also unmount by device name:

umount *device_name*

> **CAUTION**
>
> Do not use umount -a to unmount everything that the system does not require to run (or is not currently using). Unmounting *everything* is a particularly bad idea on a multi-user, networked system because your users are certain to lose access to some or all of their files. So, as any good sysadmin will tell you, do not do that.

Mounting Automatically with /etc/fstab

A special file, /etc/fstab, exists to provide the system with predetermined options and mount points so that the file systems can be automatically or manually mounted with minimal typing and without having to recall arcane Linux syntax.

The /etc/fstab file can only be written to by the super-user. The commands fsck, mount, and umount all read information from /etc/fstab. Each file system gets its own line with the information separated by tabs.

On each line of fstab, the first field indicates the block device or remote file system that will be mounted. The second field identifies the mount point on the local system where the file system will be mounted. The third field is the file system type, and the fourth field is a comma-delimited list of mount options. Options include:

- ▶ exec—If this option is specified, binaries can be executed from this file system.

- ▶ noauto—This means that the -a option does not cause the file system to be mounted and it is not mounted at bootup.

- ▶ noexec—If this option is specified, binaries cannot be executed from this file system.

- ▶ nosuid—This option does not permit set-user-identifier or set-group-identifier bits to take effect.

- ▶ ro—This option mounts the file system as read-only.

- ▶ rw—This option mounts the file system as read/write.

- ▶ sync—Reading from and writing to the files are done synchronously.

- ▶ user—This option allows a regular (not just root) user to mount the file system, but it includes the options noexec, nosuid, and nodev by default unless they are overridden by exec, dev, and suid.

35

For `iso9660` file systems, the interesting option is `unhide`, which shows hidden and associated files.

The `fstab` man pages contain an in-depth description of `fstab` and its options.

The fifth field of `/etc/fstab` is used by `dump` (a traditional Unix backup program) to determine whether the file system should be dumped (backed up); 1 is yes, and 0 is no. Default values are set for you during the initial installation. They are of concern only if you actually use `dump`; then you would set the value to 1 for the file systems you wanted to back up.

The sixth field is used by `fsck` to determine how `fsck` needs to interact with the file system—0 means that `fsck` is never run on the file system (a FAT32 file system, for example); 1 means that `fsck` will be run on the drive at a predetermined time. 2 is recommended for nonroot file systems so that `fsck` is not run on them as frequently.

Here is a simple `/etc/fstab` file from a system with a RAID0 ext3 root partition and dual-booted with MS Windows:

```
LABEL=/12      /             ext3     defaults               1 1
none           /dev/pts      devpts   gid=5,mode=620         0 0
none           /proc         proc     defaults               0 0
none           /dev/shm      tmpfs    defaults               0 0
/dev/hda11     swap          swap     defaults               0 0
/dev/cdrom     /mnt/cdrom    iso9660  noauto,owner,kudzu,ro  0 0
/dev/fd0       /mnt/floppy   auto     noauto,owner,kudzu     0 0
/dev/hda1      /mnt/win_c    vfat     auto,quiet,exec        0 0
```

Notice the two entries marked with the `kudzu` option. This is the result of the actions of `updfstab`, which keeps `fstab` synchronized with the state of any removable devices on the system such as CD-ROMs. The `quiet` option shown for the Windows partition suppresses error messages and is recommended if you use the Wine application.

NOTE

Device labels can be very useful. You can use the label in `/etc/fstab`, and if you have many devices, their labels might be easier for you to remember and track than would be their device names. You can also shuffle around partitions without editing `fstab`, just by changing their labels. The `e2label` command is easier to remember than the analogous `tune2fs` command.

The command `e2label` can display or change a device's label. (You also can change a device label with `tune2fs -L`.) For example, to change the label of `/dev/hda4` to archives, use:

```
# e2label /dev/hda4 archives
```

As mentioned earlier, you record mounting preferences in `/etc/fstab` during installation. You need to modify `/etc/fstab` only if you make changes to your mounts or desire to change the default settings to address the specific needs of your system.

As long as the super-user understands the syntax and options of the fstab file, she can edit the file with any text editor.

Relocating a File System

Many home users start with a single disk partition that mounts not only the root file system files, but also all the other files. Although this might work quite well for most home users, there might come a time when the physical disk becomes full. Adding another drive and moving part of the file system there is not difficult, but it is the source of many questions from new Linux users. This section of the chapter explains how to do this kind of file system relocation.

In this example, we install a new IDE hard drive to /dev/hdb (the primary slave drive), create a single partition on it, format it as an ext3 file system, and move all the user files located in /home to it. When done, we make it mount, by default, at the /home mount point by editing the /etc/fstab file.

Installing the New Drive

First, physically install the drive, making certain that the master/slave jumpers are set correctly to set the drive as a slave drive. Also be certain that the jumpers are set correctly on the existing master drive. (Some drives require a different jumper setting, depending on whether they are a single master drive or a master drive with a slave drive; others offer a "cable-select" option to automatically set the drive status.) Failing to ensure that the jumpers are set correctly is a common error made even by people who are familiar with computer hardware.

Most modern large drives use the LBA setting (Logical Block Addressing) to deal with the BIOS size limitations. If the drive is not detected, check the power connection, the IDE cable connection (the red stripe usually goes next to the power connector, but always double-check), and the master/slave jumpers. If all these are fine, you might have a bad drive, or the two hard drives might not be playing nicely with each other (especially if they were made by different manufacturers).

To check further, reset the jumper of the new drive to make it the master drive, disconnect the old drive, and plug in the new one in its place. If the new drive is now correctly detected, suspect some incompatibility between the drives. Always make cable changes to the drives with the power off, or you will damage the drive.

Creating the Partition Table and Formatting the Disk

After it is installed and recognized by the BIOS, a partition table needs to be created. Use fdisk (or the program of your choice) to create a single partition on the drive, remembering to write the changes to the MBR before you exit the program (refer to "Creating the Partition Table," earlier in this chapter).

Formatting the drive is next. Because we are creating a new ext3 file system, we use the j option, as:

```
# mke2fs -cj /dev/hdb1
```

Notice that we are checking the drive (using the -c option) for bad blocks as we format. Even though it adds considerable time to formatting the drive, an initial bad block check is always a good idea. The program identifies bad blocks and doesn't use them; bad blocks would only corrupt our data if we didn't mark the file system to ignore them.

Mounting the New Partition and Populating It with the Relocated Files

For the example that follows, it is assumed that /home was a directory that was part of the partition mounted at /, not a separate partition to begin with.

Here, we create a temporary mount point and mount the new partition:

```
# mkdir /mnt/newpartition
```

```
# mount -t ext3 /dev/hdb1 /mnt/newpartition
```

It is now time to copy all the files from /home to /mnt/newpartition. It is important that we preserve the time and date stamps for the files and the permissions. We're copying entire directories and subdirectories, so we use the one of three basic copying methods (tar, cpio, or cp) that best accommodates this:

```
# cp -a /home/* /mnt/newpartition
```

We need to modify /etc/fstab so that the new ext3 partition will be mounted correctly:

```
/dev/hdb1    /home ext3  defaults    1 2
```

Here, we have chosen to use the default mount options for the ext3 partition. The defaults are identical to those for the ext2 file system, and additionally selects the default data=ordered journaling mode.

Anytime we reboot, the new partition containing the copied files will automatically be mounted at /home. But before we do that, we must cd to /home and enter this:

```
# touch thisistheoldhomepartition
```

Now we can mount the new partition:

```
# umount /mnt/newpartition
```

```
# mount /dev/hdb1 /home
```

Note that if you enter:

```
# ls -al /home
```

you will not see the thisistheoldhomepartition file we created with the touch command. So, what happened to the old files? They are still there, but just hidden because we mounted a directory "over" them. When we are satisfied that all is well, we can unmount the newly created home partition and delete the files in the partition that contains the thisistheoldhomepartition file.

> **TIP**
>
> You can use the previously explained technique as a placeholder or warning for any temporarily mounted file system so that you do not mistakenly think that the file system is mounted when it is not.

Logical Volume Management

The previous example showed you how to add a new drive to overcome a lack of disk space. What if this could be done without all the mounting and file copying? That's where logical volume management (LVM) is useful. Using LVM, disk space from multiple drives can be pooled into a single logical volume.

As with any new technology, there is a steep learning curve involved in using LVM, not the least of which is its vocabulary. Within this vocabulary, partitions are known as physical volumes, or *pvs*. We add pvs to a volume group that defines a logical volume on which we can create our file system.

On a heavily used system, the files being backed up can change during the backup, and the restored files might be in an unstable condition. LVM can also make snapshots of the logical volume that can then be mounted and backed up.

For more information on LVM under Linux, read the LVM HOWTO at http://tldp.org/HOWTO/LVM-HOWTO/, which explains the terminology and provides a guide to setting up and using LVM on a Linux system.

File System Manipulation

Different people have various learning styles. For those of you who prefer examples rather than lectures, here are a few practical examples in which you learn how to create a file system within a file and mount it using the *loopback file system*—a special file system that enables you to accomplish this useful feat. You can use the file system you create to experiment with and practice almost all the commands found in this chapter with no fear of damaging your system.

Creating a File System for Testing

Because most of us do not have a spare computer or hard drive on which to experiment and practice, you can make one of your own by creating an image file containing the file system of your choice and using the loopback file system to mount it. That way, you do not run the risk of accidentally wreaking havoc on the system itself. Although you could also use a floppy drive for these same exercises, their small size limits your flexibility.

Step 1—Make a Blank Image File

Use the dd command to create a file with a block size of 1,024 bytes (a megabyte) and create a file that is 10MB in size. (You need to have enough free space on your hard drive to hold a file this big, so adjust the size accordingly.) You need 10,000 1KB (1,024-byte) blocks, so select a count of 10000.

If you wanted a floppy-sized image, you would have selected a block size (bs) of 512 and a count of 2880 for a 1.4MB floppy or 5760 for a 2.88MB floppy. Here's how to do that:

```
# dd if=/dev/zero of=/tmp/fedoratest.img bs=1024 count=10000
```

You can see the computer respond with the following:

```
10000+0 records in
10000+0 records out
```

If you check your new file command, you see this:

```
# file /tmp/fedoratest.img
/tmp/fedoratest.img: data
```

Step 2—Make a File System

Now you need to make the system think that the file is a block device instead of an ASCII file, so you use losetup, a utility that associates loop devices with regular files or block devices; you will be using the loopback device, /dev/loop0.

```
# losetup /dev/loop0 /tmp/fedoratest.img
```

Now you can format the file as an ext2 file system:

```
# mke2fs /dev/loop0
```

You can see the computer respond as follows:

```
mke2fs 1.27 (8-Mar-2003)
File System label=
OS type: Linux
Block size=1024 (log=0)
Fragment size=1024 (log=0)
2512 inodes, 10000 blocks
500 blocks (5.00%) reserved for the super user
```

```
First data block=1
2 block groups
8192 blocks per group, 8192 fragments per group
1256 inodes per group
Superblock backups stored on blocks:
    8193

Writing inode tables: done
Writing superblocks and file system accounting information: done

This file system will be automatically checked every 21 mounts or 180 days, \
whichever comes first. Use tune2fs -c or -i to override.
```

Step 3—Mount the Test File System

After your test file system has been created, you can experiment with the different options for the formatting commands you will be using. It will be useful to make a mount point for your image file:

```
# mkdir /mnt/image
```

and then mount it:

```
# mount /dev/loop0 /mnt/image
```

You can do this now because you already have the loopback file system associated with the image file. Later on, if you remount it, you must use the following format to use the loopback option:

```
# mount -o loop /tmp/fedoratest.img /mnt/image
```

After mounting the new file system, you can look at it and see that the /lost+found directory has been created on it and that the df command returns:

```
# df -h /mnt/image
File System     Size Used Avail Use% Mounted on /dev/loop0     \
9.5M 13k 8.9M   1% /mnt/image
```

To unmount it, use this:

```
# umount /mnt/image
```

Make a backup of the image just in case you break the original:

```
# cp /tmp/fedoratest.img fedoratest.bak
```

After the test file system is created, you can create directories, copy files to it, delete files, attempt to recover them, and, in general, create controlled chaos on your computer while you are learning and practicing valuable skills. If you damage the file system on the image beyond repair, unmount it, delete it, and create a new one (or copy a new one from that backup).

Mounting a Partition as Read-Only on a Running System

Remember that to do almost any kind of file system manipulation (formatting, checking, and so on), you should unmount the file system; by doing so, you avoid having any writes made to the file system, which would corrupt it.

How do you remount partitions on a running system? For example, to remount the /home partition (assuming that it is on a separate physical partition from root) as read-only to run fsck on it and then remount it as read-write, use the remount option for mount:

```
# mount -o ro,remount /home
```

> **NOTE**
>
> Remounting does not work if a normal user is logged in because /home is busy (in use). You might need to switch to runlevel 1 (init 1), which is single-user mode, to remount /home.

Now you can run fsck on the partition. When done,

```
# mount -o rw,remount /home
```

puts it back in service.

If you reboot your system to mount the root file system read-only for maintenance (enter the maintenance mode, s, as described in Chapter 11),

```
# mount -o rw,remount /
```

will remount it read-write and you can continue on. That's easier than unmounting and remounting the device.

Examine an initrd Image File

The initrd.img file is automatically created during the installation process (if necessary) or with the mkinitrd command. You never need to examine it, but if you are curious about what's in the initrd.img file, just take a look: It is really just a gzipped ext2 file system. To examine it, first copy it to the /tmp directory and add the .gz suffix to it:

```
# cp /boot/initrd-2.6.7-1.478.img /tmp/initrd-2.6.7-1.478.img.gz
```

If your system does not have an initrd.img file in /boot, mount your boot floppy and see whether it has one. Next, uncompress it as follows:

```
# gunzip /tmp/initrd-2.6.7-1.478.img.gz
```

Mount it as follows:

```
# mount -o loop /tmp/initrd-2.6.7-1.478.img /mnt/image
```

and browse the directory to your heart's content.

Not every system has an `initrd.img` file. It is typically used to load device drivers for file systems (such as Reiser) or hardware (such as the Promise RAID IDE controller) that must be in place before the system can continue booting. Some floppy-disc–based Linux distributions use `initrd.img` to load a minimal operating system that can then uncompress and load the working file system from the floppy.

You can also mount `.iso` images in the same way, but remember that they are always read-only because of the nature of the underlying `iso9660` file system; you can write to the other images unless you explicitly mount them as read-only. If you want to read and write to the files in an ISO file system, you must first copy the files to a device that is mounted read-write, make your changes, and then use `mkisofs` to create a new `.iso` image. This is a common "gotcha" for many users.

Relevant Fedora and Linux Commands

You use these commands when managing file systems in Fedora:

- **df**—Shows free disk space
- **du**—Displays disk usage
- **dump**—An ext2 file system backup utility
- **dumpe2fs**—Shows information about an ext2 file system
- **e2fsadm**—Administers an LVM/ext2 file system
- **e2image**—Creates an image file of ext2 file system data
- **fdisk**—The standard Linux partition table editor
- **fsck**—Checks or repairs a file system
- **lsraid**—Displays information about Linux RAID devices
- **mformat**—Formats a DOS floppy disk; part of the Mtools suite of tools
- **mkfs**—Creates various file systems and acts as a wrapper for the actual programs that do the work
- **mkisofs**—Creates a CD-ROM file system in `iso960` format
- **mkreiserfs**—Creates a Linux `reiserfs` file system
- **mkswap**—Prepares a Linux swap device
- **mount**—Mounts a supported file system
- **parted**—The GNU partition editor and resizing utility
- **reiserfsck**—Checks a Linux `reiserfs` file system
- **resize_reiserfs**—Resizes a Linux `reiserfs` file system
- **smbmount**—Mounts an smbfs file system
- **stat**—Shows file or file system status
- **swapon**—Displays swap usage or start using system swap device

35

- ▶ **swapoff**—Turns off swap usage
- ▶ **sync**—Flushes file system buffers
- ▶ **tune2fs**—Changes file system parameters on `ext2` file systems
- ▶ **umount**—Unmounts a file systems
- ▶ **usermount**—The Fedora graphical file system mounting and formatting tool

Reference

- ▶ http://www.ibiblio.org/pub/Linux/docs/HOWTO/other-formats/html_single/Ext2fs-Undeletion.html—You deleted a file on your `ext2/3` partition? The Linux Ext2fs Undeletion mini HOWTO is there to help you out.

- ▶ http://www.ibiblio.org/pub/Linux/docs/HOWTO/other-formats/html_single/LVM-HOWTO.html—Throw away those concepts that marry physical disks to finite-sized file systems; the Logical Volume Manager HOWTO explains how to overcome that kind of restrictive thinking.

- ▶ http://www.math.ualberta.ca/imaging/snfs/—Secure NFS via an SSH Tunnel is a very interesting attempt to address a security shortcomings of NFS over a public network.

- ▶ http://www.ibiblio.org/pub/Linux/docs/HOWTO/other-formats/html_single/NFS-Root.html—The NFS-Root mini HOWTO.

- ▶ http://www.ibiblio.org/pub/Linux/docs/HOWTO/other-formats/html_single/NFS-Root-Client-mini-HOWTO.html—Explains in detail how to set up and use NFS for exporting root file systems.

- ▶ http://www.ibiblio.org/pub/Linux/docs/HOWTO/other-formats/html_single/Tips-HOWTO.html—The Linux Tips HOWTO provides some useful tips that make it worth the time to read because it addresses some file system problems such as "Is there enough free space?" and "How do I move directories between file systems?"

- ▶ http://www.ibiblio.org/pub/Linux/docs/HOWTO/other-formats/html_single/BootPrompt-HOWTO.html—The BootPrompt HOWTO informs you of boot time arguments that can be passed to the kernel to deal with misbehaving hardware, configure non-PNP devices, and so on.

- ▶ http://www.linux-usb.org/USB-guide/x498.html—The USB Guide for mass storage and other USB devices. If you have a USB device and need to know whether it is supported and how to access it, check here. (Tip: USB storage devices are emulated as SCSI devices.)

# CHAPTER 36

Kernel and Module Management

A *kernel* is a complex piece of software that manages the processes and process interactions that take place within an operating system. As a user, you rarely, if ever, interact directly with it. Instead, you work with the applications that the kernel manages.

The Linux kernel is Linux. It is the result of years of cooperative (and sometimes contentious) work by numerous people around the world. There is only one common kernel source tree, but each major Linux distribution massages and patches its version slightly to add features, performance, or options. Each Linux distribution, including Fedora, comes with its own precompiled kernel as well as the kernel source code, providing you with absolute authority over the Linux operating system. This chapter examines the kernel and so you can learn what it does both for you and for the operating system.

In this chapter, you also learn how to obtain the kernel sources, as well as how and when to patch the kernel. The chapter leads you through an expert's tour of the kernel architecture and teaches you essential steps in kernel configuration, how to build and install modules, and how to compile drivers in Fedora. This chapter also teaches you important aspects of working with GRUB, the default Fedora boot loader. Finally, the chapter's troubleshooting information will help you understand what to do when something goes wrong with your Linux kernel installation or compilation process. As disconcerting as these problems can seem, this chapter shows you some easy fixes for many kernel problems.

Most users find that the precompiled Fedora kernel suits their needs. At some point, you might need to recompile the kernel to support a specific piece of hardware or add a new feature to the operating system. If you have heard horror stories about the difficulties of recompiling the Linux kernel, you can relax; this chapter gives you all the information you need to understand when recompiling is necessary and how to painlessly work through the process.

The Linux Kernel

The Linux kernel is the management part of the operating system that many people call "Linux." Although many think of the entire distribution as Linux, the only piece that can correctly be called Linux is the kernel. Fedora, like many Linux distributions, includes a kernel packaged with add-on software that interacts with the kernel so that the user can interface with the system in a meaningful manner.

The system utilities and user programs enable computers to become valuable tools to a user.

The First Linux Kernel

In 1991, Linus Torvalds released version .99 of the Linux kernel as the result of his desire for a powerful, Unix-like operating system for his Intel 80386 personal computer. Linus wrote the initial code necessary to create what is now known as the Linux kernel and combined it with Richard Stallman's GNU tools. Indeed, because many of the Linux basic system tools come from the GNU Project, many people refer to the operating system as GNU/Linux. Since then, Linux has benefited as thousands of contributors have added their talents and time to the Linux project. Linus still maintains the kernel, deciding on what will and will not make it into the kernel as official releases, known to many as the *vanilla* or *Linus* Linux kernel.

The Linux Source Tree

The source code for the Linux kernel is kept in a group of directories called the kernel source tree. The structure of the kernel source tree is important because the process of compiling (building) the kernel is automated; it is controlled by scripts interpreted by the make application. These scripts, known as *Makefiles*, expect to find the pieces of the kernel code in specific places or they do not work. You will learn how to use make to compile a kernel later in this chapter.

It is not necessary for the Linux kernel source code to be installed on your system for the system to run or for you to accomplish typical tasks such as email, web browsing, or word processing. It is necessary that the kernel sources be installed, however, if you want to compile a new kernel. In the next section, we show you how to install the kernel source files and how to set up the special symbolic link required. That link is /usr/src/kernels/ <*yourkernelversion*>, and it is how we will refer to the directory of the kernel source tree as we examine the contents of the kernel source tree.

The `/usr/src/kernels/<yourkernelversion>` directory contains the `.config` and the `Makefile` files among others. The `.config` file is the configuration of your Linux kernel as it was compiled. There is no `.config` file by default; you must select one from the `/configs` subdirectory. There you will find configuration files for each flavor of the kernel Fedora provides; simply copy the one appropriate for your system to the default directory and rename it `.config`.

We have already discussed the contents of the `/configs` subdirectory, so now you can examine the other directories found under `/usr/src/kernels/<yourkernelversion>`. The most useful is the `Documentation` directory. In it and its subdirectories, you will find almost all the documentation concerning every part of the kernel. The `00-INDEX` file (each `Documentation` subdirectory also contains a `00-INDEX` file as well) contains a list of the files in the main directory and a brief explanation of what they are. Many files are written solely for kernel programmers and application writers, but a few are useful to the intermediate or advanced Linux user attempting to learn about kernel and device driver issues. Some of the more interesting and useful documents are

▶ `devices.txt`—A list of all possible Linux devices that are represented in the `/dev` directory, giving major and minor numbers and a short description. If you have ever gotten an error message that mentions `char-major-xxx`, this file is where that list is kept. Devices are mentioned in Chapter 35, "Managing the File System."

▶ `ide.txt`—If your system uses IDE hard drives, this file discusses how the kernel interacts with them and lists the various kernel commands that can be used to solve IDE-related hardware problems, manually set data transfer modes, and otherwise manually manage your IDE drives. Most of this management is automatic, but if you want to understand how the kernel interacts with IDE devices, this file explains it.

▶ `initrd.txt`—Chapter 34 also discusses the initial RAM disk. This file provides much more in-depth knowledge of initial RAM disks, giving details on the loopback file system used to create and mount them and explaining how the kernel interacts with them.

▶ `kernel-parameters.txt`—This file is a list of most of the arguments that you can pass at boot time to configure kernel or hardware settings, but it does not appear too useful at first glance because it is just a list. However, knowing that a parameter exists and might relate to something you are looking for can assist you in tracking down more information because now you have terms to enter into an Internet search engine such as http://www.google.com/linux.

▶ `sysrq.txt`—If you have ever wondered what that SysRq key on your keyboard is used for, this file has the answer. Briefly, it is a key combination hardwired into the kernel that can help you recover from a system lockup. Fedora disables this function by default for security reasons. You can re-enable it by entering the command `#  echo "1" > /proc/sys/kernel/sysrq` and disable it by echoing a value of `0` instead of `1`.

In the other directories found in Documentation, you will find similar text files that deal with the kernel modules for CD-ROM drivers, file system drivers, gameport and joystick drivers, video drivers (not graphics card drivers—those belong to X11R6 and not to the kernel), network drivers, and all the other drivers and systems found in the Linux operating system. Again, these documents are usually written for programmers, but they can provide useful information to the intermediate and advanced Linux user as well.

The directory named scripts contains many of the scripts that make uses. It really does not contain anything of interest to anyone who is not a programmer or a kernel developer (also known as a *kernel hacker*).

After a kernel is built, all the compiled files wind up in the arch directory and its subdirectories. Although you can manually move them to their final location, we will show you later in this chapter how the make scripts will do it for you. In the early days of Linux, this post-compilation file relocation was all done by hand; you should be grateful for make.

> **NOTE**
>
> The make utility is a very complex program. Complete documentation on the structure of Makefiles, as well as the arguments that it can accept, can be found at http://www.gnu.org/software/make/manual/make.html.

The remaining directories contain the source code for the kernel and the kernel drivers. When you install the kernel sources, these files are placed there automatically. When you patch kernel sources, these files are altered automatically. When you compile the kernel, these files are accessed automatically. Although you never need to touch the source code files, they can be useful. The kernel source files are nothing more than text files with special formatting, which means that we can look at them and read the programmers' comments. Sometimes, a programmer will write an application, but cannot (or often does not) write the documentation. The comments he puts in the source code are often the only documentation that exists for the code.

Small testing programs are even hidden in the comments of some of the code, along with comments and references to other information. Because the source code is written in a language that can be read as easily—almost—as English, a nonprogrammer might be able to get an idea of what the application or driver is actually doing (see Chapter 28, "C/C++ Programming Tools for Fedora"). This information might be of use to an intermediate to advanced Linux user when he is confronted by kernel- and driver-related problems.

> **NOTE**
>
> The interaction and control of hardware is handled by a small piece of the kernel called a *device driver*. The driver tells the computer how to interact with a modem, a SCSI card, a keyboard, a mouse, and so on in response to a user prompt. Without the device driver, the kernel does not know how to interact with the associated device.

Types of Kernels

In the early days of Linux, kernels were a single block of code containing all the instructions for the processor, the motherboard, and the other hardware. If you changed hardware, you were required to recompile the kernel code to include what you needed and discard what you did not. Including extra, unneeded code carried a penalty because the kernel became larger and occupied more memory. On older systems that had only 4MB–8MB of memory, wasting precious memory for unnecessary code was considered unacceptable. Kernel compiling was something of a black art as early Linux users attempted to wring the most performance from their computers. These kernels compiled as a single block of code are called *monolithic kernels.*

As the kernel code grew larger and the number of devices that could be added to a computer increased, the requirement to recompile became onerous. A new method of building the kernel was developed to make the task of compiling easier. The part of the kernel's source code that composed the code for the device drivers could be optionally compiled as a module that could be loaded and unloaded into the kernel as required. This is known as the *modular* approach to building the kernel. Now, all the kernel code could be compiled at once—with most of the code compiled into these modules. Only the required modules would be loaded; the kernel could be kept smaller, and adding hardware was much simpler.

The typical Fedora kernel has some drivers compiled as part of the kernel itself (called *in-line* drivers) and others compiled as modules. Only device drivers compiled in-line are available to the kernel during the boot process; modular drivers are available only after the system has been booted.

36

> **NOTE**
>
> As a common example, drivers for SCSI disk drives must be available to the kernel if you intend to boot from SCSI disks. If the kernel is not compiled with those drivers in-line, the system will not boot because it will not be able to access the disks.
>
> A way around this problem for modular kernels is to use an initial RAM disk (`initrd`) discussed later in section "Creating an Initial RAM Disk Image." The `initrd` loads a small kernel and the appropriate device driver, which then can access the device to load the actual kernel you want to run.

Some code can be only one or the other (for technical reasons unimportant to the average user), but most code can be compiled either as modular or in-line. Depending on the application, some system administrators prefer one way over the other, but with fast modern processors and abundant system memory, the performance differences are of little concern to all but the most ardent Linux hackers.

When compiling a kernel, the step in which you make the selection of modular or in-line is part of the `make config` step that we detail later in this chapter. Unless you have a specific reason to do otherwise, we suggest that you select the modular option when given a choice. The process of managing modules is addressed in the next section because you will be managing them more frequently than you will be compiling a kernel.

Managing Modules

With a modular kernel, special tools are required to manage the modules. Modules must be loaded and unloaded, and it would be nice if that were done as automatically as possible. You also need to be able to pass necessary parameters to modules when you load them—things such as memory addresses and interrupts. (That information varies from module to module, so you need to look at the documentation for your modules to determine what, if any, information needs to be passed to it.) This section covers the tools provided to manage modules and then look at a few examples of using them.

Linux provides the following module management tools for your use. All these commands (and modprobe.conf) have man pages:

▶ lsmod—This command lists the loaded modules. It is useful to pipe this through the less command because the listing is usually more than one page long.

▶ insmod—This command loads the specified module into the running kernel. If a module name is given without a full path, the default location for the running kernel, /lib/modules/*/, is searched. Several options are offered for this command—the most useful is -f, which forces the module to be loaded.

▶ rmmod—This command unloads (removes) the specified module from the running kernel. More than one module at a time can be specified.

▶ modprobe—A more sophisticated version of insmod and rmmod, it uses the dependency file created by depmod and automatically handles loading, or with the -r option, removing modules. There is no force option, however. A useful option to modprobe is -t, which causes modprobe to cycle through a set of drivers until it finds one that matches your system. If you were unsure of what module would work for your network card, you would use this command:

```
# modprobe -t net
```

The term net is used because that is the name of the directory (/lib/modules/*/ kernel/net) where all the network drivers are kept. It tries each one in turn until it loads one successfully.

▶ modinfo—This queries a module's object file and provides a list of the module name, author, license, and any other information that is there. It often is not very useful.

▶ depmod—This program creates a dependency file for kernel modules. Some modules need to have other modules loaded first; that is, they depend on the other modules. (A lot of the kernel code is like this because it eliminates redundancy in the code base.) During the boot process, one of the startup files contains the command depmod -a and it is run every time you boot to re-create the file /lib/modules/*/ modules.dep. If you make changes to the /etc/modprobe.conf file, run depmod -a manually. The depmod command, its list of dependencies, and the /etc/modprobe. conf file enable kernel modules to be automatically loaded as needed.

▶ /etc/modprobe.conf—This is not a command, but a file that controls how modprobe and depmod behave; it contains kernel module variables. Although the command syntax can be quite complex, most actual needs are very simple. The most common use is to alias a module and then pass it some parameters. For example, in the following code, a device name (from devices.txt) is aliased to a more descriptive word and then some information is passed to an associated module. The i2c-dev device is used to read the CPU temperature and fan speed on the system. These lines for /etc/modprobe.conf were suggested for use by the program's documentation. They were added with a text editor.

```
alias char-major-89 i2c-dev
options eeprom ignore=2,0x50,2,0x51,2,0x52
```

A partial listing of lsmod is shown here, piped through the less command, so that you can view it a page at a time:

```
# lsmod ¦ less
Module              Size  Used by
parport_pc         19392  1
Module              Size  Used by
parport_pc         19392  1
lp                  8236  0
parport            29640  2 parport_pc,lp
autofs4            10624  0
sunrpc            101064  1
```

The list is actually much longer, but here you can see that the input module is being used by the joydev (joystick device) module, but the joystick module is not being used. This computer has a joystick port that was auto-detected, but no joystick is connected. A scanner module is also loaded, but because the USB scanner is unplugged, the module is not being used. You would use the lsmod command to determine whether a module was loaded and what other modules were using it. If you examined the full list, you would see modules for all the devices attached to your computer.

To remove a module, joydev in this example, use

```
# rmmod joydev
```

or

```
# modprobe -r joydev
```

A look at the output of lsmod would now show that it is no longer loaded. If you removed input as well, you could then use modprobe to load both input and joydev (one depends on the other, remember) with a simple:

```
# modprobe joydev
```

36

If Fedora were to balk at loading a module (because it had been compiled using a different kernel version from what you are currently running; for example, the NVIDIA graphics card module), you could force it to load like this:

```
# insmod -f nvidia
```

You would ignore the complaints (error messages) in this case if the kernel generated any.

Chapter 7, "Multimedia," talked about loading a scanner module; in the example there, the scanner module was loaded manually and the vendor ID was passed to it. The scanner was not included in the lookup list because it is not supported by the GPL scanner programs; as a result, the scanner module was not automatically detected and loaded. However, the scanner works with a closed-source application after the module is loaded. Automatic module management is nice when it works, but sometimes it is necessary to work with modules directly.

When to Recompile

Fedora systems use a modified version of the plain vanilla Linux kernel (a modified version is referred to as a *patched* kernel) with additional drivers and other special features compiled into it.

Fedora has quite an intensive testing period for all distribution kernels and regularly distributes updated versions. The supplied Fedora kernel is compiled with as many modules as possible to provide as much flexibility as possible. A running kernel can be further tuned with the sysctl program, which enables direct access to a running kernel and permits some kernel parameters to be changed. As a result of this extensive testing, configurability, and modularity, the precompiled Fedora kernel does everything most users need it to do. Most users need to recompile the kernel only to

▶ Accommodate an esoteric piece of new hardware.

▶ Conduct a system update when Fedora has not yet provided precompiled kernels.

▶ Experiment with the system capabilities.

Fedora supplies several precompiled versions of the kernel for Athlon and Pentium processors, for single- and multi-processor motherboards, and for Enterprise-class systems (higher security; uses 4GB of memory). These kernel versions are provided in RPM format. Installing them is as easy as:

```
# rpm -Uvh new_kernel.rpm
```

The kernel (but not the source) RPM files include installation scripts that automatically alter your bootloader configuration, making the new kernel the default. If you do not want that to happen, just manually edit the /etc/lilo.conf or /boot/grub/grub.conf files and change them back.

> **CAUTION**
>
> You should always `rpm -U` (upgrade) a new kernel `rpm`, rather than `rpm -i` (install), to avoid overwriting the old, but still working, kernel. This is done as a safety measure. What if the new one does not work?

Kernel Versions

The Linux kernel is in a constant state of development. As new features are added, bugs are fixed, and new technology is incorporated into the code base, it becomes necessary to provide stable releases of the kernel for use in a production environment. It is also important to have separate releases that contain the newest code for developers to test. To keep track of the kernels, version numbers are assigned to them. Programmers enjoy using sequential version numbers that have abstract meaning. Is version 8 twice as advanced as version 4 of the same application? Is version 1 of one application less developed than version 3 of another? The version numbers cannot be used for this kind of qualitative or quantitative comparison. It is entirely possible that higher version numbers can have fewer features and more bugs than older versions. The numbers exist solely to differentiate and organize sequential revisions of software.

For the latest development version of the kernel at the time of writing, for example, the kernel version number is 2.6.22.

The kernel version can be broken down into four sections:

- ▶ `major version`—This is the major version number, now at 2.
- ▶ `minor version`—This is the minor version number, now at 6.
- ▶ `sublevel number`—This number indicates the current iteration of the kernel; here it is number 10.
- ▶ `extraversion level`—This is the number representing a collection of patches and additions made to the kernel by the Red Hat engineers to make the kernel work for them (and you). Each collection is numbered, and the number is indicated here in the kernel name. From the preceding example, it is 1.

Typing **uname -r** at the command prompt displays your current kernel version:

```
# uname -r
2.6.10-1
```

Even-numbered minor versions are stable kernels, whereas odd-numbered minor versions are development releases. Version 2.6.x is the stable production kernel, whereas version 2.5.x is the development Linux kernel. When a new version of the development kernel is started, it will be labeled 2.7.x.

For production machines, you should always use the kernels with even minor numbers. The odd minor numbers introduce new features, so you might want to use those on a test machine if you need features they provide.

Obtaining the Kernel Sources

The Linux kernel has always been freely available to anyone who wants it. If you just want to recompile the existing kernel, install the `kernel-sources` RPM from the CD. To get the very latest vanilla version, open an FTP connection to ftp.kernel.org, using your favorite FTP client, and log in as anonymous. Because you are interested in the 2.6 kernel, change directories to `/pub/linux/kernel/v2.6`. The latest stable kernel as of this writing is `2.6.15`.

> **NOTE**
>
> ftp.kernel.org receives more than its share of requests for download. It is considered a courtesy to use a mirror site to reduce the traffic that ftp.kernel.org bears. http://www.kernel.org/mirrors/ has a list of all mirrors around the world. Find one close to your geographic location and substitute that address for ftp.kernel.org.

A number of different entries are on the FTP archive site for each kernel version, but because you are interested in only the full kernel, it is necessary to get only the full package of source code. There are two of these packages:

`linux-2.6.15.tar.gz`

`linux-2.6.15.bz2`

Although these are the same kernel packages, they are built using different compression utilities: The `.gz` extension is the `gzip` package, found on almost every Linux system available. The `.bz2` extension is the newer `bzip2` utility, which has better compression than `gzip`. Both packages have the same content, so download the one compressed with the program you use.

After it is downloaded, move the package to a directory other than `/usr/src` and unpack it. If you downloaded the `.gz` package, the unpacking command is `tar -xzvf linux-2.6.15.tar.gz`. Otherwise, the `bzip2` unpack command is `tar -xjvf linux-2.6.15.tar.bz2`. When it is unpacked, the package creates a new directory, `linux-2.6.15`. Copy it to `/usr/src/kernels` or move it there. Then create a symbolic link of `linux-2.6` to `linux-2.6.15` (otherwise, some scripts will not work). Here is how to create the symbolic link:

```
# rm /usr/src/kernels/linux-2.6
# ln -s /usr/src/kernels/linux-2.6.15 /usr/src/kernels/linux-2.6
```

By creating a symbolic link to /usr/src/linux-2.6, it is possible to allow multiple kernel versions to be compiled and tailored for different functions: You just change the symbolic link to the kernel directory on which you want to work.

> **CAUTION**
>
> The correct symbolic link is critical to the operation of make. Always have the symbolic link point to the version of the kernel sources with which you are working.

Patching the Kernel

It is possible to patch a kernel to the newest Linux kernel version, as opposed to downloading the entire source code. This choice can be beneficial for those who are not using a high-speed broadband connection. (A typical compressed kernel source file is nearly 30MB for a download time of about 10 minutes on a 512Kb DSL connection; adjust accordingly for your connection.) Whether you are patching existing sources or downloading the full source, the end results are identical.

Patching the kernel is not a mindless task. It requires the user to retrieve all patches from her current version to the version to which she wants to upgrade. For example, if you are currently running 2.6.1 (and have those sources) and want to upgrade to 2.6.8, you must retrieve the 2.6.2, and 2.6.3 patch sets, and so on. After they are downloaded, these patches must be applied in succession to upgrade to 2.6.8. This is more tedious than downloading the entire source, but useful for those who keep up with kernel hacking and want to perform incremental upgrades to keep their Linux kernel as up-to-date as possible.

To patch up to several versions in a single operation, you can use the patch-kernel script located in the kernel source directory for the kernel version you currently use. This script applies all necessary version patches to bring your kernel up to the latest version.

The format for using the patch-kernel script looks like this:

```
patch-kernel source_dir patch_dir stopversion
```

The source directory defaults to /usr/src/linux if none is given, and the patch_dir defaults to the current working directory if one is not supplied.

For example, assume that you have a 2.6.6 kernel code tree that needs to be patched to the 2.6.8 version. The 2.6.7 and 2.6.8 patch files have been downloaded from ftp.kernel.org and are placed in the /patch directory in the source tree. You issue the following command in the /usr/src/kernels/linux-2.6 directory:

```
# scripts/patch-kernel /usr/src/kernels/linux-2.6.15
➥/usr/src/kernels/linux-2.6.15/patch
```

Each successive patch file is applied, eventually creating a 2.6.8 code tree. If any errors occur during this operation, files named xxx# or xxx.rej are created, where xxx is the version of patch that failed. You have to resolve these failed patches manually by examining the errors and looking at the source code and the patch. An inexperienced person will not have any success with this because you must understand C programming and kernel programming to know what is broken and how to fix it. Because this was a stock `2.6.6` code tree, the patches were all successfully applied without errors. If you are attempting to apply a nonstandard third-party patch, the patch is likely to fail.

When you have successfully patched the kernel, you are ready to begin compiling this code tree as if you started with a fresh, stock `2.6.8` kernel tree.

Using the `patch` Command

If you have a special, nonstandard patch to apply—such as a third-party patch for a commercial product, for example—you can use the `patch` command rather than the special patch-kernel script that is normally used for kernel source updates. Here are some quick steps and an alternative method of creating patched code and leaving the original code alone:

1. Create a directory in your home directory and name it something meaningful, like `mylinux`.

2. Copy the pristine Linux source code there with `cp -ravd /usr/src/kernels/linux-2.6/* ~/mylinux`.

3. Copy the patch file to that same directory with `cp patch_filename ~/mylinux`.

4. Change to the `~/mylinux` directory with `cd ~/mylinux`.

5. Apply the patch with `patch -p1 < `*`patch_filename`*` > mypatch.log 2>&1`.

   (This last bit of code saves the message output to a file so that you can look at it later.)

6. If the patch applies successfully, you are finished and have not endangered any of the pristine source code. In case the newly patched code does not work, you do not have to reinstall the original, pristine source code.

7. Copy your new code to `/usr/src/kernels` and make that special symbolic link described elsewhere in the chapter.

Compiling the Kernel

If you want to update the kernel from new source code you have downloaded or you have applied a patch to add new functionality or hardware support, you have to compile and install a new kernel to actually use that new functionality. Compiling the kernel involves translating the kernel's contents from human-readable code to binary form. Installing the kernel involves putting all the compiled files where they belong in `/boot` and `/lib` and making changes to the bootloader.

The process of compiling the kernel is almost completely automated by the make utility, as is the process of installing. By providing the necessary arguments and following the steps covered next, you can recompile and install a custom kernel for your use.

Here is a checklist of steps to compile and configure the kernel:

1. Verify a working bootdisk for the old kernel to be able to reboot your system in case something goes wrong with the new kernel.

CAUTION

Before making any changes to your current, working kernel, make sure that you have a backup copy on a floppy disk. This enables you to boot into your system with a known working kernel in case something goes wrong during configuration. The command to do this is as follows:

```
# mkbootdisk --device /dev/fd0 'uname -r'
```

This assumes that your floppy drive is /dev/fd0. (Here is a good shell script tip: The ' character tells the shell to execute what is within ' first and then returns that output as part of the input of the mkbootdisk command.) On this machine, the result is the following:

```
# mkbootdisk --device /dev/fd0 2.6.7-1
```

This command is not echoed to your screen, but it is what the system executes.

2. Apply all patches, if any, so that you have the features you want. See the previous section for details.

3. Back up the .config file, if it exists, so that you can recover from the inevitable mistake. Use the following cp command:

```
# cp .config .config.bak
```

NOTE

If you are recompiling the Fedora default kernel, the /usr/src/kernels/linux-2.6/ configs directory contains several versions of configuration files for different purposes. Fedora provides a full set of .config files in the subdirectory configs, all named for the type of system for which they were compiled. For example, kernel-2.6.7-i686-smp. config is a configuration file for a multiprocessor Pentium-class computer. If you want to use one of these default configurations as the basis for a custom kernel, simply copy the appropriate file to /usr/src/kernels/linux-2.6 and rename it .config.

4. Run the make mrproper directive to prepare the kernel source tree, cleaning out any old files or binaries.

5. Restore the .config file that the command make mrproper deleted, and edit the Makefile to change the EXTRAVERSION number.

NOTE

If you want to keep any current version of the kernel that was compiled with the same code tree, manually edit the Makefile with your favorite text editor and add some unique string to the EXTRAVERSION variable. You can use any description you prefer.

6. Modify the kernel configuration file using `make config`, `make menuconfig`, or `make xconfig`—we recommend the latter, but read the text following these numbered instructions for more details.

7. Run `make dep` to create the code dependencies used later in the compilation process.

TIP

If you have a multiprocessor machine, you can use both processors to speed the make process by inserting `-jx` after the `make` command, where, as a rule of thumb, x is one more than the number of processors you have. You might try a larger number and even try this on a single-processor machine (we have used `-j8` successfully on an SMP machine); it loads up only your CPU. For example,

```
# make -j3 bzImage
```

All the `make` processes except `make dep` work well with this method of parallel compiling.

8. Run `make clean` to prepare the sources for the actual compilation of the kernel.

9. Run `make bzImage` to create a binary image of the kernel.

NOTE

Several choices of directives exist, although the most common ones are as follows:

`zImage`—This directive compiles the kernel, creating an uncompressed file called `zImage`.

`bzImage`—This directive creates a compressed kernel image necessary for some systems that require the kernel image to be under a certain size for the BIOS to be able to parse them; otherwise, the new kernel will not boot. It is the most commonly used choice. However, the Fedora kernel compiled with `bzImage` is still too large to fit on a floppy, so a smaller version with some modules and features removed is used for the boot floppies. Fedora recommends that you boot from the rescue CD-ROM.

`bzDisk`—This directive does the same thing as `bzImage`, but it copies the new kernel image to a floppy disk for testing purposes. This is helpful for testing new kernels without writing kernel files to your hard drive. Make sure that you have a floppy disk in the drive because you will not be prompted for one.

10. Run `make modules` to compile any modules your new kernel needs.

11. Run `make modules_install` to install the modules in `/lib/modules` and create dependency files.

12. Run `make install` to automatically copy the kernel to `/boot`, create any other files it needs, and modify the bootloader to boot the new kernel by default.

13. Using your favorite text editor, verify the changes made to `/etc/lilo.conf` or `/boot/grub/grub.conf`; fix if necessary and rerun `/sbin/lilo` if needed.

14. Reboot and test the new kernel.

15. Repeat the process if necessary, choosing a configuration interface.

Over time, the process for configuring the Linux kernel has changed. Originally, you configured the kernel by responding to a series of prompts for each configuration parameter (this is the `make config` utility described shortly). Although you can still configure Linux this way, most users find this type of configuration confusing and inconvenient; moving back through the prompts to correct errors, for instance, is impossible.

The `make config` utility is a command-line tool. The utility presents a question regarding kernel configuration options. The user responds with a Y, N, M, or ? (it is not case sensitive). Choosing M configures the option to be compiled as a module. A response of ? displays context help for that specific option, if available. (If you choose ? and no help is available, you can turn to the vast Internet resources to find information.) We recommend that you avoid the `make config` utility, shown in Figure 36.1.

36

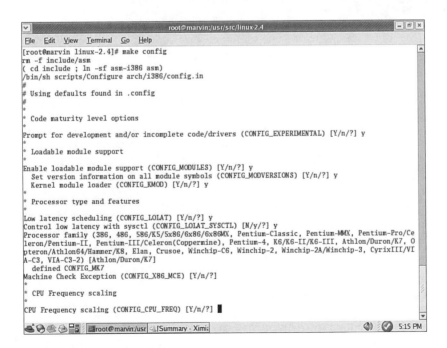

FIGURE 36.1   The `make config` utility in all its Spartan glory.

If you prefer to use a command-line interface, you can use make menuconfig to configure the Linux kernel. menuconfig provides a graphical wrapper around a text interface. Although it is not as raw as make config, menuconfig is not a fancy graphical interface either; you cannot use a mouse, but must navigate through it using keyboard commands. The same information presented in make config is presented by make menuconfig, but as you can see in Figure 36.2, it looks a little nicer. Now, at least, you can move back and forth in the selection process in case you change your mind or have made a mistake.

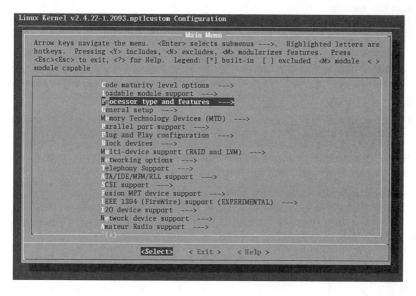

FIGURE 36.2   The make menuconfig utility, a small improvement over make config.

In make menuconfig, you use the arrow keys to move the selector up and down and the spacebar to toggle a selection. The Tab key moves the focus at the bottom of the screen to Select, Exit, or Help.

If a graphical desktop is not available, menuconfig is the best you can do. However, both menuconfig and xconfig (see later discussion) offer an improvement over editing the .config file directly. If you want to configure the kernel through a true graphical interface—with mouse support and clickable buttons—make xconfig is the best configuration utility option. To use this utility, you must have the X Window System running. The application xconfig is really nothing but a Tcl/Tk graphics *widget set* providing borders, menus, dialog boxes, and the like. Its interface is used to wrap around data files that are parsed at execution time. Figure 36.3 shows the main menu of xconfig for the 2.6.7 kernel.

After loading this utility, you use it by clicking on each of the buttons that list the configuration options. Each button you click opens another window that has the detail configuration options for that subsection. Three buttons are at the bottom of each window: Main Menu, Next, and Prev(ious). Clicking the Main Menu button closes the current window and displays the main window. Clicking Next takes you to the next configuration section. When configuring a kernel from scratch, click the button labeled Code Maturity Level Options, and then continue to click the Next button in each subsection window to proceed through all the kernel configuration choices. When you have selected all options, the main menu is again displayed. The buttons on the lower right of the main menu are for saving and loading configurations. Their functions are self-explanatory. If you just want to have a look, go exploring! Nothing will be changed if you elect not to save it.

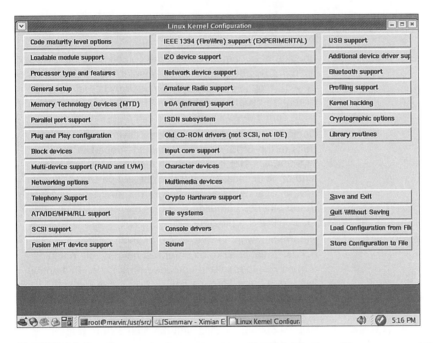

FIGURE 36.3   The much nicer make xconfig GUI interface. We recommend that you use this interface if you are able.

If you are upgrading kernels from a previous release, it is not necessary to go though the entire configuration from scratch. Instead, you can use the make oldconfig directive; it uses the same text interface that make config uses, and it is noninteractive. It just prompts for changes for any new code.

Using xconfig to Configure the Kernel

For simplicity's sake, during this brisk walkthrough, we assume that you are using make xconfig. Prior to this point, we also assume that you have completed the first five steps in the kernel compilation checklist shown previously.

As you learned in the preceding section, you configure the kernel using make xconfig by making choices in several configuration subsection windows. Each subsection window contains specific kernel options. With hundreds of choices, the kernel is daunting to configure. We cannot really offer you detailed descriptions of which options to choose because your configuration will not match our own system and setup.

Table 36.1 provides a brief description of each subsection's options so that you can get an idea of what you might encounter. We recommend that you copy your kernel's .config file to /usr/src/kernels/linux-2.6 and run make xconfig from there. Explore all the options. As long as you do not save the file, absolutely nothing will be changed on your system.

TABLE 36.1   Kernel Subsections for Configuration

Name	Description
Code maturity level options	Enables development code to be compiled into the kernel even if it has been marked as obsolete or as testing code only. This option should only be used by kernel developers or testers because of the possible unusable state of the code during development.
General setup	Contains several different options covering how the kernel talks to the BIOS, whether it should support PCI or PCMCIA, whether it should use APM or ACPI, and what kind of Linux binary formats will be supported. Contains several options for supporting kernel structures necessary to run binaries compiled for other systems directly without recompiling the program.
Loadable module support	Determines whether the kernel enables drivers and other nonessential code to be compiled as loadable modules that can be loaded and unloaded at runtime. This option keeps the basic kernel small so that it can run and respond more quickly; in that regard, choosing this option is generally a good idea.
Processor type and features	Several options dealing with the architecture that will be running the kernel.
Power management options	Options dealing with ACPI and APM power management features.
Bus options	Configuration options for the PCMCIA bus found in laptops and PCI hotplug devices.
Memory Technology Devices (*MTDs*)	Options for supporting flash memory devices, such as EEPROMS. Generally, these devices are used in embedded systems.
Parallel port support	Several options for configuring how the kernel will support parallel port communications.
Plug-and-play configuration	Options for supporting Plug and Play PCI, ISA, and plug-and-play BIOS support. Generally, it is a good idea to support plug-and-play for PCI and ISA devices.
Block devices	Section dealing with devices that communicate with the kernel in blocks of characters instead of streams. This includes IDE and ATAPI devices connected via parallel ports, as well as enabling network devices to communicate as block devices.

TABLE 36.1   Continued

Name	Description
ATA/IDE/MFM/RLL support	Large collection of options to configure the kernel to communicate using different types of data communication protocols to talk to mass storage devices, such as hard drives. Note that this section does not cover SCSI.
SCSI device support	Options for configuring the kernel to support Small Computer Systems Interface. This subsection covers drivers for specific cards, chipsets, and tunable parameters for the SCSI protocol.
Old CD-ROM drivers	Configuration options to support obscure, older CD-ROM devices that do not conform to the SCSI or IDE standards. These are typically older CD-ROM drivers that are usually a proprietary type of SCSI (not SCSI, not IDE).
Multi-device support	Options for enabling the kernel to support RAID devices in (RAID and LVM) software emulation and the different levels of RAID. Also contains options for support of a logical volume manager.
Fusion MPT device support	Configures support for LSI's Logic Fusion Message Passing Technology. This technology is for high-performance SCSI and local area network interfaces.
IEEE1394 (firewire) support	Experimental support for FireWire devices.
I2O device support	Options for supporting the Intelligent Input/Output architecture. This architecture enables the hardware driver to be split from the operating system driver, thus enabling a multitude of hardware devices to be compatible with an operating system in one implementation.
Networking support	Several options for the configuration of networking in the kernel. The options are for the types of supported protocols and configurable options of those protocols.
Amateur radio support	Options for configuring support of devices that support the AX25 protocol.
IrDA (infrared) support	Options for configuring support of the Infrared Data Association suite of protocols and devices that use these protocols.
Bluetooth support	Support for the Bluetooth wireless protocol. Includes options to support the Bluetooth protocols and hardware devices.
ISDN subsystem	Options to support Integrated Services Digital Networks protocols and devices. ISDN is a method of connection to a large area network digitally over conditioned telephone lines, largely found to connect users to ISPs.
Telephony support	Support for devices that enable the use of regular telephone lines to support VOIP applications. This section does not handle the configuration of modems.

TABLE 36.1   Continued

Name	Description
Input device support	Options for configuring universal serial bus (*USB*) human interface devices (*HIDs*). These include keyboards, mice, and joysticks.
Character devices	Configuration options for devices that communicate to the server in sequential characters. This is a large subsection containing the drivers for several motherboard chipsets.
Multimedia devices	Drivers for hardware implementations of video and sound devices such as video capture boards, TV cards, and AM/FM radio adapter cards.
Graphics support	Configures VGA text console, video mode selection, and support for frame buffer cards.
Sound	Large subsection to configure supported sound card drivers and chipset support for the kernel.
USB support	Universal Serial Bus configuration options. Includes configuration for USB devices, as well as vendor-specific versions of USB.
File system	Configuration options for supported file system types. Refer to Chapter 34 for a description of the file systems supported by the kernel.
Additional device driver support	Third-party patches.
Profiling support	Profiling kernel behavior information to aid in debugging and development.
Kernel hacking	Determines whether the kernel will contain advanced debugging options. Most users do not want to include this option in their production kernels because it increases the kernel size and slows performance by adding extra routines.
Security options	Determines whether NSA Security Enhanced Linux (SELinux) is enabled.
Cryptographic options	Support for cryptography hardware (Fedora patches not found in the vanilla kernel sources).
Library routines	Contains zlib compression support.

After you select all the options you want, you can save the configuration file and continue with step 7 in the kernel compiling checklist shown earlier.

Creating an Initial RAM Disk Image

If you require special device drivers to be loaded to mount the root file system (for SCSI drives, network cards or exotic file systems, for example), you must create an initial RAM disk image named /boot/initrd.img. For most users, it is not necessary to create this file, but if you are not certain, it really does not hurt. We covered the initrd.img in Chapter 34. To create an initrd.img file, use the shell script /sbin/mkinitrd.

The format for the command is the following:

```
/sbin/mkinitrd filename kernel_version
```

where *filename* is the name of the image file you want created.

mkinitrd looks at /etc/fstab, /etc/modprobe.conf, and /etc/ raidtab to obtain the information it needs to determine which modules should be loaded during boot. For our personal systems, we use the following:

```
# mkinitrd initrd-2.6.7-1.img 2.6.7-1
```

When Something Goes Wrong

Several things might go wrong during a kernel compile and installation, and several clues will point to the true problem. You will see error messages printed to the screen, and some error messages will be printed to the file /var/log/messages, which can be examined with a text editor. If you have followed our directions for patching the kernel, you will have to examine a special error log as well. Do not worry about errors because many problems are easily fixed with some research on your part. Some errors may be unfixable, however, depending on your skill level and the availability of technical information.

Errors During Compile

Although it is rare that the kernel will not compile, there is always a chance that something has slipped though the regression testing. Let's take a look at an example of a problem that might crop up during the compile.

It is possible that the kernel compile will crash and not complete successfully, especially if you attempt to use experimental patches, add untested features, or build newer and perhaps unstable modules on an older system. For example, the kernel compile will fail on an older-stock Red Hat 7.2 installation using the 2.4.9 kernel when the NTFS file system is selected, either as a loadable module or inline, as shown here:

```
gcc -D__KERNEL__ -I/usr/src/kernels/linux-2.4.9/include -Wall -Wstrict-prototypes
-Wno-trigraphs -O2 -fomit-frame-pointer -fno-strict-aliasing -fno-common
-pipe -mpreferred-stack-boundary=2 -march=athlon  -DMODULE -DMODVERSIONS
-include /usr/src/kernels/linux-2.4.9/include/linux/modversions.h
➥-DNTFS_VERSION=\"1.1.16\" Â\
   -c -o unistr.o unistr.c
unistr.c: In function 'ntfs_collate_names':
unistr.c:99: warning: implicit declaration of function 'min'
unistr.c:99: parse error before 'unsigned'
unistr.c:99: parse error before ')'
unistr.c:97: warning: 'c1' might be used uninitialized in this function
unistr.c: At top level:
unistr.c:118: parse error before 'if'
```

```
unistr.c:123: warning: type defaults to 'int' in declaration of 'c1'
unistr.c:123: 'name1' undeclared here (not in a function)
unistr.c:123: warning: data definition has no type or storage class
unistr.c:124: parse error before 'if'
make[2]: *** [unistr.o] Error 1
make[2]: Leaving directory '/usr/src/kernels/linux-2.4.9/fs/ntfs'
make[1]: *** [_modsubdir_ntfs] Error 2
make[1]: Leaving directory '/usr/src/kernels/linux-2.4.9/fs'
make: *** [_mod_fs] Error 2
```

At this juncture, you have two options:

▶ Fix the errors and recompile

▶ Remove the offending module or option and wait for the errors to be fixed by the kernel team

Most users will be unable to fix some errors because of the complexity of the kernel code, although you should not rule out this option. It is possible that someone else discovered the same error during testing of the kernel and developed a patch for the problem: Check the Linux kernel mailing list archive. If the problem is not mentioned there, a search on Google might turn up something.

The second option, removing the code, is the easiest and is what most people do in cases in which the offending code is not required. In the case of the NTFS module failing, it is almost expected because NTFS support is still considered experimental and subject to errors. This is primarily because the code for the file system is reverse-engineered rather than implemented via documented standards. Read-only support has gotten better in recent kernels; write support is still experimental.

Finally, should you want to take on the task of trying to fix the problem yourself, this is a great opportunity to get involved with the Linux kernel and make a contribution that could help many others.

If you are knowledgeable about coding and kernel matters, you might want to look in the MAINTAINERS file in the /usr/src/kernels/linux-2.6/ directory of the kernel source and find the maintainer of the code. The recommended course of action is to contact the maintainer and see if he is aware of the problems you are having. If nothing has been documented for the specific error, submitting the error to the kernel mailing list is an option. The guidelines for doing this are in the README file in the "If Something Goes Wrong" section under the base directory of the kernel source.

Runtime Errors, Boot Loader Problems, and Kernel Oops

Runtime errors occur as the kernel is loading. Error messages are displayed on the screen or written to the /var/log/messages file. Bootloader problems display messages to the screen; no log file is produced. *Kernel oops* are errors in a running kernel, and error messages are written to the /var/log/messages file.

Excellent documentation on the Internet exists for troubleshooting just about every type of error that LILO, GRUB, or the kernel could give during boot. The best way to find this documentation is to go to your favorite search engine and type in the keywords of the error you received. You will need to adjust the keywords you use as you focus your search.

In this category, the most common problems deal with LILO configuration issues. Diagnosis and solutions to these problems can be found in the LILO mini-HOWTO found on the Linux Documentation project's website at http://www.ibiblio.org/pub/Linux/docs/ HOWTO/other-formats/html_single/LILO.html.

If you have GRUB problems, the GRUB manual is online at http://www.gnu.org/software/ grub/manual/.

TIP

For best results, go to http://www.google.com/linux to find all things Linux on the Internet. Google has specifically created a Linux area of its database, which should allow faster access to information on Linux than any other search engine.

Usenet newsgroup postings are searchable at http://www.google.com/grphp.

Mail list discussions can be searched in the Mailing listARChives (MARC) at http://marc.theaimsgroup.com/.

Relevant Fedora and Linux Commands

You will use the following commands when managing the kernel and its modules in Fedora:

► **gcc**—The GNU compiler system

► **make**—GNU project and file management command

► **mkbootdisk**—Fedora's boot disk creation tool

► **sysctl**—The interface to manipulating kernel variables at runtime

► **mkinitrd**—Create a RAM-disk file system for bootloading support

36

Reference

► **http://www.kernel.org/**—Linux Kernel Archives. The source of all development discussion for the Linux kernel.

► **http://www.kerneltraffic.org/kernel-traffic/index.html**—Linux Kernel Traffic. Summarized version and commentary of the Linux Kernel mailing list produced weekly.

► **http://www.gnu.org/**—Free Software Foundation. Source of manuals and software for programs used throughout the kernel compilation process. Tools such as make and gcc have their official documentation here.

▶ **http://slashdot.org/article.pl?sid=01/08/22/1453228&mode=thread**—The famous AC Patches from Alan Cox, for whom they are named.

▶ **http://www.digitalhermit.com/linux/Kernel-Build-HOWTO.html**—The Linux Kernel Rebuild Guide; configuration, compilation, and troubleshooting.

▶ **http://www.ibiblio.org/pub/Linux/docs/HOWTO/other-formats/html_single/ KernelAnalysis-HOWTO.html**—KernelAnalysis HOWTO. Describes the mysterious inner workings of the kernel.

▶ **http://www.tldp.org/HOWTO/Module-HOWTO/**—Kernel Module HOWTO. Includes a good discussion about unresolved symbols.

▶ **http://www.ibiblio.org/pub/Linux/docs/HOWTO/other-formats/html_single/ Modules.html**—The Linux Kernel Modules Installation HOWTO; an older document discussing recompiling kernel modules.

▶ **http://www.tldp.org/**—The Linux Documentation Project. The Mecca of all Linux documentation. Excellent source of HOWTO documentation, as well as FAQs and online books, all about Linux.

▶ **http://www.minix.org/**—The unofficial minix website. It contains a selection of links to information about minix and a link to the actual homepage. Although minix is still copyrighted, the owner has granted unlimited rights to everyone. See for yourself the operating system used to develop Linux.

▶ **http://jungla.dit.upm.es/~jmseyas/linux/kernel/hackers-docs.html**—A web page with links to Linux kernel documentation, books, hacker tomes, and other helpful information for budding and experienced Linux kernel and kernel module developers. This list also will be found in the `/usr/src/kernels/linux-2.6/Documentation/ kernel-docs.txt` file if you install the Fedora kernel sources.

PART VII

Appendices

APPENDIX A

The History of Red Hat and Fedora

The main object of this book has been to give you practical advice on getting up and running with Fedora 8, and as such we haven't really spent any time looking at the origins of Fedora and how it got to where it is today. This appendix gives you information that will enable you to put Fedora into context and understand the history behind Fedora 8.

Fedora represented an evolution in the business direction of its sponsor, Red Hat. Red Hat itself is the largest commercial Linux developer in the world, and is based in Raleigh, North Carolina. For nearly 10 years, Red Hat provided copies of its commercial Linux distribution, Red Hat Linux, free over the Internet and also sold boxed copies to consumers and businesses. All that changed in October 2003, when Red Hat discontinued the sale and free distribution of the commercial Red Hat Linux.

As the company has since its inception, Red Hat then released all its work on the open source software in the former commercial distribution. The work, which was to be a new version of Red Hat Linux, was then merged with an existing Fedora Linux project and was reborn as Fedora Core. Red Hat now focuses its efforts on enterprise and corporate Linux-based products and services, but again, continues to make source code available for all its products that are under an open source license.

Red Hat's Enterprise Linux is a series of software products aimed for corporate and enterprise migration, deployment, and use. Although all Linux distributions could be considered the same underneath because all use the Linux kernel, Red Hat takes special pains to create, test, sell, and support commercial Linux distributions optimized for deployment on multiple hardware and CPU architectures. These high-performance enhancements include hardware-tweaked Linux kernels, failover and load-balancing clustering, and integrated Java support—essential for mission-critical applications and production environments.

About Red Hat

Red Hat is one of the world's foremost open source development houses and returns nearly all its development efforts back to the Linux development community.

The company has been involved in many open source and GNU GPL projects, such as the Apache web server, the `glibc` software libraries, the *GNU Network Object Model Environment (GNOME)*, various GNU software tools and packages, the Linux kernel and device drivers, the PostgreSQL database system, and the *Red Hat Package Manager (RPM)*.

Red Hat also supports many other projects by providing FTP service and web hosting and is one of the few companies actively promoting and using the open source business development model. This means that, although many of its products are free, revenue streams are derived from spin-off and related technologies and services.

One possible reason for the success of Linux could be "best hack wins." In other words, software that works well, fills a critical need, is readily available in source form, and is distributed under a free software license (such as the GNU GPL) will quickly spread and see extensive use. The growth in popularity and widespread adoption of Linux around the world is a testament to quality, licensing, and need for Linux.

UNIX enjoyed a similar rapid-fire adoption after it was distributed in the early 1970s and fulfilled user needs on a number of fronts. However, its licensing was restrictive, caused much grief in some open source communities (such as education), and continues to spawn problems to this day.

It was not long ago that any new major project involving use of Linux by big business, government (on any level), or academia would have been big news. Today, Linux is increasingly used by IS/IT strategists for computing solutions. Linux and related open source software rule the Internet. It is the host platform of choice for traditional server operations. Linux is poised to take over the desktop, occupying the number two spot behind a monolithic software entity.

NOTE

The list of Linux projects, efforts, and partnerships reads like a *Who's Who* of the software industry: Amazon, Ameritrade, Borland, Computer Associates, Dell, Hewlett-Packard, IBM, Oracle, and SAP are just some of the enterprise-level players using Linux. Linux is also a key ingredient and shares an ever-increasing portion of server hardware sales from all large vendors, such as IBM, Hewlett-Packard, and Dell.

What Is Fedora?

Fedora is the heir to Red Hat Linux and incorporates many of the features and software tools included with previous Red Hat Linux distributions, along with many enhancements. Red Hat Linux spawned many imitators in the Linux world in the past decade, and many of these imitators have gone on to create credible products and distributions.

Thanks to the different ways you can get Fedora, you no longer need to worry about downloading multiple CDs. Included with this book is a DVD that contains 3GB of packages just waiting to be installed onto your hard drive. Alternatively, you could snag either the Live CD (with the Gnome interface) or the KDE Live CD (with the KDE interface, funnily enough) if you want a usable yet light installation. More than 5,000 separate software packages are in Fedora. This distribution comprises the Linux kernel, installation utilities, thousands of pages of documentation, several thousand fonts, a comprehensive graphical networking interface, and several thousand individual commands and clients.

Fedora provides a base, or core, framework operating system and desktop composed entirely of free software. Fedora includes the Nodoka desktop theme and has an improved consistency in the two major graphical desktops available for use: Gnome and KDE.

You can expect an extensive amount of Linux software to be supported by Fedora, and in fact an extensive library of software packages outside the Fedora release is available through third-party repositories. This means your first Fedora CD-ROMs or DVD are just the beginning of a large collection of Linux software!

Fedora provides the latest version of the X Window System and its server, X11R7, which sports improved and integral font handling. The Linux desktop has never looked better, and you will notice the difference when you browse the web, use one of the dozen or so word processors and text editors included with Fedora, or view text at the command line in a terminal window.

Fedora is slated for upgrades two or three times a year, according to the Fedora Project. In reality, however, work never ceases on the distribution because open source developers, along with Red Hat engineers, cross-pollinate Red Hat's Enterprise Linux and Fedora with software package upgrades, security updates, and bug fixes. Fedora's free, online upgrade system is available via the Internet.

Red Hat works to an approximate 18-month release cycle for Enterprise Linux. This cycle is required to provide third-party application developers time to test, deploy, and market products. In the past, Red Hat has used a 6-month release schedule for the consumer version of Red Hat Linux, with a 3- to 4-month beta cycle for development and testing. Fedora will have a similar schedule; the Fedora Project has stated it intends to "produce time-based releases of Fedora about two times a year."

Distribution Version and Kernel Numbering Schema

There is a specific numbering system for Linux kernels, kernel development, and Fedora's kernel versions. Note that these numbers bear no relation to the version number of your Fedora Linux distribution. Fedora distribution version numbers are assigned by the Fedora Project, whereas most of the Linux kernel version numbers are assigned by Linus Torvalds and his legion of kernel developers.

To see the date your Linux kernel was compiled, use the uname command with its -v command-line option. To see the version of your Linux kernel, use the -r option. The numbers, such as 2.6.23-1.49, represent the major version (2), minor version (6), and patch level (23). The number 1 is the developer patch level, while the final number (49) is the distro-specific version and is assigned by the Fedora Project.

Minor numbers that are even are considered "stable" and generally fit for use in production environments, whereas odd minor numbers (such as a Linux 2.7 source tree) represent versions of the Linux kernel under development and testing. You will find only stable versions of the Linux kernel included with this book. You can choose to download and install a beta (test) version of the kernel, but this is not recommended for a system destined for everyday use. Most often, beta kernels are installed to provide support and testing of new hardware or operating system features.

Fedora for Business

Linux has matured over the past 10 years, and features considered essential for use in enterprise-level environments, such as CPU architecture support, file systems, and memory handling, have been added and improved. The addition of virtual memory (the capability to swap portions of RAM to disk) was one of the first necessary ingredients, along with a copyright-free implementation of the TCP/IP stack (mainly due to BSD UNIX being tied up in legal entanglements at the time). Other features quickly followed, such as support for a variety of network protocols.

Fedora includes a Linux kernel that has the capability to use multiple processors. This allows you to use Fedora in more advanced computing environments with greater demands on CPU power. In reality, small business servers typically use only dual-CPU workstations or servers, but Fedora has the capability to run Linux on more powerful hardware.

Fedora automatically supports your multiple-CPU Intel-based motherboard, and you can take advantage of the benefits of *symmetric multiprocessors (SMPs)* for software development and other operations. The Linux kernels included with Fedora can use system RAM sizes up to 64GB, allow individual file sizes in excess of 2GB, and host the demands of—theoretically—billions of users.

Businesses that depend on large-scale, high-volume, and high-availability systems can now turn to Red Hat's Enterprise Linux products for stable, robust, scalable, and inexpensive solutions for various platform hosting. Storage requirements in the terabyte range, no lengthy file system checks, and no downtime are just a few of the minimum requirements in such environments.

However, Fedora can be used in many of these environments by customers with widely disparate computing needs. Some of the applications for Fedora include desktop support; small file, print, or mail servers; intranet web servers; and security firewalls deployed at strategic points inside and outside company LANs.

Commercial Red Hat customers will benefit from Red Hat's engineering and support teams because Red Hat works closely with many computer industry leaders, such as HP, Fujitsu Limited, and IBM. This enables Red Hat Enterprise Linux to work well on a wide range of computers such as laptops, mid-range Intel Xeon and Itanium platforms, and some of the most powerful enterprise-class servers in the world.

Red Hat also develops platform and development tools for other CPUs, such as the Xstormy16 CPU from Sanyo, NEC's VR5500 MIPS, Motorola's 128-bit AltiVec and Book E PowerPC e500, SuperH's SuperH SH-5, and Intel's XScale-based chips.

Red Hat Enterprise Linux in Government

Red Hat Enterprise Linux has a presence in many government entities at various levels across the world. For example, the New Jersey State Police use a Red Hat–based Oracle system, whereas India's Centre for Development of Advanced Computing uses Red Hat Linux in its high-performance computing lab.

Use of Linux is expanding rapidly in the U.S. federal sector. Red Hat Enterprise Linux is on the General Services Administration Schedule, and the U.S. National Security Agency has offered a series of kernel patches to assist in building secure versions of Linux. This has quickened the development of SELinux within both Fedora and Red Hat Enterprise Linux. Other agencies and departments, such as the U.S. Air Force, U.S. Marine Corps, Federal Aviation Administration, NASA, and the Departments of Defense, Agriculture, and Energy also use Linux-enabled platform solutions from IBM and Hewlett-Packard.

Small business owners can earn great rewards by stepping off the software licensing and upgrade treadmill and adopting a Linux-based solution. Using Fedora not only avoids the need for licensing accounting and the threat of software audits, but also provides viable alternatives to many types of commercial productivity software.

Using Fedora in a small business setting makes a lot of sense for other reasons, too, such as not having to invest in cutting-edge hardware to set up a productive shop. Fedora easily supports older, or *legacy*, hardware, and savings compound over time as unnecessary hardware upgrades are avoided. Additional savings will be realized because software and upgrades are free. New versions of applications can be downloaded and installed at little or no cost, and the office suite software is free.

Fedora is easy to install and network and plays well with others, meaning it works well in a mixed-computing situation with other operating systems such as Windows or Mac OS X. A simple Fedora server can be put to work as an initial partial solution or made to mimic file, mail, or print servers of other operating systems. Clerical help will quickly adapt to using familiar Internet and productivity tools, while your business gets the additional benefits of stability, security, and a virus-free computing platform.

When monies spent on server hardware are allocated carefully, a productive and efficient multiuser system can be built for much less than the cost of comparable commercial software. Combine these benefits with support for laptops, PDAs, and remote access, and you will find that Fedora supports the creation and use of an inexpensive yet efficient work environment.

Fedora in Your Home

Fedora's basic install option copies a special set of preselected software packages onto your hard drive; these are suitable for *small office/home office (SOHO)* users. This option provides a wealth of productivity tools for document management, printing, communication, and personal productivity.

The basic installation option requires nearly 2GB of hard drive space but should easily fit onto smaller hard drives in older Pentium-class PCs. The install also contains administrative tools, additional authoring and publishing clients, a variety of editors, a Gnome-based desktop, support for sound, graphics editing programs, and graphical and text-based Internet tools. You can customize the selection to include or sidestep installation of unwanted software.

Connecting to the Internet is a snap, and Fedora supports modem dialup and other broadband connections, such as cable modems or *Digital Subscriber Line (DSL)*. When you do connect, you can do so in relative confidence because the in-built firewall offers you protection from outside attacks and malicious intruders.

If you have a digital camera, run F-Spot client to download, organize, and manage your digital images. You can then fine-tune your pictures by editing them with one of the finest digital image editors in the world: the GIMP.

Fedora can be used for a variety of purposes, and every user has different needs. Fortunately Fedora and Linux offer many different programs to assist you in what you are attempting to do. I personally use Fedora mainly as a server to hold an extensive collection of OGG music files, as well as a growing collection of digital images. They are all available to my local network, and I can also upload files from wherever I am in the world by using the FTP server, or retrieve photos when I am visiting family and friends abroad.

64-Bit Fedora

Advances in computing saw the introduction of 64-bit, x86-compatible CPUs from AMD in the spring of 2003. The only platform at launch to support the new technology was Linux. Intel's EM64T extensions for x86, which largely mirror the advances made by AMD, have further increased the availability of commodity x86-64 hardware.

As a direct response to the growing 64-bit user base, Fedora released a 64-bit version, allowing the use of Fedora on AMD64 and Intel hardware. If you have a 64-bit CPU, you are strongly encouraged to get involved and give it a try—just bear in mind that, because the architecture is still quite new, there might not be a 64-bit version of all the software you require.

However, because the Intel Itanium platform uses a radically different set of instructions that are not compatible with the x86 instruction set, the 64-bit version of Fedora does not support Itanium or Itanium2. There are members of the community who are working toward making the Itanium a supported platform, but the niche nature of the platform means that this is unlikely.

Fedora on the PPC Platform

In recognition of the wide availability of the Power architecture, The Fedora Project decided to simultaneously release a PPC version of Fedora starting with Fedora 4. Fedora 8 continues in this vein, and you are able to run Fedora natively on Apple power-based hardware such as PowerMacs, iMacs, and the Mac mini, not to mention the very tasty PowerBooks.

Of course, now that Apple has moved across to Intel processors, it will leave a large gap in the market. Vendors such as IBM and Genesis will still produce and in IBM's case, develop the PowerPC platform beyond the current crop of G4- and G5-based machines.

You maybe didn't realize it, but your PlayStation 3 can run Fedora, because the Cell processor is part of the PPC family. Check out the release notes for more information on using your PS3 console.

Fedora on Multicore Machines

The second half of 2005 brought significant availability of dual-core processors from Intel, AMD, and Power. As always, Linux was at the forefront of support for new computing platforms, and dual-core processors were no different. Fedora natively supports multi-core, and significant speed enhancements can be had from using such machines. Dual-core processors are prevalent today, but four-way processors are starting to appear in mainstream PCs, most notably in the dual quad-core Mac Pro (a total of eight cores), which is supported by Fedora.

APPENDIX B

Installation Resources

Installing a new operating system is always a major event, especially if you have never had to install an OS before. This is especially true if you are used to running Microsoft Windows XP or Windows Vista that has been preinstalled for you on your computer. In many cases, "recovery" discs are supplied that contain a mirror image of how your system was the day it rolled off the production line; so in reality you are not actually installing Windows, just copying some files. With Fedora you get a lot of options that you can choose from, making it easy to tailor make your installation to suit your end goals. This appendix is all about helping you prepare for installing Fedora, taking you through some of the considerations that you perhaps do not realize are important to think about.

Linux has a formidable reputation as being difficult to install. You had to know every conceivable fact and specification about all the components of your computer to ensure that the installation went smoothly. Thankfully, for the most part that reputation is in the past, and now Fedora does most of the hard work for you, having much improved hardware detection and autoconfiguration. This is definitely a good thing, and vastly reduces the time needed to install Fedora. Another good thing is the advent of Live CDs for Fedora, which give you a fully functional operating system on a CD. If you have ever been concerned about whether your system is compatible with Linux, take one of these Live CDs for a spin to help you make your decision.

This appendix is intended to prepare you for installing Fedora on your computer. We start off with a look at some of the things you should take in to account when considering moving to Linux, including what your aims and objectives are for using Fedora. We also take a look at the hardware requirements of Fedora, along with information on how to check whether your hardware is compatible with Fedora. By the end of this appendix, you should recognize just how flexible Fedora really is, both in the software it provides and also in the many ways in which you can install it.

Planning Your Fedora Deployment

The first thing you need to decide is why you are installing Fedora. By working out the "end-use scenario" for the proposed installation, you then can begin to make choices and decisions about hardware specifications and software options. Before planning the specific steps of an installation, you need to make decisions about the type of deployment you want to undertake. For example, if you were going to use Fedora for 3D graphics work, you would need to factor in the amount of space needed to store the sometimes intricate 3D models and graphics, as well as the graphics card needed for rendering, not to mention the amount of system memory and processor speed. On the flip side, if all you are doing is providing an elderly relative with a quick and easy way to access the Internet, RAM, hard drive storage, and processor speed are less likely to be important rather than a decent monitor, keyboard, and mouse. You learn more about these issues in the sections that follow. These sections also include a table you can use as a predeployment planning checklist and some final advice for planning the installation.

Business Considerations

Making a choice of operating system for business can often be a thorny issue. Certainly there is a monopoly already in place from Microsoft, and a lot of users have only ever used Microsoft products. This alone is a powerful argument to go down the Microsoft path, but there are other ways to implement Fedora in business. Your company may have been the target of a virus attack, or perhaps you have had to deal with one too many spyware and adware outbreaks on users desktops. Making the switch to Linux can eradicate many of these problems, increasing the uptime of users and reducing the security risk. The important thing is to work closely with the business to ensure that whatever is delivered is in line with the business requirements. If you consider that Linux is still in a minority, you need to think about how other companies will be able to work with you. Staff training and overall cost of change needs to be closely monitored at all times to ensure a smooth delivery. However, don't expect it to be perfect; anyone who has worked on a project knows that unexpected problems can and will occur, and you need to be as prepared as possible to deal with them. Bear in mind that what works for your company may not work for another, so when swapping stories over a beer with other long-suffering sysadmins, think about how their successes can be adapted to your enterprise, but also pay close attention to things that went wrong. Even better, get one of their business users to present to your users and management to demonstrate the impact that moving to Linux has had. It's surprising how much good a relationship with other companies can do for your own IT infrastucture.

NOTE

As an example of inter company relationships, most of the large law firms in London have their own soccer teams that regularly meet to do battle on the soccer field. They also meet to discuss IT issues and swap ideas between each other which benefits all of them. Why not set up a local corporate Linux user group in your area? You don't have to make it a sports-related meeting; just make it clear that you want to share ideas and best practice.

NOTE

Browse to Red Hat's Migration Center at http://www.redhat.com/business/utol/success/ to read success stories, market analyses, and technical reports on using Red Hat's Enterprise Linux products for business.

One of the great things about Linux is that it allows you to try it before committing yourself. What other operating system do you know that can be booted up from a single CD and allow you to have a fully operational system, complete with applications? Although it sound like black magic, this kind of thing actually exists in the form of Live CDs and there are plenty to choose from, including the two that are available for Fedora (Gnome and KDE based). Boot your system with one of these CDs to give you an idea of how well your hardware will cope with Linux.

Of course, if you are happy with the move to Linux, you can ease the change by downloading versions of OpenOffice.org, Firefox, and Thunderbird for your existing platform so that users can test them out before the migration.

Sometimes it is not always the visible changes that make the most difference. Give careful thought to the potential deployment of Linux into such areas as web servers and file and print servers. You can extend the life of existing hardware long beyond its useful "Windows" life by deploying them as print or web servers. Thankfully, Linux and open source software is pervasive enough to provide plenty of flexibility should you decide to test the water before diving in. Nowadays, popular open source applications such as OpenOffice.org are available for both Windows and Mac platforms, enabling you to try the software before deciding to switch. Also consider changing back-end systems across to Linux-based alternatives. There are many Linux equivalents to Microsoft Exchange, for example, that can handle email and calendaring. Other popular servers ripe for moving across to Linux include file and print servers, web servers, and firewalls.

Of course, if you use Fedora, you largely go it alone in terms of support, having to rely mainly on community forums and message boards (although if you go down the Red Hat Enterprise Linux route, doing so opens up commercial support channels from Red Hat).

Do not think that you have to switch everything over in one go. Linux works well in a mixed environment (including Mac OS X and Windows XP), so you can quite safely plan a step-by-step migration that allows you to implement each phase one at a time. Moving servers across to new operating systems should be done on a server-by-server basis.

Luckily, Linux can easily co-exist in a multi-OS environment, being compatible with Mac OS X, Windows, and UNIX.

We have collated some of the questions that need to be asked when considering a move to Fedora in Table B.1, "Deploying Fedora." As mentioned earlier, you need to identify the need that is going to be satisfied by moving to Fedora. Any project needs to meet a specific objective to be considered a success, so having this clear right at the start is essential. Another area of consideration is the impact to the existing computing environment. How will users cope with moving onto Linux? Are they dyed-in-the-wool Windows users who will resist any move to a different platform? Do you have the full support of management (something that is critical for projects of all sizes)? Successful changes behind the scenes, demonstrating the flexibility and choice of open source, can win management over quickly.

One of the key buzzwords to have come out of the dot-com era is *total cost of ownership*, and it is one that is fiercely debated when people talk about Linux. Those against Linux argue that although the software is free, the real cost comes in the amount of retraining and support necessary to move users to a new operating system. This can be circumvented by implementing Linux in situations where the end users are not directly affected, such as that web server that you have been planning to retire or the file and print server that needs more drive space. What is also often unseen is the increased availability that Linux-based systems offer companies. Quite simply, they very rarely go down, unlike their Windows counterparts. Stability counts for a lot in this modern world of e-commerce where even a few minutes can cost thousands of dollars in lost orders and new customers. Talking about stability, one of the great things about Linux is that it does not necessarily need the latest hardware to function effectively—I have a router at home that is based on an old 486 machine that I bought sometime in 1994, coupled with a minimalist Linux distribution! Think how many computers are needlessly disposed of that could be used as print servers or Internet gateways. The savings generated by sensibly recycling existing hardware are very tempting, and easily obtainable if you choose the Linux route.

In all of this, you need to be very clear what the objectives are. Specify exactly what you want to achieve from the project, what the Linux implementation will deliver, and how it will be used to replace any existing machines. What is the Linux machine replacing and what resources will be needed to maintain and support it? If you are rolling out to end users, what specific applications will they be using that you will have to provide support for?

Research is definitely a must before you embark on any project. It is also sensible to set up a test environment so that you can examine the performance of the new machine under set conditions to ensure that it functions in the way that you require. It is crucial that you spend a decent amount of time on testing because doing so will pay off in the long run with fewer bugs to fix and more positive user feedback and end-user experience.

System Considerations

Fedora is flexible enough to cope with a wide range of computing needs, but with any switch of operating system you need to be aware of some of the issues that switching might cause. Table B.1 lists some of these. For example, how you choose to use Fedora could affect your choice of computer hardware, might affect your network configuration, and could dictate software policy issues (such as access, security, and allowable protocols).

Linux-based operating systems can be used to provide many different services. For example, one server might be boot management for a thin-client network in which workstations boot to a desktop by drawing a kernel and remotely mounted file systems over a network. This mechanism is not supported out of the box, so some effort can be expended if such a system is required. Other services more easily implemented (literally in an hour or less) could be centralized server environments for file serving, web hosting for a company intranet, or bridging of networks and routing services.

Linux supports nearly every network protocol, which enables it to be used to good effect even in mixed operating system environments. The security features of the Linux kernel and companion security software also make Linux a good choice when security is a top priority. Although no operating system or software package is perfect, the benefit of open source of the kernel and other software for Linux allows peer review of pertinent code and rapid implementation of any necessary fixes. Even with the secure features of Linux, some effort will have to be made in designing and implementing gateways, firewalls, or secure network routers.

Fedora can serve as a development platform for applications, e-commerce sites, new operating systems, foreign hardware systems, or design of new network devices using Linux as an embedded operating system. Setting up workstations, required servers, source code control systems, and industrial security will require additional effort.

Hardware compatibility can be an issue to consider when setting up a Linux server or building a Linux-based network. Fortunately, most of the larger server manufacturers such as IBM, HP, and even Dell realize that Linux-based operating systems (like other open source operating systems such as BSD) are increasingly popular, support open standards, and offer technologies that can help rapid introduction of products into the market (through third-party developer communities).

Fedora can help ease system administration issues during migration. The latest suite of Fedora's configuration utilities provides intuitive and easy-to-use graphical interfaces for system administration of many common services, such as networking, printing, and Windows-based file sharing. Fedora can also be used to support a legacy application environment, such as DOS, if required.

User Considerations

Humans are creatures of habit. It can be hard to transition a workforce, customer base, or other community to a new environment. The Fedora desktop, however, provides a friendly and familiar interface with menus and icons that new users can readily learn and put to work.

Part of the migration process can involve addressing user concerns, especially if Linux will take over the desktop. Fedora can be deployed in stages to make the migration process a bit easier, but the issue of user training must be addressed early on. This is especially true if users will be required to develop new skills or be aware of any caveats when using Linux (such as deleting all files in one's home directory). Although Fedora can be configured to provide a "turn-key" desktop in which only several graphical applications (such as a web browser, organizer, or word processor) can be used, some users will want and need to learn more about Linux.

You can turn to formal Linux training from commercial vendors. System administrators can get training directly from Red Hat (go to http://www.redhat.com/training). For other issues concerning Linux in larger computing environments, browse to Linas Vepstas's Linux Enterprise Computing pages at http://linas.org/linux/.

A Predeployment Planning Checklist

Table B.1 provides a minimal checklist you can use to help plan a deployment.

TABLE B.1   Deploying Fedora

Consideration	Description
Applicability	How is Fedora going to be used?
Boot management	Will remote booting be required?
Connectivity	Will the system be used in an internal network, or connected to the Internet? Is there a requirement for wireless connectivity? What about bandwidth?
Context	How does this install fit in with academic, business, or corporate needs?
Consensus	Are managers and potential users on board with the project?
Comparison	Is this install part of platform comparison or benchmarking?
Development platform	Will development tools be used?
Embedded device	Is it an embedded device project?
Hardware	Are there any special hardware or device interfacing requirements?
Finance	How much is in the budget? Will cost comparison be required?
Marketing	Will a product or service be offered as a result?
Networking	What type of networking will be required?
Objective	Is there a specific objective of the install?
Pilot project	Is this a pilot or test install?
Power management	Any special power or energy requirements?
Public relations	Does the public need to know?
Quality of service	Is high availability or data integrity an issue?
Roadmap	What other steps might precede or follow the install?
Reporting	Are follow-up reports required?
Security	What level or type of security will be required?
Server	Is this a server installation?
Site considerations	Does the location provide needed temperature and security, or does it even matter?
Software	Are any special device drivers needed for success?
Storage	Are there size or integrity needs? Has a backup plan been devised?

TABLE B.1   Continued

Consideration	Description
Timeline	Are there time constraints or deadlines to the install?
Training	Will special training be required for users or administrators?
Users	How many and what type of users are expected?
Workstation	Is this a workstation or personal desktop install? Is the workstation portable?

Do not forget to address follow-up issues on your migration roadmap. Pay attention to how satisfied or how well new users, especially those new to Linux, are adapting if a new desktop is used. However, if Fedora is deployed in a mixed environment, many users might not even know (or need to know) that Linux is being used!

Planning the Installation

There are many factors in favor of using Fedora as a computing solution. Fedora can fill many different roles on various tiers and hardware platforms because of the huge variety of software on offer.

Addressing software concerns beforehand can help quell any worries or fears felt by new users. Some key factors for a successful installation include the following:

▶ **Preparation**—Thoroughly discuss the migration or deployment, along with benefits, such as greater stability and availability of service.

▶ **Preconfiguration**—If possible, give users a voice in software choices or categories and poll for comments regarding concerns.

▶ **Correct installation**—Ensure that the installed systems are working properly, including access permissions, password systems, or other user-related issues and interaction with the deployment.

▶ **The right hardware to do the job**—Make sure that users have the hardware they need for their work, and that computers match the tasks required. For example, developers have workstation requirements vastly different from those of administrative personnel.

Hardware Requirements

Fedora can be installed on and will run on a wide variety of Intel-based hardware. This does not include pre-Pentium legacy platforms, but many older PCs, workstations, rack-mounted systems, and multiprocessor servers are supported. Small-, medium-, and even large-scale deployments of specially tuned Linux distributions are available through a number of companies such as IBM, which offers hardware, software, and service solutions.

> **TIP**
>
> It is always a good idea to explore your hardware options extensively before jumping on board with a specific vendor. You can buy computer hardware with a Linux distribution preinstalled. At the time of this writing, Dell Computer offered systems complete with Red Hat Enterprise Linux (such as desktop PCs and workstations) through http://www.dell.com/redhat/. IBM also offers Linux on its product line, and more information can be found through http://www.ibm.com/linux/. To find HP and preinstalled Linux systems, browse to http://www.hp.com/linux/. You can also buy low-cost desktop PCs with Linux through Wal-Mart's online store at http://www.walmart.com (click to select the electronics department).

The type of deployment you choose also determines the hardware required for a successful deployment of Linux—and post-deployment satisfaction. The range of Linux hardware requirements and compatible hardware types is quite wide, especially when you consider that Linux can be used with mainframe computers as well as embedded devices.

Meeting the Minimum Fedora Hardware Requirements

The Fedora Project publishes general minimum hardware requirements for installing and using its base distribution in a file named RELEASE NOTES on the first CD-ROM or DVD, or available at http://fedora.redhat.com/docs/release-notes/. For the current release, your PC should at least have a 200MHz Pentium CPU, 620MB of hard drive space, and 128MB of RAM for using (and installing) Fedora without a graphical interface. For obvious reasons, a faster CPU, larger-capacity hard drive, and more RAM are desired. Servers and development workstations require more storage and RAM.

Using Legacy Hardware

If you have an older PC based on an Intel 486 CPU with only 32MB RAM and a 500MB hard drive (which can be hard to find nowadays), you can install other Linux distributions such as Debian from the Debian Project at http://www.debian.org/.

Installing Fedora on legacy hardware is easier if you choose to use more recent Pentium-class PCs, but even older Pentium PCs can be used and purchased at a fraction of their original cost. Such PCs can easily handle many mundane but useful tasks. Some of the tasks suitable for older hardware include the following:

- Acting as a firewall, router, or gateway
- Audio jukebox and music file storage server
- Handling email
- Hosting a remote printer and providing remote printing services
- Network font server
- Providing FTP server access
- Remote logging capture

- ▶ Secondary network-attached backup server

- ▶ Serving as an intranet (internal LAN) web server

- ▶ Unattended dialup gateway, voice mailbox, or fax machine

- ▶ Use as a "thin-client" workstation for basic desktop tasks

Older PCs can handle any task that does not require a CPU with a lot of horsepower. To get the most out of your hardware, do not install any more software than required (a good idea in any case, especially if you are building a server). To get a little performance boost, add as much RAM as economically and practically feasible. If you cannot do this, cut down on memory usage by turning off unwanted or unneeded services. You can also recompile a custom Linux kernel to save a bit more memory and increase performance.

Planning for Hard Drive Storage for Your Fedora Installation

Making room for Fedora requires you to decide on how to use existing hard drive space. You might decide to replace existing hard drives entirely, for example, or you might decide to use only one operating system on your computer, making partitioning unnecessary. A full install from this book's DVD will require at least 7GB hard drive space just for the software, so if you plan to install everything, a 10GB hard drive could be ideal for a workstation. Note that depending on how you plan to use Linux, a smaller-capacity disk can be used, or a disk capacity many times the size of your system will be required.

> **NOTE**
>
> The following recommended installations and minimal storage requirements are based on a full install of the freely available version of Fedora distributed on the Internet. The copy of Fedora included with this book is the same, but you might find many additional software packages available from third-party Fedora contributors. Installing additional software affects your storage requirements.

The Fedora installer no longer provides different installation classes. Instead it allows you a lot of control over the software that you want to install. However, you can specify whether you want to install tools for productivity and development and can specific packages according to your exact requirements. Fedora computes the storage space required when you are selecting packages, so you can always be sure that you have sufficient hard drive space before it starts to install. Of course, if you are after a minimalist installation, here are some software packages you might want to consider passing up in the installation process for as small a system as possible:

- ▶ X

- ▶ Gnome

- ▶ KDE

- ▶ Any graphical Internet tools

▶ Office/productivity applications

▶ Documentation

▶ Sound and video applications and utilities

▶ Any development software or libraries

Checking Hardware Compatibility

Fedora software for Intel-based PCs is compiled for the minimum x86 platform supported by the Linux kernel.

> **NOTE**
>
> The compatibility information in this appendix relates to Fedora. Other distributions might have different storage and CPU requirements. Also bear in mind that Fedora is available for x86-64 and PPC architectures, too. Consult the release notes to get a detailed specification for these versions.

Specific issues regarding Linux hardware compatibility can be researched online at a number of sites. A pretty good place to visit if you want to know about general hardware compatibility with Linux is http://www.linuxquestions.org/hcl/index.php; this covers a wide range of hardware devices and peripherals.

Other sites, such as the Linux-USB device overview at http://www.qbik.ch/usb/devices/, offer an interactive browsing of supported devices, and printer compatibility can be researched at LinuxPrinting.org at http://linuxprinting.org/. Some hardware categories to consider in your research include the following:

▶ **Controller cards**—Such as SCSI, IDE, SATA, FireWire

▶ **CPUs**—Intel, AMD, Power, 64 Bit, and Multi-Core

▶ **Input devices**—Keyboards

▶ **Modems**—External, PCMCIA, PCI, and controllerless workarounds

▶ **Network cards**—ISA, PCI, USB, and others

▶ **Pointing devices**—Mice, tablets, and possibly touch screens

▶ **Printers**—Various printer models

▶ **RAM**—Issues regarding types of system memory

▶ **Sound cards**—Issues regarding support

▶ **Specific motherboard models**—Compatibility or other issues

▶ **Specific PCs, servers, and laptop models**—Compatibility reports, vendor certification

▶ **Storage devices**—Removable, fixed, and others

▶ **Video cards**—Console issues (X compatibility depends on the version of X or vendor-based X distribution used.)

If you have a particular laptop or PC model, check with its manufacturer for Linux support issues. Some manufacturers such as HP now offer a Linux operating system prein-stalled, or have an in-house Linux hardware certification program. Laptop users will defi-nitely want to browse to Linux on Laptops at http://linux-laptop.net/.

> ### TIP
>
> A company called EmperorLinux in the United States supplies laptops from prominent manufacturers with Linux preinstalled complete with support. They have been in busi-ness for a few years now, and ensure 100% compatibility with the laptops that they sell. Check out their range at http://www.emperorlinux.com.

If you cannot find compatibility answers in various online databases, continue your research by reading the Linux Hardware HOWTO at http://www.tldp.org/HOWTO/ Hardware-HOWTO/. At that address, you will find loads of general information and links to additional sources of information.

Keep in mind that when PC hardware is unsupported under Linux, it is generally because the manufacturer cannot or will not release technical specifications or because no one has taken the time and effort to develop a driver. If you hit a roadblock with a particular piece of hardware, check the hardware manufacturer's support web pages, or Google's Linux pages at http://www.google.com/linux. You can then type in a specific search request and hopefully find answers to how to make the hardware work with Linux. This is also a good way to research answers to questions about software issues.

Preparing for Potential Hardware Problems

Fedora will work "out of the box" with nearly every Intel-or PowerPC-based desktop, server, and laptop; drivers for thousands of different types of hardware peripherals are included. But you can sometimes run into problems if Linux does not recognize a hard-ware item, if Fedora does not correctly initialize the hardware, or if an initialized item is incorrectly configured. For these reasons, some hardware items are prone to creating prob-lems during an install. In the sections that follow, you learn some important pointers for avoiding these problems or resolving those that do occur.

Controllerless Modems

As you read earlier, most Linux hardware-related installation problems stem from a lack of technical specifications from the manufacturer, thwarting efforts of open source develop-ers to create a driver. In the recent past, one hardware item that triggered both types of difficulties was the controllerless modem, also colloquially known as a *WinModem*. The good news is that modem chipset manufacturers have been more forthcoming with driver details. Some original equipment manufacturers, such as IBM, have made a concerted effort to provide Linux support. Support for the ACP Mwave modem, used in ThinkPad 600/Es and 770s, is included in the Linux kernel. Drivers have been developed for many of the controllerless modem chipsets that formally did not work with Linux.

If a driver is not available for your controllerless modem, you have a few options. You can download the driver's source code and build the driver yourself. Alternatively, you can download a binary-only software package and install the driver.

Some controllerless modems might also need to be initialized and configured through a separate utility program. The modem, if supported, should work normally after you install and configure the driver.

You can research Linux support for controllerless modems by browsing to http://www.linmodems.org/.

USB Devices

Fedora supports hundreds of different Universal Serial Bus devices. *USB* is a design specification and a protocol used to enable a host computer to talk to attached peripherals. Because of lack of manufacturer and device ID information or lack of technical specifications regarding certain chipsets, some devices might not work with Fedora. USB 1.1 devices are designed to support data transfer speeds between 1.5 and 12Mbps.

Common USB devices include cameras, keyboards, mice, modems, network interfaces, printers, scanners, storage devices, video (such as webcams), and hubs (to chain additional devices).

Although most enlightened manufacturers are aware of opportunities in the Linux marketplace, some still do not support Linux. It pays to determine Linux support before you buy any USB device; again, research Linux USB support and its current state of development by browsing to http://www.qbik.ch/usb/devices/.

The newer USB 2.0 specification enables devices (such as hard and CD drives) to use speeds up to 480Mbps. Fedora supports USB 2.0 with the ehci-hcd kernel module. This driver, in development since early 2001, enables the use of many forms of newer USB 2.0 devices as long as you have a supported USB controller. Check out the current state of Linux USB 2.0 support by browsing to http://www.linux-usb.org/usb2.html.

Motherboard-Based Hardware

Small form factor PCs, thin clients, notebooks, and embedded devices are part of a growing trend in the PC industry. Manufacturers are cramming more functionality into fewer chips to simplify design and lower power requirements. Today, many computers come with built-in video graphics, audio chipsets, and network interfaces, along with a host of peripheral support.

Common modern (1996 onward) PC motherboard form factors are designed according to industry-assigned specifications (usually from Intel), and are ATX (12–9.6 inches); MicroATX (9.6–9.6 inches); and FlexATX (9–7.5 inches). One of the newest and even smaller motherboard forms is from VIA Technologies, Inc.—the mini-ITX (approximately

6.5–6.5 inches), which has an embedded CPU. CPUs commonly used in all these mother-boards will vary, and have different socketing requirements based on chipset pins: Socket 478 for K7-type CPUs (from AMD); Socket 939 for some Athlon and Sempron processors; Socket AM2 for newer Athlon 64 and AMD FX processors; Socket 370 for Pentium IIIs and Celerons from Intel, or C3s from VIA; Socket 478 for Intel's Pentium 4s (early versions of which used a 423-pin socket); and Socket LGA775 for newer Core 2 and Pentium D processors. Older socket types are Socket A, Socket 7 (and Super 7), Slot 1, and Slot B.

Fortunately, nearly all controllers, bridges, and other chipsets are supported by Linux. Although flaky or unsupported built-in hardware can (usually) be sidestepped by the installation of a comparable PCI card component, cutting-edge notebook users are at the most risk for compatibility problems because internal components are not user replace-able. Potential pitfalls can be avoided through careful research (vote with your money for Linux-compatible hardware), or by choosing PC motherboards with a minimum of built-in features, and then using *PCI (Peripheral Component Interconnect)*, *AGP (Accelerated Graphics Port)*, or PCI Express cards known to work.

CPU, Symmetric Multiprocessing, and Memory Problems

Fedora supports all Pentium class x86 compatible CPUs. Code is included in the Linux kernel to recognize the CPU type when booting, and to then implement any required fixes to overcome architecture bugs (such as the now-infamous divide-by-zero error). After you install Fedora, you can also rebuild the Linux kernel to specifically support and take advantage of the host PC's CPU. You might not realize extreme improvements in compu-tational speed, but you'll be assured that Linux is crafted for your CPU's architecture, which can help stability and reliability. Some of the x86-based CPUs with specific supporting code for Linux include those from Advanced Micro Devices, Transmeta, and VIA Technologies.

Fedora's Linux kernel also should automatically recognize and use the amount of installed RAM. The Linux kernel should also recognize and map out any memory holes in system memory (perhaps used for video graphics).

If you are installing Fedora on a working, stable PC, you should not have any problems related to the system's memory. If you are putting together a new system, you need to avoid combining or configuring the system in ways that will interfere with its capability to process data. Some issues to be aware of include the following:

▶ Do not expect similar CPU performance across product lines from different manu-facturers, such as AMD or VIA. Some CPU models offer better floating point or integer math operations, which are important for a number of CPU-intensive tasks (such as graphics, audio, and video rendering or conversion). If you need better performance, try to find a faster CPU compatible with your motherboard, or switch to a CPU with better floating-point unit (FPU) performance.

▶ Overclocking can cause problems with overheating, memory access, and other hard-ware performance, and it is not a good idea for any Linux system. Overclocking is a popular geek pastime and a great way to get a bit of performance boost out of slower CPUs by altering voltage settings and/or clock timings via the BIOS. You can try to push your CPU to higher speeds, but this approach is not recommended if your aim is system stability. The Linux kernel reports the recognized CPU speed on booting (which you can view by using the dmesg command).

▶ Along the same lines, CPU and motherboard overheating will cause problems. Proper attachment of the CPU's heatsink using a quality thermal paste (never use thermal tape), along with one or more fans providing adequate airflow lessens the chance of hardware damage and system failure.

▶ You can run into problems if you switch the type of CPU installed in your computer, and especially if your PC's BIOS does not automatically recognize or configure for newly installed mainboard hardware and components. In some instances, a system reinstall is warranted, but BIOS issues should be resolved first.

▶ Not all CPUs support symmetric multiprocessing, or SMP. Fedora readily supports use of two or more CPUs and, during installation, automatically installs an appropriate Linux kernel. You can avoid problems by reading the Linux SMP HOWTO (available through http://www.tldp.org/). Note that some CPUs, such as the current crop of VIA C3s, might not be used for SMP. Also, SMP motherboards require that all CPUs be identical. This means that you need two identical CPUs to take advantage of SMP.

▶ Faulty or bad memory causes Linux kernel panics or Signal 11 errors (segmentation faults), causing a system crash or a program to abort execution. Linux is quite sensitive to faulty hardware, but runs with great stability in a correctly configured system with good hardware. Problems can arise from incorrect BIOS settings, especially if video memory must occupy and use a portion of system RAM. Always install quality (and appropriate) memory in your PC to avoid problems.

Preparing and Using a Hardware Inventory

Buying a turn-key Linux solution is one way to avoid hardware problems, and many vendors are standing by, ready to prescribe solutions. However, managing deployments aimed at using existing hardware requires some information collection.

If you are a small business or individual user, you are well advised to prepare detailed checklists of existing hardware before attempting a migration to Linux. Not only do you benefit from the collected information, but you might also be able to sidestep or anticipate problems before, during, or after installation. Problems are most likely to occur with newer hardware, cutting-edge hardware such as new motherboard chipsets and video cards, or extraneous hardware such as operating system–specific scanners, printers, or wireless devices.

Table B.2 provides a comprehensive checklist you can use to take inventory of target hardware, such as the computer and any peripherals. Veteran Linux users can take the collected information to build custom systems by adding known hardware or substituting cheaper but equivalent hardware.

TABLE B.2   System and Peripheral Inventory Checklist

Item	Errata
Audio devices	Microphone:
	Line out:
	Line in:
BIOS	Type:
	Revision:
	ACPI:
	APM:
CD-ROM drive	Brand:
	Type:
CD-RW drive	Brand:
	Type:
	CD-R write speed:
	CD rewrite speed:
	CD-ROM read speed:
DVD drive	Brand:
	Type:
DVD+/-RW drive	Brand:
	Type:
	Dual layer?:
Digital camera	Brand:
	Model:
	Interface:
CPU	Brand:
	Socket type:
	Speed:
FireWire (IEEE 1394)	Chipset:
	Device(s):
IrDA port	Device number:
	Port IRQ:
Keyboard	Brand:
	Type:
Laptop	Brand:
	Model:
	Hibernation partition:
Legacy ports	Parallel type:
	Parallel IRQ:
	RS-232 number(s):
	RS-232 IRQ(s):

B

TABLE B.2   Continued

Item	Errata
Mice	Brand:
	Type:
Modem	Brand:
	Type:
Motherboard	Brand:
	Type:
	Chipset:
Monitor(s)	Brand:
	Model:
	Horizontal freq:
	Vertical freq:
	Max. resolution:
Network card	Wireless:
	Brand:
	Type:
	Speed:
PCI bus	Version:
	Model:
	Type:
PCMCIA	Controller:
	Cardbus:
	Brand:
	Type:
Printer(s)	Brand:
	Model:
System RAM	Amount:
	Type:
	Speed:
S-Video port	X Support:
Scanner	Brand:
	Model:
	Interface type:
Sound card	Chipset:
	Type:
	I/O addr:
	IRQ:
	DMA:
	MPU addr:

TABLE B.2   Continued

Item	Errata
Storage device(s)	Removable:
	Size:
	Brand:
	Model:
	Controller(s):
Storage device controller	Type:
Tablet	Brand:
	Model:
	Interface:
Universal Serial Bus	Controller:
	BIOS MPS setting:
	BIOS Plug-n-Play setting:
	Device(s):
Video device(s)	Brand:
	Model:
	Xinerama:
	Chipset:
	VRAM:

Use the checklist in Table B.2 as a general guideline for recording your computer's hardware and other capabilities. You can get quite a bit of information through hardware manuals or other documentation included with your PC, video, sound, or network interface card. Don't worry if you cannot fill out the entire checklist; Fedora will most likely recognize and automatically configure your PC's hardware during installation. Much of this information can be displayed by the dmesg command after booting. However, some of these details, such as your video card's graphics chipset and installed video RAM, can come in handy if you need to perform troubleshooting. You can also use the list as a post-installation check-off sheet to see how well Fedora works with your system.

Preparing for the Install Process

The basic steps in installing Fedora are to plan, install, and configure. You have to decide how to boot to an install and how much room to devote to Linux. Then perform the install (a sample step-by-step installation is discussed in Chapter 1, "Installing Fedora"), and afterward configure your system to host new users and specific software services. Much of the initial work is done during the install process because the installer, Anaconda, walks you through partitioning, configuring the desktop, and configuration of any recognized network adapter.

B

> **TIP**
>
> You can use the first Fedora CD or the DVD to perform other tasks aside from installing Linux. The CD-ROM/DVD features a rescue mode and you can also use it to partition and prepare a hard drive for Linux, using `fdisk` as described earlier.

There are many different ways to install Fedora, and selecting an installation method might depend on the equipment on hand, existing bandwidth, or equipment limitations. Here are some of the most commonly used installation methods:

- **CD-ROM/DVD**—Using a compatible CD-ROM or DVD drive attached to the computer. (Laptop users with an external CD-ROM drive need PCMCIA support from a driver disk image included under the first CD-ROM's `images` directory.)

- **Network File System (NFS)**—You can install Fedora from a remotely mounted hard drive containing the Fedora software. To perform this installation, you must have an installed and supported network interface card, along with a boot floppy with network support. (You learn how to make boot floppies later in this section of the chapter.)

- **File Transfer Protocol (FTP)**—As with an NFS install, installation via FTP requires that the Fedora software be available on a public FTP server. You also need an installed and supported network interface card, along with a boot floppy with network support.

- **Installation via the Internet**—If you have the bandwidth, it might be possible to install Fedora via the Internet; however, this method might not be as reliable as using a *local area network (LAN)* because of availability and current use of the Fedora Project or other servers on mirror sites.

- **A hard drive partition**—By copying the ISO images to a hard drive partition, you can then boot to an install.

- **Preinstalled media**—It is also possible to install Linux on another hard drive and then transfer the hard drive to your computer. This is handy, especially if your site uses removable hard drives or other media.

After booting and choosing to use either a graphical or text-based install interface, the installation procedure is nearly the same for each type of install. Chapter 1 walks you through a typical installation.

Installing Fedora can be as simple as inserting the first CD/DVD into your computer's CD drive and rebooting the computer. But if you choose this method, first make sure that your system's BIOS is set to boot from CD-ROM.

You usually enter the BIOS to make this change by depressing a particular key, such as Del or F2, immediately after turning on the computer. After entering the BIOS, navigate to the BIOS Boot menu, which should look like Figure B.1.

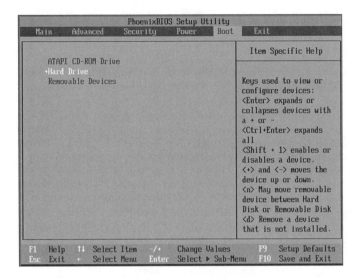

FIGURE B.1   To boot to an install using your Fedora CD-ROM or DVD, set your BIOS to have your computer boot using its CD drive.

Partitioning Before and During Installation

Partitioning your hard drive for Linux can be done before or during installation.

If you plan to prepare your partitions before installing Linux, you need to use commercial partitioning software. Some of the popular commercial software utilities you can use to create Linux partitions are Symantec's PartitionMagic or VCOM Products' Partition Commander. Alternatively, it might be possible to prepare partitions before installing Fedora by using the free FIPS.EXE command.

If you want to partition a hard drive already using an existing Linux system, you can attach the hard drive to a spare IDE channel, and then use the Linux fdisk or GNU parted partitioning utilities. Both utilities offer a way to interactively partition and prepare storage media. Linux recognizes IDE hard drives using a device name such as /dev/hda (for the master device on IDE channel 0), /dev/hdb (for the slave device on IDE channel 0), /dev/hdc (for the master device on IDE channel 1), and /dev/hdd (for the slave device on IDE channel 1). With more modern computers that use the SATA interface, Linux will refer to drives as /dev/sda (for the master device on channel 0), /dev/sdb (for the slave device on channel 0), and so on.

If a new hard drive is properly attached to your PC and you then boot Linux, you can see whether the kernel recognizes the device by viewing the output of the dmesg command. You can then use fdisk with the device name to begin partitioning like so:

```
# fdisk /dev/hdb
```

Note that you will need root permission, and in this example, the new drive is attached as a slave on IDE channel 0. Do not change partitioning on your root device; otherwise, you will wreck your system! The fdisk command is interactive, and you can press M to get help when using the utility. You can use parted in much the same way if you specify the i, or interactive option on the command line, as follows:

```
# parted -i /dev/hdb
```

To get help when using parted interactively, press ? or type **help** followed by a command keyword. The parted command has other helpful features, such as the capability to copy a file system directly from one partition to another.

Finally, you can prepare partitions ahead of installation by booting your system using a live Linux distribution (such as the LNX Bootable Business Card, available at http:// www.lnx-bbc.org/) and then using a native Linux utility such as fdisk to partition your drive. For details on using the fdisk partitioning utility and alternative software tools to partition your hard drive, see the section "Creating the Partition Table" in Chapter 35, "Managing the File System."

> **NOTE**
>
> It is possible to create a dual-boot configuration, which allows the choice of booting Fedora and another operating system, such as Windows XP. To configure your system for dual booting, you must first install Windows and then install Linux. Note that many Windows system-restore CD-ROMs wipe out all data on your hard drive, including Linux. During installation of Fedora, you install the GRUB Linux bootloader in the primary drive's *Master Boot Record*, or *MBR*. When properly configured, GRUB allows your system to reboot to Windows or Linux. Browse to http://www.gnu.org/software/grub/ manual/ to read the GRUB manual online.

Choosing a Partitioning Scheme

As with deployment and installation of Linux, partitioning your hard drive to accept Fedora requires some forethought, especially if the target computer is going to be used other than as a home PC on which to learn Linux. If Linux is to be the only resident operating system, you can have the installer automatically create and use a partition scheme according to the type of installation you select during the install. If you plan to have a dual-boot system in which you can boot Linux or another operating system, you have to manually partition your hard drive before and possibly during the install.

> **CAUTION**
>
> Before you begin partitioning your drive, get your safety nets in order. First, back up all critical data! Any changes to your system's hard drive or operating system put your existing data at risk. To prevent the loss of time and resources that inevitably follow data loss, do full backups before you make any changes to your system. Create a bootdisk during the install (you will be asked before the install finishes) so that you will be able to at least boot Linux if something goes wrong.

The simplest and most basic partitioning scheme for a Linux system requires a Linux native root partition and a swap partition. On a single-drive system with 12GB storage and 512MB of RAM, the scheme might look like this:

```
Hard Drive Partition    Mount Point    Size
/dev/hda1               /              10.74GB
/dev/hda2               swap           1GB
```

On a system running Windows, the scheme might look like this:

```
Hard Drive Partition    Mount Point      Size
/dev/hda1               /media/c_drive      4GB
/dev/hda2               /                7.74GB
/dev/hda3               swap             1GB
```

> **CAUTION**
>
> Notebook users should be careful when partitioning. Some notebooks use a special partition equal to the size of installed RAM to perform suspend-to-disk or other hibernation operations. Always examine your computer's initial partitioning scheme if configuring a dual-boot system, and leave the special partition alone! One way around this problem is to use a software suspend approach as outlined at htpp://www.suspend2.net/.

Hosting Parts of the Linux File System on Separate Partitions

Your choice of specific partitioning scheme will depend on how Fedora will be used. On a system being designed for expansion, greater capacity, or the capability to host additional software or users, you can use separate partitions to host various parts of the Linux file system. Some candidates for these separate partitions include

▶ **/home**—Users will store hundreds and hundreds of megabytes of data under their directories. This is important data, perhaps even more so than the system itself. Using a separate partition (on a different volume) to store this user data helps make the data easier to find and it segregates user and system data. You must decide ahead of time how much storage to allocate to users. For a single workstation, you should reserve several gigabytes of storage.

▶ **/opt**—As the home directory for additional software packages, this directory can have its own partition or remote file system. Fedora does not populate this directory, but it might be used by other software packages you install later. Just 1GB of storage should be adequate, depending on applications to be installed.

▶ **/tmp**—This directory can be used as temporary storage by users, especially if disk quotas are enforced; as such, it could be placed on its own partition. This directory can be as small as 100MB.

- ▶ **/usr**—This directory holds nearly all the software on a Fedora system and can become quite large if additional software is added, especially on a workstation configuration. Using a separate partition can make sense. A full install requires at least 6GB for this directory or more if additional software is added.

- ▶ **/var**—Placing this directory (or perhaps some of its subdirectories) on a separate partition can be a good idea, especially because security logs, mail, and print spooling take place under this tree. You should reserve at least 1GB of storage for /var, especially if using Fedora as a print server (as spooled documents reside under /var/spool).

TIP

As a general rule, it is a good idea to segregate user and system data. Although a Linux system can be restored quickly, user data has a much greater value and can be much more difficult to replace. Segregating data can make the job of backing up and restoring much easier. If you ever have a problem accessing your partition, we recommend that you get the excellent Knoppix distribution that boots and runs entirely from CD. This will enable you to access your partitions and make any necessary repairs.

Using Fedora's `kickstart` Installation Method

Automating the installation process can save system administrators a lot of time and effort during an initial deployment, upgrade, or maintenance cycle by managing multiple computers at one time. Fedora offers a highly automated installation technique called `kickstart`, developed by Red Hat, which can be used for unattended installation of Linux.

Fedora's `kickstart` installation uses a single configuration file with a special, extensive syntax on a server, boot floppy, or other medium to install Fedora via CD/DVD, a hard drive partition, or a network connection. Using `kickstart` is easy and involves passing a kernel argument to the Fedora Linux boot kernel. The various arguments tell the boot kernel to look for a configuration file on floppy, a designated server, via a network, specific file, or CD/DVD.

You can use `kickstart` to install Fedora on one or more computers at the same time. First, set up a web or FTP server with Fedora's installation files. Next, create a network boot floppy, using the techniques described in the next section. Follow the directions given here (choosing an FTP install), and then copy the custom `kickstart` file to the network boot floppy. You can then use this floppy (and copies) to boot one or more PCs to a network install, using your FTP server.

TIP

Fedora does not automatically install `system-config-kickstart`, the utility used to create and customize `system-config-kickstart` files. Be sure that you install it, using either yum or the Add/Remove Programs tool.

To begin the automated installation process, you create the configuration file that will be used by kickstart as an installation profile. You can configure the complex configuration file with Fedora's Kickstart Configurator. To start the configuration, click the Kickstart item from System, Administration menu, or enter the system-config-kickstart command, like so:

 # system-config-kickstart

After you press Enter, you see the Kickstart Configurator dialog box, as shown in Figure B.2.

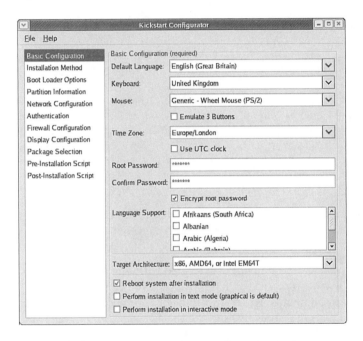

FIGURE B.2   Fedora's kickstart configuration tool, system-config-kickstart, can be used to quickly and easily create installation profiles for use in automated installations.

Click to select various options, and then enter the specifics desired for the target system. Start by selecting the default system language, type of keyboard, mouse, and so on. Of course, automated installations work best when they are done on similar equipment. When finished, press Ctrl+S, or use the Save File item from the File menu. The configuration will be saved with the name ks.cfg. When you use the kickstart installation method, the kickstart file will be read by computers booting to the install. The kickstart language covers nearly every aspect of an install with the exception of sound card, printer, or modem setup.

For example, a portion of a kickstart file generated for an install might look like this:

```
#Generated by Kickstart Configurator

#System language
lang en_US

#Language modules to install
langsupport en_US

#System keyboard
keyboard us

#System mouse
mouse genericps/2

#System timezone
timezone --utc Europe/London

#Root password
rootpw --iscrypted $1$/n3yjyDV$AWoBZgRQq/lAxyRhX1JSM1
...
```

Note that not all the output of a sample ks.cfg is shown. However, you can see that this file feeds kickstart directions for an install, including an encrypted root password to be installed on the target system.

The next step is to copy your new ks.cfg to a boot disk created with one of the boot floppy images (found at http://www.thisiscool.com/fcfloppy.htm). You can do this with Linux by using the mount and cp commands. For example, insert your boot disk into your PC, and then use the mount command (as root) like so:

```
# mount /mnt floppy
```

If Fedora has mounted your floppy automatically, you'll receive an error message such as /dev/fd0 already mounted. You can then simply copy the ks.cfg file to your floppy, as follows:

```
# cp ks.cfg /mnt/floppy
```

You can verify the contents of the floppy by using the ls command like this:

```
# ls /mnt/floppy
boot.msg       general.msg      initrd.img      ks.cfg          ldlinux.sys
options.msg    param.msg        rescue.msg      snake.msg  splash.lss
syslinux.cfg   syslinux.png     vmlinuz
```

Then unmount the floppy, using the `umount` command:

```
# umount /mnt/floppy
```

Remove the disk. It is now ready for use. When you use the disk to boot a PC, tell the install boot image that you want to perform a `kickstart` install:

```
linux ks=floppy
```

The installer then uses the specifications you outlined in the Kickstart Configurator and saved in `ks.cfg` to install Fedora.

Reference

The following is a list of references you can use to learn a bit more about partitioning, installation tools, and installing Fedora and Linux variants on a variety of hardware. You'll also find information about installation on hardware employed for embedded and mainframe solutions.

- ▶ **https://www.redhat.com/en_us/USA/rhel/migrate/**—Red Hat's helpful Migration Center, with news, views, whitepapers, and other tips and research on migrating to a Linux solution.

- ▶ **http://www.yale.edu/pclt/BOOT/DEFAULT.HTM**—A basic primer to partitioning that is operating system nonspecific.

- ▶ **http://www-1.ibm.com/linux/**—Home page for Linux at IBM, with links to products, services, and downloads.

- ▶ **http://www-124.ibm.com/developerworks/opensource/linux390/**—Home page for IBM S/390 Linux solutions.

- ▶ **http://www.dell.com/linux/**—Dell Computer's Linux information pages.

- ▶ **http://hardware.redhat.com/hcl/**—Entry point to Red Hat's hardware compatibility database.

- ▶ **http://www.linux1394.org/**—Home page for the Linux FireWire project, with information regarding the status of drivers and devices for this port.

- ▶ **http://www.linux-usb.org/**—Home page for the Linux USB project, with lists of supported devices and links to drivers.

- ▶ **http://elks.sourceforge.net/**—Home page for Linux for x286 and below CPUs, ELKS Linux.

- ▶ **http://www.lnx-bbc.org/**—Home page for the Bootable Business Card, a 50MB compressed Linux distribution that offers hundreds of networking clients, a live X session, web browsing, PDA backup, wireless networking, rescue sessions, and file recovery.

B

▶ **http://www.coyotelinux.com/**—Home page for several compact Linux distributions offering firewalling and VPN services. The floppy-based distribution works quite well on older PCs and does not require a hard drive.

▶ **http://www.freesco.org/**—Home page for a floppy-based Linux router solution that works on 386 PCs, requires only 6MB of RAM, and provides bridging, firewalling, IP masquerading, DNS, DHCP, web, telnet, print, time, and remote access functions.

▶ **http://www.bitwizard.nl/sig11/**—A detailed overview of some root causes of Linux Signal 11 errors.

▶ **http://www.gnu.org/software/parted/parted.html#introduction**—Home page for the GNU parted utility.

▶ **http://www.linux.org/vendors/systems.html**—One place to check for a vendor near you selling Linux preinstalled on a PC, laptop, server, or hard drive.

APPENDIX C

Fedora and Linux Internet Resources

Linux enjoys a wealth of Internet support in the form of websites with technical information, specific program documentation, targeted whitepapers, bug fixes, user experiences, third-party commercial technical support, and even free versions of specialized, fine-tuned clone distributions.

This appendix lists many of the supporting websites, FTP repositories, Usenet newsgroups, and electronic mailing lists that you can use to get more information and help with your copy of Fedora.

If You Need Help 24/7

If you are a small business, corporate, or enterprise-level Red Hat Enterprise Linux user, do not forget that you can always turn to the source, Red Hat, or third-party companies, such as Dell and HP, who supply Red Hat servers for commercial technical support on a 24/7 onsite basis, by phone, by electronic mail, or even on a per-incident basis. Red Hat offers a spectrum of support options for its software products. You can read more about support options when you purchase Red Hat software at https://www.redhat.com/apps/commerce/. Remember that Fedora is not an officially supported product from Red Hat. If you want help, try http://fedoraforum.org.

This appendix also lists websites that might be of general interest when using Fedora or specific components such as Xorg. Every effort has been made to ensure the accuracy of the URLs, but keep in mind that the Internet is always in flux!

Keep Up-to-Date with yum

Keeping informed about bug fixes, security updates, and other errata is critical to the success and health of a Fedora system. To keep abreast of the most important developments when using Fedora, be sure to register with the Fedora Announcements mailing list. The list tells you about updates that have been issued and what has been fixed as a result. Go to http://www.redhat.com/mailman/listinfo/fedora-announce-list to register for this mailing list. At the very least you should use the updater applet, or *puplet* as it's affectionately known, to ensure that you are up-to-date with all the patches, bug fixes, and security updates that are available for your system. Alternatively, if you are taken with the command line, you could also use the yum update command (as root) to do the same thing.

Websites and Search Engines

Literally thousands of websites exist with information about Linux and Fedora. The key to getting the answers you need right away involves using the best search engines and techniques. Knowing how to search can mean the difference between frustration and success when troubleshooting problems. This section provides some Internet search tips and lists Red Hat, Fedora, and Linux-related sites, sorted by various topics. The lists are not comprehensive, but have been checked and were available at the time of this writing.

Web Search Tips

Troubleshooting problems with Linux by searching the web can be an efficient and productive way to get answers to vexing problems. One of the most basic rules for conducting productive searches is to use specific search terms to find specific answers. For example, if you simply search for "Fedora Linux," you end up with too many links and too much information. But if you search for "Fedora sound," you are more likely to find the information you need. If you receive an error message, use it; otherwise, use the Linux kernel diagnostic message as your search criterion.

Other effective techniques include the following:

▶ Using symbols in the search string, such as the plus sign (+) to force matches of web pages containing both strings (if such features are supported by the search engine)

▶ Searching within returned results

▶ Sorting results (usually by date to get the latest information)

▶ Searching for related information

▶ Stemming searches; for example, specifying returns for not only link but also linking and linked

Invest some time and experiment with your favorite search engine's features—more productive searches will result. In addition to sharpening your search skills, also take the time to choose the best search engine for your needs.

Google Is Your Friend

Some of the fastest and most comprehensive search engines on the Web are powered by Linux, so it makes sense to use the best available resources. Out of the myriad number of websites with search engines, http://google.com stands out from the crowd, with at least 81 million users per month. Google makes use of advanced hardware and software to bring speed and efficiency to your searches, although at its heart is a heavily customized Linux distro. If you are looking for specific Linux answers, take advantage of Google's Linux page at http://google.com/linux.

Why is Google (named after a math number) so powerful? You can get a quick idea from the company itself at http://www.google.com/technology/index.html. Part of its success is because of great algorithms, good programming, and simple interface design, but most users really seem to appreciate Google's uncanny capability to provide links to what you are looking for in the first page of a search return. Google's early success was also assured because the site ran its search engine on clusters of thousands of PCs running a customized version of Red Hat Linux!

Google has the largest database size of any search engine on the web, with reputedly more than eight billion web pages searched and indexed. The database size is important because empty search results are useless to online users, and the capability to return hits on esoteric subjects can make the difference between success and failure or satisfaction and frustration. Some of Google's features include a GoogleScout link to return similar pages on the results page, the capability to see the exact version of a web page as returned to a search engine (known as a *cached* feature), advanced searches, and more recently, a link to an active Usenet news feed!

To get a better idea of what Google can offer you, browse to http://www.google.com/options/. You will find links to more than two dozen different services and tools covering specialized searches, databases, information links, translators, and other helpful browsing tools.

Fedora Package Listings

You can quickly and easily view a list of the installed RPM packages installed on your Fedora system, along with a short description of each package, by using the rpm command:

```
$ rpm -qai ¦ less
```

Fedora users can also use the yum command to view package names and information about not only installed packages, but any available updated packages, like this:

```
$ yum info ¦ less
```

If you use Fedora and want to see info about only your installed packages, use the yum command's installed list option like so:

```
$ yum info installed ¦ less
```

However, because this will generate a lot of information, you might want to generate a text file that contains all this information for your records. This is fairly easy to do by piping the output from the yum command into a file, as follows:

```
$ yum info available > ~/availablepackages.txt
```

or

```
$ yum info installed > ~/installedpackages.txt
```

Certification

Linux certification courses are part of the rapidly growing information technology training industry. Hundreds of different vendors now offer courses about and testing of Linux skill sets. However, because Linux is open source software, there are no formal rules or mandates concerning what knowledge or level of expertise is required for certification. If you are interested in certification using Red Hat Linux and would like to pursue a career or obtain employment with a company using Red Hat Linux, you really should seek training from the best and most qualified company: Red Hat.

That said, the following websites might be of interest if you would like to pursue a certification track for Red Hat or other Linux distributions:

▶ http://www.lpi.org—The Linux Professional Institute, with Linux vendor- and distribution-neutral programs

▶ http://www.redhat.com/training/—Entry page to Red Hat's Global Learning Services and information about the Red Hat Certified Engineer program

Commercial Support

Commercial support for Linux and Red Hat Linux is an essential ingredient to the success of Linux in the corporate and business community. Although hundreds, if not thousands, of consultants well versed in Linux and UNIX are available on call for a fee, here is a short list of the best-known Linux support providers:

▶ http://www.redhat.com/apps/support/—Red Hat's main support page with links to its various support programs.

▶ http://www.ibm.com/linux/—Linux services offered by IBM include e-business solutions, open source consulting, database migration, clustering, servers, and support. In addition to service-oriented support companies, nearly every commercial distributor of Linux has some form of easily purchased commercial support. There are various ways in which to take advantage of support services (such as remote management, onsite consulting, device driver development, and so on), but needs vary according to customer circumstances and installations.

> **The Benefits of Joining a Linux User Group**
>
> Join a local *Linux Users Group (LUG)*! Joining and participating in a local LUG has many benefits. You can get help, trade information, and learn many new and wonderful things about Linux. Most LUGs do not have membership dues, and many often sponsor regular lectures and discussions from leading Linux, GNU, and open source experts. For one great place to start, browse to http://www.tux.org/luglist.html. Another great place to meet up with like-minded people is at one of the numerous Linuxworld shows held around the world. Head on over to http://www.linuxworldexpo.com/flash/ for a list of international shows.

Documentation

Nearly all Linux distributions include thousands of pages of documentation in the form of manual pages, HOWTO documents (in various formats, such as text and HTML), mini-HOWTO documents, or software package documentation (usually found under the /usr/share/doc/ directory). However, the definitive site for reading the latest versions of these documents is the Linux Documentation Project, found at http://www.tldp.org.

Linux Guides

If you are looking for more extensive and detailed information concerning a Linux subject, try reading one of the many Linux guides. These guides, available for a number of subjects, dwell on technical topics in more detail and at a more leisurely pace than a HOWTO. You can find copies of the following through the web:

▶ "Advanced Bash-Scripting Guide," by Mendel Cooper; a guide to shell scripting using bash

▶ "LDP Author Guide," by Mark F. Komarinski; how to write LDP documentation

▶ "Linux Administration Made Easy," by Steve Frampton

▶ "Linux Consultants Guide," by Joshua Drake; a worldwide listing of commercial Linux consultants

▶ "Linux from Scratch," by Gerard Beekmans; creating a Linux distribution from software

▶ "Linux Kernel Module Programming Guide," by Peter J. Salzman, Michael Burian, and Ori Pomerantz; a good guide to building 2.4 and 2.6 series modules

▶ "Securing and Optimizing Linux," by Gerhard Mourani

▶ "The Linux Network Administrator's Guide, Second Edition," by Olaf Kirch and Terry Dawson; a comprehensive Net admin guide

The Fedora Project

▶ **http://fedoraproject.org/**—The community home page for the Fedora Project. Also includes an ever-growing Wiki that provides a lot of tutorials and HOWTOs for Fedora.

▶ **http://planet.fedoraproject.org**—Find out what's going on in the lives of people closely connected with Fedora.

▶ **http://fedoraforum.org**—A good place to go if you need specific Fedora support.

Red Hat Linux

▶ **http://www.redhat.com**—The home page for Red Hat's distribution of Red Hat Enterprise Linux for multiple processors and architectures.

▶ **http://www.redhat.com/apps/support/documentation.html**—A web page with links to current official Red Hat manuals and guides, FAQs, HOWTOs, whitepapers, free books, mailing list archives, hardware compatibility lists, and other documentation.

Mini-CD Linux Distributions

Mini-CD Linux distributions are used for many different purposes. Some distributions are used to boot to a read-only firewall configuration; others are used to provide as complete a rescue environment as possible; whereas others are used to either install or help jump-start an install of a full distribution. Mini-CDs are available in a wide variety of sizes, such as 3" CD-Rs (or CD-RW) with sizes ranging from 185MB to 210MB. You can also download an ISO image and create a Linux bootable business card, typically fitting on a 40MB or 50MB credit card–sized CD-R (consider using a mini–CD-RW, especially if you want to upgrade your distribution often). Here are some links to these distributions:

▶ **http://www.lnx-bbc.org**—The home page for the Linux BBC, a 40MB image hosting a rather complete live Linux session with X, a web browser, and a host of networking tools.

▶ **http://crux.nu/**—The home page of the CRUX i686-optimized Linux distribution.

▶ **http://www.trustix.net/**—The home page for the free version of the Trustix Secure Linux distribution, which currently uses the latest 2.6 kernel. Trustix is RPM based.

▶ **http://smoothwall.org/get/**—The 34MB SmoothWall distribution, which easily fits on a bootable business card and is used to install a web-administered firewall, router, or gateway with SSH, HTTP, and other services.

Floppy-Based Linux Distributions

▶ http://floppix.ccai.com/index.html—Debian-based floppy

▶ http://www.toms.net/rb/—Tom's root and boot disk distribution

▶ http://www.coyotelinux.com/—Secure routing and embedded Linux disk distributions

▶ http://trinux.sourceforge.net—Ultra-secure Linux distribution on floppy

▶ http://PenguinBackup.sourceforge.net/—Unique, floppy-based distribution that allows quick backup of your Palm-type PDA

Various Intel-Based Linux Distributions

Choosing a Linux distribution (*distro*) for an Intel-based PC is generally a matter of personal preference or need. Many Linux users prefer Red Hat's distro because of its excellent support, commercial support options, and widespread use around the world. However, many different Linux distributions are available for download. One of the best places to start looking for a new distro or new version of your favorite distro is http://www.distrowatch.com. Typically each distro will have a x86_64 version available for download:

▶ http://www.xandros.net—The new home of the original and improved version of Corel's Debian-based Linux

▶ http://www.debian.org—The Debian Linux distribution, consisting only of software distributed under the GNU GPL license

▶ http://www.slackware.com—The home page for download of the newest version of one of the oldest Linux distributions, Slackware

▶ http://www.opensuse.com—The home page for SuSE Linux, also available for the PowerPC and x86_64 platforms

▶ http://www.ubuntu.com—A popular Linux distribution that is based on Debian

▶ http://www.mandrivalinux.com—A Pentium-optimized, RPM-based distribution, originally based on Red Hat's Linux distribution

PowerPC-Based Linux Distributions

▶ http://penguinppc.org/—Home page for the PowerPC GNU/Linux distribution

▶ http://www.opensuse.com—SuSE PPC Linux

▶ http://www.yellowdoglinux.com—Home page for Terra Soft Solutions' Yellow Dog Linux for the PowerPC, which is based on Fedora

Linux on Laptops and PDAs

One of the definitive sites for getting information about running Linux on your laptop is Kenneth Harker's Linux Laptop site. Although not as actively updated as in the past, this site (http://www.linux-laptop.net) still contains the world's largest collection of Linux and laptop information, with links to user experiences and details concerning specific laptop models.

Another site to check is Werner Heuser's Tuxmobil-Mobile UNIX website at http://www.tuxmobil.org. The site contains links to information about topics such as IrDA, Linux PDAs, and cell phones. Linux Zaurus PDA users can browse to http://www.openzaurus.org to download a complete Open Source replacement operating system for the Zaurus 5000 and 5500 models.

If you want to purchase a laptop with Linux already installed, then we highly recommend Emperor Linux, one of the leading suppliers of Linux laptops. They take laptops from the likes of Dell, Sony, and Lenovo and install a customized version of Fedora (called EmperorLinux) that fully supports the capabilities of the laptop. You can find them at http://www.emperorlinux.com.

X

Although much technical information is available on the Internet regarding the X Window System, finding answers to specific questions when troubleshooting can be problematic. If you are having a problem using X, first try to determine whether the problem is software or hardware related. When searching or asking for help (such as on Usenet's comp.os.linux.x newsgroup, which you can access through Google's Groups link; see the next section for other helpful Linux newsgroups), try to be as specific as possible. Some critical factors or information needed to adequately assess a problem include the Linux distribution in use; the kernel version used; the version of X used; the brand, name, and model of your video card; the names, brands, and models of your monitor and other related hardware.

This section lists just some of the basic resources for Linux XFree86 users. Definitive technical information regarding X is available from http://x.org:

- ▶ **http://www.lesstif.org/**—Home page for the GPL'd OSF/Motif clone, LessTif

- ▶ **http://www.motifzone.net**—Site for download of the open source version of Motif for Linux, Open Motif

- ▶ **http://www.rahul.net/kenton/index.shtml**—Ken Lee's X and Motif website with numerous links to tutorial, development, and other information about X

- ▶ **http://www.x.org**—Home page for X.org, the X server used in Fedora

- ▶ **http://www.xig.com/**—Home page for a commercial version of X for Linux (along with other software products)

Usenet Newsgroups

Linux-related Usenet newsgroups are another good source of information if you're having trouble using Linux. If your ISP does not offer a comprehensive selection of Linux newsgroups, you can browse to http://groups.google.com/.

The primary Linux and Linux-related newsgroups are the following:

- **alt.os.linux.dialup**—Using PPP for dialup

- **alt.os.linux.mandriva**—All about Mandriva Linux

- **alt.os.linux.redhat**—Alternative discussions about Red Hat Linux

- **alt.os.linux.slackware**—Using Slackware Linux

- **alt.os.linux.suse**—Using SuSE Linux

- **alt.os.linux.ubuntu**—Using Ubuntu Linux

- **comp.os.linux.advocacy**—Heated discussions about Linux and other related issues

- **comp.os.linux.alpha**—Using Linux on the Alpha CPU

- **comp.os.linux.announce**—General Linux announcements

- **comp.os.linux.answers**—Releases of new Linux FAQs and other information

- **comp.os.linux.development.apps**—Using Linux development tools

- **comp.os.linux.development.system**—Building the Linux kernel

- **comp.os.linux.embedded**—Linux embedded device development

- **comp.os.linux.hardware**—Configuring Linux for various hardware devices

- **comp.os.linux.m68k**—Linux on Motorola's 68K-family CPUs

- **comp.os.linux.misc**—Miscellaneous Linux topics

- **comp.os.linux.networking**—Networking and Linux

- **comp.os.linux.portable**—Using Linux on laptops

- **comp.os.linux.powerpc**—Using PPC Linux

- **comp.os.linux.redhat**—All about Red Hat Linux

- **comp.os.linux.security**—Linux security issues

- **comp.os.linux.setup**—Linux installation topics

- **comp.os.linux.x**—Linux and the X Window System

- **comp.windows.x.apps**—Using X-based clients

- **comp.windows.x.i386unix**—X for UNIX PCs

- **comp.windows.x.intrinsics**—X Toolkit library topics

- **comp.windows.x.kde**—Using KDE and X discussions

- **comp.windows.x.motif**—All about Motif programming

- **comp.windows.x**—Discussions about X

- **linux.admin.***—Two newsgroups for Linux administrators

- **linux.debian.***—30 newsgroups about Debian

- **linux.dev.***—25 or more Linux development newsgroups

- **linux.help**—Get help with Linux

- **linux.kernel**—The Linux kernel

- **linux.redhat.***—Red Hat-based discussions: linux.redhat.announce, linux.redhat.list, linux.redhat.applixware, linux.redhat.misc, linux.redhat.devel, linux.redhat.pam, linux.redhat.development, linux.redhat.ppp, linux.redhat.digest, linux.redhat.rpm, linux.redhat.install, linux.redhat.sparc, linux.redhat.axp

Mailing Lists

Mailing lists are interactive or digest-form electronic discussions about nearly any topic. To use a mailing list, you must generally send an email request to be subscribed to the list, and then verify the subscription with a return message from the master list mailer. After subscribing to a mailing list, each message sent to the list appears in your email inbox. However, many lists provide a digest form of subscription in which a single- or half-day's traffic is condensed in a single message. The digest form is generally preferred unless you have set up electronic mail filtering.

The main Fedora Project mailing lists are detailed here, but there are quite a few Linux-related lists. Red Hat's offerings are also provided here. You can search for nearly all online mailing lists by using a typical mailing list search web page, such as the one at http://www.lsoft.com/lists/list_q.html.

GNOME and KDE Mailing Lists

GNOME users and developers should know that more than two dozen mailing lists are available through http://mail.gnome.org/. KDE users can also benefit by perusing the KDE-related mailing lists at http://www.kde.org/mailinglists.html.

Fedora Project Mailing Lists

The Fedora Project is always expanding, with many users finding Fedora for the first time. You can find many other knowledgeable users with answers to your questions by participating in one of Fedora's mailing lists. The lists are focused on using, testing, developing and participating in Fedora's development:

- **fedora-devel-list@redhat.com**—Developer information exchanges

- **fedora-announce-list@redhat.com**—Announcements concerning Fedora

- **fedora-docs-list@redhat.com**—Fedora users working on project documentation

- **fedora-list@redhat.com**—Discussions among users of Fedora releases

- **fedora-test-list@redhat.com**—Queries and reports from testers of Fedora test releases

Red Hat Mailing Lists

Red Hat provides a comprehensive archive and mailing list management web page at http://www.redhat.com/mailman/listinfo/. You can use this page to subscribe to one of more than 40 mailing lists related to Red Hat and Fedora. Some of the more pertinent lists are the following:

- **redhat-devel-list**—Information for developers using Red Hat Linux

- **redhat-install-list**—Installation issues about Red Hat Linux

- redhat-list—General Red Hat Linux discussion list

- **redhat-ppp-list**—Issues regarding PPP and dialup under Red Hat Linux

- **redhat-secure-server**—Using Red Hat, Inc.'s secure server

- **redhat-watch-list**—Announcements of bug fixes and updates for Red Hat Linux

- **rpm-list**—Using the Red Hat Package Manager

Internet Relay Chat

Internet Relay Chat (IRC) is a popular form and forum of communication for many Red Hat Linux developers and users because it allows an interactive, real-time exchange of information and ideas. To use IRC, you must have an IRC client and the address of a network and server hosting the desired chat channel for your discussions.

You can use the `irc.freenode.net` IRC server, or one listed at http://www.freenode.net/ to chat with other Fedora Project users. Two current channels are the following:

▶ **#fedora channel**—General chat about Fedora

▶ **#fedora-devel**—Hangout for a number of the Fedora Project developers

Sadly, the list of active IRC channels that has been referred to in previous editions of this book has disappeared from the Internet. However, Google can once again be your savior. Just enter in the distribution name and IRC into the search options to retrieve information on any IRC channels relevant to your requirements. To get started with IRC, browse to http://www.irchelp.org/. Some of the channels of interest might be the following:

▶ **#linux**—General discussions about Linux

▶ **#linuxhelp**—Help chat discussion for new users

Most IRC networks provide one or more Linux channels, although some providers require signup and registration before you can access any chat channel.

Symbols

A

B

How can we make this index more useful? Email us at indexes@samspublishing.com

How can we make this index more useful? Email us at indexes@samspublishing.com

How can we make this index more useful? Email us at indexes@samspublishing.com

How can we make this index more useful? Email us at indexes@samspublishing.com

F

How can we make this index more useful? Email us at indexes@samspublishing.com

How can we make this index more useful? Email us at indexes@samspublishing.com

How can we make this index more useful? Email us at indexes@samspublishing.com

How can we make this index more useful? Email us at indexes@samspublishing.com

How can we make this index more useful? Email us at indexes@samspublishing.com

N

How can we make this index more useful? Email us at indexes@samspublishing.com

How can we make this index more useful? Email us at indexes@samspublishing.com

How can we make this index more useful? Email us at indexes@samspublishing.com

How can we make this index more useful? Email us at indexes@samspublishing.com

Z

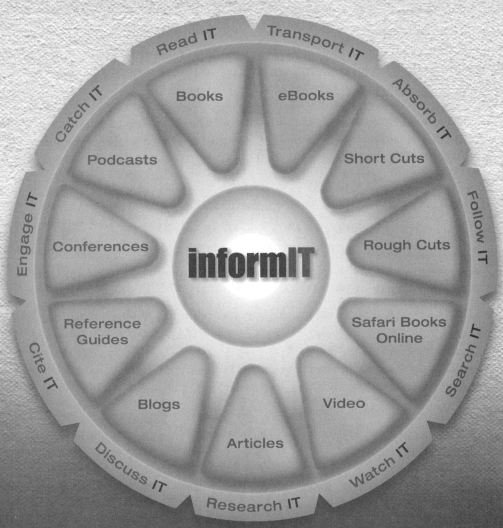

BOOKS ONLINE

ENABLED

THIS BOOK IS SAFARI ENABLED

INCLUDES FREE 45-DAY ACCESS TO THE ONLINE EDITION

The Safari® Enabled icon on the cover of your favorite technology book means the book is available through Safari Bookshelf. When you buy this book, you get free access to the online edition for 45 days.

Safari Bookshelf is an electronic reference library that lets you easily search thousands of technical books, find code samples, download chapters, and access technical information whenever and wherever you need it.

TO GAIN 45-DAY SAFARI ENABLED ACCESS TO THIS BOOK:

- Go to **informit.com/safarienabled**

- Complete the brief registration form

- Enter the coupon code found in the front of this book on the "Copyright" page

If you have difficulty registering on Safari Bookshelf or accessing the online edition, please e-mail customer-service@safaribooksonline.com.

What's On the DVD

This book's DVD includes the full binary version of the Fedora Linux distribution—the equivalent of at least four CDs.

DESKTOP ENVIRONMENTS
- GNOME Desktop Environment
- K Desktop Environment 3

APPLICATIONS

Authoring and Publishing
- DocBook slides, styles, and utilities
- Linux Documentation Tools
- Scribus
- TeX

Editors
- Emacs (base + X11)
- Vi IMproved (base + X11)

Engineering and Scientific
- NetCDF

Games and Entertainment
- GNOME games
- GNU Chess
- Joystick

Graphical Internet
- Ekiga
- Evolution
- Evolution Webcal
- Firefox
- K FTP Grabber
- Konversation
- Pidgin
- Transmission

Graphics
- Dcraw
- Digikam
- F-Spot
- GIMP
- ImageMagick
- Kdegraphics
- Kipi-plugins
- Libsane-hpaio
- Netpbm-progs
- SANE/XSANE
- Xsane-gimp

Office/Productivity
- Evince
- Kdepim
- OpenOffice.org Calc
- OpenOffice.org Draw
- OpenOffice.org Graphic-filter
- OpenOffice.org Impress

Office/Productivity
(continued)
- OpenOffice.org Math
- OpenOffice.org Writer
- OpenOffice.org Xslt-filter
- Planner

Sound and Video
- Akode
- Amarok
- Cdparanoia
- Codeina
- Festvox
- Genisoimage
- Gstreamer
- Icedax
- Jack-audio-connection-kit
- Kaffeine
- Kdemultimedia
- MikMod
- Rhythmbox
- Sound Juicer
- Sox
- Totem
- Vdr
- Wodim

Text-based Internet
- BitTorrent
- Cadaver
- ELinks
- Fetchmail
- Lynx
- Mutt
- Slang Read News (slrn)
- W3m

DEVELOPMENT

Development Libraries
- Binutils
- Boost
- Coolkey
- Curl
- Cyrus
- DB4
- Dbus
- Expat
- Gdbm
- GMP
- GPM
- Hesiod
- Kerberos
- Kudzu
- Libacl

Development Libraries
(continued)
- Libattr
- Libcap
- Libogg
- Libselinux
- Libusr
- Libvorbis
- Libxml2
- Lockdev
- Newt
- OpenLDAP
- OpenSSL
- Pciutils
- Pcsc Lite
- Perl
- Python
- RPM
- Slang

Development Tools
- Automake
- Byacc
- Ccache
- Cscope
- Ctags
- Concurrent Versions System (CVS)
- Diffstat
- Doxygen
- elfutils
- Frysk
- GCC
- Imake
- Indent
- Ltrace
- Lua
- Oprofile
- Patchutils
- Process Stack Dumper (pstack)
- Python-ldap
- Revision Control System (RCS)
- Ruby
- Subversion
- SystemTap
- Valgrind

GNOME Software Development
- Assistive Technology Service Provider Interface (at-spi)
- Devhelp
- Eel 2

GNOME Software Development
(continued)
- Evolution
- Firefox
- GAIL
- Glade2
- GNOME Desktop
- GNOME Panel
- GNOME Pilot
- Gtk
- HAL
- Libart lgpl
- Libgnomeprintui

Java Development
- Ant
- Byte Code Engineering Library (Bcel)
- Jakarta
- Java_cup
- Ldapjdk
- Libgcj
- Log4j
- Mx4j
- Regexp
- Xalan
- Xerxes
- XML Commons

KDE Software Development
- Kdbg
- KDE Base
- KDE Graphics
- KDE Network
- KDE PIM
- KDE SDK
- KDevelop
- PyQT
- Qt Designer

X Software Development
- FreeType
- Gd
- Giflib
- LibDMX
- LibDRM
- LibJPEG
- LibMNG
- LibPNG
- LibSM
- LibTIFF
- LibXau
- LibXcomposite
- LibXcursor

X Software Development
(continued)

- LibXdamage
- LibXdmcp
- LibXevie
- LibXext
- LibXfontcache
- LibXft
- LibXkbfile
- LibXmu
- LibXrandr
- LibXrender
- LibXres
- LibXScrnSaver
- LibXTrap
- LibXtst
- LibXvMC
- Mesa libGL
- Mesa libGLU
- NetPBM
- Simple DirectMedia Layer (SDL)
- Xaw3d
- X.Org
- X Resource Monitor

SERVERS

DNS Name Server

- bind-chroot

Mail Server

- Cyrus SASL
- Dovecot
- Esmtp
- Exim
- Postfix
- Sendmail
- SpamAssassin
- Spambayes

MySQL Database

- Libdbi-dbd-mysql
- Mod_auth_mysql
- MySQL ODBC Connector
- MySQL Python
- MySQL Server
- Perl-DBD-MySQL
- PHP MySQL
- UnixODBC

Network Servers

- Cyrus SASL
- DNS Masq
- Virtual Network Computing (VNC)

PostgreSQL Database

- Lib-DBI-pgsql
- Perl-DBD-Pg

PostgreSQL Database
(continued)

- PostgreSQL Python
- PostgreSQL Server
- Rhdb-utiils
- UnixODBC

Printing Support

- A2ps
- Enscript
- Gutenprint
- Hal Cups
- HP Linux Imaging and Printing Project (hplip)
- HP Printer Drivers (hpijs)
- Samba Client

Server Configuration Tools

- Apache
- Firewall
- NFS
- Printer
- Samba
- Services

Web Server

- Apache Manual
- Apache Top
- Awstats
- Boa
- Cryptoutils
- Dap Server
- Distcache
- Drupal
- Light Tpd
- Media Wiki
- Mod_auth_kerb
- Mod_auth_MySQL
- Mod_auth_PGSQL
- Mod_authz_LDAP
- Mod_cband
- Mod_extract_forwarded
- Mod_fcgid
- Mod_geoip
- Mod_perl
- Mod_python
- Mod_security
- Mod_ssl
- MoinMoin
- Namazu
- Perl-HTML-Mason
- Perl-Kwiki
- PHP
- PHP LDAP
- PHP MySql
- PHP ODBC
- PHP Pecl APC

Web Server (continued)

- PHP PGSQL
- Pound
- Squid
- Tcl HTTPD
- Tht Tpd
- Tiquit
- Tomcat
- VDR
- Webalizer

Windows File Server

- SAMBA

BASE SYSTEM

Administration Tools

- Authconfig
- Pirut
- System configuration tools

Base

- Anacron
- Aspell
- Autofs
- Bluez utils
- Bridge utils
- Ccid
- Coolkey
- CPU Speed
- Crypt setup
- Device mapper
- Dhclient
- DHCPv6 client
- Dmraid
- Dos2unix
- Dosfstools
- Dump
- Eject
- Fbset
- Finger
- Firstboot
- Ftp
- Gnupg
- GPM
- IP Tstate
- Irda utils
- IRQ balance
- iSCSI Initiator
- JFS utils
- Logwatch
- Man
- Mdadm
- Mingetty
- Microcode
- Mlocate
- Mtools
- Mtr

Base (continued)

- Nano
- Nc
- NetworkManager
- NFS
- NSS
- NTFS
- Numa CTL
- OpenSSH
- Pam
- Pax
- RSH
- Rsync
- Smartmon tools
- Stunnel
- Sudo
- Talk
- Telnet
- Yum
- Zip

Dial-up Networking Support

- ISDN4k-utils
- Irzsz
- Minicom
- PPP
- Wvdial

System Tools

- Audit
- BackupPC
- Createrepo
- Festival
- Fuse
- Gnokii
- Ipsec tools
- Jigdo
- Network Manager
- Nmap
- Ntp
- OpenLDAP Client
- OpenVPN
- SAMBA Client
- Screen
- Virtual Network Computing (VNC)
- Xdelta
- Zisofs
- Zsh

Virtualization

- GNOME Applet VM
- Kernel Xen
- Kvm
- Qemu
- Virt-manager
- Xen

Related Linux and Open Source Titles

Ubuntu Linux 7.10 Unleashed

Andrew and Paul Hudson
ISBN-10: 0-672-32969-7
ISBN-13: 978-0-672-32969-2

openSUSE Linux Unleashed

Michael McCallister
ISBN-10: 0-672-32945-X
ISBN-13: 978-0-672-32945-6

FreeBSD 6 Unleashed

Brian Tiemann
ISBN-10: 0-672-32875-5
ISBN-13: 978-0-672-32875-6

Red Hat Enterprise Linux 5 Administration Unleashed

Tammy Fox
ISBN-10: 0-672-32892-5
ISBN-13: 978-0-672-32892-3

Sams Teach Yourself PHP, MySQL and Apache All in One
Julie Meloni
ISBN-10: 0-672-32873-9
ISBN-13: 978-0-672-32873-2

Linux Phrasebook
Scott Granneman
ISBN-10: 0-672-32838-0
ISBN-13: 978-0-672-32838-1

MySQL Phrasebook
Zak Greant and Chris Newman
ISBN-10: 0-672-32839-9
ISBN-13: 978-0-672-32839-8

PHP Phrasebook
Christian Wenz
ISBN-10: 0-672-32817-8
ISBN-13: 978-0-672-32817-6

Apache Phrasebook
Daniel Lopez
ISBN-10: 0-672-32836-4
ISBN-13: 978-0-672-32836-7

SUSE Linux Enterprise Server 9 Administrator's Handbook
Peter Kuo and Jacques Béland
ISBN-10: 0-672-32735-X
ISBN-13: 978-0-672-32735-3

Linux Firewalls, Third Edition
Steve Suehring
and Robert L. Ziegler
ISBN-10: 0-672-32771-6
ISBN-13: 978-0-672-32771-1

Linux Kernel Development
Robert Love
ISBN-10: 0-672-32720-1
ISBN-13: 978-0-672-32720-9

Sams Teach Yourself MySQL in 10 Minutes
Chris Newman
ISBN-10: 0-672-32863-1
ISBN-13: 978-0-672-32863-3

SAMS

www.samspublishing.com